Ref
Z
7551
P54

OCT 20 1980

CONTENTS

Introduction
 i: The Communist Legacy in Central
    and Eastern Europe 1
 ii: Why Hungary, the Czech Republic and Romania? 3
 iii: A Strategy for Comparison 5
 iv: Historical Continuities 8
 v: The Historical Position of Central
    and Eastern Europe 17
 vi: Communism: The Soviet Model 21

CHAPTER 1
Communism in Central and Eastern Europe
after World War Two 25
 1.1.1: The Jewish Factor 33
 1.1.2: De-Stalinisation 38
 1.1.3: Relations with the Soviet Union 41

1.2: The Hungarian Revolution 1956 44
 1.2.1: The 'Secret Speech' 44
 1.2.2: Nagy becomes Prime Minister 51
 1.2.3: Rakosi Returns 54
 1.2.4: Revolution 58
 1.2.5: Repercussions from the Revolution 60

1.3: The 1968 Prague Spring 65
 1.3.1: Late Novotnyism 68
 1.3.2: Dubcek becomes First Secretary 72
 1.3.3: The Warsaw Pact Invasion 75

1.3.4: Ideological De-legitimisation 78
1.3.5: Reactions to the Events 79
1.3.6: Consequences for Czech Development 86
1.4: Ceausescu's Renegade Position 90
1.4.1: The Romanian Communists 93
1.4.2: Stalinisation and Systemisation 97
1.4.3: Ceausescu's Personality Cult 102
1.4.4: Demonstrations of Discontent 104
1.4.5: Political Relations with Ceausescu 106

1.5: Reform Communism and Democratisation 109

CHAPTER 2
Regime Collapse and the Role of the Soviet Union 113
2.1.1: Soviet Subsidies to Eastern Europe 121
2.1.2: Perestroika and Glasnost 123
2.1.3: The Brezhnev Doctrine is Abandoned 126

2.2: Hungary's Negotiated Revolution 132
2.2.1: The Standard of Living Falls 136
2.2.2: Ideology is Weakened 138
2.2.3: Democratisation 140
2.2.4: Independent Opposition 143
2.2.5: Reform within the Socialist Workers Party 147
2.2.6: The Roundtable Negotiations 149
2.2.7: Hungary becomes a Republic 152
2.2.8: Continuity and Change 154

2.3: Czechoslovak Regime Immobility 156
2.3.1: Normalisation 159
2.3.2: The Dissident Movement 162
2.3.3: Economic Failure 164
2.3.4: Ideological Degeneration 167
2.3.5: Moral Disorientation 168
2.3.6: The Velvet Revolution 173
2.3.7: Collapse and Change 177

2.4: Romania's Tangled Revolution 178
   2.4.1: Ceausescuism 180
   2.4.2: Regime Opposition 182
   2.4.3: Economic Collapse 188
   2.4.4: The Timisoara Uprising 193
   2.4.5: Ceausescu Falls 197
   2.4.6: Confusion and Conspiracy 199
   2.4.7: Continuity within Revolution 204

2.5: The Importance of the Revolutions 209

CHAPTER 3
Political Democratisation 213
3.1: Conservative Parties 221
   3.1.1: Hungarian Democratic Forum 221
   3.1.2: Christian Democratic People's Party 225
   3.1.3: Independent Smallholders Party 226
   3.1.4: National Peasant Party/Christian Democracy 230
   3.1.5: Democratic Convention of Romania 232
   3.1.6: Democratic Federation of Hungarians in Romania 233
   3.1.7: Civic Forum 235
   3.1.8: Civic Democratic Alliance 236
   3.1.9: Christian Democratic Union/
         Czech People's Party 237
   3.1.10: Christian Democratic Party 238
   3.1.11: Civic Democratic Party 238
   3.1.12: Czech Agrarian Party 242

3.2: Liberal Parties 243
   3.2.1: National Liberal Party 243
   3.2.2: Liberal Party-93 245
   3.2.3: Civic Alliance Party 246
   3.2.4: Alliance of Free Democrats 247
   3.2.5: Alliance of Young Democrats-Civic Party 249
   3.2.6: Movement for Self-Administrative Democracy-
         Association for Silesia and Moravia 253

3.3: Social Democratic Parties 253
    3.3.1: Czech Social Democratic Party 254
    3.3.2: Romanian Social Democratic Party 258
    3.3.3: Hungarian Social Democratic Party 259
    3.3.4: Hungarian Socialist Party 260
    3.3.5: Democratic Party 265

3.4: Successor Communist Parties 266
    3.4.1: Hungarian Socialist Workers Party 266
    3.4.2: Communist Party of Bohemia and Moravia 266
    3.4.3: Party of Social Democracy in Romania 268
    3.4.4: Party of Socialist Labour/
           Romanian Communist Party 277

3.5: Extremist Parties 278
    3.5.1: Extremist Romanian Parties 278
        3.5.1.1: Greater Romania Party 281
        3.5.1.2: Party of Romanian National Unity 283
    3.5.2: Hungarian Justice and Life Party 286
    3.5.3: Czech Assembly for the Republic/
           Republican Party 288

3.6: Election Results 290
    3.6.1: Hungarian Election Results 290
    3.6.2: Czech Election Results 293
    3.6.3: Romanian Election Results 296

3.7: Democratisation and Political Parties 301

CHAPTER 4
Dealing with the Communist Economic Legacy 307
4.1: Economic Transformation 310

4.2: Economic Reform in Hungary 313
    4.2.1: Rejection of Reform
           in Czechoslovakia and Romania 319

4.3: Privatisation ... 329
    4.3.1: The Hungarian Programme ... 332
        4.3.1.1: Spontaneous and Self-Privatisation ... 334

    4.3.2: Radical Czech Transformation ... 340
        4.3.2.1: Czech Privatisation ... 345
        4.3.2.2: The Voucher Scheme ... 349
    4.3.3: The Contradictory Romanian Programme ... 352
        4.3.3.1: Romanian Privatisation ... 358

4.4: Restitution and Compensation ... 365
    4.4.1: Hungarian Compensation Vouchers ... 366
    4.4.2: Czech and Romanian Restitution ... 369

4.5: Problems of Transformation ... 377
    4.5.1: Unemployment ... 378
    4.5.2: Industrial Restructuring ... 385
    4.5.3: Agriculture ... 391
    4.5.4: Bad Debts ... 396

4.6: Hungarian Economic Problems ... 405
    4.6.1: The Bokros Austerity Package ... 407

4.7: Czech Economic Difficulties ... 414

4.8: Romanian Radicalism ... 421

4.9: The Impact of Economic Transformation ... 436

CHAPTER 5
Formation of a Democratic and Civil Society ... 443
5.1: Historical Truth and Personal Responsibility ... 450
    5.1.1: Hungarian Reconciliation ... 453
    5.1.2: Czech Lustration ... 457
    5.1.3: Delayed Romanian Confrontation ... 461

5.2: The Media 466
   5.2.1: Hungarian Media Autonomy 466
   5.2.2: The Czech Media 468
   5.2.3: State Domination of the Romanian Media 469

5.3: The Role of the Church 474
   5.3.1: Roman Catholic Conservatism in Hungary 475
   5.3.2: Czech Secularism 477
   5.3.3: Romanian Orthodox Complicity 479

5.4: Ethnic Prejudice and Nationalism 482
   5.4.1: The Roma 483
   5.4.2: The Magyar Minorities 492

5.5: NATO and European Union Membership 496
   5.5.1: Czech and Hungarian Membership
        of NATO and the EU 498
   5.5.2: Future Romanian Accession 504

5.6: Trust in State Institutions 511
   5.6.1: Support for Transformation 515

5.7: Civil Society and Democratic Consolidation 517

Conclusion 525
Final Analysis 537

APPENDIX 539
BIBLIOGRAPHY 575

INTRODUCTION

'It is a strange sad story that remains to be told.'
Hannah Arendt, *On Revolution*.

*

i: The Communist Legacy in Central and Eastern Europe
The Revolutions which occurred in 1989 in Central and Eastern Europe were unexpected and truly momentous[1]. They swept away the Communist regimes which had been imposed upon the states of Central and Eastern Europe after the Second World War. The people of Eastern and Central Europe broke the shackles of control and threw off the mantle of fear and lies in which the Communist regimes had cocooned them. However, the euphoria of Revolution served to disguise the enduring legacy which Communist rule has bestowed onto these countries, their populations, economies and ecology. It is only now, after the collapse of the Communist regimes, that the true extent of their penetration of all levels of society, and cultural and economic life has been gradually revealed.

The Party aimed to control all the activities of its citizens and thus ensure their activities were useful for the Communist cause. As demonstrated by the *Small Political Dictionary*, citizens were to have no time in which to occupy themselves with unsupervised and perhaps 'useless' activities:

> *'In socialism the contradiction between work and free time, typical of capitalism, is removed. Free time must be purposefully and effectively deployed by all members of the socialist community.'*[2]

---

[1] For an eyewitness account, see Ash, Timothy Garton, *We the People*, Granata Books 1990.
[2] Ash, Timothy Garton, *The Uses of Adversity*, Penguin Books 1991, p. 9.

The logic behind this penetration of personal space is inherent in Communist ideology because it strives to create not only a new society, but also a new man[3]. Thus, people must be re-educated socially in order to be capable of functioning in the future reality. As Nicolae Ceausescu stated:

'...we want to improve nature's best creation – man,' ...'permanent, steady and patient activity [is necessary] to delete from people's minds the remains of the past, the obsolete conceptions, mentalities and customs, and to cultivate a new attitude towards work, life and society.'[4]

This self-appointed task is one of the reasons why ideology, propaganda and outward measures of success towards this goal form an integral part of the Communist system of rule. It also helps to explain why control over cultural and intellectual life was necessary, since these are the means of dissemination of the new ideology and therefore actually contribute to the formation of the new man and society. Marxist ideology also motivated and justified interference in the economy[5]. However, the command system developed under Lenin and perfected by Stalin in the Soviet Union included an ideology which encouraged fast industrialisation as a means of 'catching up' and overtaking capitalist governments[6]. Since the value of actual work done was measured in physical units, an ideological imperative developed which measured progress in increasing industrial production. Stalin himself realised that the Soviet system was distorted, and wrote in 1951:

'Engels ...does not speak at all in favour of those who think that under socialism existing economic laws can be

---

[3] For an evaluation of 'Homo Sovieticus', see Heller, Mikhail, *Cogs in the Wheel*, Alfred A. Knopf Inc. 1988.
[4] Almond, Mark, *The Rise and Fall of Nicolae and Elena Ceausescu*, Chapmans 1992, p. 184. For original quotes, see Ceausescu, N., *Builder of Modern Romania*, p. 113, pp. 117-118.
[5] An interesting examination of Marx and Engels' economic theories about state intervention can be found in Barbaria, Frank, A., *Modern 'Asiatic' Despotism*, IDEAS 1980.
[6] For an excellent analysis of Stalinism, see Tucker, R., C., *Stalinism: Essays in Historical Interpretation*, W. W. Norton & Co. Inc. 1977.

Introduction 3

abolished and new ones created. On the contrary, it demands, not the abolition, but the understanding of economic laws and their intelligent application.[7]

The ideological nature of economic policy led to over-investment in heavy industry and under-investment in consumer and service industries. Moreover, the ideological necessity of exhibiting progress towards the goal of a new society led to disregard of the ecological consequences of industrialisation.

Communist ideological penetration has as its legacy economic chaos, political uncertainty and personal and moral crisis[8]. As Vaclav Havel aptly described in his 1990 New Year's Day speech:

'The worst thing is that we are living in a decayed moral environment. We have become morally ill, because we have become accustomed to saying one thing and thinking another ...all of us have become accustomed to the totalitarian system, accepting it as an unalterable fact and thereby kept it running. None of us is merely a victim of it, because all of us helped to create it together.'[9]

Havel provides us with an insight into the complex relationship and *modus vivendi* which the Communist regime formed with its subjects. It is the legacies of the Communist system which this dissertation aims to examine and evaluate in respect to their effect on the transformation and democratisation process in the countries of Hungary, the Czech Republic and Romania.

ii: Why Hungary, the Czech Republic and Romania?
The Central European region, from which the countries of Romania, Hungary and the Czech Republic have been chosen as a base for comparison, faces the legacies which forty years of Communist rule have left behind. Unfortunately, it is not possible in the space of this dissertation to undertake a comprehensive study

---

[7] Swain, G., Swain, N., *Eastern Europe since 1945*, Macmillan 1993, p. 226.
[8] For a detailed account of the moral crisis the Communist system evinced, see Havel, Vaclav, *Versuch in der Wahrheit zu leben*, Rowohlt Taschenbuch Verlag 1989.
[9] Brogan, Patrick, *Eastern Europe 1939-1989*, Bloomsbury 1990, pp. 109-110.

of the whole Central European region, much as this may be desirable. However, this factor was not the sole guiding reason for the choice of these three countries.

A regional comparative analysis of this kind requires that the countries compared exhibit both a level of similarity and dissimilarity. The countries must be sufficiently similar to make a comparison possible, and yet also display certain differences in the pattern of development which make comparison desirable and useful. The Central European region displays a number of similarities of historical, cultural and social experience which provide the basic foundation of shared characteristics which make such a regional study possible. But, in addition to this, Central Europe also displays a variety and difference of policy and action, which implies that certain important factors are crucial in explaining this difference. This is particularly true for Hungary, the Czech Republic and Romania which, as the sub-region under discussion, stretch from the heart of Central Europe into South-Eastern Europe and down into the Balkans.

In many respects these countries continue to suffer from the 'historical backwardness', which has plagued East-Central Europe[10]. The roots of this 'backwardness' lie in the pre-feudal peasant commune and the distribution of land, in favour of large landowners, which effectively bound peasants to the land as subsistence farmers, and in the specific peasant culture and way of life, which in some areas is still visible today. All were parts of supranational empires before the First World War, were subject to increasing German influence and power during the inter-war period and were subsequently confronted with similar situations following the Second World War. They experienced increased Soviet influence in the region and had Communist regimes, modelled on the Soviet system, imposed upon them. During the Communist period, protest against the regimes was discernible and was consistently dealt with using similar methods of terror and intimidation. Furthermore, all the regimes collapsed almost simultaneously in 1989. These three countries are therefore faced with many similar historical legacies, as well as a Communist legacy. However, the nature and influence of the Communist legacy

---

[10] See Chirot, D., *The Origins of Backwardness in Eastern Europe*, University of California Press 1989.

seems to differ. During the course of this dissertation, factors which may cause this will be examined.

iii: A Strategy for Comparison

These countries are diverse and display many seemingly unique features. This is true, but at the same time it is also true that, features of one country only obtain meaning when compared with differing features of another country. As Frank H. Aarebrot and Pal H. Bakka state in the chapter 'Die Vergleichende Methode in der Politikwissenschaft'[11]:

'...*so besteht doch eine Skepsis gegenüber dem Vergleich verschiedener, scheinbar einzigartiger Phänomene. Andererseits ist es richtig, daß jede Beobachtung ohne Bedeutung ist, wenn man sie nicht mit anderen Beobachtungen vergleicht ...Ein Ding bekommt nur dann eine individuelle Identität, wenn man es mit anderen vergleicht.*'[12]

This tension between uniqueness and similarity forms part of the dynamic behind this dissertation. Adam Przeworski and Henry Teune describe two differing strategies for this type of research in their chapter 'Research Designs' in *The Logic of Comparative Social Inquiry*[13]. The aim is to explain certain patterns observed in the countries, or systems, studied. The 'Most Similar Systems Design' is based on the belief that:

---

[11] Berg-Schlosser, D., Müller-Rommel, F., *Vergleichende Politikwissenschaft*, Opladen 1992, p. 51. For information on the application of this method to Central and Eastern Europe, see also Berg-Schlosser, D., Müller-Rommel, F., *Vergleichende Politikwissenschaft (3. Auflage)*, Leske & Budrich 1997.

[12] Ibid Berg-Schlosser, D., Müller-Rommel, F., *Vergleichende Politikwissenschaft*, p.51. '...a certain skepsis exists in respect to the comparison of different, seemingly unique phenomena. On the other hand, it is true to say that every observation is without meaning unless it is compared with other observations.....A thing only gains an individual identity when one compares it with others.' Translated by Wendy Hollis.

[13] Przeworski, A., Teune, H., *The Logic of Comparative Social Inquiry*, Wiley-Interscience 1970, pp. 31-46.

'*...systems as similar as possible with respect to as many features as possible constitute the optimal samples for comparative enquiry.*'[14]

In this design, the number of features, 'experimental variables', with an unknown effect is minimised, but still remains large. Thus:

'*It is anticipated that if some important differences are found among these otherwise similar countries, then the number of factors attributable to these differences will be sufficiently small to warrant explanation in terms of those differences alone.*'[15]

In this design, inter-systemic similarities and differences are examined. It is the system which is analysed and variations within systems are explained using systemic factors. Common systemic characteristics are sought because they are 'controlled', whereas inter-systemic differences are viewed as possible explanatory factors, 'variables'. Thus, characteristics which are not shared are kept at a minimal level, whereas shared characteristics are maximised. Differences which are discovered between the systems studied imply that:

'*...factors that are common to the countries are irrelevant in determining the behaviour being explained since different patterns of behaviour are observed among systems sharing these factors ...[and further that] any set of variables that differentiates these systems in a manner corresponding to the observed differences of behaviour (or any interaction among these differences) can be considered as explaining these patterns of behaviour.*'[16]

However, although the number of differences among countries which are similar is low, it will invariably be large enough to 'over-determine' the differences observed. In view of this, Przeworski

---

[14] Ibid Przeworski, A., Teune, H., *The Logic of Comparative Social Inquiry*, p. 32.
[15] Ibid Przeworski, A., Teune, H., *The Logic of Comparative Social Inquiry*, p. 32.
[16] Ibid Przeworski, A., Teune, H., *The Logic of Comparative Social Inquiry*, p. 34.

Introduction

and Teune also suggest another research design, a 'Most Different Systems Design'.

The goal remains the same as that of the 'Most Similar Systems Design', but systemic factors do not occupy a preferential position as possible factors explaining certain patterns of behaviour. The initial assumption is that the population of the countries to be studied is basically homogenous, and that systemic factors do not play a role in determining behaviour. This assumption is then tested by further cross-systemic research. If this initial assumption is not rejected, then the analysis remains at an 'intra-systemic level', but if this assumption is rejected, systemic factors must once again be taken into consideration. In this way, independent factors, or 'variables', which do not contradict the original assumption are identified within the systems. The samples, although derived from different systems are treated as one. If the groups of population from different systems do not differ with regard to the factor, 'dependent variable', being studied, then systemic differences do not play a role in describing the factor, 'variable'. For example, if suicide rates are the same among Russians and Swedes, factors which distinguish these societies are not significant in explaining the suicide rate[17].

Whereas the 'Most Similar Systems Design' focuses on isolating relevant systemic factors, the 'Most Different Systems Design' concentrates on eliminating irrelevant systemic factors. However, the two research designs do not oppose each other and the difference between them is a matter of emphasis. In short:

> *'The most similar systems design is based on the belief that a number of theoretically significant differences will be found among similar systems and that these differences can be used in explanation. The alternative design, which seeks maximal heterogeneity in the sample of systems, is based on a belief that in spite of inter-systemic differentiation, the populations will differ with regard only to a limited number of variables or relationships.'*[18]

---

[17] Ibid Przeworski, A., Teune, H., *The Logic of Comparative Social Inquiry*, p. 35.
[18] Ibid Przeworski, A., Teune, H., *The Logic of Comparative Social Inquiry*, p. 39.

In this way, the nature of the Communist legacy will be analysed in an attempt to explain and evaluate its differentiated influence on transformation and long-term democratic consolidation.

iv: Historical Continuities
The three countries chosen for study display various aspects of historical similarity which precede Communism. These similarities make the differing influence of the shared Communist experience on the transformation process more striking and the factors which cause this more intriguing.

Romania, along with parts of Hungary, was subjected to many years of Ottoman rule which affected its development and can still be seen to have some lingering influence even today[19]. But, in Romania, Ottoman rule did not entail conversion to Islam. Unlike the situation in southern and central Hungary, no mosques were erected, there was no *sharia* law and Muslims were not allowed to settle there. However, the native rulers of Romania were expected to pay a tribute to the Sultan. At times this tribute was refused[20]. In order to try and prevent this, the Romanian principalities were later ruled by princes from Greek families who were appointed by the Sultan. They had no hereditary rights over the land they ruled and had an average reign of three years in Moldavia and two and a half in Wallachia[21]. Their main concern was to extract as much wealth from their principality as possible before they were replaced. It was this period of Phanariot rule which embedded practices of corruption and *baksheesh*. The Romanian principalities of Moldavia and Wallachia were not united until 1859, and had to wait for international recognition until 1878[22]. It was widely recognised that Romania had been one of the worst ruled regions of Europe. In

---

[19] For a comprehensive history of the Balkans, see Castellan, G., *History of the Balkans*, Boulder 1992.
[20] Vlad Tepes Dracul, who ruled the Voevod of Wallachia, impaled alive two of the Sultan's commanders who had come to collect the tribute outside his castle. At the time this was a common practice, but this was an open act of defiance. It is from this incident that accounts of Count Dracul's bloodthirsty habits stem. They were circulated to discredit the Count. He was imprisoned and later hacked to death in Wallachia as he tried to regain his throne in 1462. Ibid Castellan, G., *History of the Balkans*, p. 148.
[21] Ibid Castellan, G., *History of the Balkans*, p. 206.
[22] Ibid Almond, Mark, *The Rise and Fall of Nicolae and Elena Ceausescu*, p. xv.

Introduction 9

1907, the peasants finally lost their patience and revolted[23]. It is estimated that between 10-12 000 were killed during the uprising. The entire Romanian army had to be mobilised in order to regain control[24]. It was this situation which forced the Romanian government to undertake a massive land reform after the First World War which finally destroyed the great landowning class.

After the Battle of Mohács in 1526, during which the Hungarian army was annihilated and the Hungarian King killed, the central and southern regions of Hungary, including the capital Buda, also fell under Ottoman rule. The Kingdom of Hungary was divided. For the next 150 years, the western and eastern parts were under Ottoman rule, while the northern and western regions, all that remained of the 'Old Kingdom', fell to the Habsburgs and became part of the Habsburg Empire ruled from Vienna. The south eastern region, Transylvania, which had become an organic part of the Hungarian Kingdom, albeit with a residual amount of administrative autonomy, became an independent country which was governed by Hungarian princes. Although Transylvania became a vassal of the Sultan in 1566 and paid him taxes[25], it remained independent and the Turks refrained from interfering in its internal affairs[26]. Once Ottoman rule began to crumble, the western lands elected the Habsburg Ferdinand as their King, while the eastern lands elected Janos Zapolyai. His successors gave up the royal title, but continued to rule the independent state of Transylvania[27]. Transylvania's period of independence contributed to the rival claims of Hungary and Romania over the territory.

In 1690, Transylvania rejoined the Kingdom of Hungary and thus became part of the Habsburg Empire. However, the Habsburgs did not allow Transylvania's reunion with the other parts of the Hungarian Kingdom. Although it was one of the Hungarian Crown Lands, Transylvania was ruled from Vienna and considered part of

---

[23] It is estimated that in 1907, 24 % of the land in Romania was owned by 6 700 large landowners, while 28% was owned by 2 500 000 poor peasants. Ibid Castellan, G., *History of the Balkans*, p. 429.
[24] For a comprehensive account of the revolt, see Ilincioiu, Ion, *The Great Romanian Peasant Revolt of 1907*, The Romanian Academy 1991.
[25] Ibid Castellan, G., *History of the Balkans*, p. 208.
[26] For an account of Transylvanian history, see Benda, Kalmán, 'From St. Stephen to Post-Ceausescu', *The Hungarian Quarterly*, Vol. 35, No. 133, Spring 1994.
[27] Sugar, P., F., *A History of Hungary*, Indiana University Press 1990, pp. xi-xiii.

the Habsburg Empire. To compensate for its loss of independence, Transylvania was granted Grand Duchy status. The Hungarian Revolution of 1848 destroyed the old feudal system and reunited Transylvania with Hungary once more. However, although the Hungarians of Transylvania supported the Revolution, the Transylvanian Saxons and Romanians did not. They supported the Habsburgs in defeating Hungarian aims. The feudal system was re-imposed and the union with Hungary annulled[28].

After the Compromise of 1867, which created the Dual Monarchy of Austria-Hungary, the union was reinstated and Transylvania came under Magyar control. While the Empire stood, the Transylvanians were content to strive for an improvement of their position within it. They showed no particular inclination for national unification with the other two Romanian principalities[29]. However, this position began to change after the Compromise as the various nationalities in the Empire who had been hoping for a such a solution for all nationalities realised that only the Magyar nation was to be elevated to the position of equal partner.

After the First World War, Translyvania came under Romanian control, but since the population of Transylvania is ethnically heterogeneous, consisting of Romanians, Hungarians, Germans and Roma, this issue has retained its political relevance. Indeed, it was this issue and the prospect of border revision which was one of the reasons for Hungary and Romania's wartime alliance with the Third Reich[30].

In addition to sharing its experience of Ottoman rule with Romania, Hungary also shares a history of Habsburg rule with the Czech lands and in this respect acts as an important link between Romania and the Czech Republic. The Czech Republic, consisting of Bohemia, Moravia and parts of Silesia had been united under the

---

[28] Ibid. Benda, Kalmán, 'From St. Stephen to Post-Ceausescu', *The Hungarian Quarterly*.
[29] For further information, see Fischer-Galati, S., *Twentieth Century Romania*, Columbia University Press 1970, especially pp. 10-19.
[30] Constant squabbling between Romania and Hungary over this issue forced Hitler to solve the question in the Second Vienna Award of 30 August, 1940. Transylvania was split into two; 43 000 km^2 was given to Hungary and the rest to Romania. One million Romanians came under Hungarian rule and 400 000 Hungarians under Romanian. Held, Joseph, *The Columbia History of Eastern Europe in the Twentieth Century*, Columbia University Press 1992, p. 186.

Introduction

Bohemian crown. However, after the Battle of White Mountain in 1620, during the course of which almost the entire native nobility perished, no attempts were made to restore the Kingdom and the Czech Lands became an integral part of the Habsburg Empire. The independent state of Czechoslovakia was created in the aftermath of the First World War in 1918[31]. The territory included in the new state had never before been under one administration. It included numerous minorities, the Slovaks, Hungarians and the Sudeten Germans forming the majority of these[32]. It proved increasingly difficult for the Hungarians and Sudeten Germans, who had been used to the privileges connected with power, to adjust to the new situation. This state of affairs was complicated by Czech efforts to consolidate the new state in a unitary rather than a federal structure, and by the active agitation of Nazi Germany, which aimed to incorporate the Sudetenland into the Reich. Problems concerning ethnic minorities within national borders and outside national borders still exist today.

Although the individual histories of Romania, Hungary and the Czech Republic differ, there are interesting parallels and points of contact. One of the most striking is that all were subject to foreign domination and were parts of supranational empires until the end of the First World War. They have all had to deal with the effects of imperial collapse at some time in their history, and remain subject to the effects of swings in the balance of power in Europe which favour Germany or Russia.

They also suffered from the effects of land shortage, which resulted in the majority of peasants cultivating merely at a subsistence and not at a commercial level. As peasants were subsistence farmers, they were tied to the land as the only means of survival for the family. Thus, there was a very limited supply of manpower which could be directed into industrial labour. Land shortage and the lack of land reform, which furthered the continued existence of a specific 'peasant' way of life and the mentality this

---

[31] For an account of the history of Czechoslovakia, see Hoensch, Jörg, K., *Geschichte der Tschechoslowakischen Republik*, Verlag Kohlhammer 1978.

[32] In 1921, the population of the new Republic consisted of 66% Czechs and Slovaks, 23.4% Germans, 5.4% Hungarians and an unknown number of Roma. Wolchik, S., *Czechoslovakia in Transition*, Pinter Publishers 1991, p. 6.

engendered, are viewed by many as the main cause of Eastern Europe's late development, or 'backwardness'[33].
But, on the eve of the First World War, the Czech Lands were one of the most industrialised and prosperous regions in Europe[34]. In 1921, 336.4 people per 1000 were occupied in industry. The figure in Bohemia was 406 per 1000 and in Moravia 378[35]. Even so, large sections of the population remained tied to the land[36]. In 1921, 395.6 people per 1000 were involved in agriculture[37]. In 1930, 48% of the population was urban[38]. In Romania in 1901, only 37 000 people worked in the 600 enterprises which employed more than 25 employees. Not only was industrialisation lagging, but land shortage was chronic. In 1895, half of the agricultural land in Romania was owned by 6500 landowners, while 300 000 peasants, or 20% of the population, remained landless[39]. In addition to this, the Romanian population increased drastically[40], but remained primarily involved in agriculture. In 1911, 75% of the Romanian population was primarily employed in agriculture[41]. The situation was similar in Hungary, where 2000 landowners held estates of 2850 acres or more. This amounted to 23% of the land. Of these landowners, 1200 were magnates who owned 92 large estates. 20%

---

[33] Ibid. Chirot, D., *The Origins of Backwardness in Easter Europe*.
[34] In 1920, the new Czechoslovak Republic consisted of approximately 1/5 of the land area, a 1/4 of the population and 3/4 of the industry of the old Dual Monarchy. In 1914, the future Republic had 64% of the monarchy's manufacturing industry and almost 100% of the glass and porcelain industry. Ströbinger, R., S., *Schicksalsjahre an der Moldau*, Casmir Katz Verlag 1988, p. 25.
[35] Ibid Wolchik, S., *Czechoslovakia in Transition*, p. 7.
[36] Servile labour was only abolished in Bohemia and Moravia in 1848, well after initial mechanisation. A report in 1902 showed that the 0.5% of the rural population with farms larger than 100 hectares owned almost one third of the land, whereas smallholders with farms under 5 hectares, who consisted of 71.6% of the population, owned only 14.7% of the land. Berend, Ivan, T., Ranki, György, *Economic Development in East Central Europe in the Nineteenth and Twentieth Centuries*, Columbia University Press 1974, p. 32.
[37] Ibid Held, Joseph, *The Columbia History of Eastern Europe in the Twentieth Century*, p. 123. This figure applies to the territory of Czechoslovakia.
[38] Ibid Held, Joseph, *The Columbia History of Eastern Europe in the Twentieth Century*, p. 120.
[39] Ibid Castellan, G., *History of the Balkans*, p. 342.
[40] The population increased from 4.6 million in 1880, to 7 million in 1910. Ibid Castellan, G., *History of the Balkans*, p.344.
[41] Ibid Castellan, G., *History of the Balkans*, p. 348.

Introduction 13

of the large estates were owned by members of the industrial middle class, but the majority, 35%, belonged to the Hungarian nobility and were therefore considered as indivisible and inalienable from the family to which they belonged. In contrast, approximately 2.5 million Hungarian peasants lived from less than 5 acres of land. The land redistribution scheme of 1920 gave 1 346 000 acres of land to 411 000 peasants, mostly those who had been previously landless. This meant that approximately two million families received small plots of land, but Hungary's social structure remained unchanged[42].

Hungary was more industrialised than Romania, but less so than the Czech Lands. By 1941, approximately 40% of the Hungarian population lived in towns and 71% of the population had electricity. The population of Budapest had topped one million, but this was by far Hungary's largest metropolis and remains so today[43]. The largest cities after Budapest have populations in the 100 000's. The first traffic lights were erected in Budapest in 1928 and by 1930 there were 13 000 cars registered[44]. But, there remained a tension between the city and the countryside; between the agrarian peasant population and the urban, often foreign and, or, Jewish population. As in much of the region, the city was often viewed as a hostile, foreign environment. Thus, much of the urban population retained close links with the countryside and many workers in the city depended on agricultural produce from the family smallholding for their survival. In 1913, 57% of Hungarian workers were involved in agriculture and 21% in industry. By 1938, 50% were still involved in agriculture and 25% in industry. As industrialisation progressed, so urbanisation increased. In 1919, 19% of the Hungarian population was urban. This figure rose to 30% in 1930 and reached 35% in 1941[45]. However, the tendency to retain a family smallholding remained and was even strengthened during the

---

[42] Ibid. Sugar, P., F., *A History of Hungary*, pp. 275-317.
[43] The population in Budapest accounted for 12.5% of the country's population; if one includes the Budapest suburbs this figure rises to 18%. Ibid Held, Joseph, *The Columbia History of Eastern Europe in the Twentieth Century*, p. 191.
[44] Hanak, Peter, *Die Geschichte Ungarns*, Reimar Hobbing Verlag 1988, pp. 232-233.
[45] Ibid Held, Joseph, *The Columbia History of Eastern Europe in the Twentieth Century*, p. 191.

Communist regime as industrial plants were specifically placed roughly evenly throughout Hungary, ironically as a means of destroying the traditional agricultural, peasant way of life.

As a result of the introduction of compulsory schooling for children between 6 and 12 in the Czech lands in 1774, the population was one of the most literate in Europe. In 1842, 95% of all children of school age attended school regularly[46]. In contrast, 40% of the Romanian population was illiterate at the start of the twentieth century[47]. The 39 daily newspapers printed in Budapest in 1906 demonstrate the vitality of the capital[48], but the situation in the countryside was rather less inspiring.

During the inter-war period, economic difficulties ensuing from the collapse of the internal market of the Dual Monarchy and the Depression of the 1930's combined with regional territorial disputes and served to direct these countries into the economic and political orbit of Nazi Germany[49]. Hungary was catastrophically affected by economic dislocation as a result of its defeat in 1918. It lost 64% of its energy resources, 80% of its iron ore and iron production facilities, 88% of its forests, 20% of its paper producing capability and all of its salt mines[50]. Although the Czech lands were incorporated into the Third Reich in 1938 as a result of the Munich Agreement, Czechoslovakia was the only state in the whole of Eastern Europe to retain its democratic structures. Romania and Hungary failed to consolidate democracy and reintroduced authoritarian structures. The Hungarian population and elite could not come to terms with the Treaty of Trianon and a national

---

[46] Koralka, J., *Tschechen im Habsburgerreich und in Europa 1815-1914*, R. Oldenburg Verlag 1991, p. 205.

[47] Ibid Castellan, G., *History of the Balkans*, p. 349.

[48] In London there were 25, in Vienna 24, and in Berlin 36. Lendvai, Paul, *Hungary: The Art of Survival*, I B Tauris and Co. Ltd. 1988, p. 17.

[49] As a result of the collapse of the Dual Monarchy, trade between its former constituent parts declined. In 1920, the Treaty of Trianon reduced Hungary in size from 282 000 km^2 to 93 000 km^2. As a result, 60% of pre-war mining and 45% of other industrial production was situated outside Hungary. Of Hungary's original territory, 124 000 km^2 had been inhabited by non-Magyars and 138 000 km^2 by ethnic Magyars. Ibid Held, Joseph, *The Columbia History of Eastern Europe in the Twentieth Century*, p. 167, p. 175.

[50] Ibid Held, Joseph, *The Columbia History of Eastern Europe in the Twentieth Century*, p. 189.

Introduction

consensus based on revisionism was established[51]. The conservative, landed elite was able to keep power and fill the political vacuum left by the failure of liberalism, exemplified by the Depression, the failure of Communism, demonstrated by the disastrous 1919 Communist coup, which ended in Romanian occupation of Budapest, and by the general disillusion which the destruction of the First World War evoked.

In Romania, the legacy of corruption left by Ottoman and Phanariot rule adversely affected the political system and, combined with other factors, also favoured the establishment of authoritarian rule[52]. The morass of politicians and political parties were perceived to be incapable of ruling the country. Indeed, they themselves did little to dispel this image. In many cases it was a reality:

> *'A patriarchal multitude of priests, provincial lawyers, doctors with small practices and professors to whom Bucharest had long represented a sort of Jerusalem, and the Parliament a Solomon's Temple, in which it was not dignified or proper to make too much noise ...a bizarre conglomeration of the ambitious and the discontented ...[many of whom were ready to] exchange their political skins.'*[53]

Unlike Romania, which was astute enough to abandon the Axis, Hungary suffered a total defeat at the end of the Second World War and lost Transylvania for good. It was given to Romania partly as a means of revenge on Hungary, and partly as a reward for Romania for leaving the Axis and declaring war on Germany, although of course as a collorary Bessarabia was once more incorporated into

---

[51] The historian Gyula Szekfü tells of a school prayer which was recited every day during this period, 'I believe in one God: I believe in one Fatherland: I believe in one eternal Godly justice: I believe in the resurrection of Hungary.' Ibid Held, Joseph, *The Columbia History of Eastern Europe in the Twentieth Century*, p. 175.

[52] The election results were tampered with as early as 1928. Instead of the people electing government, 'In Romania...this happens the other way round: the head of state chooses the government; the government arranges the parliamentary majority and then calls on the electorate to endorse it.' Longworth, Philip, *The making of Eastern Europe*, Macmillan 1992, p. 74.

[53] Ibid Longworth, Philip, *The making of Eastern Europe*, p. 75.

the Soviet Union[54]. It is interesting to note that of all Germany's allies, Romania had been the most supportive in the war effort and had thus suffered the most troop casualties[55]. Paradoxically, Hungary had been one of Germany's least accommodating allies; but it failed to renounce its alliance with Germany. Hungary thus suffered great destruction as German troops withdrew and Soviet troops advanced[56]. Although the Czech lands had been formally incorporated into the Reich, together with Romania, which managed to abandon the Axis, it suffered comparatively little physical destruction[57]. Much of Czech industry survived the War intact. In the immediate aftermath of the War this was an advantage, however, in the long term it turned out to be a 'poisoned chalice' as its industrial base was not modernised and quickly became outdated following advances made in the 1950's.

The chaos and destruction caused by the Second World War is difficult to imagine today. Millions of homeless refugees and expellees crowded the roads together with Allied troops. The infrastructure of the region was in many cases severely damaged, if not totally destroyed, and agricultural production had been seriously interrupted. The state had to take the commanding role in many aspects of the economy and society to ensure order and promote recovery. As Germany had commandeered most of its allies' industry, the post-war administrations were obliged to recover it and place it under state control. Disillusion with the

---

[54] Romania received 102 000 km² territory, although the Romanian population formed a majority only on 65 000 km² territory. Ibid Held, Joseph, *The Columbia History of Eastern Europe in the Twentieth Century*, p. 168.

[55] From the start of the war until 23 August, 1944, Romania lost 642 000 troops. 71 000 were killed, 243 000 wounded and 310 000 disappeared. In 1944, the total Romanian population stood at 14 million. From the start of the War until 31 December 1944, Hungary lost 300-310 000 troops. 120-160 000 troops were killed, and 256 431 missing. Lengyel, György, *Hungarian Economy and Society during World War Two*, Columbia University Press 1993, p. 9.

[56] As a result of the War, Hungary lost 39% of its horses, 44% of its cattle, 78% of its pigs, 90% of its large railway bridges, 63% of its medium bridges, 60% of its locomotives and 86% of its freight cars. Budapest was besieged and all its bridges destroyed. Simons, Thomas, W., *Eastern Europe in the Postwar World*, Macmillan 1991, p. 39.

[57] However, the Gestapo killed 38 000 Czechs, mostly intellectuals, effectively destroying the country's potential leaders. Ibid Simons, Thomas, W., *Eastern Europe in the Postwar World*, p. 40.

Introduction

politics which were perceived to have led to National Socialism formed a general post-war consensus accepting an increased role for the state. In addition, the real need for drastic land and social reform, and the fact that all of the countries in question were liberated by the Red Army, enabled the foundations for the Communist system to be laid. These foundations formed the basis for forty years of Communist rule in the region.

These historical experiences constitute the foundations of similarity for this comparative study. The Communist regimes in Hungary, the Czech Republic and Romania shared the same ideology and imposed the same administrative centralism. The system affected the region in a similar way and evoked similar reactions from the populations; there were several attempts to reform, or overthrow the system before the Revolutions of 1989. However, the nature of the Communist legacy seems differentiated. The factors which contribute to the different nature of the Communist legacies will therefore be examined to determine the influence of the Communist legacy on transformation and democratic consoldiation.

v: The Historical Position of Central and Eastern Europe

In order to understand the relevance of this differing influence, it is necessary to keep in mind the controversy surrounding Central and Eastern Europe's historical, geographical and cultural position within the European framework. The position of Central and Eastern Europe, in both the cultural and geographical sense, has always been the subject of intense intellectual and political debate[58].

At the heart of this debate lies the question of where Europe's borders are to be drawn and which countries are to be considered part of the European cultural-historical tradition, and which are not. The debate has been revived as a result of the end of the ideological division of Europe, and one of the cardinal factors in deciding this issue may well become the existence, or not, of democratic structures, institutions and society. The Revolutions in 1989 demonstrated that the states and people of Central and Eastern Europe view themselves as an integral part of Europe. Indeed,

---

[58] See Schöpflin, G., Wood, N., *In Search of Central Europe*, Polity Press 1989.

awareness of their European identity, a desire to return to 'Europe' and what they perceived as a more 'European' development contributed to the collapse of the Communist regimes. 'Western' Europe is now confronted with the task of reassessing its 'cold-war' perception of Europe.

Before the Second World War, the Central and East European area was considered an integral part of the European tradition; indeed, the metropolitans of Central and Eastern Europe, such as Prague, Vienna, Budapest, and Bucharest, were important actors on the European cultural stage. However, it had long been recognised that, in comparison to its western neighbours, Central and Eastern Europe was lagging behind in political and social development.

The reasons for this phenomenon are manifold. Part of the problem was the fact that the Central European states were all members of supranational empires which did not necessarily act in the best interests of the individual regions or nations[59]. Another reason was the relative over-population of Eastern Europe and the lack of land available to the peasants as a result of the absence of a land reform[60]. In this region of Europe, the majority of the land was controlled by a small landed elite, while the majority of the population, the peasants, remained smallholders, if not landless. The relative abundance of peasant labour for agricultural work contributed to the worsening situation. Peasants, tied to small plots of land as subsistence farmers, became enserfed to the landowners as a means of obtaining access to more land, in return for labour on the estate. Thus, paradoxically, although the countryside suffered from over-population, there was a lack of manpower available to work in industry. However, the landed elite remained opposed to

---

[59] An example of this were Austrian trade policies, which ensured that manufacturing industries were based in the Austrian lands while Hungary remained an agricultural producer. Maria Theresa introduced a differential tariff for Austrian industrial goods and Hungarian agricultural produce which favoured Austrian finished goods and Hungarian agricultural goods. Ibid. Chirot, D., *The Origins of Backwardness in Eastern Europe*, p. 220.

[60] In the period 1801-1911, the population in Hungary rose from 13 192 million to 20 886 million. In the Austrian lands the population rose form 13 881 million to 28 572 million. Before 1880, the Balkans had a lower than average rate of population growth, but between 1880 and 1914 the rate of population growth was above the European average. Zeman, Z., A., B., *Pursued by a Bear*, Charto and Windus 1989, p. 16.

land reform as it threatened to destroy their position of power and influence. These factors combined to stall the process of modernisation in Eastern Europe. Yet, although this meant differentiation from 'western' Europe, the region's ties to Europe were not severed and it retained a basically European identity.

Modernisation was further disrupted by the collapse of the multi-national empires in the region, and by the two World Wars. After the Second World War, socialist policies, often with Communist overtones, were viewed by many as a means of overcoming the effects of the War and Eastern Europe's historical backwardness via rapid industrialisation and modernisation; as had been effectively achieved in the Soviet Union. Unfortunately, at this stage, no one was fully aware of the price the Soviet people had paid for this initial success and which Eastern Europe would also have to pay[61].

The crucial point is that, if Central and Eastern Europe is viewed as an integral part of Europe, sharing its cultural and historical heritage of liberalism, humanism and freedom for the individual, this can be viewed as a positive factor favouring a successful transition to democracy. If one comes to the conclusion that Eastern Europe was historically and culturally separate from the rest of Europe, this would by definition exclude Central and Eastern Europe from specifically 'European' organisations and perhaps lead to a more pessimistic assessment of the possible success of democratic transition. Related to this discussion is the question as to the nature of the Communism imposed on Central and Eastern Europe and what influence it has exerted on the region, that is whether Communism exerted a fundamentally non-European influence, and how far this influence has been internalised in the region. As Communism in Eastern Europe was directly transplanted from the Soviet Union, an evaluation of Russia's position in relation to Europe is also necessary to determine the nature of Eastern Europe's experience of Communism, and whether rejection

---

[61] Milan Kundera maintains the tragedy of Central Europe is that it has remained aware of its European history, culture and identity but that, as a result of Communist rule, 'western' Europe has forgotten Central Europe is an integral part of Europe and sees it merely as a part of the Soviet, or rather Russian sphere of influence. Kundera, M., *The Tragedy of Central Europe*, The New York Review of Books, 26 April 1984.

of it can be viewed as an affirmation of the region's European identity. George Schöpflin submits the theory that:

'...Russia may have had European elements in its culture, that it certainly contributed ideas and values to Europe and its culture, and that individual Russians may indeed be Europeans, but it was not a part of the current of European cultural development and, most significantly, excluded itself from that current by the Russian Revolution and its aftermath.'[62]

This seems to confirm that the Russian model of Communism imposed on Central Europe was essentially a non-European model of society, and that in rejecting Communism, Central Europe is returning to a more fitting European model. György Konrad agrees with the view that Russia cannot be classed as European, but comes to the more differentiated conclusion that Russia cannot not simply be classed as European or Asiatic, but is rather a combination of both:

'Die russische Elite denkt in zwei Wertsystemen. Das eine ist das westliche Christliche, europäische, pluralistische, rationalistische, Veränderungen anstrebende Wertsystem, das andere ist das asiatische, autokratische, imperiale, dogmatische, Veränderungen gegenüber fanatische argwöhnische Wertsystem.' ...'Obwohl es zeitweise so aussah, als sei der westliche Ruf schwächer geworden, melden sich neue Westler zu Wort, die das Grundparadoxon der rusischen Seele auffrischen, nämlich daß sie auf asiatische Weise europäisch ist und auf europäische Weise asiatisch.' ...'Die russische Elite konnte sich bis auf den heutigen Tag nicht entscheiden, auf welches der beiden Wertsysteme, ...sie festlegen soll, denn die Antimonie dieser beiden Prinzipiensysteme prägt ihre historische Wirklichkeit, und sie kann auf keines davon verzichten.' ...'Die Russen werden nie eindeutig Asiaten oder eindeutig Europäer sein.

---

[62] Ibid Schöpflin, G., Wood, N., *In Search of Central Europe*, p. 7.

Sie werden höchstens den Akzent zugunsten der einen oder der anderen Seite verlagern.[63]

This description seems to be more fitting, but does not solve the problem of the nature of the Communist regimes imposed on Central and Eastern Europe; for if Russia is a European-Asiatic mix, then the Soviet model of Communism cannot have symbolised a caesura with Central Europe's 'European' development; after all, Communist theory was originally developed in Europe. It is thus important to clarify the nature of Communism in Eastern Europe if one is to study the differing influences of the Communist legacy in Eastern Europe today.

vi: Communism: The Soviet Model

At their inception, the Communist systems in Central and Eastern Europe were a series of blue-prints of Soviet Communism, or rather Stalinism. Although over the course of time they developed in a rather different way to the Soviet system, they still maintained many of its fundamental features.

Lenin was profoundly influenced by, among others, Tkachev (1844-1885). Tkachev believed that the Russian Revolution would be carried out by a small, elite body of professional revolutionaries. This minority revolutionary party would seize power and transform society. However, Tkachev was aware that this task would not be possible without the support of the population. Thus, he advocated organising a national uprising to coincide with the Revolution and conducting a propaganda policy once the Revolution had occurred. The social revolution which he proposed included nationalisation of

---

[63] Konrad, G., *Antipolitik*, Suhrkamp 1985, pp. 85-86. 'The Russian elite thinks in two value systems. One is the western, Christian, European, pluralist, rationalist system which strives for change, the other is the Asiatic, autocratic, imperial, dogmatic system which is fanatically opposed to change.'...'Although it at times looked as if the appeal of the western system had become weaker, new westerners have come to light. They refresh the basic paradox of the Russian soul, that it is European in an Asiatic way and Asiatic in a European way.'....'The Russian elite has not been able to decide to this day on which of the two values systems it should settle upon...since the antipathy of the two systems has shaped their historic reality and they cannot do without one or the other.'....'The Russians will never truly be Asiatic or European. At most, emphasis oscillates from one to the other.' Translation Wendy Hollis.

the land and the means of production. The concept of freedom does not appear anywhere in his works.

Although Tkachev had been severely criticised by Engels, Lenin decreed that Tkachev's works should be read by all Bolsheviks. A more extreme position was advocated by Bakunin (1814-1876). He rejected any kind of order at all and saw salvation in the complete overthrow and destruction of the present society and order. He believed that from the chaos would arise a new brotherhood of man. Thus, his followers prepared for revolt and destruction[64].

Marx and Engels observed several ancient Asiatic systems from which they concluded that the key to their success was the fact that there was no private property and that the state, or rather the King, had control of the means of production, that is the water supply. However, as Frank Babaria notes, the systems were all centralistic and despotic[65]. He concludes that there is a powerful relationship between a nationalised economy and the despotic state it nourishes. In addition to this, Lenin's theory of the unity of will at the work place is in reality only possible via the appointment of a dictator. This is exposed in his pondering over the question of how to ensure the unity of will of the workers:

> '...How can strict unity of will be ensured? By thousands subordinating their will to one...But be that as it may, unquestioning submission to a single will is absolutely necessary for the success of labour processes that are based on large-scale machinery.'[66]

Thus, he advocates, 'the appointment of individual persons, dictators with unlimited powers'. Regarded in this light, socialism as defined by the Russian Revolution and experience will invariably result in a form of despotism.

Stalin introduced further modifications and perfected the system of administrative centralism. However, this was not necessarily an aberration of Communism. The Communist Manifesto declares

---

[64] Schapiro, L., *The Communist Party of the Soviet Union*, Methuen and Co Ltd 1963, pp. 4-5.
[65] Ibid Barbaria, Frank, A., *Modern 'Asiatic' Despotism*.
[66] Ibid Barbaria, Frank, A., *Modern 'Asiatic' Despotism*, p. 15. Original in Lenin, V., I., *Selected Works Vol. VII*, New York, pp. 342-344.

that, 'in Communist society, the present dominates the past'[67]. Thus, even time would be subject to the dictates of the Party according to its needs. Vladimir Tismaneanu believes that herein lies the fundamental problem with Marxism:

> *'It seems to me that there is a voluntaristic, almost irrational undercurrent in Marxism that could account for many of the perversions this doctrine was bound to undergo. Together with the romantics, Marxism emphasises the ontological superiority of the community over the individual. I regard Marxism as a most elaborated form of ethical realism and I consider therefore that both Leninism and Stalinism are not alien to the ideological intentions of the founding fathers.'*[68]

Kenneth Minogue comes to the conclusion that the realisation of a Communist society is an impossible dream because, in attempting to realise it, one must negate life and enter a suicide pact which aims to destroy in order that something better may come into being:

> *'A condition of things in which all strife between essence and existence had been removed might possibly be a thing of beauty, but there would be no one to contemplate such beauty ...It is not a possible condition for human beings, and this means that ideology poses an essentially insoluble problem for the West. In pronouncing the rottenness of a civilization, it is actually declaring a hatred of any possible human life. What it proposes is the cosmic equivalent of a suicide pact.'*[69]

Stalin erected a tyranny, but it was a tyranny that was accepted as a means of preventing a return to capitalism. He also perfected an ethical revolution in which traditional values of good and evil, of

---

[67] Tismaneanu, Vladimir, *The Crisis of Marxist Ideology in Eastern Europe*, Routledge 1988, p. 16. Orignal in *Marx Engels Reader*, p. 485.
[68] Ibid Tismaneanu, Vladimir, *The Crisis of Marxist Ideology in Eastern Europe*, p. 3.
[69] Minogue, Kenneth, *Alien Powers: The Pure Theory of Ideology*, St. Martin's Press 1985, p. 222.

vice and virtue were re-evaluated. Thus, reprehensible deeds were commended by the Party if they furthered the cause of Communism. The Party fused itself with this new morality and, using this ideology, effectively freed itself from any moral constraints.

And yet, despite the glaring contradiction between the reality of the Stalinist system and the professed ideals of Communism, the system did not lose its attractiveness to those who believed in the ideology, even to those who were affected by the Purges. As Goldstücker realises:

> *'You see: it is the problem of the conflict of rational criticism and belief. The stronger you believe, the weaker becomes your rational criticism or your critical faculties and your readiness to apply them.'*[70]

The willingness to believe absolutely in Communist ideology is a fundamental prerequisite of the Communist system, since it requires that one trust the Party absolutely and obey without question.

This was the system which was passed on to Eastern Europe. Although Communism inevitably underwent a certain 'Russification', these modifications were not necessarily incompatible with the original Communist doctrine. Thus, although it was extremely hostile to the 'European' system of social and state organisation, the Communism which was imposed on Eastern Europe cannot be viewed as a totally non-European model of society. The extent to which the Communist legacy still effects the countries chosen for study may be regarded as the measure of the possible success of democratisation; of Europeanisation. The process of democratisation and transformation can therefore be viewed as a test of Central and Eastern Europe's 'Europeanness' in the sense that a successful transition is an affirmation of the region's European identity. Thus, differentiated influence of the Communist legacy may affect the ability, or not, to achieve a successful transformation.

---

[70] Charlton, Michael, *The Eagle and the Small Birds*, BBC 1984, p. 89.

CHAPTER ONE

COMMUNISM IN CENTRAL AND EASTERN EUROPE AFTER WORLD WAR TWO

'The first and most important quality of a Soviet man is his total commitment to Communist ideas and his devotion to the Party.'
Alexander Zinoviev, *Homo Sovieticus*.

*

Since the end of the Second World War and until the Revolutions of 1989, Central Europe had been frozen within the confines of the Soviet Bloc. Although this situation initially contributed to the stabilisation of the post-war *status quo*, it became the main source of European instability and immobility as the Soviet system of politics was incapable of dealing with the deepening economic, political and social crises facing it both at home and in Central Europe. It is difficult to asses the extent to which the system itself caused these crises, but it is clear that the Soviet system, which had retained its Stalinist command administration[1], was not only completely incapable of reacting to the needs and demands of the modern society and industrial base it

---

[1] Khrushchev started de-Stalinisation at the XX Congress of the Communist Party of the Soviet Union (CPSU) in 1956 with his 'Secret Speech', but the programme was mainly aimed at exposing the personality cult and stressed Stalin's personal responsibility for the excesses of his rule. It did not aim to change the fundamentals of the Stalinist System. Thus, the Warsaw Pact and the CMEA were reactivated, ideology was stressed and bilateral ties were increased as a means of ensuring Soviet control. Albania's defection in 1961, the Sino-Soviet split, and the Cuban Crisis of 1962 discredited de-Stalinisation under Khrushchev and contributed to his downfall in 1964. See Brown, J., F., *Eastern Europe and Communist Rule*, Duke University Press 1988, pp. 7-9.

had helped create, but also of creating the conditions required for the further development necessary in the post-industrial age. Gorbachev recognised this, but could not make the necessary ideological break with Communism, so he tried to reform rather than transform. Indeed, attempts at reform have been a repeating occurrence within the Soviet Bloc. Unfortunately, they invariably led to a general de-stabilisation of power, which in turn evoked retreat from reform.

The Soviet Stalinist system imposed on Eastern Europe after the Second World War had never been stable. Continuous ferment erupted periodically in revolt; 1948 witnessed the break with Yugoslavia, caused by the rather paradoxical fact that Tito was, initially at least, more eager for immediate implementation of full-blown Stalinist policies than Stalin himself[2]; the Berlin Uprising and the Pilsen riots took place in 1953; 1956 saw the Posnan riots in Poland and the Hungarian Uprising; Albania defected from the Soviet Bloc in 1961; the Prague Spring and the ensuing Romanian deviation led by Ceausescu occurred in 1968; and the Polish crisis of 1977 was ongoing until the complete collapse in 1981[3]. Viewed in this light, the period of Soviet rule in Eastern Europe was not a factor of stability, but rather a factor which contributed to the continuation of instability and crisis. This development, or rather non-development, in Central and Eastern Europe stands in stark contrast to Western Europe, which experienced continuously increasing stability and welfare in the post-war period.

The countries under discussion, Hungary, the Czech Republic and Romania, all had Communist governments which were more or less installed and kept in power by the occupying Soviet military forces. Any popular support they enjoyed was often due to general disillusion with pre-war political forces, to the Communist Party's impressive organisation and discipline, and to the policy of land redistribution, which had been long overdue and which the Communists ensured they controlled at local level. They were also initially at pains to keep more radical policies, such as collectivisation, if not secret, than at least out of the public arena.

---

[2] The Cominform had been established in 1947 to curtail outbreaks of 'domesticism'.
[3] Ibid. Brown, J., F., *Eastern Europe and Communist Rule*, pp. 5-6.

All embarked on a rapid policy of reconstruction based on extensive production, heavy industry and nationalisation. By 1947, 45% of Hungarian industry had been nationalised. This figure rose to 81% by 1949. In Romania, the figure stood at 11% in 1947, but had risen to 95% by 1948. In Czechoslovakia, 80% of industry was nationalised by 1947, and the figure increased to 92% by 1950[4]. Collectivisation of the newly redistributed land proved more problematical and took much longer than anticipated because the peasants were not eager to give up their recently obtained land to the collectives envisaged by the Parties.

Although Romania boasted the highest rate of investment in industry, 34% of the produced national income in 1953, it also had the slowest rate of collectivisation[5]. Forced collectivisation disrupted agriculture and in 1953 agricultural production in Romania was lower than pre-war levels[6]. By 1958, Romania had collectivised 55% of its farmland, but Czechoslovakia had collectivised 75%[7]. In 1961, Gheorghe Dej ordered the army be used to impose collectivisation[8]. Collectivisation was finally completed in 1962. Although collectivisation of the land was an ideological imperative, the Stalinist Romanian Communist Party leaders believed fervently in the supremacy of heavy industry as a symbol of progress and modernisation. This reinforced their determination that Romania, a country traditionally specialised in agriculture, should not become a 'vegetable garden'[9] and concentrate on agricultural production, as had been proposed at the 1962 June meeting of the newly revived Council for Mutual Economic Assistance (CMEA)[10]. This suggestion offended Gheorghe Dej's Stalinist concept of progress being synonymous

---

[4] Fowkes, Ben, *Aufstieg und Niedergang des Kommunismus in Osteuropa*, Decaton Verlag 1994, p. 28.
[5] Simons, Thomas, W., *Eastern Europe in the Postwar World*, Macmillan 1991, p. 94.
[6] Harrington, Joseph, F., Courtney, Bruce, J., *Tweaking the Nose of the Russians*, Columbia University Press 1991, p. 148.
[7] Revesz, Gabor, *Perestroika in Eastern Europe*, Westview Press 1990, p. 46.
[8] Brogan, Patrick, *Eastern Europe 1939-1989*, Bloomsbury 1990, p. 219.
[9] Crampton, R., J., *Eastern Europe in the Twentieth Century*, Routledge 1994, p. 313.
[10] Rothschild, J., *Return to Diversity*, Oxford University Press 1989, p. 162.

with industrialisation, concentrated on heavy industry, and therefore also his nationalism. Thus, the huge industrial monoliths built during the Communist period were viewed by the Romanian Party as symbols of progress and national pride, and were presented to the population as such.

In 1949, at the end of Imre Nagy's tenure as Minister of Agriculture, 2% of Hungarian peasants were members of cooperatives. It is partly as a consequence of this that he vanished from Hungarian government in 1948, a fact which enabled him to survive the Purges. Between 1950 and 1953, 23% of Hungarian peasants were forced to join cooperatives or collectives, but increased tax burdens and compulsory state deliveries left 800 000 peasants with no seed for the 1953 crops. Indeed, Hungarian agriculture was on the verge of collapse when Imre Nagy was recalled to become Prime Minister in 1953[11]. During the 1956 Revolution, the peasants left the cooperatives. Starting in 1957, they were induced to rejoin, but not by force. By 1961, 94% of the land had been collectivised[12]. Thereafter, Hungarian agriculture became one of the more successful in the Soviet Bloc. This was partly due to the numerous reforms it underwent, which gave the cooperatives almost full independence and control over their marketing policies. The cooperatives also paid the peasants rent, albeit minimal, for the use of their land. This preserved the illusion that the land still belonged to the peasants and not the state.

The governments all shared a Communist pedigree, but they also exhibited a considerable degree of variety, not in their ultimate policies and aims, but in the means and ways in which they exercised and defended their power and dealt with the consequences of their policies. In this sense they had a differentiated effect on their respective populations and economies.

Although totalitarianism is arguably an absolute state, for want of a better expression, it is differences in the degree of Communist totalitarianism practised which contribute to an understanding and explanation of the current variations in transformation and levels of democratic consolidation observable in Hungary, the Czech

---

[11] Ibid. Revesz, Gabor, *Perestroika in Eastern Europe*, p. 36.
[12] Ibid. Revesz, Gabor, *Perestroika in Eastern Europe*, p. 46.

Republic and Romania. Differences between the personalities involved and the historical experiences and levels of social, political and industrial development influenced and moulded the characters of the Communist Parties which gained power after the Second World War. Their different histories affected their modes of operation and the members who were attracted to them.

The fact that the Communist Party of Czechoslovakia had been able to operate legally during the inter-war period and also enjoyed a measure of genuine domestic support amongst the industrial work force most certainly influenced the way it operated[13]. Although Gottwald started bolshevisation of the Party in 1929, the majority of Party members were accustomed to, and mostly abided by, democratic parliamentary procedure. In the 1946 elections, the Communist Party obtained 38% of the vote[14]. It seemed to be quite content to await success in a parliamentary election, in accordance with the legalistic traditions of democracy in the Czech Republic and amongst its own members. At this stage it could almost be compared, at first glance at least, to the Italian Communist Party of the time.

Unlike the Romanian, and to a lesser extent the Hungarian Party, the Czechoslovak Party was already in possession of a reasonably large, and moreover relatively intact, industrial base. This meant that, in contrast particularly to Romania, it did not have to rely entirely upon the Stalinist programme of forced industrialisation to reconstruct and modernise. This economic factor also contributed to the relative stability of the Stalinist regime and was in part responsible for the delayed de-Stalinisation of the Party. The Czech Communist Party only changed its original policy of gradualism when ordered to by Stalin. Even then, the Party remained tied to its earlier legal traditions and legislated meticulously. It was the only Communist country to have an official law governing the Labour and Internment Camps which the Communist Party subsequently set up.

---

[13] The strong domestic position of the Czech Communist Party, an estimated 38% of workers in industry and the mines supported the Communists in 1934, may have influenced the decision to withdraw the Red Army by November 1945. Ibid. Fowkes, Ben, *Aufstieg und Niedergang des Kommunismus in Osteuropa*, p. 24.
[14] Ibid. Brogan, Patrick, *Eastern Europe 1939-1989*, p. 80.

When the Coup came in 1948, it was a legal Coup and the Party made sure that the new Communist government was officially sworn in by the President. This was an attempt to gain domestic support and ensure that the government was justifiable on legal grounds. And yet ironically, the Czech Communist Party, although one of the most legalistic, became one of the most disciplined, orthodox Stalinist Parties in the region and was even planning new Purges after Stalin's death in 1953[15]. So, those who obtained the confessions for the Prague Show Trials of the 1940's were themselves tried in 1955; although the three of their victims still alive were not released until the late fifties, and none of the victims were rehabilitated until 1963[16]. The Czech Party's belated de-Stalinisation programme, which gained momentum in 1968, was halted and reversed by the Warsaw Pact invasion, which left it completely paralysed until its collapse in 1989.

The Communist Party elites initiated Stalinist Purges on Moscow's orders, but they also used them to rid themselves of rivals for power. Specific factions within the Party emerged during the ensuing power struggle. Defeated groups were consequently most affected by liquidation. One group consisted of the Party's Jewish members. The large number of Jewish Communists affected by the Purges, especially in Czechoslovakia[17], could have been a consequence of their high numbers within the Party and a perceived need to gain domestic support by purging 'foreign' elements. The Jewish Communists had frequently spent the War years in exile in Moscow. They represented a 'muscovite' faction within the Party and were totally loyal to Stalin and the Soviet Union. They competed for power with a 'national' group. The 'national' grouping within the Communist elite had not been in exile in the Soviet Union during the War. They had remained at home, often in prison or concentration camps. Some had also fought in the Spanish

---

[15] For an insight into the reasons for this, see Skilling, H., Gordon, 'Stalinism and Czechoslovak Political Culture'. In Tucker, R., C., (Ed.), *Stalinism: Essays in Historical Interpretation*, W. W. Norton & Co. Inc. 1977, p. 257.
[16] Ibid. Brogan, P., *Eastern Europe 1939-1989*, p. 91.
[17] The anti-Jewish character of the Czechoslovak Trials can also be traced back to the Soviet campaign against Zionism and Israel during Stalin's last years. Ibid. Skilling, H., G., 'Stalinism and Czechoslovak Political Culture'. In Tucker, R., C., *Stalinism: Essays in Historical Interpretation*, p. 273.

Civil War. As it was necessary to uncover 'enemies' as evidence of one's own reliability, the Purges gained a momentum of their own and ran out of control. One of the most notorious examples of this is the Trial of Rudolf Slansky.

Rudolf Slansky was a stalwart Stalinist, but had spent the War in Czechoslovakia. He had been a close associate and personal friend of Klement Gottwald and had helped to organise the 1948 Coup which brought the Communists to power. He supervised the arrest of non-Communists and set up the first Czech Concentration Camps in 1948. He had set the Purge in motion on Beria's orders and heralded it as a necessary 'purification' of Party members:

> *'The enemy is penetrating our ranks: it is necessary to examine every Party member. Our Party must pass through a purification process.'*[18]

As Secretary General of the Party in charge of security, he presumably considered himself above suspicion. It was he who ordered the arrest of Vladimir Clementis, Arthur London and Eugen Loebel. However at the trial, which opened on 20 November, 1952, the main defendants were Clementis and Slansky. Gottwald had been forced to order Slansky's arrest after Stalin's direct intervention[19]. Further delay would have thrown suspicion onto Gottwald himself. Of the fourteen members of the Czechoslovak Communist Party accused at the 'Slansky Trial', eleven were Jewish. All 14 defendants pleaded guilty to all the charges. Eight of them, all Jewish, were sentenced to death, and three to life imprisonment[20]. They had been liquidated by the rival 'muscovite' group who had spent the War in exile in Moscow.

---

[18] Ibid. Brogan, P., *Eastern Europe 1939-1989*, p. 86.
[19] On 11 November, 1951, Stalin wrote to Gottwald insisting Slansky be arrested. The letter was delivered personally by Anastas Mikoyan. Gottwald wrote a draught reply insisting on Slansky's innocence, but this letter was never sent. After a brief hesitation, Gottwald entrusted himself to Stalin's judgement and concluded Stalin must have some information he did not possess. Ibid. Skilling, H., G., 'Stalinism and Czechoslovak Political Culture'. In Tucker, R., C., *Stalinism: Essays in Historical Interpretation*, p. 272.
[20] Ibid. Brogan, P., *Eastern Europe 1939-1989*, pp. 86-90.

As previously mentioned, many members of the 'muscovite' faction within the Communist Parties were themselves Jewish and had fled the National Socialist terror. They had completely assimilated the Stalinist mentality and ideology and no longer regarded themselves as Jewish. This enabled them to treat all rivals for power with equal brutality. Triumph of the 'muscovite' Stalinist faction meant that only those Stalinists who were absolutely loyal to Stalin were left in power.

The groupings within the Party often overlapped and personal rivalries also played a role in the struggle. Thus, Imre Nagy was not Jewish, but had spent the War in exile in Moscow and had worked at a Radio Station where he was able to survive the Purges[21]. He originally held the post of Minister of Interior in the 1945 Hungarian coalition government, but was soon replaced by László Rajk who proved more suited to the task. Nagy became Minister of Agriculture and gained much personal popularity as he became identified with the land redistribution of 1945, during which no attempts were made to collectivise[22]. Although associated with the 'muscovite' group, Nagy was not in close association with Rakosi. Indeed, Rakosi increasingly came to view him as a rival. Partly as a result of his reluctance to collectivise agriculture, and his fall from favour with Rakosi, Nagy was demoted and expelled from the Central Committee in 1948, and later the Party. Ironically, Nagy's fall from power, and consequent distance from it, facilitated his survival of the Purges.

So, in the case of the Hungarian Party, it was the Jewish faction within the 'muscovite' grouping which triumphed as a result of the Purges, whereas in Czechoslovakia it was the non-Jewish 'muscovite' faction. In Romania the 'national' non-Jewish faction liquidated both its Jewish and 'muscovite' rivals.

The Romanian and Hungarian Communist Party had operated illegally in the inter-war period and had achieved limited success. At the end of World War Two, there were only an estimated 2500 members of the Communist Party in Hungary and a mere 1000 in

---

[21] Ibid. Brogan, P., *Eastern Europe 1939-1989*, p. 118.
[22] Ibid. Brogan, P., *Eastern Europe 1939-1989*, p. 119.

Romania[23]. The Communist Party in Romania was viewed almost universally as an alien force partly because of its links with Soviet Russia[24]; it supported the Soviet claim to Bessarabia, but more significantly because the overwhelming majority of its members came from minority groups, notably Jews and Hungarians[25]. The overwhelmingly rural Romanian peasant population was also mainly interested in providing for its own needs and was highly suspicious of outside political interference in daily life.

1.1.1: The Jewish Factor
It is interesting to note that Jews were prevalent in all the Communist Parties. They had been particularly active in the Hungarian Party. Of the fifteen members of the first Central Committee in Hungary in 1918, ten were Jewish, and of the 200 highest ranking officers of Bela Kun's Hungarian Soviet Republic in 1919, three quarters were Jewish. This trend continued after the Second World War. Every Secretary General of the Hungarian Communist Party from Bela Kun to Ernö Gerö was Jewish. Jews were particularly well represented amongst the members of the political police; they accounted for approximately 70-80% of its leaders[26]. They, along with the majority of Hungarian Jews, had attempted to assimilate themselves into Hungarian culture and society and had adopted Hungarian identities and names as a means of confirming their Hungarian, and concealing their Jewish, identity. For the Communists this was not only a final symbolic severance from the Jewish tradition, but in the light of continuing

---

[23] Gati, Charles, *The Bloc that Failed*, Indiana University Press 1990, p. 15. See Appendix II.
[24] Although the Party was founded in Bucharest on 8 May, 1921 as a 'Section of the Communist International', it was directly subordinated to the Moscow based Comintern. Indeed, so intense were the personal factional struggles within the Party between 1928-1930, that the Comintern appointed a foreigner, the Pole Alexander Stefanski, as Secretary General of the Romanian Communist Party. This practice was continued until Gheorghe Dej became Secretary General. For a history of the Romanian Communist Party, see Tismaneanu, Vladimir, 'Ceausescu's Socialism', *Problems of Communism*, January-February 1985.
[25] Held, Joseph, *The Columbia History of Eastern Europe in the Twentieth Century*, Columbia University Press 1992, p. 11.
[26] Gati, Charles, *Hungary and the Soviet Bloc*, Duke University Press 1986, pp. 100-101.

discrimination and prejudice against Jews even after the experience of the War, a political necessity. The alternative group identity and promise of equality in a new society which the Communist Party offered was attractive to many Jews who had survived the War. Thus, Rakosi was originally Roth, Gerö was Singer, Farkas was Wolf, Vas was originally Weinberger, and Gábor Péter, the Head of the political police, the *AVO*, was in reality Benö Auspitz[27].

The Hungarian Communist Party enjoyed a very limited appeal, partly due to its connection with Bela Kun's disastrous Hungarian Soviet Republic of 1919, and partly due to the prominent number of Jews amongst its members, which gave the impression that it was a foreign element in Hungarian politics[28]. As a result, anti-Semitism continued to be a force in Hungary after the Second World War, but it took on a rather different character as it was directed against the political authority of the Jews as symbolised by the Communist Party. Stalin was aware of this problem and as a consequence no Jews were present in Hungary's Provisional Government. However, it was the 'Jewish-muscovite' faction centred around Matyas Rakosi[29], Ernö Gerö, Mihaly Farkas and Gábor Péter[30] which initially triumphed over the 'national' group of László Rajk, János Kádár and Gyula Kallai[31].

The Romanian Communist Party was almost non-existent at the end of the Second World War. Military personnel outnumbered civilians in the Romanian government of August 1944, and it was Andrei Vyshinski who, having arrived from Moscow on 23 February 1945 to decide the new Romanian government, presented King Michael with an ultimatum forcing him to accept Petru Groza

---

[27] Ibid. Gati, Charles, *Hungary and the Soviet Bloc*, p. 100.

[28] Grebing, Helga, *Der Revisionismus: Von Bernstein bis zum Prager Frühling*, Verlag C. H. Beck 1977, p. 203.

[29] Rakosi spent 16 years in the Horthy's jails before escaping to the Soviet Union. It is difficult to understand how he survived for such a long time in what must have been unbearable conditions. The answer may lie in the Communists belief that everything is justified as long as the cause of Communism is furthered. Rakosi spoke nine languages and had worked in London, but was in Petrograd for the October Revolution. His own position was based on his relationship to Stalin.

[30] Bela Kun was liquidated as a Trotskyite in the Soviet Union during the Stalinist Purges.

[31] Staar, Richard, F., *The Communist Regimes in Eastern Europe (2nd. Edition)*, Hoover Institute Press 1971, p.116.

as the new Prime Minister[32]. Although given the situation, the King's approval was not strictly necessary, the Communists recognised the importance of a seemingly legal take-over of power as a means to profess legitimacy. For all practical purposes, Romania was under direct Soviet control. Indeed, the Allied Control Commission documents in Romania, bear the title 'Allied (Soviet) Commission of Control'[33].

The weakness of the Romanian Party made it a source of unpredictability for the Soviet Union. In addition, the history of violent factional struggles amongst the Romanian Communist leaders made them appear unreliable. Soviet advisors supervised the Plan for Reconstruction[34] and were in direct control of the coordination of the Purge Trials until 1954[35]. In this situation, the Soviet Union viewed it as imperative to install a reliable Communist government in Romania as soon as possible. In the elections held in Romania in 1946, 75% of the votes were cast for Iuliu Maniu of the National Peasant Party. However, after a recount two days later, the Romanian Communist Party was declared the winner[36].

Romania was to suffer the most intense 'Sovietisation' of all three countries. The cause of this can be seen as a result of the total lack of indigenous theoretical Communist discourse within Romania and the specific characters and peasant background of the poorly educated 'national' Stalinist faction of the Communist Party which eventually gained control. This doomed the Party to adopt a simplified and fixed form of Stalinist dogma from the Soviet Union. Nicolae Ceausescu's cousin Flora remembers Ceausescu's

---

[32] Almond, Mark, *The Rise and Fall of Nicolae and Elena Ceausescu*, Chapmans 1992, p. 50.
[33] Interview with Liana Petrescu, *România Libera*. Bucharest 15.3.96.
[34] The Romanian Recovery Plan was finally presented in 1948, it was a source of embarrassment for the Romanian government as the other countries had managed to draft plans in 1946. Ibid. Simons, Thomas, W., *Eastern Europe in the Postwar World*, p. 59.
[35] See Hodos, G., H., *Show Trials, Stalinist Purges in Eastern Europe 1948-1954*, New York 1987.
[36] Golea, Traian, *Romania beyond the Limits of Endurance*, Romanian Historical Studies 1988, p. 26.

father asking him why he had been to prison. Ceausescu is said to have replied:

> *'I went to jail so we can work the land with heavy machinery and we can raise production.'*[37]

Weakness of ideology was a factor which contributed to the Romanian political elite's obsession with retaining absolute power, and the brutality with which they went about achieving it. This weakness afflicted all the countries under consideration and became a crucial factor determining reform. Ideology was instrumental in mobilising the masses and legitimising the dictatorship of the Party, but increasingly became purely a means to maintain power.

Despite the weakness of the domestic Communist movement in Romania, the faction of 'national' Stalinist leaders grouped around Gheorghe Dej managed to liquidate not only their 'muscovite' contemporaries, but also other rival 'national' groupings within the Party, and remained in power right up until 1989. The 'muscovite' group were mostly Jewish or non-ethnic Romanians[38]. Its most prominent members included Ana Pauker, originally Rabinovici, a Rabbi's daughter from Bessarabia. It was she who propagated the policy of recruiting former Fascists to increase the number of Communist Party members. She had demonstrated her loyalty to the Party in Moscow by denouncing her husband as a Trotskyite in the 1930's. Thereafter he was shot. Vasile Luca, originally László Lucas, an ethnic Hungarian from the Bukovina, and Emil Bodnaras, a Ukrainian from the Bukovina were also members of this faction[39].

The credit for the dubious achievement of complete liquidation of an entire faction within the Party elite must go to Gheorghe Gheorghiu Dej. He benefited from Moscow's decision to improve the national base of the Romanian Communist Party to counter the negative impression which had been created by the succession of

---

[37] Ibid. Almond, Mark, *The Rise and Fall of Nicolae and Elena Ceausescu*, p. 37. Original from *The Independent*, 8.1.90.
[38] For an explanation of the nature of Romanian Communism and the Romanian Communist elite, see Tismaneanu, Vladimir, 'The Tragicomedy of Romanian Communism', *East European Politics and Societies*, Vol. 3, No. 2, Spring 1989.
[39] Ibid. Brogan, P., *Eastern Europe 1939-1989*, p. 217.

Communism in Central and Eastern Europe... 37

foreign Party leaders. However, once installed in power, Dej liquidated all his remaining potential rivals. Having demonstrated Romania's loyalty to the Soviet Union by holding Imre Nagy in prison until his return to Hungary, Gheorghe Dej managed to effect the withdrawal of the Red Army in 1958. Interestingly, it was none other than Nicolae Ceausescu whom Gheorghe Dej chose to deal with the Hungarian situation[40]. Ceausescu had already shown his ability for ruthlessness in his position in charge of organising collectivisation. Indeed, in 1946, as supervisor of the elections in Slatina, the local newspaper, *Glasul Adverarului*, reported him as stabbing and killing Vasile Lupu, a Bank Manager who had refused to contribute to Communist Party funds[41]. It was this ruthlessness which enabled the 'national' faction of the Romanian Communist Party to achieve power, and it was ruthlessness which was the means by which it retained that power.

The situation was similar in Hungary. The Hungarian elections of November 1945 gave the Smallholders 57% of the votes, while the Communists obtained only 17%[42]. However, the Smallholders were forced into a broad coalition by the Allied Control Commission and Matyas Rakosi began his infamous 'Salami tactics', gradually slicing off potential rivals for power. Hungary was declared a People's Democracy in 1948[43]. However, the Hungarian Communist Party, aware of its limited appeal, was initially careful to present itself as a party of democratic reform and called upon Kossuth's national ideals rather than those of socialism[44]. Bela Kun was labelled a 'left-wing deviationist'. Continued electoral failure led to Stalinisation and radicalisation of

---

[40] Ibid. Almond, Mark, *The Rise and Fall of Nicolae and Elena Ceausescu*, p. 60.
[41] Ibid. Almond, Mark, *The Rise and Fall of Nicolae and Elena Ceausescu*, p. 54.
[42] Ibid. Gati, Charles, *The Bloc that Failed*, p. 11.
[43] For more information on the nature of the take-over, see Hammond, T., T., *The Anatomy of Communist Take-overs*, Yale University Press 1975, p. 398.
[44] Kossuth had led the Hungarian army to victory over the Austrians in 1848-49. Kaiser Franz Joseph had to call on the Russians to restore order and save his monarchy. The young poet Alexander (Sandor) Petöfi died in 1849 at the age of 27 during service in Kossuth's army. Thus, Kossuth and Petöfi represent Hungarian nationalism combined with anti-Russian sentiment. Petöfi became the national figure associated with the Hungarian Uprising of 1956.. In Singer, Ladislaus, *Der ungarische Weg*, Seewald Verlag 1978, pp. 16-17.

the Party, although it remained aware of the need to maintain the mantle of legality.

The Hungarian Party elite was extremely sectarian and also engaged in an internal power struggle which divided those returning from exile in Moscow and those who had spent the war in Hungary. As in Czechoslovakia, the most loyal Stalinist faction gained the advantage, but in contrast, the Hungarian 'muscovite' faction was overwhelmingly Jewish. Ironically, only in Romania, the country with the weakest domestic Communist tradition and the greatest level of direct Soviet control, did the 'national' Stalinists manage to completely liquidate the rival, mostly Jewish, 'muscovite' grouping. Once this had been achieved and Romania's 'deviation' set in motion, the Soviet Union could no longer be relied upon to provide a guarantee for their power. So, the Romanian Communist Party elite increasingly manipulated nationalism as a means of gaining limited domestic legitimacy and securing their power base.

1.1.2: De-Stalinisation

The illegal and conspiratorial nature of the Hungarian and Romanian Communist Parties shaped their political character. Their internal power struggles were exceedingly brutal and savage, as were the regimes they installed. Whereas the Czechoslovak Communist Party took on the form of a well-disciplined and ordered Stalinist Party, the Hungarian and Romanian Parties, although just as Stalinist, were wracked by internal battles between rival power groupings. The power struggle amongst the Hungarian Party elite, combined with increased pressure for de-Stalinisation[45], caused the Party's total collapse in 1956.

The Romanian Party managed to avoid any form of de-Stalinisation at all. Gheorghe Dej manipulated the de-Stalinisation programme to his own advantage in the internal power struggle amongst the Party elite. Although himself a convinced Stalinist, Dej had rid himself of the rival 'muscovite' group of Stalinists within

---

[45] Rakosi was both President and Prime Minister in 1953. He was summoned to Moscow with Imre Nagy, who had survived the Purges, and was forced to give up the post of Prime Minister to Nagy. Ibid. Brogan, P., *Eastern Europe 1939-1989*, p. 122.

the Party during the Purges. In contrast to the other countries, the Romanian Show Trials were not as spectacular, and the victims were not chosen by the Soviet advisors, but suggested by the General Secretary, that is Dej, and accepted by his advisors. Under the guise of de-Stalinisation Dej's remaining potential rivals amongst the 'national' Communist elite were liquidated[46].

In order to avoid falling foul of de-Stalinisation himself, Dej temporarily relinquished his post as First Secretary on 5 October, 1955, although he remained Prime Minister, and distanced himself from Stalin, with whom he was associated[47]. He increased the minimum wage and closed a number of concentration camps, but after the Hungarian Uprising had been put down they were re-opened. Autonomous districts for the Szeklers, a Hungarian minority, were founded, but the Romanian and Hungarian Universities in Cluj were ordered to merge in 1959[48]. Indeed, one year after relinquishing his post as First Secretary of the Party, he was re-elected to it[49]. Dej successfully employed both the Purges and de-Stalinisation to secure his own power base. Having secured personal power, his rigid Stalinist policies, now tinged with nationalism, were continued. It could therefore be claimed that Romania's 'deviation' from the Soviet model began the moment the Romanian 'national' Communists secured their power under Gheorghe Dej.

The disciplined and united Czech Communist Party elite was able to delay de-Stalinisation until the 1960's. Ironically, this delay made de-Stalinisation even more problematical when it was finally introduced. Its effects and conceivable consequences caused the exogenous intervention carried out by the Warsaw Pact. In the

---

[46] The most distinguished of these was Lucretiu Patrascanu. He had been appointed Minister of Justice by King Michael following the 1944 Coup. In February 1948, he was denounced as a Menshevik and expelled from the Communist Party. He was tried and executed secretly in 1954. De-Stalinisation, made him a potential alternative to Gheorghe Dej. Ibid. Tismaneanu, Vladimir, 'Ceausescu's Socialism', *Problems of Communism*.
[47] Rothschild, J., *Return to Diversity*, Oxford University Press 1989, p. 161.
[48] Ibid. Brogan, P., *Eastern Europe 1939-1989*, pp. 221-222.
[49] Hartmann, Jürgen, *Politik und Gesellschaft in Osteuropa*, Campus Verlag 1985, p. 148.

aftermath of the 1968 intervention, the belated de-Stalinisation programme was reversed.

Although in Hungary the Stalinist faction led by Rakosi was able to gain the upper hand, it was not a united faction. As a result, the Purges were particularly brutal, reflecting the numerous internal struggles and also the brutal Stalinism which Rakosi propagated[50]. László Rajk was the Hungarian Interior Minister who began the Purges in 1948. To demonstrate loyalty to the Soviet Union, which had just terminated its relations with Yugoslavia and Tito, the Hungarian Show Trials were based entirely on various charges of 'Titoism' and espionage for Yugoslavia.

As Chief of the secret police, László Rajk had liquidated the democratic opposition in preparation for the Communist take-over. He had also spoken out for a quicker move towards dictatorship and thus come into conflict with Rakosi, who favoured more gradual tactics. As in the Slansky case, Rajk became a victim of his own Purge as it gathered momentum. He was demoted to Foreign Minister and arrested in May 1949. Rajk was tried in September 1949 along with seven other prominent Communists in the first 'Show Trial' in Eastern Europe. Five of the accused were sentenced to death[51]. Rajk was hanged in October 1949. The new Interior Minister supervising the Rajk Trial was none other than János Kádár. Kádár himself fell victim during the second Purge in 1951[52].

During the course of the Purges an estimated 2000 Hungarian Communist Party members were executed and 150 000 imprisoned. A further 300 000 were expelled from the Party. Since Party membership was required for access to almost every conceivable aspect of life, this was also a brutal form of punishment[53]. However, the Party remained divided and it was these divisions which, under the pressure of de-Stalinisation, contributed to its total

---

[50] Between 1948-1950, the Czechoslovak Communist Party expelled 250 000 members, the Romanian Communist Party 192 000 members, no mean feat considering its minimal membership immediately after the War. The Hungarian Communist Party expelled 483 000 members during this period. See Anderson, Andy, *Die ungarische Revolution 1956*, Verlag Association 1977, p. 56.
[51] Maderthaner, W., Schafranek, H., Unfried, B., *Ich habe den Tod verdient*, Verlag für Gesellschaftskritik 1991, p. 18.
[52] Ibid. Brogan, P., *Eastern Europe 1939-1989*, pp. 119-121.
[53] Ibid. Simons, Thomas, W., *Eastern Europe in the Postwar World*, p. 67.

collapse and precipitated the 1956 Hungarian Revolution. The unforeseen consequence of the Hungarian Revolution was that the Hungarian Communist Party was completely de-Stalinised.

However, despite the differences in their histories and the various ways in which they came to power, all three Communist governments were initially intent on implementing the Soviet Stalinist model of society and economics. The effects of this policy soon led to various symptoms of crisis which erupted periodically in revolt. The problem was that the population and economic structure in Eastern Europe were not the same as those for which the Soviet Stalinist model had been devised[54]. The population was also aware of the imported nature of the Communist system. As Gert-Joachim Glaessner notes, the Soviet system was a model for forced industrialisation and modernisation of a backward economy[55]. For the achievement of its aims, the model may have been initially appropriate for an underdeveloped, rural country such as Romania[56], the society and economy were revolutionised and modernised by the Stalinist policies inflicted upon them, but the policies themselves underwent no development. The real problem and the root cause of the recurring crises which affected Eastern Europe during the period of Communist rule was the dogmatic nature of Communist ideology which guided all areas of policy.

1.1.3: Relations with the Soviet Union

Another problem for the governments of Eastern Europe was that as they had become more dependent on the Soviet Union, so their isolation from each other had increased. This was a direct result of Stalinism.

---

[54] For a discussion on the prerequisites of Soviet Stalinism, see Lewin, Moshe, 'The Social Background of Stalinism'. In Tucker, R., C., (Ed), *Stalinism: Essays in Historical Interpretation*, W. W. Norton & Company Inc. 1977.

[55] Glaessner, Gert-Joachim, *Demokratie nach dem Ende des Kommunismus*, Westdeutscher Verlag 1994, p. 17.

[56] The Stalinist model for modernisation is controversial, and it is not certain that such a model of forced industrialisation is any more efficient than a more gradual, albeit slower, development. Thus, it can be argued that the Stalinist model is not appropriate for any country, regardless of its level of industrial or social development.

'Stalinism had tried to atomize society, to force each individual to face the state alone. In the same way, Stalin had separated the states of Eastern Europe, discouraging inter-regional cooperation and forcing the Soviet policy line upon each country.'[57]

This state of affairs made it difficult for the states of East-Central Europe to form normal relations with each other. The Party elite was more interested in ensuring good relations with Moscow than with its neighbours. This fostered a culture of self-interest which resulted in a complete lack of solidarity amongst the Communist regimes in Eastern Europe when dealing with the Soviet Union. Each tried to gain favour at the expense of another. Attempts at reform in one country often caused popular unrest and outbursts of solidarity amongst neighbouring populations, but this did not extend to government, which was more interested in ensuring its own power was not jeopardised by events in a neighbouring country. This helps to explain the Czech government's flow of false information to the Soviet Union about the Hungarian crisis, and the invasion of the Warsaw Pact into Czechoslovakia in 1968[58].

In the same way, Ceausescu's denunciation of the Warsaw Pact invasion was not a demonstration of solidarity, or sympathy with Czechoslovakia's cause. Ceausescu himself was not in favour of reform, and criticised the Czechoslovak Party's reform plans. His 'independent' policy was designed to ensure his domestic position could not be threatened in a similar fashion. The show of defiance against the Soviet Union gained him a measure of real, albeit short-lived, domestic popularity. Once it became clear that Ceausescu had no intention of introducing even a modicum of reform into the Romanian Stalinist system, he rapidly lost support and was increasingly forced to rely on coercion to maintain power. It is also important to note that Ceausescu's defiance was tolerated by the

---

[57] Ibid. Simons, T., W., *Eastern Europe in the Postwar World*, p. 193.
[58] This action was no doubt greeted with a certain amount of *Schadenfreude* by those who had already had their hopes of reform dashed, although, for the same reason, it also evinced a great deal of sympathy for the plight of the Czechoslovakian population.

Soviet Union, partly because of his orthodoxy in domestic politics[59], and partly because of Romania's limited strategic importance to the Soviet Union. In addition, Romania's deviancy could be employed by the Soviet Union to demonstrate its leniency and tolerance towards wayward allies. After the invasion of Hungary in 1956 and subsequently of Czechoslovakia in 1968, this contrived public image was not unwelcome.

Attempts to moderate, change or modernise the ideology in order to deal with the demands of a modern society and economy invariably resulted in crisis; since this threatened to reveal the illegitimate nature of Communist power. Subsequent retreat was the only means of retaining power, and this in turn led to further crisis as problems were left unsolved and so became worse. A vicious circle of reform and retreat became a noticeable feature of East European politics. It is the effects of the Communist regimes' periods of reform and subsequent retreats which will be examined here: specifically, the effects of the 1956 Hungarian Revolution, the 1968 Prague Spring and the noticeable lack of spectacular crisis in Romania throughout Ceausescu's regime.

The cyclical periods of reform and retreat affected the regimes in a similar fashion, but they employed subtly different methods to deal with them. The methods chosen have their roots in the origins and histories of the Communist Parties in question. They also had a long-term effect on society and played a role in determining the form of Revolution which occurred in 1989. Indeed, they still have an influence on the transformation and consolidation process today. As Gorbachev stated in 1987:

> *'The roots of the present situation go back far into the past . . .There should be no forgotten names or blank spots in either history or literature ...History must be seen as it is.*[60]

---

[59] Ironically, it was Ceausescu's Stalinist orthodoxy which became his main liability. He became increasingly out of touch and unable to cope with the domestic situation in Romania and with the rapid chain of events which swept the Soviet Bloc from 1985 onwards.

[60] See Daniels, Robert, V., *The End of the Communist Revolution*, Routledge 1993, p. 18. Original in *Pravda*, 14.2.87.

Although this statement refers to the Soviet Union, it is applicable to Central Europe, which, in the midst of transformation, finds itself confronted with the past in the form of the Communist legacy.

1.2: The Hungarian Revolution 1956

'There is no life without growth,
There is no growth without change,
There is no change without controversy.'
H. Puckrose and P. Wilby[61].

Hungary was the first country under discussion to experience a serious crisis. It was precipitated by the calamitous state of the Hungarian economy and society in general. As a result, the wisdom of the Stalinist path began to be doubted. The confusion which Khrushchev's 'Secret Speech'[62] on the excesses of Stalinism caused was the final link in a long chain of events leading to the Hungarian Uprising. In this chain, external influences were as influential as internal developments. The 1953 Pilsen strikes and riots in Czechoslovakia in response to a proposed currency devaluation which would entail a 20% reduction in the standard of living[63], the Berlin Uprising in June 1953 and the Austrian Treaty, signed in 1955, which ensured Austrian independence, all served to increase tensions within the Hungarian population and the Party. These tensions could not be resolved within the confining strait-jacket of Stalinist dogma.

1.2.1: The 'Secret Speech'
The 'Secret Speech' was of specific importance because it destroyed the monolithic unity of the Communist Party of the

---

[61] Puckrose, H., Wilby, P., *Education 2000*, Maurice Temple Smith 1980.
[62] For the text of Khrushchev's 'Secret Speech', see *Die Geheimrede Chruschtschows*, Dietz Verlag 1990.
[63] Ibid. Anderson, Andy, *Die Ungarische Revolution 1956*, p. 59.

Soviet Union. This in turn paved the way for disintegration of unity within the Parties in Central Europe. The tacit admission that the Party was fallible, at least in respect to Stalin, raised the spectre that other policy mistakes may have been made. This posed a question mark over the validity of the Soviet model and led to a discussion of whether separate 'national' roads to Communism were more appropriate. The speech was not a criticism of Communism itself, rather of certain excesses which occurred during the Stalinist period[64]. It had never been intended to keep the speech secret and copies of it were sent to all local Party Headquarters in the Soviet Union and to East European leaders. In his report at the Twentieth Congress in 1956, Gheorghe Dej was careful to distance and exonerate himself from any connection with Stalinism[65]. Even though the Romanian Party had carried out a Purge of its members as late as June 1953[66], Dej had shrewdly indulged in some self-criticism at the Central Committee meeting of 19-20 August, 1953. He even proposed a form of collective leadership and halted some monumental Stalinist projects, such as the Black Sea Canal in 1954[67]. The question is, why did the tensions caused by these events lead only to the Hungarian Party's disintegration and popular uprising in Hungary?

The Hungarian Uprising was the spontaneous reaction of a people who could see that the Communist regime was floundering and that freedom was thus within reach. A United Nation's Commission Report stated:

---

[64] For an indication of the scale and brutality of Stalin's 'Great Terror', it is interesting to note, that of the 139 Central Committee members at the XVII Party Conference, 98 of them, or 70% were shot between 1937-1938. Of the 1966 delegates at the Conference, 1108 were arrested or worse. Ibid. *Die Geheimrede Chruschtschows*, pp. 25-26.
[65] Fischer-Galati, S., *Twentieth Century Romania*, Columbia University Press 1970, p. 145.
[66] On 23 June, 1953, it was announced 192 000 members had been purged. Ibid. Fischer-Galati, S., *Twentieth Century Romania*, p. 123.
[67] Ibid. Rothschild, J., *Return to Diversity*, p. 161.

'Sie war nicht organisiert und nicht zentral gelenkt. Der Wille zur Freiheit war die treibende Kraft bei jeder Aktion.[68]

The Hungarian Communist Party subsequently took note of the tensions which contributed to the Revolution and attempted to mould its policy to fit Hungarian needs. This entailed continuing a reform process as a means of pacifying the population. The Revolution also had the singular effect of de-Stalinising the Hungarian Communist Party. It was to have the opposite effect on the Communist Parties in Romania and Czechoslovakia which, as a result, became more determined to avoid de-Stalinisation and reform.

In contrast to the Hungarian Party elite, Gheorghe Dej and Antonin Novotny were able to consolidate their position after Stalin's death. They used the tensions visible within the Hungarian Party as an excuse to delay de-Stalinisation. The Revolution itself provided them with the perfect reason to avoid such a course of action. In the immediate aftermath of 1956, the Soviet leaders, reluctant to risk another eruption of popular discontent, were content with the stability and reliability provided by Dej and Novotny. In return, Dej and Novotny became staunch upholders of Stalinist orthodoxy and postponed reform for as long as possible. But this policy only delayed the inevitable crisis which was called forth once de-Stalinisation could no longer be delayed, be it for political, social or economic reasons.

The position of the Communist Party in Hungary had always been precarious. Its members had been decimated during the brutal Purges, but unlike their Czech counterparts, its leaders had not become united as a result. Stalin's death on 6 March, 1953 caused confusion and uncertainty. This was linked to the ensuing power struggle which took place in the Soviet Union. An indirect result of this struggle was a perceptible loosening of control, since it was not clear which group in the Kremlin would gain the advantage and

---

[68] Arendt, Hannah, *Die ungarische Revolution und der totalitäre Imperialismus*, R. Piper & Co. Verlag 1958, p. 12. 'It was not organised and not centrally controlled. The will for freedom was the propelling force behind every action.' Translation Wendy Hollis.

secure power. The Hungarian Party had been just as reliant on Stalin and the Communist Party of the Soviet Union to direct policy, if not by actual intervention then by example, as the Romanian and Czechoslovak Parties. Stalin's death and the confusion it caused proved fatal only to the Hungarian Party because it re-ignited the internal power struggle.

Uncertainty as to which group within the Kremlin would gain power made it impossible for the Hungarian Party to react to the growing domestic crisis, since it was not sure which policy was favoured by the Soviet leaders or indeed which leaders were favoured at any given time. Combined with the intensifying internal divisions, this served to paralyse it. The Party elite found it impossible to formulate policies which would be acceptable to the various factions within the Soviet Union's leadership, suitable for the specific Hungarian situation and acceptable to themselves. Thus, for the duration of the power struggle in the Soviet Union following Stalin's death, the Hungarian Party was immobilised and underwent a process of disintegration[69].

The Communist Parties of Eastern Europe were faced with an insoluble dilemma. They had to chose between policies which were more suited to domestic conditions, which offered them the chance of achieving a modicum of popular support and independence from Moscow; and policies which were acceptable to the Soviet Union and followed the Soviet model, but which led to a complete loss of domestic support. The former course carried with it the risk of incurring Moscow's wrath and thus losing personal power as a result, while the latter would ensure power but result in total dependence on the Soviet Union. This dilemma was to plague the Communist regimes in Eastern Europe. It is also one of the factors which contributed to the pendulum of reform and counter-reform during the Communist period. These are representative of the regimes' swing from one option to the other. Inability to combine rational policy with Communist ideology, as interpreted by the

---

[69] An example of this is the fact that the Party was unable to agree on a suitable Five Year Plan for 1953-1958. This was also a reflection of the internal struggle taking place within the ranks of its leaders. See Timmermann, Heiner, (Ed.), *Ungarn nach 1945*, Dadder 1990, p. 205.

Soviet Union, ultimately made the regimes incapable and incompetent. The Hungarian Communist Party was the first to confront this problem. The experience of 1956 was to influence the other Communist regimes in the region when confronted by the same dilemma. The Czechoslovak Party tried to make de-Stalinisation more palatable by extolling a modified form of socialism in 1968, but it too collapsed. Its attempt failed more completely than even the Hungarian. Gustav Husak, Alexander Dubcek's successor, introduced a form of neo-Stalinism, whereas Imre Nagy's replacement, János Kádár, de-Stalinised the Hungarian Party, its politics and Hungarian society by introducing gradual, albeit limited, reform.

The Communist regime in Romania was singular in that it managed to turn this dilemma to its own uses. Romanian 'national' Communism did not embody a reform movement within the Party, rather it was a policy employed to ensure personal power and the continuation of Stalinist policies. The Romanian Party did not follow the Soviet Union's instructions to embark on de-Stalinisation. De-Stalinisation was a mere facade which served to consolidate Dej's personal power. The continuation of Stalinist policies was justified by claiming that, as an independent Communist state, Romania was free to decide its own policy. Taking historical Romanian antipathy towards Russia into account, it was an easy task for the Party to present this as an independent course of action in Romania's national interest. In reality, it was only in the interests of the Party elite, which was determined to stay in power and implement its Stalinist policies.

Hungary suffered terrible damage to and destruction of its industrial base and cities during the War. The retreating Germans and subsequently the advancing Red Army dismantled and carried off the majority of what little had remained intact. In addition to this, Hungary was obliged to pay reparations to the Soviet Union, Czechoslovakia and Yugoslavia. The reparations amounted to $300 million. The Soviet Union received two thirds of this and the rest was divided between Czechoslovakia and Yugoslavia. The costs of occupation by the Red Army were also carried by the Hungarian government. Thus, for the period of the Red Army occupation, the total costs to Hungary were approximately 30-35% of the national product[70]. The War and its aftermath placed an extreme burden on the already struggling Hungarian economy. In June 1946, Hungary registered a world record inflation rate. Farmers refused to sell produce in return for a currency which soon became worthless[71]. The Marshall Plan, proposed in 1947, was initially welcomed as a means of stabilising and rejuvenating the Hungarian economy. After initial acceptance, the Hungarian Politburo was summoned to Moscow where Stalin instructed them, in the same way he did the Czechs, to reject the Marshall Plan. Romania needed no prompting, its first Five Year Plan of 1951-1955 was Stalinist in its conception and implementation.

Hungary, in common with Romania and Czechoslovakia, had been an area of high German investment. All German property in Hungary, Romania and Czechoslovakia was taken over and put under direct Soviet control. Although it was later returned to the respective governments, the Soviet Union retained a large, direct interest in, and therefore influence over, the economies of the area. It became the main export and import partner of the region. Hungary is a small country poor in raw materials. It became totally dependent on raw material imports from the Soviet Union to supply its new industrial complex. Thus, in 1955, 71% of the iron ore, 80% of pig iron, 30% of foundry lead, 81% of sulphur, 81% of raw phosphate, 77% of native soda, 30% of synthetic rubber, 80% of pine timber, and 55% of raw cotton imported by Hungary came from the Soviet Union[72]. Romania, a country with many raw materials and substantial oil reserves, exported most of these to the Soviet Union. Indeed, as many of the oil companies had been foreign owned[73] and were taken over by the Germans during the

---

[70] Ibid. Anderson, Andy, *Die Ungarische Revolution 1956*, p. 43.
[71] Hungary had experienced economic problems even before the War due to the collapse of the Austro-Hungarian Empire and the resultant loss of markets for Hungarian produce. As a result, in 1931, one gold Pengo was worth 1.3 quintillion paper Pengos (i.e. 1.3 with 30 zeros afterwards). Ibid. Brogan P., *Eastern Europe 1939-1989*, p. 119.
[72] Berecz, Janos, *1956: Counter-Revolution in Hungary*, Budapest 1986, p. 12.
[73] In 1946, 51% of the Romanian oil industry was Anglo-Dutch and 11% was owned by companies in the United States. Joint Soviet-Romanian companies

War, much of the Romanian oil industry was placed under direct Soviet Control. Although joint Soviet-Romanian companies were later organised, so called *SovRoms*, they served to ensure that the Soviet Union retained a controlling interest in crucial areas of Romanian industry[74]. In this way, the Soviet Union created an area of political and economic interest in which it had considerable influence and power.

Although the policy of nationalisation of heavy industry and land reform initially found support amongst the Hungarian population, the nationalisation of small and medium-sized enterprises did not, and collectivisation proved a disaster. In March 1948, 25% of heavy industry and 80% of small and medium-sized industry was still in private hands. A law was hastily drafted which nationalised all enterprises employing over 100 workers. In this way, nationalisation was virtually completed by 1949[75]. However, the government, or rather the Agricultural Ministry under the leadership of Imre Nagy, was hesitant to implement collectivisation. Agricultural policy was only changed in 1948, once Imre Nagy's influence began to decline.

The Cominform suggested implementation of collectivisation at the September 1947 meeting, but Imre Nagy had subsequently rejected the policy at the Political Committee meeting in December 1947[76]. By November 1949, only 7% of land had been transferred to cooperatives or state farms[77]. The government was afraid of the farmers' opposition and its potential de-stabilising effects, yet it was ideologically bound to complete collectivisation in some manner, especially since one criticism levelled at Yugoslavia was that its collectivisation programme was too slow. In addition to ideological considerations, the small size of the plots distributed as

---

accounted for 28% of the industry. This was mostly confiscated German property. Ibid. Simons, Thomas, W., *Eastern Europe in the Postwar World*, p. 60.
[74] In 1946, the Soviet Union owned 46% of Romanian industry and financial enterprises. Ibid. Staar, Richard, F., *The Communist Regimes in Eastern Europe (2nd Edition)*, p. 171.
[75] Ibid. Anderson, Andy, *Die Ungarische Revolution 1956*, p. 48.
[76] Swain, Nigel, *Hungary: The Rise and Fall of Feasible Socialism*, Verso 1992, p. 41.
[77] Ibid. Anderson, Andy, *Die Ungarische Revolution 1956*, p. 49.

a result of the land reform, the average size was 2.9 hectares, did not provide a realistic base for efficient agricultural production[78]. But collectivisation based on the Soviet Stalinist model did not alleviate the problem. Emphasis on heavy industry, both in the ideological and economic sphere, led to neglect of agriculture and increased migration from the land. Only 13.8% of total investment was given to agriculture between 1950 and 1954. In 1949 it had been 17.5%. In the period during which Nagy was Prime Minister, between 1954 and 1957, investment in agriculture increased to 17%[79]. One result of the low level of investment was that agricultural targets for 1950-54 were not met. Consequently less bread was produced than in 1911-1915, although the population had increased by 25%[80]. In addition, the workers were showing signs of unrest. There was an increase in absenteeism and the number of days of work lost due to illness.

The fact was that the Hungarian economy, which was already struggling from the aftermath of the War and the burden of reparations, was on the verge of total collapse at the start of the 1950's[81]. The first Five Year Plan was modified secretly in 1951, but only 150 copies of the new Plan were produced[82]. Only the highest circles of the Party elite were aware that the Plan targets being extolled were totally unrealistic and could not be fulfilled. Despite this knowledge, the Party elite in charge was not prepared to change its Stalinist policies, even after Stalin's death. Neither was it willing to relinquish its power.

1.2.2: Nagy becomes Prime Minister

Matyas Rakosi, unlike Comrade Gottwald, who died shortly after returning from Stalin's funeral, was unprepared to leave the stage gracefully. In addition to being a convinced Stalinist, he was

---

[78] Ibid. Swain, Nigel, *Hungary: The Rise and Fall of Feasible Socialism*, p. 36.
[79] Ibid. Swain, Nigel, *Hungary: The Rise and Fall of Feasible Socialism*, p. 83.
[80] Ibid. Staar, Richard, F., *The Communist Regimes in Eastern Europe (2nd. Edition)*, p. 122.
[81] In the period between 1949-1953, real wages decreased by 22%. They increased three times between 1956-1970. Sugar, P., F., *A History of Hungary*, Indiana University Press 1991, p. 395.
[82] Ibid. Swain, Nigel, *Hungary: The Rise and Fall of Feasible Socialism*, p. 81.

too deeply implicated in the direction and implementation of the 'Titoist' Purges and brutal repression which had swept Hungary and Eastern Europe[83] from 1948 onwards[84]. As the battle for power in Moscow progressed, Beria seemed to gain the initial advantage. Beria had been Stalin's security chief and as such was considered extremely dangerous by the majority of the Kremlin leadership. Their common fear of Beria united them and they collectively ensured Beria's arrest in the summer of 1953. He was subsequently shot. However, Beria's fall from power did not signal an end to internal struggle. It was now centred around Khrushchev and Malenkov.

Malenkov was Imre Nagy's supporter within the Kremlin, and Nagy's rise and fall from power is linked to that of Malenkov. Khrushchev replaced him as First Secretary in September 1953, although Malenkov was to remain Prime Minister for a time. It was during Malenkov's time as Prime Minister that Rakosi was called to Moscow and forced to relinquish his post as Prime Minister to Imre Nagy.

From the 13-14 June, 1953 the members of the Hungarian Politburo were summoned to Moscow where they met their Soviet counterparts. The Hungarians were informed that their policies were unsatisfactory. Rakosi had accumulated too much personal power; the economy was in a state of collapse; the Purges and

---

[83] The Czechoslovak Communist Party set up a Commission headed by Jan Piller to re-examine the Show Trials. It was given access to the Czechoslovak Party Archives, but not those of the Soviet Union. The report, produced by a group of historians headed by Karel Kaplan, was prevented from being published. It documented Stalin's and other foreign Party leaders' direct intervention in the Trials. Thus, on 3 September, 1949, Rakosi sent Gottwald a letter warning that the names of spies would be revealed in the Rajk trial and that they were at liberty in Czechoslovakia. He also laid suspicion on leading Communist officials, the Minister of the Interior, Vaclav Nosek, the Minister of Foreign Affairs, Vladimir Clementis and two other economists. Ibid. Skilling, H., G., 'Stalinism and Czechoslovak Political Culture'. In Tucker, R., C., *Stalinism: Essays in Historical Interpretation*, pp. 271-272.

[84] Hungary was the first East European country to employ Show Trials. László Rajk was tried in 1949. He was a veteran of the Spanish Civil War and had been a Titoist partisan. After the 1948 break with Yugoslavia, Hungary was the first and most vocal in denouncing 'Titosim', the charge which would become standard during the Purges.

Show Trials had been particularly vicious and had decimated the Party; and collectivisation had been incorrectly and inefficiently carried out. Rakosi was ordered to resign as Prime Minister and Imre Nagy was 'proposed' as his successor[85]. Since Nagy had been absent from government since 1948, he was not tarnished by responsibility for the Purges. He had also spent ten years in the Soviet Union and had married a Soviet citizen[86]. He was therefore considered reliable. However, Rakosi remained First Secretary of the Communist Party where, surrounded by loyal functionaries, he re-formed his power base.

The fact that this meeting took place at all illustrates the extent of control exercised by the Soviet Union over the Communist governments in Eastern Europe. It was the Soviet Politburo members who decided policy and selected personnel, but they blamed Rakosi for the results of their policy and for the catastrophic state of affairs in Hungary. This was significant because it became clear for the first time that the leaders in Eastern Europe would be held accountable if policies failed. In accordance with this development and the admittance of fallibility in the case of Stalin, the extent of independence of action permitted to East European leaders was increased, but the limits remained unclear. It was into this new, undefined sphere which Imre Nagy and the Hungarian population blundered.

Nagy's inaugural speech as Prime Minister heralded the beginning of a 'New Course' for 1954. He had already closed the internment camps in July 1953[87]. The first Five Year Plan had failed, and the revised 1951 Plan was criticised. Nagy proposed an increase in investment given to light and consumer industry. He also accepted the dissolution of cooperatives if a majority of members voted in favour. Four months after his speech 10% of all cooperatives had been dissolved[88]. Investment in heavy industry was 40% lower in 1954 than in 1953 and the standard of living increased by 15%. 1954 also saw many of the remaining Purge

---

[85] Ibid. Gati, Charles, *The Bloc that Failed*, p. 32.
[86] Ibid. Sugar, P., F., *A History of Hungary*, p. 375.
[87] Ibid. Sugar, P., F., *A History of Hungary*, p. 376.
[88] Ibid. Anderson, Andy, *Die Ungarische Revolution 1956*, p. 61.

victims freed and, in March 1954, Gábor Péter, the chief of the *AVO*, was tried and sentenced to life imprisonment for his role in the Purges[89]. The emergency One Year Plan for 1955 continued the reformist trend[90]. A new period of relaxation and limited liberalisation was introduced. It came as a great relief to the majority of the population and Party members.

But, Rakosi had been allowed to keep his post as First Secretary, and the Central Committee, indeed the whole Party apparatus, remained unchanged. This was a fatal miscalculation, since it provided Rakosi with an alternative power base from which to challenge Nagy. Rakosi still enjoyed support among the ranks of the *nomenklatura*, Party functionaries and certain members of the Central Committee. They were all implicated in the direction and control of the Purges and the crimes connected with them. Many of the Party functionaries were reluctant to support Nagy and thus expose themselves in a de-Stalinisation campaign. They had a personal interest in keeping Rakosi in power. Since Rakosi was also implicated and compromised by the Purges, he was the only person who could be relied upon not to initiate a de-Stalinisation which would cost all of them their positions and power. Imre Nagy represented exactly the opposite and was viewed as a threat. He was hindered by the fact that he was the only 'new face' in the Party elite. Although the Central Committee unanimously approved all Nagy's new policies, there was continual debate about the New Course.

1.2.3: Rakosi Returns

Malenkov's replacement by Bulganin in February 1955 gave Rakosi the opportunity he had been waiting for to regain power. Nagy's protector in Moscow, although still influential, was no longer in a position of power. In January 1955, Malenkov summoned Nagy and Rakosi to Moscow where he criticised Nagy. Rakosi regained power to all intents and purposes in March 1955,

---

[89] Ibid. Sugar, P., F., *A History of Hungary*, p. 376.
[90] The Hungarian Party leaders were unable to agree on a Five Year Plan, a catastrophe for an economy dependent on Plan targets to function. Ibid. Staar, R., F., *The Communist Regimes in Eastern Europe (2nd. Edition)*, p. 125.

thus ending the reformist interlude under Nagy. Nagy was relieved of his post as Prime Minister on 18 April, 1955 by the Central Committee under the pretext of exhibiting 'nationalist tendencies'[91]. After a brief period as an ordinary member of the Party, one of the founder members of the Communist Party in 1918, was expelled from it in November 1955[92]. He had been Prime Minister for a mere 18 months, but these had made a lasting impression on the Hungarian population.

Although Rakosi managed to regain power, he became a liability for sections within both the Hungarian and the Soviet Communist Parties. This was especially true after Khrushchev had made the 'Secret Speech' and embarked on a policy of de-Stalinisation. This was due to Rakosi's rigid, orthodox Stalinist mentality and the singular duplicity which he had displayed during the 'Titoist' Purges[93]. He even proposed a new wave of Purges on 16 July, 1956. They were to begin with the arrest of Nagy and 400 other Communist Party members[94].

Stalin's death had offered an opportunity for change but it had been bungled. As the Soviet Union embarked on a policy of relaxation after the Stalinist terror and of reconciliation with Tito, Rakosi became impossibly compromised. Indeed, Tito demanded Rakosi's removal from power before a reconciliation between Yugoslavia and the Soviet Union be formally agreed. After finally signing the 'Moscow Declaration' on 20 June, 1956, Tito said of the Rakosi regime:

> *'These men have their hands soaked in blood; they have staged trials, given false information, sentenced innocent men to death. They have dragged Yugoslavia into all these trials, as in the case of the Rajk trial, and now they find it difficult to admit their mistakes before their own people.'*[95]

---

[91] Ibid. Anderson, Andy, *Die Ungarische Revolution 1956*, p. 62.
[92] Nagy was 60 years old when the Revolution took place in 1956. Ibid. Gati, Charles, *Hungary and the Soviet Bloc*, p. 127, p. 135.
[93] Raksoi had acted as Moscow's hatchet-man in the tirade against Tito.
[94] Ibid. Sugar, P., F., *A History of Hungary*, p. 377.
[95] Swain, G., Swain., N., *Eastern Europe since 1945*, Macmillan 1993, p. 84.

Indeed, it would be one of Ernö Gerö's first tasks as Rakosi's successor to travel to Yugoslavia and end the quarrel with Tito. Experience of the reform interlude associated with Nagy made Rakosi's return and his rigid Stalinist policies unbearable to the majority of Hungarians. In addition, certain victims of Rakosi's Purges, including János Kádár, began to appear in public once more. They had been freed under the amnesty proclaimed by Nagy. In the Summer of 1956, the *Petöfi Circle* was formed as a discussion forum by young members of the Communist Party and writers. They demanded Nagy's return and even managed to persuade Rajk's widow to speak at their last public meeting on June 27, 1956. Géza Losonczy, a member of the editorial board of *Hungarian Nation*, openly supported the call to reinstate Nagy. The Communist Party, completely unprepared and unused to dealing with such situations, disintegrated in indecision. The radicalism which Rakosi's return precipitated is demonstrated by Nagy's statement that, he saw the crisis as stemming from the time when:

> *'...the clique headed by Rakosi ...crushed the basis of Hungary's young democracy and liquidated our people's democratic forms and the democratic partnership of socialism.'*[96]

This also points to the democratic direction Hungarian reforms were taking. Rakosi[97] was finally removed from power on 18 July, 1956 after a visit from Mikoyan and Suslov[98], who ordered him to

---

[96] Ibid. Swain, G., Swain, N., *Eastern Europe since 1945*, p. 85.

[97] On relinquishing his position as First Secretary, Rakosi fled to the Soviet Union where he lived and died in exile. Ibid. Brogan, P., *Eastern Europe 1939-1989*, p. 124.

[98] On 25 October, 1956, Mikoyan travelled to Budapest with Suslov and ordered the replacement of Gerö as First Secretary by Kádár. They remained to observe the situation. By 29 October, 1956, transition to a multi-party democracy was being discussed, as well as the withdrawal of all Soviet troops. Ibid. Sugar, P., F., *A History of Hungary*, pp. 380-381.

go[99]. His successor was named as Ernö Gerö, one of his loyal Stalinist supporters[100]. Although a limited programme of de-Stalinisation was set in motion, Gerö offered no hope of a return to the reform course started by Nagy. He had been party to all Rakosi's decisions since 1945. The Soviet Union expected him to be capable of establishing some kind of order. At the same time, Nagy demanded to be re-admitted into the Party. The Central Committee eventually re-admitted him on 13 October, 1956. It also rehabilitated László Rajk, blaming Rakosi for his execution[101]. These events increased the frustration and division within the Party between the Stalinist faction and those favouring de-Stalinisation, and amongst the population at large. Ernö Gerö's appointment was the final catalyst needed for the Hungarian Revolution of 1956. Since Stalin's death in 1953, the Hungarian Communist Party had been grappling with looming disintegration bought about by the conflict between its leaders. The Revolution occurred when this process was complete.

László Rajk was re-buried on 6 October, 1956[102]. The event turned into a mass demonstration and a political event. Approximately 200 000 people were present at the funeral. It was a means by which the population could express its rejection of Rakosi, Gerö, and indeed the whole Stalinist system which had been forced upon it. Unlike the Prague Spring of 1968, the Hungarian Revolution had profoundly anti-Communist and nationalist aims. The people wanted to be free to choose a non-communist, Hungarian government in a democratic manner and were prepared to pay for this dream with their lives. Approximately 20-50 000 Hungarians and 3500-7000 Russians were killed during the course of the Revolution[103]. But, tragic as it was, this blood-

---

[99] The fact that Mikoyan stopped off in Budapest on the way to Belgrade must have been an extra humiliation. He also alighted on his return trip on 21 July to see Nagy. Ibid. Gati, Charles, *Hungary and the Soviet Bloc*, pp. 136-137.
[100] Ibid. Anderson, Andy, *Die Ungarische Revolution 1956*, p. 76.
[101] Ibid. Brogan, P., *Eastern Europe 1939-1989*, p. 124.
[102] Ibid. Sugar, P., F., *A History of Hungary*, p. 379.
[103] Ibid. Anderson, Andy, *Die Ungarische Revolution*, p. 183.

shed taught the Communist Party to respect, and fear, the population over which it ruled.

1.2.4: Revolution

The Revolution sprang spontaneously from a demonstration in support of the Posnan workers in Poland called by the *Petőfi Circle* for 23 October, 1956. The demonstration was initially approved, but on the day it was due to take place, approval was withdrawn. The demonstration would have occurred without official approval, so at the last minute, approval was re-issued. Such indecision was to characterise both the Hungarian and Soviet Communist Parties' actions during the Revolution. It is a vivid demonstration of the total disarray in the Hungarian state apparatus at the time, and the new Soviet leaders' uncertainty as to how to deal with the situation. As the Revolution broke out, Russian soldiers remained confined to their barracks. They were mobilised, only to be de-mobilised, withdrawn and then re-grouped and reinforced to invade Hungary a few days later.

Nagy had Moscow's cautious support until 30-31 October. This fact is demonstrated by the presence of Mikoyan, who stayed in Budapest from 24-31 October in the hope of finding a political solution to the crisis. It was during this period that the Soviet Union agreed to withdraw its troops, accepted the formation of a new cabinet and *de facto* the creation of a new multi-party system in Hungary. Nagy announced the formation of the new cabinet on the radio at 2.28 p.m. on 30 October, 1956:

> *'In the interest of the further democratisation of the country's life, the cabinet abolishes the one-party system and places the country's government on the basis of the democratic cooperation between the coalition parties as they existed in 1945. In accordance with this decision, a new national government with a smaller inner cabinet has been established, at the moment with only limited powers. The members of the new cabinet are Imre Nagy, Zoltán Tildy, Béla Kovács, Ferenc Erdei, János Kádár, Géza Losonczy,*

and a person to be appointed by the Social Democratic Party.,[104]

Nagy also declared Hungary's intention to become a neutral state and withdraw from the CMEA. The United Nations (UN) was requested to acknowledge Hungary's new status. Unfortunately, at the same time, the Suez Crisis was reaching its climax. The Hungarian request was not put on the agenda because there was an emergency debate on Suez. In addition, the United States and the Soviet Union found themselves united in their opposition to the old colonial powers of France and Britain over the Suez question. The failure of the UN to act on behalf of Hungary brought home the realisation that the countries of Central Europe had to deal with the Soviet Union on their own and could expect no intervention on their behalf by the Western powers. Relations with the Soviet Union took priority over relations with the other states in the Soviet Bloc.

At the same time Soviet troops officially withdrew from Hungary, the *AVO*, the Hungarian secret police, was dissolved. But, on the night of the 30-31 October, the Soviet Union changed its policy and Soviet troops re-grouped and re-entered Hungary. They were reinforced by fresh troops on 4 November and the invasion began. The Soviet Union was afraid of losing control of the situation and its grip on Hungarian politics. The speed with which the Communist Party apparatus and Party discipline collapsed was also cause for alarm, since these formed the foundations of all the Communist regimes in Eastern Europe.

Although the invasion was a political success, the Nagy government was removed and an alternative installed, it was a military disaster. Many Russian troops were unwilling to fire on the Hungarian population, and the Russian army needed three weeks to fully restore order. The invasion was a salutary warning that any changes to the system must not go beyond the limits of reform. Reform also had to be harmonious with the Soviet Union's own interests. This meant that the basic tenets of Communism, that is

---

[104] Ibid. Gati, Charles, *Hungary and the Soviet Bloc*, p. 146.

one-party rule, membership of the Warsaw Pact and the CMEA, had to be left untouched by any reform movements.

1.2.5: Repercussions from the Revolution

Antonin Novotny used the situation to vindicate the Czechoslovak Party's refusal to embark upon wholesale de-Stalinisation. He had already suffered embarrassment at the hands of the workers in Pilsen in 1953. As a result of this, various measures, both political and economic, had been introduced to stabilise the regime. Wages were increased, the standard of living improved and with it the regime's legitimacy. Novotny had also been in Moscow on 27 February, where he had learned of the 'Secret Speech'. The Czechoslovak Communist Party only heard of it on 24 March. This gave Novotny the time he needed to consider his course of action[105]. Combined with the salutary example of Hungary, this contributed to the Czechoslovak Party's ability to deal with the problem of de-Stalinisation without disintegrating into warring factions.

There were no mass Czech demonstrations in support of the Hungarian cause and the Communist Party retained its grip on power. Indeed, Novotny increased his own power base by using the example of Hungary to vindicate his policy of limited de-Stalinisation. The victims of the Show Trials had the charges against them reduced from 'Treason' to 'Sabotage'. None of the sentences were changed to not guilty, and none of the victims were rehabilitated. Rehabilitation was not on the agenda since it would entail re-examination of the Trials and would so expose the duplicity and guilt of the leadership at the time. At the June Party Conference in 1956, Novotny made it clear that he saw no reason to rehabilitate Rudolf Slansky[106]. An amnesty for political prisoners

---

[105] Beyram, Dietrich, Bock, I., (Hrsg.), *Das Tauwetter und die Folgen*, Temmen 1988, p. 76.
[106] Novotny had been a member of the Political Secretariat and had approved Slansky's arrest on 24 November. He also took part in the preparation and supervision of the Trial. He was also First Secretary during eight subsequent Show Trials. Thus, he had no interest in exposing himself by embarking upon a discussion of the Trials. Ibid. Skilling, G., H., 'Stalinism and Czechoslovak Political Culture'. In Tucker, R., C., *Stalinism: Essays in Historical Interpretation*, p. 275.

was only issued on 9 May, 1960. As a result, the majority of the 8708 prisoners still held in detention were released[107]. Ironically, this event was a forebear of the Prague Spring, since those released were a living example of the entire leadership's guilt and the inhuman nature of the Stalinist system they had imposed upon the country.

The crisis of 1956 caused the Czechoslovak Party elite to close ranks and unite in the face of the prospect of losing power altogether. They managed to keep the truth about the Show Trials secret and completely out of the public arena. As a result, the Party functionaries suffered no public pressure to reveal the truth about the Purges and remained loyal to the regime. Thus, with the help of the correction made between 1953-55 and the limited programme of de-Stalinisation, the Party power elite was able to stabilise the situation for a period of time. The problem was that, while Novotny resisted any substantial alterations to the Stalinist system and formally retained it, much of the essence which was required to keep it intact was removed. Although they were still present, terror and faith in Communist ideology decreased, while public awareness gradually increased. These were both results of the 'Secret Speech' and events in Hungary in 1956, and were to lead to the Czechoslovak crisis in 1968, which was in its essence a delayed de-Stalinisation of the Party, politics and the economy.

Although the events in Hungary had caused some disturbances in Transylvania, the home of the large Hungarian minority in Romania, they had not been serious. The Hungarian crisis provided Gheorghe Dej with an opportunity to increase his level independence from Moscow. Once Nagy had been arrested, he was taken to Romania and held there until his secret return to Hungary and execution in June 1958. In return for this service, Dej was rewarded with the withdrawal of Soviet Troops in 1958. He had been shrewd enough to distance himself publicly from Stalin and present the liquidation of his personal rivals as the liquidation of the

---

[107] Ibid. Beyram, Dietrich, Bock, I., (Hrsg.), *Das Tauwetter und die Folgen*, pp. 82-103.

Stalinist faction within the Party[108]. This was hailed as proving that the Romanian Party had successfully completed a de-Stalinisation programme, without the complications which arose in Hungary. But, although the Communists who had been liquidated were all Stalinists, so were those who had liquidated them.

Ironically, the only Party which was successfully de-Stalinised as a result of the 1956 Hungarian Revolution was the Hungarian Party itself. The invasion also demonstrated that Communist ideology was a facade erected to conceal the Soviet Union's real aim of keeping control of Eastern Europe. From this moment, Communism in Hungary lost its 'true believers' and evolved into a mechanism for maintaining power in the hands of a political elite acceptable to the Soviet Union. However, the experience of the Revolution had another salutary effect on the Hungarian Communist Party. As the former Hungarian President, Joseph Antall noted, it forced the realisation that a new form of Communist government had to be introduced in Hungary. The policy of gradual reform which the Hungarian Party followed under Kádár would not have been possible without the sobering experience of 1956:

> 'Die Revolution von 1956 vermittelte den ungarischen Kommunisten bzw. der ungarischen sozialistischen Arbeiterpartei eine große Lehre. Diese Lehre bestand darin, daß dieses Land und sein Volk nicht mehr so behandelt werden konnten wie zuvor. Das wußte auch die sowjetische Regierung. Und so wäre dieses Land nicht die fröhlichste Baracke im kommunistischen Lager geworden, wenn es nicht die furchtbare Erfahrung von 1956 gegeben hätte, die sich für die Machthaber, obwohl sie zuächst zu grausamer Rache führte, als eine unvergeßliche Lektion erwies.'[109]

---

[108] Lucretiu Patrascanu and Vasile Luca were tried in April and October 1954 respectively. Ibid. Skilling, H., G., 'Stalinism and Czechoslovak Political Culture'. In Tucker, R., C., *Stalinism: Essays in Historical Interpretation*, p. 269.

[109] From a speech at the Hungarian State Opera on the 30th Anniversary of the Revolution. See Antall, J., 'Remembering the Revolution', in *Current Policy*, No. 41, 1991, p. 7. 'The Revolution of 1956 taught the Hungarian Communists, that is the Hungarian Socialist Workers' Party, a great lesson. This lesson consisted of the fact that the country and its people could no longer be treated as they had been in the past. The Soviet government also realised this. Thus, this country would never

János Kádár learned from this lesson and managed to regain the trust of the Soviet leaders, rebuild the Hungarian Communist Party[110] and form a *modus vivendi* with a hostile population. György Konrad aptly describes the Kádár regime as practising an, 'enlightened, paternalistic authoritarianism, accompanied by a willingness to undertake gradual liberal reforms[111]. So, after an initial period of consolidation, the political atmosphere was relaxed and police terror was reduced. Although collectivisation was re-started in 1959 and completed by 1961, it was not forced in the earlier Stalinist style, rather the peasants were offered inducements to join the cooperatives. Once collectivisation was completed, democracy within cooperative structures was increased and the peasants' private plots were not only protected, but also encouraged.

At this time, Khrushchev began a second wave of de-Stalinisation. Even though Kádár was himself implicated in the Show Trials; he had cajoled Slansky into confessing his 'crimes', he purged Party dogmatists and embarked upon a programme of national reconciliation. In 1963, an amnesty for political prisoners was announced; the policy of internal exile and imprisonment without trial was abandoned; the number of Labour Camps was reduced and the jamming of Western radio broadcasts was stopped. It was during this period that the right to education was extended to everyone, regardless of class background, and that Kádár coined the phrase, 'everyone who is not against us is with us'. The year 1967 even saw the end of single list voting[112]. The Party also laid increasing importance on competence, rather than possession of a

---

have become the 'happiest barrack' in the socialist camp if the terrible experience of 1956 had not occurred. Although those in power at first engaged in a terrible revenge, the experience of 1956 proved to be an unforgettable lesson for them.' Translation Wendy Hollis.

[110] One month after the Revolution, Communist Party members numbered 38 000. After a recruiting drive, this figure had risen to half a million by 1962. See Heinrich, Hans-Georg, *Hungary: Politics, Economics and Society*, Pinter 1986, pp. 45-47.

[111] Bugajski, Janusz, Pollack, Maxine, *East European Fault Lines*, Westview Press 1989, p. 62.

[112] See Crampton, Richard, *Eastern Europe in the Twentieth Century*, p. 317.

Party Card, as a criterion in deciding who should occupy important positions. The Kádár regime did not insist on public denunciations of belief in Communism and renounced its control over a considerable sphere of private life. The Communist regime in Hungary was thus tolerated. In comparison with those in the neighbouring countries of Czechoslovakia and Romania, it was much more humane and tolerable:

> *'Dort gibt es aber auch das am besten organisierte, am wenigsten irrationale, zudem zweckrationale, nun:* in gewissem Maße *erträgliche Unterdrückungssystem.'*[113]

However, reconciliation with the population was bought at the price of increased living standards and availability of consumer goods. It was this policy, vital to the survival of the regime and thus untouchable, which caused Hungary's foreign debt to increase at such an exponential rate[114]. In order to fulfil this imperative the Hungarian Party was forced to rid itself of the Stalinists and dogmatists within its ranks and embark upon a programme of continuous, if cautious, reform. The events of 1956 clearly demonstrated that the population was not willing to accept a Stalinist government any longer. De-Stalinisation was therefore necessary to make the country governable and to enable the introduction of reforms which would placate the population. Another result of the Revolution was that belief in Communist ideology in Hungary was completely destroyed. Communism was officially practised, but not believed. The Hungarian government and population had to come to terms with the fact that although they had rejected Communism, the Soviet Union was intent on keeping a Communist regime in Hungary. Everything depended on the Soviet Union. Kádár's talent lay in being able to judge

---

[113] Heller, Agnes, Fehér, Ferenc, *Ungarn 1956*, VSA Verlag 1982, p. 178. 'There also exists the best organised, the least irrational, or rather rational for the purpose, and also in a certain sense the most bearable system of repression.' Translation Wendy Hollis.

[114] Importing foreign consumer goods increased the Hungarian Foreign Debt from $1 Billion in 1970 to a staggering $9.1 Billion by 1980. This in itself made reform imperative. Ibid. Brown, J., F., *Eastern Europe and Communist Rule*, p. 213.

accurately where the limits lay and in some instances being able to convince the Soviet leaders to increase the room for manoeuvre. So, although 'Kádárism' recognised the need for change, it was at the same time aware of its limits. Reform was therefore limited lest it threaten the weakened Communist ideology which emerged in the wake of de-Stalinisation.

1.3: The 1968 Prague Spring

'Communism in Eastern Europe was doomed when it became irreformable'
J., F., Brown, *Surge to Freedom*.

At the start of the 1960's, the Czechoslovak Communist Party experienced a situation similar to that which had arisen in Hungary. Antonin Novotny had survived Khrushchev's de-Stalinisation and remained in power. He had stubbornly refused to de-Stalinise the Party and rehabilitate the victims of the Purges. In addition to this, it was becoming clear that the Stalinist concept of extensive growth based on large, heavy industrial complexes was having a crippling effect on the Czechoslovak economy and population. Czechoslovakia's 'poisoned chalice' of heavy industry which had survived the War intact was beginning to take its toll. Although this industrial base had initially enabled the Czechoslovak economy to recover relatively quickly, especially in comparison with the economies of Hungary and Romania, by the 1960's it was as outdated and old as the Stalinist mentality of the Communist Party leaders.

This combination created a rather peculiar situation in Czechoslovakia. As Gordon Skilling notes:

'The case of Czechoslovakia is particularly paradoxical, since, in spite of the relatively late establishment of Stalinism and the antecedent democratic political culture, it lasted long after the death of Stalin and in many cases was not basically modified until 1968.'[115]

The Czechoslovak Communist Party had initially endorsed a democratic path to socialism. This attitude was no doubt influenced by the legal history of the Party and by the real popular support it enjoyed amongst the population in the immediate aftermath of the War. This policy had been approved not only by the Soviet Union, but also by the core of the Bolshevist leadership under Gottwald. It was partly due to this that the democratic parties in Czechoslovakia were able to defend their position within the coalition government for three years. However, this period and the seeming transformation of the Communist Party lulled them into a false sense of security. In the same way as President Benes, they could not comprehend the Communist mentality and thus misunderstood the real motives behind Communist policy. They made the fatal mistake of applying democratic standards and norms to Communist behaviour. Although the blatant Communist seizure of power in Slovakia in late 1947 warned of the coming storm, it seemed that the Communist Party had been drawn into the traditional Czechoslovak institution of coalition government and thus into the framework of the pre-war democratic political system.

The Communist Coup in February 1948 was an unpleasant and unexpected shock. However, President Benes' official acceptance of the new Communist government served to give it a mantle of legality and legitimacy. It seems that the Czechoslovak Communist Party had been instructed to seize power as a result of its slow progress towards gaining it democratically. Subsequently, the Stalinist system was meticulously and brutally applied. Czechoslovakia's early economic policy had not been fully Stalinist, it had publicly accepted the Marshall Plan, before being humiliated in Moscow and having to withdraw from it. Czechoslovakia was also one of the last countries to stage Show Trials although, paradoxically, of the eight major Show Trials set in motion, the majority took place after Stalin's death[116]. In addition,

---

[115] Ibid. Skilling, H., G., 'Stalinism and Czechoslovak Political Culture'. In Tucker, R., C., *Stalinism: Essays in Historical Interpretation*, p. 268.

[116] Due to unwillingness to cooperate, or unreliability in performing before the Court, many people were tried in secret. In 1968, the estimated number of death

the staging of the Trials was so complete and perfect that none of the defendants withdrew their confession or used the opportunity provided by the Court to defend themselves[117]. All the trials enjoyed wide publicity and were broadcast live from Court. This phenomenon of 'over-correction' may have been an attempt to comopensate for earlier reluctance to introduce Stalinist policies.

The Hungarian Revolution in 1956 facilitated the prolongation of the Stalinist system in Czechoslovakia. In addition to being personally implicated in the Purges, as was the rest of the Czechoslovak leadership, Novotny was unwilling to risk a comprehensive de-Stalinisation programme that could precipitate the same situation which had developed in Hungary. As long as de-Stalinisation was not on the agenda, the Party elite and functionaries remained united. De-Stalinisation would destroy this precarious stability because those implicated would not give up power willingly and an internal struggle would ensue.

The problem was that, much as Hungary had found itself at the start of the 1950's, Czechoslovakia was facing an economic crisis by the start of the 1960's. The economic and political problems collided in the Purges. The Purges had specifically aimed to discredit the idea of a 'national' path to socialism which had initially been sponsored by the Czechoslovak Party, including Gottwald. Of course, during the Purges Gottwald had ensured that other leaders took the blame for this policy. Therefore, the Purges also served to justify the subsequent policy of applying the Soviet model of development, which was introduced after 1948. However, by the 1960's it was clear that this model was neither suitable for the Czechoslovak economy or society. So, if it were to deal with the economic problems, the Czechoslovak Communist Party would be

---

sentences issued by the State Court from 1948 to the end of 1952 was 233, of which 178 had been carried out. Ibid. Skilling, H., G., 'Stalinism and Czechoslovak Political Culture'. In Tucker, R., C., *Stalinism: Essays in Historical Interpretation*, p. 270.

[117] Bukharin had tried to defend himself during his trial in the Soviet Union, and Kerensky retracted his confession in open Court. Ibid. Skilling, H., G., 'Stalinism and Czechoslovak Political Culture'. In Tucker, R., C., *Stalinism: Essays in historical Interpretation*, p. 270.

forced to deal with the question of the Purges and thus of de-Stalinisation.

Economic difficulties became obvious as early as 1958. These came partly as a result of the concessions made to the workers in 1953, but were mainly a result of the Planning System. Czechoslovakia experienced negative economic growth in the 1950's. In 1958 the Plan and the Planning mechanism were reorganised, but this proved confusing and pointless as those involved in the system were not economists and did not understand the programme. In addition to this, the central price mechanism was left untouched. The root of the problem lay in the system of bureaucratic orders which were directed from the centre to the periphery, that is in the Stalinist command administration. No one was willing to take any personal responsibility and this led to stagnation and late fulfilment of the Plan. In addition to this, Plan Targets were often unrealistic. By the start of the 1960's it was clear that some kind of reform and de-Stalinisation was necessary.

1.3.1: Late Novotnyism

In the light of the economic situation, and especially after Khrushchev started his second de-Stalinisation campaign in the Soviet Union in 1961[118], Novotny was no longer in a position to block reform. Thus, 'late Novotnyism', i.e. the period between 1963-1968, was characterised by relaxation in the public sphere, encouragement of Party debate about economic and political problems, and the cautious beginnings of a de-Stalinisation programme. An amnesty for political prisoners came into effect on 9 May, 1960. As a result, most of the 8708 remaining political prisoners were freed to bear witness to the crimes of the regime[119].

The third Five Year Plan of 1960-1965 was finally abandoned in August 1962[120]. At the subsequent 12th Conference of the Czechoslovak Communist Party in 1962, Novotny was forced to change course. Stalin's statue was removed form the centre of

---

[118] The second wave of de-Stalinisation was heralded at the XXII Congress of the CPSU in 1961. See Golan, Galia, *Reform Rule in Czechoslovakia*, Cambridge University Press 1973, p. 4.
[119] Ibid. Beyram, D., Bock, Ivo, (Hrsg.), *Das Tauwetter und die Folgen*, p. 97.
[120] Ibid. Golan, Galia, *Reform Rule in Czechoslovakia*, p. 3.

Prague and Novotny got rid of some of his Stalinist supporters. The Interior Minister, Barak, was dismissed in an attempt to place the majority of the blame for the Show Trials on his shoulders. In addition, some of those who had been tried between 1948-54 were to be rehabilitated. Specialist groups were also contracted to work on new programmes aimed at solving the economic and political problems. A group headed by Zdenek Mlynar was set up to examine the development of the political system in socialism. A further group, led by Radovan Richta, was designated to analyse the effects of the scientific-technological revolution on the socialist system. However, the most important was the group of economists led by Ota Šik[121]. They were charged with presenting a reform programme for the economic system. In his final report, Šik criticised the administrative planning system. He proposed a 'New Economic Model' aimed at reforming the bureaucratic system to enable the economic planning system to optimise quantitative economic growth. This programme was finally accepted by the Central Committee in 1965, but had to wait for final approval from the Party Congress before implementation. During this period of limbo, it was watered down and changed. As Novotny continually tried to slow down the reforms undertaken between 1963-67, the reformist faction within the Party began to agitate for his removal. These were the first signs of a split within the Party elite.

At the same time, the Party also set up a Commission to review the Show Trials. It was headed by Jan Piller and had access to the Czechoslovak Party archives. Its draft report was so damning that, even in a moderated form, it was not published prior to the invasion[122]. However, during the Prague Spring, Karel Kaplan published a series of articles in the journal *Nova Mysl* which contained the major findings of the report[123].

In addition, the Slovak Party began to reiterate its demands for more independence. Alexander Dubcek replaced Bacilek as First

---

[121] Grebing, Helga, *Der Revisionismus: Von Bernstein bis zum Prager Frühling*, Verlag C. H. Beck 1977, p. 215.
[122] Ibid. Skilling, H., G., 'Stalinism and Czechoslovak Political Culture'. In Tucker, R., C., *Stalinism: Essays in historical Interpretation*, p. 272.
[123] Kaplan, Karel, 'Reflections on the Political Trials', *Nova Mysl*, Nos. 6, 7, 8, 1968.

Secretary of the Slovak Party in 1963, the same year in which Gustav Husak was rehabilitated. The de-Stalinisation programme within the Slovak Party structures he initiated complemented Slovak demands for more independence from Prague and for more democracy within Party structures, but the system of democratic centralism was at no time called into question. As a result, Dubcek became viewed as a possible alternative to Novotny. During the three years before the 13th Party Congress in June 1966, there was an increasingly public struggle between the Party conservatives and the group of reformists over the proper course required to deal with the crisis. Although the 13th Congress accepted Šik's 'New Economic Model', it decided not to implement it until 1967[124].

Although the economists who had worked out the economic reform programme were Marxists, they had come to the conclusion that the system was based on unrealistic premises. It was taken for granted that the production of many thousands of products, which coincided with the needs of a continually changing population, could be achieved by giving the factories an economic plan. It was also assumed that, without the incentives of the market, factory managers would still opt for an optimal level of production. These were utopian ideals. In reality, it was impossible to regulate exactly the necessary quantity of each product produced. In addition, factory managers often acted 'irrationally' in that they opted for a low level of production to ensure the Plan target would not be raised and thereby increase their personal work-load. They were also only interested in the quantity of goods produced, not the quality.

Ota Šik proposed that only a few products be set in figures in the Plan, allowing the others to be aggregated. It was also proposed that pay should depend on Plan fulfilment. The problem was that the enterprises did not react to the reforms by producing goods which coincided with consumer expectations, but simply to fulfil Plan targets[125]. In addition, the programme was changed before implementation and, even though it was officially sponsored by the

---

[124] James, Robert, Rhodes, *The Czechoslovak Crisis 1968*, Weidenfeld & Nicolson 1969, pp. 5-6.
[125] For more information about Ota Šik's economic reforms, see Miller, Tilly, (Ed), *Prager Frühling und Reformpolitik heute*, Olzog Verlag 1989, pp. 19-23.

government, in many cases was only partially implemented by the hostile local bureaucracy. Thus, the results hoped for did not materialise. The system itself was hindering the implementation of the economic reform programme. Wlodimir Brus identifies one of the main problems of the Communist economic system as:

'...*the lack of political pluralism 'as' the major cause of blockage of information flows in Eastern Europe, and hence the major cause of misallocation of resources on a long-term scale.*'[126]

Brus expands that the 'planned chaos' which results is peculiar to this 'form of socialism and seems to be firmly rooted in the political system.'[127]

The de-Stalinisation of state structures was therefore vital for successful economic reform. On 1 January, 1967, a new Press Law, which was effectively a more severe censorship law, was issued[128]. It sparked the Writer's Union revolt against the Party and Novotny at its 4th Congress on 27 June, 1967. The speakers leading the revolt included Vaclav Havel, Milan Kundera and Ludvik Vaculik[129]. Pavel Kohout also read out Solzhenitsyn's open letter concerning Soviet censorship[130]. The Party representatives present, including Vasil Bilak, the Minister of Education and Culture, left the podium during the speeches. This public defiance caused an irreconcilable spilt in the Party leadership. The 11 member Praesidium remained deadlocked between 30-31 October, 1967 over the question of Novotny's replacement[131]. The problem was finally resolved by the Central Committee on 19 December,

---

[126] Gomulka, Stanislav, *Growth, Innovation and Reform in Eastern Europe*, Wheatsheaf, p. 28.
[127] Ibid. Gomulka, Stanislav, *Growth and Innovation in Eastern Europe*, pp. 28-29.
[128] Ibid. James, Robert, Rhodes, *The Czechoslovak Crisis 1968*, p. 7.
[129] Ludvik Vaculik was the author of the '2000 Words Manifesto', which was published on 27 June, 1968. Valenta, J., *Soviet Intervention in Czechoslovakia 1968*, John Hopkins University Press 1991, p. 40.
[130] Schwartz, H., *Prague's 200 Days*, Frederick A. Praeger Publishers 1969, p. 42.
[131] Renner, Hans, *A History of Czechoslovakia since 1945*, Routledge 1989, p. 42.

1967[132], but during the interim period the government was effectively paralysed.

1.3.2: Dubcek becomes First Secretary

Novotny was blamed for failure to de-Stalinise and for the debacle surrounding the economic reform programme. He had to renounce his position of First Secretary, but remained President. Alexander Dubcek replaced him as First Secretary on 5 January, 1968[133]. Novotny was too compromised by the Show Trials to receive support from the Soviet Union. The Soviet leaders realised that he had to go and effectively abandoned him. During his visit to Prague on 8 December, 1967, Brezhnev had assured the Czechoslovak leaders that dealing with the crisis and getting rid of Novotny was their own business[134]. The problem was that, in the final analysis, it obviously was not.

Born in 1921, Dubcek had grown up in the Soviet Union and was considered absolutely loyal by the Soviet leaders. He presented an 'Action Programme' for 1968 which included rehabilitation for the Purge victims and a revival of the Parties which had been members of the 'National Front' before the Communist take-over. Dubcek also started to reform and de-Stalinise the Party structures. This was an admittance that the Communist Party was unable to cope with the situation in its present form and that sweeping reform was necessary if the Party was to govern competently. However, the socialist nature of the government and country was not questioned. The Parties of the 'National Front' were to be revived as discussion forums via which the Communist Party would be able to involve the population more directly in government. The Party would listen and act on those proposals which it thought appropriate. There was to be pluralism, but it would be limited, and the basic security interests of the Soviet Union would not be called into question. That is, Czechoslovakia would remain a member of the Warsaw Pact and the CMEA and thus within the Soviet sphere

---

[132] Ibid. James, Robert, Rhodes, *The Czechoslovak Crisis 1968*, p. 10.
[133] Ibid. Brogan, P., *Eastern Europe 1939-1989*, p. 94.
[134] He is said to have stated, 'It is your own affair'. Ibid. Valenta, J., *Soviet Intervention in Czechoslovakia*, p. 29.

of influence. Unlike the position in Hungary in 1956, Dubcek proposed to reform the Communist system, not to replace it.

Economic reform was vital not only to the economy, but also as proof that the Party was capable of competent government. The Party elite wanted to become politically legitimate in the eyes of the population. In order to gain legitimacy, the Party had to reform the economy, reform itself and recognise particular interests within the population. Problems could then be solved on the basis of a democratic consensus. Real political legitimacy would therefore facilitate the resolution of the crisis which faced Czechoslovakia. It is important to note that the aim of the Party elite and the population at large was not the resurrection of capitalism. In a survey carried out in 1968, 89% of those questioned wanted socialist development to continue; a mere 5% were in favour of a return to capitalism. 71.4% supported the Party's Action Programme and a further 78% trusted Dubcek and the Party leadership. 86% supported the abolition of censorship, this included 67% of Communist Party members[135]. The Czechoslovak Communist Party was gaining genuine legitimacy in the eyes of the population. Domestic legitimacy of course meant it would no longer have to rely on the Soviet Union for support. It would also mean that the Czechoslovak Party could become independent from the Communist Party of the Soviet Union.

Ota Šik's 'New Economic Model' was revised and proposed for implementation. Market prices were to be introduced, wage policy was to be reviewed, enterprise independence increased and conditions of competition to be created. Plan targets would no longer be binding, but would act as production guides. However, many factories interpreted the new guidelines in the same way they had done binding Plan targets, thus emphasising the basic problem that the bureaucratic-centralist system could not readily adapt itself to embrace reform.

Censorship was abandoned and a press campaign was initiated to support the reform movement by exposing the failures of the former regime. A serious problem with this strategy was that, once it was free, the Press tended to criticise the Communist regime per

---

[135]. Ibid. Miller, Tilly, (Ed.), *Prager Frühling und Reform Politik heute*, p. 52.

se. Neither the Party nor Dubcek had foreseen the extent and vitality of debate. Dubcek and the group of reformers within the Party still believed in Communist ideology, but wished to reform the system so that it could function efficiently. The delicate balance between reformers and conservatives was destroyed by the defection of General Jan Sejna, who revealed the full extent of the Novotny regime's corruption[136]. Novotny resigned as President on 23 March, 1968. He was replaced by General Svoboda. Novotny and Gottwald were held personally responsible for the crimes of the Stalinist period. Novotny was eventually expelled from the Party on 30 May, 1968[137]. On the same day Novotny was relieved of his position as President, the Warsaw Pact met in Dresden to discuss the situation in Czechoslovakia. Indeed, during May and June, a series of manoeuvres were carried out along the Czechoslovak border.

Dubcek's difficulties were similar to those which Imre Nagy had encountered twelve years before. Although Dubcek had replaced Novotny, Novotny's supporters still held the most influential positions within the Party. It was imperative to call the 14th Party Congress as soon as possible in order to rid the Party of the anti-reform grouping and elect a new Central Committee and Praesidium. An Extraordinary Congress was called, but was scheduled to take place on 26 August for the Slovak Party and 9 September for the whole Czechoslovak Party. Failure to call the Congress earlier and place reformers in the Party's leading positions meant that after the Warsaw Pact invasion Dubcek was effectively abandoned.

It was the task of reforming the Party, combined with pressure to reform the economic system, which caused the Czechoslovak Party to split. It was at no time clear that Dubcek was in control of the Party or the situation in the country. He called on the population to engage in the reform debate and examine the crimes of the past in the hope that the popular support this generated could be used to his advantage in the internal Party struggle over the reform programme. On 27 June, 1968, Ludvik Vaculik issued the '2000 Word

---

[136] He defected in order to avoid arrest. Novotny's son was also implicated. Ibid. Brogan, P., *Eastern Europe 1939-1989*, p. 95.
[137] Ibid. Brogan. P., *Eastern Europe 1939-1989*, p. 97.

Manifesto', which was signed by 70 writers and intellectuals. It was a call to support reform and Dubcek's government[138]. Unfortunately, Dubcek's call for a Czechoslovak 'Socialism with a Human Face' implied that the Soviet variety was inhuman and inferior. This was of course unacceptable to the Soviet Union.

1.3.3: The Warsaw Pact Invasion

The Soviet Union and the members of the Warsaw Pact were worried by the possible consequences of the Czechoslovak reforms. However, they seemed reluctant to intervene directly and attempted to influence events by employing psychological and political pressure. Although there were numerous meetings and consultations, both bilateral and multilateral, the Czechoslovak government was not intimidated. Dubcek was invited to a Warsaw Pact meeting on 15 July, 1968, but declined the invitation. A further invitation was extended from the Soviet Politburo to the Czechoslovak Praesidium to meet in Moscow, but this too was declined. However, this strategy may have increased the Soviet Union's fears that the Czechoslovak government was intent on going its own way without taking Soviet interests into account.

The Soviet Union was not prepared to allow another Communist country to follow a course which differed from its own interpretation of Communism, and yet it was painfully aware of the political consequences of another invasion. This contributed to indecision amongst the Soviet Politburo members. Preparations for an invasion were taken during June and July, but it seems they were part of a 'worst case scenario' strategy[139]. A consensus facilitating the political decision to invade was only reached on 21 August, 1968[140]. The invasion was a military success, but a political failure. No one stepped forward to take over from Dubcek and the Soviet

---

[138] Ibid. Brogan, P., *Eastern Europe 1939-1989*, p. 97.

[139] 16 000 Warsaw Pact troops had remained on Czechoslovak territory after the end of the joint manoeuvres in July 1968. Ibid. Valenta, J., *Soviet Intervention in Czechoslovakia*, p. 13.

[140] The Warsaw Pact invaded Czechoslovakia on the night of 20-21 August, 1968 with approximately 400 000 troops. 50 000 of these were from Polish divisions, 20 000 from the German Democratic Republic, 20 000 from Hungary and 10 000 from Bulgaria. Romania did not take part in the invasion. Ibid. Brogan, P., *Eastern Europe 1939-1989*, pp. 98-99.

Union was forced to negotiate with him and the very same government it had hoped to depose. The government was flown to Moscow on 21 August where, on 26 August, Dubcek signed the 'Moscow Protocol' accepting the invasion as an offer of help from the Warsaw Pact. He remained First Secretary and continued to be, at least nominally, in charge of government.

The Czechoslovak population practised sullen, passive resistance in the face of the invading troops, but did not rise up in arms. Dubcek remained First Secretary until 17 April, 1969 when, at Dubcek's own request, Gustav Husak took over the post. Dubcek became Chair of the National Assembly, the position he was to hold once again after the 'Velvet Revolution' in 1989[141]. Gustav Husak had become First Secretary, but had to wait until 1975 before he was able to rid himself of General Svoboda and become President as well. Dubcek was eventually removed from the National Assembly and sent to Turkey as Ambassador in September 1969, where he remained until 1970. He was finally expelled from the Communist Party on 27 June, 1970. Thereafter he slipped into anonymity as a forestry worker in Slovakia[142]. Although during his tenure as First Secretary from August 21, 1968 to 12 April, 1969[143], Dubcek attempted to save some of the reforms, his acceptance of this role in the new Soviet approved government meant he was also party to their reversal. New censorship laws were introduced as early as September 1968. Indeed, the only reform to survive the invasion was the Federalisation of the Czechoslovak state. Ironically, this was not to survive the transition to democracy.

Dubcek's fate demonstrates a feature which was common to all the Communist regimes in Eastern Europe. The system oppressed the population, but at the same time was reliant on the people to maintain it. Consequently there was no clear division between those who supported the regime and those who opposeed it, since everyone was compromised by the system. As Vaclav Havel notes:

---

[141] Hejzlar, Zdenek, *Reform Kommunismus*, Europäische Verlagsanstalt 1976, p. 335.
[142] Ibid. Brogan, P., *Eastern Europe 1939-1989*, p. 102.
[143] Ibid. Hejzlar, Zdenek, *Reform Kommunismus*, p. 334.

'In the post-totalitarian system, this line runs de facto through each person, for everyone in his or her own way is both a victim and a supporter of the system.'[144]

The invasion was a brutal reminder that the Communist regimes in Eastern Europe were maintained by the Soviet Union and served not national interests, but those of the Soviet Union. It demonstrated the basic dilemma between demonstrating loyalty to the Soviet Union and acting in the national interest - a dilemma which confronted all the Communist regimes in Eastern Europe. As Richard Staar notes, not only did the Soviet military guarantee, or 'Brezhnev Doctrine'[145] as it became known, de-legitimise the governments of the region in the eyes of the indigenous populations, it also decreased the willingness and indeed the necessity to tackle the economic and social problems facing the regimes. The Warsaw Pact guarantee secured the ruling political elites' power regardless of the state of the economy. In addition, any attempt to deal with problems which led to a reform movement not in accord with Soviet ideology could lead to an invasion which would topple the elite:

'Paradoxically, the USSR military guarantee had the long term effect of undermining these Parties. The Warsaw Pact security guarantee undercut the legitimacy of the pro-Moscow Parties by emphasising their roles as Soviet viceroys. The USSR security guarantee also diminished the incentive for the ruling Parties to manage their societies and economies efficiently.'[146]

However, the 1968 invasion was to have another, more wide reaching, effect on the Communist movement as a whole.

---

[144] Ash, Timothy Garton, *The Uses of Adversity*, Penguin Books 1991, p. 173.
[145] Brezhnev stated that, 'The weakening of any links in the world socialist system directly affects all the socialist countries, which cannot look on indifferently when this happens.' Ibid. Brogan, P., *Eastern Europe 1939-1989*, p. 202.
[146] Staar, Richard, F., (Ed), *East-Central Europe and the USSR*, St. Martin's Press 1991, p. 25.

1.3.4: Ideological De-legitimisation

In harmony with their Communist world view, many Communist reformers could justify the invasion of Hungary because the Communist system had been on the verge of collapse. The Hungarian population had taken violent revenge on certain members of the Communist apparatus, notably members of the *AVO*, and had actively resisted intervention, thus emphasising their anti-Communist sentiments. Whereas the Hungarian Revolution of 1956 had been a violent attempt to get rid of the Communist system, the Prague Spring of 1968 was a peaceful attempt at structural reform as a means to retain a more effective Communist system. However, Radoslav Selucky notes that the invasion of Czechoslovakia in 1968:

> '...*proved something most Czechoslovak reformers ...did not even dare to believe at the time, namely, that the established Marxist-Leninist theory is incompatible with a genuine, modern, democratic, economic and political system and, what is more, that it is not even open to reform.*'[147]

He also believes that the Prague Spring was, 'the last attempt to rejuvenate Communism in Central Europe'[148]. The experience of 21 August, 1968 led the majority of the reformers to break completely with Communism as they perceived its imperial and despotic nature. The invasion of Czechoslovakia demonstrated that, in the absence of democratic pluralism a form of totalitarianism would evolve. However, this was not the only consequence. Leszek Kolakowski realised that once the prospect of reform was crushed:

> '*Communism ceased to be an intellectual problem and became merely a question of power.*'[149]

He also states that the reformers themselves were partly to blame for the collapse of Communist ideology by the sheer power of their criticism. Once ideology had been destroyed as an

---

[147] Selucky, Radoslav, *The Plan that Failed*, Nelson 1970, p. xii.
[148] Ibid. Selucky, Radoslav, *The Plan that Failed*, p. 142.
[149] Ibid. Selucky, Radoslav, *The Plan that Failed*, p. 227.

intellectual problem, it became an instrument employed to legitimise the system of power:

> *'Der politische Revisionismus ist 1968 endgültig zu Ende gegangen zusammen mit seinem Gegenspieler und Widersacher: der Ideologie des kommunistischen orthodoxen Dogmatismus. In Osteuropa hat seitdem der Kommunismus als ideologisches Phänomen zu existieren aufgehört. Die offizielle Staatsdoktrin ist nun zum unentbehrlichen Ritual geworden, das dem Machtsystem die Legitimation zu schaffen hat. Der Kommunismus aber ist intellektuell tot und hat keine Gläubigen mehr, weder die Regierten noch die Regierenden glauben an ihn. Daß es dazu gekommen ist, liegt zum Teil an der zerstörenden Kraft, die von der revisionistischen Kritik ausgelöst wurde.'*[150]

1.3.5: Reactions to the Events

The Soviet leaders' fears about the consequences of allowing the Czechoslovak experiment to continue were exacerbated by the other members of the Warsaw Pact who feared for their own power[151]. Although Nicolae Ceausescu had taken over power from Gheorghe Dej in Romania after his death in March 1965[152], he had still not fully consolidated his position within the Party. The reform movement in Czechoslovakia threatened his attempts at consolidation since it provided an example which could lead to

---

[150] Ibid. Grebing, Helga, *Der Revisionismus: Von Bernstein bis zum Prager Frühling*, p. 240. 'Political revisionism was buried for good in 1968 together with its opponent and adversary: the ideology of Communist orthodox dogmatism. Since then Communism has ceased to exist as an ideological phenomenon in Eastern Europe. The official State doctrine has degenerated into a necessary ritual which has as its only aim the legitimisation of the power structure. Communism is intellectually dead and no one believes in it anymore; neither those who are ruled nor those who rule believe. That it has come to this lies in part with the destructive force which was set free by revisionist criticism.' Translation Wendy Hollis.
[151] Demonstrations in Poland in March, 1968 had witnessed students chanting 'Poland is waiting for its own Dubcek'. Czechoslovak papers had already been banned in Poland and in the Spring of 1968 a number of Czech students and journalists were expelled. Ibid. Valenta, J., *Soviet Intervention in Czechoslovakia*, p. 24.
[152] Ibid. Almond, Mark, *The Rise and Fall of Nicolae and Elena Ceausescu*, p. xi.

reform tendencies in Romania. But, the Czechoslovak crisis also provided Ceausescu with the means he needed to secure his own position within the Party, and he used the situation to his own advantage. Theoretically, the Czechoslovak reforms could have provided support to Kádár's 'New Economic Mechanism'. Presented in 1968, this programme was in many ways similar to the Czechoslovak Party's 'Action Programme'. Kádár may have viewed the developments in Czechoslovakia with sympathy, but they represented a threat to the Hungarian programme as they attracted unwanted attention to the whole question of systemic reform.

Hungarian troops invaded Czechoslovakia with the Warsaw Pact on 21 August, 1968, but no Romanian troops took part in the operation and Ceausescu was the only East European leader to denounce the invasion. Both Kádár and Ceausescu acted out of fear for their own position, but chose different methods by which to preserve it. This paradox can be explained by examining the Romanian Communist Party's attempts to increase independence from Moscow, and the Hungarian Party's complete dependence on Moscow since 1956.

Gheorghe Dej had already steered Romania on a course of independence from Moscow. This culminated in Romania's 'Declaration of Independence' in April 1964. It had taken the form of 'A Statement on the stand of the Romanian Workers' Party concerning the problems of the World Communist Movement'. The declaration stated Romania's determination to decide its own course of development:

> *'It is up to every Marxist-Leninist Party, it is a sovereign right of each socialist state to elaborate, choose or change the forms and methods of socialist construction.'*[153]

Of course this declaration was necessary if the Romanian Communist Party was continue its Stalinist policies during Khrushchev's second wave of de-Stalinisation. As the Soviet Union preached de-Stalinisation, it would be difficult for it to defend a

---

[153] Ibid. Crampton, R., J., *Eastern Europe in the Twentieth Century*, p. 313.

direct intervention, à la Stalin, in Romanian affairs. In addition, the easiest, and indeed only, means of securing a limited domestic legitimacy for the Romanian Communist Party was to manipulate Romanian nationalism. As Romanian nationalism had always contained a substantial amount of anti-Russian sentiment, it was relatively simple to portray the Romanian Communists' striving for an independent policy from Moscow as in the national interest, irrespective of its content.

On coming to power, Ceausescu needed to consolidate his personal position within the Party and legitimise his power to the population. He gradually rid himself of Dej's supporters and initiated a limited liberalisation programme. There had in fact been a continuous trend towards liberalisation in Romania from 1962 onwards. The hope was that Ceausescu would continue this trend, and indeed cultural and literary freedom was initially increased. Ana Pauker had died a non-person in prison in 1961, but Lucretiu Patrascanu was posthumously rehabilitated. Dej was blamed for their deaths. The paradox was that at the same time as Ceausescu denounced Dej, in an attempt to obliterate his memory and usurp his position of absolute power, he continued Dej's policies. Thus, a new Constitution was drafted in which Romania was described as a, 'unitary socialist state' and at the 9th Party Congress in July 1965, the Romanian Workers' Party was named the Romanian Communist Party once more[154]. Ceausescu used the Czechoslovak crisis to demonstrate his own independence from Moscow in the hope that such a policy would gain him domestic support and so increase his personal power base.

Although no Romanian troops took part in the Warsaw Pact invasion of Czechoslovakia, the Bulgarian contingent travelled across Romanian territory, and to avoid voting against its allies within the Warsaw Pact, the Romanian delegation had simply not attended the meetings which dealt with the Czechoslovak crisis. However, Ceausescu's policy reaffirmed Romania's independence at precisely the moment when the limits of Eastern European independence had been demonstrated. On the 21 August, 1968, the fifty year old Ceausescu spoke from the Balcony of the Central

---

[154] Ibid. Bugajski, Janusz, Pollack, Maxine, *East European Fault Lines*, p. 26.

Committee building in Bucharest to a large and ecstatic crowd. He explained that no Romanian troops had taken part in the invasion, and that the Romanian army had been mobilised and would resist a Soviet invasion[155]. It was at this time that Paul Goma, a well-known Romanian dissident, joined the Communist Party in the belief that reform would soon sweep the Romanian system. He was to be sorely disappointed.

Ceausescu's action, however brave it might have appeared, was misunderstood by the Romanian population and the world at large. First of all, such action would not have been possible without the Soviet Union's tolerance, if not tacit approval. Secondly, in denouncing the Warsaw Pact invasion, Ceausescu was not, as assumed, acting in support of the reforms associated with the Prague Spring. Although he had travelled to Dubcek two days before the invasion to give his moral support to the Czechoslovak strivings for more independence, he was totally opposed to any reform of the Stalinist system. Ceausescu was aware that the East European countries were subject to Soviet control, but was determined that he alone should hold power in Romania. Ceausescu's denunciation of the invasion was a demonstration of independence, but also an expression of his own fears concerning Soviet intervention in Romanian affairs.

Objection to the Warsaw Pact invasion of Czechoslovakia gave Ceausescu prestige and genuine popularity at home and abroad, in the same way his refusal to sever relations with Israel during the Six Day War in 1967 had done. The period of euphoria which the action precipitated gave Ceausescu the time he needed to secure his own power base within the Party. Ironically, he was aided in this by the public support of the misled population. Although multi-candidate elections were introduced, candidates had to be approved by the Communist controlled 'Social Democratic and National Unity Front'[156]. In this way, Ceausescu persuaded the population he was a reformer, although the electoral system was a means by which he could remove those Communists he disapproved of. Once Ceausescu had obtained absolute power within the Party, the vague

---

[155] Ibid. Almond, M., *The Rise and Fall of Nicolae and Elena Ceausescu*, p. 1.
[156] Ibid. Almond, Mark, *The Rise and Fall of Nicolae and Elena Ceausescu*, p. 68.

but perceptible movement towards reform was immediately halted. The dissolution of the autonomous areas for the Szekler minority in late 1968 was a foretaste of what was to come. The Warsaw Pact invasion presented Ceausescu with the perfect opportunity to consolidate his personal rule. Consolidation was achieved by instrumentalising Romanian nationalism and insisting on a policy independent from Moscow. This combination was to form the foundation of Ceausescu's rule.

In contrast, the Czechoslovak crisis came at a particularly inopportune moment for Kádár who, having consolidated his regime[157], had also started on a programme of reform at the start of the 1960's. The relaxation began with Kádár's famous phrase, 'all those who are not against us are with us'. This was a subtle play on the phrase employed during Rakosi's regime that, 'all those who are not with us are against us.' This example aptly demonstrates the new strategy which Kádár employed to co-opt the population into passive support of the regime. In 1963, all those who had been interred as a result of the Revolution were released. All forced labour camps were closed and the policy of internal exile and imprisonment without trial was stopped. At the same time, press censorship and book restrictions were reduced and western radio was no longer jammed. It also became easier to travel abroad to the West. In 1960, 35 000 Hungarians received exit visas. This figure rose to 143 000 in 1967 and during the course of the 1970's as many as one million Hungarians travelled to the West[158].

Although domestic policy seemed to be largely Kádár's own affair, he was careful to follow the Soviet Union's lead in foreign policy. This was due to the experience of 1956, which left the Hungarian Party broken and totally dependent on the Soviet Union. In order to avoid a repetition of 1956, Kádár accepted that Hungarian foreign policy remain in total harmony with that of the Soviet Union. So, in 1970 relations with Israel were broken off and two Hungarian divisions were sent to join the Warsaw Pact invasion of Czechoslovakia in 1968.

---

[157] Between 1957-1959, an estimated 2000 people were executed, 20 000 were imprisoned and 200 000 fled to Austria. Ibid. Brogan, P., *Eastern Europe 1939-1989*, Bloomsbury 1990, p. 135.
[158] Ibid. Brogan, P., *Eastern Europe 1939-1989*, p. 137.

In return, the Hungarian regime was allowed to embark on gradual reform of the system. Kádár managed to convince the Soviet leaders that his initiatives did not consist of system threatening reform, but rather were necessary corrections. His position was strengthened by the experience of 1956, which pointed to the possible outcome if no measures were undertaken. Thus, at the same time as the Prague Spring was reaching its climax in 1968, a 'New Economic Mechanism' was quietly being implemented Hungary. This programme had as its aim a reorganisation of the Planning System, but made no attempt to reform the central planning mechanism. Conceived by Reszö Nyers, a Central Committee Secretary, it had originally been presented to the 8th Congress of the Hungarian Socialist Workers' Party in November 1962. In May 1966, the Central Committee Plenum accepted the programme and scheduled implementation for 1 January, 1968[159]. In addition to liberalisation of the economic sphere, a more general liberalisation of the cultural sphere was undertaken. At the same Plenum György Aczel, who was in charge of Cultural Affairs, set up a cultural study group. This group came to the conclusion that it was acceptable to publish literature which was:

> *'Ideologically debatable and more or less in opposition to Marxism or socialist realism, as long as they [possessed] humanistic value and [were] not politically hostile.'*[160]

But the limits of criticism were never clearly defined and, in the final analysis, depended on the whims of the Minister of Culture and Education at any given time. Although the virtual absence of censorship was to be welcomed, the regime still retained an arbitrary right to withdraw from publication any work which it considered hostile. In this way the regime successfully co-opted the majority of intellectuals into passive support. The policy also had the consequence that, in the absence of an official censor and censorship law, everyone became an unofficial censor. Censorship

---

[159] Ibid. Brown, J., F., *Eastern Europe and Communist Rule*, pp. 208-209.
[160] Kovrig, Bennet, *Communism in Hungary*, Hoover Institute Press 1979, p. 402.

was internalised and practised by everyone since they had to gauge for themselves the limit of the regime's tolerance[161].

As a result of the 'New Economic Mechanism', planning was de-centralised and 50% of prices were market determined. Enterprises were given more independence and had to operate in a semi-free market environment. Small scale private enterprise and cooperatives were encouraged. However, all the safety nets of the Central Planning System remained unchanged and the Communist Party retained its political and economic monopoly[162]. In this way, all the essential characteristics of a centrally planned Communist economy were preserved. Vasil Bilak, the Czechoslovak Minister in charge of Culture and Education, criticised the 'New Economic Mechanism' but the Hungarian government continued its implementation, carrying on even after August 1968. The programme was only officially withdrawn by Reszö Nyers at the Central Committee Plenum of November 1972, after the Soviet Union had expressed its misgivings about the pace of Hungarian reform[163]. In lieu of reform, the Central Committee Plenum decided to raise the wages of the half a million lowest paid workers. This policy was subsequently repeated the next year.

However, events in Czechoslovakia did not have an immediate negative effect on Hungarian developments. This was due to the fact that Kádár enjoyed the Soviet leaders' confidence. Although he travelled numerous times to see Dubcek and discuss the situation, he was careful not to become associated with Dubcek's 'Action Programme' as this would jeopardise his own reforms[164]. Although five Hungarian intellectuals, Agnes Heller, Maria and György

---

[161] For an good description of this see, 'A Hungarian Lesson: The Maze'. Ibid. Ash, Timothy Garton, *The Uses of Adversity*, pp. 130-141.

[162] Although the aim was to create a semi-competitive market, no enterprise could be allowed to go bankrupt, thus budget constraints remained 'soft' and the main enterprise aim remained fulfilment of the Plan.

[163] This was the beginning of the period of stagnation under Brezhnev in the Soviet Union. It meant that Hungarian reform had to be halted until the situation in the Soviet Union was more favourable. The 'New Economic Mechanism' was re-implemented in 1977, after the oil crisis highlighted the continuing difficulties of the Hungarian economy.

[164] Kádár was employed as a go-between in an attempt to bring political pressure to bear on Dubcek. Although Kádár expressed sympathy for Dubcek's situation, he also warned Dubcek not to underestimate the people he was dealing with.

Márkus, Vilmos Sos and Zandor Tordai, issued a statement concerning the invasion on 21 August, 1968, the reaction of the general population was subdued. The Hungarian population had been thoroughly defeated in 1956 and had resigned itself to the continuance of a Communist regime. It had also accepted Kádár and was not to willing to jeopardise his programme of gradual reform in order to support the Czechoslovak cause. As stated by E. J. Czerwinski and Jaroslav Piekalkievicz:

> *'In Hungary's case it may be argued that the sum total of the Kádár regime's reformist innovations ...amounted to a* de facto *revisionist model whose sheer momentum and apparent success have, in effect, inhibited the elites from going beyond muted expressions of sympathy with the goals of the Czechoslovak liberalisation programme.'*[165]

Hungary's participation in the invasion, although a rather macabre spectacle since the Hungarian population had already tried to rid itself of the Soviet system, provided an opportunity to demonstrate loyalty to the Soviet Union[166]. Such a demonstration was necessary to convince the Soviet leaders that the continuation of Hungary's policy of gradual reform, or 'goulash Communism', did not represent a potentially dangerous deviation from Soviet norms. However, Kádár's reluctance to intervene in Czechoslovakia can be inferred from his two month absence from public life following the invasion[167].

1.3.6: Consequences for Czech Development

Unlike Kádár, Dubcek was unable to continue a reform programme after the invasion. During the period in which he remained in government, he attempted to salvage the remains of the 'Action Programme', but failed. He had been unable to gain the

---

[165] Czerwinski, E., J., Piekalkiewicz, Jaroslav, (Eds.), *The Soviet Intervention of Czechoslovakia: Its Effects on Eastern Europe*, Praeger 1972, p. 151.
[166] The Hungarian contingent consisted of two divisions from Slovakia. Having nominally participated in the invasion in August, they were hastily withdrawn two months later in October. Ibid. Kovrig, Bennet, *Communism in Hungary*, p. 410.
[167] Ibid. Kovrig, Bennet, *Communism in Hungary*, P. 411.

trust and confidence of the Soviet leaders. They turned to Gustav Husak, the new Slovak Party leader, to restore order. After becoming First Secretary of the Czechoslovak Party in April 1969, he began a programme of 'normalisation' which aimed to eliminate the last remnants of the reform programme. Although he had been sentenced to life imprisonment under Novotny for 'national deviation', Husak successfully re-Stalinised the Czechoslovak Party, economy and society.

A Party Purge was initiated in 1970. It involved exchanging old Party Cards for new ones[168]. In the process a questionnaire had to be filled out. If the answers were unsatisfactory, a new card was not issued. In this way, 327 000 Communist Party members lost their Party card and another 150 000 voluntarily resigned. In addition, the Writer's Union, which had subjected the Party to public humiliation, was purged. Two out of every three members of the Union lost their jobs. The educational system was also affected. Social science subjects were struck from the curriculum and 900 University lecturers lost their jobs. Twenty-one academic institutions were closed as a result. For the first time since 1821, not a single journal was published between 1969-1971[169]. In addition, a new Criminal Code was introduced which was, in Husak's own words:

'Especially designed to facilitate swift persecution of political and ideological deviance.'[170]

When the Party met in May 1971 for its 14th Congress, only 26 of the 137 strong Central Committee had been members in 1968. The Congress denounced the 1968 'Action Programme' and reinstated a Stalinist economic model[171]. The Party elite decided

---

[168] The person in charge of the process was Milos Jakes, who was presented as the new Prime Minister in 1989.
[169] Ibid. Crampton, R., J., *Eastern Europe in the Twentieth Century*, p. 346.
[170] Kusin, Vladimir, V., 'Husak's Czechoslovakia and Economic Stagnation', *Problems of Communism*, Vol. 31, No. 3, May-June 1982, p. 26.
[171] Ibid. Kusin, Vladimir, V., 'Husak's Czechoslovakia and Ecconomic Stagnation', *Problems of Communism*, p. 26.

against co-opting the population by means of a policy of reconciliation and opted instead to revert to the traditional methods of the Stalinist system, that is coercion, intimidation and fear. This policy was preferred partly because, in contrast to Kádár, Husak was not prepared for any compromise, and partly because of the passive reaction of the Czechoslovak people in the face of invasion. Unlike the Hungarians, they had not completely rejected the system and its methods. As the population had already demonstrated stoic acceptance of invasion, reinstatement of the old system was obviously a possibility. It was therefore the safest policy option for the embattled Party as it strove to regain not only the Soviet Union's confidence, but also its own.

However, re-Stalinisation doomed the Czechoslovak Party and society not only to a creeping ossification, but also to an increasingly desperate psychological crisis. 'Normalisation', or at least the appearance of it, was viewed as indispensable by the Czechoslovak Party leaders. Nevertheless, as Vaclav Havel succinctly states, the outward appearance of normalisation was achieved at the expense of the spiritual crisis of society:

'Es wurde die äußere Konsolidierung geschaffen - für den Preis der geistigen und moralischen Krise der Gesellschaft.'[172]

The Prague Spring of 1968 and its consequences remained a traumatic experience for the Communist Party and it endeavoured to obliterate all memory of it. This was the only means by which the Party could continue to rule and implement the very policies which had been rejected in 1968. Therefore, pseudo-history and public demonstrations of loyalty to the Party became the norm in Husak's Czechoslovakia. Vaclav Havel describes the situation in which a never-ending round of State Holidays and Party Congresses signified the passing of time:

---

[172] Havel, Vaclav, *Am Anfang war das Wort*, Rowohlt 1990, p. 52. 'The outward appearance of consolidation was achieved - at the price of the spiritual and moral crisis of society.' Translated by Wendy Hollis.

'Die Geschichte wurde durch Pseudogeschichte ersetzt, durch rhythmisierte kalendarische Jahrestage, Kongresse, Feiern und Spartakiaden.'[173]

Milan Kundera also realised that; 'Forgetting is the key to the so-called normalisation of Czechoslovakia'[174]. But by forgetting, the population sentenced itself to living an interminable lie which led to a moral and psychological crisis. In accepting the 'lie', the people become part of the system, but they also condemn themselves to a double existence which leads to a moral and psychological crisis, for they must do and act something which they do not believe. As Vladimir Tismaneanu states:

'Individuals must not believe all the mystifications, but they must behave as though they did, or they must at least tolerate them in silence, or get along well with those who work with them. For this reason, however, they must live within a lie. They need not accept the lie. It is enough for them to have accepted their life with it and in it. For by this very fact, individuals confirm the system, fulfil the system, make the system, are the system.'[175]

Interestingly, this leads to the conclusion that on being confronted by the truth, that is by someone unwilling to play the game and live according to the Communist Party's rules, the system will be unable to face the reflection of its own image and will collapse. The treatment which dissidents received from the Communist regime bears witness to the truth of this observation. Despite the harshness of the Husak regime, it was Czechoslovakia which developed the most organised, public and successful opposition groups. This was because in Romania the Stalinist system had been implemented so thoroughly there was no

---

[173] Ibid. Havel, Vaclav, *Am Anfang war das Wort*, p. 162. 'History has been replaced by pseudo-history, by a rhythmical calendar of Anniversaries, Congresses, Holidays and Athletic Tournaments.' Translated by Wendy Hollis.
[174] Ibid. Ash, Timothy Garton, *The Uses of Adversity*, p. 55.
[175] Tismaneanu, Vladimir, *Reinventing Politics*, The Free Press Inc. 1992, p. 139.

possibility of forming the personal relationships necessary to create dissident groupings. In the same way as the general population was isolated and had to face the state alone, so dissidents had little option but engage in individual, isolated acts of disobedience. The intellectuals in Hungary had been co-opted into passive support of the regime and saw little gain in open opposition.

Although the situation in Hungary was similar to Czechoslovakia in that the events of 1956 were officially forgotten, they were not expunged in the same way, since the Hungarian Party took note of the reasons behind the explosion. But, the Hungarian population suffered from the same symptoms of psychological crisis which affected the populations in both Romania and Czechoslovakia. The degree of affliction may have been differentiated, but the cause of the illness was the same. One important difference was that, while Kádár's regime attempted in some ways to alleviate this crisis, the Czechoslovak and Romanian Communists actively contributed to it. Whereas the population in Hungary was not forced to continually demonstrate its belief in Communism, the Party and its version of history, the opposite was true in Czechoslovakia and in Romania. In this sense, the normalised regime in Czechoslovakia bore more resemblance to that of Ceausescu's in Romania.

1.4: Ceausescu's Renegade Position

'It's Cold, Dark and You can't leave.'
The Economist.

Romania is the only country under consideration which did not experience a significant reform movement and where, consequently, no de-Stalinisation was carried out. The Communist regime retained all its Stalinist features right up until the Revolution at the end of 1989. The Romanian regime was unique due to the personality of Nicolae Ceausescu, but as events in Hungary and Czechoslovakia demonstrate, Romania did not have a monopoly of tyrants. Such a development was just as feasible in Czechoslovakia or Hungary and was only averted by the reform movements which swept the countries in 1968 and 1956 respectively. Hungary rid itself of Rakosi during 1956, and the ensuing violence of the Revolution ensured that no further neo-Stalinist policies could be implemented. The Prague Spring did not represent a complete rejection of socialism or its methods. Therefore, it was easier for Husak to re-introduce a more moderate form of Stalinism after the invasion of 1968. Husak's 'normalised' Czechoslovakia was in many ways a neo-Stalinist state.

The Communist, specifically the Stalinist, system of government creates conditions which enable a minority to gain power. While the role of individual tyrants must not be ignored, it must also be remembered that tyrants do not rule alone:

'Dictators don't become dictators by themselves; they don't dominate countries simply because they have dictatorial tendencies. People make a dictator - the people who advise him, the people who take orders from him and especially the people in society at large who support him.'[176]

It is not only individual partiality which determines whether a dictator will be born, but also the prevailing political culture of a country which accepts such a development. Romania is the only one of the countries under consideration where the logics of Communist dictatorship combined with the personality of Ceausescu and prevailing political culture to produce such an extreme form of tyranny. There was no de-Stalinisation and no attempt to reform the Stalinist system. Romania became completely subjected to Ceausescu's will. As Daniel Nelson stated:

'Romania has become, in less than one generation, a chaotic autocracy - where the rule of one man and his family

---

[176] Ibid. Tismaneanu, Vladimir, *Reinventing Politics*, p. 250.

is unquestioned, but where policies that emanate from such a regime evoke images of entropy.[177]

The question is, why was this possible in Romania and not in Czechoslovakia or Hungary? The answer lies in the combination of Romania's agrarian history, its political culture, the nature of the Romanian Communist Party and Ceausescu's personality.

Romanian society and culture was still in the process of Europeanisation and modernising itself when the Second World War broke out. The first Romanian state was declared in December 1918 and aimed to emulate the European democracies. It embarked upon a massive land redistribution scheme which effectively eliminated the former landowning class. The necessity of such a programme had been brutally demonstrated by the last 'Great Peasant Revolt' in 1907[178]. The peasants received land, but remained impoverished by the financial burden of redistribution; they had to buy the land they were allotted[179]. The Romanian economy was to remain basically agrarian and peasant orientated until after the Second World War. So, the majority of the population was rural, illiterate and uninterested in politics[180]. Its main concerns consisted of ensuring daily needs were met and that life was not subject to interference. Considering that, at this time, the average size of the peasants' plot was a mere 3.6 hectares, this was not surprising. The average area of a large estate was 900 hectares, but there were 1500 estates, representing 38% of the total arable land, with an area over 500 hectares[181].

---

[177] Nelson, Daniel, N., *Romanian Politics in the Ceausescu Era*, Gordon & Breach Science Publishers 1988, p. 155.
[178] For more information, see Ilincioiu, Ion, *The Great Romanian Peasant Revolt of 1907*, The Romanian Academy 1991.
[179] Ibid. Held, Joseph, *The Columbia History of Eastern Europe in the Twentieth Century*, p. 279.
[180] Before World War Two, only one fifth of the population lived in towns, while two thirds lived in the countryside. Until the Second World War, grain was Romania's most important export. See Rafael, Edgar, R., *Entwicklungsland Rumänien*, R. Oldenbourg Verlag 1977, p. 21.
[181] Ibid. Ilincioiu, Ion, *The Great Romanian Peasant Revolt of 1907*, p. 12.

The concerns of the peasants were a sharp contrast to those of the emerging middle class in the towns and cities, and even more so to the social and political elite which had been almost completely assimilated into French culture[182]. In addition to this, the Romanian King played an exceedingly important role in the country's politics and was idolised by the vast majority of the population. The Orthodox Church of Romania was too concerned with obedience and its own position within the power structure to engage itself fully with the concerns of the poorest peasants.

1.4.1: The Romanian Communists

The first political group to make use of this situation were the Fascists. In 1930, there were an estimated 34 000 Iron Guard cells serving approximately 350 000 supporters[183]. They were successful in mobilising the population because they used symbols and concepts the population could easily understand. They instrumentalised traditional resentment against Jews and foreign elements of domination. Not only did the minute Communist Party have to try and explain a completely new and foreign ideology, it was allied to the Soviet Union, arch enemy number one in the eyes of many Romanians. Furthermore, it supported Russia's claim to Bessarabia. These were obstacles which prevented it from ever gaining any measure of real support amongst the population at large. In addition, the members of the Communist Party were drawn almost exclusively from minority groups.

It is interesting to note that, on coming to power, the Communist elite increasingly employed means similar to those of the Fascists in order to gain support. Although Ceausescu's propaganda legitimised Stalinist ideology, its emphasis on the Romanian nation, lavish ceremonies and even the use of the title *Conducator*, was reminiscent the Iron Guard's propaganda methods. As Anneli Ute Gabanyi states, Ceausescu's personality cult:

---

[182] I have seen a family portrait in Bucharest which depicts the husband in Turkish and the wife in European finery. This was in no way an exception. Interview with Prof. Neagu Djuvara. Bucharest, 10.3.96.
[183] Ibid. Almond, Mark, *The Rise and Fall of Nicolae and Elena Ceausescu*, p. 31.

'...is clearly trying to keep deep rooted feelings, aligning itself with the political culture of a peasant society that has embarked upon a road of modernisation.'[184]

Nicolae Ceausescu and Gheorghe Dej were members of the 'national' faction which gained power within the Communist Party. Both came from poor peasant families and in many ways retained their peasant mentality[185]. They both shared a mystical, almost religious, faith in Communism. Ceausescu left school at the age of eleven to go to Bucharest as an apprentice to a shoemaker. He had already come into contact with the Communist movement through his elder brother Marin and was convinced enough to stammer, 'I am a Communist' to Gheorghe Klein[186]. He went to prison at the age of 16 after being arrested for supposedly acting as a courier for the Communist group he was associated with. In prison he met Gheorghe Dej. Ceausescu became his most loyal disciple. Amongst his cell mates were Chivu Stoicu, Gheorghe Apostol and Alexandru Draghici. After Dej's death, Ceausescu gradually got rid of all these possible rivals until only he was left to accept Dej's mantle of power.

The fact that Ceausescu and his wife, Elena, did not complete their statutory schooling was not uncommon at the time. Perhaps this explains Elena's aspirations to erudition. She chose a most complex and incomprehensible branch of chemistry, 'the stereoscopic polymerisation of isoprene', as the subject in which she was officially to excel. Maybe the sheer unintelligibility of the

---

[184] Gabanyi, Anneli Ute, 'Ceausescu's Personality Cult: An Analysis', *RFE/RL Research: Romanian Situation Report*, 6 February 1987.
[185] For an example of this mentality, see Crane, Keith, *The Romanian Economic Mess After Ceausescu*, The Rand Corporation December 1986, p. 11. Ceausescu's desperate debt repayment policy is an example of this mentality. When times are good, a peasant can afford to borrow money which improves his standard of living, since he knows he can repay it with the harvest. However, when times are bad the peasant will try to repay the debt he has incurred as it is an added burden which he cannot afford. This mentality, combined with Ceausescu's obsession with complete control, caused him to insist on repaying all Romania's external debt as soon as possible at the start of the 1980's.
[186] Ibid. Almond, Mark, *The Rise and Fall of Nicolae and Elena Ceausescu*, p. 27.

subject was appealing[187]. The poor intellectual quality of the Communist elite in Romania also helps to explain why there was no domestic ideological discussion about Communism. The Soviet Union's model of dogmatic Stalinism was simply adopted and never reformed. There was no reform movement within the Party and there was little possibility of a Communist reform movement forming outside the Party, since the majority of the population was opposed to the Communist regime. In addition, the Party embarked upon a policy aimed at eliminating not only the former political elite, but also the entire intellectual elite; that is, all its potential opponents. This policy has been accurately described by Katherine Verdery as:

'The decisive alteration or destruction of values, structures, and behaviours which are perceived by a new elite as compromising or contributing to the actual or potential existence of alternative centres of power.'[188]

Given that the intellectual and political elite in Romania was smaller, less developed and thus rather more exposed than in Czechoslovakia and Hungary, its extermination was an easier proposition and was successfully achieved[189]. In addition, the Romanian Communist Party embarked upon a deliberate policy of restructuring the Romanian social environment in the hope of restructuring the citizens themselves.

There was never any question of the Romanian Communist leaders following a 'national' road to socialism in the sense that Nagy and Dubcek had proposed. The Romanian Communist leaders were intent on realising a Stalinist reality in the image of its contemporary Soviet reality. In an interview with *Newsweek* four months before his death, Ceausescu stated:

---

[187] Ibid. Almond, Mark, *The Rise and Fall of Nicolae and Elena Ceausescu*, p. 86.
[188] Verdery, Katherine, *National Ideology under Socialism*, University of California Press 1991, p. 108.
[189] The historian Ghita Ionescu has estimated that as many as 60 000 people were executed by the regime as a result of their political beliefs. Ibid. Brogan, P., *Eastern Europe 1939-1989*, p. 220.

> 'Stalin did everything a man in his position should have done ...in twenty years, Stalin raised Russia from an underdeveloped country to the most powerful country in the world ...He won a war, he built nuclear weapons. He did everything a person should do in his position.'[190]

This statement demonstrates Ceausescu's simplistic Stalinist world view. In his own way, Ceausescu attempted to achieve the same things Stalin had done. The aim was to modernise the Romanian economy using Stalin's 'tried and tested' methods. Ceausescu was obsessed with heavy industry and the centralisation and control of all areas of economic and social life. This was in keeping with his primitive understanding of the best means by which to modernise a country and create a new 'socialist man'. He aimed to create a new society in Romania, and in some respects he succeeded. However, the longer Ceausescu remained in power, the more irrational he became. This irrational element was amplified by the very structure of power which he had constructed. Ceausescu had the last word in all areas of policy and his personal decisions were not to be debated. As a result of this, the irrational element of his behaviour became more and more obvious, especially towards the end of his regime. And yet, it is virtually impossible to quantify this phenomenon. As J. F. Brown comments:

> 'Political science reveals its limitations with a man like Ceausescu. So does sociology, however interesting the insights it might give into the peasant mentality of Romania's rulers. Psychology might be more appropriate and revealing. Ceausescu's last twenty years can best be described in terms of obsessional and paranoidal disorder. Quite simply, he became mad, viciously so.'[191]

---

[190] *Newsweek*, 8 January 1990.
[191] Brown. J., F., *Surge to Freedom*, Duke University Press 1991, p. 201.

Whether Ceausescu was really mad or was simply intellectually incapable of developing a more sophisticated Communist ideology and was therefore deluded as to the real effect of the policies he pursued in order to create a Communist society in Romania, is open to debate. In any event, the Stalinist system which was introduced served to increase the irrationality of his policies.

1.4.2: Stalinisation and Systemisation

As a traditional exporter of agricultural produce, Romania did not comply with the Stalinist ideal. It did not possess much heavy industry, and the peasants cultivated small plots. Collectivisation was an ideological imperative, but proved a long and fruitless project[192]. The peasants continued to view the land which was in the collective as their own and took crops from it as they had always done, albeit at night. They were simply taking what was rightfully theirs back from the state. In an attempt to create a heavy industrial base, numerous monolithic 'Stalinist' projects were started. These included the Black Sea Canal project[193], which Ceausescu revived after its abandonment by Dej in the 1950's, and the completion of the largest steel complex in the world at Galati in 1962[194]. Many new towns were built around heavy industrial complexes, or had complexes built near them[195]. In addition to their monolithic size,

---

[192] More than 80 000 peasants were brought to trial as a result of their resistance to collectivisation. Dej blamed Pauker for the failure and placed Ceausescu in charge of the project. Ibid. Brogan, P., *Eastern Europe 1939-1989*, p. 219.
[193] An estimated 180 000 Romanians were employed to build the Canal. They were political prisoners and worked under conditions of forced labour. Many of them died during its construction. Ibid. Brogan, P., *Eastern Europe 1939-1989*, p. 220.
[194] Ibid. Staar, Richard, F., *The Communist Regimes in Eastern Europe (2nd. Edition)*, p. 175.
[195] An unfortunate consequence has been a deterioration of the general health of the population due to the abysmal industrial standards which prevail. Environmental protection was not high on the Communist Party's list of priorities. One of the most infamous examples of this is the chemical factory in the Romanian town of Giurgiu on the Danube border with Bulgaria. The chemical factory produces clouds of toxic yellow smoke which settle on the buildings of the Bulgarian town of Russe on the opposite side of the river. See Beckherrn, Eberhard, *Tal der Wende*, Knaur 1991, p. 279. The Bulgarian authorities registered an alarming increase in the rate of lung cancer in the town from 965 per 100 000 in 1975, to 17 386 per 100 000 by 1985. They have consistently demanded the

many of the new industries required raw materials which Romania did not possess. This led to the situation in which Romania, a country relatively rich in raw materials, consistently increased its imports of raw materials. Thus, by 1988, imports of iron ore had increased twenty times since 1960, and 3.6 times since 1980[196].

The workers in the industrial complexes formed a new *proletariat* but, as first generation town dwellers, the majority of them maintained close contact with the countryside and in this way retained their peasant mentality. In many cases this remains true even today. Many people work in city enterprises, but travel to their private plot or home to their parents or grandparents at the weekend to work on the family land and obtain produce from it. Interestingly, this phenomenon is also prevalent in Hungary where a tendency for workers in the cities to live in the country, and thus have access to a plot of land developed. This is especially feasible in Hungary due to its small size and the relatively short journey time required to travel from a small town, or village, to a city. The Romanian peasant population as a whole was extremely conservative and had little or no experience of democracy. They were suspicious of towns and accustomed to power being misused. This meant that the abuses of the Communist regime were born with the same stoic acceptance as those which the Ottomans had inflicted.

It was partly to rid the workers of their peasant traits and create a socialist society and suitable socialist man, as Ceausescu understood it, that he decided on the 'systemisation' of Romania in 1972. The plan became law in 1974, but its implementation was continuously delayed by reluctant officials. The delay was facilitated by Ceausescu's consequent disinterest in the project until 1986.

Systemisation aimed 'to reduce the number of villages radically, from about 13 000 to between 5000 and 6000 at the most'[197]. This was deemed necessary in order to obliterate the differences between

---

closure of the Romanian factory. Ibid. Crampton, R., J., *Eastern Europe in the Twentieth Century*, p. 412.
[196] Ratesh, Nestor, *Romania: The Entangled Revolution*, Praeger 1992, p. 4.
[197] Ibid. Brown, J., F., *Surge to Freedom*, p. 202.

the town and countryside. It was also a means by which the population could be controlled and re-moulded into the image of 'man' which Ceausescu strove to attain. An *RFE/RL Situation Report* on Romania stated that:

> 'Life in apartment blocks is helping to create a collective consciousness in the people's minds. It means living under the close scrutiny of your neighbours. It is a new way of life in which the behaviour and requirements of the collective body are present at every moment. It is a new social environment in which priority is given to the community over the individual.'[198]

The distinct houses in Romanian villages and old areas of the towns represented an individualism which offended Ceasescu's ideological understanding. In destroying the villages and houses, Ceausescu hoped to destroy the European tradition of individualism they represented and create a new homogenous, Communist society[199]. This aim was clearly stated by Stefan Dactu, the architect of the blocks, in July 1988:

> 'The designing of [internal] spaces is in keeping with a unitary legislation. The living room, the bedrooms, the bathroom, the rooms' height and other dimensions are therefore the same in a small or a big town.'[200]

Systemisation would have the effect of gradually obliterating all perceivable differences in every aspect of social life. Although Ceausescu viewed this as the ultimate prerequisite of a Communist society, it would make life in Romania unbearably monotonous,

---

[198] *RFE/RL Situation Report on Romania*, 'An Underground Essay on Urban and Rural Development'. 3 February 1986.
[199] For a more in-depth account and analysis of Ceausescu's systemisation policy, see Ronnas, Per, 'Turning the Romanian Peasant into a New Socialist Man: An Assessment of Rural Development Policy in Romania', *Soviet Studies*, Vol. 41, No. 4, October 1989.
[200] *Romanian News*, 22 July 1988.

dull and grey. It was also a means of increasing control over the population, both directly via the increased information network which could be more easily accessed by the *Securitate*, and indirectly by the deterrent effect living in such close quarters, where every action could be observed, had on 'deviant' behaviour. The Polish philosopher Leszek Kolakowski also realised the deeper significance of this development:

> *'The object of a totalitarian system is to destroy all forms of communal life that are not imposed by the state and closely controlled by it, so that individuals are isolated form one another and become mere instruments of the state.'*[201]

It was Ceausescu's obsession with control and the creation of a new society, which led him and his wife, who was in charge of women's affairs, to introduce Romania's pro-natalist policy. The aim was to increase the population from 20 million to 30 million by the year 2000[202]. This was necessary because the Stalinist economy suffered from a chronic shortage of workers, although ironically most workers were under-employed[203]. As a result of this and Ceausescu's obsession with the creation of a new society, population growth ceased to be a spontaneous phenomenon in Romania and became the concern of the Party. Family life became a 'socialised private problem'. Every three months, women were subjected to gynaecological examinations at their place of work by 'Demographic Control Units'. In this way it could be ascertained if they were pregnant. If a woman was pregnant, the examinations ensured that an abortion was not carried out. Even so, by the 1980's the number of legal abortions exceeded the number of live births and unwanted babies were often abandoned at birth.

---

[201] Ibid. Tismaneanu, Vladimir, *Reinventing Politics*, p. 29.
[202] For this figure to be reached, it would have been necessary for every woman to have five children. Ibid. Brogan, P., *Eastern Europe 1939-1989*, p. 226.
[203] The average Romanian enterprise employed 1480 people, twice as many as the average Soviet factory, and ten times as many as the average enterprise in the Federal Republic of Germany. See Bidelux, Robert, *Communism and Development*, London 1985, p. 147.

Unfortunately, the regime's concern with population management did not extend to those unwanted children who were produced as a result. Romanian orphanages were home to approximately 15 000-40 000 children[204]. The form of society which Ceausescu nurtured had a detrimental effect both on the population and economy. Its long-term effects on the psychological health of the population remain unknown.

At the time the Communist Party came to power, Romania suffered from rural over-population. It therefore possessed a surplus of workers from the countryside who could be employed in the new industrial enterprises constructed by the Communist regime. As a result, the strain which the Stalinist system placed on the economy only really began to be felt in the 1970's. The slightly later signs of dysfunction can be explained by the fact that the deficiencies of the Stalinist system become more apparent when dealing with a more developed industrial sector. In comparison with Hungary and Czechoslovakia, Romania originally possessed a relatively underdeveloped industrial base. Therefore systemic dysfunction became apparent at a later date.

The apartment blocks which were built for the new class of industrial workers were often a great improvement on conditions which had existed in the villages. However, the blocks were poorly constructed, poorly maintained and made the population dependent on the provision of consumer goods and food in state shops. Whereas apartment blocks had originally represented an increase in the standard of living, they soon became associated with the opposite. As Laura Thyson notes

> *'By 1977-78 the Romanian economy began to exhibit the traditional characteristics of shortage associated with an excessive investment drive, including disruptions in raw material and fuel supplies, a sharp increase in the number*

---

[204] They were the official responsibility of the Ministry of Public Works, the ministry in charge of Sewage and drains. *Washington Post*, 7 June 1990.

and volume of incomplete investment projects and shortages too in consumer goods markets . . .'[205]

Continuous over-investment in heavy industry led to the neglect and under-development of Romanian agriculture and the consumer industry. As a result of under-investment in agriculture, the countryside became de-populated and incapable of meeting the needs of the growing town populations. By 1989, archaic methods of agricultural production, combined with the disincentive to produce for the state, left Romania with the lowest level of agricultural production in Europe.

1.4.3: Ceausescu's Personality Cult

At the same time as economic problems were beginning to make themselves felt, tensions also arose in the cultural sphere. It became clear that Ceausescu had completely abandoned any pretence of wanting to reform the system. Indeed, after his trip to North Korea and China in 1971[206], he became fascinated with the idea of a 'Cultural Revolution'. It was during this period of perfection of the Stalinist regime that the first obvious signs of Ceausescu's irrationality became noticeable. The Romanians' Dacian-Roman ancestry was extolled, as was Romanian nationality as a whole. A personality cult depicting Ceausescu as the, 'genius of the Carpathians' was set in motion[207], and repression increased. Ceausescu also began, in true Byzantine style, to promote members of his own and his wife's family into positions of power[208]. This

---

[205] See Tyson, Laura, 'Economic Adjustment in Eastern Europe', *Rand*, September 1984, pp. 84-92.
[206] Ibid. Brown, J., F., *Eastern Europe and Communist Rule*, p. 278.
[207] Ceausescu also dressed up and engaged in television conversations with important figures from Romanian history.
[208] Ceausescu's brother, Nicolae A. Ceausescu, was Secretary of the Political Council of the Ministry of the Interior. Another brother, Ilie, was a General and Deputy Head of the Higher Political Council in the Ministry of Defence and a member of the Central Committee; brother Ion was the Vice Chairman of the State Planing Committee, Secretary of the National Council for Agriculture, Food Industry, Sylviculture, and Water Management, and a member of the Central Auditing Commission; brother Marin held a position in the Foreign Trade Department, and brother Florea was a member of staff at *Scînteia*, the Party

was a well-known tradition amongst earlier rulers and the Romanian political elite; the Bratianu family had dominated politics in the inter-war period. But, Ceausescu's elevation of his wife was something completely new and foreign to Romanian political culture, and her prominent position was resented by the vast majority of Romanians.

Ceausescu's policy of constantly re-shuffling his closest officials caused the remaining Communist veterans, Apostol, Barladeanu, Voitec and Constantin Pirvulescu, to complain about his methods[209]. However, their complaints served to ensure that they were removed from power. They did not form an alternative grouping within the Party, and even if they had, they were not interested in reforming the basic tenets of the system either. Their main concern was the loss of their own power under Ceausescu. In fact, at no time was there a perceivable reform movement within the Romanian Party. This was due to the weakness of theoretical discourse within the Party. The Stalinist ideology had been accepted *volte face* and all that mattered was to ensure one's own position of power remained secure. In order to achieve this it was necessary to obey without question, which is what the vast majority of the political elite did. This meant that it was the Romanian workers, the object of Stalinist adulation, who were the main source of opposition to Ceausescu's Stalinist regime, and that the political elite never supported any of the workers' demonstrations of discontent.

Newspaper. Ceausescu's sister was a Deputy Minister of Education until her husband, Vasile Barbulescu, a Central Committee member, became Party First Secretary in Olt County in 1983. Elena Ceausescu's brother, Gheorghe-Petrescu, was a Deputy Chairman of the General Union of Trade Unions and a member of the Central Committee, the Council of State and the Executive Bureau of the Socialist Democracy and Unity Front. In addition, Ceausescu promoted associates from his native village, Scornicesti in Olt County. Ibid. Tismaneanu, Vladimir, 'Ceausescu's Socialism'.

[209] Constantin Pirvulescu publicly called for Ceausescu not to be renominated at the 12th Party Congress in 1979. Ibid. Brown, J., F., *Eastern Europe and Communist Rule*, p. 279.

1.4.4: Demonstrations of Discontent

Resentment against the regime boiled over in 1977 amongst the workers in the mines of the Jiu Valley. Although there were often small stoppages, the Jiu Valley strike was supported by 35 000 coal miners and it required Ceausescu's personal intervention, and that of the regular army, to regain control of the situation. The representatives of the Party, Prime Minister Ile Verdet and Gheorghe Pana, who were originally sent to calm the situation were taken hostage. The threats issued against their persons forced Ceausescu to fly personally to the miners. Ceausescu was held hostage in a similar fashion until he promised to improve working conditions and pay. Of course the promises were never kept, and once he had returned to Bucharest the *Securitate* weeded out the leaders of the strike and dispersed them[210]. A substantial number of them died in 'accidents'. The *Securitate* also organised a dense network of informers which prevented another outbreak on such a scale.

It was also in 1977 that Paul Goma and a few other intellectuals attempted to organise some sort of open opposition to the regime[211]. Paul Goma published an open letter of support for the Czechoslovak group of dissidents, led by Vaclav Havel, who had formed *Charter 77*. Letters in the spirit of *Charter 77* were published from January-April 1977. They were signed by up to 200 people[212]. Although this attempt at opposition occurred at the same time as the workers' strikes, there was no contact between the two groups, and protest remained mainly an individual affair. The totalitarian system inhibited the dissidents from forming a bond which could have lessened their isolation in the face of the state. This, combined with the sheer misery of life, made repression an easier task for the regime. Paul Goma was eventually forced to emigrate to the West in April 1977[213]. In 1979, he announced the

---

[210] Ibid. Brown, J., F., *Eastern Europe and Communist Rule*, p. 287.
[211] The most prominent of them were the historian, Vlad Georgescu; the mathematician Mihai Botez, and the poet, Dorin Tudoran. Ibid. Nelson, Daniel, N., *Romanian Politics in the Ceausescu Era*, p. xiv.
[212] Ibid. Ratesh, Nestor, *Romania: The Entangled Revolution*, p. 12.
[213] Ibid. Brown, J., F., *Eastern Europe and Communist Rule*, p. 288.

formation of a *Free Trade Union of the Working People of Romania (SLOMR)*. It officially had 2000 members, but the public nature of the Union made its infiltration and harassment of its leaders an easy task and it was quickly liquidated. It therefore had little real impact[214].

1977 was also the year in which Romania was hit by an earthquake. This seriously disrupted all areas of the economy. The peasants continued to practise their policy of endemic passive resistance, destroying stock and withholding food deliveries to the state. As a result, compulsory state deliveries were reintroduced in 1983. In order to try and increase agricultural production[215], apatite concentrates (fertilisers) were also imported. These imports increased annually and had risen to 100% of all consumption in 1980[216].

Brasov was the scene of a major demonstration and riots on 15 November, 1987. The unrest started during elections in the Red Flag Tractor Factory, one of the regime's prestige enterprises, where conditions and rations were above the average. The workers marched to the centre of the city and demanded more rations and pay. The demonstrators were joined by the townspeople and proceeded to storm the local Party Headquarters and the Town Hall chanting, 'Down with the Dictator!' and, 'Down with Ceausescu!'. Order had to be re-enforced by the security forces and in the process a policeman was killed. In the aftermath of the unrest there were many arrests and reports of torture. Despite this, the *Steagul Rosul* factory workers went on strike to demand the release of the 110 demonstrators still held in custody and the workers of the Brasov munitions factory threatened to blow up the Party

---

[214] Of the fifteen original founders, Vasile Paraschiv, Gheorghe Brasoveanu and Ionel Cana were incarcerated in psychiatric units until 1980. Paul Goma was forced to emigrate. Ibid. Nelson, Daniel, N., *Romanian Politics in the Ceausescu Era*, p. 52.
[215] Although the regime wanted to increase food production, this was not intended to alleviate the food shortage, but to increase food exports as a means of paying off Romania's external debt. Ironically, it was this policy which had caused the food shortage.
[216] Ibid. Ratesh, Nestor, *Romania: The Entangled Revolution*, p. 4. See Appendix XII.

Headquarters[217]. But, in December 1987, the leaders of the riots were tried and sentenced to between six months and three years in prison[218]. The local Party leaders were also removed as they had initially tolerated the demonstration[219].

1.4.5: Political Relations with Ceausescu

Ceausescu's reaction to the growing economic and social unrest was not to introduce reform, but to increase centralisation and coercion. By this stage the whole system was completely under Ceausescu's personal control. The Party elite was hopelessly compromised by its association with Ceausescu and individuals tried to retain personal power by any means they could, i.e. by ensuring they remained in Ceausescu's favour. Indeed, as early as 1975, Trond Gilberg commented:

> '...the most important decisions in Romania today are being made in response to Ceausescu's personal initiative ...The apparatchiks either wait for an initiative from the General Secretary or attempt to anticipate his wishes.'[220]

Those who criticised the development of Ceausecu's personality cult and direction of policies were marginalised and removed from power[221]. This development, combined with Ceausescu's policy of rotating cadres, paralysed and left little room for diversity amongst the Communist political elite.

However, Ceausescu's increasingly chauvinistic, nationalist propaganda excluded the Romanian minorities from inclusion in the mythos of the creation of the Romanian state. Since Transylvania had only been acquired from Hungary after the Second World War,

---

[217] Golea, Traian, *Romania: Beyond the Limits of Endurance*, Romanian Historical Studies 1988, p. 44.
[218] Ibid. Ratesh, Nestor, *Romania: The Entangled Revolution*, p. 10.
[219] Gabanyi, Anneli Ute, *Die Unvollendete Revolution*, Piper 1990, p. 49.
[220] Gilberg, Trond, *Modernization in Romania since World War II*, Praeger 1975, p. 84.
[221] Such people include those who were instrumental in removing Dej's 'barons' from power. These include Niculescu-Mizil, Virgil Trofin, Ion Iliescu and Ilie Verdet. Ibid. Tismaneanu, Vladimir, 'Ceausescu's Socialism'.

it was particularly important for the regime to prove that the region was really Romanian.

Hungary and Romania are still embroiled in a historical discussion as to which people actually settled the Transylvanian basin first. As a result, the large Hungarian minority in Romania was particularly victimised by the Ceausescu regime. The Hungarian Party's continued policy of gradual reform meant the issue of the treatment of the Hungarian minority in Romania became a legitimate subject of public interest. Indeed, it was a means by which the Kádár regime could gain popular support and legitimacy. Paradoxically, both the Romanian and Hungarian regimes employed nationalist policies, albeit diametrically opposed, to gain domestic support. For this reason, the Transylvanian issue is still of great importance to both governments. It also demonstrates the different experiences which define Romanian and Hungarian national identity. The Romanian experience of centuries of foreign domination has led to over-sensitivity to any incursion into Romania's realm of sovereignty. On the other hand, the Hungarian experience of decline of a once powerful Kingdom has resulted in fear of the final disappearance of the Hungarian nation[222].

In the case of the Hungarian regime, concern for Human Rights in Romania was one of the reasons which compelled it to respect Human Rights within its own borders, a rather unforeseen consequence[223]. The Hungarian regime found it impossible to compromise itself by appearing to tolerate Romanian policy and consequently the Ceausescu regime. Between 1988 and 1989, Hungary accepted 30 000 refugees from Romania[224]. The Hungarian domestic political necessity of making a public issue over the situation in Romania led to an increasingly public disagreement and quarrel over the treatment of the Hungarian

---

[222] For an apt description of Romanian and Hungarian nationalism, see Hartl, Hans, *Nationalismus in Rot*, Seewald Verlag 1968, pp. 24-25.

[223] It was partly this fact which forced the Hungarian regime to open the Iron Curtain and allow citizens of the German Democratic Republic free travel across its borders to the West. This signalled an end to the Honecker regime, contributed to the demise of Husak and also of Ceausescu.

[224] Ibid. Gabanyi, Anneli Ute, *Die unvollendete Revolution*, p. 159.

minority and eventually resulted in a break-down in Romanian-Hungarian relations.

In contrast, the Czechoslovak Party increasingly found itself allied with the Romanian regime. In view of the fact that Ceausescu had not taken part in the Warsaw Pact invasion in 1968, and by this omission had provided passive support for Husak's forerunner and rival, Alexander Dubcek, this was a rather ironic situation. It demonstrates both the real motives behind Ceausescu's refusal to participate in the invasion and the similarities between the regimes. Both Ceausescu and Husak were dogmatic Stalinists with respect to domestic policy. Once it became clear during the 1980's that the rest of the Soviet Bloc was in the process of considering reform of the system, they called upon the principles of state sovereignty to defend their hard-line position. By 1989, together with the Honecker regime in the German Democratic Republic, Husak and Ceausescu formed the last bastion standing in the way of systemic reform in the whole Eastern Bloc.

In Czechoslovakia and Hungary, although systemic reform had failed in 1968 and 1956, it had entailed a serious discussion about change both within and without the Party, and a well-organised and well-known dissident movement had formed as a result. In contrast, the population and the Communist Party in Romania had never embarked upon a critical examination of the Stalinist system, or attempted to reform it. There was no organised dissident movement and no opportunity to publish anything which did not coincide with the regime's propaganda. As a consequence, Romania seemed to be completely paralysed in Ceausescu's iron grip.

Ceausescu was the only person who decided policy. Nothing could be undertaken until he had approved the appropriate measures. Added to this difficulty was the fact that he often contradicted earlier statements. One of the consequences of Ceausescu's excessive centralisation was the increasing incidence of direct intervention by the army in the economy by the early 1980's[225]. However, increased centralisation within the realms of an already highly centralised, bureaucratic Stalinist administrative

---

[225] Ibid. Nelson, Daniel, N., *Romanian Politics in the Ceausescu Era*, p. 187.

system, reliance on coercion and binding Plan targets, and Ceausescu's increasingly erratic behaviour increased the economic and social chaos and served to make life in Romania unbearable for everyone.

1.5: Reform Communism and Democratisation

Communist systems were established in all three countries following the end of the Second World War, but they underwent different courses of development. During the course of this development, three different types of Communist system emerged. The legacy of these systems has affected transformation and democratic consolidation in Hungary, the Czech Republic and Romania.

The Communist system in Hungary underwent a severe crisis, and indeed near collapse, during the 1956 Revolution. The Hungarian Communist Party imploded, losing control as it became clear that the general population supported neither the Party, nor the form of government and society which had been introduced. The total loss of control and the violent Soviet assistance required to restore order forced the Hungarian Party to re-evaluate its role and the means by which it exercised power. Although the Revolution failed, it exposed the coercive nature of Soviet control and destroyed belief in Communism. It also resulted in the complete de-Stalinisation of the Hungarian Party and the introduction of a different system of state control. Conciliation with the population was bought at the price of Party retreat from the private sphere and the promise of ever increasing living standards; both of which required gradual reform of the ossified structures of the Stalinist command administrative system.

The gradual evolution of the specific Hungarian Communist system entailed the transformation of the unpredictable totalitarian system into a paternalistic authoritarian system which tolerated a certain amount of constructive criticism and respected a private sphere. Ideology was all but abandoned and, by embarking on reform of the centrally planned economy, living standards were increased and a wide variety of consumer goods became available.

The 1956 Revolution was the catalyst which sparked the development of the specific Hungarian Communist system. The Party's acceptance of the principle of reform and its abandonment of dogmatic ideology led to a peaceful, negotiated Revolution in 1989. The population's retreat from political life meant negotiations were carried out between the opposing elites with little popular participation. This prevented a complete break with the old system by enabling the reform-orientated Party elite to retain political influence

The Czechoslovak Communist Party managed to avoid far-reaching de-Stalinisation until 1968. In that year, a second-wave of de-Stalinisation coincided with serious economic problems to precipitate a crisis. The failure of earlier economic reform demonstrated the command system itself was the cause of the difficulties and that, to succeed, economic reform had to be accompanied by political reform. The Stalinist Czechoslovak Party split under the combined pressures for internal and economic reform. In contrast to the 1956 Hungarian Revolution, the 1968 Prague Spring was not an attempt to dismantle, but to reform the system. Nevertheless, the nature of the Prague Spring's failure destroyed the Communist system's ideological legitimacy. The Warsaw Pact invasion exposed the totalitarian nature of the regime and its total incompatibility with a modern, democratic system.

The elimination of the economic and political reform programme was achieved by normalisation. The reintroduction of traditional methods of Stalinist control and purges of opponents cowed the population into submission, but also led to the formation of a dedicated group of dissidents. A conservative, neo-Stalinist command system was re-introduced in both economic and political spheres. In contrast to the Hungarian, the Czechoslovak Party demanded public demonstrations of loyalty. In this way, the outward appearance of normalisation was achieved. However, normalisation also increased the speed of ideological decomposition and robbed the Party of its political legitimacy; the poor record of economic performance also left it bereft of professional legitimacy. The Czechoslovak regime therefore relied solely on Stalinist methods of control to retain power. The Party elite became paralysed by its ideological decomposition and awareness of its lack of legitimacy, but rejected reform and negotiations with the opposition. This left it incapable of retaining a role in the democratic system. Although the regime's reaction to the 1968 Prague Spring hindered systemic reform before 1989, the legacy of the Prague Spring ensured the peaceful nature of the Velvet Revolution and a complete break with the previous system.

The lack of any significant reform movement either within the Romanian Party or amongst the general population, meant the Romanian system retained many of its original Stalinist features. However, it was not a traditional totalitarian Stalinist system. Under Ceausescu, the Stalinist system was distorted and manipulated into something more resembling despotic sultanism[226].

The traditional methods of terror and control associated with the Stalinist system were employed to ensure general submission. In Byzantine fashion, Ceausescu promoted members of his extended family to high positions, but it was mainly the prominent position of his wife, Elena, which caused wide-spread resentment. In addition, Ceausescu demanded mass demonstrations of public adulation and gradually saturated the ideology with a distorted nationalism. In this way, a form of national Communism emerged which was manipulated and employed to atomise the population and prevent the formation of any kind of united opposition.

Along with the majority of the Romanian Communist Party elite, Ceausescu's understanding of progress and development remained primitive and Stalinist in nature. Thus, the Romanian economy was excessively centralised and unevenly developed. The lack of any internal Party initiatives aimed at reform during the entire period of Communist rule facilitated the development of Ceausescuism. Once established, there was little opportunity for an alternative power elite to form within the Party, and strict social control prevented the formation of any significant dissident

---

[226] See Linz, Juan, J., Stepan, Alfred, *Problems of Democratic Transition and Consolidation*, John Hopkins University Press 1996.

movement outside of it. The articulation of discontent was left to individual intellectuals and industrial workers, who periodically engaged in mass strikes. Ceausescu's categorical refusal to accept the failure of the Stalinist economic and social system effectively blocked any attempts at systemic reform.

The specific sultanic nature of the system meant some form of violent popular uprising was unavoidable, but at the same time prevented a complete caesura with the old regime. The inability of the uprising to affect regime transformation enabled marginalised groupings within the regime to retain power. This negatively influenced the course of the December Revolution and Romanian democratisation.

CHAPTER TWO

Regime Collapse and the Role of the Soviet Union

'Would it not then be simpler, for the government to dissolve the People and elect another?'
Bertold Brecht, *The Solution*.

*

Brezhnev's eighteen year rule was a period of stabilisation and stagnation. It was during this time that the problems associated with the planned economy of the Soviet Union and Eastern Europe became insoluble and the Soviet Bloc became incapable of supplying even basic necessities to its populations. The planned economy began to fail according to its own standards of measurement[1]. The average annual rates of growth from 1951-1988 show a gradual decline for all the individual members of the CMEA. Hungary experienced a decline in growth from 5.7% for the period 1951-1955, to 1.7% between 1986-1988. Growth in Romania declined from 14.1% between 1951-1955, to 5.1% for the period 1986-1988. The figures for Czechoslovakia are similar, showing a drop in the rate of growth from 8.2% between 1951-1955, to 2.4% from 1986-1988 (see Table 1 overleaf)[2].

Living standards in Eastern Europe also began to fall. In Romania, domestic electricity consumption was limited. The vast majority of energy was needed to fuel Romania's monolithic,

---
[1] It was also failing to keep pace with the technological revolution. See Appendix III.
[2] White, Stephen, Batt, Judy, Lewis, P., G., *Developments in East European Politics*, Macmillan Press Ltd. 1993, p. 8. Originally in *Statisticheskii ezegodnik stran-chenov SEV 1989*, Moscow: Finansy i statistika, 1989, pp. 18-28. See Appendix V, VI, VII.

energy-hungry heavy industrial base. However, despite restrictions on energy use, by 1981, as Romania's own oil reserves declined and imports increased, 30% of the Romanian petrochemical industry stood idle[3]. During the 1980's Romanian oil imports increased to a total of 16 million tons a year. This increase took place at a time when oil prices were high and therefore placed an enormous strain on the fragile Romanian economy.

Table 1
Average Annual Rates of Growth, 1951-1988 (%)

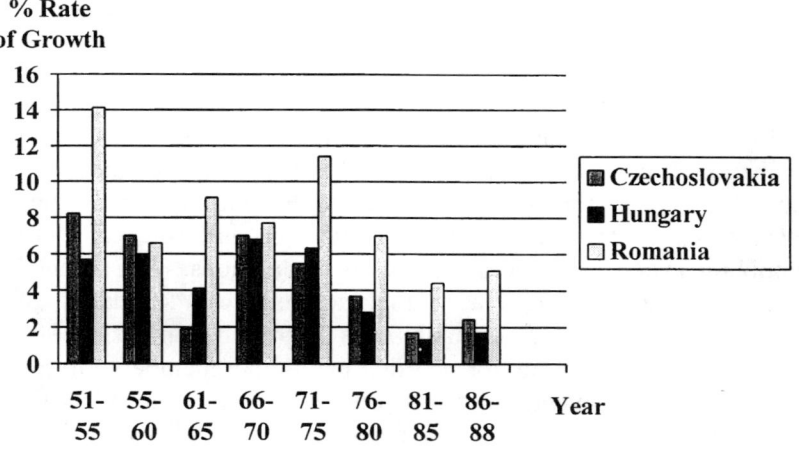

Source: Adapted from White, Stephen, Batt, Judy, Lewis, Paul, G., (Eds.), *Developments in East European Politics*, Macmillan Press 1993, p. 8. Originally in *Statisticheskii ezhegodnik stran-chlenov SEV 1989*, Moscow: Finansy i Statistika, 1989, pp. 18-28.

Increasing oil imports drained the economy of much needed capital and hard currency. As a result, Romania's hard currency

---

[3] Brown, J., F., *Eastern Europe and Communist Rule*, Duke University Press 1988, p. 283.

debt began to increase. It rose from $3.6 billion (Gross), $3.4 billion (Net) in 1977, to $10.2 billion (Gross) and $9.8 billion (Net) by 1981[4]. In 1982, at the same time as Hungary was suffering a liquidity crisis, Romania was forced to reschedule its debt repayments[5]. Indeed, all the countries suffered an increase in their foreign debt (see Table 2 overleaf)[6].

Foreign indebtedness ran contrary to Ceausescu's Stalinist ideal of autarky and he became obsessed with repaying Romania's external debt as quickly as possible. By 1986 Romania's foreign debt stood at $6 billion, low enough to improve its credit rating and facilitate a new loan of $150 million. But, by May 1986 a new rescheduling plan was required[7].

Table 2
Estimates of Gross Hard Currency Debt (Billions of Dollars)

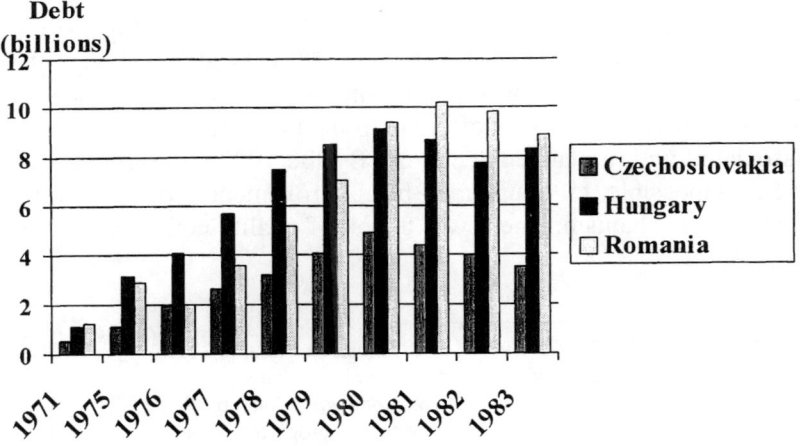

Source: Adapted from Economist Intelligence Unit, *Regional Review: Eastern Europe and the USSR, 1985*, EIU 1985, p. 16.

---

[4] Ibid. Brown, J., F., *Eastern Europe and Communist Rule*, p. 507.
[5] Ibid. Brown, J., F., *Eastern Europe and Communist Rule*, p. 285.
[6] See Appendix IV.
[7] Ibid. Brown, J., F., *Eastern Europe and Communist Rule*, p. 285.

The Romanian population suffered severely as a result of Ceausescu's debt repayment policy. Food and energy were directed away from the domestic market for export as a means of obtaining hard currency. As a result, rationing of bread and flour was introduced in October 1981 and prison sentences were introduced for hoarding. In 1982, public and shop lighting was forbidden at night and by 1984 many factories stopped producing all together due to the energy shortage[8]. Continuing lack of foreign currency forced the Romanian regime to import the cheaper oil on offer from the Soviet Union, and by 1985 it was importing 3 million tons annually[9].

Romania was an extreme case, but living standards in Hungary and Czechoslovakia were also falling. By 1980, real wages in Hungary were at the same level as ten years previously, although the country had seen an average inflation rate of 7%. Between 1980-1985, the inflation rate soared to 30%[10]. Hungary has the dubious distinction of having one of the highest rates of alcoholism, drug dependency and suicide in Europe[11]. It also has the highest per capita debt in the World; standing at $1873 in 1980[12]. Although the Czechoslovak economy was consistently one of the best performing in the CMEA, it also suffered from the structural problems associated with a planned economy. By the 1980's these problems were impossible to counteract by improvements to the central planning mechanism. There was a lack of quality consumer goods,

---

[8] Ibid. Brown, J., F., *Eastern Europe and Communist Rule*, p. 286.
[9] Ibid. Brown, J., F., *Eastern Europe and Communist Rule*, p. 283.
[10] Ibid. Brown, J., F., *Eastern Europe and Communist Rule*, p. 213, p. 224.
[11] Hungary has had the highest suicide rate in Europe for some time. By 1984 it stood at 45.6 for every 100 000. This was above the rate in the Federal Republic of Germany, which stood at 27.6 per 100 000, and above that of the German Democratic Republic. Bango, Jenö, *Die post-sozialistische Gesellschaft Ungarns*, Trofenik Verlag 1991, p. 133.
[12] Commission of the European Communities, *A Historic Challenge*, 1990, p. 23. Although the problem of foreign debt was not unknown to Romania, Hungary still topped the list and borrowed a further $3 billion in 1985, albeit under the auspices of the International Monetary Fund (IMF) which oversaw the introduction of an austerity programme. Ibid. Brown, J., F., *Eastern Europe and Communist Rule*, pp. 12-129.

a housing shortage and wasteful energy consumption[13]. Czechoslovakia was one of the world's largest energy consumers and required more energy to produce a unit of Gross Domestic Product (GDP) than any other country. It was also the largest user of steel per unit of GDP in the world. However, the products officially classified as conforming to 'world technical level' declined, as did Czechoslovakia's share in world engineering exports[14].

By the 1980's, independent information was flowing freely into most parts of Eastern Europe. Many East Europeans could tune into Western radio or television. In 1985, Austria and Hungarian television were linked by satellite with the result that 100 000 Hungarian homes could receive *3 Sat*. In May 1986, a joint Hungarian-Austrian-German radio station, *Radio Danubius*, was founded. It broadcast a 12 hour programme every day[15]. The system's failure became all the more evident in comparison to the standards which had been reached in Western Europe since the end of the Second World War. In the light of this, the luxurious lifestyles of the East European political elite also became less acceptable. The Hungarian population, which was permitted to travel abroad to the West once a year, was the most acutely aware of the discrepancy between ideology and economic reality[16]. This discrepancy was vitally important because, as Ivan Völgyes states, one of the main foundations of legitimacy for the Communist regimes was that of equality:

'One of the primary claims of the East European Communist regimes and their most frequently used argument

---

[13] By 1980, Czechoslovakia was paying five times as much for its oil imports from the Soviet Union than in 1971, and importing twice as much. Ibid. Brown, J., F., *Eastern Europe and Communist Rule*, p. 302.
[14] Sobell, Vlad, 'Czechoslovakia: The Legacy of Normalization', *East European Politics and Societies*, Vol. 2, No. 1, Winter 1988.
[15] Toma, Peter, A., *Socialist Authority: The Hungarian Experience*, Praeger 1988, p. 200.
[16] In 1984, 300 000 Hungarians visited Austria. In the same year, 2 million Austrians visited Hungary. Ibid. Brown, J., F., *Eastern Europe and Communist Rule*, p. 72.

for legitimacy has been that only Communist rule can achieve the cherished goal of equality.[17]

It was obvious that this goal had not been achieved by any of the Communist countries. By 1983, 28.2% of the Hungarian population was living on 2500 Forints a month, below the official Hungarian poverty level. At this time, the average wage was 4800 Forints a month. By 1984, approximately one quarter of the population was officially living in poverty[18].

The problem was that the Soviet Union feared the destabilising effects reform could have on the Communist system as a whole. As an *RFE/RL Report* states;

'At the origin of the blocking of economic reform in the USSR, a decisive consideration was the fear of the destabilising effect that it might have in the social sphere, through the weakening of some of the principles that help to maintain consensus around the regime substantially stable prices, job security, and so on. These are considered principles that cannot be given up, even if citizens have to pay for them through very modest salaries, inefficient services, and shops that are often half empty and in any case stocked with low-quality products. To this is added the certainty that in any case economic reform would require a political price (decentralisation of the decision making power) that the regime does not want to pay or is incapable of paying.'[19]

However, declining living standards and lower economic growth, indeed in some cases negative growth by the late 1980's, broke the tacit 'social contract' which had been formed between

---

[17] Ibid. Brown, J., F., *Eastern Europe and Communist Rule*, p. 407.

[18] Of course these are official figures and do not take into account the semi-legal and illegal activities which the majority of Hungarians engaged in to obtain a reasonable standard of living. Ibid. Brown, J., F., *Eastern Europe and Communist Rule*, p. 409.

[19] Delvin, Kevin, 'Are the East Blocs reformable?', *RFE/RL Background Report*, No. 3, November 1993.

population and political elite as a means of facilitating government. The 'social contract' promised continual growth, secure employment, low prices for energy, rents and food, and general health care for everyone in return for political quiescence. Once it became clear that the regime was unable to fulfil even these basic tenets of its political ideology, the system lost the precarious legitimacy it had gained over the years.

As long as the economic and political crisis remained under control and hidden from public view, the majority of the population was resigned to the situation and to some extent accepted the regime ideology, that is those parts pertaining to job security and subsidised prices. However, once the failure of the regime to provide even this limited level of security was exposed, legitimacy was endangered. Corrective action had to be implemented in order to pacify the population and correct the economic dysfunction. However, in the past, the Soviet Union had strongly resisted any attempts at reform. As a result of the Warsaw Pact invasion in 1968 and the means by which the Husak regime restored orthodox order, the Czechoslovak regime was unwilling to implement any new reform programme. The Romanian regime was also unwilling to implement reforms, but for somewhat different reasons. It was firmly in the grip of Nicolae Ceausescu, a convinced 'national-Stalinist'. Only the Hungarian regime had implemented gradual reforms, albeit with periodic setbacks, during the entire period since 1956.

Although the Romanian population practised a passive form of resistance, there had been no concerted effort to reform the system, partly as it was so severe and partly because it was viewed as a means by which to fend off Soviet influence and interference. In contrast, the system in Hungary had already been rejected by the population in 1956, and the Czechs and Slovaks had tried to reform it during the Prague Spring of 1968. In both cases the Soviet Union had successfully intervened to halt the processes of systemic reform. The threat of Soviet intervention therefore kept the Communist regimes in power and prevented any attempts at systemic reform. By the 1980's it had become clear that the system was unable to fulfil even its own aims and was essentially bankrupt. But it was necessary to wait until the Soviet Union itself took steps towards systemic reform before anything further could be undertaken in Eastern Europe.

As noted earlier, the role of the Soviet Union in supporting the governments of Eastern Europe was partly to blame for the catastrophic situation[20]. The political elites of Eastern Europe were torn between the need to obey Moscow in order to remain in power; and the need to implement more suitable policies, which required a more independent stance. This was a classic *Catch 22* situation which resulted in periodic rebellions within the Eastern Bloc as governments wavered between appeasing domestic demands and Moscow's insistence on obedience and loyalty. The extent of independent action undertaken was determined by the extent of crisis in which the respective society and economy found itself at the time. The deeper the crisis, the more pressing the need to increase domestic legitimacy in order to apply the necessary corrective policies; but, the more serious the crisis, the less willing Moscow was to allow independent policies and the more concerned it became to ensure Soviet influence remained undamaged. The Soviet Union's fear of losing control in Eastern Europe propelled it to intervene in East European affairs during periods of crisis. After 1968, this was justified by the 'Brezhnev Doctrine':

> *'The sovereignty of each socialist country cannot be contrary to the interests of the world socialist movement.'*[21]

Brezhnev personally emphasised this position by stating:

> *'We cannot remain indifferent to the fate of socialism in another country.'*[22]

However, once loyalty to Moscow had been restored, the government in question was even more dependent on Moscow and

---

[20] Staar, Richard, F., (Ed.), *East Central Europe and the USSR*, St. Martin's Press 1991, p. 25.
[21] Original in *Pravda*, 25 September, 1968. From Daniels, R., V., *A Documentary History of Communism: Volume 2*, University Press New England 1984, pp. 336-339.
[22] Gati, Charles, *The Bloc that Failed*, Indiana University Press 1990, p. 46.

became less capable of dealing with any future crisis. This increased the political, economic and military burden on the Soviet Union until it became untenable.

By 1985[23], the year in which Mikhail Gorbachev became Secretary General of the Communist Party of the Soviet Union, the whole of the Eastern Bloc was facing a general systemic crisis. Events of the past and bitter experience had exhausted the possibilities of reform in Eastern Europe. As a result, the region had fallen into a deep economic and psychological crisis. Developments in technology and society made it impossible to rely on traditional methods of repression to deal with social and political unrest, and in any case the Soviet Union, suffering from what has been termed 'imperial overstretch', was both unwilling and incapable of employing such methods.

2.1.1: Soviet Subsidies to Eastern Europe

The term 'imperial overstretch' was coined by Paul Kennedy in his book, 'The Rise and Decline of the Great Powers'[24]. He argues that powerful countries are forced to expand until their economies can no longer maintain their imperial commitments, especially military commitments. Devoting so much of the economy to defence and military expenditure becomes an intolerable drain on resources. As a result, economic performance declines. Imperial commitments thus become a burden, rather than a benefit to the economy[25].

Measuring the extent of Soviet economic resources devoted to defence and supporting Eastern Europe is problematical because the Soviet Union produced no precise figures concerning its Gross Domestic Product (GDP)[26]. Indeed, Moscow received its GDP

---

[23] Sakwa, R., *Gorbachev and His Reforms 1985-1990*, Philip Allan 1990, p. 1.

[24] Roskin, Michael, G., *The Rebirth of East Europe (2nd. Edition)*, Prentice Hall 1994, p. 132.

[25] There has been much discussion as to the nature and amount of Soviet subsidies to Eastern Europe and whether the latter's economic ties to the Soviet Union can thus be viewed overall as beneficial. For a more detailed account, see Desai, Padma, 'Is the Soviet Union Subsidizing Eastern Europe?', *European Economic Review*, Vol. 30, No. 1, January 1986.

[26] The Communist countries measured economic growth in terms of Net Material Product. This included the value-added output of all physical production, but did

estimates from CIA Calculations. The CIA calculated the level of defence spending as a percentage of the GDP. In this way the strain on the Soviet economy was measured. The CIA estimated that the Soviet Union spent about twice as much as the United States on defence, that is approximately 12% of its GDP. However, in the 1970's George Bush called together a group of radical academics, calling them 'Team B', and gave them the task of revising the methods employed to calculate the figure. This group came to the conclusion that the size of the Soviet GDP had been over-estimated and the level of defence spending under-estimated. They claimed that the Soviet Union's defence spending accounted for 20% of its GDP. However, during a conference in 1990, two Soviet economists claimed that Soviet Union's GDP was even smaller and defence spending even greater than anyone had thought, and set the figure of defence spending between 25%-28% of its GDP. In 1990, Edward Sheverdnadze gave the proportion of Soviet GDP spent on defence as 25%[27]. Whatever the exact figure was, it represented an enormous strain on the Soviet economy and one which, by the 1980's, it could no longer afford to sustain.

In addition, the Soviet Union subsidised the countries of Eastern Europe by providing cheap energy supplies; accepting as payment products which were un-saleable on the world market[28]. The countries of Eastern Europe could accumulate a balance of Rubles with the Soviet Union by supplying a surplus of goods, but this balance could only be used to buy other sub-standard Soviet goods[29]. Trade amongst the East European members of CMEA was carried out on a similar barter basis. In this way, the economies of

---

not count the value of non-material sectors, such as defence, banking and other services.
[27] Ibid. Roskin, Michael, G., *The Rebirth of East Europe*, p. 134.
[28] During the 1980's the Soviet Union cut its supply of oil to certain CMEA countries, particularly to Bulgaria. Bulgaria had been receiving cheap Soviet oil and was re-selling it on the world market at a profit. It was partly in response to this that the Soviet Union decided to sell all its oil at world prices in hard currency, thus ending East European subsidies.
[29] The cost of these goods had however risen substantially. In 1974 Hungary could buy 1 million tons of Soviet oil by delivering 800 *Ikarus* busses, this had risen to 2300 buses in 1981, and stood at 4000 buses by 1988. Crampton, R., J., *Eastern Europe in the Twentieth Century*, Routledge 1994, p. 410.

the Eastern Bloc were sheltered from the competitive world market and bound to the Soviet economy. Immediately after the Second World War the Soviet Union systematically drained Eastern Europe; one economist, Paul Marer, estimates the Soviet Union removed an equivalent of $14 billion from Eastern Europe[30], but by the 1980's the situation had reversed. The maintenance, politically, economically and militarily of Eastern Europe was now draining the Soviet Union's inflexible, command economy at an alarming rate[31]. Radical new policies were required to remedy the situation before the Soviet Union became totally bankrupt, both economically and ideologically.

2.1.2: Perestroika and Glasnost

At 54, Gorbachev was the youngest ever Party leader and the youngest member of the Politburo of the time[32]. His election heralded an end to the gerontocracy which had developed during Brezhnev's rule and began a new era in Soviet domestic and foreign policy. *Glasnost* and *Perestroika* were conceived as a means of rehabilitating socialism, thereby enabling it to offer a feasible alternative to capitalism. Unfortunately, systemic decay had already reached an advanced stage when Gorbachev came to power and his new initiatives further de-stabilised the already precarious situation. In addition, the new policies aimed to reform a system which had been constructed specifically to resist change.

Initiation of a new course in the Soviet Union made it impossible to deny economic and political reform to Eastern Europe. Indeed, one of the prerequisites for successful reform of the Soviet Union was complete restructuring of the Soviet Bloc. However, public admittance of the appalling state of the economy in both Eastern Europe and the Soviet Union served only to expose the total incompetence of the ruling political elites and the bankruptcy of the system as a whole. This destroyed any remaining

---

[30] Ibid. Roskin, Michael, G., *The Rebirth of East Europe*, p. 116.
[31] It has been estimated that stationing Soviet armed forces combined with economic subsidies, such as selling natural gas and oil below world prices, cost the Soviet Union $ 7 billion in 1970, and had escalated to $ 40 billion a year in 1980. Ibid. Roskin, Michael, G., *The Rebirth of East Europe*, p. 134.
[32] Ibid. Sakwa, R., *Gorbachev and His Reforms 1985-1990*, p. 2.

trust in the various political elites' competence and ability to carry out major systemic reform.

The policies of *Perestroika* and *Glasnost* were conceived as a means of modernising and thereby strengthening the Soviet system[33]. The 'Brezhnev Doctrine' would not have been abandoned if this action had been viewed as threatening vital Soviet interests in Eastern Europe. The fact was that the Soviet Union could no longer afford the political and economic costs associated with keeping the East European regimes in power. The tacit agreements which had been reached during the height of the Cold War, when the Soviet Union viewed it as imperative to support the regimes with all the means at its disposal, were no longer suitable in view of the changed international climate and domestic position of the Soviet Union. In addition, many of the regimes showed themselves to be incompetent and incapable of dealing with the growing economic crisis. Even though it was obvious that reform was necessary, Gorbachev avoided using the term during his first year of office, preferring more neutral expressions such as, 'improving the economic mechanism', 'perfecting socialist construction' and, '*Perestroika*'. It was only from 1987 onwards that he spoke of 'radical reform' and 'democratisation'. But, however radical they appeared, the reforms remained constrained by the belief that socialism could be salvaged by removing past 'deformations'.

Although Gorbachev initiated reform of the Soviet system, he over-estimated the attractions of socialism and under-estimated the strength of the reform movement. He believed that the government and Party could direct and control the reform process. However, the reform movement gained a momentum of its own and the policies of *Perestroika* and *Glasnost* themselves became redundant, as did the socialist ideology they supported. But, although they were

---

[33] Gorbachev is a member of the same generation as the 1968 Czech reformers. As a Law student in Moscow he came into contact with Zdenek Mlynar, who became responsible for ideology in Czechoslovakia during the Prague Spring. In Czech, Gorbachev's speech in Prague in 1987, during which he referred to a 'Common European Home', bore a striking, and rather eerie, resemblance to the ides which had circulated during 1968, and in some instances even employed the very same phraseology. The problem was, events had demonstrated the futility of a 'Third Way'.

undoubtedly flawed, it was these policies, discernible in the Soviet Union during the period from 1985-1990, which afforded the East European countries a further possibility for systemic reform and change.

Gorbachev realised that to reform the Soviet Union and create a sustainable economic base for further development it was necessary to reassess relations with the Soviet Union's East European Allies. Past Soviet interventions in East European affairs as well as current political and economic relations were reassessed. As part of this process, East European independence and domestic sovereignty had to be recognised. The Eastern Bloc was to remain closely tied to, but not dependent on, the Soviet Union. This subtle change of emphasis would return Eastern Europe to the international arena and enable the Soviet Union to cut costs by reducing troop numbers and subsidies. The policy would also bring with it political advantages and provide for better relations with the Western powers, from whom Gorbachev hoped to gain political and financial support. The new policy was implemented almost as soon as Gorbachev came to power, but the lack of a clear official statement concerning the degree of independence and sovereignty which was to be respected left relations unclear and open to individual interpretation. Although Gorbachev stated in November 1987:

> *'Unity does not mean uniformity... There is no model of socialism to be imitated by all.'* [34]

This statement still implied that, although variation would be tolerated, it was to remain compatible with socialism. However, it soon became clear that Gorbachev aimed to restructure completely relations with Eastern Europe and allow full independence and sovereignty. In an interview with *The Economist* in July 1989, he stated:

> *'Social and political orders in one or another country have changed in the past and may change in the future. But*

---

[34] Ibid. Crampton, R., J., *Eastern Europe in the Twentieth Century*, p. 400.

this change is the exclusive affair of the people of that country and is their choice. Any interference in domestic affairs and any attempts to restrict the sovereignty of states, both friends and allies or any others is inadmissible.[35]

2.1.3: The Brezhnev Doctrine is Abandoned

In his speech to the Council of Europe on 6 July, 1989, Gorbachev once again emphasised his commitment to respecting the independence of Eastern Europe:

'It is the sovereign right of each people to choose their social system at their own discretion.[36]

The 'Brezhnev Doctrine' had been abandoned. The Soviet Union re-examined its role in Eastern Europe during the Communist period and admitted that the intervention in Hungary in 1956 and in Czechoslovakia in 1968 had been unjustified. This action re-ignited the discussion over 1956 in Hungary and helped facilitate the rehabilitation of the Revolution and the re-burial of Imre Nagy.

After 1956, the Kádár regime had based its legitimacy on the promise of continuously increasing living standards, rising consumption and a relaxation of the Stalinist system. It had therefore been the only regime of the region to embark on a consistent programme of gradual reform. The majority of the Hungarian political elite was therefore favourably inclined towards Gorbachev's initiatives and welcomed the opportunity to gain more independence and implement more far-reaching reforms.

The regime in Czechoslovakia was completely unable to deal with a re-examination of the Warsaw Pact invasion and the abandonment of the 1968 Action Programme since it had based its whole legitimacy around the claim that the invasion was justified. In contrast to the Hungarian regime, it had introduced a form of neo-Stalinism and successfully frozen Czechoslovak politics, society and economic development. A re-examination of the events

---

[35] Mikhail Gorbachev. Interview with *The Economist*, July 15, 1989, p. 53.
[36] Ibid. Crampton, R., J., *Eastern Europe in the Twentieth Century*, p. 408.

surrounding 1968 would inevitably expose the regime's illegitimacy, something which the political elite was not prepared to contemplate. The Czechoslovak political elite was therefore unwilling to initiate any reforms. On the contrary, they manipulated the abandonment of the 'Brezhnev Doctrine' and the full recognition of national sovereignty to block reform. The regime transformed itself from being one of the regimes which followed Moscow's wishes most closely, to completely rejecting Gorbachev's new course, stating that the policies emanating from the Soviet Union were not suitable for Czechoslovak conditions.

The Romanian regime was used to following an independent course, but also employed this policy in its attempt to block reform. Ironically, the situation in Romania led to calls in support of a Soviet intervention. As reform in the Soviet Union proceeded and the rigidity of the regime in Romania hardened, Soviet intervention was seen as a means to depose Ceausescu and ensure the introduction of reform. Paradoxically, in the light of reactions to previous Soviet interventions, such a move would have been supported by the Western powers. On 24 December, 1989, the French Foreign Minister, Dumas, stated that if the Soviet Union intervened in Romania, France:

> *'Not only would not object to it, but would support this action.'*[37]

James Baker gave an interview to *NBC* on the same day and confirmed the United States' favourable perception of a Soviet intervention:

> *'We would be inclined probably to follow the example of France, who has said that if the Warsaw Pact felt it necessary to intervene on behalf of the opposition, that it would support that action.'*[38]

---

[37] Ratesh, Nestor, *Romania: The Entangled Revolution*, Praeger 1992, p. 112. Original in *The New York Times*, 25 December 1989.
[38] Ibid. Ratesh, Nestor, *Romania: The Entangled Revolution*, p. 112.

During the Romanian Revolution, a call was sent to the Soviet Embassy asking for assistance. The telephone call was recorded, as were many events concerning the Revolution, and later broadcast by Romanian Television on 23 December, 1989:

> *'We are informed that the help of the Soviet army was requested through the Embassy of the USSR, due to the fact that the terrorists have resorted to helicopters through foreign interventionists.'*[39]

Interestingly, the Soviets declined to offer military assistance. Gorbachev confirmed that such a request had been received from the *Romanian National Salvation Front Council* and stated that although the Soviet Union had been asked to replenish ammunition supplies, only humanitarian assistance was offered. Assisstence was officially refused, but the true extent of Soviet involvement in the Romanian Revolution remains unclear.

The reason for Soviet reluctance to intervene was partly explained by Edward Sheverdnadze at the February Plenum of the Communist Party Central Committee in 1990:

> *'Why did we not foresee the events in these countries? We did. And that was why, starting April 1985, we fundamentally restructured the nature of interstate ties with them, abandoned interference in their internal affairs, and stopped imposing solutions. But it is easier to change policy than to change people... After April 1985 they could not be removed from power by the current Soviet leadership, since I repeat, it had forsworn interference in other countries' internal affairs. This was the only correct decision.'*[40]

The problem which the 'hard-line' regimes in Romania and Czechoslovakia posed was that, having abandoned interference in Eastern Europe, the Soviet Union could not simply replace them.

---

[39] Ibid. Ratesh, Nestor, *Romania: The Entangled Revolution*, p. 111.
[40] Dawisha, Karen, *Eastern Europe, Gorbachev and Reform (2nd. Edition)*, Cambridge University Press 1990, p. 197. Original in *Pravda*, 8 February, 1990.

Regime Collapse and the Role of the Soviet Union

Of course, it is debatable whether the Soviet leadership foresaw all the consequences which the abandonment of the 'Brezhnev Doctrine' would have for Eastern Europe. What was probably foreseen, was the inevitable collapse of the regimes if old policies were continued. As military pressure was no longer a legitimate means of removing unwanted leaders in Eastern Europe, Gorbachev resorted to applying political pressure to those regimes, in this case Czechoslovakia and Romania, which refused to follow the Soviet lead and implement a reform programme. He visited all the Warsaw Pact countries and was greeted ecstatically by the crowds which gathered to greet him[41].

Thus, the Soviet Union once again played a decisive role in the reform movement which swept the Soviet Bloc during the late 1980's. In contrast to the crises of the past, the Soviet Union was the force behind change and reform, rather than the major hindering obstacle. However, although the Soviet Union started and encouraged the reform movement, it was unprepared for the dramatic consequences of this policy. Gorbachev expected the East European countries to remain socialist even without the threat of Soviet intervention. He was convinced that socialist development was only possible in the context of an open and democratic society. Soviet interference in East European affairs was therefore a hindrance to both East European and Soviet socialist development. However, by 1989 socialism held little attraction for the populations of Eastern Europe.

The Hungarian and Czechoslovak regimes had attempted to reform the system, but had been thwarted; partly by the system's own resilience and partly by the intervention of the Soviet Union. Gradualist reform, exemplified by Hungary's 'goulash communism', had also failed to produce the expected long-term improvement. Internal reform had thus proved incapable of solving the basic problems inherent in the Soviet system. Although the Romanian regime had never attempted reform, by 1989 the

---

[41] Gorbachev visited Romania in the summer of 1987. It was the last Warsaw Pact country to receive him, an indication of the tensions between the two leaders. Ibid. Brown, J., F., *Eastern Europe and Communist Rule*, p. 292.

situation was so desperate that the main aim was simply to get rid of the existing system by removing Ceausescu, who personified it.

Forty years of Communist totalitarian rule had increased the relative economic and social backwardness of Eastern Europe in comparison with the Western half of the continent[42]. While economic deprivation was undoubtedly an important factor which led to the Revolutions in 1989, it was the rejection of totalitarianism as such which proved the most potent force. As György Konrad states, the people of Eastern Europe were fed up of the politicisation of every aspect of life:

> *'What occupies our minds above all in Eastern Europe is not whether a policy is good or bad but the overabundance of policies everywhere the state drags countless matters, questions and decisions into politics that have no business there... Because politics has flooded nearly every nook and cranny of our lives, I would like to see the flood recede. We ought to de-politicise our lives, free them from politics as from some contagious infection. We ought to free our simple everyday affairs from considerations of politics. I ask that the state do what it is supposed to do, and do it well. But it should not do things that are society's business, not the state's. So I would describe the democratic opposition as not political but an anti-political opposition, since it is essential activity is to work for de-statification.'* [43]

By removing its security guarantee and economic subsidies, and by admitting the catastrophic state of the economy, the Soviet Union forced the regimes in Eastern Europe to rely on domestic legitimacy and deal with the crises on their own. In this way their complete lack of legitimacy and incompetence was exposed. Bloc coherence and integrity was quickly eroded as the regimes in Romania, Hungary and Czechoslovakia chose different methods to

---

[42] The population in Hungary and Czechoslovakia did not judge their standard of living against other CMEA members, but rather used Austria and Germany as a yardstick to measure success.
[43] Stokes, Gale, *From Stalinism to Pluralism*, Oxford University Press 1991, pp. 179-180. Original in Konrad, György, *Antipolitics*, Suhrkamp 1985.

deal with the crisis. Timothy Garton Ash accurately described this process:

> *'[Change] would not occur by planned reform from the imperial centre, in the context of sustained growth and comprehensive modernisation, but mainly by uncoordinated independent action, whether individual, collective, or national, by pressure from below or from outside in an overall context of growing relative backwardness in relation to much of the developed world, specifically to Western Europe.'*[44]

The Revolutions in Eastern Europe were therefore varied, but their original aims, as understood by the population and some sections of the political elite, were the same; to free the population and country from dictatorship and introduce democracy in order to return to European cultural, economic and political norms, as exemplified by the European Union. However, while the Hungarian Party embarked upon a long and time consuming 'march though the institutions'; transformation of the economy was started in the early 1980's, the Czechoslovak regime collapsed within a week. The Romanian regime suffered the last and most spectacular fall. The regime collapsed as a result of a spontaneous and violent Revolution which ended with Ceausescu's execution on 25 December, 1989. The different types of Revolution reflected the differencees between the respective regimes. The specific nature of the Revolution influenced the transformation policies which were subsequently implemented. In this way, the Commuist legacy may influence the prospects of successful democratic consolidation.

---

[44] Ash, Timothy Garton, *The Uses of Adversity*, Penguin Books 1991, p. 229.

2.2: Hungary's Negotiated Revolution

'Question: Who was Karl Marx?
Another voice: He was a Soviet philosopher; Engels was his friend. Well, what else can I say? He died at an old age. A female voice: Of course, a politician. And he was you know, he was what's his name's Lenin's, Lenin, Lenin's Works well he translated them into Hungarian.'
Radio Budapest, Interviews on Marx Square[45].

By the 1980's there was no one in Hungary who still believed in orthodox Communism. Moreover, there was little direct need to hide this fact since this condition afflicted not only the population at large, but also state functionaries and the political elite of the Hungarian Socialist Workers Party. The reasons behind this development were related to the events surrounding the 1956 Revolution and Imre Nagy's execution, but were also connected to the regime's own reformist policies. Gorbachev's acceptance of East European sovereignty freed Hungarian politics from socialist rhetoric and enabled it to embark on an open transformation programme, both economic and political.

It was not so much the 1956 Revolution itself which had become a problem for the Hungarian political elite, but Kádár's personal role in luring Imre Nagy and his companions out of the Yugoslav Embassy. Kádár had signed a written undertaking guaranteeing Nagy's safety outside the Embassy. However, as soon as Nagy had left the Yugoslav Embassy he was kidnapped, along with his companions, and taken to Romania before being secretly tried and executed in Hungary[46]. These facts had been suppressed, but were widely known. A re-examination of 1956 and rehabilitation of Nagy would therefore implicate Kádár. During the 1980's, the last surviving defendant of the Nagy trial, Miklós Vásárhelyi became a powerful symbol of the bankruptcy and illegitimacy of the Kádár

---

[45] 'Hungarian Situation Report', *RFE/RL Research Report*, 16 May 1985, pp. 39-41.
[46] Ash, Timothy Garton, *We the People*, Granata Books 1990, p. 47.

regime[47]. As long as Kádár was in power the ghost of 1956 would continue to haunt Hungarian politics. Before more radical reform could be considered it was necessary to remove Kádár from political power. By the late 1980's, it was only a question of time before he was replaced.

Moreover, the reformist policies of the Kádár regime had reached their limit by the early 1980's. Rather than producing a healthy socialist market economy, they had caused a rapid decline in health of the Hungarian economy and population. Although relative ideological freedom had developed under Kádár, the economy was tottering on the brink of collapse[48]. This was partly due to the nature of the central planning system and the reforms which had modified it, but also to the strain created by the need to import consumer goods to keep the population subdued. The Hungarian economy therefore differed from those of Romania and Czechoslovakia in that, although it suffered from the same problems associated with the central planning system[49], the administration of the economy and the psychology of the working population had been transformed[50]. Karl-Eugen Wädekin sees this as a result of the regime's policy of gradual reform:

---

[47] He had been Nagy's advisor and press spokesman during the 1956 Revolution and had remained in contact with senior Party members as well as the democratic opposition. Ibid. Ash, Timothy Garton, *We the People*, pp. 47-48.

[48] The high level of Hungarian foreign debt has already been mentioned. In addition, Hungarian growth slowed to 2.3% in the second half of the 1970's. By 1981, growth figures were negative. Although Hungary is poor in natural resources and relies on foreign trade for as much as 40-50% of its income, the Hungarian trade deficit also began to rise. In 1978, the hard currency trade balance showed a $1 billion deficit. The first six months of 1986 produced a deficit of $400 million. The Hungarian trade deficit with the Soviet Union was also increasing. This led the Soviet Union to insist that Hungary reduce its deficit by 70% in 1984. Ibid. Brown, J., F., *Eastern Europe and Communist Rule*, pp. 213-219.

[49] That is 'soft budget constraints', monopoly enterprises, chronic worker shortage, low productivity, low quality standards, over-employment within enterprises and non-fulfilment of Plan targets.

[50] The 'New Economic Mechanism', which was introduced under the direction of Rezsö Nyers in 1968, freed 50% of prices from government subsidy. But, the social safety net was not sufficient to deal with those who could not afford to pay the new market determined prices. Thus, wages for the lowest paid were increased in 1972. Ibid. Brown, J., F., *Eastern Europe and Communist Rule*, pp. 208-211.

> '*Neither tolerance toward the private sector, nor the opening up of co-operation with Western firms, which has led to the widespread adoption of Western technology and the spreading of technical innovations... nor the flexible ways of entering export markets are alone sufficient explanations of the Hungarian success. There are other elements of great importance that allowed for the successful application of these approaches: abstention from setting plan targets in physical units and subsidising them with highly aggregated, annually corrected and not absolutely mandatory ones (i.e. targets), combined with leaving considerable decision-making powers to factory managers... In that same sense, a sizeable decompression of the domestic political atmosphere... also exerted a positive influence... last but not least, this rather consistent reform has been continued for roughly two decades.*'[51]

It is necessary to define Wädekin's use of the term 'success' in this case. The reforms had changed the operation of the planning system and had also influenced working practices and workers' aspirations, but had failed to correct the basic dysfunction of the system. 'Soft budget constraints' meant monopoly enterprises exported sub-standard goods to the Soviet Union because this was the easiest way to secure employment. The state could not close unprofitable or technically out of date enterprises, thus creating unemployment, as long as a socialist ideological base, which guaranteed the right to work and state ownership of the means of production, was retained.

As the economic system began to collapse, the regime was forced to consider ways in which it could successfully reform the economy. The main difficulty was how to impose 'hard budget constraints' on enterprises and introduce effective control over enterprise activities and, more specifically, how to limit the power of enterprise managers and ensure they acted more rationally, in an economic sense. The solution was a return to private property and

---

[51] Wädekin, Karl-Eugen, 'East European Trends and Prospects: A European Perspective', *East European Economies*, Vol. 1, p. 432.

the creation of a market in property. This would increase identification with performance and at the same time create the conditions necessary for ending monopolies. In this way the regime hoped to impose 'hard budget constraints'[52].

In 1983, a bond market was established and in 1985, two new banks were founded. By 1986, three commercial banks were operating. By 1988, the Party, under the leadership of the reformist wing, initiated a property reform which re-introduced a property market. Tax reform was initiated with the introduction of Personal Income Tax, Value Added Tax and an Entrepreneurs' Profit Tax. In addition, in July 1988, the Central Committee accepted plans for liberalisation which reduced subsidies by approximately 32-35 billion Forints. Controls were ended on 67-68% of all consumer prices and 35-40% of convertible currency imports. Company and Investment Laws were passed for implementation in 1989[53]. The Company Law permitted the development of domestic capitalism by allowing legal persons to own, buy and sell shares in the means of production. It was this legislation which was used for the privatisation which occurred during 1989-1990. The Investment Law permitted foreign capitalists to repatriate profits on very generous terms and granted them various tax exemptions[54].

The decrease in real wages led the regime to encourage people to engage secondary work in addition to official state employment via the Enterprise of Economic Work Partnerships[55]. This policy was instrumental in fostering entrepreneurial spirit, enabling workers to use state equipment for their own enterprises after

---

[52] For more information on the problem of 'soft budget constraints', see Kornai, J., *The Road to a Free Economy*, W. W. Norton & Co 1990, and Szelenyi, I., *Urban Inequalities under State Socialism*, Oxford University Press 1983
[53] Swain, Nigel, *Hungary: The Rise and Fall of Feasible Socialism*, Verso 1992, p. 10.
[54] Top foreign managers were permitted to repatriate 50% of their post-tax income. Sárközy, T., (Ed.), *Foreign Investments in Hungary*, Budapest 1989.
[55] Real wages in the industrial sector dropped from being comparable to 62% of the Austrian level in 1965, to 40% in 1982. The decline was similar in the white collar sector, where they fell from being 49% of the Austrian level in 1965, to 30% in 1982. Over the period, Hungarian wages declined from being 57% of Austrian level wages to 38%. Lendvai, Paul, *Hungary: The Art of Survival*, I. B. Tauris & Co. Ltd. 1988, p. 105.

working hours. It legalised additional earnings and maximised the income of skilled workers while keeping them within the official economy[56]. But, even though equipment and manpower were often employed for private purposes during official working hours, many people still had difficulty making ends meet.

2.2.1: The Standard of Living Falls

The number of Hungarians living in poverty had generally fallen during the socialist period, but after 1980, due to a continuous fall in the standard of living and drop in the value of real wages, the numbers began to rise once more. Thus, between 1982-1987 the number of those living below the official subsistence level rose from 650 000 to approximately one million. By 1987, 20.1% of the population lived below the socially accepted minimum. A further 9.1% were living below the survival minimum[57].

Originally, only those who were employed by the state were covered by health insurance and had rights to sick pay, free health services and child-care facilities. The peasantry were excluded from all these benefits. Universal provision was introduced in the 1960's along with collectivisation. While the health service had coped as long as it had to deal with only 47% of the population, the strain of 100% health insurance could not be met without investment. However, the proportion of the state budget devoted to spending on social services declined. This resulted in the system's deterioration and ensured class remained an important factor in determining some health factors, such as suicide and mortality rates[58].

Budapest remains the largest metropolis in Hungary with one fifth of the population living there[59]. The city has the effect of draining the surrounding countryside. By 1970 there was already a large discrepancy between the provision of amenities in Budapest and in the surrounding towns and villages[60]. The housing shortage

---

[56] Ibid. Swain, Nigel, *Hungary: The Rise and Fall of Feasible Socialism*, p. 178.
[57] Ibid. Swain, Nigel, *Hungary: The Rise and Fall of Feasible Socialism*, p. 192.
[58] Ibid. Swain, Nigel, *Hungary: The Rise and Fall of Feasible Socialism*, p. 205.
[59] Timmermann, Heiner, (Hrsg.), *Ungarn nach 1945*, Dadder 1990, p. 130.
[60] In 1970, Budapest had 4.04 doctors per 1000 population, while the surrounding villages had only 0.52. Budapest had 6.57 crèche places per 1000, while the surrounding villages had only 3.18. 87% of houses in the villages around Budapest

was a further problem. An idea of the shortage can be gained by examining the number of people living as sub-tenants, or 'bed-tenants', that is sharing a room with strangers in someone else's house. In 1960, the figures stood at 173 000 sub-tenants, and 47 000 bed-tenants. By 1970, these figures had risen to 260 000 sub-tenants, and 119 000 bed-tenants. As a result of this development available living space also declined. By 1980, the available living space for the average Hungarian was 36% of that of the average Dane. An added problem was that the quality of flats was deteriorating. It has been claimed that one fifth of state flats did not meet the minimum standard[61]. In an attempt to alleviate this shortfall, the Hungarian regime re-privatised house construction and withdrew almost completely from the housing market. Unfortunately, this resulted in further deterioration of state flats; while a speculative and chaotic housing market gradually emerged. Between 1972-1982, the price of houses increased at a rate of 20% a year. This was more than twice the rate of inflation for other products[62]. It is hardly surprising that the health of the Hungarian population began to suffer under the strain of such poor living and working conditions.

Hungary has the highest suicide rate in the World. Between 1946-1950, there were 2370 recorded suicides. In 1968 this figure stood at 3370, but in 1984, 5000 suicides were recorded. It has been estimated that between 50-80 000 people attempt to take their lives every year. The incidence of alcoholism also rose from 76 000 in 1960, to 500 000 by the 1980's[63]. Every third crime in Hungary is committed while under the influence of alcohol. In addition, from 1970-1980 the number of people afflicted by nervous diseases

---

had electricity, but 62.5% used bottled gas for cooking. Only 24.4% had running water and only 4.4% were connected to the mains sewage. Ibid. Swain, Nigel, *Hungary: The Rise and Fall of Feasible Socialism*, pp. 207-208.
[61] Ibid. Swain, Nigel, *Hungary: The Rise and Fall of Feasible Socialism*, pp 208-209. The figures which relate to the housing problem are taken from Foti, P., *Röpirat a Lakashelyzetröl*, Budapest 1988.
[62] Ibid. Swain, Nigel, *Hungary: The Rise and Fall of Feasible Socialism*, p. 209.
[63] At 4.8 litres a year, Hungarians have the second highest consumption rate of hard liquor in the World, and between 1963-1983 consumption of hard spirits rose by 343%. Ibid. Toma, Peter, A., *Socialist Authority: The Hungarian Experience*, p. 164.

doubled, with 15% of Hungarians taking some form of tranquilliser. Drug addiction also increased, especially amongst the young. From 1983-1985, the number of officially registered young drug addicts rose from 10 000 to 30 000. Faced with these figures, it is not surprising that the Hungarian regime was the first in Eastern Europe to officially recognise a drug problem. By the 1980's, life expectancy for Hungarian men had fallen from 66.4 years in 1960, to 65 years[64].

2.2.2: Ideology is Weakened

The Party's own reformist policies also had the long-term effect of weakening belief in Communist ideology. After the 1956 Revolution both Party and state administration had been thoroughly de-Stalinised. By the 1980's, the majority of the Hungarian political elite and state administrators were members of the post-1956 generation; they were too young to have taken part in the Revolution themselves or to be compromised by events immediately after it. The Party's recruitment and job distribution policy also contributed to the declining importance and relevance of ideology and commitment to socialism in Hungarian society. State functionaries were appointed not as a result of loyalty or membership of the Party, but in recognition of their competence and ability. Consequently, the majority of those in the Hungarian administration were more concerned with a career than with the semantics of Communism. In addition, discrimination according to class was stopped in the educational system and everyday life was de-ideologised. The political elite's acceptance of the need to reform the system was an implicit admission that the socialist economic and social system had failed.

As a result, ideology lost its leading role and became redundant in Hungarian politics and society. The population lost faith in the system and the regime lost faith in its own legitimacy. Public opinion polls show a decline in the population's belief in the government's ability to solve the country's problems. In an analysis conducted by the *Hungarian Public Opinion Research Institute* over the ten years preceding 1988, it was discovered that a

---

[64] Ibid. Lendvai, Paul, *Hungary: The Art of Survival*, pp. 101-104.

significant change in attitude occurred in 1982 and in 1986. In 1982, 'dissatisfaction' became focused on the economy and day-to-day economic problems. In 1986, the public called into question the government's competence and felt that the economy was in decline. Declining faith in government was accompanied by increasing scepticism of the government's ability to fulfil its 'socialist' objectives[65]. Although the population remained committed to principles of public welfare, it recognised the economy was unable to fulfil such expectations. For example, belief that Hungary's education system was providing better education than in the West fell from 98% in 1981, to 87% in 1986, and plummeted to 47% on a national basis, and to 27% amongst intellectuals by 1988[66]. This was complemented by a high degree of cynicism concerning the Party's motives[67].

However, by allowing the publication of most literary works the Party had successfully co-opted a large section of the intelligentsia. The population at large had been pacified by the provision of consumer goods and recognition of a private sphere which remained untouched by the state. Therefore, many people were anxious to preserve the reforms and were reluctant to engage in open criticism of the regime. The regime was willing to allow dissent as long as criticism was not too open and certain taboo subjects, such as 1956, were not mentioned. This had the effect that a form of self-censorship was practised and that the line between intra- and extra-establishment dissent was difficult to define. However, by the 1980's this part of the system was also in the process of collapse. As Timothy Garton Ash noted:

'There is almost nothing that might not be allowed'[68]

László Rajk, the son of László Rajk, the Interior Minister killed under Rakosi, ran a *samizdat* shop from his flat for a number of years relatively unimpeded[69]. It was finally closed in 1983[70].

---

[65] See Appendix IX, X.
[66] Ibid. Swain, Nigel, *Hungary: The Rise and Fall of Feasible Socialism*, p.14.
[67] See Appendix XI.
[68] Ibid. Ash, Timothy Garton, *The Uses of Adversity*, p. 131.

In an attempt to deal with the crisis, the Hungarian Socialist Workers Party had to modernise its concept of socialism. Unfortunately, the symbolic trappings and rhetoric of socialism were the only means by which the regime was formally legitimated. As György Aczel answered the questions about Hungarian society put to him by the *New Hungarian Quarterly* in 1981, it was clear that, as a result of the economic and social crisis the country was facing, the Hungarian Party's legitimating ideology had undergone an internal review. Aczel justified the Party's increasingly radical policies by stating:

'We had to reconsider the aim of socialist policy and the means of attaining it.'[71]

2.2.3: Democratisation

The Hungarian Socialist Workers Party had to make clear that its policies were capable of bringing the country's economy and society into line with West European development. To this end, the Party stressed its commitment to switching from extensive to intensive economic development and growth. The Party realised that in order to achieve this it was necessary to place itself under the control of the population as a means of gaining legitimacy and support for its programme. Aczel stated that the Party:

'...knowingly builds on control by the masses and consistently strives to subject itself, or rather its decisions, to mass control.'[72]

In addition, it was acknowledged that to this end:

---

[69] *Samizdat* is the term used to describe independent publications in Eastern Europe. It means self-published.

[70] Skilling, G., *Samizdat and an Independent Society in Eastern Europe*, Macmillan 1989, p. 35.

[71] 'György Aczel answers questions on Hungarian Society', *The New Hungarian Quarterly*, No. 22, Summer 1981.

[72] Aczel, György, 'The Challenge of our Age and the Response of Socialism', *The New Hungarian Quarterly*.

Regime Collapse and the Role of the Soviet Union 141

'Democracy must be extended and not restricted.'[73]

Without the formal legitimisation of socialism, the regime desperately needed a new form of legitimation. It found one in a democratisation programme aimed at social and political life, but which was also originally planned to ensure the Party retained ultimate control. However, events forced the introduction of a comprehensive democratisation and transformation programme. In this sense, transformation occurred as a direct result of the decay of the old system, and was not a Party initiative. Heiner Timmermann views the Party's democratisation programme, and its protection and encouragement of system critics, as the ultimate demonstration of the system's collapse and failure.

'Die Schizophrenie der Macht wurde dann am vollkommensten, als sie, die Unmöglichkeit des ganze vier Jahrzehnte dauernden Versuchs sehend, begann, die eigene Opposition zu schützen, ja sogar zu ihrer das System kritisierenden Tätigkeit zu ermutigen.'[74]

At an extraordinary meeting from 10-11 February, 1989, the Central Committee voted 101 in favour of, and 2 against, introducing a multi-party system[75]. In conjunction with the reorganisation and de-centralisation of local administration during 1984, the Party had already passed a new Electoral Law in 1985 which allowed multiple candidate elections. At this time participation was still limited and strictly controlled by the Party. However, Article 37, Section 2, of the new law allowed candidates who had not been nominated by the Patriotic People's Front (PPF) to stand, although they had to accept the PPF's programme which

---

[73] Ibid. Aczel, György, 'The Challenge of our Age and the Response of Socialism'.
[74] Ibid. Timmermann, Heiner, (Hrsg.), *Ungarn nach 1945*, p. 97. 'The schizophrenia of those in power was at its most complete when, on realising the impossibility of the whole forty years of experiment, they began to protect their own opposition and were encouraged to take on the role of system criticism themselves.' Translated by Wendy Hollis.
[75] Ibid. Timmermann, Heiner, (Hrsg.), *Ungarn nach 1945*, p. 150.

had been decided at the 13th Party Congress[76]. Thus, candidates who were not sponsored by the Party had a chance of obtaining a parliamentary mandate. As a result of this law, a number of prominent Party members were rejected as candidates and had to be re-nominated by the PPF's electoral committees. They included such figures as the former Interior Minister, Béla Biszku, and the Secretary General of the National Council of Trades' Unions, Sándor Nagy[77]. Dissidents, such as László Rajk, used the election platforms as an opportunity to criticise the government's policies. In the elections of June 1985, 25 candidates were elected who were not of the Party's choice[78]. This was a significant development because it indicated how far the Hungarian Party had moved away from the ideology of dictatorship and how much it needed a new form of legitimisation derived from real popular support. It also demonstrated that the population was eager for an alternative.

The Hungarian Party was forced to embark upon a full-scale democratisation policy in the hope that this would bring it the legitimacy it needed to reform the economy. The Party gambled that by initiating the democratisation programme itself, it would regain the trust and confidence of the population. It aimed to instrumentalise its vast network of local branches to persuade the population that its political experience and record of gradual reform since 1956 was evidence that is was best suited to undertake the proposed transformation. The Party also possessed a further advantage in the new generation of radical reformers within its own elite. They were well-known and respected by the population.

The Hungarian system under Kádár had been tolerant of various expressions of dissent, as long as these were not criticisms of the system itself. As there had always been possibilities, albeit limited, of independent communication, the majority of intellectuals had accepted the limited autonomous political role which the Party was willing to grant them and had published in the official press. Although there were limits to openness and criticism, there was no strict totalitarian control, as in Czechoslovakia and Romania.

---

[76] Ibid. Toma, Peter, A., *Socialist Authority: The Hungarian Experience*, p. 52.
[77] Ibid. Toma, Peter, A., *Socialist Authority: The Hungarian Experience*, p. 54.
[78] Ibid. Brown, J., F., *Eastern Europe and Communist Rule*, p. 221.

Regime Collapse and the Role of the Soviet Union 143

Paradoxically, semi-freedom fostered the development of opposition, while at the same time restricting it.

This was aptly demonstrated by the appearance of semi-independent groups. Such groups were permitted; but official permission was required. Official recognition enabled the group to function relatively freely, but entailed implicit cooperation with the system and acceptance of certain restrictions relating to subjects which were not open for official discussion. Denial of official recognition automatically condemned a group to dissidence, even if this had not been the original intention. An example of this was the independent peace group, *Dialogue*, founded on 2 September, 1982 by Ferenc Kőszegi. It had moderate, non-political aims and applied for official recognition. This was refused and the group was forced to dissolve on 6 July, 1983. The original founder of the group became the leader of an official *Peace Club* sponsored by the Party, while another section of the original group dismissed official recognition and founded a more radical and overtly political group[79].

2.2.4: Independent Opposition

The most important issue which led to the formation of active opposition groups was the controversial Hungarian-Slovakian project to build a huge hydro-electric dam on the Danube[80]. The Gabcikovo-Nagymoros project had been conceived at the height of Stalinism in 1953 and was monolithic in size. A plan for its construction was agreed in 1977, but actual building had been delayed until 1985. It would not only have the effect of changing the path of the Danube, and thus altering the border between the two countries, but would also flood a greater part of the lowlands used by the Hungarian minority in Slovakia. The water of the Danube would be channelled into a canal which led to the Slovakian Dam. On return to the Danube it would be allowed to develop into a fifteen foot swell to service the Hungarian power

---

[79] Ibid. Skilling, G., *Samizdat and an Independent Society in Eastern Europe*, p. 184.
[80] For an interesting analysis of the policies of the two governments involved, see Nagy, Boldizsár, 'The Danube Dispute: Conflicting Paradigms', *The New Hungarian Quarterly*, Vol. 33, No. 128, Winter 1992.

station, Nagymaros[81]. Environmentalists feared that changing the course of the river would have unforeseen consequences for the ground water level and the wildlife of the region. Nationalists claimed, not without some justification, that the project was being employed as a means to disperse the Hungarian minority in Slovakia. A further scandal erupted when it was revealed that, because the Hungarian government could no longer afford to complete the project, the Austrian government had agreed to finance it. It was foreseen that in return, Austria would receive all the electricity produced by the Hungarian power station for the next twenty years[82]. The Austrian government had been unable to undertake a similar project in Austria due to environmental objections[83].

The Danube Circle was founded in May 1983 to protest at the building of the dam. In April 1988, it published an advertisement in *Die Presse* protesting at Austria's role in the project[84]. A more militant group, *The Blues,* also formed. During 1985 *The Blues* carried out numerous leaflet campaigns, and in 1986 sent open letters to the press in both Hungary and Austria, and even to the Austrian Chancellor. *The Blues* were also involved in the founding of the first environmental journal in Eastern Europe, *Watermark*, in June 1986[85].

By the 1980's, the Hungarian system of control had deteriorated to such an extent that more and more independent publications began to appear. In 1981, an independent publishing house, *A. B.*

---

[81] Tismaneanu, Vladimir, (Ed.), *In Search of Civil Society*, Routledge 1993, p. 77.
[82] See Judt, Tony, 'The Dilemmas of Dissidence: The Politics of Opposition in East-Central Europe', *East European Politics and Societies*, Vol. 2, No. 2, Spring 1988.
[83] Although the Hungarian government is legally bound by contract, it unilaterally stopped work on the project and took the matter to the European Court of Justice. Ibid. Tismaneanu, Vladimir, (Ed.), *In Search of Civil Society*, p. 81.
[84] The letter was signed by the most prominent figures in the Hungarian opposition; Miklós Haraszti, Andras Hegedüs, János Kenedi, János kis, György Konrád and László Rajk. Ibid. Judt, Tony, 'The Dilemmas of Dissidence: The Politics of Opposition in East-Central Europe', *East European Politics and Societies.*
[85] Ibid. Skilling, G., *Samizdat and an Independent Society in Eastern Europe*, pp. 184-185.

Independent Publishers, was formed. It later split into two houses, *A. B.* and *A. B. C.*, led by the two co-founders of the original house. Both were to suffer police harassment. The head of *A. B.*, Gabor Demszky, was beaten up by the police in December 1983[86]. This demonstrates the limited nature of the tolerance practised by the Kádár regime. It was only after the myth of unanimity as a source of legitimacy was rejected that the Party tolerated independent publishers and political parties.

By 1987 the Party had practically given up all control over cultural life and independent activity exploded. Indeed, the Writers' Union had not elected any Communists to its board since 1986[87]. Moreover, in 1986, Imre Pozsgay, one of the leading advocates of reform within the Party, published a radical manifesto calling for reform. On 8 September, 1987, he read the 66 page document entitled 'Change and Reform' to the National Assembly[88]. In June 1987, the radical journal *Beszelö*, founded in 1981, published an article headed 'A Social Contract'[89]. It detailed the pressing need for economic and political reform. Other radical journals included *The Hungarian Observer*, founded in 1982 and concerned with democratic renewal, and *The Courier*, founded in 1983 and concentrating on Human Rights[90].

In November 1988, a law governing independent organisations was passed[91]. This officially allowed the free development of reform and opposition groups. 1988 saw a dramatic increase in the number of independent groups operating in Hungary. Their number rose to 21 by 1989, of these 15 had been formed between 1988-1989. At the same time as these fledgling parties were forming,

---

[86] Ibid. Skilling, G., *Samizdat and an Independent Society in Eastern Europe*, pp. 34-35.
[87] Ibid. Skilling, G., *Samizdat and an Independent Society in Eastern Europe*, p. 186.
[88] Ibid. Skilling, G., *Samizdat and an Independent Society in Eastern Europe*, p. 187.
[89] Ibid. Crampton, R., J., *Eastern Europe in the Twentieth Century*, p. 381.
[90] Ibid. Skilling, G., *Samizdat and an Independent Society in Eastern Europe*, p. 34.
[91] Delapina, F., Hofbauer, H., Komlosy, A., Melinz, G., Zimmermann, S., *Ungarn im Umbruch*, Verlag für Gesellschaftskritik 1991, p. 20.

Party membership dramatically declined. Between January and April 1989 the Party lost 30 000 members[92].

The formation of political parties was facilitated by the enactment of a Law on Assembly and Political Parties This legalised public demonstrations and the formation of political parties other than the Hungarian Socialist Workers Party[93]. The Hungarian Democratic Forum, founded as an independent group in the village of Lakitelek in 1987, was reconstituted as a party in 1988. The Alliance of Free Democrats was founded as a political party in November 1988. It held its first Assembly in April 1989. The League of Young Democrats was founded by radical Law and Economics students in March 1988 as an independent off-shoot of the Communist Youth League[94]. However, in 1989 it transformed itself into a political party[95]. In addition to these new parties, the 'historical' parties which had been in existence before the Communist take-over in 1947 reactivated themselves. Thus, the Independent Smallholders, the Peasant Party, the Social Democrats and the Christian Democratic People's Party reappeared[96]. In addition, an *Independent Lawyers' Forum* formed on 5 November, 1988 with the aim of preparing the legal profession for a non-violent transformation in which constitutional reform would play an important role. It was this group which volunteered to organise talks and serve as mediator between the various opposition groups. The group invited all opposition parties to take part in coordinated action, so the first meeting of the Opposition Roundtable took place on 22 March, 1989 in the Law School of the Eötvös University in Budapest[97]. As a result of these developments, the Hungarian opposition groups were rather better organised than those in

---

[92] *International Science Journal*, 'Democratic Transition in the East and the South', No. 128, May 1991, Basil Blackwell 1991, p. 318.
[93] Mommsen, Margareta, *Nationalismus in Osteuropa*, Verlag C. H. Beck 1992, p. 101.
[94] East, Roger, *Revolutions in Eastern Europe*, Pinter Publishers 1992, pp. 95-96.
[95] Bozóki, András, 'Democracy Across the Negotiating Table', *The New Hungarian Quarterly*, Vol. 33, No. 125, Spring 1992.
[96] Brown, J., F., *Surge to Freedom*, Duke University Press 1991, pp. 111-112.
[97] Ibid. Bozóki, András, 'Hungary's Road to Systemic Change: The Opposition Roundtable', *East European Politics and Societies*.

Regime Collapse and the Role of the Soviet Union 147

Czechoslovakia or Romania and had taken on the characteristics of political parties.

2.2.5: Reform within the Socialist Workers Party

By 1988 it was clear that Kádár's influence and power was declining. He was removed from the Central Committee and lost his position as First Secretary on 8 May, 1988[98]. But his successor, Karoly Grosz, tried to delay the process of reform. In the rapidly changing situation he seemed outdated and unsuited for leadership. In June 1989, a four man Presidium consisting of Karoly Grosz, Imre Pozsgay, Reszö Nyers and Miklos Nemeth, who became Prime Minister, took over the government. At the same time, the Central Committee renounced the *nomenklatura* system, pledged to create a independent, professional administrative system and released society from Party control. The Party also officially placed its 60 000 strong Workers' Militia under state control[99].

Apart from Karoly Grosz, all the members of the new Presidium were reformers. Reszö Nyers subsequently took Grosz's place as First Secretary. Imre Pozsgay was one of the most outspoken advocates of reform within the Party elite. As early as 1980 he had openly stated that the Party should transform itself into a social democratic party. As a result, he had been demoted from his position as Minister of Culture to head the People's Patriotic Front. Reszö Nyers was the father of the 1968 'New Economic Mechanism' and his return to the Politburo thirteen years after his dismissal was a triumph for reformers within the Party[100].

A new Political Executive consisting of 21 members was formed and the Central Committee disbanded. The Minister of Justice, Kalman Kulscar, had carried out a Constitutional review in August 1988 and produced a radically revised Constitution. In it, the Party accepted the superiority of the Constitution and also the precedence of Parliament over the Party. This increased the power of Parliament and set the stage for the introduction of competitive

---

[98] Ibid. *International Science Journal*, 'Democratic Transition in the East and the South', p. 319.
[99] Ibid. *International Science Journal*, 'Democratic Transition in the East and the South', p. 319.
[100] Ibid. Brown, J., F., *Surge to Freedom*, p. 109.

Parliamentary politics[101]. On 10 March, 1989, the National Assembly approved the Constitution and the introduction of a multi-party system. The leading role of the Party was officially ended.

In the Spring of 1988, the relatives of those who died and the survivors of 1956 formed a Committee for Historical Justice. On the thirtieth anniversary of the execution of Imre Nagy, a small ceremony was held at the anonymous Plot 301 where he was buried. A subsequent demonstration held in the centre of Budapest was broken up by the police. The new leaders of the Party knew that the ghosts of 1956 had to be lain to rest if the Party was to have a chance of gaining real legitimacy.

In January 1989, the government announced the exhumation and identification of the remains of Nagy and his companions and proposed a proper burial[102]. Two days later, on 30 January, 1989, Imre Pozsgay, without prior consultation with Party officials, broadcast the conclusions of the Central Committee sub-committee, which had been established to examine the events of 1956, on Hungarian radio[103]. He confirmed the events had been judged not as a 'counter-revolution', as previously claimed by the regime, but rather constituted a:

'...popular uprising against an oligarchic rule that had debased the nation'[104].

The Committee for Historical Justice, in co-ordination with the opposition groups and certain leading reform figures within the Party, notably Imre Pozsgay, organised the reburial of Nagy's remains. Nagy and his four companions were reburied, together with a coffin for the Unknown Insurgent, on 16 June, 1989. This event represented the culmination of what had become a veritable 'war' about how and which historical events were to be remembered. In 1989 there had been two demonstrations

---

[101] Ibid. Brown, J., F., *Surge to freedom*, p. 113.
[102] Ibid. Garton Ash, Timothy, *We the People*, p. 48.
[103] Ibid. Delapina, F., Hofbauer, H., Komlosy, A., Melinz, G., Zimmermann, S., *Ungarn im Umbruch*, pp. 20-21.
[104] Ibid. Ash, Timothy Garton, *We the People*, p. 49.

commemorating 15 March, an official and an unofficial one[105]. It was estimated that 10 000 people took part in the official demonstration, while 100 000 attended the unofficial gathering[106]. The regime realised it was losing the new public relations battle.

Nagy's official funeral was a means by which it was hoped to regain public confidence. Although members of the government were present, they did not represent the Party. However, their presence gave the event the character of a state funeral. Leading reformers such as Imre Pozsgay, the Prime Minister, Miklos Nemeth, and the President of the Parliament, Matyas Szürös, stood guard at Nagy's coffin[107]. The whole event was broadcast live on television. But, this served to further weaken the regime as the population saw the 200 000 people who had gathered to pay their respects to Nagy at Heroes' Square and heard the speeches of various opposition leaders.

2.2.6: The Roundtable Negotiations

Negotiations between the Party, a number of 'quasi non-governmental', or rather non-Party, organisations (*Quangos*) and the Opposition Roundtable began three days before Nagy's funeral[108]. The Party insisted that the *Quangos* took part as they hoped this would ensure a majority in their favour during the negotiations[109]. Indeed, the Hungarian Socialist Workers Party continuously attempted to spilt the opposition as a means of assuring its own position within the new power structure. Unfortunately, the *Quangos* did not always side with the Party and the Opposition Roundtable proved itself more united and

---

[105] 15 March, 1848 is the date Hungary gained independence from Austria. There had also been unofficial demonstrations in 1988. Ibid. Crampton, R., J., *Eastern Europe in the Twentieth Century*, p. 380.
[106] Ibid. Mommsen, Margareta, *Nationalismus in Osteuropa*, p. 101.
[107] Ibid. Ash, Timothy Garton, *We the People*, p. 54.
[108] For a thorough account of the events leading to the formation of the Opposition Roundtable, its members and the course of negotiations, see Bozóki, András, 'Hungary's Road to Systemic Change: The Opposition Roundtable', *East European Politics and Societies*, Vol. 7, No. 2, Spring 1993.
[109] The *Quangos* consisted of nominally independent, but in reality Party controlled, groups such as the official Trade Unions, Women's Groups and Youth Organisations.

determined than supposed. The chairman of negotiations was the President of the Parliament, Matyas Szürös. As everyone was more or less agreed that the introduction of a parliamentary democratic system was desirable, the negotiations did not concentrate on the question of democratisation as such, rather they centred on the theoretical questions of what type of system, presidential or parliamentary, should be introduced. Both the opposition and the Hungarian Socialist Workers' Party were aware that parliamentary elections would follow the conclusion of negotiations. They vied for political advantage as a means of convincing their potential electorate to vote for them in the coming general election. The negotiations therefore provided an opportunity to engage in political bargaining and forge the political consensus necessary in a functioning democratic system.

During the talks a number of by-elections were held. The Hungarian Democratic Forum, a new opposition party, competed in four and won three of them[110]. Despite this, the Hungarian Socialist Workers Party tried to ensure its leading role was retained in the revised Constitution. It was also keen to ensure the President was given strong powers and was elected by popular vote. This would have probably resulted in the election of Imre Pozsgay as he was well-known, highly respected and popular due to his championing of reform. The Hungarian Socialist Workers Party also refused to unconditionally disband the Workers' Militia and was not willing to account for all its assets or withdraw its political organisations from the workplace. This position was rejected by four members of the Opposition Roundtable, the Alliance of Free Democrats, the Alliance of Young Democrats, the Social Democratic Party and the Democratic League of Independent Unions, who wanted parliamentary election of the President and dissolution of the Workers' Militia. The talks became deadlocked and in August were briefly broken off.

However, in September 1989, a document was finally presented which would ensure Hungary's transformation into a parliamentary democracy. The Party, aware that time was of the essence, had accepted the de-politicisation of the army, a new legal system and a

---

[110] Ibid. Brown, J., F., *Surge to Freedom*, p. 111.

new electoral law similar to that of the Federal Republic of Germany. In return, the majority of the Opposition Roundtable had accepted the election of a powerful President by popular vote. This election was to take place 90 days before the general elections. However, the Young Democrats and the Free Democrats refused to sign the document, although they refrained from invoking their veto which would have prevented the other members of the Opposition Roundtable from signing it. The Democratic League of Independent Trade Unions, which had taken part in the negotiations as an observer, abstained. The radical Young and Free Democrats objected to the powerful position of the President and the form of election. They collected the 200 000 signatures necessary to force a referendum on the issue. The referendum, which took place on 26 November, 1989, was a victory for the radical opposition. 58% of those who voted supported parliamentary election of the President[111]. This defeat represented a severe set-back for the Hungarian Socialist Workers Party, demonstrating that its democratic credentials had been found lacking by the population. The Party was suspected of supporting a popular vote for the Presidential election as a means of retaining its own power. This did not bode well for the coming elections which had been set for March 1990.

At its 14th Party Conference on 8 October, 1989, the Hungarian Socialist Workers Party became the first Communist Party in history to dissolve itself. Its membership had continued to shrink and at the time of dissolution the Party only had approximately 700 000 members[112]. The Hungarian Socialist Party was founded by the reform wing of the old Party and headed by Reszö Nyers. The hard-liners re-founded the Hungarian Socialist Workers Party. The Hungarian Socialist Party has stressed that it does not represent a continuation of the Hungarian Socialist Workers Party either ideologically or politically. As a means of ensuring membership was not automatically continuous with that of the Hungarian

---

[111] Ibid. Brown, J., F., *Surge to Freedom*, p. 122.
[112] Ibid. Delapina, F., Hofbauer, M., Komlosy, A., Melinz, G., Zimmermann, S., *Ungarn im Umbruch*, p. 9.

Socialist Workers Party, the Hungarian Socialist Party issued new membership cards.

2.2.7: Hungary becomes a Republic

On 18 October, 1989, the National Assembly, with the opposition members elected in the by-elections already present, approved an interim Constitution for the period until the general elections took place in 1990[113]. The Constitution pronounced Hungary a Republic, gave the Assembly far reaching legislative powers, accepted a multi-party system and officially recognised Human Rights. The principle of a market economy was also accepted and both private and public property was protected accordingly.

Having accepted the principle of Human Rights, the Hungarian government lifted all travel restrictions for its citizens and opened its borders. Travel restrictions to Austria had already been lifted on 27 June, 1989, when the then Foreign Minister, Gyula Horn[114], had cut through the barbed wire border fence[115]. In order to maintain its integrity, the government could not deny citizens from other East European countries who were in Hungary rights already granted to Hungarians. It therefore abandoned its bilateral accord with the German Democratic Republic, which prevented citizens who were on holiday in Hungary from travelling to a third destination[116] Hungary thus became the first country to officially break Bloc solidarity and raise the 'Iron Curtain'[117]. The border was officially

---

[113] Hungary officially became a Republic on 23 October, 1990, the 33rd Anniversary of the 1956 Revolution. Ibid. Mommsen, Margareta, *Nationalismus in Osteuropa*, p. 103.

[114] From 1988-1989, Gyula Horn had been a member of the Historical Sub-Committee of the Central Committee which had re-examined the events of 1956. In this way, Horn discovered the extent of repression and the brutality of the regime. Horn, Gyula, *Freiheit, die ich meine*, Hoffmann & Campe 1991, p. 21.

[115] The border with Austria had been constructed in the 1960's at a cost of 200 million Forints. Horn travelled to Vienna in June 1989 to discuss dismantling it. Ibid. Horn, Gyula, *Freiheit, die ich meine*, pp. 293-294.

[116] It has been estimated that as many as 4 500 000 German tourists visited Hungary each year. *Der Spiegel*, 20 May 1985.

[117] The Hungarian authorities stopped sending East German citizens back to the German Democratic Republic on 21 July, 1989. The Hungarian authorities granted

Regime Collapse and the Role of the Soviet Union 153

opened to East German citizens on 11 September, 1989. This action precipitated a huge emigration flow of East German citizens. Once the East German authorities stopped issuing travel visas to Hungary, many citizens wishing to leave the German Democratic Republic were stranded in Prague. They took refuge in and around the Embassy of the Federal Republic of Germany. This situation demonstrated to the Czech population how advanced Hungarian transformation was in comparison with the stagnation in Czechoslovakia.

The Hungarian government not only hoped to improve its image by recognising basic the Human Rights of all citizens in Hungary, but also to increase its possibilities of improving the situation of the various Hungarian minorities, particularly that in Romania[118]. Between 1988-1989, Hungary accepted 30 000 Romanian refugees[119], and the government was aware that the situation of the Hungarian minority, and indeed of the Romanian population in general, had become a focus for Hungarian public attention[120]. In June 1988 there had been a demonstration in Budapest against the Romanian systemisation plan[121]. The Hungarian governemt could only insist on free travel rights for Hungarian citizens in and out of Transylvania if it lessened its own travel restrictions. Hungarian

---

the East German refugees official permission to travel to the West on 10 September, 1989.
[118] The Hungarian minority in Romania numbers approximately 2 million. The total number of ethnic Hungarians living outside Hungary accounts for 10.5% of the total number of ethnic Hungarians. Ibid. Mommsen, Margareta, *Nationalismus in Osteuropa*, p. 97.
[119] Gabanyi, Anneli Ute, *Die unvollendete Revolution*, Piper 1990, p. 159.
[120] For more information on Hungarian policy and the numbers and countries of origin of the refugees, see Müller, Stephan, 'Flüchtlings- und Asylpolitik in Ungarn bis Anfang 1992', *Südosteuropa*, Vol. 42, No. 7-8, 1993.
[121] Ibid. Crampton, R., J., *Eastern Europe in the Twentieth Century*, p. 380. Systemisation involved developing some villages into agro-industrial centres and destroying others and moving their populations to the designated centres, where new apartment blocks would be built for them. The land upon which the villages had stood could then be used for agriculture. It was feared that the Hungarian minority within Transylvania would be particularly affected by this plan as homogenous Hungarian villages would be destroyed. For more information on Romanian systemisation, see Ronnas, Per, 'Turning the Romanian Peasant into a new Socialist man: An Assessment of Rural Development Policy in Romania', *Soviet Studies*, Vol. 41, No. 4, October 1989.

progress towards democracy also emphasised the seemingly hopeless Romanian situation, in particular to the population in Transylvania where the majority of the Magyar minority live. By the 1980's Romanian-Hungarian relations were almost nonexistent. Kádár had not met Ceausescu since 1976. Karoly Grosz's visit in August 1988 did little to improve the situation[122].

2.2.8: Continuity and Change

The general elections, held on 25 March and 8 April, 1990, were the culmination of a gradual, institutionalised transformation which had been initiated by the ruling Party itself in response to system decay. The transformation process was carried out by the political elite of the ruling Party and the opposition parties which had been allowed to form in accordance with the regime's own legislation. The general population was only involved in so much that it demonstrated rejection of the system. In this sense, political transformation occurred almost unnoticed and no distinct point of break with the old system was discernible.

As a result, the Hungarian political system demonstrates a certain degree of continuity. Although legal continuity should not be confused with ideological continuity, many of the former regime's late reform policies and laws remained in place and formed the basis of Hungarian transformation during the crucial period before the democratic elections[123]. Many individual reformist politicians from the old regime maintained their popularity and integrity and have remained active in political life. In this way, many of those connected with the old regime have become fully integrated in the new system. In the Hungarian case, the continuing presence of members of the political elite connected with the old regime was a stabilising factor in the democratisation process and furthered democratic consolidation. Although many

---

[122] Almond, Mark, *The Rise and Fall of Nicolae and Elena Ceausescu*, Chapmans 1992, p. 207.

[123] Hungary had put in place 75% of the laws needed to introduce a market economy during this period. In addition, these laws were some of the most liberal of the region, a fact which helps to explain Hungary's success in attracting foreign investment. 90% of prices were also market controlled. Druwe, Ulrich, *Osteuropa im Wandel*, Bettz Quadriga 1992, p. 60.

members of the former political elite in Romania have also remained active in political life, they have yet to demonstrate convincingly their commitment to democratisation and transformation. In stark contrast, the political elite of the old regime in the Czech Republic disappeared totally, to be replaced by members of the former opposition or previously unknown politicians.

Unlike Czechoslovakia or Romania, the Hungarian regime had been involved in gradual systemic reform for a long period of time. The roots of reform can be traced back to the Kádár regime's policy of gradualism, which led to an incremental decrease of the dictatorial elements in the system. As a result, opportunities arose for independent and semi-independent action. However, the reforms failed to solve Hungary's social and economic problems. Instead, they led to a decrease and eventually the final destruction of ideological conviction amongst the political elite.

The ideological conviction of the elites in Romania and Czechoslovakia is also questionable; but they were too compromised by the harshness of the system of which they had been part to harbour any realistic hope for re-election in a multi-party system. In both countries very little, if any, independent activity was officially tolerated. In Romania, Ceausescu had remained a convinced Stalinist; and after 1968 the Husak regime had successfully re-Stalinised Czechoslovakia. Neither regime had attempted reform. Although the economic situation had become critical, the elite seemed quite content with the system. This was because the system was the only mechanism by which both Ceausescu and the Czechoslovak Party remained in power. As result, both regimes opted to delay reform for as long as possible.

2.3: Czechoslovak Regime Immobility

'Time and again I have been persuaded that a huge potential of goodwill is slumbering within our society. It's just that it's incoherent, suppressed, confused, crippled and perplexed.'

Vaclav Havel, Summer Meditations on Politics, Morality and Civility in a Time of Transition[124].

The 'Velvet Revolution' was a demonstration of the Czechoslovak population's civil courage and goodwill. It was also a negation of the 'normalisation' policy which forced the majority of the population into a state of passivity as a means of destroying the traditional values of society. From the period after the 1968 'Prague Spring' until the 'Velvet Revolution', the Party had totally rejected reform and had instead implemented a 'normalisation' programme. Its aim was to isolate and subdue the individual and thereby ensure the Party's control over the country. As Gordon Skilling noted:

'For some years after the [1968] occupation, a profound malaise gripped the entire country, and the great majority of the people relapsed into what the internationally famous playwright and dissident Vaclav Havel called a state of anomie. Disillusioned by the experience of 1968 and by earlier disasters such as Munich and the Prague Coup, most Czechs saw no prospect for early change and were not ready to risk their own futures through any kind of opposition or open criticism.'[125]

But, the Czechoslovak Revolution was initiated by the population in the form of mass demonstrations. In this respect it bears similarity to the Revolution in Romania, which also represented a popular uprising against a hard-line regime. However, the Romanian Revolution was bloody and violent and did not result in a complete caesura with the old system, but rather in a rotation

---

[124] Havel, Vaclav, *Summer Meditations on Politics, Morality and Civility in a Time of Transition*, Faber & Faber Ltd. 1992, pp. 3-4.
[125] Griffith, (Ed.), *Central and Eastern Europe: The Opening Curtain?* p. 252.

amongst the political elite. So, why did the 'Velvet Revolution' in Czechoslovakia perfect an almost complete caesura with the old regime?

By late 1989 the international situation bore little resemblance to that of a few years before. Democratisation was in its final stages in Hungary and the Czechoslovak regime was in danger of being left behind in the democratisation race. The regime was immobile and unsuited to deal with the new situation. It had compromised itself by rejecting reform and reinstating a neo-Stalinist order. It had no policy other than that of repression to deal with renewed popular discontent, but by 1989 had lost the will to implement it. The reasons for this are to be found in the 'normalisation' of Czechoslovakia.

The Czechoslovak regime had embarked upon dismantling the reforms introduced as a result of the 'Prague Spring' as soon as Dubcek signed the 'Moscow Protocols' in Moscow on 26 August, 1968. This document sanctioned the intervention of the Warsaw Pact in Czechoslovakia[126]. Dubcek remained in government until 1969 and so took part in the dismantling of the 'Action Programme' and the reforms he had initiated[127]. On 22 August, 1969, General Svoboda and he signed the Emergency Laws which formed the legal base for the mass dismissals and persecutions under 'normalisation'[128]. Therefore Dubcek also bears some responsibility for the implementation of the 'normalisation' programme. However, 'normalisation' itself was carried out only after Gustav Husak became First Secretary on 17 April, 1969. On 29 May, 1969, Husak presented a report which officially denounced Dubcek's policies and introduced the 'normalisation' programme[129]. 'Normalisation' was the means employed by the Communist Party to regain control. Unlike the policy of reconciliation followed by

---

[126] James, Robert, Rhodes, *The Czechoslovak Crisis 1968*, Weidenfeld & Nicholson 1969, p. 113.

[127] The only reform to survive was the federalisation of Czechoslovakia. This was approved on 28 October, 1968. Otahal, Milan, *Der rauhe Weg zur 'samtenen Revolution'*, Bundesinstitut für Ostwissenschaftliche und Internationale Studien, Bericht No. 25, 1992, p. 1.

[128] Renner, Hans, *A History of Czechoslovakia since 1945*, Routledge 1989, p. 97.

[129] Krystufek, Z., *The Soviet Regime in Czechoslovakia*, East European Monographs 1981, p. 136.

Kádár in Hungary, Czechoslovak 'normalisation' restored the Stalinist system and Stalinist methods of control over the population and economy.

The 'Prague Spring' had been an attempt to reform socialism and create a 'Third Way' which was neither Communist nor Capitalist, but combined aspects of both. The section of the Czechoslovak political elite which supported Dubcek's reform programme had hoped to regenerate socialist ideology. After the Warsaw Pact invasion, socialism lost its attractiveness for them as it was viewed as the means by which the Soviet Union retained control over developments in Czechoslovakia. In addition, it was clear that the Soviet Union was unwilling to allow a form of socialism to develop which it had not defined itself. For those in the Party elite who had not supported the 1968 'Action Programme', the invasion meant repression and the threat of Soviet intervention became the main instruments employed to retain power. Thus, ideological development was halted and the socialist system stagnated. For these different reasons, the Party elite as a whole lost its belief in ideology and thus the sense of its legitimacy to rule. As Vaclav Havel states, although ideology supported the system, its foundations were built on sand. It was effective for only as long as the population was prepared to remain passive, accepting the regime and the 'lie' it represented:

> '[Die Ideologie] ist einer der Pfeiler der äußeren Stabilität des Systems. Dieser Pfeiler ist jedoch auf Sand gebaut nämlich auf der Lüge. Deshalb bewährt er sich nur so lange, solange der Mensch bereit ist in der Lüge zu leben.'[130]

Therefore 'living in the truth' became a simple way to expose the bankruptcy of the regime and the 'lie' which it had constructed. Vaclav Havel and a small, but well-known group of Czechoslovak dissident intellectuals, decided to 'live according to the truth' as a

---

[130] Havel, Vaclav, *Versuch in der Wahrheit zu Leben*, Rowohlt Taschenbuch Verlag 1989, p. 22. '[The ideology] is one of the columns which supports the external stability of the regime. This column is however built on sand - that is on the lie. Therefore it can only hold as long as one is prepared to live in the lie'. Translated by Wendy Hollis.

means of exposing the regime. This decision was of enormous importance since it served to expose the 'lie' which had been forced upon the population since 1968, and demonstrated that it was possible to reject the regime. Vaclav Havel compares this action to the children's fairytale, *The King's New Clothes*. The man who has the courage to say that the King is naked exposes the 'lie' everyone has accepted:

> 'Er hat die Welt des 'Scheins' zerstört, die Grundlage des Systems; er hat die Machtstruktur dadurch verletzt, daß er ihre Bindung durchlöchert hat; er zeigte, daß das 'Leben in Lüge' ein Leben in Lüge ist... Er sagt, daß der Kaiser nackt ist. Und da der Kaiser wirklich nackt ist, ist das, was passierte, unheimlich gefährlich. Durch seine Tat... hat er jedem ermöglicht, hinter die Kulissen zu schauen; er hat jedem gezeigt, daß man in der Wahrheit leben kann.'[131]

'Living in the truth' and refusing to accept the Party's rules and lies therefore represented a fundamental threat to the system. It was acceptance of the principle of 'living in the truth' and rejecting the 'lie' which enabled the Czechoslovak population to force the abrupt, but peaceful, collapse of the Husak regime.

2.3.1: Normalisation

It was not possible, as in Hungary, for there to be an elite initiated transformation since after 1968 no further attempt at reform had been undertaken by the Czechoslovak regime. This was partly because the reformers had ceased to believe in the possibility of reforming the system and had been purged from the Party; and partly because the remaining conservative Party elite had rejected reform and was too compromised by its association with

---

[131] Ibid. Havel, Vaclav, *Versuch in der Wahrheit zu Leben*, p. 27. 'He has destroyed the world of 'appearances', the basis of the system; he has thereby injured the power structure by exposing its connections; he has shown that 'living in a lie' means accepting a life of lies... He has said that the King is naked. And while the King really is naked, this is extremely dangerous. By this action... he has let everyone look back stage; he has shown everyone that one can life in the truth.' Translated by Wendy Hollis.

'normalisation' to initiate any changes. In effect, even by 1989, no alternative policy to the one which had been in place since 1968 existed in Czechoslovakia. Timothy Garton Ash aptly described the ossification of the regime:

> *'The country's politics are frozen into immobility a fifteen year winter after one Prague Spring.'*[132]

After the Warsaw Pact invasion, 'normalisation' had presented itself as the easiest means of regaining control and demonstrating the regime's loyalty to the Soviet Union. This was partly due to the reaction of the Czechoslovak population to the invasion. Unlike the Hungarian population, the Czechs had accepted the futility of resistance and remained passive. The invasion had also demonstrated that a reform of socialism was not acceptable to the Soviet Union. The regime under Husak therefore abandoned all attempts at reform and reinstated the system which was both the easiest to reconstruct and the safest politically. 'Normalisation' therefore represents the introduction of a conservative, neo-Stalinist socialist order in Czechoslovakia and its consequent stagnation, politically, economically and socially.

The Party itself was effectively purged of all reformists by introducing new membership cards. In order to obtain a new card, a personal interview was conducted and a questionnaire had to be completed relating to the respondent's reactions to the 1968 'Action Programme' and Dubcek's rule. The man placed in charge of this procedure was Milos Jakes Husak's follower as General Secretary in 1987. By this means, the Party lost 450 000 members between 1969-1971[133]. Those who remained had either been opposed to the reforms or were willing to obey the Party and publicly denounce reform. Although this procedure rid the Party of its reformist elements, it also left it unable to provide a solution to the country's

---

[132] Ibid. Ash, Timothy Garton, *The Uses of Adversity*, p. 57.
[133] Ibid. Brown, J., F., *Surge to Freedom*, p. 165.

economic and social problems[134]. The Party ceased generating new ideas.

In addition to a Purge of the Party, cultural and educational institutions were also cleansed of reformist elements. This entailed the dismissal of teaching staff, an estimated 900 university lecturers lost their jobs, and the closure of numerous University departments and 21 academic institutions[135]. At the Czech Academy of Sciences alone, five departments were closed. Journals and newspapers also came under heavy scrutiny and editorial boards were changed. Forty-five of the eighty editors at the Party Daily, *Rude Pravo*, were dismissed as well as 2000 journalists[136]. Twenty-five journals were closed and between 1969-1971 not one literary journal was published. The Writers' Union, the scene of a major rebellion against the Party in 1967, was also purged and two out of every three writers in the Union lost their jobs[137]. The theatrical community was also affected. Seventeen provincial theatres were closed and 344 actors lost their jobs. Seventeen provincial museums were also shut and 196 historical researchers, representing 80% of the total, were dismissed. Official cultural life in Czechoslovakia came to a grinding halt and the country became, in the words of Heinrich Böll, 'a cultural cemetery'[138].

Censorship had already been given an official legal framework under Dubcek in September 1968[139]. It was not possible, as in Hungary, to criticise the government and remain acceptable to the official press and publishers. Although, paradoxically, the official freedom in Hungary restricted to some extent the development of a radical dissident movement. In contrast, the severity of the regime in Czechoslovakia meant that dissident thoughts and opinions were almost impossible to avoid. But the decision to publicly criticise the regime was more difficult due to its consequences.

---

[134] It has been estimated that after the Purge, 40% of the leading figures in the Party and government were without qualifications. Ibid. Renner, Hans, *A History of Czechoslovakia since 1945*, p. 110.
[135] Ibid. Crampton, R., J., *Eastern Europe in the Twentieth Century*, p. 346.
[136] Ibid. Renner, Hans, *A History of Czechoslovakia sine 1945*, pp. 99-100.
[137] Ibid. Crampton, R., J., *Eastern Europe in the Twentieth Century*, p. 346.
[138] This is taken from Böll's speech of acceptance for the 1972 Nobel Prize for Literature. Ibid. Renner, Hans, *The History of Czechoslovakia since 1945*, p. 101.
[139] Ibid. Crampton, R., J., *Eastern Europe in the Twentieth Century*, p. 337.

2.3.2: The Dissident Movement

Dissidents, nearly all intellectuals, were forced to give up their professions and take menial jobs as unskilled manual workers[140]. It was a rather odd form of humiliation to choose for a regime which officially glorified manual work. The dissidents were periodically arrested, beaten and placed under house arrest. In addition, they and their families were harassed and were often evicted from their flats. Their children were not allowed to study at university, wives lost their jobs and other family members and friends suffered similar humiliations. The nature of this persecution subdued all but the most dedicated and convinced many that open opposition was not worth the price one had to pay.

Therefore, the majority of the Czechoslovak population passively accepted the regime and the system and withdrew into the private sphere. However, a small but well-known and very public group of activists and dissidents maintained open opposition. They consisted of intellectuals, writers, scientists, historians and former members of the Party and Dubcek's reform government. They remained a small group because the consequences of their decision to 'live in the truth' affected not only themselves and their careers, but also families, relations and friends. However, it was the efforts of this group which led to the creation of one of the most active and vocal *samizdat* in Eastern Europe.

Although the number of people actively involved remained relatively low, they were highly motivated. They published censored texts, literary works and independent reports on the situation in Czechoslovakia by typing or hand copying manuscripts. One of the most well-known *samizdat* publishers was *Petlice*, 'Padlock Publishers'. It was launched in 1972 by Ludvik Vaculik, the author of the '2000 Word Manifesto'. Another *samizdat* publisher was *Expedice*, 'Dispatch', founded by Vaclav Havel. By 1987, it had published 250 titles[141]. In addition to long-standing publishers which specialised in literary works, by the 1980's, a large number of satirical journals also appeared. In 1986 a satirical

---

[140] Approximately 75% of the expelled Party reformers were forced to do menial work. Ibid. Renner, Hans, *The History of Czechoslovakia since 1945*, p. 110.

[141] Ibid. Skilling, G., *Samizdat and an Independent Society in Eastern Europe*, p. 30.

magazine, *XXX (The Society for the Wearers of Stockings)*, was founded[142].

The *samizdat* dissident movement came into being as a result of the unbearable restraints the regime imposed upon artistic and scientific freedom. However, the movement was not only concerned with intellectual freedom, but also with general Human Rights. Human Rights gained special importance after the signing of the Helsinki Final Act of 1975. The declaration included a commitment to uphold Human Rights in the so-called fifth basket and was signed by the Husak regime in 1976.

This international agreement provided an opportunity to expose the regime by daring it to abide by its own internationally declared principles. A small group of dissidents founded the independent organisation *Charter 77* on 1 January, 1977. It was founded in accordance with the rights provided by the Helsinki Act. It published regular reports on the situation in Czechoslovakia in the form of typed open letters, communiqués and documents. The publications were confined to typed and carbon copies because this was the only form of duplication allowed by law. Circulation of the documents was also against the law, so many had a typed cover proclaiming that they were for private use only. Although it officially rejected a political role, the restrictions the regime placed upon *Charter's* activities and upon its members demonstrate its political importance. In an attempt to discredit it, the regime circulated an anti-charter, but this actually raised public awareness of *Charter 77's* existence.

The document, from which *Charter 77* gained its name, was originally signed by 242 people[143]. It authorised three spokesmen to represent it for one year and present the publications it prepared. Between 1977-1987, *Charter 77* published 350 letters[144]. At the same time as *Charter 77* was founded, other groups also came into existence. *KAN*, a group formed by non-Party activists, and *VONS*, 'The Committee for the Protection of the Unjustly Persecuted', were formed in May 1978. All *VONS'* original members were

---

[142] Ibid. Skilling, G., *Samizdat and an Independent Society in Eastern Europe*, p. 29.
[143] Ibid. Otahal, Milan, *Der rauhe Weg zur 'samtenen Revolution'*, p. 13.
[144] Ibid. Renner, Hans, *A History of Czechoslovakia since 1945*, p. 142.

Charter 77 signatories. At the time of founding *VONS* had 17 members, but by 1986 this figure had risen to 35[145]. It distributed as many as 800 leaflets detailing the illegal methods employed by the regime to persecute specific people[146]. *K321* formed as a group dedicated to helping former political prisoners who had been sentenced according to Article 231 in the Constitution.

The relatively small number of active dissidents and their close personal relations, most were members of *Charter 77*, led to allegations that they were a closed society of moral purists. The events of 1989 proved this a false accusation. In a world of lies and moral degeneration, the dissidents' commitment to moral integrity and truth made them highly respected figures. By 1989 they alone possessed the moral authority to direct the mobilised masses. In addition, Vaclav Havel's policy of reconciliation and moral healing of the whole nation demonstrates deep understanding and tolerance of those who did not have the courage to 'live in the truth' under the Husak regime. However, it would be true to say that for a long time the form of 'intellectual' opposition chosen by the dissidents remained alien to the workers and the majority of the population. They had little contact with *Charter 77* and until the late 1980's, demonstrated little interest in active opposition. In fact, it was the students who finally ended the population's passivity and the dissidents' isolation by persuading the workers to join the general strike in 1989.

2.3.3: Economic Failure

In addition to re-introducing cultural and political control, the Party also tried to raise the standard of living by increasing the availability of consumer goods and items previously considered as luxuries, for example country cottages and cars. Between 1970-1978 private consumption increased by 36.5%[147]. Social welfare benefits were increased and extended to sections of the population

---

[145] Ibid. Skilling, G., *Samizdat and an Independent Society in Eastern Europe*, p. 46.
[146] Horsky, Vladimir, *Die sanfte Revolution in der Tschechoslowakei 1989*, Bundesinstitut für Ostwissenschaftliche und Internationale Studien, Bericht No. 14, 1990, p. 15.
[147] Ibid. Crampton, R., J., *Eastern Europe in the Twentieth Century*, p. 347.

Regime Collapse and the Role of the Soviet Union 165

which had previously been excluded, such as collective and state farm workers. This policy bore similarities to the Kádár regime's attempts to pacify the population. The Romanian regime's policies forced the population to exist at subsistence level. The daily battle for survival left little time or energy for active opposition.

Although the Czechoslovak regime aimed to increase living standards, it reinstated a traditional form of central economic planning in an attempt to achieve this goal. In contrast to Hungary, it did not import large quantities of Western consumer goods, nor did it borrow large sums of money from foreign creditors to finance its policy. Czechoslovakia had one of the lowest foreign debts in the Eastern Bloc, standing between $3-4 billion in 1988. But its economy had also been one of the most isolated from the world market, conducting 80% of its trade within the Soviet Bloc[148]. The lack of incentive this fostered meant that there had been little investment in new technology, leaving Czechoslovakia with some of the oldest industrial plants in the Bloc. This in turn exacerbated the problems of high energy consumption, low productivity and poor quality which are common to centrally planned economic systems.

Czechoslovakia relied heavily on imports of crude oil from the Soviet Union. Approximately 93-98% of energy needs were met in this way[149]. Although this oil was purchased at a price well below that on the world market, by 1975 the cost had doubled. As a result, Czechoslovak terms of trade with the Soviet Union worsened by approximately 20%[150]. The resultant decrease in Soviet oil exports to Czechoslovakia in the early 1980's led to energy shortages. Although Czechoslovakia had one of the highest rates of collectivisation, production on private plots flourished. By 1985, private plots produced 60% of all fruits, 25% of poultry, 40% of vegetables and 40% of all eggs[151]. A bumper grain harvest in 1984 meant that Czechoslovakia was nearly self-sufficient in grain in

---

[148] Stokes, Gale, *The Walls came Tumbling Down*, Oxford University Press 1993, p. 148.
[149] Ibid. Renner, Hans, *A History of Czechoslovakia since 1945*, p. 114
[150] Ibid. Renner, Hans, *A History of Czechoslovakia since 1945*, p. 115.
[151] Wolchik, Sharon, L., *Czechoslovakia in Transition*, Pinter Publishers 1991, p. 230.

1987 and 1988, but this did not solve the continuing general economic decline of the 1980's. The standard of living stagnated.

Official negative growth figures for 1981-1982 and a decrease in the National Income[152] led the Party to introduce 'economic intensification' in an attempt to increase production without implementing any real reforms. However, national income and wages remained virtually static and industrial production experienced only a minimal increase. According to official figures, in 1981 and 1982 industrial production increased by just 0.3% and 0.9% respectively[153]. The annual growth rates set in the Five Year Plan 1985-1990 were not achieved in the first three years of the Plan and thereafter targets were reduced.

The Czechoslovak economy was failing even by its own standards[154]. However, at the 17th Party Conference in March 1986, the expected reform platform did not materialise. The Conference re-elected the old leadership in its entirety[155]. At this time, the first signs of a split became visible, but there was so much opposition to reform within the Party itself that potential reformists remained cautious. The old guard coud not support a re-examination of 1968 because this would compromise them. They were afraid of reform because it would inevitably undermine 'normalisation' and thus weaken Party rule.

However, by the late 1980's the economic situation was so desperate that a long term plan for economic reform was presented in January 1987. Although wholesale prices were reformed during January 1989[156], the planned nature of the economy dictated that the reform plan, such as it was, be implemented according to the 'Principles of Reconstruction' at the start of the next Five Year Plan

---

[152] Ibid. Brown, J., F., *Surge to Freedom*, p. 153.
[153] Ibid. Wolchik, Sharon, L., *Czechoslovakia in Transition*, p. 225. These figures were the official figures published by the Party. It is an indication of the severity of the crisis that, despite the inaccuracies of the statistical methods employed and the propensity to doctor figures to achieve the ideologically prescribed upward curve, they show a decline in industrial production.
[154] For a study of the Czechoslovak economic system, see Kusin, Vladimir, V., 'Husak's Czechoslovakia and Economic Stagnation', *Problems of Communism*, Vol. 31, No. 3, May-June 1982, pp. 24-37.
[155] Ibid. Brown, J., F., *Surge to Freedom*, p. 157.
[156] Ibid. Brown, J., F., *Surge to Freedom*, p. 162.

Regime Collapse and the Role of the Soviet Union   167

in 1991. But even these measures represented little more than superficial tinkering with the Plan and the central economic planning mechanism. There was no attempt at real structural reform of the centrally planned economy.

2.3.4: Ideological Degeneration

The Party's policy since 1968 had facilitated the regaining of almost total control, but the price paid for this was ideological degeneration; the psychological and moral crisis of society; and the retention of an out-dated, Stalinist command economy, which was inacapbale of functioning satisfactorily. Ideological degeneration resulted in the Party elite not only losing faith in its own legitimacy, but also being incapable of reacting to the political changes introduced by Gorbachev after 1985. By the late 1980's, the general stagnation in Czechoslovakia stood in stark contrast to the developments in Hungary, and the regime increasingly allied itself to one of the most intolerant regimes in Eastern Europe that in Romania. The failure of the system established under Husak became all the more intolerable because the external factors preventing change had disappeared.

The heart of the problem lay in the Czechoslovak political elite. In March 1985 the average tenure of the eleven member Politburo was seventeen years. There were four full members who had been present for between 18-20 years. Even by March 1989, only six of the eleven full members had been present for less than two years[157]. The Party elite remained imprisoned by the events and consequences of 1968. Although Husak had retired as Party Secretary in 1987, he retained his position as President. His replacement as Party Secretary was the 64 year old Milos Jakes, the man who had carried out the Party Purge as part of 'normalisation'. His appointment confirmed the Czechoslovak Party elite's commitment to the conservative policies which had been followed since 1968.

After 1968 reform had been abandoned. Moreover, since the implementation of the 'normalisation' programme the leaders were

---

[157] Held, Joseph, *The Colombia History of Eastern Europe in the Twentieth Century*, Columbia University Press 1992, p. 143.

too compromised for there to be any hope, as in the case of Hungary, that power would be retained in a free election. The elite was unwilling to implement reform, yet doubted its own legitimacy. Unable to find a means of regaining legitimacy which did not involve reform, the Party became paralysed. It found itself bereft of Soviet support and lacking the ideological will to employ methods of repression to control the population. Once the population demonstrated that it was no longer prepared to be intimidated and rejected the passive role required by the Party, the system simply collapsed. However, twenty one years of neo-Stalinist rule had devastated both the economy and society.

2.3.5: Moral Disorientation

The nature of the Czechoslovak system made everyone an accomplice in its support. The whole population was implicated because of its acceptance of the lie which the regime had presented. Thus, the population had become surrounded with lies and had suffered moral disorientation. For, as Milan Simecka recognised, in order to accept the pseudo-reality which the Party presented, one had to lie to oneself and disregard one's own memory:

> '*In a system in which the past is always in accord with the present, memory convicts the falsifier of lying. When a man has a memory, he can agree with a lie only at the cost of awareness of his own piteousness and cowardice.*'[158]

Although on 12 May, 1990, 100 000 people took part in a demonstration to demand justice against those who had committed crimes under the old regime, the truth is that everyone carries a portion of guilt[159]. As Vaclav Havel commented, the line of guilt and responsibility for the system cannot be drawn at the Party elite:

---

[158] Ibid. Skilling, G., *Samizdat and an Independent Society in Eastern Europe*, p. 121.
[159] Brogan, P., *Eastern Europe 1939-1989*, Bloomsbury 1990, p. 111.

'In the post-totalitarian system, this line runs de facto through each person, for everyone in his or her own way is both a victim and a supporter of the system.'[160]

It had been the dissidents' aim to demonstrate by example that it was possible to reject the system and the lie which it represented. In this way, they hoped to prevent civil society in Czechoslovakia from disappearing. By 1987, under the influence of Gorbachev's policies and the changes in Hungary and Poland, a renewal of civil society in Eastern Europe was underway. *Samizdat* publications in Czechoslovakia had increased, as had the number of independent organisations. Between 1988-1989, twenty independent groups were formed. By mid-1989 there were 27 independent groups and 40 *samizdat* journals, of which 20 had been founded in 1988. As their public profile increased, so did the number and variety of their political demands. The 1970's had seen a concentration on Human Rights' issues due to the Helsinki process and 'normalisation', which was then at its height. Although this remained a crucial issue, the 1980's saw increased concerns about the state of the economy and religious freedom. A petition campaigning for religious freedom gathered 600 000 signatures[161]. In addition, the number of those undertaking pilgrimages to Holy Shrines in Moravia and Slovakia grew to approximately 800 000 by 1988[162]. Ecological concerns about environmental damage also gained importance. The northern parts of Moravia and Silesia constitute one of the most polluted areas in Europe and the region has been named the 'black triangle'. Czech and Slovak environmentalists were also united with their Hungarian counterparts in their mutual concern about the Nagymaros Dam project.

The independent organisations united socially and politically heterogeneous groups. An example of the heterogeneity within the movements is provided by the *Movement for Civic Freedom*. It was founded in October 1988 by Vaclav Benda, Jan Carnogursky, both democrats, Rudolf Bartek, a social democrat, and Ladislav Lis and

---

[160] Ibid. Ash, Timothy Garton, *The Uses of Adversity*, p. 173.
[161] Ibid. *International Social Science Journal*, 'Democratic Transition in the East and South', p. 318.
[162] Ibid. Wolchik, Sharon, L., *Czechoslovakia in Transition*, p. 215.

Jaroslav Sabata, former reform Communists. A *Czechoslovak Helsinki Committee* was founded on 5 November, 1988 by Jiri Hajek, the former Foreign Minister and one of the founding members of *Charter 77*. Another group, *Obroda*, was formed in February 1989 by reform Communists who had been active in 1968. Other groups included, *The Democratic Initiative, The Independent Peace Society, The T. G. Masaryk Society, Friends of the USA, Bohemian Children* and *The Circle for Czech and Polish Solidarity*[163]. Another group, *The Jazz Section*, was officially affiliated to the Union of Musicians. Although the Union had tolerated its activities, it received no financial support and relied on an annual subscription fee of 40 Crowns to survive. *The Jazz Section's* affiliation with the International Jazz Fellowship and the Music Council of UNESCO since 1979 helped it overcome the difficulties it encountered. In July 1984, the regime suspended the Musicians' Union for three months as a punishment for its toleration of *The Jazz Section*. The Union was completely dissolved on 24 October, 1984, but *The Jazz Section* continued its existence as an independent organisation[164]. Despite their heterogeneity, the groups were united by their opposition to the regime's totalitarian policies and a resolve not to be intimidated.

The evaporation of fear was demonstrated by increasingly public acts of dissidence and the uncertainty on the part of the regime as to how to deal with this new phenomenon. After almost twenty years of silence, Dubcek gave an interview to the Italian Communist Party Daily, *L'Unita*, in July 1988. He also gave an interview to *Hungarian Radio* in April 1989[165]. Yet despite this, he was permitted to receive an Honorary Degree at the University of Bologna in October 1989[166]. In addition, on 6 December, 1989, Jiri Hajek was allowed to travel abroad for the first time in twenty

---

[163] Ibid. Horsky, Vladimir, *Die sanfte Revolution in der Tschechoslowakei 1989*, p. 16.
[164] *The Jazz Section* had a limited membership, approximately 4000, but as many as 100 000 followers. Ibid., Skilling, G., *Samizdat and an Independent Society in Eastern Europe*, pp. 80-82.
[165] Ibid. Brown, J., F., *Surge to Freedom*, p. 170.
[166] Ibid. Brogan, P., *Eastern Europe 1939-1989*, p. 106.

years[167]. During September 1989 the number of *Charter 77* signatories also increased from 242 to 1575[168]. An open letter entitled 'Just a Few Sentences' had been published on 29 June, 1989 calling for the introduction of democracy. It originally had 800 signatories, but within a short period of time, this figure had risen to over 10 000[169]. By 24 August, 1989 the letter had collected 20 191 signatures[170], and by November the number had risen to 40 000[171]. The majority of signatories were academics in official positions, artists and actors. The regime was becoming isolated from its own elite circles and losing its grip on power. The drop in membership of the Communist Party by 130 000 in 1989 was also a measure of its loss of power and increasing isolation[172]. As the Party's awareness of this development increased, so too did its indecision and immobility.

The confrontations with the regime which preceded the Revolution concerned the population's desire for historical truth. They took the form of mass, unofficial demonstrations. The first major demonstration took place in 1988 to commemorate the 20th Anniversary of the 1968 invasion. Approximately 100 000 people took part[173]. The next significant demonstration occurred on 15 January, 1989 to commemorate the anniversary of the self-immolation of Jan Palach[174]. Approximately 2000 people, mostly students, took part in the demonstration which was brutally dispersed by the police[175]. During the demonstration 13 members of

---

[167] *Der Fischer Weltalmanach 1990*, Fischer Taschenbuch Verlag 1989, p. 531.
[168] Ibid. Horsky, Vladimir, *Die sanfte Revolution in der Tschechoslowakei 1989*, p. 17.
[169] Ibid. Brown, J., F., *Surge to Freedom*, p. 171.
[170] Ibid. Horsky, Vladimir, *Die sanfte Revolution in der Tschechoslowakei 1989*, p. 17.
[171] Ibid. Otahal, Milan, *Der rauhe Weg zur 'samtenen Revolution'*, No. 25, 1992, p. iii.
[172] Ibid. *International Social Science Journal*, 'Democratic Transition in the East and South', p. 321. By February 1990, members had fallen by a further 500 000, that is a third of all Party members.
[173] Ibid. Wolchik, Sharon, L., *Czechoslovakia in Transition*, p. 44.
[174] On 15 January, 1969, the student Jan Palach had committed suicide on Wenceslass Square in protest at the Warsaw Pact invasion.
[175] Ibid. *Der Fischer Weltalmanach 1990*, p. 534.

Charter 77, including Vaclav Havel, were arrested and later charged with 'Rowdiness'[176].

In addition to popular discontent, the political elite was also re-awakening. The 'satellite parties' which had been co-opted by the Party were reactivated in 1989[177]. In April 1989, the Socialist Party was reactivated as an independent Party, and in June 1989 the Czech Popular Party followed suit. Unlike the Hungarian Democratic Forum, whose first Congress from 11-12 March, 1989 was officially sanctioned by the authorities, the independent groups and reactivated Parties suffered repression from the Czechoslovak regime[178]. As a result, most political parties were founded after the regime collapsed[179]. Nevertheless, the historical parties' re-activation bore witness to the Party's waning totalitarian power. Twenty years of immobility left the Party unable to cope with the new situation. As power gradually crumbled, it left behind an empty shell.

A further demonstration to commemorate the 1968 invasion was called for in 1989. The open letter of 4 August, 1989 from Dubcek and the former Prime Minister, Oldrich Cernik, asking the Warsaw Pact to review its role in the invasion; and the subsequent admission of both Hungary and Poland that their part in it had been a mistake, no doubt helped to increase public interest in the demonstration[180]. On 28 August, 1989, a further demonstration commemorated Czech independence from Austria[181]. On 28 October, 1989, the 71st Anniversary of the founding of the First Czechoslovak Republic was also commemorated[182], providing evidence that the population identified with the democratic values

---

[176] Ibid. Crampton, R., J., *Eastern Europe in the Twentieth Century*, p. 397.

[177] Ibid. *International Social Science Journal*, 'Democratic Transition in the East and South', p. 318.

[178] Ibid. *International Social Science Journal*, 'Democratic Transition in the East and South', p. 318.

[179] On 26 January, 1990, Czech Radio announced the formation of forty political parties. Ibid. *International Social Science Journal*, 'Democratic Transition in the East and South', p. 321.

[180] Ibid. *Der Fischer Weltalmanach 1990*, p. 534.

[181] Ibid. Brogan, P., *Eastern Europe 1939-1989*, p. 105.

[182] Ibid. Brown, J., F., *Surge to Freedom*, p. 173.

which President Masaryk had proclaimed at the founding of the Republic.

The regime was proving incapable of dealing with an active, politically aware population. The only response was to change leaders. In October 1988, after eighteen years in office, Lubomir Strougal retired as Prime Minister. His replacement was Ladislav Adamec, a relatively unknown functionary and member of the economic elite. His election promised economic reform, but left the question of political reform unanswered. The Party was searching for a way to break with the past and initiate economic reform, yet retain political control[183]. However, having witnessed the introduction of democratic reforms in the Soviet Union, Poland and Hungary, by the end of 1989 the population was no longer willing to accept economic without political reform.

2.3.6: The Velvet Revolution

The so-called 'Velvet Revolution' was set in motion by a student demonstration on 17 November, 1989. By the 26 November the whole of the Politburo had resigned, and by 10 December a coalition government was in place[184]. Even though the Czechoslovak system was neo-Stalinist, and the Party had stubbornly clung to its hard-line policies, it took just 24 days to affect the change.

The Revolution was set in motion and sustained by the student population. They were not affected by the trauma of 1968 in the same paralysing way as the older generation. They had experienced only the neo-Stalinist Husak regime and had no illusions about the prospects of socialist reform. In addition, the students could not be easily controlled by the usual threats and sanctions because few had families and most did not possess flats or have jobs; so they had nothing to lose. They were, however, painfully aware that their future under the Czechoslovak regime was decidedly bleak in comparison with that of their contemporaries in Western and most of Eastern Europe.

---

[183] Ibid. Brogan, P., *Eastern Europe 1939-1989*, pp. 104-105.
[184] Ibid. Brogan, P., *Eastern Europe 1939-1989*, p. 77.

The student demonstration on 17 November, 1989 drew approximately 25 000 participants[185]. They broke into different groups and walked to separate points in Prague. As the group which had set off for the city centre arrived, its numbers had risen to 50 000. The police encircled a group of 5000 demonstrators and dispersed them with extreme brutality. There were rumours that a student had been killed. These were later proved false, but precipitated a second demonstration to protest against police brutality on 20 November, 1989. This demonstration drew 200 000 participants[186]. Milos Jakes made a televised appeal for calm on 21 November and, after the Central Committee's criticism of the violence on 24 November, a Commission was set up to investigate the events[187]; but the Revolution was already underway.

The students organised a strike on 18 November, 1989 and, at a meeting chaired by Prof. Jan Lukes, the Director of the National Theatre, persuaded the theatrical community to organise a general strike for 22 November, 1989[188]. The theatres closed and schools and universities remained empty. By 24 November, the regime's censorship apparatus had completely broken down and the events of the preceding few days became widely known. At the start of each cancelled theatre performance actors read out a statement explaining the reasons for their action. In most cases they were greeted with applause.

The population had been shocked out of passivity by the brutality with which the regime had reacted to the original student demonstration. In addition, the courage of the young students shamed many into action by forcing them to re-examine their personal role in the system. The demonstrations therefore represent a mass catharsis which enabled the population to rediscover the 'truth' and the values of civil society which the regime had denied them since 1968.

---

[185] Ibid. Horsky, Vladimir, *Die sanfte Revolution in der Tschechoslowakei 1989*, p. 18.
[186] Ibid. Brogan, P., *Eastern Europe 1939-1989*, p. 106.
[187] Its findings were published on 12 December, 1989.
[188] Ibid. Horsky, Vladimir, *Die sanfte Revolution in der Tschechoslowakei 1989*, p. 23.

An umbrella organisation, *Civic Forum*, was formed on 19-20 November to co-ordinate the various independent and opposition groups in the Czech lands; while a sister organisation, *Public Against Violence*, was formed in Slovakia to co-ordinate events there. The majority of *Civic Forum's* members were also signatories to *Charter 77*[189]. The prominent role of the dissidents, in particular that of Vaclav Havel, in the Revolution and its co-ordination is unique and vindicated their chosen form of opposition. By 'living according to the truth' they were not compromised by cooperation with or tacit acceptance of the regime and were thus the only people capable of leading the opposition against it. *Civic Forum* presented its demands to the population at the demonstrations. They included the ending of the Party monopoly of power; a political amnesty for those imprisoned due to political crimes; a revision of the law to provide protection for civil and Human Rights; a new properly qualified government and free, democratic elections in 1990; and resignation of those compromised by their actions under the Communist regime.

The depth of moral degeneration and disorientation which occurred as a result of 'normalisation' is reflected in the general desire to regain moral integrity. This found expression in the Czech Lustration Law. It compelled all those accepting a position above a certain level in the state administration or becoming a member of Parliament, local or national, to obtain a Lustration Certificate, thereby revealing their activities under the old regime. In this way, functionaries and politicians who collaborated too closely with the former system of repression have been removed from public life.

By Monday 20 November, 1989, 250 000 people had gathered in Prague and a general strike was called for on 27 November. In Slovakia, Dubcek had spoken at a rally in Bratislava and was on his way to Prague, where he was to address a crowd of 500 000 with Vaclav Havel at the Letna Hill Stadium on 25 November[190]. Ladislav Adamec had overcome his aversion to talking to Vaclav Havel and was also present. He promised to rid the Party of hard-

---

[189] Ibid. Horsky, Vladimir, *Die sanfte Revolution in der Tschechoslowakei 1989*, p. 24.
[190] Ibid. Brogan, P., *Eastern Europe 1939-1989*, p. 106.

liners and initiate negotiations with the opposition. However, his assurances and the resignation of Jakes, the entire Politburo and government on 26 November could not halt the general strike which went ahead as planned for two hours on 27 November. The students managed to persuade the majority of the workers to join the strike by campaigning at factories and by promising to help after the strike to ensure that production was not too badly affected.

Karel Urbanek, a reformer, became General Secretary of the Party and negotiations with the opposition took place on 28 November. Adamec accepted a coalition government, agreed to free elections and an end to the leading role of the Party[191]. The Politburo also issued a statement condemning the Warsaw Pact Invasion of 1968 as unjustified. However, the new coalition government which Adamec presented on 3 December still had a Communist majority. This precipitated another mass demonstration on 4 December at which demands were made for the government's resignation, even though it had not officially taken office[192]. Adamec resigned on 7 December and his position as Prime Minister was taken over by an unknown functionary from Slovakia, Marian Calfa. He negotiated with the opposition once more and was able to present an acceptable coalition government on 10 December, 1989.

The Government of National Understanding consisted of 21 Ministers, of which only seven were nominal members of the Communist Party. Independent members included Jiri Dienstbier, who had to give up his job as a stoker to take on his new position as Foreign Minster; Jan Carnogursky, recently released from prison to become First Deputy Prime Minister; and the relatively unknown economist Vaclav Klaus, who became Minister of Finance. Communist Party members were given the posts of Minister of Defence, Trade and Economic Planning. The job of Interior Minister was abolished and the police force was temporarily placed under the jurisdiction of a committee of Ministers and the independent *Civic Forum*. Following Czech legalistic traditions, the new government was sworn in by the President, Gustav Husak, on

---

[191] The Party officially gave up its leading role on 29 November, 1989, when the relevant Article 4 was struck from the Czechoslovak Constitution. Ibid. Horsky, Vladimir, *Die sanfte Revolution in der Tschechoslowakei 1989*, p. 50.
[192] Ibid. Brogan, P., *Eastern Europe 1939-1989*, p. 108.

10 December, 1989. Thereafter he resigned, leaving the way clear for the dissident playwright, Vaclav Havel, to become President of Czechoslovakia. Alexander Dubcek became Chairman of the National Assembly. Soon after, Marian Calfa and two other Communist Ministers left the Party and it was forced to give up the 90 seats which had been reserved for it in Parliament[193]. The Communist Party held an extraordinary Conference on 20-21 December to elect a new Central Committee but, although it disbanded the People's Militia, it did not disband itself. As a final irony, Rudolf Slansky's son became Ambassador to the Soviet Union.

2.3.7: Collapse and Change
In contrast to Hungary, where the emerging and established political elites negotiated a gradual transformation, the Revolution in Czechoslovakia was signally abrupt. It is interesting to note that, despite the relative freedom of expression permitted under the Kádár regime, the population as a whole remained relatively passive during the process. People preferred to use the opportunities which public holidays presented to go shopping in Vienna rather than demonstrate on the streets. Thus, only 30 000 people attended the official ceremony on March 15, 1989, while 200 000 travelled the 150 miles to Vienna[194].

The Czechoslovak Revolution took the form of mass demonstrations which were organised by students and dissidents. Despite the regime's previous attempts to pacify and isolate the population by harsh sanctions against those who criticised it, a prominent and vocal minority had remained active. The regime became increasingly isolated following developments in international relations; notably the Soviet Union's recognition of East European sovereignty and its consequent rejection of direct intervention in East European affairs, and lost its grip on power. The weakened government was overthrown by a population finally shamed into action by the example provided by the dissidents and students.

---

[193] Ibid. Brogan, P., *Eastern Europe 1939-1989*, p. 110.
[194] Ibid. Stokes, Gale, *The Walls came Tumbling Down*, p. 100.

The old political system suffered a complete collapse as its incompetence and culpability were fully exposed. Whereas in Hungary the regime's own reform laws formed the basis of transition during the period of coalition government before free elections, in Czechoslovakia, lack of reform under the old regime meant that the laws had to be completely revised[195]. Furthermore, whereas prominent figures from the Hungarian regime retained their credibility and have been able to regain political power with the Hungarian Socialist Party, the lack of a prominent reform wing within the Czechoslovak Party and the historical parties' cooperation with the old regime has meant that no politicians closely associated with the old regime are still active in public life in the Czech Republic. In this sense, the Czech Revolution represents more of a caesura with the old regime than the Hungarian transition. Yet, despite the lack of continuity within the Czech political elite and the relative inexperience of the new elite, the caesura helped ensure stability. As the previous political elite did not support systemic reform, its removal from active political life furthered the transformation process and democratic consolidation. The Romanian Revolution was also a mass demonstration of popular opposition to the regime and, although it took the form of a violent popular uprising, it would also seem to represent a complete caesura with the old regime.

2.4: Romania's Tangled Revolution
'The end is a recapitulation of the means employed to obtain it'

Jean-Paul Sartre.

Given the nature and history of the Communist regime in Romania, it is hardly surprising that its end was also brutal and violent. The transition in Hungary and the dramatic collapse of the hard-line regime in Czechoslovakia left the Romanian regime alone in its determination to reject reform. By December 1989 Romania

---

[195] This revision included the negotiation of a new Federal Agreement. The negotiations were unsuccessful and led to the spilt of the Federal Republic of Czechoslovakia into its constituent Republics; the Slovak and the Czech Republic.

was the only country which retained an unreformed, totalitarian Stalinist system. The severity of the system had enabled it to resist transformation the longest, but its collapse was the most spectacular, brutal and, surprisingly, the quickest. Moral support from the hard-line regimes in the German Democratic Republic and Czechoslovakia had helped Ceausescu justify rejection of reform. But, by November 1989 this support no longer existed. Hungarian complicity had contributed to the fall of the Berlin Wall and Hungarian transition had also increased discontent within Transylvania, particularly amongst the Hungarian minority. The dramatic regime collapse in Czechoslovakia as a result of peaceful mass demonstrations completed Romania's isolation within Europe.

By 1989, the Ceausescu regime had become unbearable to the majority of the political elite and the population. The Revolution which occurred in December 1989 was a genuine popular uprising against dictatorship. Consequently, it was uncoordinated and susceptible to manipulation from various groupings within the Party elite who were opposed to Ceausescu and more inclined to implement reform Communist policies akin to those being implemented in the Soviet Union. This does not of itself constitute a hindrance for democratic consolidation; the Hungarian example demonstrates that a Party elite is capable of initiating democratic reform; but conditions in Romania were somewhat different from those in Hungary.

The Romanian system was essentially unchanged since the implementation of a Soviet Stalinist model shortly after the end of the Second World War, and under the influence of Nicolae Ceausescu had evolved into something which bore little resemblance to the reformed Hungarian system and was rather more complicated than the neo-Stalinist system in Czechoslovakia.

The Romanian regime under Ceausescu was perhaps the most repressive in the whole of Eastern Europe. It shared some characteristics with the Husak regime in its methods of repression and atomisation of the population; but although both had a basically Stalinist economic policy and central planning system, after 1968 the Czechoslovak regime had attempted to improve living standards and increase the availability of consumer goods within the parameters of the system. This was an anathema to the Romanian regime. It had succeeded in pacifying the population without making concessions to consumerism. It had never been under consistent pressure, popular or elite, to introduce reform even if it had been so inclined. As the system of dictatorship was perfected and as Ceasescu's personal control increased, so too did the obvious effects of his irrationality[196]. These were amplified by the highly centralised Stalinist command administration and by the 1980's, the almost total disintegration of the Romanian economy and society had been achieved.

2.4.1: Ceausescuism

The Romanian system which developed under Ceausescu has been described by Juan Linz as a form of 'Sultanism'[197]. Certain traditional forms of Romanian political culture which can be traced back to the Phanariot system of rule employed by the Ottomans were manipulated and combined with both nationalism and Stalinism to create a totalitarian system which covered all aspects of cultural, social and economic life, and over which Ceausescu alone had absolute control.

The Party political elite demonstrated little interest in initiating reform or curbing the development of Ceausescu's totalitarian system. Securing personal power was of more interest. In addition, the intellectual weakness of the Communist elite and the absence of ideological discussion in Romania offered little opportunity for the development of a socialist alternative. Yet despite this, Ceausescu placed members of his extended family clan in positions of power[198]. The family clan protected him and also prevented outsiders or rivals from gaining power. Ceausescu's brothers were all placed in positions of power. Ilie Ceausescu was the Deputy

---

[196] However excessive Ceausescu's policies appear, it is necessary to keep in mind that he was a product of Romanian Communist political culture and that his policies reflected the Stalinism which Romanian Communism never discarded. Calinescu, Matei, Tismaneanu, Vladimir, 'The 1989 Revolution and Romania's Future', *Problems of Communism*, Vol. 40, No. 1-2, January-April 1991.

[197] See Linz, J., Stepan, A., *Problems of Democratic Transition and Consolidation of Democracy*, John Hopkins University Press 1996.

[198] For an explanation of this phenomenon, see Tismaneanu, Vladimir, 'Personal Power and Political Crisis in Romania', *Government and Opposition*, Vol. 24, No. 2, Summer 1989.

Minister of Defence, while General Nicolae Andruta was Deputy Minister of the Interior and Head of the Ministry of Interior's Academy. Another brother, Marin, was Head of the Romanian Foreign Trade Mission in Vienna and provided for the family's everyday needs by acquiring Western goods[199]. Ion Ceausescu was a State Secretary and Deputy Minister of Agriculture. He was also Head of Party Finances[200]. Ceausescu's children occupied important academic positions. Nico Ceausescu was officially an atomic physicist who was to take charge of Romania's nuclear power programme. Fortunately the Revolution put an end to his career. Zoe Ceausescu was the Chief of the Mathematics Department at the National Institute, and Valentin Ceausescu was Scientific Secretary at the Bucharest Institute for Physics and Atomic Energy[201].

Although the Stalinist system introduced by Ceausescu aimed to modernise Romanian society, it failed to abolish pre-modern attitudes characteristic of Byzantine Romanian culture and in some aspects even reinforced them. The individual remained of limited importance. In the same way as people had been subjects of the Sultan, everyone was now a subject of Ceausescu. Protection and favours were extended to Ceausescu's family and friends in the same way as they had been to the Sultan's.

In addition, the regime provoked, manipulated and instrumentalised Romanian nationalism:

'Der rumänische Nationalismus... ist provoziert, manipuliert, kontrolliert und instrumentalisiert.'[202]

This manipulation was a means of securing power by dividing the multi-ethnic population and providing the Romanians with an exaggerated sense of national pride and unity. The system and its

---

[199] Almond, Mark, *The Rise and Fall of Nicolae and Elena Ceausescu*, Chapmans 1992, p. 72.
[200] Rados, Antonina, *Die Verschwörung der Securitate*, Hoffmann & Campe 1990, p. 43.
[201] Ibid. Rados, Antonina, *Die Verschwörung der Securitate*, p. 43
[202] Anneli Ute Gabanyi in Mommsen, Margareta, *Nationalismus in Osteuropa*, Verlag C. H. Beck 1992, p. 143. 'Romanian Nationalism... is provoked, manipulated, controlled and instrumentalised.' Translated by Wendy Hollis.

achievements were proclaimed as national triumphs. In this way attention was effectively drawn away from failures and criticism of the system became equivalent to criticising the Romanian nation. Romanian links with the Roman Emperor Trajan's legions were also emphasised, thus giving the population a sense of superiority over the other nations which surrounded them. Manipulation by the regime distorted and exaggerated Romanian national identity with the result that a vicious, chauvinistic nationalism developed. Atomisation and isolation combined with nationalism to effectively limit open opposition to the system. As a result of the divisive nationalist policy, the majority of Romania's ethnic German population chose to emigrate to the Federal Republic of Germany[203]. This in turn destroyed the ethnic balance in Translyvania and has increased tension between the remaining Romanian, Hungarian and Roma populations.

2.4.2: Regime Opposition

The most effective and disruptive opposition to the regime was carried out by the workers in the form of mass strikes; while the intellectuals engaged in sporadic individual acts of open opposition. However, both these strategies remained ineffective due to the extreme form of political control which had developed. The workers were pacified in the short-term by promises of better working conditions, increased wages and more rations. In addition, the *Securitate* infiltrated workers' groups using informers or agents and so dispersed the leaders of the infant workers' movements. The 'dispersal' took the form of actual physical annihilation in unexplained 'accidents', trials and imprisonment[204]. Workers were

---

[203] Romania was the only country after the Second World War which did not expel its German population. Approximately 3 million Germans remained in Romania; mostly concentrated in the Banat, the north western part of Transylvania. Between 1955-1985 a total of 200 000 Germans left Romania. The emigration of ethnic Germans was accepted because an agreement signed with the Federal Republic of Germany in 1978 obliged the West German government agreed to pay 8000 DM for each ethnic German who left Romania. Since 1978, 11 000 ethnic Germans were officially allowed to leave Romania each year. Totok, William, *Die Zwänge der Erinnerung*, Jurius 1988, p. 51.

[204] The leaders of the 1987 Brasov workers' demonstration disappeared or were brought to trial in December 1987. They were sentenced to between 6 months and

also moved to different factories or outlying villages away from close and trusted friends[205]. In addition, the twelve hour working day limited the time and energy available for opposition activities. The Work Law No. 24-25, introduced in 1976, obliged everyone to work from the age of 16 until pensionable age. Anyone who refused a job offered to them by the state was liable for one year's forced labour. This law was also used effectively against activists in the civil rights' movement and dissidents in general[206].

The intellectuals were easily persecuted because of their general isolation from the masses and from each other. Individual dissenting intellectuals were singled out by the regime and in most cases forced to emigrate. Such was the case of Paul Goma, who had attempted to form a *Movement for Democracy* and an independent Trade Union. He was finally forced to emigrate in 1977, having been severely beaten by the *Securitate*. Vasile Paraschiv's failed attempt to found a free trade Union in 1971 also led to his emigration. In March 1979, a *Free Trade Union of Romanian Workers* (*SLMOR*) was founded by forty people, sixteen of them workers[207]. But the leaders were all forced to emigrate. An attempt to revitalise the Union in February 1980 was effectively blocked. The workers remained alienated from the intelligentsia and the intelligentsia remained powerless. The workers could not identify with the dissidents' form of intellectual opposition, and the dissidents made little attempt to contact or cooperate with the workers.

Although there were well-known and respected members of the intelligentsia who opposed the regime, they practised a pragmatic form of passive, individual opposition. The mathematician and economist Mihai Botez lost his academic position in 1977 and was

---

3 years in prison. Ratesh, Nestor, *Romania: The Entangled Revolution*, Praeger 1992, p. 10.
[205] After the Jiu Valley strike in 1977, during which 35 000 miners went on strike and held Ceausescu hostage, 4000 miners were arrested and deported to various villages. Amnesty International, *Rumänien: Zur politischen Verfolgung seit 1970*, Nomos Verlag 1978, p. 44.
[206] Ibid. Amnesty International, *Rumänien: Zur politischen Verfolgung seit 1970*, p. 20.
[207] Ibid. Skilling, G., *Samizdat and an Independent Society in Eastern Europe*, p. 194.

expelled from the Party in 1984. He was critical of the regime's economic policies and condemned the personality cult which had grown around Ceausescu. However, he remained an isolated figure because he actively rejected the perverted society which had developed under Ceausescu and became a hermit[208]. Other well-known dissidents were the poets Ana Blandiana, Dori Tudoran and Mircea Dinescu; the school teacher, Doina Cornea; and the historian, Vlad Georgescu. The former Diplomat Dumitru Mazilu had also become a figure of dissent since his critical report to the UN Commission on Human Rights concerning the position of youth in Romania. However, the population failed to form a bond with the dissidents which would have lessened their isolation.

In the rigid, structured existence imposed by the Romanian regime, informal acts of protest or simple self-expression were more important, and more feasible, than developing a formal dissident movement such as evolved in Hungary and Czechoslovakia. However, informal resistance remained largely ineffective. Mircea Dinescu believes that its seeming passivity constitutes the most tragic failure of the Romanian intelligentsia. In contrast to the Czech dissidents, the Romanian intelligentsia allowed itself to become a servant of the regime and therefore ensured its own alienation and isolation:

> *'Dennoch: der passive Widerstand einiger bedeutender Autoren ist wirkungslos geblieben; wir haben auf radikale Forderungen verzichtet, wir haben zugelassen, daß man uns eine gehorsame Verbandsführung aufgezwungen hat, die Massen Emigration desillusionierter Künstler hat Leeräume hinterlassen, und all das hat den Schriftstellerverband unterhöhlt, der zu einer Genossenschaft für die Produktion von Entfremdung geworden ist.*'[209]

---

[208] Ibid. Skilling, G., *Samizdat and an Independent Society in Eastern Europe*, p. 195.
[209] Schirrmacher, Frank, (Ed.), *Im Osten erwacht die Geschichte*, Deutsche Verlags-Anstalt 1990, p. 202. Original from Dinescu, Mircea, *Die geknebelte Existenz eines Volkes*, pp. 196-203. 'Yet the passive opposition of a few important authors remained ineffective; we refrained from radical demands, we allowed them to put up an obedient Union leadership. Mass emigration of disillusioned artists

As a result, cultural life in Romania deteriorated and no significant dissident movement developed. Individual dissident intellectuals invariably lost confrontations with the regime due to their isolation and the brutality with which they were treated. Thus, one of the founders of the *Romanian Association for the Defence of Human Rights*, Florian Russu, was beaten and imprisoned for four months[210]. Iona Puiu, the author of a letter to commemorate the anniversary of the 1956 invasion of Hungary was also beaten and interrogated. This form of brutal and random intimidation silenced most dissidents. A joint proclamation published in Hungary in 1986 on the anniversary of the 1956 Revolution was belatedly signed by only three Romanians. The other signatories, totalling 122, included 54 Hungarians, 28 Poles, 24 Czechs and Slovaks and 16 East Germans[211].

Romania had no *samizdat* publications. All typewriters had to be registered with the police and a sample of the type-set presented. This meant *samizdat* publications were easy to trace and therefore much more difficult to produce. Independent publications by dissidents took the form of sporadic, open, typewritten letters.

This form of protest became more widespread during the early 1980's as the destruction of historical Bucharest began. The letters of protest were written by prominent members of the establishment, such as Professors, architects, cultural figures and members of the clergy. The earliest statement condemning the destruction appeared in April 1984. It was followed by others in 1985 and 1986[212]. However, unlike their Hungarian counterparts who demonstrated against the Nagymaros Dam, the Romanian protesters were unable to affect a change in the regime's policy.

Almost the whole of historical Bucharest was destroyed and a total of 40 000 people were moved to create space for Ceausescu's

---

has left behind empty rooms and hollowed out the Writers' Union, which has become a club for the production of alienation.' Translated by Wendy Hollis.

[210] Ibid. Skilling, G., *Samizdat and an Independent Society in Eastern Europe*, p. 192.

[211] Ibid. Skilling, G., *Samizdat and an Independent Society in Eastern Europe*, p. 59.

[212] Ibid. Skilling, G., *Samizdat and an Independent Society in Eastern Europe*, p. 193.

monumental *Casa Republicii*. The first stone for the Palace was laid in June 1984. The Palace has five underground storeys and is 84 metres high. It covers an area of more than 265 000m^2 and is the second largest building in the World after the Pentagon. The flag pole in front of it carries the largest tricolour in the World[213]. It represents the realisation of Ceausescu's ideology in stone. It displays many elements of fascist architecture and stands as a monument to the inhumanity of the system which Ceausescu created. It is perhaps a final irony that on completion the democratic Romanian Parliament and some Ministries moved into it.

The Hungarian minority also practised a form of opposition. The Hungarians were in many ways isolated and suffered discrimination, but they remained united as an ethnic group. Encouraged by events in Hungary, the first *samizdat* journal which appeared in Romania between 1981-1983 was a Hungarian language journal called *Counterpoints*. In February 1985, its editor, Geza Szocs, sent a memo to the UN Agency for Minority Rights complaining about the treatment of the Hungarian minority in Romania[214]. In May 1983 a *Hungarian Press of Transylvania* was formed. It publicised the plight of the Magyar minority in Transylvania and was still in operation in 1986[215].

The various Romanian minority churches also played an important role in independent opposition. As early as 1977 six evangelical priests published a 'Call for the Truth' calling for religious tolerance and freedom. In 1978, 27 Orthodox and Protestant Christians published a 'Programme of Demands'. It contained 24 Articles calling for tolerance and freedom. The Romanian Baptist Church also wrote an open letter to the regime and founded the *Romanian Committee for the Defence of Religion and Conscience*. In April 1981, five Orthodox priests published a 'Testimony of Faith' criticising the regime and calling for the

---

[213] Ibid. Almond, Mark, *The Rise and Fall of Nicolae and Elena Ceausescu*, p. 168.
[214] Ibid. Skilling, G., *Samizdat and an Independent Society in Eastern Europe*, p. 194.
[215] Ibid. Skilling, G., *Samizdat and an Independent Society in Eastern Europe*, p. 195.

release of Father Gheorghe Calciu-Dumitreasa[216]. He had spent almost half of his fifty years in prison as a result of a series of critical sermons he delivered in 1978[217]. His opposition and letters supporting him were significant because of the Romanian Orthodox Church's duplicity and willingness to cooperate with the regime. It had gained many of the buildings and land which had belonged to persecuted minority churches, in particular those of the Greek Catholic Church[218]. Romanian religious minorities coincide to a large extent with ethnic cleavages. With this in mind, calls for religious freedom and tolerance also represented a rejection of the national intolerance and prejudice propagated by the regime.

By the 1980's the intellectual opposition movement was still small and ineffective, and although the workers' antagonism towards the regime continued to express itself through strikes, sabotage and unfulfilled Plan targets, the instruments of control and manipulation remained intact and capable of sustaining Ceausescu's power. But as the economic situation worsened and the international climate changed, the irrationality of the system and of Ceasuescu himself became unbearable not only to the population, but also to the political elite. The first major public expression of discontent within the Party political elite came in March 1989 and took the form of an open letter to Ceausescu. It was signed by six Communist Party veterans who were all former members of the Political Executive Committee. They were Constantin Pirvulescu, who at the age of 94 was one of the last surviving founders of the Communist Party and had opposed Ceausescu's re-nomination as Party Leader at the 12th Party Congress in 1979; Gheorghe Apostol, who had been a member of the Politburo in 1977 before being demoted due to his opposition to Ceausescu's methods; Silviu Brucan, who had been a member of the Communist Party

---

[216] He was forced to emigrate in 1985. Nelson, Daniel, N., *Romanian Politics in the Ceausescu Era*, Gordon & Breach Science Publishers 1988, p. xv.
[217] Ibid. Skilling, G., *Samizdat and an Independent Society in Eastern Europe*, p. 193.
[218] For more information, see Cipaianu, George, *The Romanian Greek Catholic Church under Communism*. In Craciun, Maria, Ghitta, Ovidiu, (Eds.), *Ethnicity and Religion*, Cluj University Press 1995.

since 1944 and was chief editor of the Party Daily, *Scinteia*[219]; Alexandru Birladeanu; Grigore Raceanu; and Corneliu Manescu, a former Foreign Minister and former President of the UN General Assembly. The letter accused Ceausescu of attempting to dislocate Romanian development from that of the rest of Europe:

> *'Romania is and remains a European country, and as such it must move forward within the framework of the Helsinki process rather than turning against that process. You have begun to change the geography of the rural areas, but you cannot move Romania into Africa'*[220]

But Ceausescu refused to affect a policy change. He had celebrated his 70th birthday in 1987 and the prospect of his dilettante son, Nico, taking over power provided little prospect for improvement. Romania was isolated and in danger of losing contact with European developments. It was this prospect which finally proved unacceptable to the population and important sections of the political and military elite.

2.4.3: Economic Collapse

By 1989 the Romanian economy and society was on the verge of complete collapse. The standards of Romanian education had fallen steadily, as had the number of students in higher education. It was estimated that by 1989, there were only 71 students for every 10 000 Romanian citizens. Romanian intellectual potential was being wasted on a grand scale. The economic base of the country was also failing. Romania had fewer radio and television sets per capita than Zaire and Kenya. The official Committee for National Statistics estimated that 42% of scientific equipment, 39% of industrial equipment and 37% of all busses and trains were worn

---

[219] Shortly after its publication, the majority of the letter's signatories were placed under house arrest and Brucan's son was arrested on charges of espionage. Ibid. Brogan, P., *Eastern Europe 1939-1989*, p. 230.

[220] Verdery, Katherine, *National Ideology under Socialism*, University of California Press 1991, p. 133.

out[221]. By 1991, more than half of Romania's power stations were not working due to a lack of spare parts[222].

The Stalinist preference for heavy industry led to a massive distortion of the Romanian economy and the total neglect of agriculture[223]. By the late 1980's scythes were once again used for harvesting and horse drawn carts were the normal mode of transport for the peasants. Agricultural output fell and in 1983 compulsory state deliveries were re-introduced. In 1989 the grain harvest was only 17 000 000 tons, although official statistics claimed a record 60 000 000 tons[224]. In 1989, Romania produced less processed food than in 1980 and had the lowest agricultural and milk productivity levels in Europe[225]. In contrast, the country possessed three times as much oil refining capacity than it actually needed, and many factories were only running at 50% capacity. The Romanian aluminium industry consumed vast quantities of energy; one aluminium factory alone required more energy than was allocated to the whole of the Romanian population[226].

In an attempt to meet the needs of the heavy industrial base, domestic energy consumption was restricted to 530 Watts per person per hour per day and only one 40 Watt bulb was permitted per room[227]. In addition, fridges were disconnected and weather reports were falsified so that the critical temperature at which central heating was turned on for the proscribed four hours a day, was not officially reached. In winter, room temperature was not permitted to rise above 10^0 Celsius (50^0 Fahrenheit). As a result, only 5.4% of the electricity produced was consumed by household use[228].

Despite these draconian measures, Romanian industrial output had stagnated since 1985 and average output had been declining

---

[221] Ibid. Brogan, P., *Eastern Europe 1939-1989*, p. 237.
[222] Beckherrn, Eberhard, *Tal der Wende*, Knaur 1991, p. 273.
[223] In 1981, investment fell by 22.1% as money was diverted to repay Romania's foreign debt. Crane, Keith, *The Romanian Economic Mess After Ceausescu*, The Rand Corporation, December 1986, p. 4.
[224] Ibid. Ratesh, Nestor, *Romania: The Entangled Revolution*, p. 5.
[225] Ibid. Ratesh, Nestor, *Romania: The Entangled Revolution*, p. 6.
[226] Ibid. Brogan, P., *Eastern Europe 1939-1989*, p. 237.
[227] Butnaru, I., C., *The Silent Holocaust*, Greenwood Press 1992, p. 55.
[228] Ibid. Ratesh, Nestor, *Romania: The Entangled Revolution*, p. 7.

since 1980[229]. The heavy industrial base was energy and raw material intensive. As Romanian energy production faltered due to import constraints and a lack of hard currency, iron, steel and chemical production declined causing a further reduction of the country's hard currency earnings. The Romanian regime was caught in a vicious circle. Brown-outs and complete loss of energy became common place, both for industrial and residential areas. The energy shortage constrained economic growth and drained resources which had been planned for investment. The factories remained energy intensive, but could not produce enough quality goods to pay for the imports necessary to keep up production.

The economic crisis gradually affected the re-integration of the Romanian economy into the CMEA[230]. As OPEC oil became too expensive for Romania to purchase, it turned to the Soviet Union for oil and gas. It was officially estimated that by 1980, imported crude oil accounted for 67.1% of all consumption[231]. Romanian trade with the Soviet Union increased from 17% in 1982, to 22% in 1984 and had reached 26% by 1985. Between 1985-1986 alone, Romanian trade with the Soviet Union increased by 47%[232]. In 1981 food rationing had been re-introduced for the first time since 1954; and by October 1989, Romanian citizens were entitled to a mere 200g of salami a month[233]. However, the Romanian regime sold food products and consumer goods to the Soviet Union in an attempt to earn enough hard currency to repay foreign debt and fund the necessary imports of raw materials.

Ceausescu was determined to repay Romania's foreign debt as quickly as possible. However, selling poor quality Romanian products and foodstuffs did not earn sufficient hard currency to alleviate the balance of payments crisis, or indeed pay off the foreign debt. In addition, Romania was on the verge of losing its

---

[229] Ibid. Crane, Keith, *The Romanian Economic Mess After Ceausescu*, p. 2.
[230] Trade increased with the Soviet Union at a spectacular rate; from 17% in 1982, to 22% in 1984 and 26% in 1985. By 1986 the Soviet share in Romanian trade had reached 33%. Georgescu, Vlad, 'Romania in the 1980's: The Legacy of Dynastic Socialism', *East European Politics and Societies*, Vol. 2, No. 1, Winter 1988.
[231] Ibid. Ratesh, Nestor, *Romania: The Entangled Revolution*, p. 4.
[232] Harrington, Joseph, F., *Tweaking the Nose of the Russians*, Columbia University Press 1991, pp. 531-532.
[233] Ibid. Butnaru, I., C., *The Silent Holocaust*, p. 53.

Most Favoured Nation (MFN) status from the USA[234]. In the Summer of 1986, Romania was forced to reschedule its Western foreign debt[235]. The Romanian government insisted on a fast repayment schedule even though its creditors were willing to accept a slower rate. The Romanian regime itself was therefore to blame for the catastrophic effects of debt repayment[236].

Although the drastic debt repayment policy affected a reduction in Romania's hard currency debt from $6.5 billion in 1980 to $3 billion by 1985[237], the economy could not support the policy over an extended period of time. Indeed, the debt repayment policy accelerated the decline and collapse of the Romanian economy and the population's health. In accordance with Ceausescu's pro-natalist policies[238], contraception and abortion were illegal. But, although the birth rate stood at 15.9% in 1989, the maternal mortality rate had also increased from 86 deaths per 100 000 births in 1966, to 150 by 1984[239]. In addition, the infant mortality rate was excessively high at 27 per 1000 live births, that is twice the European average[240]. Thus, the quality of life in Romania deteriorated rapidly during the course of the 1980's. The population was under-nourished and life expectancy was one of the lowest in Europe. The population had been so degraded that it became

---

[234] MFN status was suspended on June 26, 1987. To avoid the ignominy of having it removed, Ceausescu renounced it in February 1988. Ibid. Harrington, Joseph, F., *Tweaking the Nose of the Russians*, pp. 572-582.

[235] In addition to its Western foreign debt, Romania also had a Ruble debt. By 1983 this debt was equivalent to approximately $197 million. Although, in comparison to Hungary's Ruble debt, which was equivalent to $1397 million, and Poland's Ruble debt of $3840 million, this sum was minimal.

[236] For more information, see 'Romania Reschedules 1986-87 Commercial Debt', *East-West*, No. 391, July 1986, p. 9.

[237] Nelson, Daniel, N., *Romanian Politics in the Ceausescu Era*, Gordon & Breach Science Publishers 1988, p. 159.

[238] For a full account of the political and social effects of this policy, see Kligman, Gail, 'The Politics of Reproduction in Ceausescu's Romania: A Case Study in Political Culture', *East European Politics and Societies*, Vol. 6, No. 3, Fall 1992.

[239] This figure was also influenced by the number of illegal abortions, which accounted for 86% of the total. Ibid. Ratesh, Nestor, *Romania: The Entangled Revolution*, p. 7.

[240] Ibid. Ratesh, Nestor, *Romania: The Entangled Revolution*, p. 7. From *Population Today*, The World Health Organisation, March 1990.

desperate and had nothing left to lose in a confrontation with the regime. Under these circumstances the regime's system of control became ineffective.

As a result of the economic crisis, Ceausescu had announced a State of Emergency in October 1985 and placed army officers in control of the economy as economic managers. They were allocated to large enterprises and important areas of the economy, such as electricity generation. Army labour had previously been called upon to help in harvesting, the building of the Bucharest underground system, the Black Sea Canal, irrigation systems and hydroelectric dams[241]. The army had also been employed to quell popular disturbances, such as the strikes in the Jiu Valley in 1977 and the riots in Brasov in 1987. These policies increased resentment against the regime within the army which felt degraded by performance of such tasks it did not consider its responsibility. In addition, the Ceausescu regime consistently favoured the *Securitate* and the Communist Party Patriotic Guards over the conventional military establishment[242]. Military expenditure decreased steadily from 1979-1981 due to budget constraints. At the Party Conference in December 1982, Ceausescu proclaimed that Romania's military expenditure would remain limited at its 1982 level until 1985. The Romanian army was left disillusioned, ill-equipped and discontented.

At the 14th Party Conference on 20 November, 1989, Ceausescu was greeted enthusiastically by the 4000 delegates and proceeded to give a five hour opening speech which was continuously interrupted by 'spontaneous' applause[243]. The Conference reinforced Ceausescu's hard-line position and confirmed his own personal position as leader. The curious 'non-event' of the Party Congress was a public demonstration that the Party would not initiate reform. But large sections of the population, both inside and outside the power structures, were reaching the limits of their endurance. Under these conditions, it would only require a seemingly insignificant event to ignite popular discontent.

---

[241] Ibid. Nelson, Daniel, N., *Romanian Politics in the Ceausescu Era*, p. 187.
[242] Ibid. Nelson, Daniel, N., *Romanian Politics in the Ceasuescu Era*, p. 185.
[243] Ibid. Rados, Antonina, *Die Verschwörung der Securitate*, p. 47.

2.4.4: The Timisoara Uprising

The revolution began in the town of Timisoara. It is the most western town in Romania and is the capital town of Timis county and the Banat region. In November 1884, it became the first European city to have its streets lit by electricity[244]. Until 1919 it had been part of Hungary and was home to various ethnic minorities; German, Hungarian and Serbian. Its close vicinity to the borders of Hungary and the former Yugoslavia gave its inhabitants access to foreign television and radio programmes, so they were better informed than other regions in Romania. The University had become a centre for discontent, but its expression had remained low-key. Thus, the vigil outside the Reformed Church of Pastor Tökés was not treated as anything exceptional and was initially tolerated by the local authorities.

Pastor Tökés had been in Timisoara since 1986[245]. On 1 May, 1989, he had been ordered to leave Timisoara and go to the outlying village of Mineu, in the County of Salaj. This decision was justified by Laszlo Papp, the Bishop of Oradea, in an 'Explanation'. The 'Explanation' stated that Laszlo Tökés had entered:

> ... into contact with political activists, foreign radio and TV stations in order to denigrate and present in a tendentious way the realities of our country.[246]

But Tökés refused to leave, and the Church was forced to ask the local authorities to remove him. After the Sunday service on 10 December, 1989, Pastor Tökés told his congregation that he had been given until 15 December to leave or face eviction. The congregation agreed to help him resist and started a vigil outside the entrance of the Church. The Reformed Church is a Hungarian Church, so the few hundred people holding vigil were Hungarians.

---

[244] Neumann, Victor, *Orizont*, 9 February 1990, p. 4.
[245] He was the son of the Pastor Ivan Tökés, who had been a Professor of Theology at Cluj University before being dismissed as a Pastor and banned from the Pulpit in 1984. Laszlo Tökés had been excluded from the clergy at the same time because of 'indiscipline', but was re-admitted two years later and sent to Timisoara.
[246] Ibid. Ratesh, Nestor, *Romania: The Entangled Revolution*, p. 20. Original in 'Explanation', *Agerpress*, 21 December 1989.

As the deadline approached people from the town came by to see what would happen. By the time darkness fell on the night of 15 December, a large crowd had gathered outside the Church. Pastor Tökés spoke to them from his window, first in Hungarian and then in Romanian. The deadline passed and Pastor Tökés remained in his Church.

About 1000 people had surrounded the Church and brought traffic to a halt. On Saturday 16 December, the Mayor of Timisoara went personally to Tökés' house. He stated that the eviction order had been rescinded and that Tökés would be allowed to stay. This led some people to leave the vigil, but the majority remained. The crowd now included younger people, mostly students, and many Romanians. Part of the crowd moved on from the Church in the direction of the town centre chanting, 'Down with Ceausescu', 'Down with the Dictator'. The Revolution had begun.

Those who remained at the Church were sprayed with water by a fire engine, while those who had set off for the centre of the town were greeted by the militia. The demonstrators now numbered 5000, having been joined by more students from the University Campus. They made their way to the Communist Party Headquarters and destroyed the two fire engines which had been placed there to protect the building. Pastor Tökés was arrested by the *Securitate* on 16 December, but the crowds continued to gather outside the town Cathedral and at 9 p.m. on 16 December, the Party Headquarters was ransacked and partly destroyed by the demonstrators. The Communist flag was burned along with Ceausescu's books and pictures[247].

After this troops from the Interior Ministry arrived and fought with the demonstrators, who by now numbered approximately 10 000, but no shooting took place. The Communist Party Headquarters was once again attacked and, in an act reminiscent of the 1956 Hungarian Revolution, the Communist symbol was cut out of the Romanian flag. The Hungarian flag was also hung from the balcony of the building. During the course of the ever more violent confrontations with the security forces, several people were crushed by tanks and injured by water cannons. The fact that such

---

[247] Ibid. Ratesh, Nestor, *Romania: The Entangled Revolution*, pp. 22-23.

Regime Collapse and the Role of the Soviet Union 195

disturbances had taken place at all was a treasonable act, so there was little incentive for the citizens to end their action and the situation threatened to run out of control.

At the Political Executive Committee meeting in Bucharest called to discuss events, Ceausescu berated the Minister of Defence, Vasile Milea and the Minister of the Interior, Tudor Postelnicu for their incompetence:

> 'It is grave and you are to blame, I, as Commander-in-Chief, think you have betrayed the interests of the country, of the people, of socialism, and did not act responsibly.'[248]

Such an accusation from the 'Genius of the Carpathians' meant that their careers, if not their lives, were over. Ceausescu summarily dismissed both Ministers and the Head of the *Securitate* and personally took control:

> 'As of this moment, if the Political Executive Committee agrees, we dismiss the Minister of National Defence, the Minister of the Interior and the Commander of the Securitate forces. As of this moment, I take over the command of the army... I trust such men no more. We cannot go on like this... They should have killed the hooligans, instead of being beaten by them... You know what I should do? Put you in front of a firing squad! This is what you deserve, because what you have done means joining forces with the enemy.'[249]

In this way, Ceausescu alienated the highest commanders within the very forces he relied upon to sustain his power[250]. He also

---

[248] Ibid. Ratesh, Nestor, *Romania: The Entangled Revolution*, p. 27. Verbatum manuscript published in *România Libera*.

[249] Ibid. Ratesh, Nestor, *Romania: The Entangled Revolution*, p. 27. Verbatum Manuscript published in *România Libera*.

[250] It is interesting to note the presence of General Victor Atanasie Stanculescu, First Deputy Minister of Defense and a liason officer between the army and *Securitate*, at Ceausescu's trial. He was not only in charge of security at the Central Committee Building on 22 December, 1989 and one of the last people to speak to Ceausescu before his flight, but may even have organised the helicopter

exposed his brutality and simplicity. He immediately ordered that the troops be armed with live ammunition and that they fire on the crowd. Heavy firing into the demonstrators commenced at 5 p.m. that evening. On hearing the shooting, further crowds gathered in the suburbs and disarmed tanks which were heading for the centre of Timisoara. But by Monday 18 December, the city was fully occupied and access to it was restricted. Telephone contact was cut off and the postal service interrupted. Army units across the country were put on full alert and foreign tourists were banned from entering Romania. Despite this, on Monday, 18 Decemebr, Ceausescu went ahead with his scheduled visit to Iran. It may be that he was advised not to alter his plans as his absence could facilitate the coordination of some sort of coup.

Evidence of the army's and some sections of the *Securitate's* reluctance to put down the rebellion in Timisoara is provided by the fact that as soon as Ceausescu left the country the troops stopped shooting. Rumours also spread that Ceausescu had fled the country and disturbances and strikes began once more. On 19 December, a general strike affected the whole of Timis county and on Wednesday, 20 December, the people once more went to the centre of the city. The army let them pass and crowds filled the town squares. A delegation of 18 people representing the demonstrators was assembled to present a list of demands to the Prime Minister, Constantin Dascalescu, who had flown in from Bucharest. However, he could not guarantee the most fundamental demand, that Ceasuescu resign. He returned to Bucharest leaving Timisoara under the full control of the crowds and the *Popular Democratic Front* which had been formed. In the light of army fraternisation and the number of demonstrators, this was the only possible course of action, although it could also be that Dascalescu travelled to Timisoara to gain the support of the army and *Securitate* for a coup. Although a news blackout was enforced in the Romanian press, the *BBC* and *RFE/RL* reported the events the same evening. In this way, news about the events in Timisoara reached the rest of the country.

---

which evacuated Ceausescu. Ibid. Calinescu, Matei, Tismaneanu, Vladimir, 'The 1989 Revolution and Romania's Future', *Problems of Communism*.

2.4.5: Ceausescu Falls

On returning from Iran, Ceausescu broadcast a radio report dealing with the events in Timisoara. He described the demonstrators as, 'a gang of hooligans' and played down the seriousness of the situation. At the same time he announced a mass demonstration to take place the next day in Bucharest on the Palace Square. The reason why Ceausescu decided to hold a mass rally at such a time of crisis remains a mystery. It seems likely that his advisors deliberately convinced him that it would demonstrate political strength, knowing that it would prove the exact opposite. Indeed, it was this rally, broadcast live throughout Romania, which finally exposed the fatal fragility of Ceausescu's power.

On the day of the rally, 21 December, Bucharest was under quasi martial law. Troops patrolled the city as thousands of people made their way to the Palace Square. Ceausescu stood on the balcony of the Central Committee Building along with Elena and the other members of the Political Executive Committee. However, after just one minute of his speech there was a commotion followed by screams from the back of the crowd. The television and radio broadcast was briefly interrupted, but after a few minutes it resumed. Ceausescu resumed his speech, but was interrupted once more by screams and chants of 'Timisoara' and 'Down with Ceausescu'.

It seems that the original group who started the chants came from the *Turbomecanica* Factory[251]. The chants caused the people near the group to move away in panic. This created more confusion as the protesters used the space thus created to rush forward into the crowd. Ceausescu was obviously shaken and hurriedly left the balcony. The majority of the crowd left the Square, gathered at other points around the city and some built barricades blocking the streets. During the night the security troops launched a full attack on the barricades. But, as the city was being cleaned up on the morning of 22 December, thousands of workers appeared in Bucharest to demand Ceausescu's resignation. A State of Emergency was called and it was reported that the former Defence Minister, Vasile Milea, the General who had refused to order the

---

[251] Ibid. Ratesh, Nestor, *Romania: The Entangled Revolution*, p. 39.

troops to fire on the crowds in Timisoara, had committed suicide. Subsequent speculation has centred on the belief that he may have been executed.

On 22 December, the gathered crowds stormed the Central Committee building and Ceausescu, who had been on the balcony trying to calm the demonstrators, was forced to flee from the roof by helicopter. Prime Minister Dascalescu stayed behind and announced the resignation of the government. Petre Roman, a Professor and the son of a leading Communist, Valter Roman, was also present and read a declaration announcing the formation of a People's Unity Front. Romanian television and radio broadcast a statement by the dissident poet Mircea Dinescu which announced Ceausescu's flight to the country:

'These are moments when God turned his face towards Romania. Let's look to God! The army in Bucharest is with us! The dictator has run away!'[252]

Ceausescu was finally arrested by a traffic policeman, Sergeant Paise Constantin. He was taken to Tirgoviste and there stood trial before a military court. It was little more than a show trial designed to officially sanction an execution which had already been decided. Nicolae and Elena Ceausescu were executed on 25 December, 1989. In order to prevent groupings still loyal to Ceausescu from fighting, the new government ensured everyone knew the dictator was dead by broadcasting pictures of the trial and the couples' bloodied bodies. However, as Paul Goma stated, the main consequence of the show trial was that it:

'...accomplished the extraordinary, the unheard and undeserved feat of turning the Ceausescus into human beings.'[253]

---

[252] Ibid. Ratesh, Nestor, *Romania: The Entangled Revolution*, p. 67.
[253] Paul Goma, Lumea Libera, New York, 16 June 1990. From Ratesh, Nestor, *Romania: The Entangled Revolution*, p. 77.

2.4.6: Confusion and Conspiracy

The fact that the army supported the uprising was important during the days of confusion which followed Ceausescu's disappearance. The *Securitate* had kept a low profile during the events, tacitly supporting the revolt by their inaction. However, there were various nebulous groups who were determined to retain their personal position by supporting Ceausescu. It was they who posed the immediate threat to the Revolution and whom the army was called upon to fight[254]. However, it is not clear exactly who these people, or 'terrorists', were.

After Ceasuescu's flight from Bucharest, battles commenced outside the Ministry of Defence, the Television Station and at Otopeni Airport. After the fighting was over the bodies of the 'terrorists' disappeared. Although there was heavy fighting on the Palace Square, the Central Committee building remained untouched and completely undamaged. In contrast, the Royal Palace and the University Library were almost completely destroyed. Although the Television Station was supposedly the centre of a fierce battle it was virtually untouched, while the buildings surrounding it were almost completely destroyed. On 23 December, the new government had appealed to the population to repel these attacks, but by the time people arrived the fighting had stopped. There have been varying estimates as to the number of casualties the fighting caused. The first estimate claimed a total of 4000 dead in Timisoara, 5000 in Sibiu and many thousands in Bucharest. The government estimated the number of casualties at 10 000. However, it has subsequently reduced the official number of casualties on a number of occasions. Immediately after the revolution it published an official report claiming 889 dead and 1471 wounded. By June 1990, the numbers had decreased to 144 dead and 727 wounded[255]. Despite this, the controversy over the exact number of people killed during the Revolution remains. If so few were really killed, then

---

[254] The army's willingness to support the Revolution has been ascribed by some to the football match between the *Securitate* team, *Dynamo Bucharest*, and the army team, *Steaua Bucharest*. The crowd is said to have shouted for *Steaua*, not *Dynamo*. Schirrmacher, Frank, (Ed.), *Im Osten erwacht die Geschichte*, Deutsche Verlags-Anstalt 1990, p. 215.

[255] Ibid. Ratesh, Nestor, *Romania: The Entangled Revolution*, p. 78.

doubts must be raised as to the seriousness of the 'battles' fought against the so-called 'terrorists'.

In August 1990, Silviu Brucan claimed that the army had fought approximately 4000 'terrorists', mostly elite trained troops from the *Securitate* school headed by Ceasusesu's brother, but also members of Ceasuescu's personal body guard and the Bucharest police force[256]. Although there were undoubtedly certain groups who fought in support of Ceausescu, there is also little doubt that the battles which took place after 23 December were partly staged. The reasons for this remain unclear. Some have speculated that the terrorists were mercenaries from Libya. This suspicion was strengthened by the arrival of a plane from Libya on 25 December, 1989. It arrived empty but left with an unspecified human load[257]. Others believe the army staged the battles to discredit the *Securitate* and regain public support and prestige after the events in Timisoara. While others claim that the battles were planned to endow the new government with legitimacy and enable it to project its members as saviours of the Revolution.

The suspicion that the battles were staged, at least in part, by the group which took power after the Revolution is strengthened when one examines its membership[258]. A video camera recorded the formation of the new government inside the Central Committee building in the hours following Ceausescu's flight. Those present included Ion Iliescu, Petre Roman, General Stefan Guse, the Deputy Minister of Defence and the Army Chief of Staff, General Nicolae Militaru, who had officially retired, Colonel Ardeleanu, the Head of the Special Units for Anti-Terrorist Warfare, Colonel Parcalabescu, the Head of the National Committee of Patriotic Guards, and two of Ceausescu's Executive Secretaries, Dumitru Apostoiu and Vasile Nicolcioiu. Also present were two authors of the 'Letter of Six', Silviu Brucan and Alexandru Birladeanu. A

---

[256] Ibid. Ratesh, Nestor, *Romania: The Entangled Revolution*, p. 60. Original in *Adevarul*, 23 August 1990.

[257] Ibid. Ratesh, Nestor, *Romania: The Entangled Revolution*, p. 63.

[258] For an insight into continuity in the Romanian political elite, see Neagoe, Stelian, *Istoria Guvernelor Romaniei: de la inceputuri - 1859 pana in zilele noastre - 1995*, Machiavelli 1995.

third signatory, Gheorghe Apostol, was refused entry to the building[259].
It was at this meeting that the *National Salvation Front* was formed. Although the well-known dissidents Doina Cornea, Ana Blandiana, Mircea Dinescu, Dan Desilu, Gesza Domkos, Aurel-Dragos Munteanu and László Tökés were also members of the *Front*, the new leader who emerged in the wake of Ceausescu's departure was Ion Iliescu. He was a leading figure under Ceausescu and had even been named as a possible successor. His father had been a member of the pre-war Communist Party, which made him one of the few people who possessed a true Communist pedigree. He had also studied engineering in Moscow, specialising in hydro-electric power. He had fallen from favour in the 1970's and had been sent to Iasi as the First Secretary of the Party organisation, but he remained a candidate member of the Political Executive Committee until 1984 and never broke with the regime[260]. As Nestor Ratesh notes:

'Iliescu may have been an opponent to Ceausescu, but never a dissident that is someone who took a public stand against the dictator or any of his policies.'[261]

Iliescu was accepted as leader mainly because there was no one else available to take the position. Another important factor was no doubt the army. It may be that army support for the Revolution was conditional on professional politicians taking over after Ceasuescu had been removed. It was Iliescu who prompted the official formation of a *National Salvation Front*. The *Front* was officially formed on 22 December with Ion Iliescu as its Chairman and Dumitru Mazilu as First Vice Chairman. However, it seems likely that the *Front*, or a similar grouping, had secretly been in existence for some time before the Revolution. This suspicion was strengthened by the film of the meeting inside the Central

---

[259] Ibid. Ratesh, Nestor, *Romania: The Entangled Revolution*, p. 53.
[260] For a short summary of Iliescu's biography, see Calinescu, Matei, Tismaneanu, Vladimir, 'The 1989 Revolution and Romania's Future', *Problems of Communism*, Vol. 40. No. 1-2, January-April 1991.
[261] Ibid. Ratesh, Nestor, *Romania: The Entangled Revolution*, p. 52.

Committee building. It shows the discussion concerning the name of the new organisation. On hearing the name of the new group, General Militaru says in an aside that the *National Salvation Front* had already been in existence for six months[262].

Further evidence of a coup by marginalised groupings within the regime is provided by the fact that although in the list published on 22 December, dissidents appeared as members of the *Front* along with the army Generals, Victor Stanculescu, Stefan Gusa and Gheorghe Voinea, none of the dissidents or Generals were members of the *Front's* Executive Bureau. However, after the new government had been formed a number of generals were promoted and others who had been retired by Ceausescu were recalled. In addition, General Stanculescu, who had cunningly avoided being involved in the repression of the Timisoara demonstrations by feigning a broken leg and having it put in plaster, was appointed as Economics Minister, so continuing the trend of militarisation of the economy begun under Ceausescu. Positions in the Executive Bureau seemed to be reserved for functionaries and other members of the *nomenklatura*. Its members included, Cazimir Ionescu, Karoly Kiraly, Dan Martian, Bogdan Teodoriu, Vasile Neacsa, Silviu Brucan, Gheorghe Manole and Nicolae Radu[263]. In this sense, Ion Iliescu can be seen as representing the interests of the state bureaucracy, Party functionaries and the *nomenklatura* who saw their competence and careers compromised under Ceasuescu, but who feared losing their position as a result of transformation and democratisation.

There is some evidence that groupings within the elite had attempted a coup as early as 1984[264]. The confusion surrounding the events which led to Ceausescu's fall has increased because the statements of those involved are contradictory. Silviu Brucan claimed that the Revolution was 100% spontaneous but also that a spontaneous Revolution was impossible under the system

---

[262] Ibid. Ratesh, Nestor, *Romania: The Entangled Revolution*, p. 89.
[263] Nicolae Radu has since become associated with the extreme nationalist right-wing. Gabanyi, Anneli Ute, *Die unvollendete Revolution*, Piper 1990, p. 61.
[264] Pacepa, Ion, *Red Horizons*, Coronet books 1989.

Regime Collapse and the Role of the Soviet Union

developed by Ceausescu[265]. In addition, the extent which the Soviet Union was involved in any actual preparations for a coup remains unclear. There is no doubt that Ceausescu had become a liability to the Romanian political and military elite and to the Soviet Union. An alternative grouping within the Romanian Party which promised to implement a reform programme similar to that proposed by Gorbachev would no doubt have been welcomed and received moral support, but hard evidence of actual Soviet interference in Romanian affairs is lacking.

Silviu Brucan has claimed he travelled to Moscow in November 1988 to seek Soviet support for a coup, although he also admits that the Soviets were concerned to avoid involvement in Romanian affairs. However, Soviet interest in Romanian developments is demonstrated by the fact that the *Pravda* correspondent in Bucharest visited Brucan regularly[266]. Some have interpreted the video of the first meeting of the *National Salvation Front* in the Central Committee Building on 22 December, 1989 as evidence of a more active Soviet interest. Iliescu's remarks concerning the Soviet Embassy reveal his concern to gain Soviet approval:

> '*I want to tell you that I got in touch with the Soviet Embassy and I already let them know the situation in which we find ourselves in that they convey to Moscow for them to know who we are and what we want. That I already told them.*'[267]

However, a Soviet interest in Romanian affairs was totally legitimate and Iliescu's report to the Soviet Embassy may merely

---

[265] On 22 December he stated: 'The idea that this 180 Degree change would have been made spontaneously is entirely mistaken.' On 4 January, 1990, he claimed: 'The truth is that there never was... a plan. The making of such a plan would have been impossible. Surveillance was so effective that no political group could possibly take shape inside that Party or outside it, an even less so to involve the military. The revolution was 100% spontaneous'. Shafir, Michael, 'Ceausescu's Overthrow: Popular Uprising or Moscow-Guided Conspiracy?', *Report on Eastern Europe*, No. 3, 19 January 1990, pp. 15-19.
[266] Ibid. Ratesh, Nestor, *Romania: The Entangled Revolution*, p. 104.
[267] *România Libera*, 12 May 1990. Ibid. Ratesh, Nestor, *Romania: The Entangled Revolution*, p. 109.

have been an indication of his desire to obtain Soviet support, rather than confirmation of it. However, as rumour has mixed with truth and truth has been manipulated for personal and political gain, the actual events surrounding the Revolution and have become more and more difficult to discern.

2.4.7: Continuity within Revolution

It seems that the popular uprising which started spontaneously in Timisoara and found expression at the mass demonstrations in Bucharest on 21-22 December was used by factions within the political elite, the military, the *nomenklatura* and the *Secutritate* to ensure that Ceausescu was removed but that they retained their own positions[268]. Although the Revolution started as a genuinely spontaneous popular uprising, given the conditions in Romania, it would probably never have been able to topple Ceausescu without at least the complicity, if not actual support of sections of the army, *Securitate* and political elite. However, these same conditions most probably prevented the organisation of an active plan of power seizure. It seems more likely that plans of action, or inaction, were discussed amongst friends and trusted associates in the event of Ceausescu's departure, but that a coordinated plan to remove him did not exist[269]. The lack of an organised opposition or dissident movement enabled the sections of the elite who opposed or had been marginalised by Ceausescu to become involved in the uprising and thereby secure their positions[270]. This was also facilitated by the fact that in the immediate aftermath of the Revolution there was

---

[268] Evidence to support this theory is provided by the case of Commodore Nicolae Radu. He had been retired by Ceasuescu in 1984, the year of the supposed attempted coup, and in 1987 had been sentenced to 10 years in jail after anti-Ceasuescu leaflets were found at his home. As a result of a general amnesty, he had only spent one year in prison, and although he refrained from resuming contact with the conspiracy, he re-appeared as a member of the *National Salvation Front* after the Revolution. Ibid. Ratesh, Nestor, *Romania: The Entangled Revolution*, p. 97.

[269] Tismaneanu, Vladimir, 'The Quasi-Revolution and Its Discontents', *East European Politics and Societies*, Vol. 7, No. 2, Spring 1993.

[270] For an insight into the personalities and ideology of the *National Salvation Front*, see Almond, Mark, 'Romania since the Revolution', *Government and Opposition*, Vol. 25, No., 4, Winter 1990.

simply no one else available who possessed the competence to take power and prevent further chaos. Thus, the Revolution represents less a complete caesura and more an elite rotation.

The grouping within the political elite which gained power as a result of Ceausescu's overthrow supported reform along the lines of that proposed by Gorbachev[271]. The *National Salvation Front* published a Ten Point Programme promising to introduce a new Constitution and a pluralistic political system; ensure the separation of powers; guarantee national minority rights; and hold free elections in April 1990. However, a few months later Dumitru Mazilu, along with the former dissidents, left the *Front* complaining about its lack of commitment to democratisation and transformation. Despite these misgivings, the first free elections since 1946 were successfully held on 20 May, 1990 and Romania became, at least officially, a democracy[272].

As the realities of the Ceausescu regime became more widely publicised, the Romanian population gained a great deal of sympathy from the rest of Europe, but this sympathy dissipated somewhat due to the policies of the *Natioanl Salvation Front*. Romania was already at a disadvantage in comparison to Hungary and the Czech Republic, whose transformation was well underway by the time Ceausescu was removed from power. Continuing confusion and questions concerning the nature of the Revolution and those who subsequently gained power has lent Romania a 'bad image'. This, combined with the calamitous state of the Romanian economy and society, has made it difficult to find companies and institutions willing to invest money in Romania.

Iliescu's calls to the miners to come to Bucharest and protect the regime were reminiscent of policies employed by Ceausescu and caused many to doubt his democratic credentials. The miners came to Bucharest twice and engaged in an orgy of violence which was at

---

[271] This may help explain the fact that the economy remained, for all intents and purposes, planned. Although the Plan for 1990 was not binding, its existence, combined with the *Front's* obvious reluctance to implement the changes required for the introduction of a full market economy, caused confusion and increased distrust. Ibid. Calinescu, Matei, Tismaneanu, Vladimir, 'The 1989 Revolution and Romania's Future'.

[272] Ibid. Gabanyi, Anneli Ute, *Die unvollendete Revolution*, p. 77.

the same time random and focused. The miners' first appearance was in February 1990 during a demonstration on Victory Square. Demonstrators were able to enter the government building unhindered by the police, but were later brutally beaten by miners who had been transported to Bucharest to restore order.

In June 1990 the miners appeared again. They were used to break up a student demonstration on University Square. Originally held on 22 April to draw attention to the regime's neo-Communist tendencies, the demonstration developed into a sit-in. A police attack on 24 April had already failed to break it up. Between April and May as many as 40 000 demonstrators gathered in the, 'neo-Communist free zone'[273]. Tents were erected and some students went on hunger strike. On 13 June, the police carried out a dawn raid on the demonstrators during which several police trucks were set on fire. During the same night, the Ministry of the Interior was attacked, along with the television station and the offices of the Romanian Intelligence Service. Iliescu's televised appeal called for the miners' help to foil the:

> *'...attempt by fascist extremists to overthrow the government through vicious acts.'*[274]

As a result, between 10-20 000 miners from the Jiu Valley arrived in Bucharest and terrorised the city for two days. Since the Jiu Valley strikes of 1977, the miners had been thoroughly infiltrated by intelligence agents and informers. It is probable that such people spread rumours as to the nature of the disturbances in Bucharest. The student leader, Marian Munteanu, was badly beaten and the offices of the main opposition parties were destroyed. The population of Bucharest was generally shocked and cowed by the brutality of events. At the end of it all, Iliescu thanked the miners for their help. One must point out, that in a state ruled by Law it is the task of the police force, and not other organised groups, to disperse crowds and prevent such mob rule.

---

[273] Ibid. Ratesh, Nestor, *Romania: The Entangled Revolution*, p. 132.
[274] Ibid. Ratesh, Nestor, *Romania: The Entangled Revolution*, p. 134.

Regime Collapse and the Role of the Soviet Union

The publication of the 'Proclamation of Timisoara' on 11 March, 1990 confirmed many doubts as to the nature of the regime[275]. The proclamation claimed that, although the uprising had succeeded in removing Ceausescu from power, it had not rid the nation of Communism:

'Timisoara initiated a revolution against the entire communist regime and its entire nomenklatura, *and by no means in order to give an opportunity to a group of anti-Ceausescu dissidents within the Romanian Communist Party to gain power.'*[276]

In addition to the use of methods of intimidation, the policy of manipulation and radicalisation of Romanian nationalism, which had proved so effective as an instrument of control under Ceausescu, continued to be employed for political aims and as means of preserving the power structures which Ceausescu developed. Indeed, the manipulation of nationalism continues to hinder consolidation of Romanian democracy.

The specific role of the Hungarian minority in the uprising provided a golden opportunity to end the alienation between the Hungarian and the Romanian population and their respective governments. The Hungarian minority was proud to have made such an important contribution to Ceausescu's overthrow. In contrast to the German minority, the majority of the Magyar population do not wish to leave Romania.

Immediately after the Revolution, Hungary sent large quantities of humanitarian aid to Romania and relations between the two countries looked set to enter a new phase. However, events such as the riots in Tîgru Mures on 19-20 March, 1990, during which several Hungarians were killed and a prominent Hungarian political figure blinded in racially motivated violence, led to a rapid deterioration of relations between the two governments and populations[277]. In this respect, a historic opportunity was missed.

---

[275] Ibid. Ratesh, Nestor, *Romania: The Entangled Revolution*, p. 133.
[276] Ibid. Calinescu, Matei, Tismaneanu, Vladimir, 'The 1989 Revolution and Romania's Future'.
[277] Ibid. Gabanyi, Anneli Ute, *Die unvollendete Revolution*, p. 223.

Evidence has since come to light that this violence was itself manipulated and staged by extremist groupings in Transylvania. These groups have no interest in a Hungarian-Romanian reconciliation because this would mean the loss of their political power. The retention of the old power structures upon which such power is based requires continued ethnic tension. This ensures the electoral success of ultra-nationalist political parties such as *România Mare*, 'Greater Romania', and of extreme nationalists such as Gheorghe Funar, who is the mayor of Cluj, the city which has the highest concentration of Magyar inhabitants in Transylvania.

Although the Romanian population can now change its ruling political elite in democratic elections, the specific nature of the Romanian Revolution strengthened some elements of Ceausescu's system which pose a threat to democratic consolidation. Confusion and doubts as to the nature of the Revolution and the character and intentions of the government which was initially elected hindered the transformation process in Romania. The extreme nature of the Romanian system meant that in the immediate aftermath of the Revolution there were few alternatives to the established political elite. But, it is precisely these people who are most compromised by their activities under Ceausescu. Their attempts to remain in power by continued use of structures established under Ceausescu's dictatorship therefore presented a particular danger to democratic transformation and consolidation.

2.5: The Importance of the Revolutions

The Revolutions which occurred in 1989 led to democratisation and economic transformation in Hungary, the Czech Republic and Romania. However, analysis shows that differences between the respective Revolutions influenced the course of democratisation and transformation in various ways.

It can be argued that the Revolution in Hungary was the culmination of the Party's own programme of gradual reform which was initiated in response to events in 1956; but this is only partly accurate. Although the regime was eager to reform the economic system, the democratic elements introduced into the political system before 1989 were limited and not intended to precipitate systemic change. The willingness to negotiate with the opposition was born of the realisation that by 1989, the whole system was on the verge of collapse. After the 1956 Revolution, the traditional Stalinist system and its methods of control had been abandoned. Therefore the majority of the Hungarian Party elite was not ideologically committed to Communism and favoured some form of democratisation. Negotiations with the opposition presented the only means by which the Party could influence the structure of the new political system. The negotiations ensured legal continuity and a smooth transition, but in many respects prevented a complete break with the old system. This is demonstrated by the presence of prominent members of the former regime in Parliament and the administration. On the other hand, the majority of the old administration supported transformation and constituted a professional elite desperately needed during transformation. Their inclusion in the new system also reduced potential elite opposition.

However, the complex electoral system remains weighted in favour of the Party elites. This is one of the legacies of the Negotiated Revolution and demonstrates the concern of both the Party and opposition to ensure prominent members enter Parliament regardless of actual electoral performance. The political landscape is therefore often dominated by elite party politics which have no direct relevance for the general population.

Despite this, the Roundtable Negotiations represent the acceptance of two of the most important principles in a democratic system; negotiation and concession. They created the basic consensus necessary for a functioning democracy, providing a firm foundation for Hungarian democratic consolidation.

The Velvet Revolution in Czechoslovakia was carried through by the general population via peaceful, mass demonstrations. After 1968 the Czechoslovak regime had maintained control by blocking reform and implementing a policy of normalisation. As submission implied acceptance of the regime, the population was forced into complicity and support of the system, but a small, dedicated group of dissidents refused to cooperate. This group was well organised and published numerous critical writings, which discredited the system and exposed the official 'lie' to which the majority of the population had acquiesced. The fact that the regime was incapable of silencing its critics also demonstrated the limits of its power.

The success of the Roundtable Negotiations in Hungary and the speed of reforms in the Soviet Union itself emphasised the Czechoslovak regime's immobility. Stalinist methods of control had succeeded in pacifying the population after 1968, but by 1989 the system was no longer effective. Members of the Party elite feared reform would lead to their removal from power, but they no longer possessed the ideological commitment to implement the harsh methods needed to sustain the *status quo*. The mass demonstrations of discontent which led to the regime's collapse was the means by which the population restored its moral integrity. The population's direct role in the regime's demise and the process of democratisation re-awakened interest in politics. The people's personal role in the Revolution helps explain why support for transformation and democratisation has remained high in the Czech Republic.

The abrupt collapse of the Czechoslovak regime and the inability of its elite to participate in the new system was a result of the total rejection of reform after 1968. The Party elite was discredited and thus barred from participating in the formation of a democratic system; but the respected and organised dissident movement provided alternative figures capable of carrying out transformation. Lack of previous reform meant more radical transformation in the legal, political, administrative and social arenas was essential. The neo-Stalinist character of the Czechoslovak regime therefore forced a complete break with the old system. This caesura was necessary to ensure the legitimacy of the democratic system and thereby furthered democratic consolidation in the Czech Republic.

The violence of the Revolution in Romania also seems to indicate a complete caesura with the regime. But, the severity of Ceausescu's dictatorship prevented the formation of an organised dissident movement; while the culpability and ideological commitment of the Party elite meant there were no internal Party reform initiatives. The Romanian economic and political system was therefore excessively centralised and bureaucratic. It had not undergone any serious reform since its installation after the Second World War. By the end of 1989, the increasing irrationality of Ceausescu's policies and the collapse of the economic system threatened to isolate Romania completely from European development. The population's despair at the inhumanity and immobility of the regime therefore found expression in a popular uprising.

The Revolution was a demonstration of the population's rejection of the regime and of Ceausescu himself. Ceausescu's willingness to use violence to force capitulation not only failed to suppress the uprising, but also encouraged the spread of open opposition throughout the country. In addition, it led sections of the army, *Securitate* and political elite to seize the moment and turn against Ceausescu. Some of those who had been marginalised by Ceausescu thus became involved in the Revolution. After years of submission and passivity, mass participation in the Revolution served to conquer the population's fear and restore a degree of personal and moral integrity, but the lack of a significant dissident movement and internal Party reformers left the Revolution disorganised and without leadership.

Marginalised groups within the regime were therefore able to use the Revolution to remove Ceausescu while retaining their own personal positions of power. Preoccupation with personal power, combined with limited intellectual capabilities, had served to stifle the development of reformist groupings within the Romanian Party. Thus, the elite which took control of the Revolution was not interested in systemic transformation. Their positions of power and influence were based on the structures of Ceausescu's system, so they were more inclined to seek reform rather than initiate radical transformation. In this way they hoped to retain their power base, while at the same time ensuring the system functioned more effectively. Consequently, the Romanian Revolution did not result in a complete break with the old regime, but rather a rotation of the ruling elite. Although a democratic political system was introduced, numerous economic, administrative and governmental structures from Ceausescu's system were retained. The Revolution therefore precipitated democratisation, but its specific form delayed democratic transformation and consoldiation in Romania.

CHAPTER THREE

POLITICAL DEMOCRATISATION

'The Naming of Cats is a difficult matter,
It isn't just one of your holiday games;
You may think at first I'm as mad as a hatter
When I tell you, a cat must have *three different names*'

T. S. Eliot, Old Possum's Book of Practical Cats[1].

*

The collapse of the Communist regimes in Hungary, the Czech Republic and Romania allowed the formation of independent political parties and free competition for political power in democratic elections. The first election campaigns in 1990 demonstrated the inexperience of many of the parties and their ineptitude in dealing with political opponents in accordance with democratic norms but, despite this, political plurality has become the norm in Hungary, Romania and the Czech Republic. Political programmes have become more complex and party behaviour has, in most cases, been modified to conform with democratic norms.

In order to understand the nature of the political parties which have been formed and the political choices of the population, it is necessary to keep in mind the nature of the former Communist regimes and the democratic Revolutions which caused their collapse. The Czech Revolution was initiated by mass public demonstrations and led to a total implosion of the system. It is perhaps not surprising therefore that one of the main Czech parties which formed in the immediate aftermath of the Revolution, Civic

---

[1] Eliot, T., S., *Old Possum's Book of Practical Cats*, Faber & Faber 1988, p. 11.

Forum, did not resemble a political party at all, but was an umbrella movement – diverse and decentralised. Under Communism politics had become associated with corruption and opportunism, and many dissidents who wished to become politically active did not want to associate themselves with, or be a member of, a political party. In addition, the Czech intellectual dissident movement owed much of its success to its rejection of politics as immoral. However, the attempt to replace political parties with a loosely coordinated umbrella movement failed, as the disintegration of Civic Forum demonstrated. It is clear that to act and govern effectively in a democracy, it is necessary to organise a disciplined political party.

Hungarian transformation, on the other hand, was negotiated between opposing political elites and did not really involve the population. Dissidents had, to a large extent, been co-opted by the regime and had therefore not been in a position to engage in either outright condemnation or dissent. Negotiated transition enabled the political elite as a whole to ensure its position within the new political system. It is hardly surprising therefore that the Hungarian political system is extremely party and elite orientated; although the electoral system itself has strengthened this tendency. However, as stability within the political landscape is an important factor contributing to democratic consolidation, this should not necessarily be viewed as an excessively negative aspect of Hungarian transformation.

The Romanian dictator, Nicolae Ceausescu, was executed as a result of a violent Revolution, but important elements of the system he created survived. This helps to explain the initial electoral success of the Romanian National Salvation Front under the leadership of Ion Iliescu. It may also help to explain Iliescu's personal success in the presidential elections; and ultimately the Romanian population's dissatisfaction with Iliescu's government and person. Immediately following the Revolution it was necessary for someone take responsibility to ensure the situation did not deteriorate further. The lack of an alternative political elite in Romania facilitated a rotation of the existing Communist elite as a result of which a formerly marginalised faction within the Romanian Communist Party came to power. However, merely reforming the old system did little to solve the crisis in Romanian society, agriculture and industry. As this became increasingly obvious and as the passing of time allowed alternative political elites and parties to organise themselves more effectively, Iliescu's popularity decreased and the 1996 elections resulted in his defeat.

The electoral systems have also influenced the course of consolidation. Hungary's electoral laws are the most complicated[2], combining majority and proportional representation, and emphasising the importance of a unicameral Parliament in relation to the President, who, however, retains some important powers of intervention[3]. The Hungarian Parliament has 386 seats which are apportioned by simple majority, proportional representation and compensation. Of these 386 seats, 176 are directly elected by single-member constituencies in individual contests on a two-round majority basis. A further 152 Deputies are elected from 20 County Party Lists using a proportional system with a 5% hurdle. The remaining 58 seats are allocated from National Party Lists using the remaining votes which were not needed to win. Each voter casts two votes, one for the local constituency and one for the County List. If neither vote is needed to elect a representative it is added to a pool from which the 58 seats are filled using the National Party Lists[4].

However, this system of mixed proportional and majority voting has caused a problem of legitimacy because it results in the majority of parliamentary seats being apportioned according to Party Lists rather than actual constituencies won. Thus, in the 1990 elections, of the 386 Deputies, only 176 won their constituency while 210 were nominated from Party Lists[5]. In addition, the system exaggerates the number of parliamentary seats gained in

---

[2] For more information on the Hungarian Electoral Law, see Arato, Andrew, 'Election, Coalition and Constitution in Hungary', *The Hungarian Quarterly*, Vol. 35, No. 135, Autumn 1994.
[3] For a comparison of presidential terms of appointment and powers, see Appendix XIII, XIV, XV, XVI.
[4] Grey, Jason, *Hungary*. Taken from the Internet on 26.11.96.
Http: //ww2.artsci.wustl.edu/~ps4271/hungary.html.
[5] Merkel, Wolfgang, Sandschneider, Eberhard, Segert, Dieter, (Hrsg.), *Systemwechsel II: Die Institutionalisierung der Demokratie*, Leske & Budrich 1996, p. 231.

relation to the percentage of votes. Table 3 (overleaf) shows the disproportionate effect the system has on election results.

This causes a lack of transparency which has led to the perception that the system ensures party elites remain in Parliament regardless of their actual performance in an electoral constituency. Although by limiting the number of parties in Parliament, the electoral law has furthered democratic consolidation; it has at the same time hindered systemic legitimisation and popular identification with political parties.

Table 3
Vote-Mandate Relationship of the Hungarian Parties

1990 Elections

Party	% Votes	% Mandates	% Disproportion
MDF	24.7	42.7	+18
SZDSZ	21.4	24.4	+3

1994 Elections

Party	% Votes	% Mandates	% Disproportion
MSZP	33.0	54.1	+21.1
SZDSZ	19.7	17.9	-1.8

MDF: Hungarian Democratic Forum
SZDSZ: Alliance of Free Democrats
MSZP: Hungarian Socialist Party

Source: Adapted from Merkel, Wolfgang, Sandschneider, Eberhard, Segert, Dieter, (Hrsg.), *Systemwechsel II: Die Institutionalisierung der Demokratie*, Leske und Budrich 1996, p. 231.

Hungary has suffered regularly from exceedingly low turn-outs at elections, especially in local elections[6]. The lack of interest in local elections can partly be traced to the highly centralised nature of the Communist state. Local and district councils had virtually no powers or areas of competence which were not supervised by central government. This has produced a legacy of disinterest in local elections. Although a reorganisation of Hungarian administration, giving local authorities more powers and independence, has begun, it has yet to affect voter behaviour and perceptions. In addition, at the time of the elections, local party organisation was still at a low level and candidates suffered not only from a lack of financial resources, but also from the lack of clarity surrounding the electoral process and the future role of the administration itself.

The low turn-out can also be explained by the extraordinarily complicated Hungarian electoral law which serves to discourage voters who cannot understand the system and are unable to determine the effect their vote will have on the overall outcome of an election. In addition, the population had already been to the polls several times by the time the local elections were held and had become weary of the election process. However, despite these problems, the system has ensured stability in Hungarian parliamentary politics and the same six parties entered Parliament after the 1990 and 1994 elections.

The Romanian and Czech systems also employ proportional representation and rely on a 5% parliamentary hurdle, but both are far less complicated than the Hungarian and incorporate a bicameral system consisting of a Parliament and a Senate.

After the dissolution of the Czech and Slovak Federative Republic on 1 January 1993, the 200 strong Czech National Council became the Chamber of Deputies, the Czech Republic's Parliament[7]. The Parliament is elected using multi-member

---

[6] The local elections on 30 September-14 October, 1990 produced a turn-out of 40% in the first round and 29% in the second. As a result, half the local seats were filled from party slates and half were filled from candidate lists. Ibid. Grey, Jason, *Hungary*. Http: //ww2.artsci.wustl.edu/~ps4271/hungary.html.
[7] *Open Media Research Institute (OMRINet)*. Taken from the Internet on 26.11.96. Http: //www.omir.cz.

constituencies of similar size. Voters cast their votes among Party Lists, but maintain a preference vote for the choice of candidate within a Party List. Seats are assigned within the constituency by dividing the total number of valid votes cast plus the number of seats plus one. The remainders are recovered by applying the same system to the whole national territory[8].

The Senate, consisting of 81 members, is elected according to relative majority in single member constituencies at a later date[9]. One third of the Senators are elected every other year and serve a six year term. According to the Constitution (Article 106), the Federal Assembly is responsible for creating the Senate. However, as long as no Senate exists, its powers lie with the Federal Assembly, that is the Czech Chamber of Deputies. Because the Assembly was originally conceived as a subordinate body within the Federation, the leading political role it gave itself after the dissolution of the Federation was not originally legitimated by popular consent or legal powers. There has been speculation that the Chamber's fear of losing political powers contributed to the four year delay in formation of the Senate. The first senatorial elections finally took place in November 1996.

The creation of a Senate has been strongly criticised, and both Klaus and the leader of the Social Democratic Party, Milos Zeman, have called for its abolition[10]. Although the Constitution requires that three fifths of all Deputies and three fifths of all Senators register their approval before international treaties concerning Human Rights and fundamental freedoms are accepted; and that an absolute majority of Senators approve a declaration of war, the stationing of foreign troops on Czech soil or changes to the electoral law, the Senate possesses few real powers[11]. The perceived unimportance of the Senate was reflected in the low 35%

---

[8] *CIA World Fact Book 1993*. Taken from the Internet on 26.11.96.
Http: //physig.ph.kd.ac.uk/local/cia/1994/65.html.
[9] 'Die Partei von Ministerpräsident Klaus liegt in Führung', *FAZ*, Montag, 18 November 1996.
[10] Ibid. 'Die Partei von Ministerpräsident Klaus liegt in Führung', *FAZ*, Montag, 18 November 1996.
[11] Senechal, David, A., *Czechoslovakia*. Taken from the Internet on 26.11.96.
Http: //ww2.artsci.wustl.edu/~ps4272/czs-ds.html.

electoral turn-out in the first round of the 1996 senatorial elections[12].

The Romanian Parliament, the Chamber of Deputies, originally had 396 members[13], but after the 1990 elections this number was reduced to 343, of which 15 are set aside for minority organisations, while the Senate was increased in size from 119 to 143 members[14]. The Deputies and Senators are elected using a system of proportional representation, while the President is not elected by Parliament as in Hungary and the Czech Republic, but by popular vote. In addition, the Romanian President also fulfils an important political role, making Romania unique in this respect as far as this study is concerned. Presidential candidates must register at least one month before elections are due and must collect at least 100 000 signatures in order to be included in the ballot. This is intended to limit the number of presidential candidates and prevent the electoral campaign from becoming too fragmented and confusing. But, the initially very low parliamentary threshold and number of signatures, 251[15], which parliamentary candidates had to produce to stand for election, meant that a wide range of parties and interests were represented, to the extent that the 1990 Romanian Parliament was excessively fragmented.

Although the electoral law provides that all parties have equal access to the Romanian media, this has not always been the case, especially during the first two electoral campaigns. At this time, the majority of the Romanian media was still state-controlled, dependent on and sympathetic to the incumbent government. However, despite certain irregularities in the Romanian elections, foreign observers have generally agreed that they have been valid and accurate.

---

[12] Although the ruling coalition maintained its majority in the Senate, the strongest party within the coalition, the Civic Democratic Party, was deprived of an outright majority. For the results of the senatorial elections, see Appendix XXVI.
[13] Staar, Richard, F., (Ed.), *The 1991 Yearbook on International Communist Affairs*, Hoover Institution Press 1991, p. 336.
[14] Press Department of the Romanian Embassy, Bonn.
[15] Grey, Jason, *Romania*. Taken from the Internet on 26.11.96.
Http: //ww2.artsci.wustl.edu/~ps4271/rom-jg.html.

Despite numerous changes of allegiance by Deputies within the Parliaments, all three national systems have succeeded in providing relative parliamentary stability. In 1994, the governing Hungarian Democratic Forum was defeated, and in 1996 the Romanian government under Prime Minister Nicolae Vacariou and President Ion Iliescu was forced to relinquish power. To date, only the Czech coalition government has remained undefeated, although with a minimal one seat majority[16]. Despite their differences, the electoral systems have succeeded in forming an accepted legal basis for a democratic system of competitive politics.

The nature of the political groupings which formed after the 1989 Revolutions have also to a large extent been dependent on the nature of the previous regime and the Revolution which removed it, although some have formed themselves on the basis of a pre-Communist historical tradition. Therefore, although similar patterns of development can be discerned between the countries and in relation to West European party cleavages, there remain some important differences. Political elites which were active in inter-war and pre-1948 parties have returned to political life, but found it difficult to adapt to the present-day situation and conditions of transition. Thus, in all of the historical parties a damaging generation conflict, often ending in fragmentation, has occurred. Some parties have succumbed to a populism and right-wing extremism which is reminiscent of the inter-war period, but which also includes elements of left-wing ideology. These parties have been able to identify the fears and insecurities of a population in social and economic flux and, by using well-known names and proposing simple solutions, they have been able to secure a certain amount of popular support and attention.

In addition, the names of some parties do not reflect the true nature of their political programme and therefore cause confusion. Although this confusion is often intentional, it is also true to say that many people in Central and Eastern Europe see no contradiction in proclaiming themselves to be at the same time a

---

[16] After being expelled from the Social Democratic Party, Tomas Teplik and Jozef Wagner both voted with the government. Jozef Wagner was expelled for accepting the coalition's 1997 budget proposal. *OMRI Daily Digest*, No. 59, Part II, 25 March 1997.

nationalist, a liberal, in favour of a market economy, but also of state intervention in strategic areas of the economy to ensure social welfare. In addition, many political parties advocate policies which stem from the inter-war period, or before. This 'freezer effect' and resultant confusion seems to be a reflection of the confusion of political identity which the experience of Communism has left behind. But it is a confusion which must be confronted and overcome if democratic consolidation is to be successful in the long term. The following comparison aims to overcome some of this confusion and place the main Hungarian, Czech and Romanian political parties in a recognisable cleavage pattern to facilitate an evaluation of their contribution to democratic consolidation.

3.1: Conservative Parties

In the immediate aftermath of the 1989 Revolutions, conservative and christian democratic parties enjoyed the advantage of embodying the political antithesis to the Communist Party and its ideology in the popular conscience. However, the conservative parties in the region which specifically incorporated nationalism and the myth of a nation united after Communism in their political programme have found it difficult to distance themselves from more extreme conservative-nationalist elements. The nationalist-populist extremist groupings subscribe to a national ideology which is more reminiscent of the inter-war period and demand an active interventionist role for the state. If these extreme elements are not dealt with, conservative parties risk becoming populist and anti-modern[17].

3.1.1: Hungarian Democratic Forum

This has been particularly true of the Hungarian Democratic Forum (MDF – *Magyar Demokrata Fórum*). The Hungarian Democratic Forum was originally founded in 1987 in Lakitelek by

---

[17] For an interesting discussion on conservatism in post-Communist societies, see Schöpflin, George, 'Konservative Politik und konservative Faktoren in den postkommunistischen Gesellschaften', *Transit*, No. 4, Summer 1992.

a group of Hungarian intellectuals who were sympathetic to traditional Hungarian nationalist-populist ideas[18]. They propagated not only a national-Christian ideology similar to that of the inter-war period, but had also incorporated folkish ideas and were interested in the idea of a 'Third Way'[19]. They were mainly concerned with the fate of the Hungarian nation, both in the existential and physical sense, and were therefore opposed to the urban opposition grouping of radical intellectuals in Budapest, who were in favour of radical transformation and westernization and would later form the Alliance of Free Democrats (SZDSZ). The MDF's opposition to the Free Democrats was also tinged with anti-Semitism. The rivalry between the MDF and the Free Democrats served to reawaken the historical Hungarian urban-populist debate, and it is this historical cultural division of values which, to a large extent, still dominates Hungary's political landscape.

Although the MDF was originally orientated towards a 'Third Way', as a political party it incorporated diverse elements and attempted to create a right of centre conservative party. It increased its support amongst the traditional Christian middle class, but continued to harbour radical nationalist-populist groupings. Initially, the christian democratic faction within the party, supported by Joszef Antall, later to become Prime Minister, managed to marginalise the radical nationalist-populist faction, but after the 1990 elections this group successfully exerted increasing pressure.

This was possible because the MDF aimed to develop a new national identity based on the Christian morals of a Hungarian middle class which would form the base of its support. As this class no longer existed, the MDF attempted to recreate it while enforcing an organic ethnic solidarity and cultural distinctiveness via its homogenising authority, which would enable the Hungarian nation to fulfil its collective destiny. Therefore, having promised stability

---

[18] Segert, Dieter, Machos, Csilla, *Parteien in Osteuropa*, West Deutscher Verlag 1995, p. 65.
[19] Márkos, György, G., *Party System and Political Cleavage Translation in Hungary*, Working Papers of Political Science, No. 3, Institute for Political Science of the Hungarian Academy of Sciences 1996. The 'Third Way' describes the attempt to combine the best aspects of both Communism and Capitalism.

and a non-radical transformation, after its victory in the 1990 elections the MDF embarked on a *Kulturkampf*. MDF supporters increasingly came to occupy important positions within Parliament, the state and other public organisations. By appointing persons sympathetic to it to oversee the State Property Agency's operations, the MDF intervened in the privatisation process, thereby hoping to recreate a propertied middle class which in the past had formed the national-conservative electoral basis. However, this led to clientilism and an economically damaging compensation programme[20].

The MDF also found it difficult to tolerate individualism and criticism of its historic mission. An independent, critical media was interpreted as damaging the cause of the nation and national-conservative and radical national-populist elements within the MDF united in their attempts to purge it. This culminated in the 1991 'media wars', during which the Heads of Hungarian Television and Radio were dismissed[21].

In addition, a campaign with decidedly anti-Semitic traits was started against 'Cosmopolitan Liberal-Bolshevik' intellectuals with the aim of enforcing Hungarian Christian ideas and morals. As early as June 1990, one of the founders of the MDF, S. Csoóri, had published an essay which claimed that following the Holocaust, Hungarian Jewry was incapable of assimilation and was instead attempting to assimilate Hungarians via the Alliance of Free Democrats[22]. It was the presence of anti-Semitic elements in the political system which led to the rapprochement between the Hungarian Socialist Party and the Alliance of Free Democrats in the form of a *Democratic Charta 91*; a civic movement which publishes papers on anti-democratic trends in the new system[23]. The *Democratic Charta* represents the end of the Socialists' isolation and, by its refusal to become part of it, the start of FIDESZ's move

---

[20] Ibid. Márkos, György, *Party System and Political Cleavage Translation in Hungary*.
[21] Ibid. Márkus, György, *Party System and Political Cleavage Translation in Hungary*.
[22] Ibid. Márkus, György, *Party System and Political Cleavage Translation in Hungary*.
[23] Ibid. Segert, Dieter, Machos, Csilla, *Parteien in Osteuropa*, p. 87.

towards the right and the national-conservative bloc. The expulsion of several extreme nationalists from the MDF made this option more attractive to FIDESZ and strengthened its belief that such a move would lead to its inclusion in government.

Although restoration of the nation's organic identity was the MDF's acknowledged historical mission, it also aimed to restore a capitalist social market economy and integrate Hungary into the European Union and NATO. This dualism led to conflict with the more radical national-populist grouping within the party. A radical nationalist group had been present within the MDF from its inception. It crystallised around István Csurka, vice-president and eminent party leader, who created the Hungarian Road Movement as a faction within the MDF[24]. It was an ultra-nationalist, radical right-wing group with anti-Semitic features which organised demonstrations and meetings to publicise its ideology. Csurka refused to support the ratification of the Hungarian-Ukrainian Basic Treaty because it recognised the inviolability of national borders. As a result, he and six others were expelled from the MDF's parliamentary faction and three new extreme right-wing groups were created. The most important of them was Csurka's Party of Hungarian Justice and Life (MIEP – *Magyar Igazság és Elet Pártja*).

The MDF's concern with the Hungarian nation's destiny led to over emphasis of symbolic issues and the neglect of practical issues in the political discourse. Its clumsy attempts to ideologise life was a stark contrast to the de-ideologised pragmatic years of the Kádár era and served to alienate a population socialised under 'Goulash Communism' to whom material welfare, rather than ideological purity, was the main concern.

Although the MDF government survived until the scheduled elections in 1994, it lost the confidence and support of the majority of the population and suffered electoral defeat (see 3.6.1)[25]. Despite the fact that the population demonstrated its hostility towards ideology, and it was precisely the nationalist stance and

---

[24] Ágh, Attila, Kurtán, Sándor, (Eds.), *Democratization and Europeanization in Hungary: The First Parliament (1990-1994)*, Hungarian Centre for Democracy Studies 1995, p. 204.

[25] For detailed election results, see Appendix XVII, XVIII, XIX, XX.

Kulturkampf which were the main causes of its electoral defeat, the MDF has continued to use anti-Semitism as a means of discrediting the coalition government led by the Socialist Party. The Free Democrats are presented as a demonic minority manipulating the Socialists. This interpretation is also employed by those within the Socialist Party who cannot come to terms with government policy.

Despite this, the MDF did make a positive contribution to the institutional consolidation of the new democratic system and the introduction of a capitalist market economy. However, the MDF's self-perceived historical mission to rejuvinate the Hungarian nation led to the loss of the initial advantage which, as a result of reforms introduced by the previous regime, Hungary had possessed at the start of transformation, and prevented Hungarian citizens forming a positive relationship with government.

3.1.2: Christian Democratic People's Party

From 1990-1994, the MDF's coalition partners were the Independent Smallholders (FKGP) and the Christian Democratic People's Party (KDNP – *Kereszténydemokrata Néppárt*). The KDNP descended from the historic Democratic People's Party, which was founded in November 1944. It was transformed into the Democratic People's Party in September 1945 and in the 1947 elections, the last free elections before the 1948 Communist takeover, the party gained second place. However, by 1949 the majority of its leaders had emigrated and it dissolved itself. It was the last of the historical parties in Hungary to re-establish itself on 30 September, 1989[26].

From the start of the 1990 election campaign the KDNP presented itself as the MDF's potential coalition partner and, as a member of the government coalition from 1990 until 1994, it has had great difficulty in developing an independent profile. Its programme claims to be christian democratic and, although the KDNP supports the creation of a social market economy, it also contains nationalist elements and strongly emphasises state intervention to correct the failures of the free market and ensure that social benefits are provided. It also emphasises the moral

---

[26] Ibid. Segert, Dieter, Machos, Csilla, *Parteien in Osteuropa*, p. 66.

importance of work in contrast to capital[27]. As a result of its ideologisation of work, the KDNP has increasingly become identified with the Unionist lobby. Particular importance is also placed on the position of pensioners, families with children and the poor. The party aims to revive the Hungarian nation by instigating a renewal of Christian morals which, in areas such as education, the media and culture, the state is expected to encourage and support. It is therefore also strongly linked to the Roman Catholic Church and is perceived by many as a Church lobby. Its main support is based regionally in eastern Hungary and in the Catholic vote, pensioners, poor families with numerous children and those who are involved in the most physical forms of labour in industry and agriculture[28].

Although the KDNP has a relatively stable voter base, as its policies are based on a particular world view, rather than a specific political programme, this base remains limited. The current leadership is divided as to the best means to increase its voter base. One group favoured joining the far-right National Alliance, which is led by the Smallholders and whose president is a member of the KDNP, while another group advocated forming an alliance with the more moderate conservative parties. However, the attempt to form a Civic Alliance with FIDESZ and the MDF failed, mainly due to the opposition of the KDNP chairman, György Giczy. The ensuing dispute within the KDNP culminated in Giczy's refusal to accept a Supreme Court's ruling which annulled his 1996 election as party chairman[29]. His re-election as party chairman on 21 June, 1997, with 133 votes to his rival, Zsolt Semjen's, 102 votes, would seem to indicate that the more radical faction within the KDNP has succeeded in gaining influence[30]. However, as the moderate platform may be unwilling to accept an electoral alliance with the Smallholders, the party may split.

3.1.3: Independent Smallholders Party

The Hungarian Independent Smallholders Party (FKGP – *Független Kisgazda-, Földmunkás-és Polgári Párt*) was originally

---

[27] Ibid. Segert, Dieter, Machos, Csilla, *Parteien in Osteuropa*, p. 67.
[28] Ibid. Segert, Dieter, Machos, Csilla, *Parteien in Osteuropa*, p. 74.
[29] *RFE/RL Newsline*, Vol. 1, No. 24, Part II, 5 May 1997.
[30] *RFE/RL Newsline*, Vol. 1, No. 58, Part II, 23 June 1997.

founded in 1930 and was one of the most important political parties in Hungary until it was disbanded in 1948[31]. During the Horthy regime it was the main opposition party and in the 1945 elections it gained 57% of the votes. The historical Smallholders Party represented the interests of small farmers and was orientated towards the family group, but collectivisation and industrialisation have drastically reduced this traditional support base. This has forced the contemporary FKGP, which was re-founded in November 1988, to search for a relevant political agenda, which it thought to have found in the issue of land restitution[32].

The FKGP became a single issue party whose main aim was the privatisation and restitution of land to the owners of 1947[33]. In this respect it differed from all the other political parties in Hungary. The major problem with this strategy was that, since 1947 houses, roads and other buildings have been built on what was originally agricultural land and the implementation of such a restitution policy would inevitably cause new injustice. The FKGP's insistence on land restitution led to its gradual radicalisation and internal conflict. In addition, the party has suffered from a generation conflict with many of the older leaders insistent not only on land restitution, but also on lustration policies aimed at revealing those who cooperated with the Communist Party. These conflicts caused the FKGP to split into two factions; a more authoritarian coalition of right-wing conservatives and a civic-liberal grouping, which has since left the party.

The split was catalysed by the election of József Torgyán, a radical conservative nationalist, as party president. However, a more moderate group, although representing a minority within the party, managed to gain the support of the majority of the party's Deputies. This group comprised of 33 Deputies and was referred to as the '33 Smallholders'. Thus, although from October 1991, there was only one *de jure* Smallholders faction in Parliament, *de facto* there were two groups, each proclaiming itself to be the rightful faction. The chaos was further increased when, on 24 February,

---

[31] Ibid. Segert, Dieter, Machos, Csilla, *Parteien in Osteuropa*, p. 67.

[32] Ibid. Segert, Dieter, Machos, Csilla, *Parteien in Osteuropa*, p. 68.

[33] Ibid. Segert, Dieter, Machos, Csilla, *Parteien in Osteuropa*, p. 68.

1992, Torgyán, still the legal party leader, announced that his faction, consisting of twelve members, would leave the government coalition[34].

This decision was partly a result of the Constitutional Court's decision in October 1990, which prohibited the restitution of land to the former owners of 1947[35], and enabled Torgyán's faction to avoid sanctioning the government's compensation programme. Torgyán announced that his group had formed a new opposition faction. It can be described as a right-wing opposition grouping. This forced the group of '33' Smallholders, which had in the meantime increased to '36', to form another Smallholders Party. They remained within the government coalition and in November 1993, in order to distinguish themselves from the Torgyán's group, founded, along with three other breakaway Smallholder grouplets, the United Smallholders Party (EKGP – *Egyesült Kisgazdapárt*)[36]. Although Torgyán's more radical group of ten MPs revived the Independent Smallholder's Party, this party bears little resemblance to the historical party whose name it bears.

The FKGP has become increasingly populist and susceptible to anti-democratic, authoritarian tendencies. Its voter base is similar to that of the other people's party, the KDNP, and comes mainly from those who are engaged in hard physical labour in industry and agriculture. It supports the introduction of a presidential system and the reduction of the Constitutional Court's importance and significance. Land restitution remains its central programmatic point, but it also supports the disbanding of agricultural collectives. It has acquired a strong nationalist character which forms a curious partner for its increasingly populist, left-wing economic policies. It supports the right of every family to live in a flat and the right of every citizen to work. It does not accept the existence of unemployment. As a radical anti-intellectual party representing extreme nationalist positions, its increased popularity must be a cause for concern.

---

[34] Ibid. Ágh, Attila, Kurtán, Sándor, (Eds.), *Democratization and Europeanization in Hungary: The First Parliament (1990-1994)*, p. 204.
[35] Ibid. Segert, Dieter, Machos, Csilla, *Parteien in Osteuropa*, p. 93.
[36] Ibid. Segert, Dieter, Machos, Csilla, *Parteien in Osteuropa*, p. 93.

The FKGP does not represent modern conservatism or christian democracy. It is obsessed with the Hungarian nation's destiny and the establishment of Christian morals, aiming to purge Hungary of liberal and Communist evil. Along with radical sections of the MDF and the KDNP, it advocates a strong state and promotes state intervention in the economy to create social justice. All three parties support a Hungarian nationalist-populist ideology which is increasingly inappropriate to modern Hungarian society. Thus, Hungary lacks a strong, modern conservative party, and the right-wing of the party system remains in flux.

The election of an anti-liberal, radical populist candidate as MDF party leader with a 60% majority at the MDF Congress in February 1996, indicated that the new leadership would be more interested in forming a strategic alliance with the extreme right-wing Smallholders rather than the more moderate FIDESZ and KDNP. As a result, half of the MDF parliamentary faction resigned and formed the Independent Hungarian Democratic Party (FMDP – *Független Magyar Demokrata Párt*), led by I. Szabó[37]. This party has since renamed itself the Hungarian Democratic People's Party (MDNP – *Magyar Demokrata Neppart*)[38]. Although committed to the nation, the MDNP has rejected the radical national-conservatism which the MDF and FKGP now represent. However, as it still lacks a clear political profile, apart from being 'not the MDF', it must form a strategic alliance with the other moderate conservative parties to be assured of a place in the next Parliament. Another party which may gain importance as a member of the moderate right-wing in the future, is the Conservative Party-Union of Farmers and Citizens (KP-GPSZ – *Konzervatív Párt-Gazdák és Polgárok Szövetsége*) which was founded in September 1993. It views itself as the legal successor of the historical Hungarian Conservative Party, which was in turn founded as a result of a split in the Independent Smallholders Party in 1846[39].

---

[37] Ibid. Márkus, György, *Party System and Political Cleavage Translation in Hungary*.
[38] Central European Online, *Hungarian Democratic People's Party*. Taken from the Internet on 7.3.97. Http: //www.centraleurope.com.
[39] Ibid. Segert, Dieter, Machos, Csilla, *Parteien in Osteuropa*, p. 92.

Thus, at present, there are two right-wing blocs in the Hungarian party system; a radical, populist, anti-liberal bloc led by the FKGP and radical sections of the MDF and KDNP, and supported by extra-parliamentary parties of the nationalist far-right; and a more moderate bloc led by FIDESZ in alliance with the liberal wing of the MDF and the KDNP. In an attempt to regain political influence, the MDF and FIDESZ have agreed to run joint candidates in the 1998 elections, but it is doubtful whether either will be a significant force in the next Parliament[40].

3.1.4: National Peasant Party/Christian Democracy

The conservative bloc in Romania is headed by the Romanian National Peasant Party (PNTCD – *Partidul National Taranesc Crestin Democrat*). The historical National Peasant Party was founded on 26 October, 1926 as the result of the alliance between the Peasant Party, which had been founded in the Old Kingdom in 1918, and the National Party, founded in Transylvania on 14 December, 1881[41]. It was Romania's largest inter-war political party and in the last free elections in 1946, won an estimated 70% of the popular vote, before being banned by the Communist Party in 1947[42]. The National Peasant Party/Christian Democracy is somewhat unique because it has consolidated itself, evading the disintegration which has befallen the majority of the historical parties.

The party merged with the Christian National Peasant Party and with the Christian Democratic Youth movement, which had been founded by students a few days after Ceausescu's fall. The Christian Democratic Youth Movement has become the youth wing of the National Peasant Party. Thereafter, the party was renamed the National Peasant Party/Christian Democracy and began

---

[40] *RFE/RL Newsline*, Vol. 1, No. 172, Part II, 4 December 1997.
[41] Gabanyi, Anneli Ute, 'Politische Parteien in Rumänien nach der Wende', *Südosteuropa*, Vol. 44, No. 1-2, 1994, p. 32.
[42] Ibid. Staar, Richard, F., (Ed.), *The 1991 Yearbook on International Communist Affairs*, p. 336.

publishing a daily newspaper, *Dreptatea*, 'Justice', on 7 February, 1990[43].

The PNTCD is a traditional christian democratic party and is one of the best organised political parties in Romania. Its members tend to be either very old, or very young. Although the advanced age of many of the party's leading figures caused tension with the younger generation, some of whom left to found new parties, it is the party's highly motivated young members who have been instrumental in setting up territorial organisational structures, such as worker's, youth, women's and union organisations, as well as study circles.

Despite its good organisation and active membership, the PNCTD has been unable to regain its traditional voting base in Transylvania and amongst the peasants and has a low peasant membership, approximately 15%[44]. The votes of the Romanian population in Transylvania have been captured by the nationalist parties and the majority of the peasant population still votes for Iliescu and the Party of Social Democracy in Romania. The PNCTD's main support now comes from the well-educated urban population and workers.

The PNTCD aims to establish a functioning market economy by increasing the pace of privatisation and investment and by providing government support for agricultural restructuring. It advocates the separation of Church and state, but wants to re-establish Christian values to fill the vacuum Communism has left behind, planning to reinstate religion as a subject at school and university. It recognises the right to strike and equal rights for all ethnic minorities and religious groups[45]. It promotes an enlightened patriotism and considers a constitutional monarchy could act as a guarantor of stability and democratic consolidation. It is also, along

---

[43] Ibid. Staar, Richard, F., (Ed.), *The 1991 Yearbook on International Communist Affairs*, p. 336.
[44] Ibid. Gabanyi, Anneli Ute, 'Politische Parteien in Rumänien nach der Wende', *Südosteuropa*, p. 33.
[45] The Programme was published in *Adevarul* on 27 January, 1990 and in *Dreptatea* on 14 April, 1990. Ibid. Staar, Richard, F., *The 1991 Yearbook on International Communist Affairs*, p. 336. See also The National Christian Democratic Peasant Party, Departments for Studies, Doctrine and Programs, *Synthesis of the Political Program (Draft)*, Bucharest January 1996.

with all Romanian political parties, in favour of union with Moldova[46]. The Peasant Party's presidential candidate in the 1992 elections was the wealthy businessman, Ion Ratiu, who had spent four decades in exile in London[47]. Consequently, he was completely unknown and the population was unable to identify with him. Having failed to win a significant majority in the 1990 elections, the PNCTD was instrumental in the formation of the electoral pact, the Democratic Convention of Romania (CDR), which aimed to avoid the repetition of a fragmented opposition splitting the votes against Iliescu and his party.

3.1.5: Democratic Convention of Romania

The Democratic Convention of Romania (CDR – *Conventia Democratica din România*) is a forum party consisting of 19 parties, the most important of which are the National Peasant/Christian Democratic Party, the Democratic Federation of Hungarians in Romania (UDMR), various Liberal Parties, the Social Democratic Party, Ecological Parties and various other non-party organisations[48]. Although the CDR is dominated by the PNCTD, it is not a homogenous group, containing classic parties, forum parties, historical parties and new parties, some of which are represented in Parliament and some not. Its supporters are young, well-educated, urban dwellers. They are often academics and represent a new middle class. In addition, the CDR has a great deal of support amongst workers and skilled craftsmen[49]. Its initial problem was that its members lacked the experience and political finesse to compete effectively with Iliescu, but since being in government, constant squabbles and tensions amongst its members are the main problems threatening the CDR's stability.

---

[46] Moldova, formerly Bessarabia, was annexed by Stalin after the Second World War. It was partly to regain control of Moldova that Romania became a member of the Axis.

[47] Ibid. Staar, Richard, F., *The 1991 Yearbook on International Communist Affairs*, p. 336.

[48] For a full list of the CDR's members, see Gabanyi, Anneli Ute, 'Politische Parteien in Rumänien nach der Wende'.

[49] Ibid. Gabanyi, Anneli Ute, 'Politische Parteien in Rumänien nach der Wende', p. 30.

Political Democratisation 233

In the 1992 parliamentary elections, the CDR gained 20.1% of the votes and had 82 Deputies. It gained 20.16% of the votes in the senatorial elections and had 4 Senators[50]. During the parliamentary term between 1992 and 1996, it presented itself convincingly as an alternative power with a clear political concept. In 1992 it had refused to join a PDSR led government, and the PDSR's subsequent coalition with three extremist parties served to increase the CDR's credibility. As one of its most important members is the Democratic Federation of Hungarians in Romania, the CDR categorically refused to work with the extremist parties.

3.1.6: Democratic Federation of Hungarians in Romania

The Democratic Federation of Hungarians in Romania (UDMR – *Uniunea Democrata Maghiara din România*) is in essence an ethnic interest group. It was founded on 25 December, 1989 as an umbrella organisation for all the political and non-political organisations of the Hungarian minority in Romania and aims to represent the Hungarian minority's national interests. Its most important members are the Magyar Christian Democratic Party, the Magyar Smallholders Party, the Independent Party, various Jewish organisations, the Cluj Liberal Circle, the Platform of Christian Democratic Unity and the Magyar Initiative of Transylvania[51].

The UDMR defines itself as a centre-right organisation. It supports swift reform and the introduction of democratic institutions, administrative de-centralisation and increased autonomy for local authorities. It alone demands that the Magyar minority in Transylvania be recognised as a national minority and be given personal, local and administrative autonomy. The UDMR has a stable voter basis which resembles that of a people's or a regional party. Its supporters are drawn from all members of the Hungarian minority. In addition, it has a large number of well-educated, highly motivated and experienced leaders. After the 1990 elections the UDMR was the second strongest party in the

---

[50] Ibid. Gabanyi, Anneli Ute, 'Politische Parteien in Rumänien nach der Wende', p. 28. See Appendix XXX.
[51] Ibid. Gabanyi, Anneli Ute, 'Politische Parteien in Rumänien nach der Wende', p. 43.

Romanian Parliament, but it was not accepted into the opposition faction and had to form a faction on its own.

In 1991 the UDMR joined the Democratic Convention, although its candidates still run separately in elections. This enabled the CDR to distance itself effectively from the extremist parties and legitimise itself as a democratic power in the Romanian political system. However, tensions remain between the UDMR and the CDR's members as, somewhat radicalised by the provocation of the extremist parties, the UDMR insists on a Constitutional revision to describe Romania as a multi-ethinc state and accept Hungarian as a second language.

In November 1996 the CDR won the parliamentary and senatorial elections. Its presidential candidate, the history Professor Emil Constantinescu, also won the 17 November run-off presidential election against the incumbent, Ion Iliescu. Constantinescu gained 54.4% of the votes and Iliescu 45.9% (see 3.6.3)[52]. Although the CDR won the elections, it does not possess an absolute majority in the Assembly of Deputies or the Senate. In order to form a stable government, the largest parliamentary party, the PNCTD formed a coalition with its fellow CDR member, the UDMR, and Petre Roman's opposition Democratic Party[53]. The success of the CDR is an expression of the Romanian population's yearning for change in the face of the relative stagnation under President Iliescu and the Party of Social Democracy in Romania. Unfortunately, the coalition has not proved to be as stable as had been hoped. Economic results have not been as good as predicted and the coalition has been plagued by in-fighting and constant bickering, all of which have served to plunge it from one crisis to another and limit the effectiveness of its transformation programme[54]. The Democratic Party's withdrawal from the

---

[52] *Open Media Research Institute (OMRINet)*, 'Romanian Election Results'. Taken from the Internet on 26.11.96. Http: //www.omri.cz. See Appendix XXXI, XXXII,. XXXIII.

[53] Shafir, Michael, 'Romania opts for Political Change', *Open Media Research Institute (OMRINet)*, Analytical Brief 436. Taken from the Internet on 26.11.96. Http: //www.omrinet.cz.

[54] Shafir, Michael, 'Romanian President puts Ball back into Democrats' Court', *RFE/RL Newsline*, Vol. 2, No. 11, Part II, 19 January 1998. The 1997 inflation rate remained over the 100% target.

coalition would leave a minority government and could result in early elections, which would further delay the implementation of the transformation programme. However, the Democratic Party itself recognises that there are no other alternative partners if transformation and democratisation are to be successful. Therefore, it is in its own interests to remain within the coalition or, failing this, give its support to a minority government led by the PNTCD[55].

3.1.7: Civic Forum

In contrast, the Czech umbrella movement, Civic Forum (OF – *Obcanské fórum*) disintegrated. But, in the same way that the consolidation represented by the CDR was necessary if stable political parties were to form in the excessively fragmented Romanian party system; Civic Forum's disintegration was necessary to facilitate the formation of structured political parties more suited to the tasks of government. Thus, paradoxically, both developments represent a consolidation of the party system.

The Czech Civic Forum movement was formed ten days after the fall of the Berlin Wall and encompassed several Czech opposition groups, including *Charter 77*. Its main leaders were dissident intellectuals who had distanced themselves from the immoral world of politics in favour of 'living the truth'. It was a loose organisation with no official membership structure or political programme. It included people of varying political convictions who were united by their opposition to the Communist regime. Although Civic Forum gained the most votes in the 1990 elections, it was generally accepted that the elections constituted a plebiscite on democracy. It set up a stable coalition with its sister organisation in Slovakia, Public Against Violence (VPN – *Verejnost proti násiliu*) and the Christian Democratic Movement. However, arguments over the future nature of the Czechoslovak state and the form of economic transformation, combined with the debate after the 1990 elections over whether to turn the movement into a political party, led to its disintegration in January 1991.

---

[55] *RFE/RL Newsline*, Vol. 2, No. 9, Part II, 15 January 1998. Also *RFE/RL Newsline*, Vol. 2, No. 23, Part II, 4 February 1998.

Although the loose organisational structure Civic Forum adopted was optimal for the purposes of the Velvet Revolution, a grouping within the movement centred around Vaclav Klaus, the Finance Minister and first chairman of Civic Forum, became convinced that in order to achieve electoral and governmental success, it was necessary to enter the arena of competitive politics as an organised and disciplined political party with a more traditional conservative orientation. But, as a result of their experience of 1968 and normalisation, many of the dissident intellectuals who had contributed to the formation of Civic Forum were disenchanted with political parties and wanted to maintain a broad based movement. In addition, they did not support Klaus' conservative orientation, which included a programme of shock therapy for the Czech economy.

The group around Vaclav Klaus left Civic Forum and formed the Civic Democratic Party (ODS). A Civic Movement, led by Jiri Dienstbier, then Foreign Minister, tried to present itself as a centrist liberal party, but failed to convince the electorate. Dienstbier is now the leader of the extra-parliamentary Free Democrats (SD – *Svobodní demokraté {Obcanské hnuti}*) who merged with the Liberal National Socialist Party (LSNS – *Liberalní strana národné sociální*)[56] in the hope of facilitating the clearance of the 5% hurdle in the 1996 elections. Another group, the Civic Democratic Alliance (ODA) also decided to become an independent political party, while another, Battek's Association for Social Democracy, tried to form an alliance with the revived Czechoslovak Social Democratic Party.

3.1.8: Civic Democratic Alliance

The Civic Democratic Alliance (ODA – *Obcanská demokratická aliance*) was one of the Civic Democratic Party's coalition partners and is politically closest to it. It identifies with British conservatism and is an avid supporter of the free market, placing social responsibility above social justice. It aims to reduce the state sector to an absolute minimum and hand over as many elements of the social welfare system as possible to the non-state sector.

---

[56] Although bearing a similar name, this is not a fascist party.

Unlike the ODS, the ODA is intellectually orientated and has an elite, rather than a mass membership. It relied on its competent leadership; Jan Kalvoda was vice-Prime Minister; V. Dlouhý was the Minister of Industry and Trade; and J. Skalický was the Minister for Privatisation, to increase its voter base. Its main support comes from the urbanised areas of central Bohemia and Prague, while it is poorly represented in south Bohemia and Moravia[57]. However, the departure of nearly all the former leadership figures as a result of a scandal concerning ananymous donations, threatens to obliterate the party from political life. Indeed, according to a public opinion poll carried out by *Sofres-Factum* and published on 24 February, 1998, support for the ODA had plummeted to 4.9%, lower that the 5% required to enter Parliament[58].

3.1.9: Civic Democratic Union/Czech People's Party

The Christian Democratic Union/Czech People's Party (KDU-CSL – *Krestanská a demokratická unie-Ceskoslovenská strana lidová*) was also one of the ODS's coalition partners. Its four main ideological tenets are the guarantee of personal freedom, the erection of a social market economy, and the importance of social and moral responsibility. Although it supported Klaus' economic policies, it consistently emphasised the necessity of a moral and spiritual renewal, and placed more emphasis than its coalition partners on federal, social and rural problems. It has been particularly active in its attempts to reactivate rural life, and suggested a federation of three Republics which would ensure Silesian and Moravian autonomy. In 1991, it split its party organisation into two, creating a Bohemian and a Silesian-Moravian organisation[59]. Its policy emphasis is reflected in the

---

[57] Hatschikjan, Magarditsch, A., Weilemann, Peter, R., (Hrsg.), *Die Parteienlandschaften in Osteuropa*, Schöningh 1994, p. 116.
[58] The former deputy chairman, Vladimir Dlouhy, and founder, Pavel Bratinka, have resigned, along with five other ODA Deputies. The scandal concerns a fictitious firm in the Virgin Islands which directed anonymous donations to the Party in 1996. *RFE/RL Newsline*, Vol. 2, No. 38, Part II, 25 February 1998.
[59] Ibid. Hatschikjan, Magarditsch, A., Weilemann, Peter, R., (Hrsg.), *Die Parteienlandschaften in Osteuropa*, p. 116.

regional structure of its support. It is weak in urban areas, in Prague and the highly industrialised north Bohemia, drawing most of its support from the rural population, especially in the Catholic parts of south Moravia.

3.1.10: Christian Democratic Party

The Christian Democratic Party (KDS – *Krestanskodemokratická strana*) is a small Christian party which was founded in December 1989. It aims to promote Christian morals in public life. It was the smallest of the ODS' coalition partners and has had difficulty forming a separate identity to the ODS. Its attempts to do so included a programme to revitalise agricultural production by supporting family farms and, although wholly in favour of the free market, it spoke out against selling agricultural land and woodland to foreigners. It also promoted an employment policy which focused on retraining the work force and providing subsidised work places for the long-term unemployed. Although it profited from the influence of its leader, *Charter 77* founder, Vaclav Benda, it has been unable to widen its social base and remains limited to the Catholic vote[60].

However, despite the fact that the KDS did not gain significant support in the 1992 elections, it secured two Ministerial positions, Education and the Environment as a result of its pre-election pact with the ODS, and on 18 November, 1995, at its annual conference, voted 101 in favour, to 69 against, to merge with the ODS. As a result of this decision, five of the ten KDS Deputies defected to the KDU-CSL. Thus, on September 12, 1995, the KDU-CSL became the third strongest party in the Czech Parliament[61].

3.1.11: Civic Democratic Party

The Civic Democratic Party (ODS – *Obcanská demokratická strana*), headed by Vaclav Klaus, has achieved the most sustained electoral success of all the political parties under discussion (see

---

[60] Ibid. Hatschikjan, Magarditsch, A., Weilemann, Peter, R., (Hrsg.), *Die Parteienlandschaften in Osteuropa*, p. 115.
[61] Ibid. Senechal, David, A., *Czechoslovakia*.
Http: //ww2.artsci.wustl.edu/~ps4271/czs_ds.html.

3.6.2)⁶². It successfully presented itself as a pragmatic, competent and realistic party. It promoted a modern idea of society and conservatism along with economic liberalism and a rapid transformation policy. It is firmly against state intervention, trusting the market to solve problems of distribution on its own. However, the actual policies pursued by Klaus' government demonstrate that the ideal of shock therapy and an absolutely free market is a flexible concept. Unemployment on the scale seen in Hungary and Romania was largely avoided by keeping workers employed using government sponsored employment and retraining schemes. Enterprises which were loss-making or bankrupt, but which had potentially good prospects, were kept afloat using government subsidies. Unemployment statistics were also low because large sections of the workforce, particularly women and the elderly, left the job market. Although it must also be noted that many of those who have left the official job market are engaged in the unofficial economy.

The ODS draws its votes mostly from those with a higher level of education who earn above average wages. Nevertheless, it managed to widen its social base and took on the character of a mass party, as its electoral success and membership numbers demonstrate. Although it defines itself as a centre-right conservative party, it has been able to collect votes from the liberal centre. It gains above average support in Prague, reflecting its urban nature, and below average support in Moravia, especially in the Catholic south where the KDU-CSL, the KDU and the Movement for Self Administrative Democracy-Association for Moravia and Silesia (HSD-SMS – *Hnutí za samosprávnou demokratická-Spolecnost pro Moravu a Slezko*) are strongly represented[63].

The initial success of Klaus' economic strategy convinced the Czech electorate that only a government led by the ODS was capable of effectively transforming the economy. Although the ODS had a much reduced majority after the 1996 parliamentary elections, the results of the senatorial elections shortly afterwards

---

[62] For electoral results, see Appendix XXII, XXIII, XXIV, XXV, XXVI.
[63] Ibid. Hatschikjan, Magarditsch, A., Weilemann, Peter, R., (Hrsg.), *Die Parteienlandschaften in Osteuropa*, p. 114.

confirmed its dominance of Czech politics and demonstrated the opposition's inability to present itself as a viable alternative. Indeed, the collapse of the government was mainly a result of internal party and coalition strife, rather than pressure from the opposition. It was the ODS' inability to deal effectively with ongoing economic difficulties, caused by the very policies which initially ensured its electoral success, which forced the resignation of Vaclav Klaus and the Czech government on 30 November, 1997[64].

Following the debacle, disillusioned members of the Civic Democratic Alliance founded a new party, the Party of Democratic Accord[65]. The ODS also split and on 17 January, 1998, 28 disgruntled ODS Deputies founded the Freedom Union and set up an official parliamentary faction. On 28 January, 1998, the Defence Minister, Michal Lobkowicz, left the ODS and joined the Freedom Union. The ODS chairman, former Foreign Minister Josef Zieleniec, has also left the party[66]. The fragmentation of the moderate conservative parties in the Czech Republic limits their prospects of electoral success at the next general election and they need to re-group if they are to retain political influence. But, if the process of consolidation is too lengthy or fraught, it may lead conservative voters who feel unable to support the Social Democratic Party to turn to the more radical right-wing in protest, thus causing polarisation of the Czech political landscape.

The polarisation already present in Czech politics was demonstrated during the 1998 presidential election. On 20 January, 1998, Vaclav Havel was successfully re-elected for his last term of office as President of the Czech Republic. However, he failed to gain the required majority in the first round ballots of the Chamber of Deputies and the Senate, and only gained a one vote majority in the second round ballot[67]. In addition, the mainstream parties'

---

[64] *RFE/RL Newsline*, Vol. 1, No. 169, Part II, 1 December 1997.
[65] *RFE/RL Newsline*, Vol. 2, No. 8, Part II, 14 January 1998.
[66] *RFE/RL Newsline*, Vol. 2, No. 13, Part II, 21 January 1998.
[67] Naegele, Jolyon,. 'Havel narrowly wins Re-election', *RFE/RL Newsline*, Vol. 2, No. 14, Part II, 22 January 1998. In the first round ballot, Havel received the support of 91 of the 200 Deputies in the Chamber of Deputies and 39 of the 81

decision not to present any other candidates meant Havel's opponents were the leader of the extremist Republican Party, Miroslav Sladek, who spent the day of the election in detention as a result of ignoring summonses over alleged incitement of ethnic hatred during a visit by Chancellor Kohl, and the Communist astrophysicist, Stanislav Fischer[68]. Despite the obvious unsuitability of such candidates, many Deputies did not vote for Havel in the first round ballot. The result was described by the KDU-CSL Chairman, Josef Lux, as an:

> '...expression of Czech political pettiness... an effort at humiliating someone before he is elected.'

Vaclav Klaus and Milos Zeman both stated the election was a reflection of the divisions in Czech society and the balance of forces as represented in Parliament. The collapse of Klaus' government seems to support this view, but the lack of any viable alternative presidential candidate also indicates the vindictive intent behind the lack of support for Havel in the first round ballot. Such behaviour has been encouraged by the ongoing political uncertainty. If political pettiness and uncertainty continue and affect other parliamentary votes, transformation will be delayed and create unwelcome uncertainty for the Czech Republic's accession negotiations with the European Union and NATO.

Another feature of the systems under discussion is the existence of Peasant Parties which were historically strongly averse to Communism, but which now promote an essentially Communist ideology in the form of large-scale state intervention in the market, the retention of large strategic sections of the economy in state ownership, absolute job security, collective values and social egalitarianism. Thus, many parties which describe themselves as Peasant, Agrarian or People's, are often left-wing and adhere to an ideology of state intervention and what is essentially a limited socialist market economy.

Senators. In the second ballot, 99 Deputies and 47 Senators supported Havel's re-election. See Appendix XXVII.
[68] Ibid. Naegele, Jolyon,. 'Havel narrowly wins Re-election', *RFE/RL Newsline*.

Although a small party, the Czech Agrarian Party provides an interesting example of a reactivated party which was historically opposed to Communism, but which now promotes an essentially Communist ideology in the form of large-scale state intervention in the market, a limited the private sector, permanent employment and social egalitarianism.

3.1.12: Czech Agrarian Party

Originally founded in 1899, the Agrarians were the strongest political party in the inter-war years[69]. The historical Agrarian Party's electoral base was focussed on the individual, small-scale farmer and during the early post-war period it defended the rights of independent farmers against nationalisation. Now the party defends cooperatives faced with privatisation. It has changed its ideological stance from favouring independent, individual farmers, to supporting the very cooperatives it once fought against. Yet, paradoxically, this policy has enabled it to continue to represent the interests of its traditional voter base, the farmers. In 1991 it merged with the unsuccessful Socialist Party (CSS – *Ceskoslovenská strana socialistická*) and Green Party to form a Liberal Social Union (LSU – *Liberální sociální unie*) chaired by Frantisek Trnka. Analysts have pointed out that the 1992 vote for the Liberal Democratic Union reproduced almost exactly the distribution of votes which was characteristic for the Agrarians before the Second World War[70].

In this case then, the Agrarian Party, now promoting a programme more similar to that of the Czech Social Democratic Party, has adapted rather successfully to the contemporary concerns of its traditional voters. However, since the formation of the LSU, the Socialist Party has partly disintegrated. The party's chairman, Jiri Vyvadil, left and, along with three Deputies from the extreme Republican Party, formed a Party of Independent Liberals. The

---

[69] Ibid. Senechal, David, A., *Czechoslovakia*.
Http: //ww2.artsci.wustl.edu/~ps4271/czs_ds.html.
[70] Pridham, Geoffry, Lewis, Paul, G., *Stabilising Fragile Democracies*, Routledge 1996, p. 37.

Socialsit Party secretary, Pavel Hirs, wants to re-name and reform the party and has called for the LSU's dissolution[71].

3.2: Liberal Parties

After the collapse of Communism, many hoped that the liberalisation of the economic and political system would also incorporate a general liberal renaissance. However, Communist ideology had emphasised the importance of the collective and social egalitarianism rather than the individual, so it has proved difficult for a radical liberalism to gain currency. In addition, historical liberal parties have been plagued by internal strife and fragmentation which discredited them and confused the electorate.

3.2.1: National Liberal Party

The National Liberal Party of Romania (PNL – *Partidul National Liberal*) was originally founded on 24 May, 1875[72]. It was re-established on 31 December, 1989 at a conference of former party members and younger activists and thereafter resumed publication of its daily newspaper, *Liberalul*, 'The Liberal', which had been closed down in 1947[73]. During the inter-war period and before the Communist take-over, the Liberal Party had been one of the main political parties in Romania, governing for the longest period of time and producing some of Romania's most prominent political figures. Although the Party was forcefully disbanded in 1948, some of its leaders remained in Romania and towards the end of the Ceausescu regime had issued a few statements of protest.

The PNL of 1990 supported the de-collectivisation of agriculture and aimed to introduce more private ownership of land and industry, ensure Trade Union rights, respect for Human Rights and equal rights for all the national minorities in Romania. It advocated

---

[71] Orbman, Jan, 'Czech Opposition Parties in Disarray', *RFE/RL Research Report*, Vol. 2, No. 16, 16 April 1993.
[72] Ibid. Gabanyi, Anneli Ute, 'Politische Parteien in Rumänien nach der Wende', p. 35.
[73] Ibid. Staar, Richard, F., (Ed.), *The 1991 Yearbook on International Communist Affairs*, p. 336.

the separation of Church and state and the resumption of traditional economic, political and cultural ties to Western Europe[74]. But it was also staunchly monarchist. Its 1990 presidential candidate, Radu Campeanu, had been imprisoned under Ceausescu and had later emigrated to Paris, where he had been living in exile for seventeen years. Although he came second in the first round elections, with 10.64% of the vote, he failed to beat Iliescu in the run-off[75].

Although after the 1990 elections the PNL was the third strongest party, in the 1992 parliamentary elections, after a bitter internal generation conflict, it only managed to gain 2.63% of the vote, and in the senatorial elections, gained 2.67% of the vote[76]. As a result of this dismal showing, a multitude of new liberal parties formed making distinction amongst them virtually impossible. The National Liberal Party was re-founded, a National Liberal Party-Democratic Convention (PNL-CD – *Partidul National Liberal-Conventia Democratica*) and a Liberal Party-93 (PL93), formed by younger activists, all came into being[77].

Thus, despite its strong historical tradition and respected politicians, both past and present, the PNL failed to consolidate its position in the Romanian political system. The reason for this lies in the complicated pattern of personal and political conflicts within the Liberal Party itself. There was not only a generation conflict between older political figures who had experienced inter-war democracy and younger members who had only experienced Ceausescuism, but also between those who had emigrated and those who had remained in Romania.

Since its 1993 fusion with the New Liberal Party, which enjoyed the support of members of the economic elite, the PNL has lost the

---

[74] The Programme was published in *Adevarul* on 12 January, 1990. Ibid. Staar, Richard, F., *The 1991 Yearbook on International Communist Affairs*, p. 336.

[75] Ibid. Staar, Richard, F., (Ed.), *The 1991 Yearbook on International Communist Affairs*, p. 336.

[76] Ibid. Gabanyi, Anneli Ute, 'Politische Parteien in Rumänien nach der Wende', p. 35.

[77] On 31 October, 1997, the National Liberal Party called on the Liberal Party and the Civic Alliance Party to merge with it. The Liberal Party is in favour of such a merger and the Civic Alliance Party's decision to rejoin the Democratic Convention indicates it is not averse to increased cooperation. *RFE/RL Newsline*, Vol. 1, No. 151, Part II, 3 November 1997.

sympathy of its nostalgia voters. The party's votes are now drawn from the new elites, most of whom have a high standard of living. Although the PNL is not represented in Parliament and is of marginal political importance, it was a founding member of the CDR and, having left in 1992, rejoined in 1994.

After continuously failing to gain significant electoral support, the Liberal Party-93 formed an electoral alliance with Nicolae Manolescu's Civic Alliance Party (PAC). Both parties left the CDR: the Civic Alliance in June 1996, as a result of the internal struggle over the CDR's presidential candidate; the Liberal Party-93 in March 1995, due to tensions with other Liberal factions within the CDR. The local election results of 1996 demonstrated that neither PAC nor the Liberal Party-93 were strong enough to make a political impression on their own. Although after the local elections in June 1996, in which close to half of those who were eligible to vote failed to do so[78], PAC gained Mayors in important municipalities such as Iasi and Sighet; overall it only secured 3% of the votes. Whilst assuring it a place in the next legislature, it was left with little real influence[79].

3.2.2: Liberal Party-93

The Liberal Party-93 (PL93 – *Partidul Liberal 93*) is a right of centre movement based on the middle class. It emphasises the necessity of political and enterprise freedom and is in favour of quick reforms and privatisation of state property. Its members and voters stem from the new elites and represent the most dynamic economic actors. Its leaders are young and its voters enjoy a high standard of living, making it in many respects a cadre party. Although it has a narrow base of support, it receives generous financial support from the banking sector.

The liberal parties' continuing lack of electoral success has led them to the inevitable conclusion that they must at least form an

---

[78] Shafir, Michael, 'Is the Romanian Opposition Heading towards Victory?' *Open Media Research Institute (OMRINet)*, Analytical Brief 260. Taken from the Internet on 26.11.96. Http: //www.omri.cz.
[79] Shafir, Michael, 'Romania's 'Different' Presidential Candidate: Nicolae Manolescu', *Open Media Research Institute (OMRINet)*, Analytical Brief 227. Taken from the Internet on 26.11.96. Http: //www.omri.cz.

alliance, if not attempt to merge into a single party once more. The Liberal Party-93 officially merged with the National Liberal Party-Democratic Convention on 14 June, 1997. The PNL-CD chairman, Nicolae Cerveni was elected leader, and the Liberal Party-93 chairman, Dinu Patriciu, was elected executive chairman of the new party. The party plans to call itself the Liberal Party, but must await the ruling of a tribunal on the internal dispute in the PNL-CD before it can do so; a faction within the PNL-CD led by Senator Alexandru Popivici does not recognise the merger. As a result, the National Liberal Party-Campeanu has decided to wait until the dispute has been resolved before joining the new party.

To further complicate matters, although the leader of the new party claims CDR membership carried on from the PNL-CD, as the Liberal Party-93 was not a member of the CDR, the leader of the National Liberal Party, Mircea Ionescu-Quintus, the largest liberal grouping within the CDR, has said that the joint leadership of the CDR must approve the membership of the new party before it can be accepted in the CDR[80]. Despite these problems, the consolidation of Romanian liberal groupings seems set to continue and is evidence of stabilisation in the Romanian political and party system.

3.2.3: Civic Alliance Party

The Civic Alliance Party (PAC – *Partidul Aliantei Civice*) was formed as the political party of the Civic Alliance (AC – *Alianta Civica*). The Civic Alliance is an anti-party intellectual grouping which was founded in 1990. It aims to create a civil society, a legal state and infuse democratic values, tolerance and public morals into state institutions and the Romanian population. It also promotes a critical examination of Romania's past. Although the Civic Alliance was a founding member of the CDR, it has forsworn political power; but the influence of its prominent members, such as Ana Blandiana, should not be underestimated.

The Civic Alliance Party is neo-liberal and, along with Petre Roman's Democratic Party, was one of the first parties to develop a practical concept of how to privatise Romania's bankrupt state

---

[80] *RFE/RL Newsline*, Vol. 1, No. 53, Part II, 16 June 1997.

enterprises. The initial lack of practical policy programmes was partly due to the enormity of the problems facing the Romanian economy and the fact that solving them demands a complicated programme which will inevitably cause further social hardship and therefore be unpopular. PAC emphasises the importance of Human Rights, civil society, the legal state and political pluralism. It aims to create a competitive market economy and reduce the role of the state. It also proposes to reform the institutions of the legal state and social security provisions. It is firmly opposed to nationalism of both majority and minority groups and is neutral concerning the reinstatement of the Monarchy, although it is in favour of accepting King Michael as a Romanian citizen. It also favours quick and decisive integration into the European Union and NATO. It draws its support from members of the urban middle class who have both high and low living standards. They are mostly employed in the cultural or academic sphere, are students, or connected with the Church. PAC is also the party which has the largest membership between the ages of 19 and 29 and under 60[81].

3.2.4: Alliance of Free Democrats

The two main Hungarian liberal parties are not historic parties and have enjoyed consistent electoral success. The Alliance of Free Democrats (SZDSZ – *Szabad Demokraták Szövetsége*) was founded as a political party in November 1988. It is not a historical party, rather it developed from the *Network of Free Initiatives* which was founded in May 1988[82]. After the 1990 elections, it formed the largest opposition party in Hungary and since the 1994 elections, is the coalition partner of the Hungarian Socialist Party. It was originally founded by radical Budapest intellectuals who had been Marxists, before following Gyorgy Lukás, accepting revisionism and finally becoming radical liberals. Most of them came from *nomenklatura* families and were of Jewish descent. They propagated moral opposition to the regime, westernization and radical democratisation. However, like most of the parties

---

[81] Ibid. Gabanyi, Anneli Ute, 'Politische Parteien in Rumänien nach der Wende', p. 39.
[82] Ibid. Segert, Dieter, Machos, Csilla, *Parteien in Osteuropa*, p. 69.

within the Hungarian party system, the SZDSZ was not based upon common political priorities, but was a heterogeneous collection of people of liberal inclination who shared general values, common experiences, a socio-cultural background, personal sympathies and friendships. Strong social democratic trends were represented alongside a social-liberal grouping, an anti-clerical liberal faction, a group advocating traditional intellectual radicalism, those in favour of liberalism for the 'man on the street' and an intellectual neo-conservative group.

Although the formation of contacts with society was initially hindered by the fact that the SZDSZ did not possess a country-wide organisational infrastructure, it did not remain an elite intellectual grouping and from August 1989, organised public demonstrations and engaged in a political campaign which increased public awareness of its existence and confirmed its image as a party which advocated radical systemic change.

The SZDSZ gave priority to the swift introduction of a market economy and recognition of private property, stressing the necessity of increased investment and an open economy. It also proposed to transform the relationship between state and society. In contrast to the KDNP, the MDF and the FKGP, it firmly opposed laws which strove to impose moral principles and economic justice. It trusted the market to solve social problems and emphasised the supremacy of the individual over the nation, or collective. However, the Hungarian population, accustomed to the gradual reform of the Kádár years, was not ready to take such a great leap forward. Thus, the SZDSZ's voter base remained limited to those in favour of radical change, that is urban intellectuals and entrepreneurs.

After the 1990 elections, the social-liberal faction gained more influence within the party and it moved slightly leftwards, placing more emphasis on policies designed to correct the failures of the market, although the importance of individual initiative continued to be stressed. Although the main aim of this adjustment was the widening of the SZDSZ social base, it also enabled it to contemplate political cooperation with the Socialist Party. In 1991, the SZDSZ helped the Socialist Party out of its enforced isolation by working with it in the *Democratic Charta*. As the SZDSZ was not willing to enter the conservative-nationalist camp, it was forced to change its attitude towards the Hungarian Socialist Party.

Although SZDSZ politicians enjoy consistently high popularity ratings, President Arpad Gnöncz, is highly respected, while the Lord Mayor of Budapest, Gabor Demszky, was one of the few to be re-elected in his post in the 1994 elections, it has failed to increase its share of the vote and, although it is the second largest party in Parliament, in both the 1990 and 1994 elections it won approximately the same number of seats[83].

As the Socialist Party's coalition partner, the SZDSZ has an opportunity to prove itself a responsible party capable of governing while ensuring the Socialist Party continues democratic and economic transformation. The problem is that if this strategy fails, the SZDSZ may be unable to retain a separate political identity and will not only be perceived simply as a potential coalition partner for the Socialists, but will also be held responsible for failures of government policy.

3.2.5: Alliance of Young Democrats-Civic Party

The second major Hungarian liberal party, the Alliance of Young Democrats (FIDESZ – *Fiatal Demokraták Szövetsége*) is a unique Hungarian product. It is neither historical, nor was it originally a traditional political party. It began as a youth movement and was founded by university Law students in March 1988 as an alternative to the Communist Youth organisation[84]. It transformed itself into a political party for the young and although it originally had a membership age limit of thirty, has developed into a viable political party concerned with the social problems of the whole of Hungarian society.

FIDESZ was spontaneously a radical liberal party because it is the young who gain the most opportunities from transformation and therefore placed most trust in the market. Thus, social policies initially played a limited role in its programme. It argued, not without some logic but perhaps a little naively, that for social

---

[83] *Central European Online*, 'Alliance of Free Democrats'. Taken from the Internet on 3.7.97. Http: //www.centraleurope.com.
[84] Ibid. Segert, Dieter, Machos, Csilla, *Parteien in Osteuropa*, p. 70.

policies to be effective it was essential the economy function effectively. As a sound economy formed the basis for all social policies, solving economic problems was its first priority. FIDESZ presented itself as radical, liberal and alternative. It was radical in the sense that it was uncompromisingly anti-state and aimed to work actively to reduce the state's activities. It was also determined to get rid of the Soviet troops stationed on Hungarian soil. It was alternative in that it criticised the whole system, both state and society, and showed some interest in alternative political currents, such as the ecology movement, although it remained somewhat ambivalent towards sex discrimination. It was liberal in the sense that it aimed to realise the values of liberal democracy, ensure respect for Human Rights and create an open economy and society; but, it also placed importance on the right of national self-determination. As the position of the Hungarian minorities abroad and the Hungarian nation as a whole became a political issue, FIDESZ developed a more conservative, patriotic stance. It developed into a more pragmatic party and moved away from its original radical liberal stance to become moderately conservative.

A study carried out in 1991 showed that 40% of FIDESZ voters lived in small provincial towns and were members of the lower middle class. A further 21% were members of the lower class and only possessed a minimum education. But FIDESZ also attracted those who had higher education and were involved in teaching or were office workers. These heterogeneous groups have three things in common; their earnings are below average; they find it difficult to use the opportunities presented by the free market; and, if FIDESZ's radical policies were implemented, approximately 72% of them would not benefit in any way[85]. A further 5% of FIDESZ supporters were students, also with low incomes, but with links to the private sector and more able to utilise market opportunities. Approximately 8% of its supporters came from the established, financially secure, provincial middle class. This group was older than the average FIDESZ supporter and, although employed in the state sector, also engaged in private enterprise. Some 3% were

---

[85] Machos, Csilla, 'FIDESZ - Der Bund Junger Demokraten', *Südosteuropa*, Vol. 42, No. 1, 1993, p. 18.

members of the upper class with extremely high incomes and a higher education. Only 12% of FIDESZ supporters could be said to form a traditional liberal voter base. These were well-earning managers and highly qualified intellectuals, often from Budapest or other large towns[86].

In the light of these figures, it is less surprising that following the election of Viktor Orbán as party leader[87], in an attempt to consolidate its voter base, FIDESZ began to change its profile from being radically liberal to moderately conservative, aiming to become a 'Liberal People's Party'. From April 1993 onwards, it began to place more emphasis on national concerns and on the creation of a socially orientated market economy. It advocated a strong state to ensure stability and drew up a new economic programme, which accepted state intervention in the economy if necessary. In this way it hoped to make itself attractive to conservative voters, and to the MDF, as a possible coalition partner.

However, this strategy ignored the fact that by the time of the 1994 elections, the MDF was in a deep crisis and had lost the confidence of the electorate. In addition, this policy failed to take note of the fact that much of FIDESZ initial success was due to its youthful, fresh image and the fact that its members were perceived as people of the future. Nationalist-conservative voters were not in favour of the radical liberal policies FIDESZ had previously advocated and its radical image made it difficult for them to accept the conservative swing as genuine. On the other hand, FIDESZ's original supporters were not prepared to accept such a radical programmatic change. Consequently, it lost the confidence of its original supporters and was unable to convince potential conservative voters to support it. This resulted in a massive loss of popularity and party fragmentation when three of its leading figures left in November 1993[88]. One of these was the party's vice-president, Gábor Fodor, a founder member of FIDESZ and one of Orbán's rivals. Fodor was a representative of the social-liberal

---

[86] Ibid. Machos, Csilla, 'FIDESZ - Der Bund Junger Demokraten', *Südosteuropa*, p. 19.
[87] Ibid. Segert, Dieter, Machos, Csilla, *Parteien in Osteuropa*, p. 71.
[88] Ibid. Ágh, Attila, Kurtán, Sándor, (Eds.), *Democratization and Europeanization in Hungary: The First Parliament (1990-1994)*, p. 201.

current within FIDESZ and was the party's most popular politician. He subsequently joined the SZDSZ and in June 1994 became the Minister for Culture and Education[89]. His departure represents the culmination of FIDESZ's identity change.

However, the question remains whether FIDESZ can remain a liberal party while attempting to become a moderately conservative people's party. Because its success to date has been based less on an organisational or social base, and more on public image and reputation, such an attempt seems likely to fail. Although its disappointingly poor showing in the 1994 elections seemed to confirm this forecast, the MDF and FKGP's move towards the more extreme nationalist right has enabled FIDESZ to gain support from more moderate right-wing conservative voters as well as those liberals who are disappointed with the SZDSZ's performance in the government coalition. FIDESZ new name, the Alliance of Young Democrats-Hungarian Civic Party (FIDESZ-MPP – *Fiatal Demokraták Szövetsége-Magyar Polgari Part*), is an attempt to further this development and increase its attractiveness to moderate conservative voters[90]. Although FIDESZ has recognised the need for a moderate conservative force in Hungarian politics, the speed with which it changed its political profile seriously damaged its credibility, and it will take time for the party to regain the voters' trust and political significance.

In contrast, despite the fact that many politicians and members of the Czech electorate consider themselves liberal, there are no significant liberal parties in the Czech Republic. The Liberal Democratic Party was founded in 1991 by Emanuel Mandler after Civic Forum's dissolution, but remained an obscure grouping and split before the 1992 elections. One of the factions joined the Civic Democratic Alliance and the rest of the party disintegrated[91]. The Civic Movement also aspires to be a liberal party but it is not unified, encompassing both left and right of centre currents. It also

---

[89] He has since resigned this post. Bingen, Dieter, *Die revolutionäre Umwälzung in Mittel- und Osteuropa*, Göttinger Arbeitskreis, No. 10, Duncker & Humblot 1993.

[90] *Central European Online*, 'Alliance of Young Democrats - Hungarian Civic Party'. Taken from the Internet on 3.7.97. Http: //www.centraleurope.com.

[91] Ibid. Orbman, Jan, 'Czech Opposition Parties in Disarray', *RFE/RL Research Report*.

presented itself as an elite intellectual party and has therefore been unable to attract a significant number of votes. But although not represented in Parliament, it still sits on local councils.

3.2.6: Movement for Self-Administrative Democracy-Association for Silesia and Moravia

Since the election of the moderate Jan Kryer as its leader and the departure of several of its more nationalistic and left-wing Deputies, the Movement for Self-Administrative Democracy-Association for Moravia and Silesia (HSD-SMS – *Hnutí za samosprávnou demokratická-Spolecnost pro Moravu a Slezko*) also claims to be liberal. Although after the 1992 elections the party had 14 Deputies, its support is limited to Moravia and Silesia. With this in mind, it united forces with Rudolf Beranek's Entrepreneurs Party in 1994 and formed a new party, the Czech-Moravian Party Centrist Party (CMSS – *Ceskomoravská strana lidová*), aiming to form a stronger centrist liberal group less reliant on a regional voter base[92].

The Independent Liberals consist of several former members of the Czechoslovak Socialist Party and Sladek's extreme nationalist Republican Party. They are led by the former chairman of the Socialist Party, Jiri Vyvadil, and can hardly be said to represent traditional liberal values.

3.3: Social Democratic Parties

Although the social democratic movement has a long democratic history, cooperation with the Communist Party under the previous regime has made the formation of a modern identity distinct from Communism very difficult. In addition, respective Communist Parties have re-formed and often re-named themselves Social Democratic. Historic social democratic parties also suffered from an ideological crisis following the discrediting of left-wing policies under the Communist regimes. Thus, the main feature of the social democratic parties which formed after the collapse of Communism has been their confusing multiplicity. In addition, the ideological

---

[92] Ibid. Orbman, Jan, 'Czech Opposition Parties in Disarray'.

confusion created a dearth of internal cohesion which led to lack of attention being given to the electorate. Bitter internal disputes led to multiple fragmentation, further weakening the parties' electoral appeal. With the exception of the Czech Social Democratic Party, which since the 1996 election constitutes the main opposition party (see 3.6.2)[93], historic social democratic parties have failed to attract any substantial support.

3.3.1: Czech Social Democratic Party

Founded in 1878, the Czech Social Democratic Party (CSSD – *Ceská strana sociálné demokratická*) is the oldest political party in the Czech Republic. It traditionally maintained a left-wing socialist position. In 1921 the radicals within the Social Democratic Party left and founded the Communist Party of Czechoslovakia[94]. After the Velvet Revolution the Czechoslovak Social Democratic Party was reactivated[95]. Although in the Czech lands some prominent social democrats, including Rudolf Battek, the vice-Chairman of the Parliament and a founder of *Charter 77*, became parliamentary Deputies after the 1990 elections, they did so as Civic Forum candidates. The CSSD did not pass the 5% threshold. As a result, contacts with Battek's Social Democratic Association were terminated and he was expelled from the CSSD. In addition, the Association was forced to leave its offices in the CSSD headquarters in Hybernská. Relations were further worsened as the Association, originally one of the clubs within the Civic Forum, laid claim to part of the property which was restored to the CSSD after 1989. Since its dispute with the CSSD, the Social Democratic Association has become further marginalised.

The failure of the CSSD in the first elections was due to the fact that the population was principally voting against Communism, rather than for a specific political party. In addition, the population was generally averse to left-wing phraseology, which was associated with the Communist regime. The 1990 elections also

---

[93] For election results, see Appendix XXV, XXVI.
[94] Ibid. Senechal, David, A., *Czechoslovakia*.
Http: //ww2.artsci.wustl.edu/~ps4271/czs_ds.html.
[95] Waller, Michael, Coppieters, Bruno, Deschouwer, Kris, (Eds.), *Social Democracy in a Post-Communist Europe*, Frank Cass & Co Ltd. 1994, p. 120.

Political Democratisation

demonstrated that the traditional working class social democratic vote had become divided amongst non-socialist parties and the Communist Party of Bohemia and Moravia. The Communist Party gained more votes than the CSSD and was the second strongest party in Parliament. Its programme appealed to those in rural areas and industrial centres where unemployment was rising. Interestingly, it also retained considerable support amongst radical left-wing Prague intellectuals[96].

Although the CSSD did not enter Parliament after the 1990 elections, by March 1992 it had gained fifteen Deputies as six parliamentary Deputies and some of the *Obroda* group joined it[97]. *Obroda*, 'Renewal', consists of reform Communists from 1968 and aims to find a 'Third Way' between Capitalism and Socialism.

In the 1992 elections the CSSD increased its percentage of the vote to 7.7% for the Federal Assembly, gaining ten Deputies, and to 6.6% for the Czech National Council, gaining six Deputies[98]. Yet despite the fact that some adverse side-effects of economic reform were becoming visible, the CSSD was unable to attract the more educated urban middle class, failing to convince them that it would successfully carry out economic reform. In addition, many industrial workers continued to vote for the Communist Party because they were afraid that economic reform would bring unemployment. Therefore, the CSSD gains more support in rural areas from farm labourers than from industrial workers. The traditional social democratic vote has been captured by the Communist Party, which consistently gains approximately 10% of the vote, and the Left Bloc, which gains most support in the heavily industrialised northern parts of Bohemia[99].

Since 1992, the CSSD has profited from the fact that several popular politicians, such as Zdenek Jicinsky, the former vice-

---

[96] Ibid. Waller, Michael, Coppieters, Bruno, Deschouwer, Kris, (Eds.), *Social Democracy in a Post-Communist Europe*, p. 123.
[97] Ibid. Waller, Michael, Coppieters, Bruno, Deschouwer, Kris, (Eds.), *Social Democracy in a Post-Communist Europe*, p. 126.
[98] Ibid. Waller, Michael, Coppieters, Bruno, Deschouwer, Kris, (Eds.), *Social Democracy in a Post-Communist Europe*, p. 126.
[99] Ibid. Waller, Michael, Coppieters, Bruno, Deschouwer, Kris, (Eds.), *Social Democracy in a Post-Communist Europe*, p. 127.

Chairman of the Federal Assembly; Valtr Komárek, the former vice-Prime Minister of the first post-Communist government; Milos Zeman, the chief author of Civic Forum's electoral programme and now chariman of the CSSD; and Petr Kucera, a member of Civic Forum's secretariat, joined the party. Between 1992 and 1996, the number of working people who voted for the CSSD increased five-fold, and the number of small business people supporting it increased six-fold. The Czech middle class turned towards the left as a result of continuing difficulties associated with economic transformation and government policies which seemed to penalise small business. The CSSD gained 26.44% of the votes in the 1996 parliamentary elections, but was unable to gain power and became the strongest opposition party. The point is that although many people in the small business community chose to vote for the CSSD, the majority had not become left-wing but were merely expressing their discontent with Klaus and the government. Indeed, a study by the *Czech Sociological Institute* suggests that this group remained the most right-wing of all[100]. They chose the CSSD as there was the no other acceptable alternative to the ODS. However, by the time the senatorial elections were held in November 1996, they had decided against experimentation and the ruling coalition gained a majority in the Senate.

The CSSD's failure to take full advantage of the protest vote against Klaus led to an internal party dispute. The problem is that the CSSD has been unable to completely modernise itself. Indeed, the party chairman, Milos Zeman, has initiated a shift to the left, thus polarising the party. It is mainly due to this that the CSSD found it difficult to present an economic policy which is convincing, clearly differentiated from that of the ruling coalition and attractive to both workers and the middle class. The CSSD's limited faith in the market and its ability to distribute wealth effectively and justly is reflected in policies which are interventionist and protectionist towards the welfare state. In addition, it has not welcomed Czech membership of NATO. Although its environment has become more centre-right, the CSSD

---

[100] See 'Disenchanted Entrepreneurs resorting to coalition or apathy', *The Prague Post*, 27 November-3 December 1996.

has remained faithful to left-wing policies. The disarray amongst the conservative parties means the CSSD leads opinion polls; 28% of those who took part in a poll carried out by *Sofres-Factum* and published on 24 February, 1998, supported the CSSD. The discredited ODS, led by Vaclav Klaus, still commanded 10.8% support, while the Freedom Union gained the support of 10.3% of those asked. The Communist Party received 9.3%[101].

Although this level of support would ensure the CSSD came to power after the next elections, the former deputy chairman of the party, Karel Machovec, has criticised Zeman for failure to distance the CSSD from the Communist Party[102]. He also criticised the fact that a number of former highly placed Communists are members of Zeman's leadership circle and has called for the CSSD to move towards the political centre:

'If the Social Democrats want to be successful in the long run, they will have to realise that the value orientation of their voters is different to that of the party. Pre-1989 political divisions of left and right cannot be used anymore... The voters are clustered more around the centre, and I would like to see a situation where we included more votes form the centre.'[103]

The necessity of modernisation to attract and retain the votes of an electorate no longer interested in the ideological divisions between left and right is a task which is being faced by social democratic parties across Europe. Although to date the Hungarian Socialist Party has embarked on the most embracing modernisation of policy, Machovec's calls for modernisation within the CSSD and his open challenge for leadership seem to point to the fact that the

---

[101] *RFE/RL Newsline*, Vol. 2, No. 38, Part II, 25 February 1998.
[102] The Communist Party's donation of approximately 10 million Crowns ($292 000) in 1990 demonstrate its continued relationship with the CSSD. Large discrepencies between the financial report the CSSD presented at its National Conference in March 1996 with that presented to the Chamber of Deputies two weeks later have also come to light. *RFE/RL Newsline*, Vol. 2, No. 27, Part II, 10 February 1998.
[103] 'Zeman deputy calls for a party right turn', *The Prague Post*, 27 November-3 December 1996.

CSSD may soon find itself forced to modernise and face a similar identity crisis.

3.3.2: Romanian Social Democratic Party

The historic Romanian and Hungarian social democratic parties have all but disintegrated. The Romanian Social Democratic Party (PSDR – *Partidul Social-Democrat Român*) was a small, but well-known political party in the inter-war period. It was founded in 1893 as the Social Democratic Party of the Workers of Romania. It was banned in 1938 but allowed to function once more in 1944. In 1948, the Social Democratic Party merged with the Romanian Communist Party and the majority of its leaders were marginalised or annihilated, though it was never officially dissolved and some activists remained underground[104]. After the December Revolution, the Social Democratic Party was re-established by a group of anti-Communist social democrats, Trade Union members and younger activists. It supported a moderate social democratic doctrine and was in favour of a social market economy. It focused on the establishment of parliamentary democracy and a market economy, advocated the use of experts to manage the economy, supported independent Trade Unions, the right to strike and the improvement of social and economic benefits for society[105].

However, its monarchist leader, Sergiu Cunescu, and most active members were old functionaries from the pre-war party, which served to limit electoral appeal and caused tension with the younger members[106]. In addition, the party was unable to compete with the populist parties for the votes of its traditional base, the workers. There was also confusion over its identity due to the existence of a number of similarly named 'phantom' parties. The party has practically disintegrated under the strain of internal strife and personal conflict and no longer represents a significant force in Romanian politics.

---

[104] Ibid. Staar, Richard, F., (Ed.), *The 1991 Yearbook on International Communist Affairs*, p. 336.
[105] The Programme was published in *Adevardul* on 6 February, 1990. Ibid. Staar, Richard, F., *The 1991 Yearbook on International Communist Affairs*, p. 336.
[106] Ibid. Gabanyi, Anneli Ute, 'Politische Parteien in Rumänien nach der Wende', p. 41.

3.3.3: Hungarian Social Democratic Party

The Hungarian Social Democratic Party (MSDP – *Magyarországi Szociáldemokrata Párt*), lacking a social base, has also disintegrated. Until 1992 it was led by an undemocratic clique around Anna Petrasovits. During the 1990 electoral campaign, the Party was allied to the radical liberal camp and indulged in heavy criticism of the Communist regime. But, after it became clear that this policy had not increased its popularity, it declared an alliance with the most reactionary Trade Unions. In this way it hoped to gain access to the vast wealth and assets which the Unions still possessed from the Communist period. However, this abrupt change of policy caused a break with the liberal parties and destroyed the party's credibility. Subsequently, it offered itself as a partner to the national-conservative parties, the Independent Smallholders and the People's Party. In the 1990 elections, Anna Petrasovits' Social Democratic Party gained a mere 3.6% of the vote, failing to enter Parliament. In the municipal elections, it gained only 0.5%[107]. In June 1992 the Supreme Court proclaimed Petrasovits' leadership illegitimate. The party has since disintegrated into a multitude of secessionist groupings and mini-parties. All attempts to unite or create a new party have failed. Although there is a considerable reservoir of social democratic potential within the Hungarian population, the Social Democratic Party has been unable to utilise it[108]. Thus, what remains of the historic Social Democratic Party seems destined to political obscurity. Nevertheless, the Hungarian Socialist Party is undergoing a social-democratisation which, if successful, will

---

[107] Ibid. Waller, Michael, Coppieters, Bruno, Deschouwer, Kris, (Eds.), *Social Democracy in a Post-Communist Europe*, p. 167.

[108] Iván Szelényi claims empirical evidence demonstrates that industrial workers and less-educated people, the traditional electoral base of social democratic parties, were over-represented in the number of non-voters in the 1990 elections. Szelényi believes this occurred because of a lack of a social democratic alternative. But, this group not only demonstrates a strong preference for the welfare-state, but also a preference for law and order in social issues, thus reflecting the new political reality in which traditional divisions of left and right are no longer applicable. Ibid. Waller, Michael, Coppieters, Bruno, Deschouwer, Kris, (Eds.), *Social Democracy in a Post-Communist Europe*, p. 167.

enable it to take the place of a social democratic party in the political system.

3.3.4: Hungarian Socialist Party

The Hungarian Socialist Party (MSZP – *Magyar Szocialista Párt*) is the legal, but not political, successor of the Hungarian Socialist Workers Party. It accepted legal continuity to facilitate more readily the return of former Party property and assets to the state or to private persons. It was founded at the XIV Conference of the Hungarian Socialist Workers Party in October 1989, immediately after the Party had voted to disband itself[109]. Its formation represented the victory of reformers and pragmatists within the Party and ensured the political marginalisation of any remaining hard-line Communists. The conservative hard-line faction within the Hungarian Socialist Workers Party revived the old party under its original name ten days later. Although they thereby unwittingly helped the MSZP to distance itself from the former regime and increased its democratic credentials, the MSZP's main problem has remained its discrediting link to the Communist Party and former regime. This link is demonstrated by the structure of its supporters within the population. In 1994, approximately 57% of former Communist Party members supported the MSZP, although the percentage of former Party members of the total of MSZP supporters was 28%[110]. However, the MSZP has undertaken measures designed to distance itself from its totalitarian past. It avoided membership continuity with its legal predecessor and in October 1989, its membership totalled approximately 50 000[111]. It also passed a new Party Statue, abandoned the system of democratic centralism and the principle of a party-state bureaucracy.

Although the hard-line, orthodox faction did not join the new party, the MSZP encompasses a variety of platforms, including reform Communist, socialist and social democratic groupings. These groups remain in the MSZP because it constitutes their only

---

[109] Ibid. Segert, Dieter, Machos, Csilla, *Parteien in Osteuropa*, p. 72.
[110] Ibid. Pridham, Geoffry, Lewis, Paul, G., *Stabilising Fragile Democracies*, p. 115.
[111] Ibid. Segert, Dieter, Machos, Csilla, *Parteien in Osteuropa*, p. 72.

realistic means of gaining power. The moderate social-liberal grouping is at present strongest and has proved vital in the political renewal of the party. At the time of the 1990 elections this renewal was still incomplete and the MSZP was orientated towards freedom of the individual, but also advocated social solidarity. It aimed to introduce a social market economy while at the same maintaining the existing Hungarian welfare state. Legal equality was to be guaranteed for all forms of property, but the further development some of the well-functioning collective forms of property, particularly those operating in agriculture, was also advocated. It was recognised that transition would require certain sacrifices and importance was placed on the need for compromise and responsibility in the form of collective bargaining. The party was notably moderate when dealing with the national question, favouring the state as a definition of nationality and allowing anyone to apply to become a Hungarian citizen[112].

Despite its history and the decidedly anti-Communist nature of the electoral campaign, the MSZP successfully entered Parliament after the 1990 elections. Its strong, disciplined faction increased its positive image as a party of professional, competent and pragmatic politicians. It was this image and the fact that its politicians presented familiar faces and were associated with the stability and security of the Kádár years but were not directly involved in the ideological battle of the *Kulturkampf*, which helped it to win the 1994 elections. And yet, despite the contrasting results of the two elections, both reflect the Hungarian electorate's desire for a government which would implement change in the tradition of Hungarian gradualism. The 1994 vote also expressed rejection of ideological penetration and support for westernization.

Another important factor which helped the MSZP to victory was its link to the Hungarian Trade Union lobby. Until this was forged, Hungarian workers had no effective mechanism through which they could influence the course of transformation. In effect, their interests had been almost completely ignored by the MDF. Although new Trade Unions, such as the League of Independent Workers' Councils, had been founded their membership remained

---

[112] Ibid. Segert, Dieter, Machos, Csilla, *Parteien in Osteuropa*, p. 73.

low. The Association of Hungarian Trade Unions, the successor to the Communist Unions, has retained almost half of its members and is the only organisation with a mass membership. By accepting the Association as a partner, the MSZP established itself as a party which represented workers' interests. The President of the Association of Hungarian Trade Unions, Sándor Nagy, entered the Hungarian Parliament after the 1994 elections as a result of his nomination by the Socialist Party leader, Gyula Horn, for the Socialist Party National List. He was in fact second on the List after Gyula Horn[113]. However, it cannot be denied that the Association preserves some of the former regime's structures in its organisation and aims to preserve some elements of the previous economic structure as a means of guaranteeing job security.

Although the characteristics which made the Socialists attractive to the Hungarian voter; their pragmatism, professionalism, dedication to the task of producing a functioning economy, the atmosphere of order and discipline they projected and commitment to finding a national compromise with Hungary's neighbours, combined with a certain nostalgia for the Kádár regime, seemed to promise social harmony and a more acceptable transformation, this has not proved to be the case. The MSZP gained an absolute majority in Parliament, but formed a coalition with the SZDSZ. It was wary of becoming the single ruling party, fearing that this would conjure up uncomfortable images from the past; and was unwilling to accept sole responsibility in the face of the crisis facing the Hungarian economy.

It is ironic that the MSZP, a party which defines itself as social democratic, specifically aimed to represent workers' interests and which offered stability and professional pragmatism after the ideological conflict during the *Kulturkampf*, should embark on shock therapy in the form of a strict stabilisation package and implement neo-liberal economic policies. Although the economic situation demanded immediate and decisive action, the coalition was forced to rely on the rational technocratic pragmatism of the post-Communist managerial elite during the nine month stalemate over the economic stabilisation package, known after the Finance

---

[113] Ibid. Segert, Dieter, Machos, Csilla, *Parteien in Osteuropa*, p. 95.

Minister as the 'Bokros Package'. The package was finally introduced on 12 March, 1995, but has been the cause of conflict ever since[114]. The delay in implementation of the package meant that the MSZP lost the political advantage it enjoyed immediately after the elections and was unable to utilise the population's initial goodwill to cushion the inevitable shock which implementation of the package would entail.

The MSZP and the SZDSZ were forced to tackle the problem of Hungary's huge public debt and budget deficit, problems which the previous national-conservative government did not have the power or will to undertake. The introduction of the Bokros Package was the only option available which presented the possibility of successfully transforming the economy. Hungary's welfare state provisions were exceedingly generous and the economy was unable to support them. This exacerbated Hungary's high level of public spending and increased the budget deficit. The Bokros Package reduced public spending on social welfare and health services by introducing means testing of benefits, limiting public consumption and reducing employment in the public sector, including education. The general monetary restriction restored equilibrium – a precondition for economic growth. Bokros himself described the package as representing the first real break with the Communist economic system because it ended the redistribution by the state which had distorted market forces[115]. Paradoxically, this argument places the MSZP more on the right than on the left of the political spectrum.

Thus, a rather odd reversal of roles has occurred in which the MSZP, a self-acknowledged social democratic party and member of the Socialist International, is implementing neo-liberal policies aimed at ensuring the market functions without state interference; while the conservative-nationalist opposition, in its criticism of government, advocates left-wing social democratic protectionist policies for the welfare state. This contradiction has caused a crisis within the MSZP.

---

[114] Ibid. Márkos, György, *Party System and Political Cleavage Translation in Hungary*.

[115] Ibid. Márkos, György, *Party System and Political Cleavage Translation in Hungary*.

The MSZP is undoubtedly the best organised political party in Hungary. In the 1994 elections, it drew support from all sections of society and attracted voters with completely different values, making it Hungary's first 'catch-all', mass party. It gained the support of urban and rural dwellers, intellectuals, managers, entrepreneurs, pensioners and blue collar workers in industrial centres. However, this means that it has great difficulty in presenting a single and constant identity. The majority of the MSZP is pro-western and is committed to the traditional values of social democracy. Unlike the MDF and the SZDSZ, it does not stem from the cultural cleavage between populists and westernizers, but is a coalition of generation, social and interest groups, of personal allegiances and ideological rivalries. Its main ideological currents are social-liberal, Trade Union and national anti-capitalist. Some Marxists and a powerful bureaucratic lobby are also present. These cleavages are in many cases cross-cutting and, although the moderate social-liberal group has gained dominance, the modernisation of the party is not yet fully complete.

The Trade Unionists and those on the national and Marxist left-wing of the party are critical of the economic stabilisation package and liberal coalition partner. They are opposed within the MSZP by the technocrats and the social-liberals. To date, the conflict between the left-wing social democratic grouping and the more moderate and modernising social-liberal grouping has not been resolved. Although the stabilisation package has been accepted, the left-wing of the party cannot envisage a long-term acceptance of such a state of affairs. Indeed, in February 1996 Finance Minister Bokros resigned[116], and the left-wing social democratic grouping within the party has called for the resignation of Gyula Horn as party leader and Prime Minister[117].

While the Socialist Party remains divided, increased support for the extreme FKGP and right-wing KDNP may have the effect of uniting the party, if only temporarily, for the 1998 elections. Although at a meeting of the left-wing group within the party, the

---

[116] Ibid. Márkos, György, *Party System and Political Cleavage Translation in Hungary.*
[117] *RFE/RL Newsline*, Vol. 1, No. 21, Part II, 29 April 1997.

leader of the MSZP parliamentary faction, Imre Szekeres, demanded that the Socialist Party build democratic socialism rather than capitalism, he also emphasised the threat which the right-wing parties represent for democratic consolidation and stressed the necessity that the MSZP present a united front and work together to ensure victory in the 1998 elections[118].

3.3.5: Democratic Party

The Democratic Party (PD – *Partidul Democrat*), formerly the Social Democratic Union (USD), is led by Petre Roman and is the only major party in Romania to advocate a social democratic programme[119]. The PD defines itself as a moderate social democratic party of the centre-left and enjoys guest status at the Socialist International. It proposes quicker privatisation, increased competition and a more effective tax system. It is also in favour of autonomous local budgeting. It proceeds from the premise of social equality and is in favour of increasing social security provisions. It is not monarchist, but does not object to a referendum on the matter. It also proposes to secure internal stability by promoting inter-ethnic peace. It is eager to see Romania incorporated into the European Union and NATO. Although it has been prepared to work with the CDR in the government coalition, it has not joined the Convention.

Its leaders and members are recruited from the pre-1989 technocratic and dissident elites, as well as from the new elites, and are on average 38 years old. Its voters are drawn from the new, young middle class of the cultural and technical elites, many of whom are women or involved in the Union movement. The leaders of the party are well-educated professionals and so also appeal to the emerging managerial class. The party shows promise of increasing in importance and developing into a Social Democratic Party. However, it continues to support itself financially, not from membership contributions, but from irregular bloc payments from

---

[118] *RFE/RL Newsline*, Vol. 1, No. 43, Part II, 2 June 1997.

[119] After his resignation from the PDSR in June 1997, Teodor Melescanu founded a new political party, the Alliance for Romania, which also has a specifically centre-left, social democratic profile. But, this political grouping is in its infancy, and a future alliance with the Democratic Party, cannot be ruled out.

anonymous private sponsors[120]. Although it supports the coalition's transformation programme, constant personnel quarrels with its main coalition partner, the PNTCD, have stalled the programme and hindered successful economic transformation.

3.4: Successor Communist Parties

In addition to successor parties which have reformed themselves, orthodox Communist Parties have also been revived. These parties still adhere to Communist ideology and their programmes contain familiar language and solutions.

3.4.1: Hungarian Socialist Workers Party
The Hungarian Socialist Workers Party (MSZMP – *Magyar Szocialists Munkáspárt*) was the only Communist Party to officially dissolve itself; but a hard-line faction which still adhered to an orthodox Communist ideology re-founded it. Although it did not manage to get into Parliament in the 1990 elections, it became the strongest extra-parliamentary political party. However, it has since fragmented with a rather more moderate faction which supports some form of 'Third Way' forming the Worker's Party, while the hard-core Communists once more re-founded the MSZMP[121]. Its policies have little appeal to the majority of Hungarians and it seems doomed to marginalisation.

3.4.2: Communist Party of Bohemia and Moravia
The Communist Party of Bohemia and Moravia (KSCM – *Kommunistická strana Cech a Moravy*) is an orthodox Communist Party which relies heavily on former members of the Communist Party for its quite considerable electoral success. It has been estimated that in 1994, approximately 70% of KSCM supporters

---

[120] Ibid. Gabanyi, Anneli Ute, 'Politische Parteien in Rumänien nach der Wende', p. 47.
[121] Ibid. Segert, Dieter, Machos, Csilla, *Parteien in Osteuropa*, p. 72.

were former Party members[122], and a poll has indicated that 82% of the party's supporters were against changing its name[123]. Its first chairman, Jiri Svoboda, left having been unable to transform the party into a modern socialist movement and has since founded the Party of Democratic Socialism[124]. One of the orthodox groups opposing modernisation was founded by Miroslav Stepan, and the former Minister for Internal Affairs, Jaromir Obzina, who were re-admitted into the party against Svoboda's wishes[125]. This platform aims to return the country to the conditions which prevailed before 1989. Although it has a limited following, it has considerable influence within the party and its spokesman, Vaclav Papez, is a member of the party's Policy Committee. The KSCM Executive Committee recommended Obzina's and Stepan's dismissal, but another orthodox group, led by Mirolsav Grebencik, now leader of the party, has since gained influence[126].

The KSCM consistently gains approximately 10% of the popular Czech vote and during the 1990 elections was the only party other than Civic Forum to receive more than 10% of the votes[127]. This percentage is roughly similar to that which the party gained in the inter-war period and is also similar to the level of support it gained in the last democratic elections before the Communist take-over in 1948. As a result of the June 1996 elections, during which the Party secured 8.08% of the vote, it has 22 Deputies in the Czech Parliament[128]. To maintain this level of support, it has formed an alliance, the Left Bloc (LB – *Levý blok*),

---

[122] For more information on the actual percentage of former Party members who support the KSCM, see Pridham, Geoffry, Lewis, Paul, G., *Stabilising Fragile Democracies*, p. 115.
[123] Ibid. Orbman, Jan, 'Czech Opposition Parties in Disarray'.
[124] Ibid. Orbman, Jan, 'Czech Opposition Parties in Disarray'.
[125] Stepan, a former Politburo member, was the chairman of the Communist Party Municipal Council in Prague and was responsible for ordering brutal police repression of student demonstrations in 1988 and 1989. Ibid. Orbman, Jan, 'Czech Opposition Parties in Disarray'.
[126] Ibid. Orbman, Jan, 'Czech Opposition Parties in Disarray'.
[127] Ibid. Senechal, David, A., *Czechoslovakia*.
Http: //ww2.artsci.wustl.edu/~ps4271/czs_ds.html.
[128] *Open Media Research Institute (OMRINet)*, 'Czech Election Results'. Taken from the Internet on 13.6.96. Http: // www.omri.cz.

with the Democratic Left, chaired by Maria Stiborova. Thus, there remains a not insignificant section of the Czech population which still adheres to orthodox Communist ideology. Indeed, in a poll carried out by *Sofres-Factum* and published on 24 February, 1998, the percentage of those asked who claimed they would prefer to live under Communism once more increased from 18.1% in 1996, to 28.7% in 1998[129]. Although this is most probably an indication of the population's weariness with the current disarray on the polical stage, it demonstrates that excessive political fragmentation and pettiness can increase support for extreme solutions by way of protest and in this way can endanger democratic consoldiaiton

3.4.3: Party of Social Democracy in Romania

In contrast, the Romanian Communist Party's *de facto* successor, the National Salvation Front (FSN – *Frontul Salvarii Nationale*), has tried to deny its links to the Communist Party. But, while the MSZP has embarked upon social democratisation, the Romanian National Salvation Front and its successor, the Party of Social Democracy in Romania (PDSR – *Partidul Democratiei Sociale din România*), has been unwilling to modernise itself.

The FSN is the *de facto* successor of the Romanian Communist Party and inherited a significant portion of the Communist Party's membership, leaders, assets and ideological baggage. The National Salvation Front came into existence on 22 December, 1989 and took on the role of provisional government in the wake of the Revolution. Ion Iliescu was officially named as its leader on 29 December, 1989. After his election as President on 20 May, 1990, he resigned as chairman on 5 July, 1990[130].

The Front's first conference was held in Bucharest from 7-10 April, 1990[131]. Although it stressed its links with the December Revolution and emphasised its oppositional role, it absorbed many of the organisational structures of the disintegrating Romanian Communist Party. Although an all party agreement on 1 February,

---

[129] *RFE/RL Newsline*, Vol. 2, No. 38, Part II, 25 February 1998.
[130] Ibid. Staar, Richard, F., (Ed.), *The 1991 Yearbook on International Communist Affairs*, p. 332.
[131] Ibid. Staar, Richard, F., (Ed.), *The 1991 Yearbook on International Communist Affairs*, p. 332.

Political Democratisation

1990 reorganised the Front's provisional government and formed a provisional Council of National Unity, consisting of 180 members, the Front continued to dominate government as half of the Council's members belonged to it. The Front's original intention to serve only as an interim government was soon renounced and on 6 February, 1990 it became a political party, able to participate in the elections which were planned for 20 May, 1990[132]. It dominated the 1990 electoral campaign and won a landslide victory, obtaining approximately a two thirds majority in the Romanian Assembly of Deputies (see 3.6.3)[133].

The Front endorsed freedom of speech, political and religious freedom and the protection of Romania's ethnic minorities. Although it supported political pluralism, the introduction of a free market and economic reform in principle, it remained sceptical of the market; continuing to place trust in the planned economy. Thus, it was not in favour of privatisation of large, heavy industrial complexes, athough it is questionable whether investors could have been found. Nor did it initially support the privatisation of land, although in practice farmers took matters into their own hands and affected the dissolution of state farms via wild privatisation. The Front used the considerable financial and organisational resources it inherited from the Communist Party and its control of the state-owned media in a concerted campaign to persuade the masses that it had been one of the main forces behind the Revolution and would implement gradual change. In addition, the FSN sponsored the formation of a number of 'phantom' parties which succeeded in splintering opposition votes. Once the election was over these parties invariably merged with the FSN. One such example was the Republican Party founded by Ion Manzatu. He had given private tuition in physics to Ceausescu's children and had a position on the National Council for Science and Technology, which was headed by Elena Ceausescu. After the 1990 elections, his party fused with the FSN and although Manzatu stood as an independent presidential

---

[132] Ibid. Staar, Richard, F., (Ed.), *The 1991 Yearbook on International Communist Affairs*, p. 334.
[133] Ibid. Merkel, Wolfgang, Sandschneider, Eberhard, Segert, Dieter, (Hrsg.), *Systemwechsel II: Die Institutionalisierung der Demokratie*, p. 244. For detailed election results, see Appendix XXVIII, XXIX.

candidate in September 1992, thereby contributing to the exponential increase of candidates, he subsequently became one of the vice-presidents of the FSN[134].

However, dissatisfaction with its policies and the lack of turn over of personnel led many of the intellectuals and dissidents who initially associated themselves with the Front to leave its ranks and move into opposition. Indeed, in the country as a whole virtually no new faces appeared in the administration. For instance, the Prefect of Cluj, Grigore Zanc, who was nominated by the government, had been the head of the local Communist Party and his position as Prefect enabled him to continue his functions under a new name[135]. Within the FSN itself, there was also little evidence of the emergence of a new political elite. The vice-president of the FSN's successor, the Party of Social Democracy in Romania (PDSR), Dan Martian, was the Deputy for Vaslei County. He had been Ion Iliescu's replacement as Minister for Youth on 17 May, 1971 and had also been First Secretary of the Central Committee of the Communist Youth Union[136]. In addition, Adrian Nastase, a former member of the *Securitate* and son-in-law to two of Ceausescu's Ministers, became the executive chairman of the PDSR and, from 28 June, 1990 until 16 October, 1992, was the Minister of Foreign Affairs[137].

In the immediate years after the Revolution it was almost impossible to find capable politicians who were not in some way compromised by their activities under the old regime. But, extremely prominent functionaries and politicians from the Ceausescu regime also remained in powerful positions without attempting to explain their previous activities and refusing to accept personal responsibility. They did not demonstrate any remorse for their previous roles and the FSN did not embark on any programme which would force a critical examination of Romania's past and thus help the population to come to terms with its experience under Communism.

---

[134] Interview with Liana Petrescu from *România Libera*. Bucharest, 15.3.96.
[135] Interview with Professor Mario. Cluj, 23.2.96.
[136] Interview with Liana Petrescu from *România Libera*. Bucharest, 15.3.96.
[137] Interview with Liana Petrescu from *România Libera*. Bucharest, 15.3.96.

The Front encompassed not only those who were intimately linked to the old regime, but also included those in secondary positions within the *nomenklatura* who were less compromised and more technocratically inclined. This led to internal tensions and the crystallisation of two ideologically and politically opposed groups within the FSN; an orthodox and a reformist, technocratic faction. The reformist faction, headed by the then Prime Minister, Petre Roman, supported quicker liberalisation and privatisation of the economy, increased administrative de-centralisation and more local autonomy. They were also unequivocally in favour of Romanian membership of NATO and the European Union. The orthodox grouping, centred around President Iliescu, wanted to preserve certain specific values and institutions which had been formed under the Communist regime. They supported the principle of large-scale state intervention in the economy and aimed to keep as much of the economy as possible under state control. They viewed the highly centralised state which Ceausescu had developed as necessary for the effective administration of such an economy and so were not in favour of de-centralisation or administrative restructuring. In addition, the orthodox group demonstrated a strong anti-west sentiment and encouraged the xenophobic Romanian nationalism which Ceausescu had instrumentalised.

The internal dispute was ended by an orchestrated mass demonstration of miners, during which Parliament was stormed, which forced Petre Roman out of office. He was replaced as Prime Minister by Nicolae Vacariou, the former Chief of Department of the State Planning Council[138]. Roman formed an alternative National Savlation Front, forcing the faction supported by Iliescu to found a rival Democratic National Salvation Front (PD{FSN} – *Partidul Democrat{Frontul Salvarii Nationale}*). Both organisations took part in the 1992 elections, with the Democratic National Salvation Front retaining its majority. On winning the elections, the Democratic National Salvation Front renamed itself the Party of Social Democracy in Romania (PDSR – *Partidul Democratiei Sociale din România*). Petre Roman's party, the Social Democratic Union (USD – *Uniunea Social Democrat)*, agreed to

---

[138] Interview with Liana Petrescu from *România Libera*. Bucharest, 15.3.96.

cooperate with the Democratic Convention of Romania in 1992[139]. The USD has since changed its name to the Democratic Party[140].

Although Roman left the FSN taking many reformers with him, some remained. Led by Vaslie Secares, this group formed another reformist faction, 'A Future for Romania' (*GUVR*). Secares is the head of the 'National School for Administration and Politics', the former Party School, *Stefan Gheorghiu*. He is also vice-president of the EX-IMP Bank, the state Commercial Bank[141]. The group consists of young professionals aged between 40-45 who have studied abroad and whose main interest is ensuring everything functions effectively to enable them to fulfil their ambitions of attaining wealth and influence. Although the orthodox members of the party share this interest in power and money, they retain an ideological commitment to Communism because it is the only system which they have experienced and can therefore imagine. Their thinking patterns are simple and remain conditioned by Stalinism and Bolshevism. Iliescu plays the interests of the reformers and the hard-liners within the party against each other as a means of retaining personal control over the party. However, it is the hard-line, orthodox group which has gained the advantage.

This group aims to retain those elements of the previous system it deems ideologically justified and politically useful. Thus, the PDSR attracts those who are afraid that change will rob them of their power and position, be it political in the form of party administration, or economic in the form of managers of state enterprises. This policy is also comforting to those who are afraid of the unknown and the chaos transformation might entail. Gradual change, coupled with the retention of certain elements of the old system, also promised to keep the number of those who would become unemployed as a result of economic transformation to an absolute minimum. Thus, in the 1990 and 1992 elections, the majority of the population, especially those in rural areas with

---

[139] Ibid. Merkel, Wolfgang, Sandschneider, Eberhard, Segert, Dieter, (Hrsg.), *Systemwechsel II: Die Institutionalisierung der Demokratie*, p. 244.
[140] Ibid. Shafir, Michael, 'Romania's 'Different' Presidential Candidate: Nicolae Manolescu', *Open Media Research Institute (OMRINet)*. Http: //www.omri,cz.
[141] Interview with Gabriel Jeflea from *Institution for a Democratic Romania*. Bucharest, 4.3.96.

virtually no access to a source of information other than state-controlled media in the form of television, voted for FSN candidates, many of whom they knew had been Deputies under the Communist regime.

However, the attempt to incorporate elements of the old system into the new hampered both economic transformation and democratic consolidation. Half-hearted reform led to continuing economic stagnation and did not prevent the social hardships associated with more radical transformation policies. Privatisation was slow due to the government's own ambiguity and the fact that since 1992, it had no official programme and took decisions on a day to day basis, frequently following the whims of its extremist coalition partners. In turn, the lack of a clear government policy made it difficult for the opposition to formulate distinct alternative polices.

Although the PDSR came a close second to the Democratic Convention in Romania in the June 1996 local elections[142], due to its political skills, it managed to get more of its members elected as head of a local council than the CDR. Thus, the urban-rural divide in Romania continues to be an important factor in political life, with the PDSR sustaining its influence in rural areas, leaving the CDR more concentrated in urban constituencies[143]. Despite this, the PDSR needed to revitalise its image for the parliamentary and presidential elections scheduled for November 1996. The Vacariou government announced the successful conclusion of negotiations concerning the Hungarian-Romanian Basic Treaty and ended its coalition with the extremist parties, the Party of Greater Romania (PRM), the Party of Romanian National Unity (PUNR) and the Party of Socialist Labour (PSM). It also engaged in a mini-reshuffle.

---

[142] The CDR gained 19.58% of the votes for County Councillors on 2 June, and 17.56%. in the repeated ballot on 16 June. The PDSR came second gaining 16.28% and 16.35% respectively. Ibid. Shafir, Michael, 'Is the Romanian Opposition heading towards Victory?' *Open Media Research Institute (OMRINet)*. Http: //www.omri.cz.

[143] Ibid. Shafir, Michael, 'Is the Romanian Opposition Heading towards Victory?' *Open Media Research Institute (OMRINet)*. Http: //www.omri.cz.

The Health Minister, Iulian Mincu, who had been in charge of the portfolio since 1992, and the Culture Minister, Viorel Marginean, were forced to resign. Mincu had been one of Ceausescu's personal physicians and had administered his last insulin injection. He was also linked to the 'rational nutrition programme', the means by which Ceausescu medically rationalised the ever dwindling calorie intake which the Romanian population received[144]. And yet, it was not due to his past that Mincu was forced to resign, at the time Romania had no Lustration Law, but rather due to present misdemeanours. His name was linked to several damaging scandals, the most sensational of which concerned mismanagement of World Bank funds worth $180 million. These funds were supposed to be used to improve the Health system, but found their way into Mincu's own pockets. He was also responsible for the export of contaminated plasma to Germany and for the mismanagement of the distribution of free medicine which led to the suspension of the European Union's Romanian PHARE Programme. Despite this, he continues to represent the PDSR in Parliament[145]. Viorel Marginean had been a particularly servile artist under Ceausescu and, before taking up his position as Minister of Culture in May 1995, had been director of the National Museum of Arts. He used large amounts of public money to organise exhibits of his own work abroad. But his resignation, the seventh Minister of Culture to resign since 1989, did not attract much attention[146].

However, the PDSR continued to employ nationalist ideology to discredit the opposition and has been unable to fundamentally change its policy. This is because its most important source of support remains those party *apparatchiks* and former *nomenklatura* administrators who fear a new system will entail loss of position. In addition, it continues to rely heavily on the uninformed rural vote –

---

[144] Shafir, Michael, 'Mini-Reshuffle of Romanian Government', *Open Media Research Institute (OMRINet)*, Analytical Brief 295. Taken from the Internet on 26.11.96. Http: //www.omri.cz.

[145] Ibid. Shafir, Michael, 'Mini-Reshuffle of Romanian Government', *Open Media Research Institute (OMRINet)*. Http: //www.omri.cz.

[146] Ibid. Shafir, Michael, 'Mini-Reshuffle of Romanian Government', *Open Media Research Institute (OMRINet)*. Http: //www.omri.cz.

on those who are engaged in subsistence farming and rely on television for information. But, the duplicity and corruptibility of its Ministers and Deputies, and the PDSR's inability to present fruitful results or formulate new and more appropriate policies led to a decrease in its appeal amongst the young and workers, especially in urban areas. The PDSR and its presidential candidate, Ion Iliescu, were defeated in the 1996 elections (see 3.6.3)[147]. Yet despite defeat, the PDSR vote only decreased by about 3% when compared with the 1992 election results; its rural supporters had remained faithful in both the parliamentary and presidential elections. On the basis of exit polls, the critical 3% reduction in the PDSR's support was due to a loss of its appeal to those under 65, particularly the young and the workers[148].

After its electoral defeat, the PDSR became entangled in increasingly bitter internal disputes as the remaining reform grouping within the party urged those responsible for defeat to accept responsibility and resign to allow the party to rid itself not only of its outdated and corrupt image, but also to renew its ideology. The group, headed by the former Foreign Minister, Teodor Melescanu, called for the PDSR to restructure itself and allow a democratic debate on the future of the party, with the aim of moving the party towards the centre-left. Restructuring implies that those associated with corruption and the electoral defeat of the party in 1996 resign.

One of those held responsible for the defeat of the PDSR in the 1996 elections and seen as representing corruption is Adrian Nastase, PDSR chairman from 1992 until 1996, and now deputy chairman. Ironically, the majority of those calling for reform within the party were promoted by Iliescu shortly before the 1996 elections in an attempt to improve the PDSR's image. But as restructuring also implied Iliescu's replacement, he supported Nastase and indulged in bitter attacks on the reformers. This strategy, aimed purely at maintaining his personal position within the PDSR, reveals Iliescu's Communist-Bolshevist mentality and

---

[147] For detailed results, see Appendix XXXI, XXXII, XXXIII.
[148] Shafir, Micheal, 'Romania Opts for Political Change', *Open Media Research Institute (OMRINet)*, Analytical Brief 436. Taken from the Internet on 26.11.96. Http: //www.omri.cz.

conviction that, *my enemy's enemy is my friend*. Interestingly, this conviction is also evident in Iliescu's renewed cooperation with the opposition neo-fascist Greater Romania Party and its leader, Vadim Tudor, who was present at the PDSR national conference to express his regret over previous criticism of Iliescu[149].

Iliescu used the party conference to criticise party factionalism and move the PDSR further towards the left. The reformist group was not allowed to present its arguments at the conference and Iliescu and Nastase were re-elected as chairman and deputy chairman respectively. Iosif Boda, former Ambassador to Switzerland, and the economist, Viorel Salagean, were expelled from the PDSR on 20 June, 1997. Teodor Melescanu and the former Deputy Prime Minister, Mircea Cosea, resigned on 21 June, 1997. Mugurel Vintila and Marian Enache had resigned on the eve of the National Conference, and on 24 June, 1997, Ioan Pintea followed suit[150]. On 25 June, 1997, Melescanu declared his intention to found a new political party, the Alliance for Romania, which will fight corruption and form a new centre-left, social democratic party[151].

The internal dispute in the PDSR followed much the same pattern as that which led to the resignation of Petre Roman and his reformist grouping in 1991. The resignations and expulsions surrounding the national conference represent the final departure of reformist groupings from the PDSR and leave it firmly in the grip of the hard-line, neo-Communist, clienitlisitc groupings around Iliescu and Nastase. However, it is doubtful whether the PDSR's renewed alliance with the left-wing, nationalist opposition parties will achieve the same electoral success it enjoyed in 1992[152].

---

[149] *RFE/RL Newsline*, Vol. 1, No. 60, Part II, 25 June, 1997.
[150] *RFE/RL Newsline*, Vol. 1, No. 60, Part II, 25 June, 1997.
[151] *RFE/RL Newsline*, Vol. 1, No. 61, Part II, 26 June, 1997.
[152] On 16 September, 1997, the PDSR, the Greater Romanian Party and the Party of Socialist Labour agreed an electoral alliance. *RFE/RL Newsline*, Vol. 1, No. 119, 17 September 1997. The PDSR has also decided to give priority to 'national' concerns in its political discourse. *RFE/RL Newsline*, Vol. 1, No. 166, 24 November 1997.

3.4.4: Party of Socialist Labour/Romanian Communist Party

The Party of Socialist Labour (PSM – *Partidul Socialist al Muncii*), founded by Ilie Verdet, Prime Minister under Ceausescu from 1979-1982, and one of those held hostage in the Jiu Valley during the 1977 miner's strike[153], has proclaimed itself official successor to the Romanian Communist Party. Indeed, at its national conference, which took place from 1-2 November, 1997, it renamed itself the Romanian Communist Party[154]. Before joining the PDSR led coalition, it had called for those who were instrumental in causing the collapse of Ceausescu's regime to be brought to justice.

The party aims to protect the population from unemployment by giving everyone the right to work. It does not approve of cooperation with international financial institutions and is violently anti-western. It advocates limited economic transformation, aiming to retain state control over the majority of the economy and limiting forms of private ownership. At the same time, it is extremely nationalist and broke its coalition with the PDSR to support the two other extreme nationalist coalition partners in their opposition to the Hungarian-Romanian Basic Treaty. The PSM caters for those of extreme nationalist convictions who are unhappy with the social costs of reform and who have themselves lost out in the process. Its voters are mostly men in low income groups with a low level of education. Two thirds of its supporters are over 40 years old and many live in rural areas[155]. Although the party split in January 1995, with a less orthodox faction of six prominent party functionaries forming a new socialist party under Tudor Mohora, it maintained its level of support in the 1996 elections[156].

---

[153] de Nève, Dorothée, 'Die Parlamentarische Opposition in Rumänien', *Südosteuropa*, Vol. 35, No. 4, 1995, p. 322.
[154] *RFE/RL Newsline*, Vol. 1, No. 151, Part II, 3 November 1997.
[155] Ibid. Gabanyi, Anneli Ute, 'Politische Parteien in Rumänien nach der Wende', p. 23.
[156] Ibid. Gabanyi, Anneli Ute, 'Politische Parteien in Rumänien nach der Wende', p. 24.

3.5: Extremist Parties

The extremist parties share a common belief that society must be subordinated to the ideal of a mythical nation. A prominent role for a paternalistic state in the economy and in the distribution of resources is the favoured means of ensuring the welfare of the citizens. Therefore, a gradual transformation and the retention of state control over strategic areas of industry is promoted with the ultimate aim of creating a mixed economy. All tend to view foreign investment with suspicion and have an anti-Western orientation. In addition, ethnicity is the only criterion judged important in deciding citizenship. Thus, anti-Semitism and fears about other outside groups such as the Hungarian minority in Romania and the Roma population are all pervasive. Such parties do not put much faith in democratic institutions or pluralism, but rather in corporatism and the idea of a strong leader who embodies the nation and is endowed with far-reaching powers.

All the extremist parties use populism and demagogic slogans to appeal to an electorate uncertain and disadvantaged by transformation. Within their ranks are included those whose only aim is personal enrichment and influence as well as those whose xenophobia is all consuming. Although such views are often shared by the remaining orthodox Communist Parties, Romania is the only country which has witnessed cooperation between former Communists and ultra-nationalists in the form of a 'red-brown' coalition.

3.5.1: Extremist Romanian Parties

The Party of Romanian National Unity (PUNR), the Greater Romania Party (PRM) and the Party of Socialist Labour (PSM) were the coalition partners of the PDSR from 1992 until 1996. Although the PDSR announced a coalition break with the PUNR on 22 March and 16 May, 1996, no action followed and it was only on the eve of the 1996 parliamentary elections, on 2 September, that the PDSR finally broke its coalition with the PUNR[157]. The decision was officially due to the vicious attacks on the PDSR which the PUNR had launched following the joint announcement by the Romanian and Hungarian Deputy Foreign Ministers, Marcel Dinu and Ferenc Somogyi, on 14 August, 1996, that agreement over the form of the Basic Treaty between Romania and Hungary had finally been reached[158].

As negotiations had been dragging on for over two years without any real prospect of a successful conclusion, the announcement came as a surprise. The document was finalised as a result of a change in Bucharest's position concerning the European Council Recommendation 1201[159]. Previously the Romanian government had opposed any mention of the Recommendation, but finally agreed to it on condition that an attachment of joint specifications relating to it was also included. It insists that the inclusion of the Recommendation in the Treaty does not grant national minorities 'collective rights' or territorial autonomy based on ethnicity. The mention of national minority problems in the text of the Treaty is understood by the Romanian government as being strictly within the specifications of the Framework Convention for the Protection of National Minorities[160]. However, some on the Romanian side still fear that Recommendation 1201 could be interpreted to give the Hungarian minority collective rights and legal powers to set up autonomous structures based on ethnic criteria. These suspicions have been given a certain amount of credence by the progressive radicalisation of the Democratic Federation of Hungarians in Romania. Although it must be noted that such radicalisation occurred as a result of persistent rejection and hostility on the part of the PDSR-led government. But, despite the PDSR's decision to

---

[157] Shafir, Michael, 'Romanian Coalition Breaks', *Open Media Research Institute (OMRINet)*, Analytical Brief 314. Taken from the Internet on 26.11.96. Http: //www.omri.cz.

[158] Shafir, Michael, 'Light at the End of the Hungarian-Romanian Tunnel?' *Open Media Research Institute (OMRINet)*, Analytical Brief 283. Taken from the Internet on 26.11.96. Http: //www.omri.cz.

[159] Recommendation 1201 regulates national minority collective rights.

[160] Ibid. Shafir, Michael, 'Light at the End of the Hungarian-Romanian Tunnel?' *Open Media Research Institute (OMRINet)*. Http: //www.omri.cz.

sign a Basic Treaty[161] and the nationalist parties' predictable objection to any concession granted to the Hungarian minority, such internal coalition conflict was not new. The PUNR's chairman, Gheorghe Funar, had in the past called for Iliescu to be removed from office on grounds of treason.

After the announcement concerning the Basic Treaty, the PUNR accused the PDSR of selling out to the Hungarian minority. The PDSR's other extremist coalition partners allied themselves with the PUNR and refused further cooperation within the coalition. This meant important legislation could not pass Parliament before the end of the legislation period. This included the new Penal Code, which had already twice failed to pass Parliament, a law covering the Ombudsman, one clarifying Ministerial Responsibility, and a law dealing with the privatisation of state trading companies and banks. The latter was considered by the World Bank and the International Monetary Fund (IMF) to be absolutely essential for the success of economic reform. The PDSR had to rely on the opposition in order to pass this legislation[162].

By signing the Basic Treaty and distancing itself from its coalition partners, the PDSR was hoping to present itself as a mature and moderate party in the 1996 electoral campaign. However, after its defeat in the elections on 3 November, 1996, it reverted to a nationalist campaign, stirring anti-Hungarian sentiment. Following the power-sharing agreement between the Democratic Convention of Romania (CDR) and the third placed Democratic Party (PD), which involved the transfer of support from the PD presidential candidate, Petre Roman, to the CDR candidate, Emil Constantinescu, the PDSR secretary general, Miron Mitrea warned of an alliance between the CDR and the UDMR, presenting it as a serious threat to Romanian national security. On 9 November, in Alba Iulia, Iliescu presented himself as the only guarantor of stability in Romania and accused the UDMR of plotting a Yugoslav-style secession of Transylvania. This attack

---

[161] Ionescu, Dan, 'The Romanian-Hungarian Basic Treaty', *Open Media Research Institute (OMRINet)*, Analytical Brief 334. Taken from the Internet on 26.11.96. Http: //www.omri.cz.

[162] Ibid. Shafir, Michael, 'Romanian Coalition Breaks', *Open Media Research Institute (OMRINet)*. Http: //www.omri.cz.

came in response to the UDMR's decision to support Emil Constantinescu, the CDR's candidate in the run-off presidential election[163].

The PDSR's willingness to form a coalition with extreme nationalist parties rather than make political concessions to the opposition and its use of nationalist propaganda as a means of retaining political power demonstrate its dubious democratic credentials. Although it accepted the results of the 1996 elections, the PDSR does not demonstrate the characteristics of a democratic political party; but neither is it extremist in the sense of the PUNR or PRM, since it is willing to renounce nationalist propaganda if this would help it retain power. The members of the PDSR follow the tradition of the Romanian Communist Party and are quite simply opportunist; willing to use every means at their disposal to ensure they remain in power, as the exposure of the party's secret telephone bugging of the opposition shortly before the 1996 elections demonstrated. In this sense they remain Bolshevists. Although the main interests of the Greater Romanian Party and the Party of Romanian National Unity also undoubtedly lie in retaining political power, they are ideologically committed to extreme nationalism.

3.5.1.1: Greater Romania Party

The Greater Romania Party (PRM – *Partidul România Mare*) is led by Corneliu Vadim Tudor and was founded on 20 June, 1991[164]. He is well-known for his previous work as 'court poet' under Ceausescu, and for his virulent nationalism and anti-Hungarian and anti-Semitic views. His views are published regularly in *Politica* and *România Mare*. Under Ceausescu, Tudor was notorious as the editor of the weekly journal, *Saptamana*, 'The Week', in which he attacked those intellectuals who were critical of the regime[165]. However, it is not only Tudor who is linked to the former regime;

---

[163] Mato, Zsolt-Istvan, 'Iliescu and His Party Play the Nationalist Card', *Open Media Research Institute (OMRINet)*, Analytical Brief 461. Taken from the Internet on 26.11.96. Http: www//omri.cz.
[164] Ibid. Gabanyi, Anneli Ute, 'Politische Parteien in Rumänien nach der Wende', p. 26.
[165] Interview with Liana Petrescu from *România Libera*. Bucharest, 15.3.96

the PRM Deputy for Bucharest, Iuliu Ioan Furo, is known to be a former member of the *Securitate* who tortured prisoners[166]. In addition, the PRM had important contacts within the PDSR government; although officially non-affiliated, the Prime Minister Nicolae Vacariou was a PRM supporter[167].

Interestingly, in 1992 the PRM's voters were mostly young, 90% being urban dwellers under the age of 40. They had a good standard of education and enjoyed a comfortable or high standard of living[168]. It seems that the extremist parties have carefully avoided intruding into each others social base. Thus, the PRM mobilises those of a higher educational level, whereas the PSM gains the support of the lower class. In order to avoid competition with the PUNR, the PRM is not active in Transylvania, concentrating its activities in the Old Kingdom, that is in areas which were part of Romania from its formation. In these areas the PRM uses the population's lack of knowledge about the situation in Transylvania to inflame anti-Hungarian sentiment. However, as the situation of the Hungarian minority is not such a pressing concern outside Transylvania, the PRM concentrates on instrumentalising prejudice against the Roma population. It is a Stalinist party which also promotes the ideology of the fascist Iron Guard. It is anti-Semitic, racist, anti-Western, anti-democratic and anti-reform. It glorifies the achievements of Communism and wants the release of the members of the Ceausescu elite who were arrested after 1989. It aims to introduce a strong, perhaps even a military state. It is strongly averse to cooperation with Western financial organisations and does not approve of selling large industrial enterprises to foreigners. It wants to rid Romania of the foreign capital already invested and aims to increase Romania's exports to China, the Soviet Union and the Third World.

Although it emphasises the Hungarian and Western threat, it plays down difficulties concerning the Moldovan question. This is because too much public support for a border revision with

---

[166] Interview with Liana Petrescu from *România Libera*. Bucharest, 15.3.96.

[167] Ibid. Gabanyi, Anneli Ute, 'Politische Parteien in Rumänien nach der Wende', p. 27.

[168] Ibid. Gabanyi, Anneli Ute, 'Politische Parteien in Rumänien nach der Wende', p. 26.

Moldova could also justify any Hungarian calls for a border revision in Transylvania. The Party of Romanian National Unity's position towards union with Moldova is therefore also somewhat nebulous and, while supporting the principle of the unification of all Romanians, it tends to avoids the issue.

3.5.1.2: Party of Romanian National Unity

The Party of Romanian National Unity (PUNR – *Partidul Unitatii Nationale Române*) was led by the Mayor of Cluj, Gheorghe Funar, until his removal from that post at the PUNR national convention on 24, March 1997. Although the Party's Central Committee had already removed him on 22 February, Funar had not recognised the legality of his dismissal. The interim president of the party, Valeriu Tabara, immediately removed Ioan Gavra, one of Funar's opponents, from the post of secratary general[169]. The party's internal machinations and the ridiculousness of Funar, who has claimed he was the victim of an assassination attempt after a stone was thrown at him as he sat in a Restaurant in Cluj[170], would be comical if the PUNR was not a parliamentary party with the potential to disrupt the course of Romanian transformation and democratisation.

The PUNR is an extreme nationalist, xenophobic party which manipulates the anxieties of ordinary Romanians as a means of preserving its members own personal power. It is closely connected to the neo-fascist organisation, *Vatra Românеasca*, 'Romanian Hearth', led by Ion Coja[171]. Although *Vatra Românеasca* is not a political party, it has published a manifesto and is politically active.

The PUNR concentrates its activities on the Romanian population in Transylvania, particularly those who were settled there during the Communist regime. They were sent to

---

[169] *OMRI Daily Digest*, No. 58, Part II, 24 March 1997. The in-fighting has continued with a meeting of the PUNR National Council invalidating Funar's expulsion. It also suspended Valeriu Tabara and 11 other Council members and called an Extraordinary Congress. But, as only 128 of the Council's 243 members attended the meeting, the Party's Executive Secretary declared it illegal. *RFE/RL Newsline*, Vol. 1, No. 166, Part II, 22 November 1997.

[170] *RFE/RL Newsline*, Vol. 2, No. 16, Part II, 26 January 1998.

[171] Ibid. Staar, Richard, F., (Ed.), *The 1991 Yearbook on International Communist Affairs*, p. 354.

Transylvania partly to dilute the numbers of the Hungarian minority, but also to work in the new industrial complexes[172]. This group had little experience or knowledge of its Hungarian neighbours and was most influenced by the Communist regime's nationalist propaganda. It has also been particularly susceptible to the PUNR's populism because its members fear economic reorganisation and privatisation of state industry. Thus, the majority of the PUNR's support comes from this group of old and new functionaries in the administration and the military, all of whom earn relatively good wages[173].

The PUNR presents the Hungarian minority, rather than the economic and administrative structure, as the major threat to Romanian stability. This task has been made easier by the radicalisation of some sections within the Hungarian minority. The Hungarians feel threatened by radical Romanian nationalism and have drawn together, becoming more aware of their ethnic identity, and thus presenting a more united and theoretically dangerous group for the nationalists to attack. By presenting the Hungarian minority as the root cause of all Romania's problems the PUNR aims not only to harm the minority, but also to prevent the transformation of the economic and social structure, which in turn would adversely affect the personal interests of many of its members and supporters.

However, once forced out of the ruling coalition the PUNR was unable to reward its supporters and members or obtain extra funds for the 1996 election campaign from the PDSR. As funds and the chance of gaining any real power became scarce, many members of the PUNR moved on to potentially more generous and powerful benefactors and its support declined. The first to go was Aurel Novac, the Transport Minister in Nicolae Vacaroiu's government. Next was Iosif Gavril Chiuzbaian, vice-chairman of the PUNR and former Justice Minister. In October, Valer Suian, the general secretary of the PUNR left, saying he could no longer agree with

---

[172] For more information on Ceausescu's policy concerning work placements and minority rights, see Shafir, Michael, *Romania: Politics, Economics and Society*, Frances Pinter Publishers 1985, pp. 158-168.
[173] Ibid. Gabanyi, Anneli Ute, 'Politische Parteien in Rumänien nach der Wende', p. 25.

Funar's extremist policies. However, his resignation seems to have actually been caused by the fact that his first place on the PUNR Bucharest Party List for the Senate had been taken by Pavel Corut[174]. This in turn may have been a result of Suian's standing against Funar in the 1995 election for the party chairmanship. The chairman of the Brasov branch of the PUNR, Gheorghe Dosinescu, along with other important members in Iasi and Prahova counties also resigned, followed on 21 October, 1996 by the chairman of the Bucharest branch, Emil Pop[175].

Although most prominent members of the PUNR seemed to be deserting the party, Ion Coja literature Professor at Bucharest University, infamous anti-Semite, founder of *Vatra Românesca*, 'Romanian Hearth', and admirer of Romania's inter-war fascist movement, the Iron Guard, returned and ran as a PUNR candidate for the Senate. He began his political career in the National Salvation Front, before moving to the PUNR. He left the PUNR after quarrelling with Funar and became a member of the Democratic Agrarian Party (PDAR), for whom he was presidential candidate in 1996. However, after the 1996 elections, the PDAR formed a National Centrist Alliance (ANC) with the Romanian Ecological Movement and the New Romania Party, electing Ion Pop de Popa as the chairman of the Alliance. Coja left in a fit of pique and returned to the PUNR[176].

The willingness of even the most prominent members of the PUNR to change their allegiances so quickly after their links to power and money were severed demonstrates that their real interest lies in the maintenance of their own personal power base. Although they may be committed to the xenophobia they preach, they are opportunists and will immediately discard that which can no longer provide them with any immediate political benefit. Thus, once removed from the governing coalition, the PUNR suffered a rapid disintegration and with the exception of Cluj and a few other

---

[174] Pavel Corut is a successful author of spy thrillers which present Romania as the victim of Hungarian, Israeli or American plots.
[175] Ibid. Shafir, Michael, 'Is the Party of Romanian National Unity Disintegrating?' *Open Media Research Institute (OMRINet)*. Http: //www.omri.cz.
[176] Ibid. Shafir, Michael, 'Is the Party of Romanian National Unity Disintegrating?' *Open Media Research Institute (OMRINet)*. Http: //www.omri.cz.

Translyvanian counties, support for the PUNR has generally declined. This trend has been strengthened by the behaviour of the PUNR's former leader, Funar, who has refused to recognise his dismissal as leader or expulsion from the party[177].

In the 1996 elections, the PUNR share of the vote fell from approximately 8% to 5%. The PSM maintained its percentage share at about 3%, and the PRM managed to slightly increase its vote from 4% to nearly 5%[178]. The Romanian extremist parties do not compete for votes, rather they work in tandem. This may help to explain their continued electoral success. Although the extremist parties have lost their political influence at a national level, they have retained a significant amount of electoral appeal and have representatives in both Parliament and the Senate. It is therefore possible that at some time in the future they will once again hold the balance of power in the Romanian Parliament.

3.5.2: Hungarian Justice and Life Party

The only extremist party in Hungary to gain notoriety is Ivan Csurka's Hungarian Justice and Life Party (MIEP – *Magyar Igazság és Elet Pártja*). The name of the party demonstrates its affinity with Hungarian populist writers of the 1930s and 1940s who glorified Hungarian traditions, rejected outside influences and advocated a paternalistic role for a state which would serve the Hungarian nation. Csurka's political theses, which appeared in the main MDF publication of policy in August 1992, was the first openly neo-fascist manifesto published in Central Europe after 1989[179].

Csurka views the nation as a living entity which faces a number of threats to its survival. One of these threats is an international Jewish conspiracy, emanating from Western bankers and

---

[177] Funar was expelled after he initiated numerous law suits against other PUNR leaders. The PUNR has expelled a further nine members who continue to support Funar. *RFE/RL Newsline*, Vol. 1, No. 154, Part II, 26 November 1997.
[178] Ibid. Shafir, Michael, 'Romania Opts for Political Change', *Open Media Research Institute (OMRINet)*. Http: //www.omri.cz.
[179] Szayna, Thomas, S., 'Ultra-Nationalism in Central Europe', *Orbis*, Vol. 37, No. 4, Fall 1993. For an analysis of the 'Treatise', see Pataki, Judith, 'Istvan Csurka's Tract: Summary and Reactions', and Oltay, Edith, 'A Profile of Istvan Csurka', *RFE/RL Research Report*, 9 October 1992.

Communists. The Roma represent another threat because as they are viewed as causing the deterioration of the Hungarian genetic pool. Csurka reserves the right to speak for the nation for himself and his followers and views the creation of a paternalistic state which would care for the poor and ensure a 'Third Way' between Capitalism and Communism as the party's goal. However, tolerance and democracy play no part in this concept.

Csurka founded the MIEP after he was expelled from the Hungarian Democratic Forum. It had the support of twelve former MDF Deputies and was thus able to create a parliamentary faction. This faction was officially recognised and given places on four Parliamentary Committees, but its status was rather nebulous. Although officially not a member of the government coalition, it often supported government initiatives and so was responsible for the survival of the MDF government until the 1994 elections[180]. Csurka's important position within the MDF and its initial subdued reaction to the publication of his theses demonstrates his influence and strong following within the MDF.

Lajos Für, former chairman of the MDF and former Minister of Defence, is a member of the nationalist-populist faction within the MDF and remains one of Csurka's allies. As Minister of Defence, he was subject to criticism for failing to act decisively against increasing neo-fascist incidents. In addition, his placement of MDF activists in high posts in the Ministry of Defence caused the Soldiers' Interest Protection Union to complain about the politicisation of the military. Although the MDF abolished the institution which had been in charge of military political education during the Communist regime, it attempted to introduce a new form of 'patriotic education'. Für's public remarks to the effect that it was the Hungarian army's task to defend all Hungarians, even those outside Hungarian borders, questioned the validity of existing borders and coincided with Csurka's nationalist agenda[181]. Csurka appealed for cross-party action to prevent the signing and ratification of the Hungarian-Romanian Basic Treaty.

---

[180] Ibid. Ágh, Attila, Kurtán, Sándor, (Eds.), *Democratization and Europeanization in Hungary: The First Parliament (1990-1994)*, p. 204.
[181] Ibid. Szayna, Thomas, S., 'Ultra-Nationalism in Central Europe', *Orbis*.

The MIEP relies on support from disaffected youth, the older population in rural areas and traditionally inclined workers with a low level of education. While the results of the 1994 elections demonstrate that Csurka's extremist position is not shared by the majority of the Hungarian population, the continued success of the radical populist FKGP shows that continuing economic hardship may lead to the formation of an ultra-nationalist, neo-fascist political movement whose potential lies in the 'protest vote'.

This potential has been captured by the radical populist FKGP, which is the only extremist party represented in the Hungarian Parliament. In reaction to the economic hardship and social tension caused by the Socialist Party's austerity programme, support for FKGP has increased. In an opinion poll carried out by *Szoda Ipsos* in March 1997, the FKGP gained 29% support, FIDESZ 24% and the Socialist Party 22%[182]. In the same way as the participation of extremist parties in the government coalition between 1992-1996 hindered democratic consolidation and created political instability in Romania, FKGP participation in government would also threaten political stability and democratic consolidation in Hungary.

3.5.3: Czech Assembly for the Republic/Republican Party

The extremist Czech Assembly for the Republic/Republican Party (SPR-RSC – *Sdruzeni pro republiku-Republikánská strana Ceskoslovenska*) is a neo-fascist party which occupies the fringes of the political spectrum. It aims to create an ethnically pure 'Greater Czechoslovakia'. It favours a paternalistic state and corporatism, job protection and the creation of a mixed economy. Although the party is anti-Semitic, it concentrates its attention on the Roma minority, calling for their 're-settlement'. It has however proved incapable of controlling radicalised groups of skinheads who have been responsible for violent attacks on Roma. Unusually for an extremist party, the SPR-RSC has little interest in the military, calling instead for the abolition of military service and the formation of a professional army. It is pathologically anti-Communist and maintains that all the other Czech political parties have remained tools in the hands of Communists. It calls for the

---

[182] *OMRI Daily Digest*, No. 48, Part II, 10 March 1997.

trial and sentencing of all those involved with the Communist regime. Rather embarrassingly, it seems that the party's leader, Miroslav Sladek, worked as a censor in the Communist regimre's Information and Propaganda Department[183]. Despite this rather murky past, Sladek has continued to dominate the party and those who come into conflict with him either leave or are expelled.

Sladek has courted the media and increased his notoriety with outrageous actions, such as planting a Czechoslovak flag in the Transcarpathian region belonging to the Ukraine; submitting himself to a psychiatric test, supposedly under government pressure; delivering racist public speeches; and indulging in rabid denunciations of every other party, politician, and even Vaclav Havel, as 'pigs' and 'traitors'. In this way he aims to disrupt the democratic political system and attract public attention. The SPR-RSC further mobilises support by organising public demonstrations and meetings. One such event was the demonstration called to protest at the signing of the German-Czech Treaty in January 1997.

The SPR-RSC's draws most support from male adults who are under thirty. Its greatest regional strongholds are the cities of northern Bohemia which suffer from high unemployment. It has very limited appeal for the intelligansia and in Prague and those areas less affected by unemployment. Its radical actions have also created a negative image and effectively limited its scope of appeal, while its attacks on all the other parties in the Czech political system have robbed it of any possible coalition partners and the possibility of any real political influence. Thus, it has remained a protest grouping. Despite this, it increased its share of the vote and seats in the Czech Parliament from 14 after the 1992 elections, to 8.01% of the vote and 18 seats after the 1996 elections[184]. Although this should be considered more as a protest vote than a demonstration of support for Sladek, the possibility remains that if the economic and political situation does not improve, support for the SPR-SRC will increase and pose a real threat to democratic consolidation.

---

[183] Ibid. Szayna, Thomas, S., 'Ultra-Nationalism in Central Europe'.
[184] *Open Media Research Institute (OMRINet).* Taken from the Internet on 26.11.96. Http: //www.omri.cz.

3.6: Election Results

Although political parties have to cope with similar problems during transformation, the Hungarian, Romanian and Czech electorates have chosen representatives of different political views to govern them. This differentiated response can be traced partly to historical experiences; the different forms of Communist rule which the population experienced; and the differing conditions of the countries' economies and social structure, but must also be seen as the natural effect that democratisation has had on the region.

At least two democratic elections have occurred in all the countries; and in Hungary and Romania these have resulted in a change of government. Although the governing coalition remained in power in the Czech Republic, its parliamentary majority was much reduced and it suffered numerous political crises, culminating in Prime Minister Klaus' resignation in December 1997. Interestingly, especially in the case of Hungary where an ecological movement was instrumental in the formation of independent groups and organisations, green and ecological parties have failed to gain any substantial electoral support. This is no doubt due to the population's more pressing economic concerns. The following election results reveal the volatility of voter behaviour and the persistence of historical, ethnic, religious and regional cleavages, and extremist tendencies, all of which hinder democratic consolidation.

3.6.1: Hungarian Election Results

Democratic elections took place in Hungary in two rounds on 25 March and 8 April, 1990, and recorded a turn-out of 65.77% for the first round and 45.44% for the second round[185]. The elections resulted in victory for the Hungarian Democratic Forum (MDF) which, although it only received 24.7% of the popular vote, gained 42.5% of the parliamentary seats and formed a coalition government with the Independent Smallholders (FKGP) and the Christian Democratic People's Party (KDNP) (see Table 4)[186].

---

[185] Ibid. Segert, Dieter, Machos, Csilla, *Parteien in Osteuropa*, p. 63.
[186] For the results of the 1990 elections, see Appendix XVII, XVIII.

Table 4
Seats in the Hungarian Parliament, 25 March-8 April, 1990

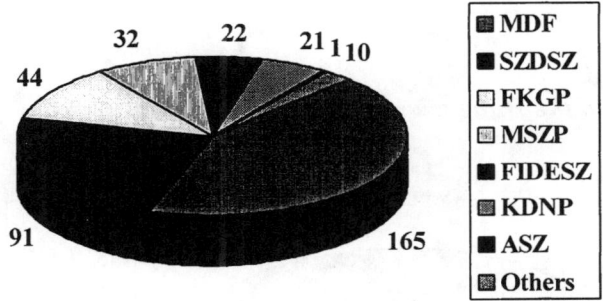

MDF: Hungarian Democratic Forum
SZDSZ: Alliance of Free Democrats
FKGP: Independent Smallholders
MSZP: Hungarian Socialist Party
FIDESZ: Alliance of Young Democrats
KDNP: Christian Democratic People's Party
ASZ: Agrarian Alliance

The Candidate of the Agrarian Alliance and the 10 Independent MP's won their seats outright in the first round elections, even though their parties did not cross the 4% threshold to enter Parliament.

Source: Adapted from White, Stephen, Batt, Judy, Lewis, Paul, G., (Eds.), *Developments in East European Politics*, Macmillan Press Ltd 1993, p. 73. Original in *Magyar Kozlony*, No. 25, 1990.

The same phenomenon occurred during the 1994 elections, which were held on 8 May and 29 May[187]. They resulted in the Hungarian Socialist Party gaining 54% of the parliamentary seats

---

[187] See Appendix XIX.

with 33% of the popular vote (see Table 5 and Table 6 overleaf)[188]. This has increased discussion over the problem of systemic legitimacy and political identification already mentioned.

Table 5
Seats in the Hungarian Parliament, 8-29 May, 1994

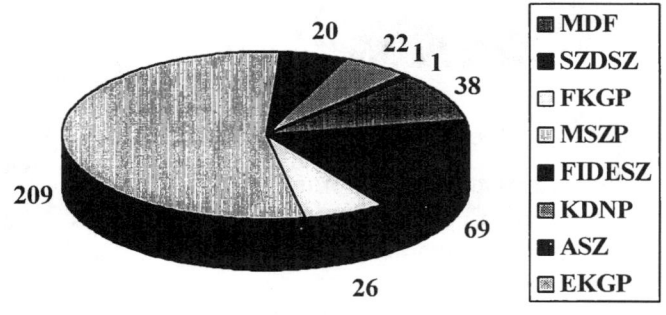

Table 6
% Votes gained by each Party

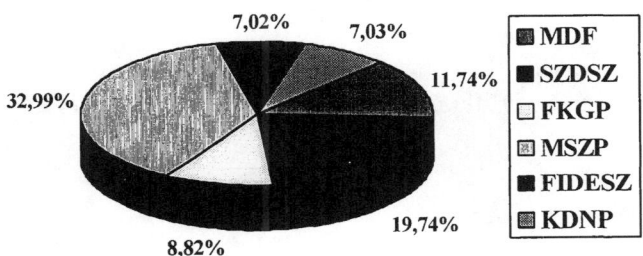

MDF: Hungarian Democratic Forum
SZDSZ: Alliance of Free Democrats
FKGP: Independent Smallholders
MSZP: Hungarian Socialist Party
FIDESZ: Alliance of Young Democrats
KDNP: Christian Democratic People's Party

Source: Adapted from Segert, Dieter, Machos, Csilla, *Parteien in Osteuropa*, Westdeutscher Verlag 1995, p. 98.

Despite this, the Hungarian system seems to be relatively stable. Extremist parties have been politically marginalised and although the major parties are still in the process of developing their political identity, they have not suffered from fragmentation and have remained in Parliament.

3.6.2: Czech Election Results

The Czech Republic is the only one of the three countries in which the same coalition has managed to remain in power. The first elections held in 1990 were effectively a referendum on Communism and the pending radical transformation of the system.

They resulted in an overwhelming majority for the Civic Forum[189]. After the dissolution of Czechoslovakia, the Czech Republic's course of rapid reform under the government led by Vaclav Klaus was endorsed by the population in the 1993 elections (see Table 7)[190].

Table 7
Seats in the Czech Assembly of Deputies, 1 January, 1993

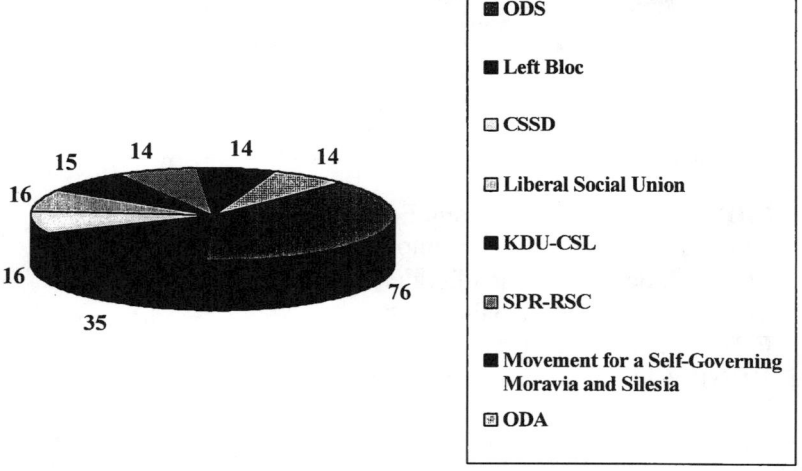

ODS: Civic Democratic Party
CSSD: Social Democratic Party
KDU-CSL: Christian Democratic Union-Czechoslovak People's Party
SPR-RSC: Assembly of the Republic-Czechoslovak Republican Party
ODA: Civic Democratic Alliance

Source: Adapted from Senechal, David, A., *Czechoslovakia*. Taken from the Internet on 29.2.96. Http: //ww2.artsci.wustl.edu/~ps4271/czs-ds.html.

---

[189] For election results, see Appendix XXI.
[190] For election results, see Appendix XXIII.

Political Democratisation

The 1996 elections resulted in victory for the ODS, but with a much reduced majority[191]. Its coalition with the KDU-CSL and the ODA had no overall parliamentary majority until two Deputies, who were expelled from the CSSD, decided to vote with the government, thus giving it a parliamentary majority of 101 in the 200 seat Parliament (see Table 8 overleaf)[192].

Table 8
Seats in the Czech Assembly of Deputies, 31 May-1 June, 1996

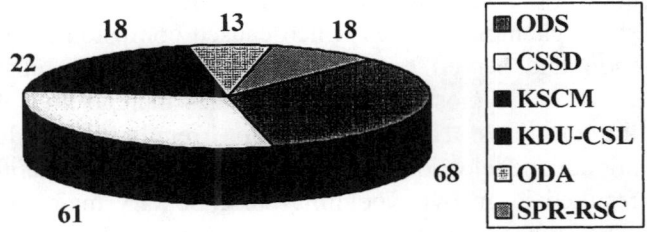

ODS: Civic Democratic Party
CSSD: Social Democratic Party
KSCM: Communist Party of Bohemia and Moravia
KDU-CSL: Christian Democratic Union-Czechoslovak People's Party
ODA: Civic Democratic Alliance
SPR-RSC: Assembly of the Republic-Czechoslovak Republican Party

Source: Adapted from *Open Media Research Institute (OMRINet)*. Taken from the Internet on 13.7.96. Http: \\www.omri.cz.

---

[191] For election results, see Appendix XXV, XXVI.
[192] *OMRI Daily Digest*, No. 59, Part II, 25 March 1997.

In the light of the fragmentation of the conservative parties following the collapse of the coalition led by the ODS, the success of the extremist SPR-RSC is a cause for concern. It demonstrates the potential of a protest vote in the face of economic hardship and political uncertainty. The current lack of feasible alternatives for disgruntled conservative voters and the rather left-wing orientation of the CSSD could lead to an increase in the protest vote and polarise the Czech political landscape. This would hinder transformation and represent a set-back for democratic consolidation.

3.6.3: Romanian Election Results

The first Romanian elections held after the December Revolution were surrounded by controversy. The FSN set up a number of 'phantom' parties which caused confusion amongst the population and served to decrease the opposition's chances of gaining power. In most cases, these parties merged with the FSN after the elections. However, despite irregularities and certain reservations, the elections were considered to be generally fair. They resulted in an overwhelming parliamentary majority for the FSN. The opposition was extremely fragmented and unable to present an effective alternative (see Table 9)[193]

---

[193] For election results, see Appendix XXVIII, XXIX.

Table 9
Seats in the Romanian Chamber of Deputies, 20 May, 1990

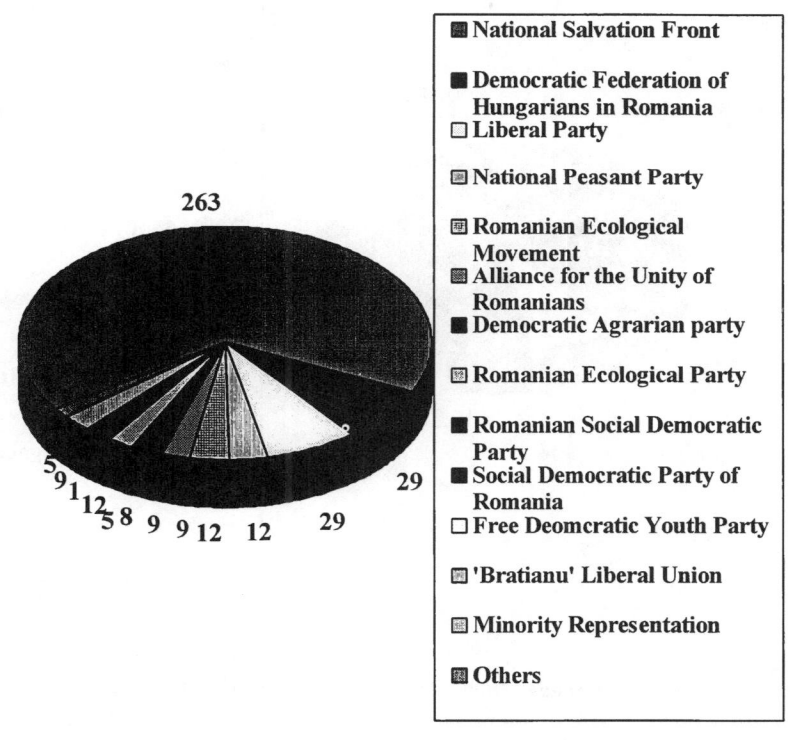

Source: Adapted from Staar, Richard, F., (Ed.), *The 1991 Yearbook on International Communist Affairs*, Hoover Institute Press 1991, p. 337. Also Grey, Jason, *Romania*. Taken from the Internet on 26.11.96.
Http: //ww2.artsci.wustl.edu/~ps4271/rom-jg.html.

The Romanian Senate presented a similar picture of opposition fragmentation and domination by the FSN (see Table 10 overleaf).

Table 10
Seats in the Romanian Senate, 20 May, 1990

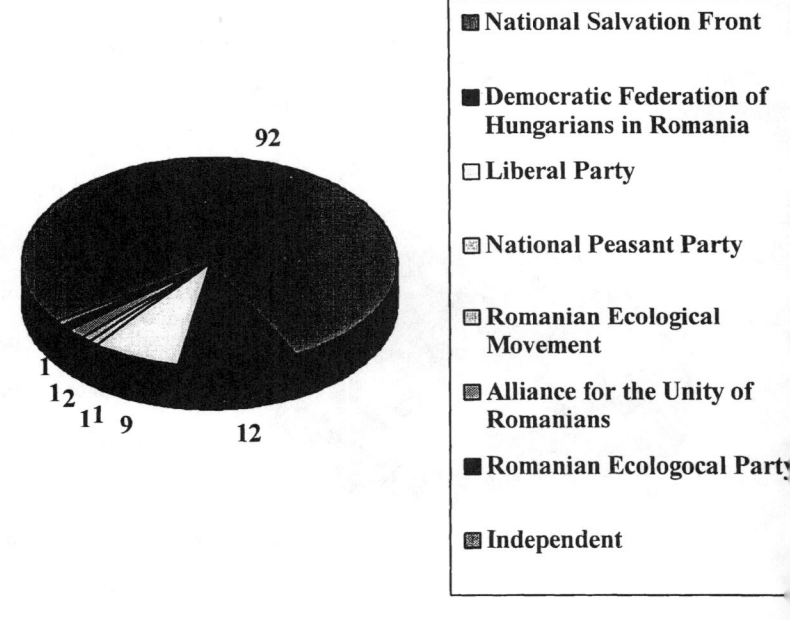

Source: Adapted from Staar, Richard, F., (Ed.), *The 1991 Yearbook on International Communist Affairs*, Hoover Institute Press 1991, p. 337. Also Grey, Jason, *Romania*. Taken from the Internet on 26.11.96.
Http: //ww2.artsci.wustl.edu/~ps4271/rom-jg.html.

The FSN's successor, the PDSR, continued to dominate Romanian politics until the 1996 general elections, which resulted in victory for the Romanian Democratic Convention (see Tables 11 and 12 overleaf)[194]. The victory of the CDR represents a new stage in Romanian democratic consolidation.

---

[194] For election results, see Appendix XXXI, XXXII, XXXIII.

Table 11
***Seats in the Romanian Chamber of Deputies,
3 November, 1996***

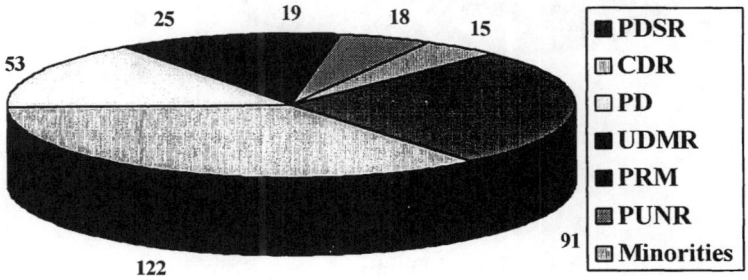

Source: Adapted from *Open Media Research Institute (OMRINet)*. Taken from the Internet on 26.11.96. Http: //www.omri.cz. Also Press Department of the Romanian Embassy, Bonn.

Table 12
Seats in the Romanian Senate, 3 November, 1996

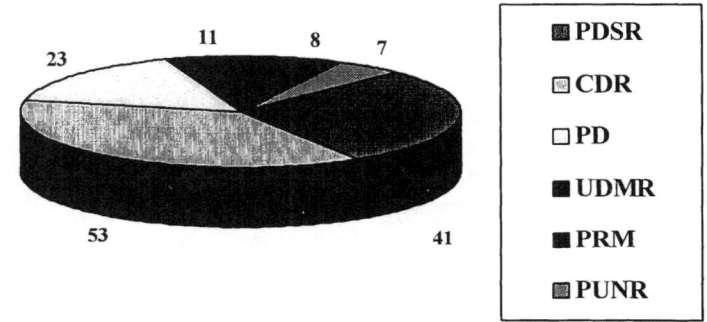

PDSR: Party of Social Democracy in Romania
CDR: Democratic Convention of Romania
PD: Democratic Party
UDMR: Democratic Federation of Hungarians in Romania
PRM: Party of Greater Romania
PUNR: Party of Romanian National Unity

Source: Adapted from *Open Media Research Institute (OMRINet)*. Taken from the Internet on 26.11.96. Http: //www.omri.cz. Also Press Department of the Romanian Embassy, Bonn.

Although the PDSR promised stability and gradual reform, it was unable to halt Romania's economic decline. The population voted for an opposition which advocated radical transformation, westernization, and which took a clear stand against the extreme nationalism which had threatened to dominate Romanian policy making. However, in view of the internal strife which has racked the coalition since its formation, the continuing presence and political influence of the extremist parties, the PRM and the PUNR, in the Romanian Chamber of Deputies and the Senate is a cause for concern. In addition, the constant coalition crises threaten the desperately needed radical economic transformation programme and have created political uncertainty which could lead to popular disillusion and an increase in the extremist vote.

3.7: Democratisation and Political Parties

Since the Revolutions of 1989, numerous political parties have formed and democratic elections have been held resulting in changes to political coalitions and governments. In this sense, formal democratisation has been achieved in all three countries However, the specific Communist legacy has had a differentiated influence on the course of development of the respective political parties.

The Negotiated Revolution in Hungary led to the creation of a complicated electoral system which is weighted in favour of the party elites. This has placed its long-term legitimacy in question and contributed to low turn-outs in both national and local elections. Although the system effectively limits the number parliamentary parties and has thereby ensured the parliamentary stability necessary for democratic consolidation, reform is required if the system is to maintain long-term popular support and legitimacy.

One of the legacies of Ceausescu's personal dictatorship has been expressed in the excessive importance of personalities in Romanian political life. The far-reaching powers of the Romanian President and popular form of election mean democratisation and transformation have been excessively reliant on the President's personal political preferences. This has had a negative influence on Romanian democratisation. Limitations on presidential powers and parliamentary election of the President would reduce the current political influence of the Romanian President.

The positive influence personalities can exert on democratic consolidation is exemplified by the Czech President, Vaclav Havel. The total collapse of the Czechoslovak Communist Party meant well-known personalities from the previous regime disappeared from public life. The public example necessary to overcome the moral disorientation which normalisation and the reintroduction of a neo-stalinist system caused has therefore been supplied by the Czech President. Although he has a representative role, Havel's personal integrity and dedication to the cause of democratisation and national healing has had an immensely positive influence on Czech transformation and democratic consolidation.

The major Hungarian, Czech and Romanian parties can be placed along a recognisable political spectrum, but differentiation between parties is considerable. These differences can be traced to the specific nature of the Communist regime and have affected the course of transformation and democratisation. But, while the Communist legacy has affected the development of political parties in various ways, a general lack of acceptable political choices can be observed in all three countries. This hinders democratic consolidation because it can lead to disillusion with the democratic system and may increase the extremist vote.

The policy of gradual reform which the Hungarian regime implemented after the 1956 Revolution encouraged the belief that a Hungarian 'Third Way' was feasible. The Hungarian Democratic Forum was formed as an opposition grouping by populist intellectuals who supported this idea. Its advocation of state intervention and increased social protection is therefore closer to a left-wing, rather than a conservative, political programme. Despite this, the MDF has found it difficult to distance itself from extreme national-conservative elements.

The historical parties' attempts to recapture a traditional voter base has limited their ability to modernise their political programme. All the Hungarian conservative parties share the extremists' concern for the Hungarian nation and are hostile to foreign influences which harm their national ideal. They run the risk of embracing anti-Semitism and propagating a national-conservative ideology which, in the age of political, economic and military European integration, is no longer appropriate. The extremism of sections within the MDF and the Independent Smallholders means Hungary lacks an established, modern conservative party.

In order to combat this development and gain a wider, stable voter base, the Alliance of Young Democrats, originally a radical liberal party, has transformed itself into a moderate conservative party; changing both its name and its policies. The Alliance of Young Democrats-Hungarian Civic Party hopes to attract moderate conservative voters and those liberals disillusioned by the Free

Democrats' performance in the government coalition. However, the speed of its political transformation has seriously damaged its credibility and it will take time for it to regain the voters' confidence.

The Hungarian Communist Party's pragmatism and policy of gradual reform led to a general loss of ideological commitment. Its legal successor, the Hungarian Socialist Party, was therefore forced to find a new political agenda and transform itself into a modern centre-left party. The negotiations which led to the 1989 Revolution enabled the radical reformist wing within the Communist Party elite to retain its professionalism and maintain public respect. Political modernisation and the retention of well-known professional politicians helped ensure the Socialist Party's electoral success, but economic reality and its own transformation prevent the implementation of traditional left-wing policies. In coalition with the Alliance of Free Democrats, it introduced a stabilisation package and austerity policies aimed at regaining economic equilibrium. This has led to a seemingly paradoxical role reversal. The opposition conservative parties advocate left-wing policies, such as increased social protection and state intervention in the economy; while the Socialists defend radical liberal policies aimed at ensuring the introduction of a free market, the state's retreat from the economy and the reduction of the excessive social obligations the state acquired under the previous regime.

The lack of a credible conservative alternative meant that the population's initial shock at the Socialist's radical reform programme was expressed in increased support for the extreme right-wing nationalist party, the Independent Smallholders. This is a cause for concern, because the Smallholders' rejection of aspects of economic and political transformation represents a threat to Hungarian democratic consolidation.

The Czechoslovak Communist Party's rejection of reform robbed it of public support and prevented its elite from participating in the democratic system. The lack of reform meant a radical transformation programme was required to ensure the destruction of the command administrative system's structures. However, the total ideological collapse left the traditionally left-wing Czech Social Democratic Party shocked and confused, and so it is the conservative parties in the Czech Republic which successfully modernised themselves and implemented the programme deemed necessary for rapid transformation.

Led by the Christian Democratic Party, the conservatives presented themselves as pragmatic, competent and professional parties capable of completing transformation. All advocate the state's retreat from the economy and emphasise the necessity of personal and social responsibility above social justice. The conservative parties' successful modernisation, their pragmatism and emphasis on professionalism secured a wide range of voters encompassing not only moderate conservatives, but also liberals and disillusioned social democrats. Therefore, despite the fact that many politicians and members of the electorate consider themselves liberal, there are at present no significant liberal parties in the Czech Republic.

The Czech Social Democratic Party provides the major opposition in Parliament, but is having difficulty finding a new political agenda suited to the contemporary situation. The CSSD has been unable to modernise itself completely and lacks convincing policies which are both attractive, but different from those of the ruling conservative coalition. Its limited faith in the market is demonstrated by its support for interventionist and protectionist policies. In view of the continued electoral success of the Communist Party of Bohemia and Moravia, the CSSD's presentation of traditional left-wing policies may indicate its desire for future political cooperation. Although the Communist Party's success demonstrates a section of the Czech population remains committed to Communism and the policies of the far-left, its following is limited. Nevertheless, in coalition with a left-wing CSSD, the Communist Party could hold the balance of power in the Czech Parliament.

The CSSD's dilemma is whether to modernise itself, and thus forfeit the opportunity of forming a government in coalition with the Communist Party, or remain committed to traditional left-wing policies and retain the option of cooperation with the Communist Party. Social democratic parties across Europe are faced with a similar task of modernisation to attract the votes of an electorate no longer interested in the ideological division between left and right.

Thus, while the moderate, centrist bloc has embraced a modern conservative political agenda, the left-wing of the Czech political spectrum, represented by the CSSD, remains in a state of uncertainty. The lack of a significant liberal party and the left-wing character of the CSSD contributed to the perception that there was no realistic political alternative to the conservative coalition. The disintegration of the governing conservative coalition and its constituent parties may therefore lead to increased support for the extremist Republican Party. The Republican Party is a neo-fascist organisation which has consistently tried to disrupt the democratic system. The lack of acceptable political choice in the Czech political system therefore threatens democratic consolidation because it could provide the extremist Republican Party with a potentially large protest vote.

The extremist parties in Romania enjoy a level of support which represents a real danger to democratic consolidation. The manipulation of chauvinist nationalism which took place under the previous regime means popular support for extreme nationalist parties has been easier to achieve. The extremist parties manipulate the fears of those sections of the population threatened by transformation and the radical changes entailed. They consistently disrupt and attempt to delay Romanian democratisation and transformation. All share contempt for the democratic system and aim to introduce either a Communist or personal dictatorship. They favour limiting forms of private ownership and increasing the role of the state in the economy. The extreme form of nationalism they advocate can be classed as neo-fascist. The extremist parties' participation in the coalition government led by the PDSR therefore had a negative impact on Romanian democratisation.

Since its 1996 electoral defeat, the PDSR has cooperated with the extremist parties to disrupt Parliament. While the PDSR cannot be classed as neo-fascist, its disruption of the parliamentary system and attempts to delay democratisation and transformation bear witness to its development into an extremist grouping.

The PDSR inherited a substantial amount of the Romanian Communist Party's assets, members, functionaries and ideological baggage. It presided over the introduction of the democratic system and the start of economic transformation, but reluctance to abandon certain elements of the former administrative and economic system left it unable to complete the process. The resignation of the main reformist group from the PDSR in protest at internal party corruption and lack of political renewal is symptomatic of its failure to modernise its political programme. The reformers have formed a new centre-left party which will compete with Petre Roman's Democratic Party for the votes of the moderate left.

Paradoxically, the fragmentation of two moderate social democratic parties from the previously all-enveloping PDSR has contributed to the consolidation of the moderate left. The PDSR has become an opportunist extremist grouping; ideologically neither right or left. The Bolshevik perception that, *enemies of my enemy are my friends* has led it to cooperate with the chauvinist nationalist parties of the extreme right. Their combined attempts to hinder transformation disrupt the democratic system. The unification of numerous parties in the Democratic Convention of Romania demonstrates the consolidation of the moderate right-wing of the political system. The most important member of the Convention, and the main conservative party, is the National Peasant Party/Christian Democracy.

The National Peasant Party has built on its inter-war reputation and at the same time modernised its political programme. This facilitated the consolidation of its membership and electoral base. It is the only historical party to date to achieve such electoral success and can be considered a moderate conservative party. Its government coalition with the centre-left Democratic Party and the ethnically defined Democratic Federation of Hungarians in Romania confirms this development. The inclusion of the ethnic Hungarian party demonstrates the realisation that successful democratic consolidation and economic transformation demand the inclusion of all sections of Romanian society.

The PDSR's government coalition with the extremist parties hindered Romanian democratisation, but inability to transform the political and economic system led to their electoral defeat. The moderate conservative and centre-left parties' presentation of a convincing, alternative transformation programme encouraged the electorate to vote for them. Thus, despite hindrance, democratic consolidation did occur. Nevertheless, the extremist parties' opposition role in Parliament and the activities of extremist extra-parliamentary groupings threaten long-term consolidation. The inability of the members of the coalition led by the PNTCD to put and end to internal disputes threatens the success of its radical transformation programme and has contributed to continued poor economic performance. The coalition's constant public bickering and the limited short-term benefits of economic transformation may cause popular disillusion and lead to an increase in support for the extremist parties and enable them to regain the balance of power in the Romanian Parliament. This would represent a serious set-back for Romanian transformation and democratic consolidation.

CHAPTER FOUR

DEALING WITH THE COMMUNIST ECONOMIC LEGACY

'One can turn the contents of an aquarium into fish soup, but can one turn fish soup into an aquarium?'
Adam Michnik[1].

*

In order to deal effectively with the Communist economic, administrative, judicial and military legacy, the political parties in Romania, Hungary and the Czech Republic must develop carefully designed and coherent transformation programmes. Although the demagogic, nationalist parties of the region emphasise the short-term negative economic and social aspects of transformation, and have thus gained a measure of popular support, they have no realistic alternative programme.

In their attempt to create an ideal socialist society, the Communist regimes in Eastern Europe restructured the region's economic, political and social relations. They introduced centrally planned Stalinist economies and nationalised all private property. The state, in the form of the Communist Party, held not only the political, but also the economic monopoly. Thus, at the same time as political and social transformation occurs, economic relations and structures must also be transformed.

Under the former system, economic decisions were highly centralised and subordinated to political considerations. These dictated that every worker had the right to work and created a situation in which, although there was a chronic shortage of

---

[1] See Kocsis, György, 'How to Uncook Fish Soup: Strategies for Privatization', *The New Hungarian Quarterly*, Vol. 32, No. 123, Autumn 1991, p. 35.

workers, due to the enterprise strategy of 'Plan storming' and limited worker mobility, over-employment was endemic[2]. Because different government Ministries controlled the various economic sectors, during the course of its evolution, informal bargaining came to dominate the planning system. Each Ministry aimed to ensure its sector was sufficiently supplied with investment funds, but not overly burdened by the requirements of the Plan. A separate Ministry controlled the activities of those enterprises allowed to engage in foreign trade. The banking system was centralised and a single central bank controlled all official monetary transactions. Wages were low and there was no comparable system of national insurance, Value Added Tax (VAT), or personal tax. Prices were controlled and subsidised, keeping the cost of health care, food, travel, rent, postal services, telecommunications and other essential services, such as water, electricity and gas, unrealistically low. Although the cost of subsidising these services was hidden from the population, it was visible in budget and current account deficits, and in a lack of investment.

Transformation requires the liberalisation of prices and trade, the break up of monopolistic, monolithic state enterprises and the privatisation of the majority of state assets, be they enterprises, housing, leisure facilities, utilities or sections of the health system. In addition, the service sector and small and medium-sized enterprises must be encouraged. To ensure the system of informal bargaining which governed the planning system ceases, hard budget constraints must be introduced and the Ministries which formerly controlled the economy dissolved, or given new tasks. A two-tiered banking system must be introduced to ensure competition and financial stability on the capital markets, and a new tax system implemented which provides a stable source of revenue for the government.

---

[2] Plan storming describes the practice in which the majority of the time allowed for the fulfilment of a production Plan was dedicated to acquiring the materials necessary for its fulfilment. Thus, production was concentrated into the last few months of a Plan when all materials had been acquired. Although the majority of workers were not needed all the time, enterprises kept them in full employment as they were needed during the period of Plan storming at the end of the production cycle.

At the same time, the *nomenklatura* system must be abandoned and state administration reduced in size. Civil servants must become aware of their personal responsibility within the system and corruption reduced. A legal state must be introduced, constitutional reform undertaken and the judicial system reviewed. The police and armed forces must also be reformed, their soviet style command structures replaced, and their task redefined to ensure they serve and protect the population.

Although the basic set of reforms required for systemic transformation has been agreed, the sequencing and timing of reform remains under debate. Two main currents of thought have crystallised; those who prefer a quick, radical transformation programme in the hope that, although the 'valley of tears' may be deeper, it will be shorter and thus more easily passed; and those who prefer a more gradual transformation in the hope that, although the passage will take longer, the valley will be shallower.

Although economic reform is often viewed as the most important aspect of transformation, and is certainly one of its main elements, economic reform alone will not affect the total systemic transformation desired. For this to occur, social, political and psychological transformation is also necessary. The population must learn how to function within and relate to the new system; and enterprises and institutions must operate within a new legal framework supported by an independent and competent law enforcement and judicial system.

The systemic transformation in Eastern Europe is therefore unprecedented. It is a highly complex process which must be considered in its entirety if a deeper understanding of the problems associated with it is to be gained. However, for the purposes of comprehension, this chapter will deal with the economic transformation programmes implemented in the Czech Republic, Hungary and Romania and examine the specific problems associated with them. In this way, specific factors realted to the Communist legacy which affect democratic consolidation during economic transformation will be isolated.

4.1: Economic Transformation

As indicated above, there are two main currents of thought regarding the method of economic transformation[3]. The 'Big Bang' approach foresees the immediate introduction of a capitalist system and the rapid destruction of old institutions. It entails the immediate and complete liberalisation of the economic sphere and the abandonment of government control over economic actors, accompanied by drastic market stabilisation based on tight monetary control and the introduction of hard budget constraints. Thus, all economic agents, state-controlled or private, operate under the same set of conditions, and the old institutions of the centrally planned economy, the planners and supply organisations, are made immediately redundant. All state sector assets and property rights are transferred to a government institution, which then implements a rapid privatisation programme. This approach emphasises speed: immediate destruction of old mechanisms and institutions, and swift introduction of market orientated institutions and organisations.

The alternative approach proceeds from the assumption that organisational and institutional structures cannot be removed so simply. Therefore old institutions are phased out in a gradual process. This form of economic transformation does not lead to the immediate emergence of a capitalist economy, but rather of a mixed, or dual, economy in which a relatively large and important state sector continues to exists alongside a new and more dynamic private sector[4]. The evolutionary approach envisages the gradual dissolution of old institutions and privatisation of state assets, while actively encouraging, and perhaps giving preference to private sector activity.

However, both these approaches have encountered problems in implementation. One unforeseen hindrance has been the continued existence of the semi-legal, or second economy. The Communist regimes both tolerated and, to some extent, relied on the second

---

[3] Murrell, Peter, 'Evolutionary and Radical Approaches to Economic Reform', *Economics of Planning*, Vol. 25, No. 1, 1992.
[4] See Kornai, János, *The Road to a Free Economy*, W. W. Norton 1990.

economy to supply consumers with a variety of products. However, the second economy had a symbiotic relationship with the socialist economy and therefore cannot form the basis of the market economy.

Although those involved in the second economy relied on informal relationships outside the official sphere, they had little interest in changing the economic structure, since its very inefficiency provided their source of income. Second economy activities were often linked to a state enterprise as a means of limiting the amount of capital investment required and reducing operating costs. Many involved in the second economy also enjoyed a monopoly position and were not necessarily interested in expansion. The introduction of a market economy has not changed their fundamental behaviour pattern because, to some extent, retention of state enterprises and limited competition is in their interest. In addition, they continue to operate outside the official economy to avoid paying tax on their earnings.

The *acteurs* in the second economy do not therefore form the new entrepreneurial base of the market economy. Indeed, the widespread existence of the second economy increasingly hinders the formation of a functioning market economy. Not only does it reduce tax revenues, thereby further decreasing government revenue, which is already suffering from loss of tax income from the state sector, but the informal relationships on which it relies were formed within the framework of the command economy and thus preserve some of its social and economic structures. In this way, the second economy can also act to hinder democratic consolidation.

Implementation of radical reform has proved difficult, partly because of the old institutions' tenacity, and partly because institutions which were expected to change their behaviour as a result of transformation have failed to do so. This is particularly true for large enterprises. Liberalisation does not necessarily change the monopolistic position they enjoyed in the highly centralised economy. Indeed, in order to maintain profitability, large enterprises can exploit their monopoly position by restricting output and raising prices. An assured monopoly also enables enterprises to continue exploiting the network of informal bargaining relationships which were established under the old system[5].

Consequently, liberalisation alone is insufficient to change many existing patterns of enterprise behaviour. Large enterprises must be broken up and domestic competition increased to prevent old structures determining the market.

But many of the older large enterprises have little prospect of surviving in a competitive market. Therefore, until the workers in such enterprises can be retrained and the private sector is dynamic enough to absorb them, it may be inevitable that some continue to exist under state control. However, continued subsidies to such enterprises, whether direct or in the form of a state funded restructuring plan not only preserve enterprise behaviour patterns formed under the old regime, which in turn hinder the formation of market relations, but also discriminate against more dynamic medium-sized private enterprises. The latter need access to the credit facilities enjoyed by large state enterprises in order to expand and take their place. Given the tenacity of informal relationships formed under the old regime, the ability of large state enterprises to adapt to market conditions remains in doubt, but their liquidation may prove politically unacceptable because they employ large numbers of industrial workers who encounter difficulty finding alternative employment.

It seems inevitable, therefore, that a state and private sector will co-exist for a period of time. But, if this period is prolonged, the market will be distorted as continued subsidies to large state enterprises hinder the acceptance of hard budget constraints and market norms.

As economic transformation on the scale required in Eastern Europe has never before been attempted, there is no single recipe for success. Both the radical and gradual approaches, or a combination of the two, may be equally successful. Although Hungary, the Czech Republic and Romania all share the task of transforming planned socialist economies, their development and the extent of central control exercised was differentiated at the start

---

[5] Comisso, Ellen, 'Market Failures and Market Socialism: Economic Problems of The Transition', *East European Politics and Societies*, Vol. 2, No. 3, Fall 1988.

of transformation. This has influenced the programme chosen to achieve economic transformation.

4.2: Economic Reform in Hungary

The events of 1956 forced the Hungarian Party to accept that the orthodox Stalinist economic and political system had failed, and it was compelled to embark on gradual systemic reform. The regime aimed to pacify popular unrest by ensuring an acceptable and continuously rising standard of living. Not only was this policy the main reason for the exponential increase in Hungary's foreign debt, as more consumer products were imported, it also created the situation in which, ultimately, the regime's legitimacy rested solely on its ability to fulfil the population's economic expectations. Thus, the need to avoid economic crisis and improve the functioning of the system came to occupy utmost priority, and ideological pragmatism, to the point of abandonment of socialist ideology, pervaded the Hungarian Party and state administration.

The first indication of this development was the introduction of the New Economic Mechanism (NEM) in 1968. Despite its failings, the NEM represented a decisive break from the traditional system of central planning and a move towards 'market socialism'. It replaced the traditional system of central planning with a hybrid, which has been described by Tamás Bauer as, 'neither plan nor market'[6]. Control over medium-level enterprises was abolished and the control mechanism transformed as branch Ministries were abolished and central management agencies established to oversee nation-wide enterprises. The remaining enterprises were formally freed from subordination to state administration, although directors and managers were still appointed by the Ministries. Thus, small and medium-sized enterprises were emancipated from direct central control. Penalties for non-fulfilment of Plan targets were abolished and replaced by general qualitative requirements, the need to satisfy

---

[6] Bauer, Tamás, 'The Hungarian Alternative to Soviet-type Planning', *Journal of Comparative Economics*, Vol. 7, No. 3, 1983, pp. 304-316. In Bauer, Tamás, 'Hungarian Economic Reform in East European Perspective', *East European Politics and Societies*, Vol. 2, No. 3, Fall 1988.

domestic demand, meet CMEA obligations and export to Western Europe.

Although such requirements meant that many enterprises were unable to discontinue unprofitable lines of production, they were encouraged to introduce new lines and increase profitability. Central resource allocation, one of the main components of the traditional planning system, was also abandoned and replaced by certain market factors which influenced production, although these remained monopolistic and state-controlled. While the monopolistic relationships between suppliers and customers inherited from the traditional planning system retained their importance, firms which embarked upon new activities could find a supplier without interference from state agencies.

NEM eliminated the official control hierarchy of the central administrative control mechanism, mandatory planning and centralised allocation. In addition, prices were partly liberalised and enterprises allowed to keep part of their profits. In contrast, the intermediate control agencies, or 'general directorates', in Czechoslovakia were preserved. All state firms were subordinated to one of the general directorates or a local authority. Thus, the organisational hierarchy of the planning system in Czechoslovakia remained intact; and the reintroduction of traditional central planning mechanisms after the failed reforms of 1968 meant that the power of the general directorates to interfere in enterprise activity actually increased[7].

As András Bozóki stated, the Hungarian economic and political system ceased to be based on the traditional Stalinist Soviet model:

'For a long time the system had no longer been Stalinist, that is, based on a totalitarian ideology which systematically used terror in the exercise of autocratic control over the everyday personal and professional lives of the people.'[8]

---

[7] Ibid. Bauer, Tamás, 'Hungarian Economic Reform in East European Perspective', *East European Politics and Societies*.

[8] Bozóki, András, 'Post-Communist Transition: Political Tendencies in Hungary', *East European Politics and Societies*, Vol. 4, No. 2, Spring 1990, p. 211.

Dealing with the Communist Economic Legacy

However, despite reform of the planning system, Hungarian economic performance did not improve. By the 1980's, the ever worsening economic situation led the Hungarian elite, both within and outside the regime, to the inevitable conclusion that the system itself had to be transformed. As Csaba Csáki, the Rector of the then Karl-Marx University in Budapest and Chairman of the Central Committee Commission which had the task of formulating future economic policy, stated:

> *'Wir müssen einen Modellwechsel vollziehen, der es ermöglicht, daß eine wirklich funktionsfähige, effiziente und wettbewerbsfähige Wirtschaft entsteht. Unsere Folgerungen gründen sich auf der Erkenntnis: das Stalinistische Modell ist nicht verbesserbar.'* [9]

Therefore, the Hungarian regime embarked on a programme of economic and limited institutional political reform. In this way, the basic institutional and legal foundations necessary for the transformation to a market economy were laid before political transformation occurred.

In an attempt to improve the quality and competitiveness of Hungarian products, the Communist regime introduced a centrally controlled, limited privatisation programme aimed at attracting foreign investors. It was hoped that foreign investment would bring the capital, technology and restructuring necessary for the modernisation of Hungarian industry. In turn, this would make the Hungarian economy more competitive on the world market and in the long run increase exports, thus producing the revenue needed to service the hard currency debt. By 1989-1990, Hungary's hard currency foreign debt stood at approximately $20 billion[10], so direct

---

[9] 'We must realise a model change which will facilitate the construction of a truly functional, efficient and competitive economy. Our conclusions are based on the realisation that the Stalinist Model cannot be improved.' Translation by Wendy Hollis. 'Strukturwandel, Markt, Eigentumsreform', *Népszbadság*, 25 April 1989. In Sitzler, Kathrin, 'Ungarns politische Reformen im Spiegel der neuen Verfassungskonzeption', *Aus Politik und Zeitgeschichte*, No. 23, 2 June 1989.

[10] Stark, David, 'Privatization in Hungary: From Plan to Market or From Plan to Clan?', *East European Politics and Societies*, Vol. 4, No. 3, Fall 1990, p. 357.

foreign investment was also a means of generating the hard currency required for immediate debt servicing obligations.

At a business meeting in San Francisco on 21 June, 1988, the privatisation of state enterprises was proposed by the then Party Secretary, Karoly Grosz:

> *'We would be very pleased if perhaps you would purchase some of our enterprises... even if they became 100% foreign owned.'*[11]

The incumbent regime's privatisation programme using foreign capital was relatively successful. On 31 January, 1989, the Minister of Industry announced a list of fifty one enterprises, accounting for approximately one quarter of industrial production, which were for sale to foreign buyers. According to National Bank estimates, direct foreign investment in Hungary in 1989 alone was approximately $300 million, compared with a total of $200 million in the previous decade[12]. Thus, the Hungarian economy was in the process of gradual transformation before the 1989 Revolution occurred.

Although the reforms introduced by the Communist regime in the 1980's undoubtedly placed the Hungarian economy at an advantage because the institutional framework necessary for a functioning market economy had already been created by the time political transformation occurred, the nature of Hungary's Negotiated Revolution meant that from June 1989 until May 1990, the period from the start of the Roundtable Negotiations until democratic elections were held, the economy was in a state of limbo and state institutions faced a legitimacy crisis. By negotiating with the opposition, the regime abandoned its claim to legitimacy and although the government and its officials remained in office, as a new government had not been elected, they possessed no authority. Power and authority therefore gradually dissolved and devolved.

---

[11] Ibid. Stark, David, 'Privatization in Hungary: From Plan to Market or From Plan to Clan?', *East European Politics and Societies*, p. 359.

[12] Ibid. Stark, David, 'Privatization in Hungary: From plan to Market or From Plan to Clan?', p. 358, p. 360.

The Communist Parliament agreed not to pass any laws which would hinder the new Parliament and thus relinquished power before a new body replaced it. Organisations which were not political were excluded from the Roundtable Negotiations; so leading economic actors, managers of large state enterprises, workers' representatives and corporate interest groups, were not represented. It was therefore impossible to agree on a new economic framework. In these circumstances, managers of state enterprises were able to act with almost complete independence and initiated wide-scale spontaneous privatisation.

In the Hungarian case, spontaneous privatisation utilised two unrelated pieces of legislation. The first, the 1984 Law on Enterprise Councils, had formally transferred some ownership functions from the Ministries to the Enterprise Councils. Since it was usual for approximately half of the members of an Enterprise Council to be appointed by the enterprise manager, it was firmly under management control. The second, the Law on Business Associations, passed on 1 January, 1989, made no provision for the actual transformation of state enterprises into private corporations, but allowed enterprises to found share-holding corporations and limited liability companies[13]. When combined, these laws created the legal mechanism for spontaneous privatisation.

Spontaneous privatisation was carried out by the Enterprise Council which exercised its ownership function and created one or more forms of property related to the original state enterprise. The new companies thus established issued share capital and exchanged these shares for the actual assets of the state enterprise, that is land, buildings, and equipment. Although the state enterprise held shares in the new companies, it had effectively been stripped of its assets which had become the property of its own creations; independent, limited liability corporations. In a further step, the new companies issued bonds, at a fixed rate of return, which were purchased by the state enterprise using the shares it had acquired in exchange for its assets. Thus, the state enterprise, although it held bonds, became a

---

[13] Ibid. Stark, David, 'Privatization in Hungary: From plan to Market or From Plan to Clan?', p. 364.

shell as its actual assets and shares were held by the private corporations it had established.

This meant that senior management, reporting only to the Enterprise Council, which it invariably controlled, chose the new enterprise owners. In some cases foreign owners who permitted managers to retain their positions, or gain a controlling interest in a profitable company derived from the original enterprise, were chosen. In others, managers selected themselves as the new owners. In these cases Enterprise Councils often approved large bonuses for management, which were used to buy shares in the new corporations[14].

In response to widespread criticism of spontaneous privatisation, a Law on the Defence of State Property was passed in January 1990, and in March 1990, a State Property Agency (SPA), responsible for overseeing privatisation, was established[15]. The SPA was directly responsible to the government and its managing board and director were nominated by the Prime Minister[16]. The SPA had powers of intervention and could take control of a privatisation initiative, although enterprise managers retained the right to decide if assets were sold in open bidding or whether to arrange the sale themselves[17]. But state enterprises were only obliged to inform the SPA of transformation plans if the value of a contract exceeded thirty million Forints. The value of a limited company usually remained under this limit, and so remained outside the SPA's control. Enterprises therefore created several medium-sized limited liability companies and in this way carried out spontaneous privatisation without interference. Conflict with the workers was avoided because in the new company they were no longer protected by the collective contracts which the Unions had negotiated with the state enterprise.

---

[14] Ibid. Stark, David, 'Privatization in Hungary: From Plan to Market or From Plan to Clan?', pp. 364-365.
[15] Ibid. Stark, David, 'Privatization in Hungary: From Plan to Market or From Plan to Clan?', pp. 366-367.
[16] Kiss, Yudit, 'Privatisation in Hungary – Two Years Later', *Soviet Studies*, Vol. 44, No. 6, 1992, p. 1018.
[17] Mizsei, Kálmán, 'Privatisation in Eastern Europe: A Comparative Study of Poland and Hungary', *Soviet Studies*, Vol. 44, No. 2, 1992, p. 293.

Dealing with the Communist Economic Legacy

The creation of a State Property Agency led to the seemingly paradoxical situation in which, to de-nationalise property, it was re-nationalised and the independence enterprises had gained under the old regime restricted. However, as the SPA's powers of intervention were limited and the appointment of its staff and permanent director postponed until a new government was formed, spontaneous privatisation was not halted. In this respect the Hungarian economy was out of control by the time the MDF came to power in 1990.

4.2.1: Rejection of Reform in Czechoslovakia and Romania

In contrast to the gradual economic reform which took place under the Kádár regime in Hungary, the economic structures and policies in the Czech Republic and Romania remained within the limits proscribed by the Stalinist economic model. But, whereas in Czechoslovakia the economic and political reforms implemented during the 1968 Prague Spring were reversed, in Romania no serious attempt at reform had ever been undertaken. Thus, the Czech experience of near collapse and subsequent normalisation, which entailed the restoration of Party control over social, political and economic relations and the discrediting of reformist policies, created a rather different system to that in Romania, where the Party remained unchallenged and convinced of the orthodox Stalinist economic system's legitimacy.

Normalisation in Czechoslovakia was possible because hard-line conservative factions within the Party formed a coalition in order to maintain power. Reformers were purged and strict central control reintroduced in the economic and political sphere. Although in light of the Warsaw Pact invasion, this development was perhaps inevitable, the harshness of the normalisation process is the sole responsibility of the hard-liners within the Czechoslovak Party.

Although the Czechoslovak economy grew during the first half of the 1970's and personal consumption increased, the fundamental structural deficiencies of the system, which had contributed to the pressure for reform during the period leading up to the Prague Spring, remained. The second half of the 1970's witnessed a decline in the growth rate and economic stagnation. Stagnation occurred not only as a result of political normalisation, the consequence of which had been the removal of the most innovative and competent from their posts in various sections of the administration, government and economy, but also because the traditional administrative command economy was not suited to furthering development from extensive to intensive production.

The reintroduction of the traditional Stalinist economic system led to an over-expansion of heavy industry at the cost of the service sector, light industry and agriculture. Increased administrative intervention in the economy, in the form of the general directorates, combined with strict central control, stifled innovation and removed managers' incentive to take personal responsibility. Their main interest lay not in ensuring profitability or efficiency, but in maintaining constant wage levels and ensuring the burdens of the Plan were not too excessive and could be fulfilled with the least possible exertion. Thus, economic inefficiency and indiscipline increased.

One of the symptoms of the command economy's inefficiency is excessive energy consumption. The extent of imbalance inherent in the normalised economy was therefore apparent in the level of Czechoslovak energy consumption. By 1980 Czechoslovakia was the third largest per capita consumer of primary energy in the world, after the USA and the German Democratic Republic. In addition, it consumed more energy to produce one unit of GDP than any other country in the world. In 1980, 54% of primary energy consumption in Czechoslovakia was accounted for by industry; in western countries, this share was approximately 40%. The apparent consumption of steel was also excessively high. By 1980 Czechoslovakia ranked first in the world in terms of the volume of steel used per unit of GDP and in per capita output and consumption of steel[18].

In addition to excessive production and consumption, the share of steel produced by the most modern methods (electrical furnaces, oxygen converters and continuously cast steel) was significantly below world levels, while the share produced by obsolescent methods (Siemens-Martin) was significantly above the world

---

[18] Sobell, Vlad, 'Czechoslovakia: The Legacy of Normalization', *East European Politics and Societies*, Vol. 2, No. 1, Winter 1988, p. 45.

average[19]. Thus, not only was energy wasted, but the more steel produced the bigger were the losses. The technical obsolescence of Czechoslovak products led to the loss of their share of the world market; indeed the percentage of products which conformed to the 'world technical level' declined from approximately 5% in 1970, to a mere 2% by 1980[20].

Although 'The Set of Measures for the Perfection of the Economic Mechanism' was presented in the late 1970's, it was a contradictory and superficial document which failed to deal with the fundamental systemic dysfunction at the root of the deepening economic crisis[21]. Indeed, the technological obsolescence of Czechoslovak industry actually increased during this period as, concerned by the rise of *Solidarnosc* in Poland, the regime decided to reduce its exposure to and dependence on the West. To this end, it embarked on rapid repayment of the hard currency debt, which limited investment and led to a reduction of imports of western technology[22]. Interestingly, the Romanian regime implemented a similar debt repayment policy, although the larger size of the Romanian debt and the poorer state of its economy had far more serious consequences. Both regimes believed that a reduction in their dependence on and contacts with the West would enable them to avoid reform.

However, as the reform course in the Soviet Union became more radical, the Czechoslovak regime was forced to adjust its policy and in January 1987, a document entitled 'The Principles of Restructuring the Economic Mechanism' was published[23]. Although the proposed reform was relatively comprehensive, it still refrained from attacking the planned economy's fundamental structural problems. It therefore exposed the regime's unwillingness to deal with the essentially political issues of reducing the vastly

---

[19] See Appendix XXXIV
[20] Ibid. Sobell, Vlad, 'Czechoslovakia: The Legacy of Normalization', *East European Politics and Societies*, p. 47.
[21] For a detailed account of the 'Set of Measures', see Levcik, Friedrich, 'Czechoslovakia: Economic Performance in the Post-reform Period and Prospects for the 1980's'. In *East European Economic Assessmen: Part 1*, U. S. Congress Joint Economic Committee, Washington D. C., 1981.
[22] Ibid. Sobell, Vlad, 'Czechoslovakia: The Legacy of Normalization', p. 49.
[23] Ibid. Sobell, Vlad, 'Czechoslovakia: The Legacy of Normalization', p. 54.

over-blown central bureaucracy and de-centralising the system. The problem was that after the experience of 1968 and normalisation, the regime was aware that the delegation of power and control inherent in de-centralisation would lead to its own loss of power and control.

Despite this, the normalised regime's reliance on the Soviet Union dictated that it undertake measures congruous with those in the Soviet Union to deal with economic problems and in February 1987, the 'Concretization of the Principles of Restructuring of the Economic Mechanism of the CSSR' was presented. Although the programme was not planned to come into effect until the 1991-1995 Five Year Plan, de-centralisation was to be tested beforehand in a number of enterprises and the legal and theoretical foundations for a reform programme prepared. A new Law on Socialist Enterprise was prepared for mid-1987 and the first elements of price reform were introduced at the beginning of 1988[24].

In mid-1988, the government presented to Parliament a law regulating the activities of joint ventures. However, the fear of foreign capital gaining too much influence remained. Only legal Czechoslovak persons could become members of a joint venture and the number of foreign held shares in an enterprise was restricted. In addition, the tax and profit laws provided foreign investors few incentives. Nevertheless, by 31 December, 1989, 55 joint ventures had been set up[25]. Although the prevailing political climate and the complicated process of establishing a joint venture, combined with the incompatible nature of a free market and a centrally controlled socialist economy, limited success, the gradual erosion of the state's monopoly of ownership had begun.

Thus, during an address in January 1987, while noting the errors present in the 1968 reform plans, Lubomír Strougal also criticised the excesses of normalisation and the consequent rejection of a role for the market in a socialist economy:

---

[24] Ibid. Sobell, Vlad, 'Czechoslovakia: The Legacy of Normalization', p. 54.
[25] Kupka, Martin, 'Transformation of Ownership in Czechoslovakia', *Soviet Studies*, Vol. 44, No. 2, 1992, p. 298.

Dealing with the Communist Economic Legacy

> 'Even today we can encounter the opinion that commodity/monetary relations are a product of capitalism and that there are hence no grounds for them in a social production under socialism. ...It is forgotten that commodity/monetary relations were not brought into existence by capitalism. They existed long before its birth, and their roots lie... in the origin of the social division of labour. The theory and practice of socialist construction confirm that these relations of necessity preserve their validity even at a very high level of development of socialist society.'[26]

In comparison with statements from the Hungarian Party elite concerning privatisation, economic reform and transformation, Strougal remains within the norms of socialist economic expression, not aiming to transform the system of economic relations. Nevertheless, the statement demonstrated that a faction within the Czechoslovak regime was in the process of orientating itself towards reform; and in comparison with statements made by Ceausescu during the same period, it appears veritably radical.

Despite the attempt to reorientate itself in line with Soviet reform policy, an influential hard-line faction within the regime was unwilling to accept such a course. The group was represented by people such as Vasil Bilak and his associate, the ideologist, Jaoslav Kucera, who had written on 13 February, 1987 in *Rudé Právo*:

> 'We have to take into account that, under the guise of support for the process of change, all kinds of slanderers of socialism will seek to repeat the experience of 1968 and inject into the process a 'virus' designed to bring about the demise of socialism's fundamental principles.'[27]

In the final analysis, the conversion to reform was forced as a result of external pressure, mainly from the Soviet Union, and, implemented only as a means of survival, it remained limited. The

---

[26] Ibid. Sobell, Vlad, 'Czechoslovakia: The Legacy of Normalization', p. 55.
[27] *Rudé Právo*, 13 February, 1987. Ibid. Sobell, Vlad, 'Czechoslovakia: The Legacy of Normalization', p. 62.

regime hoped its reform policy would facilitate restructuring of the economic sphere in line with Soviet wishes without abandoning the principles of normalisation. The Czechoslovak reform programme cannot therefore be considered a serious attempt to deal with the basic systemic dysfunction or compared with the radical transformation programme accepted by the Hungarian regime, and remains closer to the Romanian position.

The normalised Czechoslovak regime was forced onto a course of limited economic reform, but the orthodox Romanian regime refused to contemplate any reform at all. This differentiation occurred because the experience of economic crisis during 1968 and the subsequent process of normalisation had not only exposed the coercive nature of the system, but also initiated creeping ideological degeneration in the Czechoslovak Party. This increased the regime's reliance on the Soviet Union and, although it feared the consequences, made it incapable of resisting Soviet pressure to initiate reform. In contrast, the Romanian regime had never been effectively challenged. Therefore, the majority of the Party elite remained convinced of the orthodox Stalinist system's superiority and, believing in the infallibility of the Party's absolute control and power, could not accept the necessity of reform. Thus, during the Central Committee Plenum from 13-14 March, 1985, Ceausescu stated:

> *'Although there are some among us who think in this way... we are not a debating club.'*[28]

The Romanian economic system had not been reformed since its creation under Gheorghe Gheorghiu Dej and retained its original Stalinist features. Although between 1969-1972 some attempts were made to disguise the functional problems of the system by introducing limited institutional changes, as there was no market reform, they represent an application of different methods within the Stalinist system, rather than its reform.

---

[28] Georgescu, Vlad, 'Romania in the 1980's: The Legacy of Dynastic Socialism', *East European Politics and Societies*, Vol. 2, No. 1, Winter 1988, p. 87.

The changes in economic organisation described by Ceausescu in June 1966, and carried out between 1969-1970, did not question the directive nature of the economy, merely implied a certain amount of de-centralisation. Although new intermediary organisations acted between enterprises and Ministries, factories in the new industrial centres, which were founded after 1967, remained subject to direct central Ministerial control. Therefore, although by the Autumn of 1969 approximately 200 new industrial centres had been founded, in keeping with the prevailing Stalinist economic ideal, they were excessively large, heavy industrial complexes[29]. In addition, limited administrative de-centralisation was effectively counteracted by increased political control. Thus, it was during 1969 that abuse of Decree No. 12, which had been passed in 1965 and dealt with the medical treatment of dangerous madmen, began. Article 2 of the Decree allowed for medical treatment of all those who disturbed peaceful life or work conditions, and was systematically used to silence uncomfortable persons[30]. As the law was invoked at will, uncertainty was increased and the Party's absolute control strengthened.

The July 1972 Party Conference officially signalled the end of any attempts at de-centralisation. It was announced that the 1971-1975 Five Year Plan was to be fulfilled in four and a half years and a new wave of forced industrialisation and mobilisation was initiated[31]. Membership of the Communist Party was increased and, as a result of changes in the state administration which had started in 1967, state and Party apparatus became increasingly integrated and Party control of the state and economy increased. Party and state appointments were integrated so that the First Party Secretary of an area was also the head of the Local Administration, and the First Secretary of a town section of the Communist Party was also the Mayor. This development culminated in 1974 when Ceausescu,

---

[29] Fink, Gerhard, Tuitz, Gabriele, *Rumänien: Wirtschafts- und Systempolitik*, Bundesinstitut für Ostwissenschaftliche und Internationale Studien, Bericht No. 51, 1984, pp. 4-6.

[30] Amnesty International, *Rumänien: Zur politischen Verfolgung seit 1970*, Nomos Verlag 1978, p. 19.

[31] Ibid. Fink, Gerhard, Tuitz, Gabriele, *Rumänien: Wirtschafts- und Systempolitik*, p. 2, p. 11.

the First Secretary of the Romanian Communist Party, became President of the Romanian state[32].

Although the new wave of industrialisation and worker mobilisation led to short-term quantitative increases in production, strict centralisation furthered the Stalinist preference for heavy industry and reduced investment in the agricultural sector. Thus, during the 1970's investment in agriculture accounted for a mere 14% of total investment. The higher wages available in the industrial sector drew the younger generation away from agricultural production and by 1980, the 29% of the population employed in agriculture were overwhelmingly members of the older generation[33]. In addition, the orthodox Stalinist nature of the system and its excessive centralisation created the situation in which cooperatives were forbidden to own their own machinery and were forced to obtain it from so-called 'Stations for Mechanisation of Agriculture'. These stations were similar to the 'Machine-Tractor Stations' which Stalin introduced in the Soviet Union, but which had already been abandoned there in 1958[34]. As much of the machinery in the stations was obsolete and out of order, by the 1980's the harvest was often gathered using scythes. As a result of these developments, the share of agriculture in Romania's national product decreased from 18.5% in 1970, to 14.1% in 1980[35].

Forced industrialisation created a heavy industrial base, but the system was unable to develop the technology necessary for the creation of a successful, modern economy. The Romanian regime was therefore forced to import western technology, and by 1977 its foreign currency debt had increased to $3.6 billion[36]. In addition, as the industrial sector grew, so did its demand for raw materials and

---

[32] Ibid. Fink, Gerhard, Tuitz, Gabriele, *Rumänien: Wirtschafts- und Systempolitik*, p. 15.
[33] Ibid. Fink, Gerhard, Tuitz, Gabriele, *Rumänien: Wirtschafts- und Systempolitik*, p. 25.
[34] Ibid. Fink, Gerhard, Tuitz, Gabriele, *Rumänien: Wirtschafts- und Systempolitik*, p. 27.
[35] Ibid. Fink, Gerhard, Tuitz, Gabriele, *Rumänien: Wirtschafts- und Systempolitik*, p. 26.
[36] Ibid. Fink, Gerhard, Tuitz, Gabriele, *Rumänien: Wirtschafts- und Systempolitik*, p. 12.

Dealing with the Communist Economic Legacy 327

energy. The demand for energy was initially satiated by Romania's domestic oil reserves, but although still an exporter in 1974, by 1979 Romania was a net importer of oil. Wasteful energy consumption exposed the inefficiency of the economic system. Thus, between 1977-1980, while the amount of oil Romania produced decreased by 20%, oil consumption increased by 50% and oil imports increased by 150%. In the first half of the 1980's, more than 60% of all Romanian imports consisted of energy and raw materials, which were only available in return for hard currency[37]. This further fuelled increases in Romania's foreign debt, which by 1981 stood at $10 billion, and between 1982-1983 increased to $78.4 billion[38].

Ceausescu perceived this development as increasing Romania's dependence on external factors and could not tolerate the reduction of his own personal control which the foreign currency debt represented. Consequently, in 1982 the Romanian regime decided to meet its debt obligations as they came due and embarked on a policy of rapid debt repayment. However, by 1985 it had already fallen behind on payments and in 1986 was forced to reschedule the commercial debt[39].

The tragedy is that to earn the hard currency necessary to pay for energy imports and repay its hard currency debt, the Romanian regime exported food products and in the same period became a net exporter of food. At the same time, forced industrialisation had increased the industrial work force and its demand for food which, under the pressure of the regime's debt repayment policy, the neglected agricultural sector was unable to fulfil. Although Romania produced enough food to support itself, agricultural producers were forced to hand over two thirds of the fruit and vegetable harvest and 70% of all meat products to the state for

---

[37] Ibid. Fink, Gerhard, Tuitz, Gabriele, *Rumänien: Wirtschafts- und Systempolitik*, p. 13.
[38] Ibid. Fink, Gerhard, Tuitz, Gabriele, *Rumänien: Wirtschafts- und Systempolitik*, p. 41.
[39] Crane, Keith, *The Romanian Economic Mess after Ceausescu*, The Rand Corporation, December 1986, p. 5, p. 11.

export[40]. In 1981 food distribution failed and rationing was introduced. In 1984 the amount of agricultural production designated for the state was increased and as a consequence the meat ration was reduced by 15% and the flour ration by 13%[41].

Despite the economic and social crisis, the Romanian Party refused to reform the economic system. On 21 November, 1985, the Romanian Party Daily, *Scinteia*, rejected reform tendencies and in 1986, a further six articles critical of reform appeared in *Ela Socialista*[42]. Central control was increased and in an attempt to ensure obedience and Plan fulfilment, the military was placed in control of strategic areas of the economy, such as energy production.

The Romanian Communist Party elite remained bound to the Stalinist model of development in the belief it would transform Romania from an agricultural into an industrial country and create an ideal socialist society. Economic success was measured in simplistic Stalinist terms of levels of industrialisation and increased productivity. As reformist tendencies had been hindered by increasing central economic and political control, the prevailing Stalinist ideology remained unchallenged. Therefore, in contrast to both the Hungarian and Czechoslovak Party, Ceausescu and the majority of the Romanian Party elite remained convinced of the validity of the ideology. Although Romania became more dependent on the Soviet economy during the 1980's, earlier acceptance of a certain amount of Romanian independence, especially in domestic policy, enabled Ceausescu to resist Soviet pressure to implement reform. In this way, the Romanian leadership, convinced of its ideological supremacy and control, was able to reject both external and internal pressures to reform.

Thus, at the start of transformation, Romania and the Czech Republic had traditional command economies. While they had relatively low levels of foreign debt, both exhibited excessive levels

---

[40] Ibid. Fink, Gerhard, Tuitz, Gabriele, *Rumänien: Wirtschafts- und Systempolitik*, p. 28.
[41] Ibid. Fink, Gerhard, Tuitz, Gabriele, *Rumänien: Wirtschafts- und Systempolitik*, p. 35.
[42] Ibid. Crane, Keith, *The Romanian Economic Mess after Ceausescu*, p. 7.

of central control, neglected agricultural sectors and overblown, technologically outdated, monopolistic heavy industrial sectors.

4.3: Privatisation

Privatisation involves the selling of state-owned enterprises. Although there are various means by which this can be achieved, they result in different ownership structures: foreign or domestic; institutional or private; and concentrated or dispersed.

A State Property Agency or Fund can oversee privatisation by reasserting state property rights over enterprises. Its task is to dispose of state assets for a reasonable price. Because the level of domestic savings is initially low and the enterprises in question require a large infusion of capital to modernise production, privatisation which involves selling assets at a fair price usually relies heavily on foreign investors. However, not only is it very difficult to estimate the market value of an enterprise in a non-market environment, but it is also a lengthy process during which enterprise assets lose value due to uncertainty over the final outcome. The fact that many enterprises are technically obsolete, produce inferior quality goods, employ excessively large workforces, are financially insecure, reliant on state subsidies and indebted to banks or other firms, further complicates the process. If the price of an enterprise is too high, it will be difficult to find an investor. If the price appears too low not only is revenue from the sale limited, but the government is open to charges of undervaluing state assets and selling the nation's wealth and economic sovereignty to foreigners.

Spontaneous privatisation describes the process, usually carried out by the incumbent management, in which the assets of a particular state enterprise are transferred to a limited liability corporation, often originally established by the enterprise. Opponents claim it represents the transformation of the *nomenklatura's* and management's political influence into economic capital and propose bringing privatisation under public control in the form of a state-controlled Property Fund. However, such Funds can become bureaucratic and since the dispersal of state property lies at the heart of privatisation, a Fund's necessary accumulation of property may hinder the privatisation it aims to promote. In addition, the Ministries, faced with the prospect of losing their economic influence, could salvage their power via a centrally controlled State Property Fund. As time is of the essence, rapid spontaneous privatisation may be preferable to the lengthy process of legislating a Fund's area of competence. In addition, as long as enterprise managers and owners are competent and act according to profit-maximising criteria, who they are is largely irrelevant.

On the other hand, a State Property Fund does not accumulate; rather it disposes of property. Furthermore, spontaneous privatisation denies the state important revenue. As in many cases managers can be held at least partly responsible for enterprise failure, their personal enrichment based on the accumulation of state assets at less than a fair price using insider contacts may become unacceptable, especially as it discriminates against those without such contacts who may be equally or more able managers and owners.

Manager/Employee Buyouts and Employee Stock Ownership Programmes offer an alternative to spontaneous privatisation. The capital required for enterprise purchase can be created by offering the workforce loans at preferential rates which can be repaid from future dividends. It is hoped that as shareholders, workers will recognise the connection between performance, profitability and economic viability and therefore be motivated to increase performance and productivity. Because workers have a personal stake in long-term profitability, rather than immediately liquidating an enterprise which is unprofitable in the short-term, they may be more inclined to restructure and develop alternative production lines.

But if an enterprise employs several thousand workers, share value could still increase even if an individual shareholder does not improve personal performance. Moreover, the workers overriding interest is to retain their employment. Therefore, Employee Stock Ownership Programmes and Manager/Employee Buyouts could hinder industrial restructuring, which automatically implies rationalisation and redundancies. However, as the economic viability of enterprises is highly differentiated and workers can only obtain shares in the enterprises in which they work, one worker can receive shares in an obsolete, economically unviable enterprise, while another gains shares in a profitable company which was modernised using state subsidies. In addition, as only those working in state enterprises gain ownership rights, other state employees, such as those in museums, hospitals or schools, are discriminated against.

A voucher scheme which encompasses the entire adult population would seem to ensure equality and a measure of social justice during privatisation. Although this effectively distributes state property amongst the population, it does so without producing revenue or attracting the foreign capital necessary for restructuring. Furthermore, not all citizens enjoy equal access to information or are capable of making equally informed decisions about how to invest. But, while the ideal of absolute equality and egalitarianism, which are rooted in the former Communist ideology, may be incompatible with the principle of privatisation, which must allow for personal enrichment and a certain level of inequality; attempting to create equal opportunity does not undermine the principle of privatisation or the free market.

A voucher scheme can contribute to support for economic transformation amongst a wide section of society, but can also produce excessively dispersed ownership rights which leave individual owners incapable of applying the concentrated pressure necessary to bring about restructuring. This problem can be partly overcome by Investment Funds which manage the shares held by individuals, but as these Funds are often owned by banks or the state, which are also enterprise creditors, a pattern of cross-ownership which also hinders restructuring can arise. Excessive concentration of ownership and cross-ownership amongst institutions can also arise if citizens decide to sell their shares in the hope of making a quick profit.

Cross-ownership occurs when companies buy shares in other state enterprises during the course of transformation. Although an enterprise is transformed, it buys shares in the same company to whom it sells its shares. The 'shareholders' appoint each other to the Board of Directors of the transformed enterprises, along with representatives from the banks which extended the credit and own the shares. Cross-ownership and interlocking relationships can therefore give rise to even more powerful and monopolistic enterprises. Because the banks which issue credit and own shares in these firms have an interest in providing assistance by extending credit, lobbying for further subsidies or debt write-offs, the informal relationships formed under the old regime may continue. Therefore, this form of privatisation may not change the system of structural incentives or achieve marketisation. On the other hand, cross-ownership is a frequent phenomenon in developed market economies and in the long-term may not present a serious problem.

4.3.1: The Hungarian Programme

Although the conservative government led by the MDF opted for a gradual approach to economic transformation, continuing the policy of gradual economic transformation initiated by the previous regime, from 1993 until 1996 the Hungarian Parliament passed more than sixty new laws pertaining to property rights and ownership structures[43]. The 1991 Kupa Programme, named after the then Minister of Finance, followed the same objectives as the radical Czech economic programme, but was based on the idea of gradualism. It promised to turn around the economy, reduce inflation to single digit figures by 1994 and complete trade liberalisation by 1992[44]. But despite commitment to gradualism, Hungarian transformation involved high social costs, a drop in the standard of living and economic recession.

A 'Programme of National Revival' set forth the government's general policy targets and set the desired share of state property in the economy by 1993 at 30-35%. A more specific document, 'Property and Privatisation', described in detail the different methods of privatisation which the State Property Agency (SPA) was to employ. By privatising 500-600 large state enterprises within the first three years of transition, it aimed to reduce state

---

[43] Laki, Mihály, 'Chances for the Acceleration of Transition: The Case of Hungarian Privatisation', *East European Politics and Societies*, Vol. 7, No. 3, Fall 1993, p. 441.

[44] Adam, Jan, 'The Transition to a Market Economy in Hungary', *Europe-Asia Studies*, Vol. 47, No. 6, 1995, p. 989.

involvement in industry by 33% and in agriculture and food processing by rather more. A further 300-400 state enterprises were also encouraged to initiate their own privatisation[45].

However, the emphasis on the role of the SPA led to a gradual increase in its scope of activity and political influence. Not only did it control and organise state-led privatisation programmes, it also supervised pre-privatisation programmes and thus gained control over enterprises belonging to local municipalities. Although the SPA originally fulfilled its financial targets in terms of privatisation, its own budget was in deficit. This was due to the expanding cost of managing the increasing number of state assets under its control, to various environmental compensation schemes and the take-over of some enterprise debts during the course of privatisation[46].

A document released in March 1991 entitled, 'The Government's Strategy on Property and Privatisation', emphasised the need to speed up the privatisation process. Although it proposed to raise the share of foreign capital in the economy to 25% and lifted limitations on foreign ownership of property and land in Hungary, it also proclaimed that the state would retain a share in enterprises in strategic areas of the economy. The document described the main aim of privatisation as that of creating a new middle class and introduced various tax incentives to encourage the formation of this social group[47]. This complimented the MDF's national-cultural policy which aimed to create a middle class which would form its voter base. Despite the realisation that the speed of privatisation had to be increased, half of the laws listed in the Kupa Programme were either not submitted to Parliament or dismissed by it[48].

The government's rejection of proposals that state property be sold for a minimal amount or given away using a voucher scheme was based on the same rationale which guided the previous

---

[45] Ibid. Kiss, Yudit, 'Privatisation in Hungary – Two Years Later', *Soviet Studies*, pp. 1016-1017.
[46] Ibid. Kiss, Yudit, 'Privatisation in Hungary – Two Years Later', p. 1018.
[47] Ibid. Kiss, Yudit, 'Privatisation in Hungary – Two Years Later', p. 1017.
[48] Csaba, László, 'Macroeconomic Policy in Hungary: Poetry versus Reality', *Soviet Studies*, Vol. 44, No. 6, 1992, p. 960.

regime's initial privatisation policy. Both favoured a centrally controlled privatisation programme which aimed to sell state assets at an appropriate market value to the highest bidder. The exceedingly low level of domestic savings meant that mainly foreign investors could afford to take part in this form of privatisation, and it was specifically designed to encourage foreign investment. Both the Communist regime and the MDF hoped to use the revenue thereby gained to service Hungary's hard currency debt and finance the current account deficit. Financing the current account deficit facilitated avoidance of fundamental budget reform and therefore shielded the population from the social costs of transformation. Although it was hoped this would maintain support for transformation and further democratic consolidation, reliance on the predicted revenue generated by the privatisation of large enterprises, represented mere continuance of existing economic policy.

However, economic continuity did not prevent a fundamental restructuring of government administration. The Central Planning Office was abolished and new Ministries put in its place. A Ministry of International Economic Relations and a Ministry of Trade and Industry, which has within its resource area a new Small Business Office, were established. An Office of Competition, dealing with anti-trust regulations, was also founded[49].

4.3.1.1: Spontaneous and Self-Privatisation

Although a comprehensive voucher scheme enables the population at large to participate in privatisation and thereby increases their personal interest in successful transformation, this was never considered a serious option in Hungary due to the necessity of servicing the hard currency debt.

The MDF's political campaign against spontaneous privatisation and public scandals, such as that concerning the sale of *IBUSZ* shares in March 1990 which led to the dismissal of the first director of the SPA, gave the impression that the government would take action against spontaneous privatisation, but little actually changed.

---

[49] Ibid. Laki, Mihály, 'Chances for the Acceleration of Transition: The Case of Hungarian Privatisation', *East European Politics and Societies*, p. 441.

Dealing with the Communist Economic Legacy

Spontaneous privatisation slowed down but remained, in a somewhat modified form, the main force behind the privatisation of state enterprises. The resilience and success of spontaneous privatisation lay in its ability to attract foreign capital. Figures vary, but official Hungarian estimates maintain that approximately 50-60% of total foreign direct investment in Eastern Europe has been directed into Hungary[50].

Spontaneous privatisation presented a legal framework and business structure within which foreign investors could easily orientate themselves and find a business partner. Thus, most spontaneous privatisation occurred in the form of a joint venture with foreign capital investment. Spontaneous privatisation also required corporatisation which forced large enterprises to restructure themselves in a de-centralised process. The willingness of managers to restructure and find foreign business partners as a means of improving an enterprise's financial position was a direct result of the general financial pressure generated by transition.

Despite the relative success of spontaneous privatisation, in the Autumn of 1990 the MDF initiated a centrally controlled pre-privatisation programme aimed at selling retail trade, catering and service enterprises. An upper limit of ten employees was set for enterprises which were to be privatised within the first two years. It was presumed this project could be carried out fairly quickly because the majority of such outlets had already been leased to their respective managers in the 1980's. However, the original estimate of 50 000 enterprises was gradually reduced as pharmacies, tourist agencies, shops which sold goods for hard currency and commercial food chains were removed from the scheme. Under the old system, large state enterprises owned the retail chains which sold their products. Thus, many small shops which were part of a retail chain escaped the small privatisation programme as they had already been corporatised as part of the spontaneous privatisation of a large enterprise. Although spontaneous privatisation in this area led to the involvement of foreign capital, there have been numerous cases of underpricing and as foreign partners often contributed to

---

[50] Ibid. Mizsei, Kálmán, 'Privatisation in Eastern Europe: A Comparative Study of Poland and Hungary', *Soviet Studies*, p. 293.

the capital of a joint venture in kind with shares, they now own a considerable part of Hungarian retail trade infrastructure.

Of the 10 000 enterprises which were finally registered, approximately 2000 were already in private ownership and another 3000 were under lease for an extended period of time. Thus, only 5000 shops were privatised under the programme. By April 1992, 680 of these had been sold and 1980 leased. Another 130 enterprises were bought by corporations and 430 leased to corporations[51]. Although foreigners were excluded from the programme in an effort to encourage domestic participation, uncertainty over property rights and the lack of domestic capital limited its success. In addition, the majority of the enterprises were located in municipal buildings and were leased. This situation did not offer potential investors much motivation, especially as a successful buyer required the permission of the local council and the SPA to change the nature of a shop within the first five years of purchase. A further hindrance was the fact that original owners, that is pre-nationalisation owners, were given preference during the sales.

Between September-October 1990, the State Property Agency initiated the first large scale privatisation programme. It included twenty large and medium-sized state enterprises whose combined assets were estimated at 33 billion Forints[52]. As their annual turn over in 1989 was approximately 100 billion Forints, the SPA envisaged between 25-40 billion Forints revenue from their privatisation. The SPA did not organise the transactions itself but hired consulting firms to manage the process. The consultants were chosen in a competitive way and although no preference was officially given to foreign consulting firms, 16 foreign and two Hungarian firms were chosen, with one group gaining two cases[53]. This process was time consuming, costly and resulted in limited success; eight enterprises failed to attract any potential buyers. In spite of this, and the fact that it had fallen behind schedule, a

---

[51] Ibid. Kiss, Yudit, 'Privatisation in Hungary – Two Years Later', p. 1021.
[52] Ibid. Laki, Mihály, 'Chances for the Acceleration of Transition: The Case of Hungarian Privatisation', p. 442.
[53] Ibid. Kiss, Yudit, 'Privatisation in Hungary – Two Years Later', p. 1021.

Dealing with the Communist Economic Legacy

second programme began at the start of 1991[54]. The second programme aimed to sell the state holding companies which remained after spontaneous privatisation had transferred assets to new private companies. In the first phase, twelve 'shell' companies, with an estimated 14 billion Forints worth of assets, and 115 limited liability companies were sold[55]. The Department of Industry within the Ministry of Trade and Industry also selected thirty six enterprises for privatisation and the Ministry of Agriculture placed thirty five state farms on its privatisation list[56].

The SPA's large privatisation programmes were highly controversial. At the end of 1992 the Agency reported that, from a total of 2200 state-owned enterprises in 1989, 362 large and medium-sized enterprises had been privatised. The book value of these privatised enterprises was approximately 30-35% of the total value of all state-owned firms. But, although these firms had been privatised, the state share within them remained high. Indeed, the average share of the SPA in these firms in 1992 was 60%[57]. The majority of them were therefore joint or mixed ventures where the state remained the major shareholder.

The Agency was also criticised for over-centralising privatisation and pursuing a policy which marginalised the role of Hungarian investors. Special loans aimed at promoting domestic participation were available to the general public, but their efficiency and range was somewhat limited. As a result, in 1991, only 716 tradesmen received so-called existence-loans, totalling approximately 1 billion Forints. The National Bank also initiated a loan programme, but this was even less successful; supplying only 40 million Forints to private businessmen in 1991[58]. Domestic savings had increased, but people preferred to invest in property, gold, hard currency or government guaranteed bonds rather than

---

[54] Ibid. Mizsei, Kálmán, 'Privatisation in Eastern Europe: A Comparative Study of Poland and Hungary', p. 294.
[55] Ibid. Kiss, Yudit, 'Privatisation in Hungary – Two Years Later', p. 1022.
[56] Ibid. Laki, Mihály, 'Chances for the Acceleration of Transition: The Case of Hungarian Privatisation', p. 442.
[57] Ibid. Laki, Mihály, 'Chances for the Acceleration of Transition: The Case of Hungarian Privatisation', p. 445.
[58] Ibid. Laki, Mihály, 'Chances for the Acceleration of Transition: The Case of Hungarian Privatisation', p. 448.

participate in privatisation. Thus, approximately 85% of privatisation revenue came from foreign capital. The fact that this was not equal to the foreign share in enterprises assets, which was approximately 9%, demonstrated the continued role of the state in privatised enterprises[59].

Even though the SPA originally employed 200 people, it was simply physically unable to deal with the sheer number of enterprises under its control. In addition, it had conflicting aims: to maximise the income from privatisation, which required a lengthy privatisation process for every individual case, while at the same time speeding up the privatisation process as a whole. The rapid personnel turnover within the SPA and its financial dependence on the government were indications of the increasing politicisation of privatisation and by the end of February 1992, only one representative of the opposition remained on the SPA's eleven member governing body[60]. The Agency was further discredited because eight former officials have been charged with fraud, mismanagement, or forgery. Irregularities in SPA accounts and mismanagement led the Prime Minister, Gyula Horn, to dismiss its board and order a full scale investigation in October 1996[61].

Privatisation was both more difficult and slower than expected. Revenue from sales only amounted to 16.1 billion Forints by the end of August 1991, less than 1% of the estimated book value of state enterprises[62]. This meant that the revenue which the MDF had been relying on to service Hungary's foreign debt and balance the

---

[59] Ibid. Laki, Mihály, 'Chances for the Acceleration of Transition: The Case of Hungarian Privatisation', p. 445.

[60] Ibid. Kiss, Yudit, 'Privatisation in Hungary – Two Years Later', p. 1020.

[61] One of those charged, Marta Tocsik, a consultant, was paid over 800 million Forints ($5.3 million) for mediation between the SPA and local governments over the division of income from the sales of state enterprises. Charges have also been filed against Laszlo Boldvai, a former treasurer, Peter Liszkai, former legal counsel for the SPA, and Imre Szokai, the SPA's former board chairman. The former Privatisation Minister, Tamas Suchman, has also been criticised for interference in the SPA's personnel and professional decisions. See *RFE/RL Newsline*, Vol. 1, No. 48, Part II, 9 June, 1997, and *RFE/RL Newsline*, Vol. 1, No. 70, Part II, 10 July 1997.

[62] Estrin, Saul, Hare, Paul, Surányi, Marta, 'Banking Transition: Development and Current Problems in Hungary', *Soviet Studies*, Vol. 44, No. 5, 1992, p. 800.

current account failed to materialise. Consequently, the MDF issued an excessive number of government bonds to finance the deficit, which merely exacerbated the problem by diverting investment away from privatisation.

It was also clear, partly due to lack of domestic interest, that there were fewer interested investors than originally assumed. In addition, those enterprises officially informed they were to be privatised suffered asset deterioration for the duration of the process. This in turn made it more difficult to accurately assess value and find an investor. If SPA initiatives were perceived by managers as contrary to their individual interests, privatisation was hampered. Thus, only 60 out of 1300 firms required to draw up plans for privatisation returned them to the SPA within the prescribed six month period[63]. Moreover, as value in a market economy is determined by demand, the sheer volume of enterprises on the market during transformation also effectively lowered their market value.

In these circumstances, the actual value of the enterprise is largely irrelevant since the longer it remains under state control, the more its assets deteriorate and its value decreases. The less it is worth, the longer it takes to find an investor and the loss to the state increases. Thus, the final loss is greater; not only has the enterprise suffered asset deterioration, perhaps to the point of being forced into liquidation, but the state has also sold it at a price well below its original estimated market value, so far as this was possible to establish.

In October 1991, the SPA's centrally organised privatisation programme had to be partly abandoned and the active participation of management and workers in de-centralised, self-privatisation schemes was accepted. The SPA delegated its decision making responsibilities to 84, mainly Hungarian, private consulting firms who were charged with overseeing the privatisation of approximately 500 enterprises[64]. Although the SPA continued to receive the revenue generated, its only control over the process was the precondition that enterprises choose the legal advisors and

---

[63] Ibid. Laki, Mihály, 'Chances for the Acceleration of Transition: The Case of Hungarian Privatisation', p. 448.
[64] Ibid. Kiss, Yudit, 'Privatisation in Hungary – Two Years Later', p. 1023.

accountants needed for aneconomic assessment from the consultancy firms officially approved by the SPA. To speed up privatisation further, enterprises were given until 1994 to transform themselves into shareholding companies and look for investors or a private owner. If an enterprise had not transformed itself by this date, its Enterprise Council was abolished and it was brought under direct state control[65].

Thus, spontaneous privatisation, in the form of self-privatisation, remains unchallenged as the main form of privatisation in Hungary. It is a pragmatic programme which decreases potential opposition to privatisation from both management and workers because they are directly involved in the process. It has also been extremely successful in attracting the foreign investment necessary to modernise and restructure the economy. Although this process did not involve the general population and therefore their personal stake in successful transformation remained low; high foreign investment created the conditions necessary for restructuring and economic growth, and in this way helped further democratic consolidation.

4.3.2: Radical Czech Transformation

The legacy of normalisation meant that the Czech economy was neither fully developed nor underdeveloped. Thus, some of the economic conditions inherited from the Communist regime were relatively favourable as far as transformation was concerned; the country's international economic performance was acceptable, it had a low level of inflation and, while the workforce was relatively skilled, wages were low. In addition, it had a small hard currency debt which, although it increased during transformation, remained relatively low and in 1992 stood at $9 billion. In contrast, in 1991 the Hungarian gross foreign debt totalled $22.1 billion, approximately 63% of the Gross National Product[66]. On the other hand, excessive centralisation, only approximately 7.5% of the

---

[65] Ibid. Kocsis, György, 'How to Uncook Fish Soup', *The New Hungarian Quarterly*, p. 35.
[66] Herr, Hansjörg, Westphal, Andreas, (Hrsg.), *Transformation in Mittel- und Osteuropa*, Campus 1993, pp. 340-343.

means of production were privately owned[67], large sectoral monopolies, the low level of foreign trade, especially with the West, and the technical obsolescence of industry, especially in the most sophisticated industries, represented a considerable hindrance to transformation.

The government, led by Vaclav Klaus, opted for a radical programme of economic transformation which it was hoped would facilitate the swift and total dissolution of the entrenched bureaucratic economic system. As the Communist regime had refused to implement reform, continuity of economic policy was not feasible. In addition, lack of reform meant systemic dysfunction was so serious that a gradual programme could not achieve the radical transformation required if the ossified structures of the command economy were to be dismantled and replaced.

The Czech government placed its trust in the ability of the market to achieve transformation and create fair conditions of competition. Although Slovak reluctance to follow this policy was one of the factors which led to the dissolution of the Czechoslovak Federation, the Czech government gained the population's support for its radical programme. This was achieved in part by the voucher scheme, which not only facilitated the rapid privatisation of large state enterprises, but also enabled a large section of the adult population to participate in their privatisation and in part by specific government policies aimed at shielding the population from the social costs of transformation by preventing bankruptcy and keeping the unemployment rate low. In contrast to the majority of the Romanian population, which remained sceptical of the market, the Czechs, encouraged by the government's trust in the benefits of transformation, were eager to participate in the voucher scheme. The voucher scheme not only also increased the population's personal interest in successful transformation and maintained public support for the process, it was also a means by which to ensure the Communist economic elite did not retain their privileges in the new system. In this sense, it furthered systemic identification and democratic consolidation.

---

[67] Kupka, Martin, 'Transformation of Ownership in Czechoslovakia', *Soviet Studies*, Vol. 44, No. 2, 1992, p. 297.

The Czech government coalition led by the Civic Democratic Party remained in office throughout the initial period of transformation. This meant that the Czech Republic experienced the most consistent transformation programme and, until recently, had achieved the most successful economic results.

The government submitted its programme for economic reform to Parliament on 1 September, 1990[68]. It declared the maintenance of low inflation as its main goal, to which all other policies, including employment, would be subordinated. The programme, which was implemented on 1 January, 1991, was strongly influenced by neo-liberal economic thought and represented a form of shock treatment for the Czechoslovak economy. It aimed to stabilise the economy by ensuring market equilibrium and a long-term surplus in the balance of payments to meet debt servicing requirements. The importance of creating a competitive environment in which market prices would determine management decisions and force increased efficiency and profitability was also emphasised. Prices were fully liberalised and subsidies abolished, except for some basic foodstuffs; flour, meat, milk and energy, where a maximum price was set and liberalisation occurred in stages. The economy was opened to the world market by liberalising trade and introducing the internal convertibility of the Crown. In addition to restrictive monetary and fiscal policies, strict wage controls were also introduced, and after trilateral negotiations between the government, employers and Trade Unions, a reduction in real wages was agreed for 1991[69].

Wage regulation consisted of an allowed wage bill and heavy taxes for exceeding it. The allowable wage bill was calculated by multiplying the set wage tariff by the number of employees, plus non-tariff benefits from the previous year. The basic wage bill thus calculated could grow by a fixed percentage each quarter. In the first quarter of 1991, the percentage was set at 5%, although by the end of the year wage growth totalled 32%. To enable them to

---

[68] Ibid. Adam, Jan, 'Transformation to a Market Economy in the Former Czechoslovakia', *Europe-Asia Studies*, p. 627.
[69] *The World Bank Economic Review*, Vol. 6, No. 1, 1992, pp. 10-11. See also Bartlett, David, L., 'Democracy, Institutional Change and Stabilisation policy in Hungary', *Europe-Asia Studies*, Vol. 48, No. 1, 1996, p. 76.

increase production, enterprises were allowed to increase wages up to 3% over the limit without paying tax fines. Increases beyond this limit were heavily taxed. For increases in wages between 3-5% above the limit, the tax was 200% of the additional wages paid, while for increases above 5% of the limit, the tax was 750%. However, in combination with the 57.9% increase in consumer prices during 1991, the 24.5% decline in real wages was excessively restrictive. In reaction to this, the government introduced a new system of wage regulation for state enterprises in 1992 which linked wage increases to the average annual rate of profit. Enterprises with a profit rate of up to 12% could increase wages by up to 13% without paying any extra taxes. Enterprises with higher profit rates could increase wages by 15%, while those with over 30% foreign capital involvement were exempt from the new regulations[70].

Although liberalisation of trade increases competition, if too excessive, it can harm domestic production and have an adverse effect on the balance of payments. In order to avoid this, the government introduced a 20% surcharge, later reduced to 15%, on consumer goods and licensed certain exports. The internal convertibility of the Crown, set at 28 Crowns for one Dollar, was linked to a basket of fifteen hard currencies and caused massive currency devaluation[71]. Exporters had to surrender all the hard currency they received for their products in order to guarantee importers hard currency. In addition, Czech citizens were only permitted to buy a limited amount of foreign currency specified by the authorities.

Restrictive monetary and fiscal policies, combined with strict wage policy, were intended to ensure stabilisation and cope with the inflationary effect of liberalising prices in a monopolised economy. The balanced state budget, which was also obtained via tight fiscal policies, was aimed to keep inflation low. However, decline in consumer demand as a result of price increases and decreases in real wages led to a considerable drop in the standard of

---

[70] Ibid. Adam, Jan, 'Transformation to a Market Economy in the Former Czechoslovakia', p. 630-633.
[71] Ibid. Adam, Jan, 'Transformation to a Market Economy in the Former Czechoslovakia', p. 629.

living and the purchasing power of savings. Thus, it was estimated that during 1991, the real value of the population's savings declined by 40%[72].

Although it was hoped that a radical programme would limit the costs of transformation, in comparison with 1990, the Gross Domestic Product (GDP) declined by 25% in the fourth quarter of 1991, and national income declined by 29%. In addition, real consumer expenditure declined by 33% and although approximately 15% of the workforce was on short hours or low wages, by December 1991 unemployment reached 7%[73]. Retention of workers kept the unemployment rate low, but also contributed to an excessive decrease in productivity. Labour productivity under the previous regime had been approximately half the level of western industrial countries, but it declined by a further 15% in 1991[74]. While shock treatment caused the loss of one million jobs, the unemployment rate remained lower than the rate of decline in production. The government's policy of wage restriction had the effect of keeping the unit percentage of labour costs low and reduced pressure on managers to rationalise.

The Ministry of Finance document, 'Information for Enterprises about Economic Conditions in 1991', stated that the main instruments of economic control remained the interest rate and credit limits for individual banks[75]. In an attempt to impose hard budget constraints, credit limits for 1991 were set only slightly higher than the 1989 level. This led to an increase of only 12% in enterprise credits during the first five months of 1991. As the

---

[72] Ibid. Adam, Jan, 'Transformation to a Market Economy in the Former Czechoslovakia', p. 630.

[73] This figure refers to the former Czechoslovakia. The unemployment rate in the Czech Republic was lower. Pick, Milos, 'Quo Vadis – Homo Sapiens? Results and Alternatives for the Transformation Strategy of the CSFR', *Europe-Asia Studies*, Vol. 45, No. 1, 1993, p. 103.

[74] Ibid. Pick, Milos, 'Quo Vadis – Homo Sapiens? Results and Alternatives for the Transformation Strategy of the CSFR', *Europe-Asia Studies*, p. 104.

[75] The discount interest rate was increased to 10% and an upper ceiling of 24% for interest rates on bank loans to enterprises was introduced. Although it was hoped to achieve a positive interest rate, as the rate of inflation was higher than the expected, 30%, it remained negative. Ibid. Adam, Jan, 'Transformation to a Market Economy in the Former Czechoslovakia', p. 631.

Dealing with the Communist Economic Legacy

inflation rate for the same period was 46.7%, the credit targets were over restrictive. As fiscal policy was also tight and government subsidies to enterprises restricted, investment in the obsolete production base and infrastructure actually declined by approximately 40% during the initial period of transformation[76].

In spite of the fact that the government did not increase taxes in 1991, the tax burden remained high, profit taxes ran at 55% and taxes on wages at 50%. While increased enterprise profits enabled the government to maintain a budget surplus during the first five months of 1991, decreasing profits during the second half of the year led to a budget deficit of 18 billion Crowns, equivalent to approximately 3.9% of government revenue[77]. The gradual increase in the Czech budget deficit was caused not only by a loss of tax revenue from poorly performing state enterprises and poor tax collection; many of the consumer goods which yield high tax revenue, such as alcohol and cigarettes, are bought and sold illegally, but also by the prolonged recession which depressed consumption and led to an increase in savings.

While many managers and workers found it difficult to adjust psychologically to the market environment, the main problems encountered by the radical Czech programme were depressed consumer demand and reduced investment resulting from the restrictive monetary and fiscal policies, which aimed at ensuring stabilisation and inflation control. The belief that the market was capable of achieving transformation on its own meant that, while continuing some subsidies, the government neglected structural policy and did little to halt the decline in investment. In combination with voucher privatisation, this did not further enterprise restructuring and has delayed the transformation of economic relations.

4.3.2.1: Czech Privatisation

The Czech privatisation programme emphasised the difference between 'large' and 'small' privatisation. Small privatisation

---

[76] Ibid. Pick, Milos, 'Quo Vadis – Homo Sapiens? Results and Alternatives for the Transformation Strategy of the CSFR', p. 104.
[77] Ibid. Adam, Jan, 'Transformation to a Market Economy in the Former Czechoslovakia', p. 632.

consisted of auctions and cash sales; whereas large privatisation entailed selling shares in state enterprises in return for investment vouchers. The limited number of shares which were offered for sale in return for cash were mostly purchased by foreign investors[78].

Small privatisation was initiated as a means by which domestic businessmen could buy production assets whose value was relatively low, but which formed complete units and could immediately begin operation. Thus, small privatisation encompassed the trade and service sector, that is shops, restaurants and small workshops. Only natural individuals who were Czechoslovak citizens, or had been Czechoslovak citizens after 25 February, 1948, and legal persons or corporations representing natural individuals who fulfilled these conditions could take part[79]. In this way, the ethnic Germans and Hungarians who had been forced to leave Czechoslovakia after the Second World War were excluded.

Lists of enterprises or parts of enterprises to be privatised were published thirty days before a public auction at which they were sold to the highest bidder. People interested in buying the property had to pay a deposit equivalent of 10% of the reserve price, or a minimum of 10 000 Crowns, approximately $330. Unsuccessful bidders regained their deposit, while the winning bidder's deposit was treated as an advance payment of the auction price and was transferred to the account of the Ministry for Privatisation. If the winning bidder failed to pay the remaining amount to the Ministry within 30 days after the auction, the advance was forfeit to the Ministry. Although the stocks of a unit were not auctioned, the new owner had to take them over and pay their value within 30 days to the state organisation which had previously owned them[80].

---

[78] Kabbe, Georgy, 'Die Privatisierung in Osteuropa: Konzeptionen, Modelle, Resultate', Institut für Weltwirtschaft, p. 50. Paper at a Conference held by the Friedrich Ebert Stiftung: 'Der Schwierige Weg der osteuropäischen Länder zur Demokratie und Markwirtschaft', 23-27 September 1996.

[79] Ibid. Kabbe, Georgy, 'Die Privatisierung in Osteuropa: Konzeptionen, Modelle, Resultate', Institut für Weltwirtschaft, p. 50.

[80] Ibid. Kupka, Martin, 'Transformation of Ownership in Czechoslovakia', *Soviet Studies*, p. 306.

If bids at the auction failed to reach the reserve price, and if at least five people took part, the price was gradually reduced in 10% blocks, but not to a level lower than 50% of the reserve price. If the unit still failed to attract a buyer, or if a buyer failed to take over an auctioned unit, it was auctioned again in the second privatisation round, which began on 16 June, 1991. The conditions of second round auctions were less strict, allowing the participation of natural persons who were not and never had been Czech citizens, and a drop in price to as little as 20% of the original reserve price[81].

Many of the small enterprises involved in this form of privatisation were often leased from local authorities, so it was agreed that for a period of five years, enterprises which had been leased before 1 October, 1990 could be sold without a public auction to those who had leased them. Units and properties which were subject to restitution claims were excluded from the small privatisation scheme and were, where possible, returned to their original owners. As a result of restitution claims, many units were not auctioned with the land on which they were situated or with the property in which they operated. In these cases, the owners of the land or property were obliged to conclude minimum five year contracts with the owners of the units[82].

Foreigners and corporate bodies not consisting of natural persons were excluded from the first round of small privatisation in an attempt to further an indigenous propertied middle class and prevent state property being purchased by state-owned enterprises or enterprises which were only formally cooperatives. It was for the latter reason that, for a period of two years, the re-sale of property which had been privatised during small privatisation to corporate bodies which did not consist of natural persons was prohibited. Despite the restrictions, interested foreign parties found Czech citizens who were willing to buy units on their behalf in the first round of auctions, but not take them over. This enabled the foreign corporations or persons to buy them during the second round of auctions. This was especially the case for the larger units, which were more expensive. The more expensive units attracted a limited

---

[81] Ibid. Kupka, Martin, 'Transformation of Ownership in Czechoslovakia', p. 306.
[82] Ibid. Kupka, Martin, 'Transformation of Ownership in Czechoslovakia', p. 307.

number of prospective buyers and interested domestic parties often formed a 'ring' in advance of the auction to keep the price low, while other prospective buyers asked for compensation for not pushing the price too high. In this way, many units were sold for a relatively low price.

Despite commitment to the market, Czech law obliged the new owners of units which had been engaged in food sales to continue such business for a minimum of one year unless the local council agreed to shorten this period at an owner's request[83].

The small privatisation programme was very successful and by the end of 1992, approximately 32 000 enterprises, 9300 of them in Slovakia, had been sold. Although it was hoped to complete small privatisation in the Czech Republic by 31 December, 1992, the process was finally completed in 1995. The total revenue from small privatisation was 35.1 billion Crowns, approximately DM 2 billion. This money was used to compensate the local authorities which had given up property for their initial loss of income and to cover the costs of the scheme[84].

Large privatisation dealt with enterprises mainly involved in industry and manufacturing. The process was managed by a Privatisation Ministry in the Czech Republic and three central Funds, which dealt with assets in all parts of the Federation. In contrast to small privatisation, foreign investors were allowed to take part. It was originally planned that 2500 of the 5500 medium-sized enterprises to be privatised would be privatised in a first wave, while the rest would be privatised within five years in a second wave[85].

The first stage of privatisation entailed the preparation of a specific plan which included a detailed breakdown of the elements of the enterprise which fell under the restitution law, parts which were unsuitable for business purposes or scheduled for small privatisation and parts which were legal self-contained units. Enterprises not proposed for direct sale had to transform themselves

---

[83] Ibid. Kupka, Martin, 'Transformation of Ownership in Czechoslovakia', p. 307.
[84] Ibid. Kabbe, Georgy, 'Die Privatisierung in Osteuropa: Konzeptionen, Modelle, Resultate', p. 50.
[85] Ibid. Kabbe, Georgy, 'Die Privatisierung in Osteuropa: Konzeptionen, Modelle, Resultate', p. 50.

into joint-stock companies and set aside 3% of their stock for the Restitution Fund. Shares also had to be set aside for voucher privatisation. Projects could include all methods of privatisation; sale by auction, tender, the sale of shares on the market and the voucher method.

The first wave of enterprises involved in large scale privatisation had to forward their projects to those in charge of them by 31 October, 1991, and the projects had to be passed on to the Privatisation Ministry by 30 November, 1990. For the second wave of large privatisation, deadlines of 31 May, 1992 for enterprise privatisation projects, and 31 July, 1992 for their receipt by the Ministry were set[86]. During the second stage of privatisation assets were sold and transferred to the new owners.

4.3.2.2: The Voucher Scheme

The basic model for the voucher scheme was devised by the then Finance Minister, Vaclav Klaus, in cooperation with Dr. Triska, who took over the position of Finance Minister after Klaus became Prime Minister, and Professor Svenjar from Pittsburgh University[87]. The voucher scheme aimed to achieve the quick privatisation of the large number of state enterprises in which foreign investors had little interest and for which Czech businessmen lacked capital.

As the overriding imperative was the quickest possible transference of ownership to private individuals, cooperatives or shareholders, and as the country was not relying on income from privatisation to service foreign debt obligations, the voucher scheme was not designed to raise revenue. Under the scheme state assets were practically given away to the adult population. Allowing broad public access to property was a means of ensuring the Communist economic elite could not carry their privileges into the new economic system[88]. Because the capital markets were still underdeveloped, it was difficult to achieve the swift privatisation of

---

[86] Ibid. Kupka, Martin, 'Transformation of Ownership in Czechoslovakia', p. 308.
[87] Ibid. Kupka, Martin, 'Transformation of Ownership in Czechoslovakia', p. 309.
[88] For a discussion of this strategy, see Appel, Hilary, 'Justice and Reformulation of Property Rights in the Czech Republic', *East European Politics and Societies*, Vol. 9, No. 1, Winter 1995, pp. 22-40.

so many enterprises using more standard methods, especially as the government was reluctant to involve too much foreign capital in the process and domestic savings were low. It was hoped that this method would avoid the situation in Hungary and Romania, where the case by case approach had led to long delays. These delays discouraged prospective investors, led to the deterioration of state assets and often ended in failure to find a prospective investor.

As the whole population had contributed to the creation of state property and assets in 1948, a voucher scheme which facilitated the population's participation in its privatisation ensured a certain amount of corrective social justice. In addition, it provided people with a personal interest in transformation's success and increased support for it, thereby furthering democratic consolidation. Thus, although dispersal of ownership rights amongst the population could hinder restructuring and mass selling of vouchers could cause considerable inflationary pressure, in the absence of large foreign debt servicing obligations which could force case by case privatisation at a fair price, the Czech government preferred voucher privatisation.

During the first round of large privatisation, the voucher scheme was based on voucher booklets, issued by the Ministry of Finance, which adult Czechoslovak citizens could buy for 35 Crowns, approximately \$1[89]. The voucher booklet contained a number of vouchers of different value which were marked in investment points. These could be used in conjunction with voucher stamps, which could be purchased up to the value of 1000 Crowns, approximately \$33, to order shares in state enterprises. After a list of enterprises to be privatised had been published, those wishing to take part had to register and affix the necessary stamp on the appropriate voucher in their booklet. In each round of privatisation participants were entitled to buy shares up to the value of 1000 points. In a pre-round, investors could exchange investment points for shares held by private or state-owned Investment Funds. In this case, the shares obtained corresponded to their weight in the total points available to the Fund. The Investment Funds managed the vouchers and decided in which enterprises to invest. Approximately

---

[89] Ibid. Kupka, Martin, 'Transformation of Ownership in Czechoslovakia', p. 309.

5 million out of the total 8.5 million participants decided to put their vouchers into such Funds[90]. Thus, Investment Funds entered the privatisation process alongside individuals.

Before participants decided how many shares they wanted to order in a given round, they had to find out the current rates for the shares on offer, that is how many investment points a given share was worth. Share orders were taken at designated offices and passed to a central office where all share orders were collected. If the demand for shares was lower or equal to the supply, all orders were fulfilled. If the demand was more than 25% of supply, orders were not fulfilled and investment points were returned to the respective participants. The price of the shares was increased and they were passed on to the next privatisation round. If demand was higher than supply, but not more than 25% higher, the Federal Ministry of Finance could decide to decrease the fulfilment of Investment Fund orders by a maximum of 20% in order to meet other orders[91].

Approximately 8.5 million adult citizens, from the total Czechoslovak population of 11.5 million, took part in the scheme. By the end of 1992, 1491 enterprises in Czechoslovakia, 498 of them in Slovakia, had been privatised using the voucher method[92]. Although participation was high, the majority of people had no idea what to actually do with their shares. In addition, the number of shares any one individual could obtain in a particular enterprise was relatively low. Voucher privatisation successfully transferred ownership from the state, but the dispersed ownership structure it created led to a lack of clear ownership rights. Consequently, it facilitated continued economic irrationality and indiscipline. Although the Investment Funds concentrated ownership rights and could exert pressure to increase profitability, many are owned by the state and by banks, which are also enterprise creditors. In this way, a cross-ownership structure arose which worked to hinder restructuring.

---

[90] Herr, Hansjörg, Westphal, Andreas, (Hrsg.), *Transformation in Mittel- und Osteuropa*, Campus 1993, p. 242.
[91] Ibid. Kupka, Martin, 'Transformation of Ownership in Czechoslovakia', p. 309.
[92] Ibid. Kabbe, Georgy, 'Die Privatisierung in Osteuropa: Konzeptionen, Modelle, Resultate', pp. 50-51.

After the dissolution of the Czechoslovak Federation on 1 January, 1993, the Czech government continued the radical transformation programme and initiated a second wave of large privatisation using the voucher method. In the second wave, all adult Czech citizens were eligible to register and in return for a fee of 1050 Crowns, approximately DM 60, obtained a new voucher booklet for use with similar voucher stamps. Between April and November 1994, six rounds of voucher privatisation took place. At the end of this process, 96% of the shares in 861 enterprises, with a total capital of $5.25 billion, had been sold. In April 1995, preparations for the privatisation of the remaining 2000 enterprises began and it was announced that only ten large companies, such as the Postal Service, Railway, and *Transgas*, the company which manages the gas pipeline from Russia, would remain under state control[93].

During the course of large privatisation, approximately 4000 enterprises were privatised and 4 million Czechs, the largest proportion of all the Central and East European countries, became shareholders. The success of the voucher scheme in transferring property rights meant that by the Spring of 1996, approximately 70% of the Czech economy had entered the private sector. Having dealt with 70 000 restitution claims, overseen the auction of 22 000 enterprises as part of small privatisation, and distributed 1849 enterprises with a value of approximately DM 20 billion amongst the population using the voucher method as part of large privatisation, the Privatisation Ministry was dissolved on 1 July, 1996[94].

4.3.3: The Contradictory Romanian Programme

Although Romania had a relatively low foreign currency debt at the start of transformation, the economy in general was in a much poorer state than either the Czech or the Hungarian. Despite the complete lack of experience with any kind of reform, the 1990 Romanian economic programme was drafted without the help of

---

[93] Ibid. Kabbe, Georgy, 'Die Privatisierung in Osteuropa: Konzeptionen, Modelle, Resultate', p. 51.

[94] Ibid. Kabbe, Georgy, 'Die Privatisierung in Osteuropa: Konzeptionen, Modelle, Resultate', pp. 51-52.

Dealing with the Communist Economic Legacy

any foreign economic advisors in a mere three months, the fastest of the three countries.

Although the centrally administered economy was obsolescent and inefficient, the PDSR-led government did not implement either radical or gradual transformation, rather it attempted to increase the efficiency and performance of the existing system by introducing limited market reforms. Transformation therefore consisted mostly of the implementation of a new legal framework and little in the way of actual transformation of the institutional and functional system of relations. The sectoral Ministries remained strong, enterprise monopolies were not called into question and despite price shocks, the monetary overhang was not eliminated.

As a result of the inconsequential transformation programme, in 1990 Romanian GDP fell by 7.3% and industrial production declined by 20%[95]. The government tried to stimulate growth using the old structures and encouraged cooperation between the new power elite and the old *nomenklatura*. It increased the imports of spare and raw materials as a means of increasing production and consumption. However, after the 1990 elections this policy was abandoned because it became clear that the economy could no longer support it. But reductions in energy imports meant that by the end of 1991, 460 of Romania's furnaces, chemical works and coal mines had ceased to operate or were running at a minimal level[96].

Starting in November 1991, prices were liberalised step by step. But as monopolies were not broken up, it was prices, rather than competition, which increased. Although Romanian wages were 25 times lower than in Western Europe, and labour productivity between 12-14 times lower, prices were close to the West European level[97]. The rise in prices led to an increase in the rate of inflation from 10% at the start of 1990, to 30% at its close. Thus, despite the fact that during the same period wages increased by 160%, there

---

[95] Gregori, Ilina, Schaser, Angelika, (Hrsg.), *Rumänien im Umbruch*, Verlag Dr. Dieter Winkler 1993, p. 36.
[96] Ibid. Gregori, Ilina, Schaser, Angelika, (Hrsg.), *Rumänien im Umbruch*, p. 38.
[97] Sîrbu, Maria Cristina, 'Towards a Market Economy: The Romanian Effort', *East European Quarterly*, Vol. 28, No. 4, Winter 1994, p. 491.

was widespread social unrest[98]. Strikes and protests delayed the liberalisation of food prices from 1 January until 1 April, 1991, and forced the retention of upper price limits on basic foodstuffs. But the upper limits set on basic food stuffs were too low to achieve equilibrium; so although prices were raised, subsidies were still retained, prices remained too low and liberalisation was not achieved[99]. The issue of price liberalisation split the government and the then Minister of Finance, Teodor Stolojan, resigned in protest at the compromising of reform.

In contrast, wages were fully liberalised. To finance wage increases, managers increased forced inter-enterprise credits and, in cooperation with the Trade Unions, pressured the government into providing fresh credits at subsidised rates. The exponential increase in this form of money substitute and the danger it represented to the stability of the financial system forced the government to ration, though not refuse, credits. However, wage increases were not accompanied by an increase in productivity.

The economic crisis led to the introduction of a stabilisation programme in June 1991. It aimed to eliminate remaining price limits, while retaining subsidies for a few essential food and energy products. An accompanying compensatory increase in wages was to be prevented by the introduction of restrictions on enterprise credit. Although the section of the programme entitled 'Social Dimensions of Adjustment' created a social safety net financed by a 1% tax on workers' salaries and a 4% tax on the wages fund to protect vulnerable sections of society, particularly the unemployed, it was not very generous[100]. In late September 1991, strikes and miners protests led to the abandonment of the programme. Wages were increased and the price of essential food and energy products frozen[101].

---

[98] Ibid. Sîrbu, Maria Cristina, 'Towards a Market Economy: The Romanian Effort', *East European Quarterly*, p. 475.

[99] Ibid. Gregori, Ilina, Schaser, Angelika, (Hrsg.), *Rumänien im Umbruch*, p. 40.

[100] van Frausum, Yves, G., Gehmann, Ulrich, Gross, Jürgen, 'Market Economy and Economic Reform in Romania: Macroeconomic and Microeconomic Perspectives', *Europe-Asia Studies*, Vol. 46, No. 5, 1994, p. 738.

[101] Ibid. Gregori, Ilina, Schaser, Angelika, (Hrsg.), *Rumänien im Umbruch*, p. 40.

Former Prime Minister, Petre Roman, commented that Romanian transformation was neither gradual in the Hungarian sense, nor radical in the Czech sense, because although shocks occurred every few months, they were not accompanied by liberalisation[102]. The reason behind this lies in the fact that the majority of those in the PDSR-led government believed that the old economic system could function effectively if it were improved.

In this political and social atmosphere, the government's commitment to transformation remained ambiguous and at the start of 1991, only two laws, the Law on the Transformation of State Enterprises and the Law on Business Companies, had been passed by Parliament. During the course of 1991 further laws were passed; the Law on the Redistribution of Land was passed in February 1991, the Law on Foreign Investment in April 1991 and the Privatisation Law in August 1991, but administrative restructuring was not attempted. Although the laws represent the legal end of the centrally planned economy, in reality old institutions and practices remained intact. Thus, the Ministry of Industry remained responsible for the distribution of approximately 200 materials and semi-finished goods[103].

Although state-owned enterprises were largely self-managed, their autonomy was limited by the fact that managers were appointed by the board of directors, usually made up of shareholder representatives, that is officials from branch Ministries selected or confirmed by the Enterprise. The government's failure to clarify judicial and institutional regulations meant that managers of state enterprises had no work contracts. Under pressure from the Unions, Ministry officials often replaced better managers with others who were more willing to appease the workers and approve wage increases, while not enforcing discipline at the workplace.

Commercial state companies enjoyed more autonomy because shareholder representatives in these companies were often inexperienced. They therefore lacked influence and were unwilling to take responsibility for state capital. The government's failure to recapitalise enterprises meant that the system under which

---

[102] Ibid. Gregori, Ilina, Schaser, Angelika, (Hrsg.), *Rumänien im Umbruch*, p. 40.
[103] Ibid. Gregori, Ilina, Schaser, Angelika, (Hrsg.), *Rumänien im Umbruch*, pp. 43-44.

enterprise capital was held in the National Bank, which approved enterprise credits, was continued. Interest was gained on profits which were paid to the National Bank, but the profit tax was high, 45%, thus depressing not only profit incentive, but also investment potential[104]. Managers therefore actively contributed to the decline of state capital, for instance selling products at a price below their market value, thus lowering the value of an enterprise and reducing the cost of a Management/Employee Buyout. Although lack of financial resources and obsolescent machinery constituted obstacles to this form of privatisation, management interest in it increased as the limitations and flaws in government strategy became obvious.

Thus, the majority of state-owned enterprises and commercial companies remained unwilling to develop strategic plans. They avoided hard budget constraints by increasing inter-enterprise debts and resisted restructuring and redundancy plans. They were assisted in this by the government's own unwillingness to enforce financial discipline, hard budget constraints and liquidate loss-making enterprises. Romanian productivity declined by a cumulative 53% between 1990-1992, but few enterprises were liquidated or restructured[105]. A two-tier banking system was adopted, but the few commercial banks which operated enjoyed monopolies and often turned down small investors' applications for credit, preferring instead to continue giving credit to their largest, but least economically viable, long-standing customers. Although the old Bankruptcy Law was inappropriate and non-operational, a new Bankruptcy Law failed to pass Parliament. Allocation of credit by non-market criteria diverted finances away from private enterprises and prolonged the existence of soft budget constraints.

It was clear that the system's institutions and bureaucracy were hindering reform and prolonging the economic crisis. But the PDSR's reliance on the *nomenklatura* within the economic and administrative bureaucracy for support, and the fact that many of its

---

[104] Oschlies, Wolf, *Wirtschaftsreform und Reformdebatten in Rumänien*, Bundesinstitut für Ostwissenschaftliche und Internationale Studien, Bericht No. 42, 1994, p. 14.
[105] Ibid. van Frausum, Yves, G., Gehmann, Ulrich, Gross, Jürgen, 'Market Economy and Economic Reform in Romania: Macroeconomic and Microeconomic Perspectives', *Europe-Asia Studies*, p. 739.

leaders were not in favour of the state withdrawing completely from the economy, meant that it failed to initiate de-centralisation, structural or administrative reform.

The 1991 Privatisation Law reflected the reluctance to relinquish central control over the economy and was indicative of the government's inherent distrust of the market. It foresaw a programme of free distribution of 10.5 million vouchers, representing a 30% share in approximately 6300 state-owned companies, to all adult Romanian citizens who resided in Romania. But the shares were held by Private Ownership Funds, which were themselves state-owned and under direct government control. Thus, the transfer actually represented the distribution of 30% of the shares in the five Private Ownership Funds[106].

Reliance on the principle of central control and a centralised decision making process meant the Communist administrative system remained virtually intact. However, the centralised bureaucratic command system was not capable of solving the economic crisis. Thus, in 1991 Romanian GDP decreased by a further 15% and the trade deficit reached $1.8 billion[107]. Continued economic crisis and worsening living standards meant the population found it difficult to accept the idea of transformation and democratic consolidation was limited.

Romanian GDP increased by approximately 1% in 1993. This represented the first growth since 1990, but as production had previously declined, the increase in GDP implied stagnation. In addition, exports had decreased by 42.1% in 1990, so the 48% increase in 1993 merely indicated a return to their previous level. Although prices decreased by 50% in 1993, real wages declined by 73%, causing a significant drop in the population's purchasing power. In addition, by 1993 the annual inflation rate had risen to 300%, and the monthly rate stood at 12.1%, as compared with a monthly rate of 9.6% in 1992[108]. The basic contradiction in

---

[106] Ibid. Gregori, Ilina, Schaser, Angelika, (Hrsg.), *Rumänien im Umbruch*, p. 44. Also Embassy of Romania, *Privatization in Romania*. Taken from the Internet on 26.6.97. Http: //www.embassy.org/romania.

[107] Ibid. Gregori, Ilina, Schaser, Angelika, (Hrsg.), *Rumänien im Umbruch*, p. 45.

[108] Ibid. Sîrbu, Maria Cristina, 'Towards a Market Economy: The Romanian Effort', p. 475.

government policy between privatisation and centralisation contributed to the continued economic imbalance.

Although Ceausescu had been removed, the institutional and administrative structures he had created remained largely intact. The PDSR implemented a reform programme which aimed to improve the economic performance of the system without fundamentally changing its central administrative structure. Despite this, the reforms damaged the PDSR's power base because the opportunity to engage in independent, free enterprise destroyed the vertical dependency of the middle class on the *nomenklautra*. This ensured the autonomy of the middle class which became dissatisfied with the half-hearted reforms. Despite continued poor economic performance, the PDSR did not develop a more coherent transformation programme, rather it turned to Ceausescu's policy of manipulating nationalism to conceal economic failure and mobilise popular support.

Limited commitment to economic transformation and the lack of progress towards establishing a functioning free market caused the International Monetary Fund (IMF) to suspend its credit to Romania in 1993[109]. The new agreement, signed with the IMF in February 1994, was conditional on improved economic performance and real commitment to privatisation and restructuring. The new agreement combined with domestic difficulties, declining popularity and continuing economic turmoil, to force the PDSR to announce a series of measures aimed at reforming state finances and speeding up the privatisation of state enterprises.

4.3.3.1: Romanian Privatisation

The main problem confronting Romanian privatisation is the size and nature of the enterprises which are available. As a result of its Stalinist development, Romania has an over-blown heavy industrial sector consisting of monolithic, technologically obsolete factories, which have little realistic prospect of becoming economically viable. Although such enterprises represent a severe drain on state funds, their closure has been politically and socially

---

[109] Ibid. Oschlies, Wolf, *Wirtschaftsreform und Reformdebatten in Rumänien*, p. 7.

unacceptable as Romania's uneven development means a single monolithic industrial complex is often the major employer for a whole town or area. Under the previous regime such complexes owned and managed housing units, shops, leisure facilities, health centres, allotments and *Kindergartens*. They were not only responsible for physical output, but also fulfilled the social role of employing people and caring for their needs. This created a different managerial mentality and a system in which the social value of an enterprise, and not necessarily economic performance, became the main factor determining resource allocation. This is relevant for transformation, because the perceived social value of an enterprise increased government and management reluctance to initiate restructuring.

Privatisation of such enterprises is difficult, but the state cannot afford to invest in them. Therefore they exist in a state of limbo; their closure delayed until alternative private enterprises capable of employing their work forces develop. This has caused disillusion amongst workers and management and resulted in a massive loss of productivity and value of state assets. Continued use of the command economy's administrative structure, the PDSR's ambiguous relationship to the free market and reluctance to seek direct foreign investment, in addition to confusion over the nature of the Revolution, worsened the situation. These economic and political factors combined to make privatisation in Romania particularly problematic. This in turn has limited the personal benefits privatisation can offer the population and therefore hindered democratic consolidation.

The PDSR-led government opted for centrally controlled privatisation. The Law on the Transformation of State Enterprises stipulated that all state enterprises were to reorganise themselves into autonomous state companies, or shareholding business companies by the end of 1990. This ensured the transformation of 400 non-commercial enterprises in strategic economic sectors, such as defence, energy and transport, and representing approximately 47% of total state assets into autonomous state companies, or *regie autonomes*. A further 6300 enterprises, approximately 53% of state assets, were transformed into joint stock-holding companies. The shares of all these companies were held by the state in the form of the State Ownership Fund (*Fondul Proprietatii de stat*) or Private Ownership Funds (*Fondul Proprietatii Private*). Enterprises were assigned to one of the five Private Ownership Funds according to economic branch and gave it 30% of their registered capital. The State Ownership Fund received the remaining 70%[110]. Not only did the Funds manage state property, but they also coordinated the preparations for privatisation.

One of the Funds for Private Property was given the task of selling those sections of state enterprises which were economically viable. They accounted for approximately 46% of commercial trade, 28.3% of the tourist industry and 8.5% of the industrial sector. As they were mostly small units and represented the most profitable state enterprises, interest was relatively good and their privatisation not too problematic. A total of 68.3% of these enterprises were sold for approximately 10 million Lei, and 1.8% for over 100 million Lei[111]. Although direct foreign investment did not play a role in this process, many who bought enterprises hoped to cooperate with foreign investors.

Case by case privatisation was favoured, but mass privatisation was also envisaged. The government transferred a 30% interest in approximately 6300 state-owned companies to all Romanian citizens permanently residing in Romania. The transfer was carried out by distributing vouchers, which represented shares in the Private Ownership Funds managing state property[112]. A mass privatisation programme involving the purchase of enterprise capital using vouchers was planned for 1992.

The PDSR's lack of a comprehensive programme or concept for the privatisation of large enterprises meant that the progress of privatisation was excessively slow. The four types of ownership in Romania; state, cooperative, mixed and private, created a mixed economy which closely resembled a socialist market. At the end of

---

[110] Ibid. Embassy of Romania, *Privatization in Romania*.
Http: //www.embassy.org/romania. Ibid. Gregori, Ilina, Schaser, Angelika, (Hrsg.), *Rumänien im Umbruch*, p. 43.
[111] Ibid. Oschlies, Wolf, *Wirtschaftsreform und Reformdebatten in Rumänien*, p. 11.
[112] Ibid. Embassy of Romania, *Privatization in Romania*.
Http: //www.embassy.org/romania.

Dealing with the Communist Economic Legacy 361

1992, 200 000 privately owned non-manufacturing enterprises were registered and accounted for approximately half of all retail trade. But over 7000 state-owned enterprises or autonomous state companies operated in mining, manufacturing, construction, the utilities and distribution, and approximately 98% of industrial output still came from state-owned enterprises[113].

This model appealed to the PDSR because it promised to facilitate the retention of its role in the economy, while at the same time allowing for market enterprise. However, government sponsored programmes not only failed to achieve restructuring but, applied within the framework of a socialist market, also caused further economic imbalances. The suspension of the IMF credit and the conditions attached to the new agreement, combined with Romania's continued poor economic performance, forced the introduction of a more radical programme of economic transformation and privatisation.

During 1993, subsidies for bread, milk, butter, sugar and cooking oil were finally phased out and on 1 July, 1993, VAT was introduced[114]. It was also agreed that under a PHARE-funded programme, ownership certificates representing 30% of shares in the registered capital of state enterprises would be distributed amongst the population[115]. A further 10% of state property would be made available to state enterprise employees at a 10% discount rate, while the remaining 60% would thereafter be made available to foreign and Romanian buyers in free competition. After one year it was possible to sell the shares which were purchased with vouchers to Romanian buyers, and after two years to foreign buyers. From May 1994 property certificates could also be exchanged in public auctions[116].

---

[113] Ibid. van Frausum, Yves, G., Gehmann, Ulrich, Gross, Jürgen, 'Market Economy and Economic Reform in Romania: Macroeconomic and Microeconomic Perspectives', pp. 738-739.
[114] Ibid. van Frausum, Yves, G., Gehmann, Ulrich, Gross, Jürgen, 'Market Economy and Economic Reform in Romania: Macroeconomic and Microeconomic Perspectives', p. 737.
[115] Ibid. Embassy of Romania, *Privatization in Romania*.
Http: //www.embassy.org/romania.
[116] Ibid. Sîrbu, Maria Cristina, 'Towards a Market Economy: The Romanian Effort', p. 496.

In January 1994, the government presented a list of 2368 state enterprises which were to be privatised. Of these, 1930 were small enterprises, 403 were medium-sized enterprises and 35 large enterprises[117]. Privatisation was carried out on the basis of coupons, which replaced the vouchers which had been distributed in 1992. The vouchers had also been distributed free of charge amongst the population, but as many people were in economic difficulty, the majority had sold their vouchers without obtaining shares. In this way, a small number of people came into possession of a large number of vouchers at low prices, which they exchanged for the new privatisation coupons.

During 1994, approximately 3000 enterprises held 'open days' during which the public was invited to view assets which were to be sold in public auctions. Thereafter they had 30 days to decide whether they wanted shares or not[118]. Although generally only 30% of enterprise capital was available, if demand was great up to 60% could be privatised in this manner[119]. In addition, in November 1994 public share offers for three light industrial enterprises were initiated and in March and April 1995, all or part of the 30% capital owned by the Private Ownership Fund in a further 100 enterprises was sold by public offer[120]. But the process was slow and as only those involved in enterprise management had an idea of its real value or potential, often resulted in the cheap purchase of enterprises by members of the former *nomenklatura* and management elite.

In an attempt to speed up privatisation, Law No. 55/1995, concerning the 'Acceleration of Privatisation', stipulated that shares representing 30% of the registered capital of a further 4000 state-owned enterprises should be transferred free to eligible Romanian citizens. Vouchers which had not been used before August 1995,

---

[117] Ibid. Sîrbu, Maria Cristina, 'Towards a Market Economy: The Romanian Effort', p. 497.
[118] Ibid. Oschlies, Wolf, *Wirtschaftsreform und Reformdebatten in Rumänien*, p. 12.
[119] Ibid. Kabbe, Gyorgy, 'Die Privatisierung in Osteuropa: Konzeptionen, Modelle, Resultate', p. 54.
[120] Ibid. Embassy of Romania, *Privatization in Romania*. Http: //www.embassy.org/romania.

the date when new coupons were distributed, could be exchanged for the new privatisation coupons. Unused vouchers which had been issued in 1992 had a value of 25 000 Lei, while new coupons were worth 975 000 Lei[121]. Although it was hoped to complete the mass privatisation programme by the end of December 1995, the subscription process was only completed on 30 April, 1996, and the process was finally completed on 31 March, 1996[122].

While the voucher scheme was similar to that in the Czech Republic in that state property and assets were practically given away to the population, the number of shares available in Romanian enterprises depended on the number of people who applied for them[123]. Thus, if the number of those interested was low, the number of shares gained was high, as was their relative value. If an enterprise was not economically unviable, as was often the case, although the number of shares gained could be high, their value was low.

The speed of privatisation was also increased by simplifying the regulations governing the sale of shares to natural or legal persons. A list of 300 economically viable enterprises was prepared and presented for sale either directly or via advertisement to strategic foreign and Romanian investors. Enterprises were permitted to use up to 60% of the revenue gained by the sale of shares in this manner to service or pay off their debts. The combination of these methods enabled approximately 1600, 25% of all state enterprises, to be privatised by the end of 1995[124].

But the various methods of privatisation; share offer, auction and public bids, were on the whole poorly managed and continued to be subject to excessive bureaucratic control. As a result of the government's ambiguous attitude towards the market, it failed to attract the foreign capital necessary for industrial restructuring.

---

[121] Ibid. Embassy of Romania, *Privatization in Romania*.
Http: //www.embassy.org/romania.

[122] Ibid. Kabbe, Gyorgy, 'Die Privatisierung in Osteuropa: Konzeptionen, Modelle, Resultate', p. 54.

[123] Interview with Gabriel Jeflea from *Institute for a Democratic Romania*. Bucharest, 4 March 1996.

[124] Ibid. Kabbe, Gyorgy, 'Die Privatisierung in Osteuropa: Konzeptionen, Modelle, Resultate', p. 55.

Although mass privatisation was specifically aimed at the Romanian population and at speeding up privatisation, share prices were determined by the official book value of an enterprise and therefore remained artificially high. As the value of one coupon was equivalent to 975 000 Lei[125], the number of shares it was possible to obtain was relatively low. In combination with the residual influence of the former ideology and the PDSR's scepticism towards the market, participation in voucher privatisation remained limited. Lack of investors meant that in many cases, shares were given to the workers and pensioners of a particular enterprise[126].

Thus, of the 1100 enterprises which had been privatised by the end of 1994, approximately 1090 were privatised via a Management/Employee Buyout. Of these, 530 were small enterprises. By June 1995, a further 754 enterprises had applied to the State Ownership Fund for approval of a Management/Employee Buyout[127]. It is estimated that a further 2000, approximately 33% of all state enterprises, have since initiated a Management/Employee Buyout[128]. The poor state of Romanian enterprises and the lack of success of share offers meant that often a Management/Employee Buyout was the only feasible option remaining. However, this form of privatisation does little to change the existing economic structure, bringing neither the capital nor the will to implement rationalisation.

Romanian Management/Employee Buyouts differ from the self-privatisation process in Hungary in that they do not involve foreign capital and often rely solely on the capital of the workers and management themselves. Therefore, although worker and management buyouts can increase productivity and induce better management without forcing the immediate closure of unprofitable

---

[125] Interview with Gabriel Jeflea, from *Institute for a Democratic Romania*. Bucharest, 4 March 1996.
[126] Ibid. Oschlies, Wolf, *Wirtschaftsreform und Reformdebatten in Rumänien*, p. 12.
[127] Ibid. Embassy of Romania, *Privatization in Romania*. Http: //www.embassy.org/romania.
[128] Ibid. Oschlies, Wolf, *Wirtschaftsreform und Reformdebatten in Rumänien*, p. 13.

enterprises, in Romania they did not create the capital required for modernisation. Moreover, as the preservation of an enterprise's social function not only ensured the management respect and influence in the locality, but also retention of the work force, management and worker interests often converged to hinder restructuring. The lack of institutional reform and the government's reluctance to enforce hard budget constraints, enabled management to use the system of informal bargaining which had developed under the old regime, to pressure the government into continuing subsidies.

The PDSR-led government created the basic legal framework for economic transformation. However, its doubts concerning the free market and consequent desire to retain an element of state control in the economy meant that not only was the implementation of the transformation programme inconsistent, but the programme itself incoherent. Economic deterioration limited democratic consolidation and necessitated the implementation of a radical stabilisation and austerity programme by the government coalition led by the National Peasant Party/Christian Democracy.

4.4: Restitution and Compensation

The former Communist regimes illegally seized property and assets from the population during nationalisation and unjustly imprisoned, or sentenced to forced labour, numerous innocent persons. Thus, to ensure corrective justice and thereby increase the legitimacy of democracy as a just system, Hungary, the Czech Republic and Romania all implemented restitution and compensation policies. The relatively short length of Communist rule facilitates restitution because many of those who lost property may still be alive. Nevertheless, the process of restitution can cause new injustice if the rights of those presently in occupation or possession of affected property are ignored. Restitution is further complicated by the fact that in many cases, confiscated land and property has been developed or put to uses other than those pertaining at the time of confiscation.

The practical difficulties of implementation and prolonged uncertainty over property rights can have a negative effect on transformation and economic performance. But because restitution aimed to rectify past injustice, it gained priority. The Hungarian government favoured restitution in kind in the case of land, but for all other forms of property, compensation was given in the form of investment vouchers, which could be used to buy shares in state enterprises. While all three governments recognised the importance of some form of restitution and compensation, their different policies reflected the different political aims associated with restitution and compensation.

4.4.1: Hungarian Compensation Vouchers

During transformation, it is vital that property ownership is clear. Unfortunately, the law concerning restitution of property to individual private owners, Churches and local municipalities became excessively politicised during its passage through the Hungarian Parliament. The reason lies in the fact that the MDF's two coalition parties were more orientated towards restitution rather than compensation. The Smallholders Party aimed to restore property to its 1947 owners, while the Christian Democratic Party was concerned to restore confiscated Church property. As a result of the Constitutional Court's ruling that the initial Restitution Law, promoted by the Smallholders Party, was unconstitutional because it gave precedence to land over other nationalised assets, the Hungarian Parliament was plunged into a lengthy debate which had a significant negative impact on the privatisation process. The prolonged debate over restitution slowed down privatisation by delaying legislation. People also decided to wait until the Restitution Law was finalised before investing. It was finally decided that, with the exception of Church property, compensation vouchers would be issued in lieu of restoration of property in its original form.

Those eligible for compensation in return for confiscated property were present day Hungarian citizens and those who were Hungarian citizens at the time they suffered the injustice concerned. These included Transylvanian Romanians who became prisoners of war as soldiers of the Hungarian army and Jews deported to

Germany from annexed territory which is now part of Slovakia. The only limitation was that in the case of property damages, reparation was due only if the nationalisation, confiscation or other injury had occurred on the territory of present day Hungary. However, the real value of compensation was limited because no one person received vouchers with a nominal value in excess of 5 million Forints and the method for calculating compensation was such that, while the compensation offered to minor property owners, especially farmers, was acceptable, urban property and large estates were in effect devalued[129].

The first two Compensation Acts of 1991 dealt with compensation for damages incurred during the confiscation of Jewish property, deportation of ethnic Germans, the confiscation of large enterprises and estates between 1938 and 1944, and forced collectivisation during the nationalisation of property after 1949. A third dealt with compensation for the loss of personal freedom as a prisoner of war or due to forced labour. The compensation vouchers which were issued to successful claimants could be used to acquire shares during privatisation. From 1992 until November 1994, a total of 115 billion Forints worth of compensation vouchers were issued, accounting for approximately 90% of the total 1.3 million claims which were submitted. Although the number of applicants was rather less than expected, the one year limit was insufficient to collect and process them. Consequently, in March 1994 the deadline for claims was extended and approximately 600 000 late claims, representing 20-39 billion Forints worth of compensation, were accepted[130].

The majority of compensation vouchers were used to buy land from cooperatives forced to offer it for sale. The land was auctioned, but only those living in the villages to which the land belonged and those entitled to compensation for land confiscated in the same area were entitled to bid. This enabled those with similar interests to form cartels and gain possession of land at a fraction of its real value. Indeed, at 80% of the 21 000 auctions held land was acquired for the lowest acceptable price, that is for compensation

---

[129] Fahidi, Gergely, 'Paying for the Past', *The Hungarian Quarterly*, Vol. 35, No. 136, Winter 1994, pp. 55-56.
[130] Ibid. Fahidi, Gergley, 'Paying for the Past', *The Hungarian Quarterly*, p. 55.

vouchers with a nominal value of 500 Forints per Gold Crown, a unit which establishes soil quality. As 1000 Forints worth of compensation vouchers were given per Gold Crown, many people acquired twice as much land as they had lost. In addition, only the theoretical fertility of land was used to calculate land value. Thus, the crop the land actually carried, and therefore its real value, was not taken into account and land was often undervalued[131]. The auctions sold 37 million Gold Crowns worth of land, accounting for almost a third of Hungary's arable land. While restitution re-created small-holdings, these cannot be cultivated economically and in the future will probably be leased for cultivation to larger farms or cooperatives.

The interest on compensation vouchers was set at 75% of the Central Bank's base rate until December 1994. Therefore, the nominal value of the voucher automatically increased. Thus, by November 1994, a 1000 Forint voucher was officially worth 1690 Forints. As local authorities were obliged to accept the vouchers at their nominal value plus the amount of interest due, many tenants of state-owned homes took advantage of the increase in value of their voucher to buy their homes. In this way, vouchers with a value over 5 billion Forints came into the possession of local authorities in return for dwellings and other buildings[132]. Thus, although the case by case method employed in the privatisation of state enterprises did not facilitate popular participation, the compensation process presented the population with the opportunity to obtain property. Home and land ownership gave the majority of the population a personal stake in the new system which compensated for lack of participation in enterprise privatisation.

The compensation policy was increasingly viewed by the MDF as a means by which it could create a new property owning middle class which would form its voter base. Shares of some leading companies, such as the *Pick Salami Producing Company*, *Prímagáz*, *Globus Canning* and the *Sopron Brewery*, were offered at extremely advantageous terms in exchange for compensation vouchers. However, the MSZP-led government has not held any

---

[131] Ibid. Fahidi, Gergely, 'Paying for the Past', p. 56.
[132] Ibid. Fahidi, Gergely, 'Paying for the Past', p. 57.

such public stock sales and the shares of a pharmaceutical plant, which had been intended for holders of compensation vouchers, were sold to foreign and Hungarian buyers[133]. This means the opportunities to use compensation vouchers are dwindling and it seems likely that the vouchers still in circulation will become invalid in the near future.

The MSZP-led government reached an accord with the Holy See concerning the restitution of Roman Catholic Church property on 16 May, 1997. The accord foresees the restitution of Church assets valued at approximately $550 million and of real estate valued at $320 million by the year 2011. In return, the Catholic Church has agreed to the settlement of all remaining claims by annual payments and has renounced any further claims[134]. Despite protests by the SZDSZ over the Catholic Church's preferential treatment, the agreement, which was signed by the Vatican and the Hungarian government on 23 June, 1997, also gave Roman Catholic schools the same legal status as state schools[135].

4.4.2: Czech and Romanian Restitution

The Czech Republic and Romania opted for direct restitution of property, combined with compensation for those cases where restitution was impracticable. In the Czech Republic, this policy facilitated the re-establishment of pre-Communist property rights because it foresaw the return of property which had been confiscated under the Communist regime to its original owners. In this way, Czech restitution aimed to prevent the pattern of social privileges acquired under the Communist regime from being carried over into the new system. Restitution was therefore specifically employed as a means of ensuring anti-Communist social justice[136]. The Czech government employed the concept of corrective social justice as a means of distancing itself from the former Communist regime. In this way, the creation of long-term legitimacy and the

---

[133] Ibid. Fahidi, Gergely, 'Paying for the Past', pp. 59-60.
[134] *RFE/RL Newsline*, Vol. 1, No. 32, Part II, 16 May 1997.
[135] *RFE/RL Newsline*, Vol. 1, No. 58, Part II, 23 June 1997.
[136] Ibid. Appel, Hilary, 'Justice and the Reformulation of Property Rights in the Czech Republic', *East European Politics and Societies*, pp. 22-40.

moral integrity of the democratic system took priority over immediate economic imperatives.

The federal government of Czechoslovakia decided that those possessions which had been illegally used by the Communist Party, including state properties the Party had appropriated for its own use, should be returned first. The law concerning the restitution of Communist Party property to the people of the Czech and Slovak Republics was passed at the end of 1990; while the law dealing with the restitution of the Communist youth organisation's property was passed in the first half of 1991. On 1 January, 1990, the property possessed by the Communist Party had an estimated value of 12.6 billion Crowns, approximately $420 million. During the first half of 1990, the state regained possession of property valued at approximately 4.5 billion Crowns, and of 5.4 billion Crowns' worth in the second half. The remaining Party property, mostly that used by the Communist youth organisation, was returned to the state during the first half of 1991[137].

The Catholic Church also laid claim to property which the regime had seized after 1948. After forced evictions of monks in April 1950 and nuns in August and October 1950, the regime had seized the Monasteries, Convents and buildings where they had lived and worked. Before dissolution, monks' Holy Orders had owned 429 houses and Monasteries, and nuns' Orders had owned 670 houses and Convents[138]. In addition, the Church lost 108 holdings with an average area of 2468 hectares, although with an area of 34 000 hectares, the Archbishopric of Olomouc's estate was the largest[139].

The 1990 law relating to the property of Holy Orders, Congregations and the Olomuuc Diocese was the first piece of legislation which regulated the restitution of property to its original owners. The law also confirmed the Church's right of ownership of a further 74 landed properties and made provision for a law to deal

---

[137] Ibid. Kupka, Martin, 'Transformation of Ownership in Czechoslovakia', p. 300.
[138] Ibid. Kupka, Martin, 'Transformation of Ownership in Czechoslovakia', p. 300. From Vasko, V., *The Unsilenced,* Zvon 1990, pp. 1-3.
[139] Ibid. Kupka, Martin, 'Transformation of Ownership in Czechoslovakia', p. 300. From Vasko, V., *The Unsilenced,* Zvon 1990, pp. 17-19.

with Church claims relating to 174 other properties[140]. The problem is that as there are very few alternative landed properties which can be offered as a substitute, the museums, schools or hospitals which now occupy many former ecclesiastical buildings must first be moved before the Church regains its property. Thus, the Czech Parliament approved the restitution of 323 Church buildings on 9 April, 1997, but ruled out the restitution of another 228 and described the restitution of a further 112 as problematic[141].

Another problem with restitution, rather than compensation, was that the new owners, although descendants of the original owners, were not automatically the most competent. Restitution also prevented the state from raising revenue via property auctions and delayed privatisation because, before all claims had been received and processed, state-owned enterprises or property which stood under the suspicion of being illegally acquired could not be privatised. Nevertheless, the Czech government considered restitution more important then its short-term negative economic impact because it ensured the Communist economic elite did not maintain its privileges in the new system. It also represented a moral and symbolic means of compensation. In this way, restitution was specifically employed to further legitimation of the democratic system and democratic consolidation.

The Restitution Law, which came into force in November 1990, regulated the process of small re-privatisation, which covered all fixed and moveable property taken from natural and legal persons either by physical force or by forced sale or contract according to the legal norms after 1955. However, by this time most large enterprises were already held by the state, so this law dealt with the restitution of an estimated 80 000 buildings; flats, small shops, cafes, pubs, restaurants, workshops and other small properties or enterprises which were mainly in the service sector. The law required the return of property to its original owners or other qualified persons. Claims had to be submitted within six months of the law coming into force[142].

---

[140] Ibid. Kupka, Martin, 'Transformation of Ownership in Czechoslovakia', p. 300.
[141] *RFE/RL Newsline*, Vol. 1, No. 8, Part II, 10 April 1997.
[142] Ibid. Kupka, Martin, 'Transformation of Ownership in Czechoslovakia', p. 302.

Qualified persons were defined as the original owners, their parents and siblings if still alive, the original owner's heirs by will, their husbands or wives, children, grandchildren, and great-grandchildren. If none of these persons was still alive, the property was given to the heirs of the owners, or the heir's children. If the property had been destroyed or transferred to other natural persons who had become its owners, monetary compensation, the buying price, or a supplementary, equivalent to the difference between monetary compensation and the buying price, was offered. Until November 1991, the Ministry of Finance assessed the value of property by estimating its value at the time of seizure and adding 3% a year to this sum. The compensation sum calculated using this method was therefore often noticeably lower than the estimated market value[143].

In addition, many villas now occupied by Embassies and Consulates in Prague were affected by the legislation and the law had to be hastily amended so that in such cases only monetary compensation could be claimed. The problem was finally settled in a further amendment which enabled qualified persons to claim restitution of property held by diplomatic or consular missions after 12 April, 1991, although successful claimants were obliged to let the property to the respective mission for at least a further ten years. A similar ten year clause applied to property which was in use for public health, social welfare services, education, culture or the rehabilitation and employment of the mentally or physically handicapped[144]. The amendment also widened the scope of restitution by including property which was acquired by natural persons, or those close to them, from the state using means that were contrary to the law at that time or via preferential treatment.

The Restitution Law which came into effect on 1 April, 1991, regulated the restitution of large enterprises, so-called large re-privatisation. It dealt with the period between 25 February, 1948 and 31 December, 1989. Claims could be made on property whose seizure had infringed the UN Charter, the General Directorate on Human Rights, or any other existing agreements concerning civic,

---

[143] Ibid. Kupka, Martin, 'Transformation of Ownership in Czechoslovakia', p. 302.
[144] Ibid. Kupka, Martin, 'Transformation of Ownership in Czechoslovakia', p. 302.

Dealing with the Communist Economic Legacy 373

political, economic, social or cultural rights. However, the monetary compensation which was offered in lieu of restitution was limited to 60 000 Crowns, approximately $2000, of which up to 30 000 Crowns were usually paid in cash while the rest was paid in non-state securities. Qualified persons had a six month period in which to hand in claims. Although qualified persons were defined in the same way as for small re-privatisation, they also had to be Czechoslovak citizens and in permanent residence[145]. This clause meant that property could not be restored to political refugees who had left Czechoslovakia unless they returned. As many exiles did not wish to become permanent residents, this clause negated their restitution rights.

The law dealt with the period following the legal transfer of power to the Communist Party and therefore prevented the ethnic Germans and Hungarians who had been forced to leave Czechoslovakia before 1948 from applying for restitution. Similarly, it did not offer restitution for property seized by the regime from Czechs and Slovaks during the period between 1945-1948. As only 13.7% of the means of production remained in private ownership by 1948, a large proportion of expropriated property remained exempt from restitution. While this limited the negative economic consequences of large re-privatisation, it enabled those who had dishonestly seized Jewish property before the cut off date, but which was subsequently taken illegally by the Communist regime after 1948, could apply for restitution. Thus, the potential of restitution to ensure corrective justice was placed in doubt[146].

The restitution of forest and agricultural land, buildings and dwellings, as well as the live and dead stock, together with reserves taken from original owners and contributed to cooperatives, was dealt with in the Land Act of 21 May, 1991. It came into effect on 24 June, 1991 and regulated not only the restitution of land, but also the transformation of the 245 state farms and 1660 agricultural cooperatives into market units[147]. It therefore involved all the 4

---

[145] Ibid. Kupka, Martin, 'Transformation of Ownership in Czechoslovakia', pp. 303- 304.
[146] Ibid. Kupka, Martin, 'Transformation of Ownership in Czechoslovakia', p. 304.
[147] Ibid. Kupka, Martin, 'Transformation of Ownership in Czechoslovakia', p. 305.

million people, approximately 25% of the population, engaged in agricultural production[148]. Claims were accepted until the end of 1992, but land was not returned if it contained graves, or if buildings had been erected which were unsuitable for agricultural or forestry use. If groups of allotments, gardens, weekend houses or sports facilities were present, land was similarly not returned. Despite this, the law preferred restitution of original property, tracts of land and live or material stock to compensation. Monetary compensation was only offered if equivalent property could not be found[149].

The Land Act placed the cut off date for applications on 25 February, 1948. Although this excluded those Germans and Hungarians who were forcibly expelled after the end of the Second World War from applying for restitution, the Act did concede the restitution of large estates in their entirety, where they were expropriated with no form of compensation. Other applications concerning large estates were subject to an upper limit of 150 hectares of agricultural land, or 250 hectares of the total area of a farm[150]. By 1 February, 1992, 50 000 land restitution claims had been filed[151].

The Land Act affected more than half the total area of agricultural land, forests, farmyards and dwellings in the Czech Republic[152]. However, it proved almost impossible to assess justly the value of cooperative members' contributions in terms of land, stock or buildings, especially as by December 1989, of the 650 000 people working in agricultural cooperatives, only half had contributed land to them. On the other hand, of the total number of former owners, only 10% remained in agricultural production[153]. Thus, in many cases the new owners were not interested in

---

[148] Richter, Sandor, (Ed.), *The Transition from Command to Market Economies in East-Central Europe*, Westview Press 1992, p. 119.

[149] Ibid. Kupka, Martin, 'Transformation of Ownership in Czechoslovakia', p. 305.

[150] Ibid. Richter, Sandor, (Ed.), The *Transition from Command to Market Economies in East-Central Europe*, p. 120.

[151] Burger, Josef, 'The Politics of Restitution in Czechoslovakia', *East European Quarterly*, Vol. 26, No. 4, Winter 1992, p. 486.

[152] Ibid. Richter, Sandor, (Ed.), *The Transition from Command to Market Economies in East-Central Europe*, p. 120.

[153] Ibid. Kupka, Martin, 'Transformation of Ownership in Czechoslovakia', p. 305.

engaging in agricultural production themselves and let their land to small farmers or cooperatives.

As the concept of corrective justice was vital for Czech restitution, compensation was also available to those who suffered other forms of injustice under the Communist regime, such as imprisonment or forced labour. On 25 June, 1997, the Health Minister confirmed the government will pay a total of 400 million Crowns, $12.6 million to such persons. Each political prisoner will receive 625 Crowns, $21.50, for each month spent in a Communist prison between February 1948 and November 1989[154].

Although the Romanian government also followed a policy of restitution, it concentrated on the restitution of land, rather than other forms of property. Initially only cooperative farms were disbanded and their land divided amongst previous owners and current members. But in many cases, peasants engaged in uncontrolled privatisation and simply took possession of land. In the summer of 1990, the Mayor of the village of Sapînta, in Mamamures, dissolved the state farm before official legislation had been passed regulating the process. The ensuing argument over the division of land and assets between the peasants culminated in supporters of the Mayor barricading the village and taking school children and an off-duty army major hostage[155]. In a similar case, peasants in the Banat mountains ran all the agricultural engineers off the state farm, demolished its buildings and removed materials. They also cut down all the fruit trees and took the animals. The damages were estimated at 200 million Lei, DM 9 million[156]. It seems that many state farms were dissolved in a similar manner. Despite such problems, over four and a quarter million people, approximately 90% of those entitled, received land, and most agricultural land in Romania was returned to private ownership[157].

---

[154] *RFE/RL Newsline*, Vol. 1, No. 61, Part II, 28 June 1997.
[155] The siege was eventually bought to an end after the arrival of a police helicopter. The Mayor was arrested and charged. Beckherrn, Eberhard, *Tal der Wende*, Knaur 1991, p. 257.
[156] Ibid. Beckherrn, Eberhard, *Tal der Wende*, pp. 257-258.
[157] Ibid. Sîrbu, Maria Cristina, 'Towards a Market Economy: The Romanian Effort', p. 498.

Land restitution provided a certain amount of social justice for those whose land was confiscated by the Communist regime and increased the personal stake of the rural population in transformation, but had little economic rationale. The limit of 10 hectares which the authorities set on the size of plot which could be owned by any one person created a mass of fragmented, excessively small holdings. Not only are these economically inefficient, but also impossible to cultivate using large-scale production methods. On the other hand, the peasants lack the capital needed to buy modern machinery. Thus, while restitution successfully privatised agricultural land, it created new structural problems which compound the effects of previous neglect and lack of investment.

In order to clarify the property rights of those peasants who worked on state farms, the government led by the Romanian Peasant Party/Christian Democracy amended the Land Law to allow the restoration and privatisation of nationalised land which was incorporated into State Agricultural Enterprises. The amendment also allows Romanian citizens who are living abroad to take part in restitution. Only the original owners or first generation inheritors are entitled to land, but the amount of land available to individual families was increased to 200 hectares[158]. This aimed to increase the efficiency and productivity of Romanian agriculture.

While the majority of the rural Romanian population lived in their own homes, this was not the case in urban areas, where the majority of dwellings were sate-owned or had been seized from their owners by the Communist regime. The PDSR-led government allowed the restitution of dwellings, but the condition that original owners be resident in the building claimed and the Constitutional Clause prohibiting foreign ownership of land and property, limited the number of successful claimants because many original owners had emigrated or no longer lived in the property in question. State property is in poor condition, but the state cannot afford to renovate it. Although the state offered many dwellings for sale, the low level of private savings prevented many people from buying their homes. At the time, the inflation and interest rates were very high, so those

---

[158] *RFE/RL Newsline*, Vol. 1, No. 30, Part II, 14 May 1997.

Dealing with the Communist Economic Legacy 377

who did buy their homes now pay enormous rates of interest on their mortgages and so lack the capital required for renovation. Thus, the standard of accommodation in Romania remains poor. Although restitution aimed to include the population in privatisation, the personal stake in transformation has remained low and therefore popular support has been limited and democratic consolidation hindered.

In contrast to the Hungarian and Czech agreements dealing with the restitution of Church property, the PDSR failed to reach an agreement dealing with the restitution of property to the Romanian Orthodox Church and the Jewish population. The PNTCD-led government has agreed in principle to return Jewish, German and Church property and an announcement on 11 April, 1997, confirmed the restitution of six buildings, but did not extend to other confiscated properties[159].

Many Jewish property owners perished during the Second World War and their heirs emigrated during the Communist regime and are no longer Romanian citizens, one of the prerequisites for restitution. In the light of this, and the specific problems concerning restitution of Jewish property in the Czech Republic, the Deputy Chairman of the World Jewish Restitution Organisation to Romania, has claimed that Romania and the Czech Republic have deliberately delayed restitution of Jewish property[160].

4.5: Problems of Transformation

Although the Czech Republic, Hungary and Romania started transformation at various stages of institutional and economic modernisation and chose different transformation strategies, their development has converged. All have had difficulty implementing the specific transformation programme chosen and experienced similar effects. The continuing prevalence of bad debts and substandard loans forced comprehensive banking reform in Hungary, the Czech Republic and Romania. The agricultural sectors all

---

[159] *RFE/RL Newsline*, Vol. 1, No. 10, Part II, 14 April 1997.
[160] *RFE/RL Newsline*, Vol. 1, No. 50, Part II, 11 June, 1997.

experienced crises and remain one of the most problematic areas of the respective economies. In addition, the heavy industrial sector, particularly in Hungary, has embarked restructuring. This is necessary if a modern economy capable of sustaining growth is to develop. However, restructuring has led to high levels of unemployment, of which an increasing proportion is long-term unemployed. Thus, while only a modern economy can ensure the material well-being essential for long-term democratic consolidation, the high social costs of transformation may hinder democratic consolidation in the short-term.

4.5.1: Unemployment

Transformation of the economy entails an initial decrease in employment as rationalisation occurs. Although the Czech Republic and Romania experienced a smaller rise in unemployment than Hungary during the early stages, unemployment in all countries has increased dramatically (see Table 13 overleaf).

Table 13
Unemployment Rates in the Czech Republic, Hungary and Romania

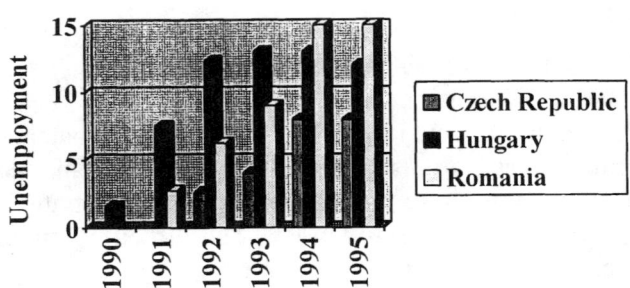

- no data available
1993 Estimated
1994/1995 Prognosis

Source: Adapted from *OECD Wirtschaftsausblick*, December 1993, p. 133.

Although the Czech government emphasised the radical nature of its transformation programme, its policy of avoiding enterprise bankruptcy by continuing state subsidies and retaining workers at lower levels of pay or reduced working hours was actually similar to that in Romania during the PDSR's term of office. Although this policy kept the unemployment rate relatively low and shielded the population from the social costs of transformation, it delayed industrial restructuring in both countries.

The relatively low level of unemployment in the Czech Republic was a result of the Czech government's specific labour policy. The employment of those above retirement age was stopped and a programme of early retirement started. In addition, many women who were made redundant left the job market. Wage restriction and the decrease in real wages also lowered the cost of keeping workers in employment. The benefit system was also radically reformed.

In 1989, those dismissed for reasons of reorganisation received 95% of the last net income for six months, and 60% for the following six months; while those dismissed for other reasons received 60% of their last income. Reforms in 1991 restricted eligibility and reduced benefits. The new system only offered benefits to those who had already worked, studied or completed military service, or those who had been sick or on maternity leave for six months during the previous two years. The benefit offered was 60% of the previous net income for the first six months and 50% for the next six months. In 1993 eligibility was further restricted to those who had worked, completed military service or taken part in school or vocational training during the previous three years. The period of benefit was restricted to six months and its amount reduced to 60% of the last net income for the first three months, and 50% during the last three months. Those who agreed to participate in a retraining scheme received 70% of the last net income for the whole period[161]. Those who are no longer entitled to unemployment benefit can apply for social benefits. The strict enforcement of the new system dramatically reduced the number of

---

[161] Koltay, J., 'Unemployment and Employment Policy in Central and Eastern Europe: Similarities and Differences', *Acta Oeconomica*, Vol. 46, No. 3-4, pp. 304-305.

the registered unemployed receiving benefit and by 1993, only 45% of those registered received unemployment benefit[162].

In this way, the government aimed to encourage the unemployed to participate in retraining schemes to facilitate re-employment and limit the long-term costs to the state. The reduction of benefits, and measures taken against those who did not cooperate with the employment office, were aimed at ensuring benefits did not reduce the incentive to work and at encouraging the unemployed to undertake a retraining programme or work scheme, thus raising their chances of finding new employment.

The Czech Republic's employment policy has therefore been much more active than those in either Romania or Hungary. By 1992, the share of Czech spending on active measures had risen to 65% of the benefit scheme's resources[163]. The authorities created jobs by subsidising the employment of trainees, school leavers and the long-term unemployed and ensured that retraining schemes were not only provided for those in employment, as was the case in Hungary, but also for the unemployed. In an attempt to create long-term jobs, employment schemes offered employers a two year subsidy for offering work placements. If employment was terminated within this period the subsidy had to be repaid, or another placement offered[164]. The recognition of the need to increase worker mobility to overcome the problem of regional unemployment, especially in areas such as Northern Bohemia and Moravia, which suffered unilateral economic development under the Communist regime, led to the introduction of grants for removal costs, rent subsidies and the creation of a national job register[165].

But the reduction of state sector employment in the Czech Republic was less dramatic than in Hungary. This was due to low wage levels and the Czech policy of restructuring enterprises rather than immediately closing them. In addition, the private sector in the

---

[162] Ibid. Koltay, J., 'Unemployment and Employment Policy in Central and Eastern Europe: Similarities and Differences', *Acta Oeconomica*, p. 307.

[163] Ibid. Koltay, J., 'Unemployment and Employment Policy in Central and Eastern Europe: Similarities and Differences', p. 307.

[164] OECD, *Review of the Labour Market in the Czech Republic*, OECD 1995, p. 93.

[165] Ibid. OECD, *Review of the Labour Market in the Czech Republic*, p. 131.

Czech Republic developed very quickly and was able to re-employ most of those made redundant. Thus, many of those employed in the private sector came from the state sector without experiencing a period of unemployment between jobs. In this way, while pursuing an officially radical transofrmation programme, the government's policies were specifically aimed to limit the social costs of transformation and thereby maintain support for economic change and further democratic consolidation. However, despite the government's labour policy, by 1992 those with only elementary education represented 37.8% of the unemployed, although they constituted 20.6% of the total labour force. This figure demonstrates the necessity for training and retraining schemes; although the situation in Romania, where people with vocational training represent 88% of the unemployed, is even more dramatic[166].

During 1989-1992, employment in Romania also decreased less than production, but by the end of 1993 the unemployment rate had reached 10.2%. Despite the fact that low wage levels, which facilitated continued over-manning, together with the widespread policy of short work and involuntary leave, delayed enterprise restructuring and rationalisation, the employment structure in Romania changed. As demand for industrial labour has decreased, the population in Romania has been forced back into agriculture, especially as cooperative and state farms have been dissolved and their land distributed to former owners and workers[167]. Thus, the proportion of the population employed in the agricultural sector has increased and agriculture now employs over a third of the Romanian work force[168]. However, the agricultural sector can only absorb a certain number of industrial workers. Seasonal agricultural unemployment has increased and as previous policies delayed

---

[166] Ibid. Koltay, J., 'Unemployment and Employment Policy in Central and Eastern Europe: Similarities and Differences', p. 300.

[167] Timár, János, 'Particular Features of Employment and Unemployment in the Present Stage of Transformation of the Post-Socialist Countries', *Europe-Asia Studies*, Vol. 47, No. 4, 1995, p. 637.

[168] Hunya, Gábor, 'The Romanian Economy in 1993/1994: From Stagnation with Inflation to Stagnation with Stabilization', *Südosteuropa*, Vol. 43, No. 11-12, 1994, p. 633.

industrial restructuring and rationalisation, further increases in unemployment must be expected.

In addition, the Romanian economy has failed to create job opportunities for the young. At the end of 1992, more than half of those registered as unemployed, excluding those not registered due to in-eligibility, were under 30 years of age. Due to the uneven nature of Romania's Stalinist economic development, there are also extreme regional differences in unemployment. The highest rates of unemployment in Romania are concentrated in Moldova. During 1993 one county registered an unemployment rate of over 28%, while in another two counties it was approximately 20%[169]. The maximum length of unemployment benefit was nine months and the benefit set at 40% of the minimum wage. However, once eligibility for unemployment benefit expired, this was reduced to 40% of the minimum pension. Thus, the situation of the unemployed in Romania, especially the long-term unemployed, was dramatic[170]. The PNTCD-led government obtained international credits for increased social protection, but the situation of the unemployed remains precarious.

The situation is made worse by the fact that Romania spends the least of the three countries on active measures aimed at creating employment; the majority of resources being allocated to fund early retirement schemes. Early retirement enables employment levels to be reduced without increasing unemployment, but does not solve the structural problems associated with high regional and youth unemployment. Nor does it encourage participation in retraining schemes, which is vital if the structure the workforce is to be successfully transformed.

Despite an officially gradual transformation programme, Hungary experienced the most dramatic rise in unemployment. Hungary also suffers from regional concentration of unemployment. The unemployment rate in Budapest and western Hungary is close to the national average, but in the less developed eastern regions and those where heavy industrial production, such

---

[169] Ibid. Koltay, J., 'Unemployment and Employment Policy in Central and Eastern Europe: Similarities and Differences', pp. 301-302.
[170] Ibid. Koltay, J., 'Unemployment and Employment Policy in Central and Eastern Europe: Similarities and Differences', p. 305.

as metallurgy, mining and engineering, are concentrated, unemployment is extremely high. In 1992, in the Szaboles-Szatmá-Bereg County unemployment stood at 17.9%, in Borsod-Abaúj-Zemplén County the rate was 16.3%, and in Nógrád County it was 15.9%. However, in some areas within these counties unemployment rates reached 24-26% in 1992[171]. The high concentration of unemployment in eastern Hungary is related to its lack of infrastructure and proximity to the depressed regions of the Ukraine, Slovakia and Romania. These factors combine to limit interest in investment, which hinders economic development. The high concentration of unemployment in eastern Hungary, and the lack of perspective of improvement in the near future, presents an increasing problem for Hungarian democratic consolidation.

Officially, the Hungarian transformation programme was gradual in nature, but in 1991 alone, the number of unemployed rose from 80 000 to 406 000, an increase from 1.9% to 7.5%[172]. Between 1990 and 1994, a total of 1.3 million jobs were lost[173]. In combination with the radical liberalisation of the import and domestic markets, the collapse of the CMEA, price liberalisation and the reduction of subsidies, this represented a severe shock which hindered the implementation of the MDF's original gradual programme and forced the population to bear more of the social costs of transformation[174].

Because job creation was consistently lower than the rate of job loss, not only did the number of unemployed rise, but increasing numbers of people left the labour market altogether. It was in the short-term interests of many women to leave the job market, though many may wish to re-enter at a later date. Labour surplus was initially reduced by stopping the employment of those above retirement age and the introduction of early retirement. The

---

[171] Molnár, Patricia, 'Unemployment: The Hard Facts', *The New Hungarian Quarterly*, Vol. 33, No. 127, Autumn 1992, p. 67.

[172] Bakos, Gabor, 'Hungarian Transition after Three Years', *Europe-Asia Studies*, Vol. 46, No. 1, 1994, p. 1192.

[173] Ibid. Timár, János, 'Particular Features of Employment and Unemployment in the Present Stage of Transformation of the Post-socialist Countries', *Europe-Asia Studies*, p. 639.

[174] Ibid. Bakos, Gabor, 'Hungarian Transition after Three Years', *Europe-Asia Studies*, p. 1193.

Hungarian Employment Act of 1991 increased the number of pensioners below retirement age. At the same time, the number of students was increased by expanding higher education possibilities.

These measures reduced labour surplus without incurring unemployment, but did not create new employment opportunities. They also forced an increase in the number of dependants in many households, particularly amongst young school leavers. In addition, while early retirement reduced the labour supply in the short-term, it increased the number of pensioners and consequently the burden on the state budget.

The rise in unemployment also increased the number of those dependent on social welfare and those living below the official poverty level. In December 1994, the official subsistence level for an average family was 56 000 Forints. It was recognised that approximately one third of the Hungarian population were living on incomes below this level[175]. However, by 1992 the number of private entrepreneurs in Hungary was 700 000. This implied that as many as 3.2 million families had direct contact to the private and more dynamic sector of the economy, or were taking advantage of the tax advantages gained from being registered as an entrepreneur[176]. Moreover, as many people are also involved in the second economy and do not fully declare their earnings, the real social costs of transformation are difficult to assess.

On the other hand, although the private sector in Hungary has grown rapidly, its structure is somewhat uneven. There are some successful Hungarian entrepreneurs whose wealth totals approximately 1 billion Forints, but such enterprises are limited in number compared with the multitude of small and medium-sized enterprises which have been established. The number of small enterprises employing less than 50 people rose from 47% in 1989 to 64% at the end of 1991, of these, those employing less than 20 people accounted for 47% of the total, compared with 26% in 1989[177]. Small enterprises struggle for survival in an environment

---

[175] Bossányi, Katalin, 'Taking Stock of the Economic Transition', *The Hungarian Quarterly*, Vol. 36, No. 138, Summer 1995.
[176] Ibid. Csaba, László, 'Macroeconimc Policy in Hungary: Poetry versus Reality', p. 949.
[177] Ibid. Kiss, Yudit, 'Privatisation in Hungary – Two Years Later', pp. 1027-1028.

of high taxation, low capital reserves, limited access to credit facilities and lack of experience. This sector of the economy is growing, but it is doubtful whether it can replace the state sector in the Hungarian economy in the near future, especially as the majority of small enterprises are not necessarily interested in expansion as they engage in tax evasion on a daily basis.

4.5.2: Industrial Restructuring

Although the level of unemployment is a cause for concern, it is an inevitable short-term consequence of the industrial restructuring which transformation requires. It is, therefore, interesting to note that while Hungary experienced the largest increase in unemployment, the decrease in Hungarian production was not as dramatic as that experienced in both Romania and the Czech Republic. The series of economic reforms carried out by the Kádár regime and the specific Hungarian programme of spontaneous, or self-privatisation, enabled Hungarian industry to adapt more easily to the market and forced a more thorough restructuring process.

Indeed, those sectors of the Hungarian economy which suffered the most significant drop in production, as much as half in some areas, are precisely those which were uncompetitive, over-sized and incompatible with future economic development. For example, since 1980 coal mining has suffered a 55.2% drop in production, production in ferrous metallurgy has declined by 53%, textiles by 56.5% and production of transport equipment has fallen by 43.7%. On the other hand, increased investment, especially in imported machinery, is an indication that remaining enterprises are modernising and restructuring their operations[178].

The greater drop in productivity, as reflected in GDP, combined with the relatively slower increase in unemployment experienced by the Czech Republic and Romania is therefore evidence of delayed industrial restructuring (see Table 14 overleaf).

---

[178] Ibid. Csaba, László, 'Macroeconimc Policy in Hungary: Poetry versus Reality', p. 959.

Table 14
Percentage Annual Change in GDP 1990-1993

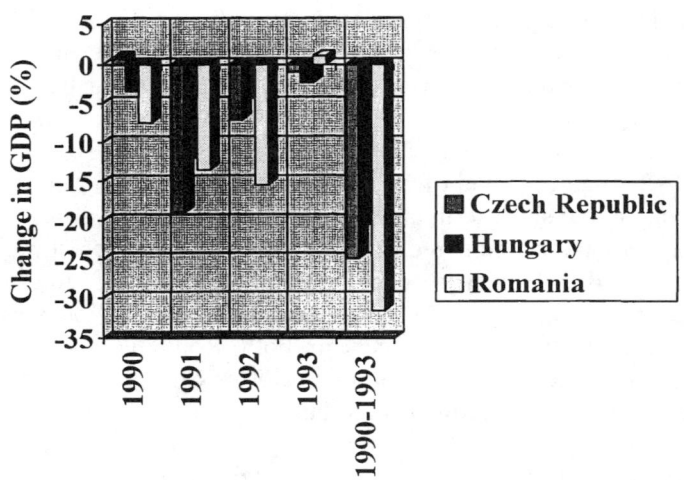

Source: Adapted from Timár, János, 'Particular Features of Employment and Unemployment in the Present Stage of Transformation of the Post-Socialist Countries', *Europe-Asia Studies*, Vol. 47, No. 4, 1995, p. 635.

This was caused by the common policy of keeping workers employed, the delaying effect the Czech voucher scheme and wage restriction policy had on restructuring within the state sector, and the PDSR-led government's reluctance to embark on restructuring. Another reason for the decrease in Czech and Romanian production lies in the fact that large sections of their economies consisted of industrial monoliths operating within a traditional Stalinist command economy, whereas the Hungarian economy had been decentralised and many large enterprises broken up before 1989.

The Czech government engaged in an anti-bankruptcy policy, but was reluctant to formulate a specific structural policy because of its preference that market forces reform the structure of the economic base. This ignored the fact that although transformation had officially put the rules of the market in place, many managers and enterprises continued to operate according to the rules of the

Dealing with the Communist Economic Legacy

old system, which was possible because of the early stage of market development. In this sense, the lack of an active structural policy contributed to the delay in the restructuring of Czech industry. The restructuring programme for the largest Czech steel producer, the forty year old *Nova Hut* plant, includes a $650 million modernisation plan to be financed in part by a loan from the International Finance Corporation (IFC), an affiliate of the World Bank which deals with the private sector, but was not agreed until 29 June, 1997[179].

Mass privatisation using the voucher method succeeded in transferring property rights quickly, and ensured popular support for transformation, but many privatised enterprises remain owned or part-owned by the Czech National Property Fund, a quasi-state institution. The state, in the form of the National Property Fund, can hold as much as 20%, and partially state-owned banks a further 40%, of an officially privatised enterprise. The government's debt consolidation scheme, which relieved private banks from their burden of sub-standard loans, made the *Konsolidacní Banka* the major creditor to most privatised enterprises[180]. The *Konsolidacní Banka* took over the loans to prevent the bankruptcies which collapse of the former system of enterprise finance threatened to catalyse. The National Property Fund also prevented bankruptcies, financing a number of specific anti-bankruptcy programmes with revenue gained from privatisation.

The Czech government aimed to create a market environment in which privatised firms succeeded or failed on their own account. However, it was decided that it was undesirable for state enterprises to fail during their privatisation. The privatisation process was expected to be completed relatively quickly, therefore it was anticipated that the economic distortion such an anti-bankruptcy policy would cause would be limited. It was also hoped that the policy would prevent social tension and a drop in support for

---

[179] The IFC has agreed approved a $75 million loan to finance the package, while a further $175 million in loans have been approved by private banks. *RFE/RL Newsline*, Vol. 1, No. 63, Part II, 30 June 1997.

[180] Brom, Karla, Orenstein, Mitchell, 'The Privatised Sector in the Czech Republic: Government and Bank Control in a Transitional Economy', *Europe-Asia Studies*, Vol. 46, No. 6, 1994, p. 894.

transformation which might result from the closure of large state enterprises and consequent dramatic increase in unemployment. Another motivation was the perception that the excessive enterprise interdependence, which had developed under the previous system as a result of various sectoral monopolies, would lead to a general economic collapse if a few large enterprises were declared bankrupt.

The programme prevented bankruptcies and kept the unemployment rate relatively low, but also delayed the reorganisation of the Czech economy and prevented the exit of unviable enterprises. As privatisation took much longer than expected, the programme increasingly served to prolong the former system's structural dysfunction by continuing direct financial support of unprofitable large enterprises. Many anti-bankruptcy programmes therefore represented little more than the continuation of state subsidies to over-manned, economically non-viable enterprises. The decision to rationalise was postponed due to management pressure on the authorities emphasising the negative social consequences of mass redundancies.

Continued support of those state enterprises which could not be immediately privatised through the anti-bankruptcy programme no doubt rescued some which were potentially profitable. The concurrent prevention of unemployment, while contributing to the high level of popular support for transformation in the Czech Republic, nevertheless postponed restructuring. In this sense, the policy was not conducive to successful transformation. On the other hand, the government's policy of wage restriction increased the competitiveness of Czech enterprises and enabled them to re-enter the European and World market. This increased the profits of state enterprises and improved their chances of successful privatisation. It also promoted the establishment of private enterprises which were capable of employing workers from the state sector. However, while the Czech policy succeeded in keeping state enterprises afloat until the nascent private sector was capable of employing a larger proportion of the workforce, it also sustained enterprises and workforce levels which were uneconomic. As the process of industrial restructuring reaches these enterprises, the level of unemployment in the Czech Republic can be expected to rise and social tension increase.

Restructuring Romanian industry has also proved particularly difficult not only because of the legacy of Stalinist development, but also because industrial complexes fulfil an important social function which makes rationalisation and closure more difficult. Although over-manning was widespread, there was initially little attempt at rationalisation. Thus, *ALOR*, an aluminium producer, employed 3644 workers, whereas a comparable plant in France employs 400; *ROMPLUMB*, a lead producer, had 1165 employees, whereas comparable West European plants only employ between 60-80 people; and the number of employees in the steel industry in 1995 was 122 809, compared with a restructuring study recommendation of 35 000[181]. However, over-manning is only one factor which contributes to low productivity and economic inefficiency.

Romanian enterprises must contend with an unsuitable product portfolio which, because of past lack of investment in Research and Development and reluctance to take the difficult decision to discontinue a line of production, continues unchanged. Products are therefore badly designed and of poor quality. This keeps sales low and contributes to poor profits, which in turn means there are insufficient resources for self-financing modernisation and the product diversification necessary to ensure economic viability. In addition, unsatisfactory products limit export opportunities and consequent possibilities of purchasing higher quality materials for production. Production of unsatisfactory products also keeps wages low and limits the incentive to increase personal productivity and maintain discipline at the work place.

Thus, many Romanian state enterprises are caught in a vicious circle. Unable to self-finance investment, they are forced to continue production of the very products which decrease enterprise profitability and constrain investment. In addition, the losses to production caused by unreliable machinery are considerable. It has been estimated that at the largest Romanian tractor producer,

---

[181] van Frausum, Yves, G., 'Industrial Restructuring in Romania: Diagnosis and Strategies', *Europe-Asia Studies*, Vol. 47, No. 1, 1995, p. 57.

interruptions of machine operation accounted for approximately 40% of total time, out of which 38% were non-scheduled interruptions. In addition, 26.4% of the plant's foundry production were rejects and 22.6% retouches[182]. Ineffective quality control combined with these problems and forced the tractor plant to sell incomplete and sub-standard tractors.

Not only are products and production methods archaic, but physical assets, buildings and machinery, are also in a poor state of repair. Floors are damaged, ceilings unpainted or unclean, water pipes leaking, lighting inadequate, factory floors are dirty and littered with components and rubbish. Machines are cannibalised and the cause of breakdowns is often not examined. It was reported that at the *Calarsi* steel plant, twenty eight ovens suffered from the same design fault. Obsolete technology adversely affects productivity and, when combined with poor maintenance, endangers worker safety. A study in the hard coal industry attributed many underground accidents, in the first half of 1993 there were 1183, to poorly constructed and maintained ladders. Not only is manufacturing technology obsolete and poorly maintained, it is, like the command economy into which it was integrated, extremely inflexible. Thus, the manufacturing capabilities at the *OLTCIT* car factory cannot be used for the production of other car models, or even for the production of a five door, rather than the present three door, car[183].

Such problems were compounded by the PDSR's continued support of inefficient enterprises. It has been estimated that subsidies in hard coal production amount to a little under 50% of the production costs, and in non-ferrous mining for over 50% of production costs. In addition, Romania has five ethylene crackers in operation, even though demand could be satisfied by one plant[184]. Failure to close economically unviable plants limited the resources available for essential repairs and retraining schemes for

---

[182] Ibid. van Frausum, Yves, G., 'Industrial Restructuring in Romania: Diagnosis and Strategies', *Europe-Asia Studies*, p. 51.
[183] Ibid. van Frausum, Yves, G., 'Industrial Restructuring in Romania: Diagnosis and Strategies', p. 55.
[184] Ibid. van Frausum, Yves, G., 'Industrial Restructuring in Romania: Diagnosis and Strategies', p. 56.

management and workers. It has therefore prolonged the economic hardships associated with transformation.

Thus, despite an officially gradual programme, it is the Hungarian economy which has witnessed the most comprehensive industrial restructuring, and as delayed restructuring occurs in Romania and the Czech Republic employment levels in these two countries may drop significantly, thus increasing social tension and hindering democratic consolidation.

4.5.3: Agriculture

Under the Communist regimes the heavy industrial sector was developed at the cost of investment in agriculture. Land was nationalised and state farms or cooperatives established, but they did not receive the resources necessary to maintain and improve the standard of agricultural equipment.

Despite years of continually declining real investment, the Hungarian agricultural system was relatively successful. State farms and cooperatives farmed the majority of the land, buy many cooperatives had diversified their activities and ran profitable food processing and packaging plants. In addition, during the 1980's more and more land was leased by cooperatives to their members who farmed it as their own and could even inherit the right of lease. A large proportion of agricultural output was exported and the domestic market was well supplied.

The Hungarian government did not adopt a general policy of restitution and compensation in kind was only given in the case of land. The majority of land passed into private hands, but only a small number of the new owners are interested in agricultural production and have the capital necessary to modernise production methods. The fragmented holdings are also unsuitable for large-scale production and as a result, the economic efficiency of agriculture in Hungary has decreased. Uncertainty during the reorganisation of property rights within collective farms also contributed to a fall in production. In addition, as the more profitable non-agricultural sectors of state farms, such as food processing, were privatised separately from cooperatives, agriculture has lost much of its attractiveness.

Hungarian compensation ensured corrective social justice and provided a large number of people a direct personal interest in the success of transformation via possession of property and land, but was not economically rational. During the compensation process the percentage of arable land decreased, as did the animal population: cattle numbers decreased by almost 50%[185]. The government aimed to revive the agricultural sector by replacing the collectives with small family farms, but the holdings are not suitable for economically viable production and many farmers have remained in cooperatives. The fall in domestic consumption and government subsidies since the start of transformation has also dramatically reduced income. In combination with the extremely high unemployment rate in agriculture, this has led many people to leave agricultural production. Consequently, in 1993 gross output was 42% lower than in 1989[186], and although plant production increased by 6% in 1994, animal husbandry decreased by 13%[187].

Agriculture plays an important role in the Hungarian economy and it is vital for economic prosperity that this sector recovers. The government led by the Socialist Party set up schemes allowing those cooperatives which had been forced to accept compensation vouchers in return for land to exchange them for shares in food or agricultural trading companies[188]. In addition, export subsidies for agricultural products were introduced and the level of investment increased.

Czech agriculture exhibited the gigantomania inherent in the Stalinist economic system. The average size of state farms in the 1980's was 7000 hectares and the average size of cooperatives 2600 hectares. Approximately 64% of agricultural land was farmed by the cooperatives, while 31% was farmed by state farms. A mere 5% was privately owned[189]. The inefficient agricultural system was supported by subsidies which ensured the average agricultural

---

[185] Ibid. Adam, Jan, 'The Transition to a Market Economy in Hungary', p. 996.
[186] Ibid. Adam, Jan, 'The Transition to a Market Economy in Hungary', p. 996.
[187] Ibid. Bossányi, Katalin, 'Taking Stock of Economic Transformation', *The Hungarian Quarterly*.
[188] Ibid. Fahidi, Gergley, 'Paying for the Past', p. 58.
[189] Ibid. Richter, Sandor, (Ed),, *The Transition from Command to Market Economies in East-Central Europe*, p. 115.

worker earned at least as much as the average wage. Indeed, in 1986, the average farmer was earning 2986 Crowns a month, while the average monthly wage was 2927 Crowns, and by 1989 the average farmer's wage totalled 3258 Crowns a month[190]. The rapid decrease in subsidies, they were halved in 1991, led to a 25% price rise for agricultural products in July 1990, but increased the general crisis in the Czech agricultural sector[191].

The Czech policy of restitution in preference to compensation, while returning the land to its original owners, failed to take into account the fact that many of them were no longer engaged in agricultural production. This created the situation in which members of cooperative or state farms were prevented from gaining possession of the land they cultivated. The general uncertainty which accompanied restitution provided little incentive for cooperative and state farm members to increase production or invest. Restitution fragmented land holdings and left many areas unsuitable for large-scale production. Many private owners are not accustomed to managing a farm single-handed and as many do not possess the necessary machinery or capital to modernise production, they are often unwilling to manage a farm alone. While voluntary cooperatives can provide a solution to the problem of fragmentation and lack of experience, the limited availability of government subsidies to finance modernisation means that the agricultural sector in the Czech Republic remains in crisis.

The Romanian government was the first to announce its intention to distribute agricultural land amongst the population. The agricultural sector in Romania was the last to be collectivised; collectivisation was finally completed in 1962, but suffered most from neglect and discrimination. The inefficiency of state farms caused by lack of investment and neglect was demonstrated by the fact that, although by the 1980's 30% of the agricultural land was cultivated by state farms and 60% by cooperatives, the mere 10% cultivated by private farmers and private agricultural producers was responsible for 57-60% of the total fruit, egg and milk production.

---

[190] Ibid. Richter, Sandor, (Ed.), *The Transition from Command to Market Economies in East-Central Europe*, p. 116.
[191] Ibid. Richter, Sandor, (Ed.), *The Transition from Command to Market Economies in East-Central Europe*, p. 119.

Private producers also accounted for 35% of grape and 40% of meat production[192].

The Romanian regime had continued the Stalinist policy, which had been used in the Soviet Union between the 1930's and 1950's, of taxing the peasants to pay for investment in industry and city infrastructure[193]. Moreover, in a drive to increase central control over private plots and cooperative farms, compulsory deliveries to the state, which had been abolished in 1956, were reintroduced in 1983. In 1986, all land, regardless of the type of property, was declared as being in temporary use. This allowed the state to include the production of private plots in the state Plan[194]. As a result, 86% of all grain produced was taken by the state[195]. In combination with a reduction in the size of private plots, this negated the peasant's incentive to produce and led to a decrease in agricultural production.

As a result of the PDSR's land reform, cooperatives, but not state farms, were liquidated and their land distributed amongst the peasants. During the reform 4.267 million people received an average of 2 hectares of land, which was split into three to five plots. In this way, 80% of arable land and 70% of agricultural land passed into private hands, and private farms now account for 80% of Romania's overall agricultural output. But, because land was fragmented and small in area, it was unsuitable for large-scale production. Many peasants formed associations to cultivate land together and in this way eliminated fragmentation on 42% of private agricultural land. However, lack of capital means that

---

[192] Ibid. Fink, Gerhard, Tuitz, Gabriele, *Rumänien: Wirtschafts- und Systempolitik*, p. 26.
[193] Ibid. Crane, Keith, *The Romanian Economic Mess after Ceausescu*, p. 3.
[194] The smallest size of a private plot was 1500 square metres, of which, after 1986, 500 square metres were cultivated by the Kolkhoz. Ibid. Georgescu, Vlad, 'Romania in the 1980's: The Legacy of Dynastic Socialism', *East European Politics and Societies*, pp. 74-75.
[195] Ibid. Fink, Gerhard, Tuitz, Gabriele, *Rumänien: Wirtschafts- und Systempolitik*, p. 26.

production methods remain archaic and many peasants farm at subsistence level[196].

Although Romanian agriculture displays the lowest technical level and most inefficient organisation of all three countries, gross agricultural production increased by 12.4% in 1993, when it reached the 1989 pre-transformation level. During 1993 cattle and sheep herds increased, as did the production of fruit, vegetables, grapes and grain. Indeed, Romania became self-sufficient in grain[197]. However, the main reasons for the improved results were favourable weather conditions and continuing soft budget constraints which subsidised inputs.

To compensate for the loss of state agricultural subsidies, the PDSR-led government provided highly subsidised credits and ensured that procurement prices remained at half the level of free market prices. Credits were linked with contracts to state procurement agencies and prolonged the agricultural sector's dependence on the state by delaying the development of private wholesalers. Although credit subsidies were phased out at the end of 1993, they were replaced with a system of producer subsidies, such as free fertilisers, for those producers willing to enter into contracts with state procurement agencies[198]. Producer subsidies were derived directly from the state budget and were transparent, but they furthered dependence on the monopolistic state procurement agencies[199]. While consolidation of property rights contributed to an increase in Romanian agricultural productivity, it remains the lowest of all three countries, and fragmentation

---

[196] Hunya, Gábor, 'The Romanian Economy in 1993/1994: From Stagnation with Inflation to Stagnation with Stabilization', *Südosteuropa*, Vol. 43, No. 11-12, 1994, p. 631.

[197] Ibid. Hunya, Gábor, 'The Romanian Economy in 1993/1994: From Stagnation with Inflation to Stagnation with Stabilization', *Südosteuropa*, p. 630.

[198] Ibid. Hunya, Gábor, 'The Romanian Economy in 1993/1994: From Stagnation with Inflation to Stagnation with Stabilization', p. 631.

[199] The subsidies were criticised by the World Bank, but refraining from subsidising agriculture would be a unique solution and place Romanian agriculture at a disadvantage on the world market.

prevents market-orientated production on approximately half the agricultural land[200].

4.5.4: Bad Debts

It is vital for successful economic transformation that the financial system is reformed to ensure enterprises operate according to market norms and do not continue using the personal relationships formed under the previous regime to avoid hard budget constraints. Only if enterprises are subject to hard budget constraints can their irrational economic behaviour be modified.

The continuing presence of soft budget constraints prevents the behavioural restructuring of former state enterprises and also hinders the growth of private enterprise based on market norms. Whereas economically based decisions favour the extension of short-term credit to new private enterprises, the persistence of old structures favours the preferential treatment of long-term customers, that is extension of further credit to already indebted enterprises. Not only does this continue soft budget constraints, it also increases bad debt. Even if banks and institutions base credit decisions on economic criteria, provided old economic structures and relationships continue to exist between enterprises, hard budget constraints can be avoided by increasing inter-enterprise credit. Consequently, the creation of a stable financial economic base has proved difficult.

The partial de-centralisation and reform of the Hungarian banking system in 1985 occurred mainly as a result of pressure from international financial organisations[201]. The banking reforms, which form the foundations of the present system, were not designed within the framework of a comprehensive transformation programme, but rather consisted of a necessary minimum and reflected the prevailing unwillingness of institutions to relinquish their monopolies.

As a result of the reforms, which came into effect in 1986, the activities of the Hungarian National Bank were split into central

---

[200] Ibid. Hunya, Gábor, 'The Romanian Economy in 1993/1994: From Stagnation with Inflation to Stagnation with Stabilization', p. 637.
[201] Ibid. Estrin, Saul, Hare, Paul, Surányi, Marta, 'Banking Transition: Development and Current Problems in Hungary', *Soviet Studies*, p. 786.

and commercial banking sections[202]. Its former Credit Department was also split into groups, which now form the core of private commercial banks. Whole Directorates, including their loan portfolio and staff, were transferred to a specific group. In this way, the Directorate responsible for financing industry, by far the largest, was assigned to one group and the Directorate responsible for agriculture to another. A third group remained a subsidiary of the National Bank[203]. In addition, the National Bank maintained a regional presence, retaining its county offices. The rest of the banking system was not reformed and many regional banks, particularly the National Savings Bank, retained their monopolies.

Major sectoral imbalances from the old system were preserved in the sectoral concentration of the new banks, and the underlying structure of the banking system in Hungary remained fragmented in three fields; domestic, wholesale and transactions related to foreign currency, and services offered to the population. In 1990, the National Savings Bank alone was responsible for 65% of the credits extended to small private businesses and controlled almost 80% of household deposits; while the four largest banks, the National Savings Bank, the Hungarian Credit Bank, the National Commercial and Credit Bank, and the Credit and Development Bank of Budapest, remained responsible for 82% of all long-term loans[204]. The sectoral fragmentation and monopolies thereby created are a result of the gradual de-centralisation started in 1986.

The banks not only inherited sectoral monopolies, but also the entire loan portfolio for their respective sectors. As a result, they came into possession of a substantial number of sub-standard, or bad loans. Although business considerations demanded financing of such loans be curtailed, this could have caused the closure of large sections of industry and created large-scale unemployment. As such

---

[202] The recent privatisation of the largest Hungarian Bank bought the State Property Agency a total of 52 billion Forints, $267 million, revenue, more than half the total revenue gained from privatisation. *RFE/RL Newsline*, Vol. 1, No. 149, Part II, 30 October 1997.
[203] Ibid. Estrin, Saul, Hare, Paul, Surányi, Marta, 'Banking Transition: Development and Current Problems in Hungary', p. 786.
[204] Ibid. Estrin, Saul, Hare, Paul, Surányi, Marta, 'Banking Transition: Development and Current Problems in Hungary', p. 792.

consequences were politically and economically unacceptable, enterprises successfully exerted pressure on the new banks to continue financing and extending new credits. In addition, the inheritance of long-term sub-standard loans weakened the banks' capital base to such an extent they were financially incapable of taking such decisions. The enterprises to which banks extended credit were often major shareholders in the banks itself and vice versa. Having bought shares in the bank, often financed by loans from the same bank, clients expected preferential treatment. Their representatives sat on the bank's board of directors and it was difficult to impose decisions which were unfavourable to them.

The decision to wind-up an indebted enterprise was also hampered by the phenomenon of queuing. This occurred as the banks handling an enterprise account queued the claims against it. The bank's own claims, as well as wages and taxes, had priority over those of other enterprises, thus queuing resulted in increased use of forced inter-enterprise credits as a money substitute. Many debtors remained in a monopoly position and their suppliers were unwilling to initiate bankruptcy proceedings against them. The majority of the debtor enterprises, while unable to pay their suppliers, were able to service their bank debt. The system therefore had the effect of removing the banks' incentive to take action against debtor enterprises.

In 1990, queuing and inter-enterprise credit was reaching dangerously high levels and the number of consistently insolvent enterprises rose by 60% to 282. Interestingly, the worst debtors were concentrated in the mining and heavy industrial sectors, where many enterprises were economically unviable and difficult to restructure. Many debtors did not pay taxes, social security payments or utility bills, and the Social Security Directorate became the biggest forced creditor in Hungary. One of its largest debtors was the Hungarian Electricity Works Trust, which was in turn unable to collect its bills from enterprises and domestic households[205]. In order to halt the increase in inter-enterprise credits, which was threatening monetary stability, an Accounting

---

[205] Ibid. Estrin, Saul, Hare, Paul, Surányi, Marta, 'Banking Transition: Development and Current Problems in Hungary', p. 803.

Dealing with the Communist Economic Legacy 399

Act and a Bankruptcy Law were passed in 1991. The Accounting Act introduced western style accounting practices and ensured that Hungarian procedures reflected international standards. The Bankruptcy Law made it compulsory to file for bankruptcy if a debt was in default for longer than 90 days from the date it fell due[206]. However, the law caused a flood of bankruptcy proceedings which swamped the judicial system. According to the Ministry of Finance, from April until September 1992, the firms which filed for bankruptcy produced a quarter of GDP, accounted for 35% of exports and employed 18% of the total labour force. Although the Bankruptcy Law has been amended, some have suggested it was responsible for the 3-5% drop in GDP in 1992[207].

The problem of bad debts, both those which were inherited from the National Bank and those which the new banks themselves created after 1990, remains. It is difficult to estimate the level of bad debt in the Hungarian system, but it could be as much as 50 billion Forints. Of this, a total of 21 billion Forints were taken over by the National Bank from long-term credits it extended before 1987. In spite of a government pledge to guarantee 50% of this amount in 1991, approximately 40 billion Forints must be written off by the banks if they are to fulfil capital adequacy ratios[208].

In contrast, the Czech banking system was not reformed by the previous regime. The banking system was totally monopolised and archaic, and the reform which was introduced after 1989 restructured the whole system. Czech banks were de-monopolised in 1990 and a new Banking Law was enacted in February 1992. At that time, 90% of all businesses were covered by the five largest state banks[209]. The new Banking Law stipulated that a bank's capital to debt ratio must reach a minimum of 2% by 1990, 4.5% in

---

[206] Ibid. Estrin, Saul, Hare, Paul, Surányi, Marta, 'Banking Transition: Development and Current Problems in Hungary', p. 803.
[207] Ibid. Adam, Jan, 'The Transition to a Market Economy in Hungary', p. 997.
[208] Ibid. Estrin, Saul, Hare, Paul, Surányi, Marta, 'Banking Transition: Development and Current Problems in Hungary', p. 804.
[209] Herr, Hansjörg, Westphal, Andreas, (Hrsg.), *Transformation in Mittel- und Osteuropa*, Campus 1993, p. 236.

1991, 6.25% in 1993 and, in line with international standards, 8% by 1996[210].

But many privatised banks, via their Investment Funds, are now significant shareholders in, as well as the major creditors of, privatised enterprises. During the first wave of voucher privatisation an estimated 72% of participants invested their vouchers in Investment Funds. More than 50% of the vouchers were invested in the 13 largest Funds, which were dominated by large Czech and Slovak financial institutions. In the second wave, 65% of all vouchers were invested in Investment Funds[211]. The Investment Funds aimed to obtain a larger interest in those enterprises in which they were specifically interested. However, the Funds are owned by banks, so in reality it is the banks which play the major role in management. Thus, situations can arise in which banks lend money to indebted enterprises with little attention to their profitability. Some Czech banks have been unwilling to bankrupt enterprises whose loans have been under performing. Although in the long-term, bank ownership and cross-ownership does not necessarily hinder the functioning of a market economy, in combination with the government's anti-bankruptcy programme, it has contributed to the low level of bankruptcies and slow progress of restructuring in the Czech Republic[212].

The government twice postponed the implementation of the Bankruptcy Law which was approved by Parliament in 1991. It was finally put into effect in April, 1993. But many large enterprises were protected from bankruptcy by a clause preventing proceedings against debtors if 50% of their shares were to be privatised using

---

[210] Ibid. Herr, Hansjörg, Westphal, Andreas, (Hrsg.), *Transformation in Mittel- und Osteuropa*, p. 243.

[211] Ibid. Brom, Karla, Orenstein, Mitchell, 'The Privatised Sector in the Czech Republic: Government and Bank Control in a Transitional Economy', p. 895.

[212] On 6 November, 1997, a new Banking Law was passed prohibiting banks from owning non-finance and non-banking institutions, such as Investment Funds, if the bank's stake exceeds more than 15% of the bank's own basic capital. Investment and Pension Funds which are controlled by a bank are not allowed to hold more than a 10% stake in a company. *RFE/RL Newsline*, Vol. 1, No. 155, Part II, 7 November 1997.

the voucher scheme[213]. This protection only lasted as long as the company was on a privatisation list and for two months after its shares had been transferred, but it further delayed liquidations and increased inter-enterprise debt.

The problem of inter-enterprise debt was compounded by the continued existence of sectoral monopolies. Enterprises were often dependent on one or a small group of other enterprises for supplies or orders, and could be forced to extend credits to continue operations. To deal with the problem, the Czech government created a computerised network of enterprise payables and receivables. The Ministry of Trade and Industry founded a new department to organise the computerised matching of all the payables and receivables in industry. The latter contracted the work out to two private firms. Although innovative, the programme achieved limited results while incurring extensive administrative costs. It was recognised that such a centralised approach could harm payment morality, but the problem of inter-enterprise debt had become so acute that even profitable firms were in danger of going bankrupt if no action was taken.

Under the previous system, the Czechoslovak Central Bank controlled enterprise operating expenses via revolving credit facilities. The interest rates for these so-called 'permanently revolving credits' oscillated between 4% and 10%[214]. After the rise in interest rates in 1989, the cheap set rates of the revolving credits threatened not only profitability, but also the stability of the Czech financial system. Cancellation of credit or debt would have caused the bankruptcy of numerous enterprises and the banks.

In order to solve this problem, as part of a debt consolidation programme, the government founded the *Konsolidacni Banka* in February 1991 and in March of that year, it took over revolving credits totalling 110 billion Crowns, $3.8 billion[215]. In addition, the *Konsolidacni Banka* purchased 15 billion Crowns worth,

---

[213] Ibid. Brom, Karla, Orenstein, Mitchell, 'The Privatised Sector in the Czech Republic: Government and Bank Control in a Transitional Economy', p. 899.

[214] Ibid. Brom, Karla, Orenstein, Mitchell, 'The Privatised Sector in the Czech Republic: Government and Bank Control in a Transitional Economy', p. 900.

[215] Ibid. Herr, Hansjörg, Westphal, Andreas, (Hrsg.), *Transformation in Mittel- und Osteuropa*, p. 246.

approximately $0.5 billion, of bad debts from other banks at 80% their nominal value. The money to purchase the credits and loans was provided at favourable interest rates by the Czechoslovak National Bank and other Czech and Slovak Banks[216]. In October 1991, the four largest commercial banks were further recapitalised in a 'debt for bond' swap which totalled 50 billion Crowns[217]. The money spent by the *Konsolidacní Banka* in 1991 represented 25% of the total of domestic credit liabilities and it has become the fifth largest in terms of capital and assets in the Czech Republic[218].

The government's interest in ensuring the success of the debt-refinancing programme was reflected in the fact that, although the average inflation rate in 1992 was 12%, the *Konsolidacní Banka* only paid 8.77% interest to the National Bank. This fact, combined with the 13% interest rate which the *Konsolidacní Banka* demanded from its customers, ensured it was able to meet all its payments and even make a small profit. The scheme offered an acceptable solution for both banks and debtors to the problem of bad and poorly performing loans inherited from the previous system. It also prevented the bad debts from burdening the newly privatised banks and de-stabilising the financial system. Although the loans taken over were deemed sub-standard, 86% of them performed in 1992 and the *Konsolidacní Banka* now collects loan payments from over 6000 firms in both Republics[219]. Despite the success of the debt-refinancing programme and the government's anti-bankruptcy policy, by 1994, 4723 enterprises, approximately 43% of all Czech enterprises, were unable to pay their accumulated debts[220]. Thus, prevention of formal bankruptcy did not prevent widespread insolvency or aid restructuring.

---

[216] Ibid. Brom, Karla, Orenstein, Mitchell, 'The Privatised Sector in the Czech Republic: Government and Bank Control in a Transitional Economy', p. 901.
[217] Ibid. Herr, Hansjörg, Westphal, Andreas, (Hrsg.), *Transformation in Mittel- und Osteuropa*, p. 246.
[218] Ibid. Brom, Karla, Orenstein, Mitchell, 'The Privatised Sector in the Czech Republic: Government and Bank Control in a Transitional Economy', p. 901.
[219] Ibid. Brom, Karla, Orenstein, Mitchell, 'The Privatised Sector in the Czech Republic: Government and Bank Control in a Transitional Economy', p. 901.
[220] Ibid. Herr, Hansjörg, Westphal, Andreas, (Hrsg.), *Transformation in Mittel- und Osteuropa*, p. 244.

The *Konsolidacní Banka* also used proceeds from the National Property Fund to purchase claims of other creditors at a 50% discount in enterprises in liquidation. The main aim of this programme was to prevent bankruptcy, but it also allowed smaller creditors to recover at least part of their losses. Being the major creditor to approximately 80% of all medium-sized and large firms in the Czech Republic, the *Konsolidacní Banka* is usually a member of the committee which decides on the future of a bankrupt enterprise and where possible initiates restructuring programmes to prevent bankruptcy[221]. In this way, the state has retained a major role in the banking sector and thereby in the economy of the Czech Republic. Although the government plans to withdraw from the privatised sector, it seems likely that until this occurs, the *Konsolidacní Banka* will continue to be used as an instrument of industrial policy.

At present, the banking and financial system in Romania is not as developed as those in Hungary or the Czech Republic. In Romania, the problems of sub-standard debt, forced inter-enterprise credits and limited incentives to file for bankruptcy, which are common to the other reforming economies, were compounded by the PDSR's reluctance to reduce the role of the state in the economy. Although a two-tier banking system was introduced in March 1991, in order to maintain its leading role in the economy, as well as to limit the number of bankruptcies, the PDSR continued the practice of allocating credits to economic enterprises directly from the National Bank[222]. The government, led by Prime Minister Victor Ciorbea, stopped this practice and credits to the economic sector of the economy must now be financed by private financial institutions[223]. However, this demonstrates the pervading role the state continued to play in the banking and financial sector until 1996.

At the beginning of 1996, Romania still had no legal mechanism for dealing with insolvent banks, either in the form of restructuring

---

[221] Ibid. Brom, Karla, Orenstein, Mitchell, 'The Privatised Sector in the Czech Republic: Government and Bank Control in a Transitional Economy', p. 901.
[222] Central European Online, *Romania: Economy*. Taken from the Internet on 29.6.97. Http: //www.centraleurope.com.
[223] National Agency of Privatisation, *Reform in Roumania*, Bucharest 1997.

programmes or an orderly process of liquidation. A Deposit Insurance Fund has been set up, but the Savings Bank, which holds the majority of domestic savings, is not currently a member. This means that savers cannot be certain to receive the full value of their deposits in case of liquidation.

The majority of banks were still state owned in 1996 and the most pressing task was to privatise them as a prerequisite for the formation of a private financial sector. The Law on Bank Privatisation, which freed three quarters of the Romanian banking sector from state control, was approved by the Romanian Parliament on 7 April, and by the Senate on 14 April, 1997. The law permits both natural and legal Romanian and foreign persons to participate in privatisation. The state will continue to hold shares, but private companies can own up to 20% of shares in a privatised bank and approximately 100 banks of international repute can hold as many shares as they wish. The law also stipulates that no one person can hold more than 5% of a bank's shares without the approval of the National Bank[224]. As a result of numerous banking scandals, no credits from other Romanian banks are accepted and payment for shares must be made in cash. Bank shares which are held by Private Ownership Funds, now State Investment Funds, must be handed over to the State Ownership Fund in exchange for suitable compensation[225].

The Bank Privatisation Law was one of the most important pieces of reform legislation introduced by the Ciorbea government. However, the original proposal, which limited the share of state ownership to 10%, was removed without any debate at the suggestion of former Prime Minister Vacariou, so the government, in the form of the State Property Fund, may continue to own the majority of shares in many banks[226]. The government also maintained its right of veto over decisions which affect national interest. Nevertheless, the law represents a major advance in the development of the Romanian financial system.

---

[224] *RFE/RL Newsline*, Vol. 1, No. 6, Part II, 6 April 1997.
[225] 'Bank Privatisation Law Update', *The Romanian Digest*, Vol. 2, No. 6, June 1997. Taken from the Internet on 26.6 97. Http: //www.centraleurope.com.
[226] Ibid. 'Bank Privatisation Law Update', *The Romanian Digest*. Http: //www.centraleurope.com.

4.6: Hungarian Economic Problems

In Hungary, the MDF was relying on predicted revenue from privatisation to service the hard currency debt and finance the budget deficit; thus protecting the population from the social costs of transformation by avoiding reform of the social security system. The revenue gained from privatisation was therefore not used to finance failing state enterprises. But revenue was lower than expected due to the slowness of the process and difficulties encountered in selling enterprises at their book value. Limited revenue from privatisation, decreasing tax revenues from failing state enterprises, increasing social costs related to unemployment and a spiralling balance of payments and trade deficit all contributed to the Hungarian economic crisis.

The sheer size of the foreign currency debt meant that its servicing preoccupied Hungarian government, especially as rescheduling, or debt forgiveness programmes, were rejected. Although this policy increased Hungary's creditworthiness and encouraged foreign investment, in combination with the current account deficit, it forced a less growth orientated policy which sacrificed investment in favour of servicing the foreign debt and the budget deficit[227].

At the end of the first half of 1992, the budget deficit had risen to 70 billion Forints[228]. By 1994, it reached 348 billion Forints, approximately 8% of GDP[229]. In an attempt to finance the deficit, the MDF channelled domestic savings into Government Bonds, thereby further restricting the capital available for investment in the private sector. The problem with this policy, apart from the fact that it failed to deal with the cause of the deficit, was that if the real interest rate on Government Bonds exceeds the real growth rate and the budget deficit remains larger than revenue, the debt to output ratio increases and it becomes impossible to sell Bonds. When this occurs, the government must either cut the deficit or print money. The interest rate on Government Bonds in 1991 was relatively high;

---

[227] Ibid. Bakos, Gabor, 'Hungarian Transition after Three years', p. 1195.
[228] Ibid. Kiss, Yudit, 'Privatisation in Hungary – Two Years Later', p. 1033.
[229] Central European Online, *Hungarian Economic Index Charts*. Taken from the Internet 2.7.97. Http: //www.centraleurope.com.

the real interest rate was 8% higher than real growth, but the MDF was unwilling to embark upon budget reform. This increased inflationary tendencies, the pressure to monetise the deficit and the deficit itself[230].

Unlike the Czech Republic, the Hungarian transformation programme did not include a strict monetary policy. Neither could the Hungarian government afford a massive currency devaluation similar to that which the Crown experienced. As a result, the money supply increased faster than GDP. This allowed enterprises to borrow more freely and contributed to the increase in indebtedness and sub-standard loans. Wage control by tax penalties was abolished in 1993. However, wage increases in Hungary were not congruent with increases in production, and real wages declined less than in either the Czech Republic or Romania. Thus, while real wages declined by 22.8% in the Czech Republic during the year of shock treatment, in Hungary they declined by 3.7% in 1990 and by 7% in 1991[231]. Indeed, in 1994 real wages actually rose by 4.5% compared with the previous year[232]. This meant that it became too expensive to retain excessive numbers of employees. Although the redundancies facilitated industrial restructuring, they also increased the social costs of Hungarian transformation.

Taxation on enterprises remained relatively high, but declining demand reduced their profits and consequently government tax revenue. The government collected 573.3 billion Forints tax revenue from enterprises in 1990, but in 1992 this figure declined to 498.7 billion Forints. At the same time, the state's contributions to the social security system increased. In 1990 social security contributions totalled 200.7 billion Forints, by 1992 they had reached 223.9 billion Forints[233]. Along with a constant balance of payments deficit equivalent to approximately 9% GDP, Hungary's trade deficit also increased[234]. Although the foreign trade balance

---

[230] Akos, Valentnyi, 'Monetary Policy and Stabilisation in Hungary', *Soviet Studies*, Vol. 44, No. 6, 1992, p. 993.

[231] Ibid. Adam, Jan, 'The Transition to a Market Economy in Hungary', p. 1000.

[232] Ibid. Bossányi, Katalin, 'Taking Stock of the Economic Transition'.

[233] Ibid. Adam, Jan, 'The Transition to a Market Economy in Hungary', p. 992.

[234] 'A Steep Road: A Conversation with János Kornai', *The Hungarian Quarterly*, Vol. 36, No. 138, Summer 1995, p. 13.

was positive in 1990, by 1991 a deficit of 91 billion Forints was recorded. By 1993 the deficit had risen to 342 billion Forints and exports had decreased by 14%[235].

A reform of the structure of GDP utilisation which increased investment as a means of increasing export production capacity became necessary. To achieve this within a given level of GDP, funds must taken from another area of the budget. As the level of social welfare and redistribution in Hungary was exceptionally high, it was this area of the budget which had to be reformed to stabilise the balance of payments and free domestic funds for investment.

4.6.1: The Bokros Austerity Package

Although the MSZP was elected on its promise to implement transformation in a more gradual and socially acceptable manner, economic reality forced the introduction of an austerity package which bore more resemblance to shock therapy than gradualism. The paradoxical nature of this situation is reflected in the fact that it took a full nine months for the government coalition to agree on an economic programme, and the vote on the new Privatisation Law was postponed until May 1995[236].

The problems associated with privatisation led to debate between different government agencies concerning its administration. The Ministry of Finance favoured giving more power to enterprise councils to organise their own privatisation, while the Government Committee on Privatisation supported a more diversified approach which included more state intervention. The Committee therefore proposed a structure in which the SPA remained responsible for the whole process of privatisation as well as for the running of the remaining state enterprises. In contrast, the Ministry of Finance aimed to set up a separate organisation, the State Privatisation Company, to supervise the privatisation of the trading sector and a State Property Holding Company to manage state assets.

---

[235] Ibid. Bossányi, Katalin, 'Taking Stock of Economic Transition'.
[236] Kocsis, György, 'Stabilization through Restriction', *The Hungarian Quarterly*, Vol. 36, No. 138, Summer 1995, p. 5.

The 1995 Privatisation Law restructured the privatisation process to accord with the Ministry of Finance's plan. Small and medium-sized enterprises with up to 500 employees under the SPA's control were privatised quickly using a competitive bidding process supervised by enterprise managers. In these cases a minimum price was set on the basis of profits and bids were accepted for up to 90 days after which time, if no offers were received, managers were able to buy up to 50% of the shares on condition they found foreign investors willing to buy the remaining shares. The government decided the percentage of the remaining state share in strategic enterprises, such as banks and large public utilities, after privatisation on a case by case basis, although management of privatisation in these cases was taken over by the State Privatisation and State Property Holding Company. A third group of enterprises, giving previous owners and shareholders preferential treatment for the purchase of up to 25% of shares before open bidding took place, was also defined[237].

The delay in the formulation of the Privatisation Law and the stabilisation package is symptomatic of the difficulty the Socialist Party had coming to terms with an economic reality which demanded the implementation of policies which not only represent a break with the Hungarian tradition of gradualism, but which are also incompatible with traditional left-wing, social democratic thought. While the majority of the MSZP has come to terms with the fact that to achieve economic growth, domestic resources must be released and therefore a more radical transformation, which demands social sacrifices, must be implemented, other influential groups within the party cannot accept this.

On 12 March, 1995, the principles of a three year stabilisation plan were published. The main aim of the programme was to avoid insolvency by cutting government spending by 170 billion Forints and to create conditions conducive to economic growth[238]. The stabilisation programme, named after the then Finance Minister, Lajos Bokros, aimed to increase the share of investment in GDP at

---

[237] Ibid. Kabbe, Georgy, 'Die Privatisierung in Osteuropa: Konzeptionen, Modelle, Resultate'.
[238] Ibid. Bossányi, Katalin, 'Taking Stock of the Economic Transition'.

the temporary expense of consumption. The 1995 budget planned that the budget deficit, which stood at 11.5% of GDP at the end of 1994[239], should not exceed 5.5% of GDP[240].

The first section of the programme, 'The 1995 Adjusting Measures of the Government to Promote Economic Stabilisation', was aimed at improving the external balance of payments and included an immediate 9% devaluation of the Forint. In addition, a daily crawling-peg devaluation of 0.06% was introduced for the first half of 1995. During the second half of 1995 the Forint was devalued by a monthly average of 1.3%, resulting in an overall devaluation of 25% for the whole year. It was hoped that this would reduce speculation and increase the international competitiveness of Hungarian firms. An import duty of 8%, abolished in 1997, was levied on all imports, except energy carriers. Firms were also permitted to hold foreign currency accounts, thus enabling them to finance the purchase of foreign products[241].

The second section of the stabilisation package dealt with measures aimed at balancing incoming revenue and outgoing expenses. In an attempt to reduce expenditure, wage-ceilings were imposed on state enterprises and central and local government authorities. These measures were designed to force a 9% drop in real wages in the state sector during 1995[242]. Local and government authorities were required to cut staff levels by 15%. The number of those enlisted in the army was reduced by 5000, and 1000 of the 4000 employees of Hungarian State Television were made redundant. The programme also introduced a wide range of radical spending cuts in welfare and can be viewed as the first serious attempt to reform the Hungarian social welfare system[243]. In this sense, it represents a radical break with the redistribution and social policies of the former Communist regime and the MDF. Means

---

[239] Ibid. Bartlett, David, L., 'Democracy, Institutional Change and Stabilisation Policy in Hungary', *Europe-Asia Studies*, p. 76.
[240] Ibid. Adam, Jan, 'The Transition to a Market Economy in Hungary', p. 1000.
[241] Ibid. Kocsis, György, 'Stabilization through Restriction', *The Hungarian Quarterly*, p. 7.
[242] Ibid. Bossányi, Katalin, 'Taking Stock of the Economic Transition'.
[243] On 27 January, 1998, the World Bank approved a $150 million loan to help implement comprehensive reform of the Hungarian pension system. *RFE/RL Newsline*, Vol. 2, No. 18, Part II, 28 January 1998.

testing of maternity and child benefits have been introduced and family allowance, previously available to all, restricted to those with an income under 25 000 Forints per head[244].

The package also attempted to raise revenue. This required an extension of social security contributions and payment of fees for certain medical services. Tuition fees of 2000 Forints a month were introduced for higher education, tax on cars was raised and tax benefits for domestic heating abolished[245]. At the same time, the running costs of the welfare system were reduced. Responsibility for sick pay was transferred from the social security system to employers and hospitals were instructed to reduce expenditure. Changes in the unemployment benefit system also reduced the level of benefit and introduced measures aimed at encouraging the unemployed to accept work and take part in retraining schemes.

The third section of the stabilisation package aimed to bring the second economy, which was estimated to account for approximately 30% of GDP, into the official realm[246]. Tax regulations were changed and additional funding made available to the Tax Authorities. However, as long as tax avoidance enjoys general acceptance amongst the population, tax collection will remain problematic.

No general programme of wage regulation was introduced, the government relying instead on a tripartite bargaining process between itself, employers and Trade Unions. Although real wages decreased by 11% in 1995, per capita real earnings had increased by 4% in 1994. The 2% cut in real wages agreed for 1996 represented the maximum concession the government could make without reducing the resources necessary for modernisation, especially as many of the planned cuts in social welfare expenditure were judged unconstitutional and not implemented[247]. But, as no clear concept existed for the future financing of the social welfare or higher education system, the 1996 budget was calculated on the basis of the old system.

---

[244] Ibid. Kocsis, György, 'Stabilization through Restriction', p. 7.
[245] Ibid. Kocsis, György, 'Stabilization through Restriction', p. 8.
[246] Ibid. Kocsis, György, 'Stabilization through Restriction', p. 8.
[247] Kocsis, György, 'Growth vs. Equilibrium: Interim Reports', *The Hungarian Quarterly*, Vol. 36, No. 140, Winter 1995, pp. 8-10.

Although a number of Union leaders are also members of the MSZP, some are actually MSZP Deputies in Parliament, they did not support the programme. The population, accustomed to more gradual policies, also had difficulty in accepting the austerity package and the programme was greeted with a wave of protest. Railway workers went on strike for four days, students demonstrated against the introduction of tuition fees, and the Farmer's Union embarked upon a series of demonstrations to protest against the increase of social security and tax contributions[248]. Controversy surrounding the stabilisation package and its rejection by large sections of the population led to an initial drop in support for the MSZP. A poll by *Szoda Ipsos* carried out in March 1997 showed that amongst those questioned, support for the Socialist Party had fallen to 22%, while support for the populist Smallholders had increased to 29%[249]. The poll indicates that the Hungarian population was not prepared for the shock of stabilisation. However, the lack of a feasible alternative on the right-wing of the political spectrum and increasingly favourable economic results, means support for the MSZP has increased once more and should enable it win the national elections in May 1998, albeit with a reduced majority. Nevertheless, the level of support for the Smallholders Party, a populist, right-wing organisation which promotes nationalism and intolerance, rather than the civic values required for a functioning democracy, represents a threat to Hungary's democratic consolidation.

The social costs of the stabilisation programme were high because the main focus of the austerity package was the reduction of the ratio of income redistribution by the state, which had been constant at 60-65%. This actually represented an increase since, despite the drop in GDP, the MDF had not significantly altered the level of welfare spending[250]. Although it is true that real wages and

---

[248] On 10 March, 1997, supported by FIDESZ, farmers held a rally to protest against increased contributions at which 300 tractors drove through the centre of Budapest. Two weeks earlier they had set up road blocks in eastern Hungary to demand the cancellation of the new regulations. See *OMRI Daily Digest*, No. 47, Part II, 10 March 1997.
[249] *OMRI Daily Digest*, No. 48, Part II, 10 March, 1997.
[250] Ibid. Kocsis, György, 'Stabilization through Restriction', p. 3.

expenditure on social security system have been consistently too high in Hungary, another important factor which contributed to the increase in the budget deficit was the rise in interest rates, which led to an increase in debt servicing costs. In addition, approximately 400-600 billion Forints of the state debt consisted of debt-cancelling transfers to former state enterprises[251].

Hungary began a programme of gradual economic transformation, but specific factors related to the Communist legacy; its large external debt and generous welfare system, combined with various policy mistakes made by the MDF and complications in the privatisation process, combined to create an economic crisis which demanded the implementation of a radical stabilisation package aimed at restoring stability and promoting economic growth. As János Kornai stated, although gradualism may have advantages, in that if a gradual step turns out to be a mistake it is comparatively easier to correct:

> 'On the other hand there are circumstances in which a drastic step is inevitable. That is the case when a measure cannot be postponed any longer, because further loss of time will cause mounting problems. That is the case in Hungary: we have to move quickly to avoid greater trouble.'[252]

Recent economic data confirming positive Hungarian economic trends testifies to the success of the Bokros Package. The current account deficit decreased from $2.5 billion in 1995, to $1.7 billion in 1996. The central budget deficit also decreased from 202 billion Forints in 1995, to 130 billion Forints in 1996. Thus, the general government deficit declined from 6.5% of GDP in 1995, to 3.8% of GDP in 1996. In addition, the net external debt decreased from $16.8 billion in 1995, to $14.3 billion in 1996. During the same period, wages remained within their set limits and decreased by 3.6%[253]. The number of those employed in industry decreased by

---

[251] Ibid. Bakos, Gabor, 'Hungarian Transition after Three Years', p. 1211.
[252] Ibid. 'A Steep Road: A Conversation with János Kornai', *The Hungarian Quarterly*, p. 16.
[253] Central European Online, *Main Figures of the Hungarian Economy*. Taken from the Internet on 3.7.97. Http: //www.centraleurope.com.

Dealing with the Communist Economic Legacy 413

6% in 1996, but worker productivity increased by 9% and total industrial sales also grew[254]. In 1996 industrial output increased by 2.3% and industrial sales increased by 3.1%. Although the decrease in real wages resulted in a 1.2% decline of domestic sales, export sales increased by 13.5%[255].

Since 1990, approximately 75% of state assets have been privatised and by the end of December 1996, the state held shares in less than 300 enterprises. Of these, one hundred strategic enterprises, such as those involved in weapons production, energy supply and transport, are destined to remain in long-term state ownership[256]. It was estimated that in 1996, private enterprise accounted for between 60-70% of Hungary's GDP. This percentage is planned to increase to 85% by 1998[257].

Figures published by the Ministry of Finance show that, although imports grew by 2.1% in the first two months of 1997, dollar exports increased by 4.1%. While real wages increased by 6% in January 1997, they only increased by 4% in February and it is forecast that wage growth will slow further. However, because consumer prices rose less than expected, this increase is not a cause for concern. At the end of March 1997, the unemployment rate stood at 11%, but the Ministry forecast the economy would grow by 2-2.5% in 1997, compared with 1% in 1996[258]. This gave rise to increased work opportunities. The gross debt of the central budget is forecast to increase from an expected 5150-5200 billion Forints in 1997, to 5600-5650 billion Forints in 1998, but as it is hoped that GDP in 1998 will increase by 4-5%, the budget deficit will not

---

[254] Central Europe Online, *Latest Figures of the Hungarian Economy*. Taken from the Internet on 17.2..97. Http: //www.centraleurope.com. Source: Press Conference given by Dr. Szabolcs Fazakaz, Minister of Industry, Trade and Tourism on 17.2.97.
[255] Ibid. Central European Online, *Main Figures of the Hungarian Economy*. Http: //www.centraleurope.com.
[256] Ibid. Central European Online, *Main Figures of the Hungarian Economy*. Http: //www.centraleurope.com.
[257] Ibid. Kabbe, Georgy, 'Die Privatisierung in Osteuropa: Konzeptionen, Modelle, Resultate'.
[258] *RFE/RL Newsline*, Vol. 1, No. 21, Part II, 29 April 1997.

exceed 3% of GDP. The government also aims to reduce the current account deficit by $1.5 billion by 1998[259].

By the end of September 1997, foreign debt totalled $10.5 billion and in November 1997, the monthly crawling peg was reduced by 0.1% to 0.9%. Furthermore, by the end of 1997 Hungary's GDP grew by 4%, and the deficit decreased to 4.9% of GDP. Although inflation for 1997 stood at 18%, foreign investment remained high[260]. These positive economic trends were confirmed by the publication of the unemployment statistics by the Central Statistics Office. For the third quarter of 1997, the unemployment rate was 8.1%, the lowest since 1989[261]. In the light of these figures, it would seem the Hungarian economy is on the road to recovery.

4.7: Czech Economic Difficulties:

Continuous government by the ODS-led coalition meant that the Czech Republic experienced a consistent programme of economic transformation. However, the 1996 elections placed the ODS in the position of forming a minority coalition government. Accustomed to an absolute majority in Parliament, the ODS and its leadership had difficulty in adapting to the new situation. Differences within the coalition combined with forced reliance on the tolerance of the major opposition party, the CSSD, to pass legislation led to constant battles over a multitude of minor problems. The result was that major issues, such as reform of the health and education system, the problematic housing situation, as well as the completion of privatisation, were not been dealt with.

In this situation, the government was unable to respond effectively and deal with negative economic developments and worsening economic indicators. Thus, although the unemployment rate was still relatively low, standing at 4.06% in February 1997, this was the highest level since 1992. The lowest unemployment rate, 0.5%, was found in and around Prague, while the highest rate,

---

[259] Ibid. Central European Online, *Hungarian Economic Index Charts*. Http: //www.centraleurope.com.
[260] *RFE/RL Newsline*, Vol. 1, No. 165, Part II, 21 November 1997.
[261] *RFE/RL Newsline*, Vol. 1, No. 148, Part II, 29 October 1997.

10.6%, was in Most. The regional nature of unemployment was also reflected in Louny, where the unemployment rate stood at 9.5%, and in Chomutov, where it was 9%[262]. Regional unemployment in the Czech Republic is related to the uneven development of the economy, similar to that in Romania, although not as extreme, which led to the dependence of whole regions on a few heavy industrial plants. Although regional unemployment in the Czech Republic is not as serious as in Hungary or Romania, it increasingly threatens democratic consolidation in all three countries.

In February 1997, the trade and balance of payments deficit, as well as the budget deficit, increased and the inflation rate reached 8.6%. The trade deficit had increased gradually during 1996, causing a balance of payments deficit equivalent to 7% of GDP by the end of the year[263]. During January 1997 the balance of trade worsened as imports increased by 8%, while exports decreased by 2.5%. The trade deficit for 1996 totalled 160 billion Crowns; for 1997 the predicted figure was 180-300 billion Crowns[264]. The negative trade balance was caused by the slowing down of growth in the Czech economy and its decreasing international competitiveness. This was partly due to the high exchange rate of the Crown and partly due to the continuing inefficiency of Czech enterprises. Imports had also been fuelled by wage increases which had increased domestic demand.

Increasing the efficiency and competitiveness of Czech enterprises has proved difficult because the privatisation method, in most cases voucher privatisation, did not attract captial and created a diffuse ownership structure which has been concentrated in Investment Funds. These are controlled by the state or banks, who are therefore both owners of and creditors to enterprises. This led to the postponement of economically rational decisions and delayed industrial restructuring and modernisation. The National Property Fund has been criticised for protracting privatisation and economists have increasingly called for its abolition.

---

[262] Czech Embassy, *Wirtschaftsbrief Tschechien*, April 1997, p. 2.
[263] Trade and Industry Ministry, *Tschechische Republik: Wirtschaftshandbuch 1997*, Prague 1997, pp. 3-4.
[264] Ibid. Czech Embassy, *Wirtschaftsbrief Tschechien*, April 1997, p. 2.

The Fund, established in 1991, is the transitional owner of the shares of enterprises which were privatised using the voucher scheme and other more standard methods. Since 1993 it has contributed directly to the state budget and is bound by Law to subsidise the activities of the Czech Land Fund (*Pozemkovy Fond CR*). However, it has no policy-making powers. It is the government which decides the method of privatisation, the Fund's task is to find an investor. It has three main portfolios, the shares it wants to sell, those it aims to keep and cash. It holds shares in 615 enterprises with a nominal value of $5.96 billion, 192.91 billion Crowns. Of these, $5.3 billion, 172.45 billion Crowns, are shares in enterprises of strategic value. The Fund holds 67% of the shares in the power utility *CEZ*, and 97% of the shares in the alcohol producer *Karlovarska Becherovka*. The Fund also manages two of the leading Investment Funds, *Restitucni Investicni* and *Nadacni Investicni*[265].

Although a large number of debt defaulters were inherited from the previous management, under whom one in four tender winners failed to pay for the property purchased, by the end of 1996 the Fund had a total of 360 debt defaulters. The largest was Vratislav Cekan who bid $9.4 million, 305 million Crowns, for the state-owned *Elektroodbyt*, but never paid anything and has since unilaterally withdrawn from the contract. He has actually demanded that the Fund pay him $24.9 million, 808 million Crowns, as compensation for the operation costs of the property between 1992-1996. Another defaulter, Alexander Komanicky, owes the Fund $3 million, 98.8 million Crowns, plus interest, for the enterprises *Stavoservis Praha* and *Graficke Tiskarny Velky Senov*. Ivo Exel, who owes the Fund $9.27 million, 300 million Crowns, for the arms factory *Vlarske Strojirny*, has threatened to take the Fund to the Court of Justice in The Hague in retaliation for its bankruptcy proceedings against *Vlarske*. The Fund also has a total of $1.08 billion, 35 billion Crowns, outstanding obligations resulting from environmental projects[266].

---

[265] Central European Online, *Czech Cabinet to Discuss National Property Fund*. Taken from the Internet on 2.7.97. Http: //www.centraleurope.com.

[266] Ibid. Central European Online, *Czech Cabinet to Discuss National Property Fund*. Http: //www.centraleurope.com.

Dealing with the Communist Economic Legacy 417

Cabinet approval is not required for the privatisation of all property, and the Fund completed a total of 4622 privatisation projects worth a total of $27.2 billion, 880.022 billion Crowns, by October 1996. The sale of a further 126 units worth $0.3 billion, 11.5 billion Crowns, is being prepared. But there is no doubt that, via the Fund, the government has maintained a considerable interest and role in the economy[267]. In this sense, privatisation in the Czech Republic has not resulted in the state's withdrawal from the economy, it has merely changed the nature of its involvement.

The government policy of preventing bankruptcy and enterprise closure by postponing the introduction of a Bankruptcy Law and continuing subsidies to economically unviable enterprises ensured popular support for transformation by keeping the unemployment rate low and limiting the social costs of transformation, but also slowed down the restructuring process and contributed to the loss of competitiveness of Czech enterprises.

Bankruptcy proceedings were started against *Poldni Kladno*, one of the Czech Republic's largest steel works employing approximately 5000 people, on 6 March, 1997, but the bankruptcy rate in the Czech Republic has been consistently low[268]. The 7.5% wage increase in 1996, which placed real wages at their 1989 level, was greater than the increase in productivity and further decreased relative competitiveness while causing additional inflationary pressure. Industrial production increased by 7.4% in 1996, but the projected growth of 5% for 1997 could not be achieved without an increase in investment to fund restructuring and modernisation programmes[269].

In 1996, the Czech National Bank experienced its first loss; approximately 20 billion Crowns[270]. The loss was caused by credits extended to a number of bankrupt financial institutions and is not likely to be recovered. As the Bank aimed to cover these losses

---

[267] Ibid. Central European Online, *Czech Cabinet to Discuss National Property Fund*. Http: //www.centraleurope.com.
[268] The steel works has suffered from economic problems for over a year. Its owners are currently under investigation. One is already in prison for fraud and dubious business deals. *OMRI Daily Digest*, No. 47, Part II, 7 March 1997.
[269] Deutsche Bank Research, *Fokus Osteuropa*, 10 March 1997.
[270] Czech Embassy, *Wirtschaftsbrief Tschechien*, March 1997, p. 2.

with its 1997 profit, it was unable to contribute any money to the state budget. This in turn made it more difficult for the government to deal with the increasing budget deficit, which reached 6.7 billion Crowns at the end of February 1997. The 1996 budget had been modified in the second half of the year and the deficit limited by reducing Ministerial budgets and premature drawing on the state Reserve Insurance Fund. Therefore both the government proposal, which foresaw a balanced budget for 1997, and its approval in December 1996, were not realistic[271].

The main reasons for the increase in the budget deficit lie in the simultaneous decrease in revenue, especially in tax revenue, which fell by 3.3 billion Crowns, and increase in expenditure, which grew by 12.8% in comparison to 1996[272]. The decrease in revenue was the result of the poor economic performance of the Czech economy. The increase in expenditure reflected not only the increase in unemployment and therefore of social expenditure, but also changes relating to the indexation of pensions and the minimum existence income. The Czech Republic has a relatively low foreign debt, it stood at $16.9 billion in 1996[273]. Therefore the budget is not burdened, as in Hungary, by large debt servicing payments and as long as measures are taken to control it, the deficit is not in itself a major cause for concern. But, in combination with the decline in economic growth and competitiveness, and increases in the balance of trade and payments deficits, it represents a threat to Czech economic stability and future economic growth. It is vital to achieve economic stability and growth because these ensure the population's material well-being and thereby increase positive identification with the system and further democratic consolidation.

The government took action to deal with the economic problems after the expulsion of two Deputies from the CSSD for their approval of the 1997 budget gave it a one vote majority in Parliament. In April 1997 an austerity package designed to reduce the trade imbalance, support the Crown and revive the economy was announced. Government budget expenditure was cut by 5%

---

[271] Ibid. Czech Embassy, *Wirtschaftsbrief Tschechien*, April 1997, p. 2.
[272] Ibid. Czech Embassy, *Wirtschaftsbrief Tschechien*, April 1997, p. 2.
[273] Ibid. Deutsche Bank Research, *Fokus Osteuropa*, 10 March 1997.

Dealing with the Communist Economic Legacy 419

and wage increases in the state sector limited. In an attempt to control the trade deficit, a new system of import deposits was introduced requiring importers of certain consumer goods to deposit money with the Czech National Bank, which they could collect after six months[274]. A new tax collection initiative was started, as a result of which, the assets of the main opposition party, the CSSD, were frozen as it had not paid any taxes since 1991[275].

But, as the programme was not accompanied by a major government reshuffle, its credibility and increasingly that of the government was questioned. An opinion poll carried out by the *Prague Institute for Public Opinion Research* showed that only 35% of those questioned had confidence in the government, and only 10% viewed the transformation as successful. Of those asked, 40% viewed the results of transformation as mixed, and 69% felt that the Ministers responsible for the economic problems should resign[276]. In an attempt to regain public confidence, the government put forward a set of stabilisation measures which included further budget cuts, wage restrictions and the possibility of new import restrictions, and engaged in a re-shuffle[277]. The Education Minister, Ivan Philip, took over as Finance Minister from Ivan Kocarnik; the Czech Ambassador to London, Karel Kuehnl, assumed the Trade and Industry Ministry from Vladimir Dlouhy; Petr Necas was appointed to the post of Interior Minister instead of Jan Ruhml; and the Czech Ambassador to Germany became Minister of Education[278].

The government decided to call for a vote of confidence on 10 June, 1997. The decision was not only aimed at restoring confidence amongst the electorate and business community, but was also a tactical decision. The Czech Constitution stipulates that a vote of confidence which is proposed by the opposition must have

---

[274] *RFE/RL Newsline*, Vol. 1, No. 13, Part II, 17 April 1997.
[275] *RFE/RL Newsline*, Vol. 1, No. 17, Part II, 23 April 1997.
[276] *RFE/RL Newsline*, Vol. 1, No. 34, Part II, 20 May 1997.
[277] Office of the Government of the Czech Republic, *Correction of Economic Policy and other Transformation Measures*, 16 April 1997. See also *CZ Government Coalition Stabilization and Recuperative Programme*, 28 May 1997. Http://www.vlada.cz.
[278] *RFE/RL Newsline*, Vol. 1, No. 41, Part II, 29 May 1997.

the support of an absolute majority of all the Deputies, whereas a confidence motion put forward by the incumbent government only requires the support of an absolute majority of Deputies present at the session. Currency speculators responded to the crisis by attacking the Crown and forced the Czech Central Bank to spend $2-3 billion in its support. The Bank eventually abandoned its 15% fluctuation band and the Crown suffered rapid devaluation[279].

On the 9 June, 1997, the eve of the no confidence motion, the Czech cabinet agreed a new set of austerity measures. These included a cut of 20 billion Crowns, $625 million, in the state budget, with certain exceptions such as defence, in view of the obligations of NATO membership[280]. In return for its support, the KDU-CSL had demanded the postponement of previously approved increases in rent and energy prices[281].

The government won the confidence vote by the narrowest of margins, 101 votes to 99, which did little to resolve the crisis. Indeed, following the vote, trust and confidence in the government and Prime Minister Klaus actually decreased[282]. In a poll by the *Prague Institute for Public Opinion Research* published on 17 June, 1997, only 22% of those questioned trusted the government; 74% did not. In comparison, in the May poll, 35% had said they trusted the government, while 61% did not. By June 1997, only 29% said they trusted Vaclav Klaus, a drop of 13% from May[283].

Despite more than $1.25 billion of budget cuts between March and May 1997, the state budget recorded a deficit of $465 million, 14.8 billion Crowns, for the first half of 1997, and the deficit actually grew by $80 million, 2.6 billion Crowns, in June 1997. Thus, while government revenue for June totalled $7.45 billion, 241.508 billion Crowns; expenditure was $7.9 billion, 256.3 billion

---

[279] *RFE/RL Newsline*, Vol. 1, No. 48, Part II, 9 June 1997. Indeed, during the first months of 1998, the Slovak Crown was worth more than the Czech Crown.

[280] *RFE/RL Newsline*, Vol. 1, No. 49, Part II, 10 June 1997.

[281] Rent increases of up to 100% for Prague and up to 62% in other cities were planned for 1 July, 1997. The proposed 35% increase in energy prices for 1997, had already been modified to 15%. *RFE/RL Newsline*, Vol. 1, No. 51, Part II, 13 March 1997.

[282] *RFE/RL Newsline*, Vol. 1, No. 50, Part II, 11 June 1997.

[283] *RFE/RL Newsline*, Vol. 1, No. 54, Part II, 17 June 1997.

Crowns[284]. However, government spending is traditionally high in June; civil servants receive their bonuses and salaries are advanced in the education and cultural sectors ahead of the summer holidays The effect of the spending cuts was further limited by the serious flooding of large parts of the Czech Republic in the summer which necessitated various government aid programmes.

The announced stabilisation package was undoubtedly necessary, but its effectiveness rested to a large extent on the level of confidence and trust the government enjoyed. It therefore remained uncertain whether the government led by Klaus could effectively combat the negative economic developments, which to a large extent resulted from its own policies. However, the resignation of Prime Minsiter Klaus and the entire Czech government in November 1997 did not resolve the crisis. The ongoing political crisis was responsible for the minimal 1.2% increase in Czech GDP in 1997, as compared to an increase of 4.1% in 1996. The crisis of confidence which the political paralysis evinced also led to a 35% drop in foreign investment in 1997[285]. If the political uncertainty, which has gripped the Czech Republic since the summer of 1997, continues it may have serious consequences for economic and democratic consolidation.

4.8: Romanian Radicalism

The economic policies of the PDSR-led government did not improve Romania's economic performance. The Gross Domestic Product declined by 12.9% in 1991, and by 8.8% in 1992. By 1993 Romania's budget deficit totalled 1178.9 billion Lei[286]. Although Romanian GDP did increase by 3.9% in 1994, the inflation rate reached an annual average of 136.7% and the unemployment rate

---

[284] Central European Online, *Czech Budget Still $465 million in the Hole*. Taken from the Internet on 2.7.97. Http: //www.centraleurope.com.
[285] Wyzan, Michael, 'Varied Economic Fortunes in Visegrad and the Balkans', *RFE/RL Newsline*, Vol. 2, No. 15, Part II, 23 January 1998.
[286] Central European Online, *Romania: Economy*. Taken from the Internet 29.6.97. Http: //www.centraleurope.com.

stood at 10.9%[287]. Economic stagnation and pressure from the IMF had forced the introduction of a more far-reaching privatisation programme and stabilisation plan, which succeeded in reducing inflation to 27.5% by the end of 1995, but the PDSR remained unwilling to privatise large sections of the economy[288].

By 1995, the private sector employed approximately half the country's workforce, yet 86% of industrial output was still produced by state-owned enterprises and the private sector only accounted for 45% of total GDP. Thus, the majority of Romania's industrial enterprises remained in state-ownership and were unaffected by transformation. The lack of restructuring was also reflected in the relatively low level of unemployment, which stood at 8.8% in November 1995[289].

On 17 February, 1997, the government led by Prime Minister Victor Ciorbea introduced a radical programme which aimed to increase the speed of reform and privatisation[290]. It was drafted in cooperation with experts from the World Bank and the IMF. Both these institutions had withheld credits in protest at the reluctance of the previous government to introduce reform, and as Bucharest requires international financial aid to complete transformation, approval from both institutions was essential if the programme was to have a chance of success. The programme detailed measures designed to combat poverty, regulate energy imports, liberalise energy prices, create new initiatives in agricultural policy, deal with the budget deficit, reform the financial and banking system, stimulate foreign investment, fight corruption and develop a social partnership. It also foresaw administrative reform and a reduction of the number of employees in the Education, Health, Justice and Agriculture Ministries.

---

[287] The Romanian Embassy, *The Romanian Business Environment: General Data*. Source: National Commission for Statistics, National Bank of Romania.
[288] U.S. State Department, *Romania: Human Rights Practices, 1995*. Taken from the Internet on 19.6.97. Http: //www.hri.org.
[289] Ibid. U.S. State Department, *Romania: Human Rights Practices, 1995*. Http: //www.hri.org.
[290] Lefter, Ion, 'Romania: Details of Economic Reforms Expected Today', *RFE/RL News*. Taken from the Internet on 27.6.97. Http: //www.rferl.org.

In the face of suspension of essential credits by international financial institutions and lack of sufficient foreign investment, one of the first priorities was to increase direct foreign investment. In order to achieve this, the overdue privatisation of the banking sector was initiated and conditions for foreign investors revised.

Foreign investment is essential for the restructuring and modernisation of the Romanian economy, and the relatively low level of direct foreign investment in Romania since 1990 was a major cause of concern. Despite the fact that the Romanian domestic market is potentially one of the largest in the region and the country enjoys a favourable strategic location, from 1990 until 1997 direct foreign investment in Romania totalled just over $2.3 billion[291]. This represents a fraction of the amount invested in the Czech Republic and Hungary. Although the PDSR's ambiguous relationship with the market and prevailing economic instability undoubtedly contributed to the reluctance to invest, it was mainly the confusing, bureaucratic and deficient legal framework governing foreign investment which deterred potential investors.

The 1991 Foreign Investment Law did provide for profit repatriation, but the main problem preventing its implementation was the lack of foreign currency available in the banking system. Romania had some of the most liberal incentives designed to attract foreign investment, such as a wide range of generous tax exemptions and holidays for investments over $10 000, but in 1994 the incentive structure was changed because the government could no longer afford to forego such large amounts of tax revenue[292].

As a result, exemptions for companies which were registered after 1 January, 1995 were limited to import customs duties on imported machinery and equipment, the installation and transportation which were utilised directly in the investment; and to import customs duties on raw materials, supplies and components imported for production purposes for a period of three years. Profit tax remained high at 38%, and tax holidays were only granted if an

---

[291] 'Proposed Revisions to Foreign Investment Laws', *The Romanian Digest*, Vol. 2, No. 6, June 1997. Taken from the Internet on 26.6 97.
Http: //www.centraleurope.com.

[292] Ibid. 'Proposed Revisions to Foreign Investment Laws', *The Romanian Digest*.
Http: //www.centraleurope.com.

investment was in excess of $50 million. Company registration was a complicated and bureaucratic procedure, including official court approval, registration with the Commercial Register and local tax authorities, and usually required four to six weeks[293].

In order to attract investors, the Foreign Investment Law was revised. On 12 February, 1997, legislation which had previously prevented foreign owned companies from owning land in Romania was overturned, although the new law does not apply to foreign individuals. In contrast to previous legislation, which restricted foreign ownership of land to those who were members of a joint venture with a Romanian enterprise, 100% foreign owned companies are now permitted to buy the land on which their offices or factories are located[294]. In addition, the new legislation made securities transactions by foreign companies easier and more flexible.

Restrictions on the repatriation of capital and profit were abolished, although the tax structure aims to ensure that investments remain in Romania for at least a year. Where a request is made to repatriate profit within three months of starting the investment, the profit tax is 75%; if a request is made for repatriation within six months, it falls to 50%; and if a request is made between six and twelve months, it drops to 30%. The profit tax falls to 18% if the request for repatriation is submitted after a year. In addition, the minimum investment which can benefit from tax advantages was lowered to $100 000. Investments which are in excess of $1 million benefit from a profit tax of 15%, a 50% custom duty exemption and more than 50% VAT reduction for five years. Furthermore, the minimum investment amount which can benefit from tax holidays was lowered from $50 million, to $10 million. Investments which exceed $10 million are entitled to profit tax exemption for up to 7 years. Such investors also have possession rights over the land, buildings and production space they use.

The changes reflected the recognition that a pro-active approach was necessary to attract foreign investment. Indeed, between

---

[293] Ibid. 'Proposed Revisions to Foreign Investment Laws'. Http: //www.centraleurope.com.
[294] *RFE/RL News*, 'Romania: Senate Approves Foreign Property Ownership'. Taken from the Internet on 29.6.97. Http: //www.rferl.org.

January and March 1997, foreign investment increased by more than 35% when compared with the same period in 1996[295]. In 1997 foreign investment totalled $1.3 billion, equal to the amount invested over the previous four years[296]. Furthermore, direct foreign investment in Romania totalled $545.0 million, compared to $92.0 million in 1996[297].

The government also introduced a system of Emergency Ordinances enabling it to introduce legislation without prior parliamentary approval[298]. This allowed swift reaction to changing conditions. Legislation could be implemented immediately, although parliamentary approval had to be gained at a later date. Emergency Ordinances were the main means by which the government implemented its radical reform programme.

In order to speed up privatisation, the process was simplified and diversified. Provided a minimum of 5%, but not more than a third of the total shares of an issuing company; a minimum of one third, but not more than half of the total shares of an issuing company ; or a minimum of 51%, but not more than two thirds of the total shares of an issuing company were sold, state-controlled joint stock companies could sell their shares on the Stock Market. The issuing companies had to gain the approval of the State Ownership Fund and issue a prospectus containing all the relevant economic data[299].

It also became possible to make a take-over bid for a state-owned company. A prospectus detailing the offer had to be presented to the company involved and to the National Securities

---

[295] Ibid. 'Proposed Revisions to Foreign Investment Laws'.
Http: //www.centraleurope.com.
[296] Embassy of Romania, 'Prime Minister's Survey of the First Ruling Year', *Press Release*, 4.12.97. Taken from the Internet on 28.1.98.
Http: //embassy.org./~romania/press/rel-0001.html.
[297] Office of the Economic Counsellor, Embassy of Romania, *Economic Bulletin: December 1997*.
[298] The Status of Foreign Investments in Romania was revised using an Emergency Ordinance on 16 June, 1997. The Ordinance ensured further benefits for foreign investors. 'Emergency Ordinance 31: Regarding the Status of Foreign Investments in Romania. 16 June 1997', *Official Monitor*, No. 125, 19 June 1997. Taken from the Internet on 29.6.97. Http: //www.centraleurope.com.
[299] National Agency for Privatisation, *Reform in Roumania*, Bucharest 1997, p. 13.

Exchange Commission. Thereafter, the company was obliged to put at the bidder's disposal all relevant information. Take-overs were effected at the par value of the issued shares, or at a higher price if a counter offer was presented[300]. Many Romanian enterprises are bankrupt, so the Employee Stock Ownership Programme, which entails the free distribution of shares of liquidated state-owned enterprises to its employees, was also simplified. In combination with Management/Employee Buyout schemes, privatisation by swapping convertible bonds for shares, debt equity swaps and leasing with an irrevocable sale clause, the speed of privatisation was increased.

The changes were implemented simultaneously in a new Privatisation Programme which affected approximately 50 enterprises a week[301]. To ensure effective implementation, on 15 April, 1997, the State Ownership Fund, which holds shares in over 6000 enterprises and was previously subject to Parliamentary control, was placed under direct government control[302]. The decision was taken as the speed and quality of the Fund's privatisation programme had come under increasing criticism.

Under the PDSR, political pressure had ensured that the Fund's main task was not to privatise enterprises, but to ensure they continued to operate. Thus, the Fund had extended credits to state enterprises without examining economic data or ensuring the implementation of a restructuring programme. At least 50 enterprises which had received funds to improve their operations had concealed bankruptcy and continued to make losses[303]. Privatisation of the enterprises under its control automatically reduces the Fund's role in the economy and will eventually lead to its dissolution. The directors of the Fund were therefore afraid that privatisation would place their personal position in jeopardy and

---

[300] Ibid. National Agency for Privatisation, *Reform in Roumania*, p. 13.
[301] Office of the Economic Counsellor, Embassy of Romania, *Economic Bulletin: February 1997*.
[302] 'State Ownership Fund Subordinated to Government', *The Romanian Digest*, Vol. 2, No. 6, June 1997. Taken from the Internet on 26.6.97. Http: //www.centraleurope.com.
[303] Ibid. 'State Ownership Fund Subordinated to Government', *The Romanian Digest*. Http: //www.centraleurope.com.

Dealing with the Communist Economic Legacy 427

acted to hinder it. Thus, they attempted to force a revision of the first privatisation list by claiming that the ten enterprises listed were not loss making[304]. In reality they accounted for 7.5% of the deficit in the state sector[305].

In April 1997, the reorganised State Ownership Fund arranged four public tenders for approximately 40% of its shares in more than 70 enterprises. A participation fee of 200 000 Lei was required and tenders were repeated after two weeks to dispose of any remaining unsold shares. Natural and legal foreign persons were entitled to participate on an equal basis as Romanian natural and legal persons[306]. On 4 June, 1997, the government issued an Emergency Ordinance which required the privatisation of all state-owned enterprises within three months and of firms owned by local government authorities within six months[307]. The *regies autonomes* are to be transformed into commercial companies. It was expected that by the end of 1997, more than 3000 enterprises would be listed on the Romanian Stock Exchange, the RASDAQ[308]. Furthermore, on 17 April, 1997, the government announced its intention to privatise sections of the defence industry[309].

In recognition of the continuing inefficiency of the Romanian agricultural sector, an amendment to the Land Law increased the amount of land individual families can own from 10 to 200 hectares[310]. The initial Land Law had only regulated the restitution of land from cooperative farms, although the dissolution of many state farms had also taken place in the form of wild privatisation. A further amendment therefore regulated the restitution of

---

[304] *RFE/RL Newsline*, Vol. 1, No. 10, Part II, 14 April 1997.
[305] *RFE/RL Newsline*, Vol. 1, No. 14, Part II, 18 April 1997.
[306] Office of the Economic Counsellor, Embassy of Romania, *Economic Bulletin: April 1997*.
[307] *RFE/RL Newsline*, Vol. 1, No. 46, Part II, 5 June 1997.
[308] Office of the Economic Counsellor, Embassy of Romania, *Economic Bulletin: January 1997*.
[309] Ibid. Office of the Economic Counsellor, Embassy of Romania, *Economic Bulletin: April 1997*.
[310] *RFE/RL Newsline*, Vol. 1, No. 24, Part II, 5 May 1997. A Parliamentary vote confirming the ammended land restitution law will take palce on 31 March, 1998. *RFE/RL Newsline*, Vol. 1, No. 119, Part II, 17 September 1997.

nationalised land which had been incorporated into State Agricultural Enterprises under the Communist regime[311].

The remaining state farms will all be privatised. Loss making state farms, particularly those in the pig and poultry sectors, are to be restructured and privatised first. Those state farms which control 20% of the best land, chiefly grain and vegetable oil producers, were divided into smaller units in 1997 and will be privatised in 1998. The National Agency of Agricultural Products was reorganised into eight commercial units and privatised in April 1997. State enterprises supplying services for agricultural producers were privatised in two stages. The first 150 enterprises were privatised in March 1997, the remaining 900 by the end of 1997. The National Seed Companies will also be restructured and privatised in May 1998[312].

As the system of direct credits allocated by the National Bank had been abandoned, agriculture remained the only sector of the economy which continued to receive direct subsidies, amounting to 2.3% of GDP in 1997[313]. Until the system of direct subsidy was fully implemented, credits were granted by the National Bank for the purchase of fertilisers and seeds. Since Autumn 1997, coupons, amounting to approximately 1400 thousand billion Lei, $180 million, have been distributed amongst farmers to enable them to buy agricultural inputs[314].

The delayed industrial restructuring was also initiated and the government published a list of 35 large public corporations to be restructured. These accounted for 85% of the total loss in the economic sector. The Trade Unions were informed that the first wave of restructuring would affect 62 state-owned enterprises and cause 85 000 redundancies[315]. Amongst them were the public utilities, 42 companies whose losses represent 20% of the total losses generated in 1996 by economic enterprises with majority

---

[311] *RFE/RL Newsline*, Vol. 1, No. 30, Part II, 14 May 1997.
[312] Ibid. National Agency for Privatisation, *Reform in Roumania*, p. 6.
[313] Ibid. National Agency for Privatisation, *Reform in Roumania*, p. 3.
[314] Ibid. National Agency for Privatisation, *Reform in Roumania*, p. 6.
[315] Ibid. Office of the Economic Counsellor, Embassy of Romania, *Economic Bulletin: February 1997*.

Dealing with the Communist Economic Legacy 429

state-ownership[316]. These enterprises will be rapidly privatised, giving primacy to ownership transfer, not sale price. In this way, the state aims to reduce its direct involvement in the restructuring process.

The non-viable *regies autonomes*, 20 enterprises classified as public service companies which accounted for 27% of total losses from state-owned companies in 1996, were subject to individual restructuring projects starting in June 1997. The remaining eight *regies autonomes* consist of the largest loss making companies, mostly operating in the mining industry. In 1996, these eight companies accounted for 25% of state-owned companies total registered losses[317]. During 1997 they were spilt up and transformed into commercial companies or companies of national interest. Restructuring should be stimulated by the creation of a more consistent economic framework and the strengthening of financial discipline, and it was hoped to offer some of these companies for sale before the end of 1997.

Although restructuring is essential, the specific Stalinist structure of the Romanian economy, particularly the over-blown heavy industrial sector, means it is a rather more complicated process than in Hungary or the Czech Republic and the associated social costs are particularly high[318].

In an attempt to ease the social hardship caused by reform, an Emergency Ordinance from April 1997 provided for severance compensation in the form of equal monthly installments for all employees who are discharged from their jobs as a result of restructuring. Employees who have worked in an enterprise for at least six months, but less than five years, receive six months wages as severance pay. Those who have worked in an enterprise at least five, but less than fifteen years are entitled to nine months wages,

---

[316] Ibid. National Agency for Privatisation, *Reform in Roumania*, p. 5.
[317] Ibid. National Agency for Privatisation, *Reform in Roumania*, p. 5.
[318] For example, the Steel Plant in Galati employs 20 000 people, making restructuring difficult.

and those who have been with the enterprise for fifteen years or more are entitled to one year's salary[319].

Severance pay is nothing unusual, and in the Romanian case is justified by the fact that the majority of redundancies due to restructuring will come from the heavy industrial sector where workers find difficulty in finding new employment. However, because the older workers, normally those most willing to take early retirement or accept redundancy, are entitled to the most severance pay, more younger workers may be laid off. More importantly, the severance pay does not represent an incentive to restructure, as its form, that of monthly installments, while spreading the financial burden, represents continued payment of salary.

Thus, the financial situation of many Romanian enterprises and workers remains fragile. The paradox is that while workers have a right to severance pay and, with the prospect of long-term unemployment ahead of them, rely on it, the burden of severance pay on massively over-staffed, financially weak enterprises hinders the very restructuring which is required if a modern industrial base capable of employing the workforce is to develop.

In a further attempt to limit the social costs of reform, approximately 10% of GDP was allocated to cover social welfare expenditure, and although the government programme introduced full price liberalisation, it affected raw materials first and basic food products last. Thus, bread subsidies were continued for eight months after the programme's introduction[320]. Child benefit was increased and unemployment benefit and pensions doubled. In addition, state pensions and salaries have been indexed. As the government aims to keep the budget deficit at a maximum of 4.4%, these programmes were part financed by loans and credits from international financial institutions and the European Union[321]. The

---

[319] 'Discharged Employees to Have Imposed Social Protections', *The Romanian Digest*, Vol. 2, No. 6, June 1997. Taken from the Internet on 26.6.97. Http: //www.centraleurope.com.
[320] Ibid. Ion, Lefter, 'Romania: Details of Economic Reforms Expected Today', *RFE/RL News*. Http: //www.rferl.org.
[321] Ibid. Office of the Economic Counsellor, Embassy of Romania, *Economic Bulletin: February 1997*.

loans were mainly used to support the social welfare programme, restructuring in the agricultural and industrial sector, environmental protection and construction.

On 21 March, 1997, the G-24 approved a package of loans for Romania. The European Union granted a $145 million loan to cover Romania's trade deficit. Japan and Switzerland granted an extra $50 million and Sweden $4 million. The European Union also released the second installment, totalling $80.5 million, of a loan which was granted in 1996[322]. On 10 April, 1997, the IMF agreed a $400 million loan to support the Romanian reforms and on 22 April, 1997, the World Bank approved a loan of $600 million[323]. Of this, $50 million was allocated to support Romania's social protection programme, increases in child benefit and food programmes for the poor; $350 million to support agricultural reform and increase the speed of privatisation; and $150 million for infrastructure improvements[324]. Despite this, the social costs of transformation are very high and it remains unclear whether the Romanian population is willing to accept them.

The Trade Union, *Fratia*, has organised demonstrations against the drop in living standards and demanded the introduction of a reasonable welfare programme[325]. Romania's largest Trade Union, the National Syndicate Block, *BNS*, has also organised demonstrations to protest against the government's economic policies[326]. The Union demands increased consultation over restructuring and has complained about the slow implementation of the social protection programme. It has also demanded pay rises and the abolition of VAT on basic food products. However, the most disturbing development has been the violence amongst the striking Jiu Valley miners who attacked a Union leader they believed had not represented them effectively. He was taken to a Timisoara hospital in a coma. The miners demanded a 45% wage increase, tax reductions and the release of their leader, Miron

---

[322] *OMRI Daily Digest*, Vol. 1, No. 57, Part II, 21 March 1997.
[323] *RFE/RL Newsline*, Vol. 1, No. 8, Part II, 10 April 1997.
[324] *RFE/RL Newsline*, Vol. 1, No. 44, Part II, 3 June 1997.
[325] *RFE/RL Newsline*, Vol. 1, No. 32, Part II, 16 May 1997.
[326] *RFE/RL Newsline*, Vol. 1, No. 51, Part II, 12 June 1997.

Cozma, who is in detention awaiting trial for his leading role in the 1991 miner's rampage in Bucharest[327].

Although the government had already approved subsidies of 24 billion Lei for the Jiu Valley mining companies, introduced measures aimed at regenerating the region, and offered the miners a 15% wage increase, it was not willing to interfere in the legal process or agree to the demand for a 45% wage increase as these were in direct contradiction to its entire reform concept[328].

The problem is that, while working conditions and wages are poor, under the previous government, the Unions and industrial workers became accustomed to having their demands fulfilled. Furthermore, as the Unions have retained the administrative structure and personnel inherited from the Ceausescu era, they cannot come to terms with the new reform programme as it threatens not only jobs, but also the important ideological position and powerful political influence which the heavy industrial sector and the Unions have until now enjoyed. Interestingly, the miners' demand that the Finance Minister, Mircea Ciumara, travel to the Jiu Valley to head negotiations was similar to those during strikes under the previous regime which had caused Ceausescu and Ile Verdet to travel there. The Trade Unions and miners were still trying to instrumentalise the orthodox command economy's structural dysfunction: its ideological commitment to an overblown heavy industrial sector, to force those in power to accept their demands. In addition, by calling for the Finance Minister to personally lead negotiations, they still displayed the rather naive belief, common amongst populations used to totalitarian regimes, that only those close to the centre of power can affect change. In this sense, the strike was not only economically damaging, but also represented a danger to democratic consolidation.

In the same way, the opposition's numerous motions criticising the reform programme cannot be viewed simply as criticism of economic policy, but of the principle of reform. They represent an attempt by the opposition, led by the PDSR, to hinder and delay the implementation of reform. This is because reform will destroy their

---

[327] *RFE/RL Newsline*, Vol. 1, No. 52, Part II, 13 June 1997.
[328] *RFE/RL Newsline*, Vol. 1, No. 53, Part II, 16 June 1997.

administrative and economic power base, which is anchored in the structures of the centrally administered economy. The Romanian opposition disapproves not only of economic reform, but also of political reforms relating to administrative de-centralisation and democratisation. Thus, the debate over economic reform in Romania remains fundamentally linked with democratic consolidation.

The opposition's total rejection of economic and political reform was demonstrated in the first proposal of two consecutive no confidence motions in the history of Romanian politics. The first was moved on 3 June, 1997 by 141 opposition members and was rejected on 6 June, 1997 by 227 to 158 votes[329]. The second was moved by 143 opposition members on 5 June, 1997. It was rejected by 268 votes to 152 on 9 June, 1997[330]. The two votes were held because the opposition proposed a no confidence motion at the same time as the government presented its future programme. The latter is deemed accepted if a no confidence motion is not tabled. In this way, the opposition was able to put forward a second motion of no confidence. Although the government won both the votes, the opposition parties cannot accept the transformation of Romanian economic and political structures. The opposition therefore represents a direct threat to democratic transformation and consolidation.

In this situation, it is all the more important that the government's economic reform programme succeed. In January 1997 the foreign trade balance showed a deficit of $134.5 million. This represents an improvement from January 1996, when the deficit stood at $158.3 million[331]. In order to ensure the continued competitiveness of Romanian exports, the National Bank purchased approximately $250 million on the foreign exchange market in

---

[329] *RFE/RL Newsline*, Vol. 1, No. 45, Part II, 4 June 1997. Also *RFE/RL Newsline*, Vol. 1, No. 48, Part II, 9 June 1997.
[330] *RFE/RL Newsline*, Vol. 1, No. 47, Part II, 6 June 1997. Also *RFE/RL Newsline*, Vol. 1, No. 49, Part II, 10 June 1997.
[331] Office of the Economic Counsellor, Embassy of Romania, *Economic Bulletin: March 1997*.

April 1997[332]. The interventions removed excess hard currency from the market and prevented an appreciation of the Lei. The accession of Romania to the Central European Free Trade Area (CEFTA) in May 1997 also reduced the customs duties on Romanian agricultural and industrial export products to the other members, Poland, the Czech Republic, Slovakia, Slovenia and Hungary. In addition, the process of harmonising the Romanian Custom Code with that of the European Union was initiated[333].

Previous support of inefficient enterprises caused pressure on fiscal and monetary policies and has led to inflation. The toleration of financial indiscipline resulted in serious financial distress for the *regies autonomes*, often utility companies such as *ROMGAZ*, whose losses were financed via the state budget[334]. Strict monetary policy managed to bring the monthly inflation rate down from 31% in March, to 6.9% in April 1997, but by May 1997 the annual inflation rate had already reached 88.7%[335]. This was higher than originally estimated and meant that for the rest of 1997 the monthly inflation rate could not exceed 2-3% if the government's aim to keep annual inflation below 110% was to be met[336]. This was not feasible and in November 1997, the National Statistics Commission confirmed that in October the annual inflation rate had reached 169.2%[337]. However, monthly inflation was pushed down from a high of 30% in March 1997, to 4.3% in November 1997. Although Romanian GDP decreased by a further 5% during 1997, the corn harvest was 11 million tonnes, the largest so far, and foreign exchange reserves reached their highest level since the end of World War Two[338].

---

[332] Ibid. Office of the Economic Counsellor, Embassy of Romania, *Economic Bulletin: April 1997*.
[333] Office of the Economic Counsellor, Embassy of Romania, *Economic Bulletin: May 1997*.
[334] Ibid. National Agency for Privatisation, *Reform in Roumania*, p. 5.
[335] *RFE/RL Newsline*, Vol., 1, No. 28, Part II, 12 May 1997.
[336] Ibid. Office of the Economic Counsellor, Embassy of Romania, *Economic Bulletin: May 1997*.
[337] *RFE/RL Newsline*, Vol. 1, No. 152, Part II, 11 November 1997.
[338] Ibid. Wyzan, Michael, 'Varied Economic Fortunes in Visegrad and the Balkans', *RFE/RL Newsline*. Also Office of the Economic Counsellor, Embassy of Romania, *Economic Bulletin: December 1997*.

At the start of the radical programme, the unemployment rate in Romania was relatively low. On 5 February, 1997 it stood at 6.7%[339]. The industrial restructuring now underway has increased unemployment and in March 1997 it reached 7.2%[340]. Although from the standpoint of economic efficiency this is a positive development, it has increased the social costs of reform and made it difficult for the population to accept the radical package. The government aims to reduce unemployment to 9.7% by 1998-2000, but the prediction that it would reach at least 10.3% by the end of 1997 severely tested its support[341].

Romania still has a trade deficit, but this has been covered by international and domestic credits. The current account deficit decreased from $2.3 billion in 1996, to $1.4 billion, 4.5% of GDP in 1997. By halving subsidies for industry, introducing partial indexation of wages for public administration, and reducing capital reallocation by 17%, the government aims to reduce expenditure by 2.5% of GDP. It is hoped to increase budget revenue by approximately 2.3% by increasing tax on alcohol, tobacco and ending certain tax preferences for some enterprises. VAT on fruit and vegetables will gradually rise to 18%, and royalties paid on domestically produced oil and gas also be increased. Social insurance contributions will be introduced for an agricultural pension fund and an accident fund, although this may be a temporary measure[342].

Despite continuing problems, the radical Romanian reform package has been a relative success. The direct foreign investment required to finance transformation has increased and international financial institutions have approved numerous loans. Privatisation has accelerated and industrial restructuring is underway. Although GDP declined in 1997, worker productivity increased, while the Lei's low exchange rate ensured Romanian exports remain competitive.

---

[339] Ibid. Office of the Economic Counsellor, Embassy of Romania, *Economic Bulletin: March 1997*.
[340] Ibid. Office of the Economic Counsellor, Embassy of Romania, *Economic Bulletin: April 1997*.
[341] *RFE/RL Newsline*, Vol. 1, No. 40, Part II, 28 May 1997.
[342] Ibid. National Agency of Privatisation, *Reform in Roumania*, pp. 3-4.

However, to maintain support for transformation and ensure the package's effective implementation, the coalition must put an end to its internal squabbles and the government must provide the workers and general population not only sufficient social protection to limit the reform's negative effects, but also sufficient incentives and opportunities to exploit the benefits which a free economy and society can provide. Only if this is achieved will the radical programme maintain the support it requires to succeed and the stable economic base essential for democratic consolidation be created.

4.9: The Impact of Economic Transformation

Hungary, the Czech Republic and Romania followed differentiated transformation strategies, but the impact of transformation on their economies and societies has been similar. The collapse of the CMEA caused specific problems at the start of transformation, but it would seem that whatever form it takes, transformation causes:

– a loss of productivity, as obsolete factories are restructured or closed:
– a realisation that many output figures were existent only in the Plan:
– a rise in prices, as subsidies are cut and prices liberalised:
– and an increase in unemployment, as surplus employees are made redundant[343].

At the start of transformation, Czech industrial and agricultural production declined dramatically, while retail prices and unemployment increased (see Table 15 overleaf).

---

[343] For an interesting study of this phenomenon, see Wineicki, Jan, 'The Inevitability of a Fall in Output in the Early Stages of Transition to the Market: Theoretical Underpinnings', *Soviet Studies*, Vol. 43, No. 4, 1991. See also Appendix XXXV.

Table 15
Impact of Transformation on the Czech Economy
(% Annual Change)

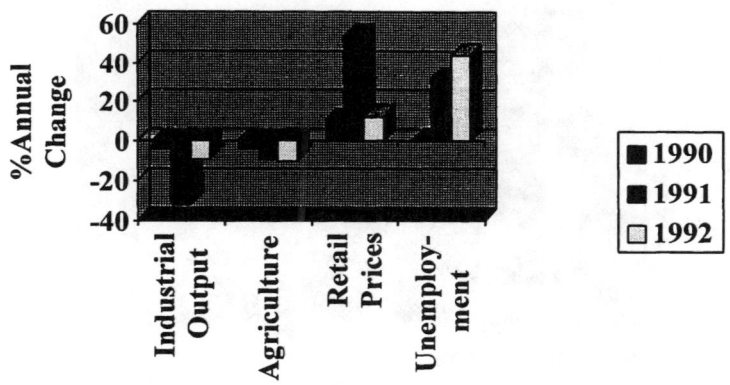

Source: Adapted from Economist Intelligence Unit Data. In White, Stephen, Batt, Judy, Lewis, Paul, G., *Developments in East European Politics*, Macmillan 1993, p. 218.

Romania suffered a similar decline in industrial production. The drop in economic activity is demonstrated by the massive decrease in port traffic in Constantza. From over 600 000 tons in 1989, traffic fell to under 300 000 tons in 1990[344]. The effects on the Hungarian economy were also similar (see Table 16 overleaf). Although transformation had a similar effect on the Czech, Romanian and Hungarian economies, as differences in transformation strategy stem from historical economic and political development, they can reveal specific factors related to the Communist legacy which may affect democratic consolidation.

---

[344] Constantza Port Administration, *Constantza Port*, 1996.

Table 16
Impact of Transformation on the Hungarian Economy
(% Annual Change)

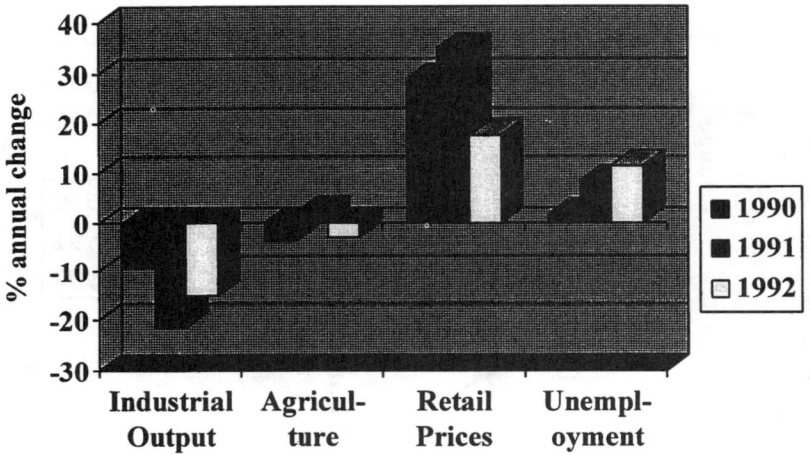

Source: Adapted from Economist Intelligence Unit Data. In White, Stephen, Batt, Judy, Lewis, Paul, G., *Developments in East European Politics*, Macmillan 1993, p. 218

The Hungarian choice to implement a policy of gradual economic and political transformation must be viewed in the light of the paternalistic, and in contrast to Czechoslovakia and Romania, enlightened character of the former regime. Under the former regime, the Hungarian population had become accustomed to gradual reform accompanied by a high level of social welfare and was only prepared to accept a transformation policy which, superficially at least, did not appear to be a radical break from this tradition. However, this prevented the restructuring of state finances which was required to free funds for the new investment transformation required. The consequences of this necessitated the introduction of an austerity package aimed at overcoming economic recession by returning the economy to equilibrium and creating the conditions for growth.

In contrast to the gradual economic reform which took place under the Kádár regime in Hungary, the economic structures of the Czech Republic and Romania retained the typical characteristics of a traditional Stalinist economy. In the Czech Republic, radical transformation was generally viewed as the only means by which to ensure the destruction of the structures formed under the old regime. The Czech government aimed to destroy the ossified structures of the command economy and prevent the privileges which had developed under the Communist regime from being carried over into the democratic system. Although the premise guiding Czech policy was diametrically opposed to that in Romania, Czech anti-bankruptcy programmes and voucher privatisation led to a situation similar to that in Romania – where insolvent enterprises continued to be subsidised and industrial restructuring was delayed. This combination of policies not only emphasised the complete break from the previous system, but also, initially at least, shielded the Czech population from the negative effects of transformation. Although this helped maintain a high level of support for transformation and in this sense furthered democratic consolidation, it also led to a neglect of economic imperatives which has caused economic difficulties. These must now be addressed in an austerity programme which the population may find more difficult to accept than at the start to transformation.

The interests of those supportive of the PDSR and of its own political elite meant that the transformation programme initially implemented in Romania was aimed at creating a mixed economy more resembling a socialist market than a free market economy. Misinformation aimed to ensure that the population remained distrustful of the market and dependent on the section of the power elite which had managed to retain its position following the Revolution. However, the short-comings of the reform programme: bankruptcy prevention and toleration of financial indiscipline, as well as a general reluctance to transform certain economic and administrative structures, were reflected in growing economic difficulties. The PDSR's conflicting policies have further complicated the already difficult task of Romanian transformation. Although the population was ill-prepared for radicalism, the Ciorbea government was forced to introduce a radical reform programme and austerity package as the only means of restoring economic equilibrium and creating a foundation for economic growth.

In the light of the various strategies employed to achieve privatisation and reduce the state's role in the economy, it seems that as long as the population is provided with an opportunity to gain a personal interest in the new system at some point during transformation, privatisation's positive contribution to democratic consolidation is not dependent on the specific form it takes. Hungarian privatisation successfully attracted foreign investment which led to thorough industrial restructuring, but the population in general was not involved and therefore their personal stake the new system remained low. Czech voucher privatisation delayed restructuring, but broad public access to national property prevented the Communist economic elite from retaining their privileges in the new economic system and also ensured the population's personal interest in the new system was relatively high. In this way popular support for transformation was maintained. Romanian privatisation under the PDSR led neither to economic rationality, nor gave the population a significant personal stake in the new system, and therefore hindered democratic consolidation. Consequently, the government led by the National Peasant Party/Christian Democracy has tried to increase the speed and breadth of privatisation.

Despite its economic disadvantages, some form of restitution or compensation is necessary if democracy is to gain legitimacy as a just and fair system. The Hungarian compensation policies effectively distributed property and land amongst the population. Corrective justice was ensured and the lack of personal involvement in the privatisation of state enterprises was compensated by home and land ownership. In this way, the population's personal stake in the new system was ensured. The

Czech population had been given an interest in the new system via voucher privatisation. Thus, Czech restitution emphasised corrective anti-Communist social justice. Returning property to its pre-Communist owners, rather than selling flats and buildings to present occupiers, ensured the pattern of social privileges obtained under Communism was broken. Corrective social justice was also an important factor determining Romanian restitution; but as privatisation of Romanian enterprises often entailed a Management/Worker Buyout or Employee Stock Ownership Programme, land distribution also became a means of increasing the rural population's stake in the new system. In this way, despite the economic problems caused, restitution and compensation contributed to democratic consolidation in all three countries.

Excessively large foreign debt, budget, current account and balance of trade deficits adversely affect the conditions required for economic growth. Because macro- and micro-economic stability ensure material well-being and thereby foster systemic support, they are essential for democratic consolidation. Although industrial restructuring and rationalisation cause unemployment, and thus carry with them social costs which can lead to a drop in systemic support, they are vital for the emergence of a successful economy. It is because of this paradox that all three governments have experienced difficulty implementing consistent policies which ensure micro- and macro-economic stability and force restructuring and rationalisation. Despite the short-term negative economic effects and possible decrease in popular support which result from introducing policies aimed at creating overall economic stability, the fact that all have now implemented similar stabilisation and austerity packages indicates the vital importance of creating the conditions necessary for sustainable economic growth. This seems to confirm, that sustainable economic growth is a crucial ingredient of democratic consolidation.

Interestingly, despite the differing influence of the specific Communist legacy on the course of transformation, the increasing similarity of economic aims seems to suggest it does not neccessarily determine the outcome of transformation. Thus, while the developmental differences caused by the various Communist legacies are still present and influence the specific choice of policy, the convergence of policy aims in Hungary, the Czech Republic and Romania demonstrates the influence of these variations may not be as significant as supposed. Economic transformation has therefore led to a convergence of political aims and economic policy, and although the difficulties associated with it cause problems for democratic consolidation in the short-term, in the long-term, the creation of conditions conducive to economic growth is vital for democratic consolidation.

CHAPTER FIVE

A DEMOCRATIC AND CIVIL SOCIETY

''Twas brillig, and the slithy toves
Did gyre and gimble in the wabe:
All mimsy were the borogroves,
And the mome raths outgrabe.'
Lewis Carrol, *Jabberwocky*[1].

*

Although the period of Communist rule was but the blink of an eye in the vastness of history and time, it nevertheless left an indelible mark on institutional structures and social relations in Central and Eastern Europe. Formal democratic structures have been introduced in Hungary, the Czech Republic and Romania, but they do not, of themselves, guarantee democratic consolidation. Dealing with the Communist legacy not only entails transformation of economic and political relationships, but also requires the formation of a personal understanding and relationship to the new pluralistic economic, political and social structures. Only if the psychological and moral legacy of Communism is successfully managed, can a democratic and civil society capable of forming such a relationship develop. The formation of a civil society is therefore essential for long-term democratic consolidation in Hungary, the Czech Republic and Romania.

The concept of civil society remains controversial. Here it is used to describe a society in which individuals have free access to information and can articulate their interests via participation in

---

[1] Blake, Quentin, (Ed.), *The Penguin Book of Nonsense Verse*, Penguin Books 1994, p. 35.

numerous activities, social and political, without government or state interference. While such groups and organisations are heterogeneous, they share a consensus of tolerance, rejection of violence and political coercion. Thus, they implicitly adhere to democratic norms and in this sense further the democratisation of society. Personal experience of democratic freedoms and the opportunities available for independent political and social organisation also help prevent anti-democratic tendencies gaining currency. In this way, the individual identification with the democratic system, which is essential for long-term systemic support, is furthered.

However, the specific Communist economic, political and social legacy means that during transformation, the countries of Central and Eastern Europe are particularly vulnerable to civil society's potential to hinder democratic consolidation[2].

The experience of Communism endowed the population of Central and Eastern Europe with a deep distrust of the state and its agents. The potential of civil society to engage in criticism of the state can consolidate the distrust which formed under the Communist regime and lead to the de-legitimisation of the new democratic system. Wide-spread social non-acceptance and distrust of the state can also lead to retreat from public and political life into the private sphere with resultant popular apathy. Although criticism of the state is legitimate, during transformation it may de-legitimise state institutions and hinder the acceptance and formation of trust in the democratic system. Furthermore, structures and forms of organisation within civil society based on networks founded in existing cleavages can consolidate lines of conflict and increase alienation between social groups. This is particularly true of ethnic cleavages which are often strengthened by organisation according to ethnic criteria. Such forms of organisation can widen existing divisions and ultimately produce violent forms of conflict resolution[3].

---

[2] For an interesting discussion of this potential, see Lauth, Hans-Joachim, Merkel, Wolfgang, 'Zivilgesellschaft und Transformation', *Forschungsjournal Neue Soziale Bewegungen*, Vol. 10, No. 1, 1997.

[3] Ibid. Lauth, Hans-Joachim, Merkel, Wolfgang, 'Zivilgesellschaft und Transformation', *Forschungsjournal Neue Soziale Bewegungen*, p. 20-22.

Thus, during transformation civil society can both hinder and promote democratic consolidation. The ability to cope with this dynamic tension is to a large extent dependent on the specific legacy of the former Communist regime and the consequent form of democratic transformation.

The paternalistic, authoritarian Kádár regime tolerated constructive criticism as a means of improving the system. In addition, the regime allowed its citizens a private sphere free from state interference. The regime's policy of gradual reform, first in the economic, and later in the political arena, encouraged the emergence of independent groups and organisations. The liberalisation which occurred during the regime's last years facilitated the formation of opposition political groupings which later transformed themselves into political parties. Indeed, the protest actions organised by independent environmentalist groups against the completion of the Gabcikovo-Nagymoros hydroelectric dam were the main cause of its unilateral abandonment by the Hungarian regime[4]. The gradual nature of reform and liberalisation during the Kádár regime allowed the *acteurs* of civil society to establish themselves firmly. This in turn facilitated their participation in the formation of the new democratic system via the Roundtable Negotiations. Thus, the existence of numerous independent groups, both economic and social, under the former regime provided a foundation conducive to the development of civil society in Hungary.

However, since democratisation many independent groupings and organisations, especially the environmentalists, have declined. They have lost the majority of their active members and thereby their potential to further the development of civil society. Distrust of the former regime was wide-spread, but passivity and apolitical behaviour ensured the state refrained from interference in the private sphere. The difficulties of economic transformation mean the majority of the Hungarian population spend most of their time trying to satisfy daily needs. In addition, mistrust of the state has

---

[4] The Hague Court has ruled that both Slovakia and Hungary broke the contract and must take all necessary measures to ensure the implementation of the 1977 accord. *RFE/RL Newsline*, Vol. 1, No. 125, Part II, 25 September 1997.

been strengthened by criticism, albeit legitimate, of government and state. Consequently, individuals have once more retreated into the private sphere and popular disinterest in political affairs has increased.

Although civil society's distrust and criticism of the state acts as a controlling function in consolidated democracies, during Hungarian transformation it has hindered democratic consolidation and limited individual identification with the new democratic institutions. Popular distrust of the state is expressed in low levels of confidence in Parliament and state institutions, limited interest in politics and low turn-outs in national and local elections[5]. Despite this, the existence, even in truncated form, of the foundations and structures of civil society under the Kádár regime had a positive effect on the development of civil society in Hungary and makes dealing with its potentially negative effects an easier proposition.

The Czechoslovak and Romanian regimes did not tolerate any form of criticism or independent organisation – social, political or economic. However, the dedication of a small group of dissident intellectuals preserved the structures necessary for the development of civil society in the Czech Republic. The group organised the unofficial publication of articles, reports and literature critical of the regime and its ideology. The wide-spread network of independent contacts which thus developed was rightly perceived by the regime as a threat to its monopoly of social organisation and control.

However, the number of dissidents remained small and the population's passive acceptance of the regime left them isolated. This isolation was only broken by the Velvet Revolution, during which the dissidents' record of criticism endowed them with the moral authority required to lead the Revolution. The numerous *samizdat* publications and the dissident's moral tenacity preserved the last fragments of civil society in Czechoslovakia, particularly in the Czech lands. But once the regime collapsed and the *acteurs* of civil society had achieved their goal, many of their organisations disintegrated and groups dispersed. Consequently, the active civil society which was present under the former regime in the Czech

---

[5] For more information, see Plasser, F., Ulram, P., A., *Transformation oder Stagnation?*, Signum Verlag 1993.

lands ceased to exist. The wide-spread perception of politics as immoral, which was furthered by the intellectual dissidents, also hindered the development of an active civil society. These factors have contributed to the low level of activity of independent groups and the continued passivity of the Czech population in general[6]. However, the Communist regime's inability to destroy the structures and networks necessary for a functioning civil society meant the foundations required for its development remained in place.

In contrast, the Romanian regime succeeded in destroying the structures of civil society. The primitive nature of Ceausescu's totalitarianism dictated Party control of all aspects of the economy and society. In Romania, the network of informers and secret police agencies was the most widespread of all three countries. No activity independent of Party supervision or control was tolerated. Not only did the regime organise public activities, it also aimed to control every aspect of its citizens' private lives. This was expressed in gynaecological examinations at work to prevent pregnant women from having an illegal abortion, and in Ceausescu's systemisation programme which entailed the replacement of individual peasant villages by uniform apartment blocks. Such extreme control forced the majority of the population into passive resignation.

The terror and nationalist propaganda employed by the regime to maintain control isolated the individual and destroyed the structure of independent social contacts which form the foundations of civil society. There were virtually no *samizdat* publications, and protest against the regime was limited to individual acts by dissident intellectuals and periodical mass strikes by industrial workers and miners to force better working conditions and wage increases. The regime's policies not only ensured individual isolation, but also alienated the workers from the intelligensia and encouraged suspicion between ethinc groups. This prevented the formation of a network of independent links between these potential opposition groups and hindered their coalescence into an

---

[6] The number of active independent groups in Slovakia is considerably higher than in the Czech Republic. See Kaldor, Mary, Vejvoda, Ivan, 'Democratisation in Central and East European Countries', *International Affairs*, Vol. 73, No. 1, January 1997, p. 77.

organised opposition. In this way, opposition to the regime was crushed and groups capable of promoting the structures necessary for the development of civil society were destroyed.

The extreme economic difficulties which the transformation of the Stalinist Romanian economy entails forces the majority of the population to concentrate on survival. Furthermore, the successful manipulation of the December Revolution by members of the former elite caused disillusion and led many individuals to cease activity in civil society. Wide-spread corruption amongst state and government agents has consolidated the population's deep distrust towards the state. Continued passivity and disinterest in political affairs hinders the development of civil society. In addition, the lack of inter-connecting structures and networks of communication within Romanian society means organisations which have developed, have often done so along existing lines of conflict.

The negative potential of this form of civil society is most visible in the social and political conflict between the Romanian and Magyar population. The exclusively ethnic nature of Hungarian organisation has led sections of the Romanian population who feel threatened by the Hungarians' concurrent increased social and political presence to form their own ethnically defined social and political groups. This in turn radicalised sections of the Hungarian minority. These developments increased the potential for social conflict, and in 1990 violence erupted between the two ethnic groups in Tîrgu Mures. Although the catalyst remains unclear, there is no doubt that the latent potential for violent conflict was increased by social and political organisation according to ethnic criteria. The paradox is, ethnic organisation of the Hungarian minority is a legitimate expression of their specific interests and bears witness to the development of an active civil society in Romania.

The destruction of the structures of civil society achieved by Ceausescu and the nature of the December Revolution prevent the rapid development of civil society in Romania. Indeed, where civil society has taken root, the shallow nature of its foundations has often enabled negative aspects to come to the fore. In the light of this, the further development of civil society in Romania will be more problematic and its potentially negative effects pose more serious problems to democratic consolidation than exist in Hungary or the Czech Republic.

The development and consolidation of civil society during transformation is influenced by various factors. Historical truth and critical examination of the Communist system, including one's individual role, is essential for the development of a healthy civil society and the restoration of moral orientation. The Communist regimes prevented independent, critical information reaching the population because it presented a danger to their power base. The presence of an independent, critical media can therefore be considered a prerequisite for the further development and consolidation of civil society. The Church, be it Roman Catholic, Protestant or Orthodox, by providing moral and spiritual guidance, can also help overcome the psychological and moral confusion caused by the Communist experience. However, the views of the Church are not always conducive to tolerance and enlightenment; the foundations of civil society. Wide-spread prejudice polarises the population and provides a demonstration of intolerance. The position of ethnic minorities, in particular the Roma and Magyar, are therefore of special interest.

Membership of the European Union and use of the European Court of Human Rights can provide a guarantee that minority and Human Rights are respected. NATO membership not only ensures integration into security structures which provide a forum for dealing with potential conflict, but also the democratic nature of the military. Soviet command structures must be discarded and civilian control accepted. Reliance on unpredictable methods of control, particularly on terror, compromised the legal system. Trust in state institutions and confidence in the rule of Law can only be restored by legal and police reform. Only if these measures are successful can a sphere independent of state control, which is necessary for the development of civil society, be guaranteed and protected. The following analysis aims to determine the influence of the Communist legacy on the current state of civil society in Hungary, the Czech Republic and Romania, and how this affects democratic consolidation.

5.1: Historical Truth and Personal Responsibility

'It is not necessary,' said the priest, 'to accept everything as true, one must only accept it as necessary.'
'A melancholy conclusion,' said K. 'It turns lying into a universal principle.'

Franz Kafka, *The Trial*.

The Communist regimes bequeathed a legacy of moral disorientation and psychological confusion to the populations of Central and Eastern Europe. The Communist Parties in Hungary, the Czech Republic and Romania relied on public displays of support to justify their claim to legitimacy. In particular, the Czechoslovak and Romanian regimes demanded public homilies and expressions of popular support to maintain pseudo-legitimacy. In contrast, the Hungarian regime abandoned excessive public demonstrations of loyalty for fear of invoking another popular uprising. Nevertheless, certain displays of loyalty, such as a Diploma from a Party College, remained essential for a successful career[7]. However, the very pragmatism which accepted limited ideological belief also contributed to growing cynicism and hopelessness in Hungarian society.

All three regimes created a pseudo-history and forced the acceptance of a version of events which was in direct contradiction to daily experience. The Hungarian regime's legitimacy rested on its claim that 1956 was a 'counter-Revolution'; while the Czechoslovak regime insisted Warsaw Pact forces had been invited into the country in 1968. The Romanian regime re-created the history of the Romanian Communist Party to emphasise Ceausescu's outstanding role and presented itself as a triumph of national independence and development.

Although the Romanian experience was the most extreme, all three populations reacted to such manipulation by distinguishing between public and personal reality and morality. Acceptance of the

---

[7] Many politicians not only held a University Degree, but also an additional Diploma from a Party College. See Machos, Csilla, 'Elitenbildung und Elitenwandel in der Ungarischen Sozialistischen Partei (1989-1996)', *Südosteuropa*, Vol. 46, No. 1-2, 1997.

pseudo-history and un-reality provided by the state meant disregarding daily experience. In this way, a dual morality and general sense of despair arose. The daily experience of two conflicting realities caused deep psychological distress and left many in Hungary, the Czech Republic and Romania confused and morally disorientated. This moral distress was acutely observed by Vaclav Havel:

> *'Alles verschwimmt in einem eintönigem Bild des immer gleichen Kreislaufs. ...Die Geschichte wurde durch Pseudogeschichte ersetzt, durch rhythmisierte Kalendarische Jahrestage, Kongresse, Feiern und Spartakiaden... Wir sind moralisch krank, weil wir uns daran gewöhnt haben, etwas anderes zu sagen als zu denken. Wir haben es gelernt, an nichts zu glauben, einer den anderen nicht zu beachten, sich nur um sich selbst zu kümmern.*[8]

Examination of the Communist past can help overcome this moral disorientation by providing historical truth. The quest for historical truth therefore contributes to the development of civil society. Indeed, it was one of the catalysts which led to the 1989 Revolutions.

Historical truth not only includes reviewing Communist interpretations of history and the actions of the Communist Party itself, but also considering and coming to terms with one's personal role in the former system. This is a necessary part of the process of moral healing. It helps individuals come to a better understanding of the flaws in the previous system; raises awareness of potential threats to democracy; and therefore provides a foundation for the development of a civil society capable of defending democracy.

---

[8] Havel, Vaclav, *Am Anfang war das Wort*, Rowohlt 1990, p. 67, p. 182, p. 236. 'Everything dissolves into a monotonous picture in an ever identical cycle.. History has been replaced by pseudo-history, by rhythmic, calendar anniversaries, Congresses, celebrations and Athletic Meetings... We are morally ill because we have become accustomed to saying something other than we think. We have learnt not to believe in anything, not to respect others, and only to look after ourselves.' Translated by Wendy Hollis.

In addition to an understanding of one's personal role in the old regime, the process of moral healing requires that the personal culpability of those most compromised by their actions under the former regime be exposed. It also demands they be prevented from holding high public office. This contributes to the democratisation of the state and facilitates the re-establishment of certain standards of behaviour. Re-examining the past and opening secret Party and Intelligence Agency files to public scrutiny reveals miscarriages of justice and leads to rehabilitation. This helps re-establish justice and facilitates the vetting of those in high public or administrative office, thereby promoting elite renewal. This confers the democratic system with moral legitimacy and increases trust in state institutions.

However, public examination cannot be allowed to deteriorate into denunciation. Many people cooperated with the regime, and the network of informers was widespread in all countries, particularly Romania. In addition, many informers were pressured into such a role; many did not submit any useful reports; and many of the reports which were submitted contained nothing of significance. Wide-spread denunciation would unjustly exclude a large group of the population from participation in the democratic system and create new social cleavages. Moreover, it is difficult to decide which public offices should be subject to a vetting procedure, and at what level individual culpability justifies exclusion. Thus, there is a fine balance to be struck between the justified desire for historical truth; the critical examination of individual actions under the former regime; and the need for social tranquillity and national reconciliation.

Despite this, there can be no doubt that some form of examination and a general coming to terms with the Communist past is a prerequisite for democratic consolidation. As Timothy Garton Ash states:

> *'Of all the ways of confronting the past... the most important comparison is surely with those post-Communist countries such as Romania and Russia which have not confronted the past in any serious way. For the less you*

confront it the more you live in conscious or unconscious continuity with it.[9]

Only if the Communist past is confronted can the moral disorientation created by Communism be overcome and a democratic, civil society capable of and willing to defend the democratic system come into being. The extent of analysis and lustration required is to a large extent dependent on the nature of the former regime, and the degree to which this has occurred has been determined by the nature of the 1989 Revolution. Thus, the form of confrontation with the past differs and the scope of lustration varies.

5.1.1: Hungarian Reconciliation

The Hungarian regime's pragmatic attempts to improve the functioning of the system via gradual reform led to specialist expertise being valued more highly than Party loyalty. This enabled a reformist group to form within the Party and many who were not ideologically committed to Communism to hold relatively high positions in state administration. Indeed, the acquiescence of the state administration and active participation of the reformist Party elite in the 1989 Negotiated Revolution facilitated a smooth transition of power. Although the continuity which the Negotiated Revolution embodied enabled many members of the former administrative elite to retain their positions, the nature of the Kádár regime, particularly during its last years, meant such people were not automatically compromised by their previous activities.

In response to the deepening systemic crisis, the regime had initiated major changes to the elite in the 1980's. This led to the removal of the majority of those from the older generation who were seriously compromised by their activities after the 1956 Revolution. Thus, whereas between 1970 and 1980 the turnover of top state personnel, such as secretaries of state, heads and deputy heads of departments, was 9.3%; between 1980 and 1984 it rose to

---

[9] Ash, Timothy Garton, 'Central Europe: The Present Past', *New York Review of Books*, 13 July 1995, p. 22.

22%, and between 1984 and 1988 it increased to 53%[10]. In this way, the old administrative elite was replaced by a younger, post-1956, university educated, specialist elite.

Furthermore, at the 1988 Party Conference approximately one third of the Central Committee was dismissed and the rate of early retirement for Party *apparatchiks* increased. Generous severance pay and six months full salary encouraged thousands more to leave the Party *apparat*. It has been estimated that by 1989, the Hungarian Socialist Workers Party and its legal successor, the Hungarian Socialist Party, had spent as much as one billion Forints on such programmes. In October 1989, the *apparat* was officially dissolved, and from February 1990, hearings were held at which all those who held sub-cabinet level offices were required to account for their homes and possessions[11]. Although the hearings were not very effective, they formed part of the general policy of elite renewal and represented an attempt to ensure certain standards of behaviour in the civil service.

Thus, during the last years of the Kádár regime, the old administrative elite was removed, replaced, or left to enter the non-state sector, and specific standards of behaviour for public servants were established. As a result, radical personnel changes in state administration was not an immediate priority for the first post-Communist government led by the Hungarian Democratic Forum. On the other hand, various corporate organisations and groups used the autonomy they had gained under the former regime to resist pressure for structural and personnel changes. This applied to a wide variety of organisations as diverse as the Trade Union Federation, the National Association of Entrepreneurs, the Academy of Sciences, journalist's, writers' and artists' unions. The Socialist Party's ability to cooperate with these sections of the remaining old elite, especially with the Trade Union Federation, has proved advantageous for the acceptance of a new social contract and economic transformation.

---

[10] Tökés, Rudolf, L., 'Hungary's New Political Elites: Adaptation and Change, 1989-90', *Problems of Communism*, Vol. 34, No. 6, November-December 1990, p. 55.
[11] Ibid. Tökés, Rudolf, L., 'Hungary's New Political Elites: Adaptation and Change, 1989-90', *Problems of Communism*, pp. 62-63.

However, some actions and forms of collaboration which occurred under the Communist regime cannot be accepted by the democratic state. In 1991, the Hungarian Constitutional Court declared as unconstitutional a law suspending the statute of limitations for all crimes of murder, treason and aggravated assault for the last forty-five years on the grounds that it was retrospective legislation to punish individuals[12]. In October 1993, it accepted a more specifically defined law which makes it possible to prosecute those involved in crimes associated with the 1956 Revolution[13]. Despite this, the legal difficulties in bringing such cases to court meant that by February 1995, only two members of the Communist Militia had been sentenced for killing civilians during the events of 1956[14]. Thus, the law's prime intention is not the prosecution of such individuals, but rather the revelation of their identity.

In addition, a law requiring the screening of top public officials and barring those who collaborated with the security services, or participated in the suppression of the 1956 Revolution, from holding high public office, was passed in March 1994[15]. The Parliamentary Commission charged with screening such officials has access to the secret files of the security services, but the law prevents public access until 1 July, 2030[16]. The denial of immediate public access to the files is based on doubts about their reliability and concern about the possible social and political disruption widespread public access could cause. The closure of the files increases the potential for political blackmail and the possibility of sensational revelations seriously compromising contemporary senior officials. But, the nature of the late Kádár regime, the elite turnover initiated in the 1980's and the work of the Parliamentary Commission limit this potential.

---

[12] *RFE/RL Research Report*, No. 1, 13 March 1992, p. 74.
[13] Morvai, Krisztina, 'Retroactive Justice based on International Law: A Recent Discussion by the Hungarian Constitutional Court', *East European Constitutional Review*, Vol. 2, No. 3, 1993/1994, pp. 32-34.
[14] *OMRI Daily Digest*, No. 34, Part II, 16 February 1995.
[15] Oltay, Edith, 'Hungary's Screening Law', *RFE/RL Research Report*, No. 3, 15 April 1994, pp. 13-15.
[16] Welsh, Helga, A., 'Dealing with the Communist Past: Central and East European Experiences after 1990', *Europe-Asia Studies*, Vol. 48, No. 3, May 1996, p. 418.

The Commission cannot force a Deputy to resign, it can merely make public an individual's activities under the Communist regime. Although the current Parliamentary Speaker, Zoltan Gal, accepted information from the domestic secret service during his period of office as Interior Minister in 1987, as State Secretary in 1989 and as acting Interior Minister in 1990, he has refused to resign. Gal has justified his refusal to resign saying his activities are general knowledge and noting that despite this, he has twice been elected to Parliament[17]. Matyas Szűrös, who as Parliamentary Speaker declared Hungary a Republic, has also been urged to resign. The Screening Panel found that during his time as a member of the Secretariat of the Central Committee, Parliamentary Speaker and acting Hungarian President in 1989, he had access to and received secret service reports on internal security[18].

The population's attitude towards the Communist regime, and to those who cooperated with it, reflects a general desire for reconciliation. Despite the tragic events of 1956, the inscrutable passage of time and the pragmatic nature of the paternalistic Communist regime meant the majority of the Hungarian population were relatively satisfied with their situation, especially in comparison with the other Soviet Bloc countries. Ironically, the most important re-evaluation of history was undertaken by the former Communist regime itself. In January 1989 a Historical Commission was called to examine the events of 1956. The Commission found the events of 1956 constituted a 'popular uprising against the existing state power'[19]. This discredited the Communist interpretation of history and placed the regime's very legitimacy in question. However, since transformation, the perception of the Kádár regime as a period of stability and material well-being has increased. This has made reconciliation with one's self, the former elite and those who cooperated with the regime much easier, but has also limited public interest in critical confrontation with the Communist past.

---

[17] *RFE/RL Newsline*, Vol. 1, No. 164, Part II, 20 November 1997.
[18] *RFE/RL Newsline*, Vol. 1, No. 168, Part II, 26 November 1997.
[19] Crampton. R., J., *Eastern Europe in the Twentieth Century*, Routledge 1994, p. 393.

The underlying feature of Hungarian policy has been reconciliation and acceptance of the old elite into the new democratic system. Given the administrative elite renewal which occurred during the final years of the Communist regime, their continued employment has not had a negative effect on transformation. Indeed, in light of the fact that potentially, in terms of power and position, this section of the former elite has the most to lose from transformation, their successful inclusion in the democratic system has furthered democratic consolidation in Hungary. Thus, the emphasis of lustration in Hungary has not necessarily been on historical justice, but rather on accountability, transparency and ensuring no one in a position of power is susceptible to blackmail.

5.1.2: Czech Lustration

In contrast, Czech policy towards dealing with the Communist past has emphasised the necessity to remove those who cooperated or collaborated with the Communist regime. The repressive nature of the former regime and the *apparat's* open resistance to transformation made it imperative that those compromised by their activities were denied access to important positions after the Velvet Revolution. Only in this way could the democratic system gain moral legitimacy and acceptable standards of behaviour be re-introduced into the public and social sphere. Vaclav Havel authorised the Ministry of Internal Affairs to screen all the candidates running in the first free elections of 1990[20]. Candidates were not required to withdraw if their names were found in the secret files, but revelations of alleged past collaboration increased fears of political blackmail and a more thorough screening process anchored in law was proposed.

On 4 October, 1991, the Czech Republic became the first country in Central and Eastern Europe to pass a Lustration Law. In addition, a Commission was established to investigate the events

---

[20] Bren, Paulina, 'Lustration in the Czech and Slovak Republics', *RFE/RL Research Report*, Vol. 2, No. 29, 16 July 1993, p. 16.

preceding the Velvet Revolution, in particular the repression of the demonstrations on 17 November, 1989[21].

The Czech Lustration Law, currently the strictest in Central and Eastern Europe, ensured those in important political or economic positions were screened for previous ties with the state security services. Anyone found guilty of collaboration was prevented from holding various positions in government, state, universities and state-controlled enterprises for a period of five years. Institutions had the right to initiate lustration if the individual concerned consented, and individuals themselves could request lustration. The lustration process entailed obtaining an affidavit, or lustration certificate, from the Ministry of Internal Affairs. Refusal of such an affidavit established guilt of collaboration and resulted in immediate dismissal or demotion. Guilt was determined according to several categories:

– state security functionaries, agents and informers, and owners of conspiratorial apartments,
– collaborators with state security who were aware of their collaboration,
– Communist Party functionaries from town level up, except those who served between 1.1.68 and 1.5.69, and members of the normalisation committees,
– members of the People's Militia,
– students and junior assistants who were in KGB schools for longer than three months.

The names of those in the first category appear in the Ministry of Internal Affair's files, which are based on the lists of the former state security apparatus. The assumption of validity of the information contained in the secret files meant those in the first category were denied appeal. Many names in the files which came under the second category, known as Category C, were registered as, 'candidates for secret collaboration'. Guilt of 'conscious collaboration' was established on the basis of evidence. Therefore,

---

[21] Ibid. Bren, Paulina, 'Lustration in the Czech and Slovak Republics', *RFE/RL Research Report*, p. 16.

individuals in this category could seek redress before an independent Commission or present their case before court[22].

The problem was, under the Communist regime those who had contact with, or relatives in, the West were often called to the Office of Passports and Visas for a 'talk' which ended with a request for collaboration. Even if those asked refused, their names remained in the register as a potential candidate for collaboration. The matter was further complicated by the lack of standard useage amongst the organs of state security. Thus, in some districts, those classed as candidates for collaboration may never have spoken to the secret services, while in other areas they could be the equivalent of agents.

As a result, the Independent Appeals Commission, which came into being in February 1992, was inundated with appeals from individuals accused of being candidates for collaboration. By October 1992, of the approximately 70 000 people registered as candidates for collaboration in the secret files, 4000 had applied for lustration and 3000 had appealed their case. The Commission had ruled on only 600 cases and only fifteen individuals were confirmed conscious collaborators. In the light of this, Jaroslav Basta, a member of the Commission, not only questioned the inclusion of Category C in the Lustration Law, but also the validity of the files as a source of evidence. In November, 1993, as a result of mounting criticism, the Lustration Law was bought before the Constitutional Court, which ruled Category C be removed[23].

The Lustration Law also did not distinguish between the nature of collaboration, that is between those who collaborated under duress and those who did so willingly. The inability to discriminate between individual cases and consequent exclusion of entire groups of individuals from certain positions implied an assumption of collective guilt, which is incompatible with the principles of a democratic, legal state. The difficulty of verifying the information contained in the files and preventing unauthorised persons gaining access to them led to the publication of illegally procured lists of

---

[22] Ibid. Bren, Paulina, 'Lustration in the Czech and Slovak Republics', pp. 16-17.

[23] Ibid. Bren, Paulina, 'Lustration in the Czech and Slovak Republics', pp. 18-19. See also Basta, Jaroslav, 'Lustration Process in the CSFR – Genesis of the Problem', Conference Paper, November 1992, Budapest.

alleged collaborators and fostered an atmosphere of political scandal[24]. Three top officials, Alojz Lorenc, former director of the Security Service, Karel Vykypel, former head of counter-espionage, and Frantisek Kincl, a former Minister of Internal Affairs, were sentenced to prison on 3 October, 1992[25], but in response to mounting international and domestic criticism, the Lustration Law was revised on 9 July, 1993[26].

On 9 July, 1993, the Czech Republic became the only country to pass legislation condemning the Communist regime as illegitimate. The legislation also lifted the statute of limitations for the period 1948-1989. This enables the prosecution of individuals for crimes in the name of Communism over the entire period of Communist rule and could affect as many as 2000 individuals[27]. In view of the Lustration Law's concentration on broadly based categories, the shift in emphasis to individuals who committed specific crimes in the name of ideology is a positive development. Public access to state security files, which was granted from January 1996 for a period of five years, facilitated the prosecution and sentencing of individuals, such as the former Prague Communist Party leader, Miroslav Stepan, for his part in the violent repression of the demonstrations on 17 November, 1989, and also furthered the process of critical evaluation[28].

Despite its shortcomings, the lustration process did prevent many of those who had collaborated with the security services from gaining influential positions. Given the repressive nature of the Czechoslovak regime and the former administration's resistance to transformation, it was vital for the success of transformation and the legitimacy of the democratic system, that those compromised by

---

[24] In the Spring of 1992, the *Anticommunist Alliance* published a list of names obtained from an illegally acquired disc of the government's lustration data base. But, certain names were incorrectly copied and others had been added by the group. A second list included the names of those who had been exonerated and of some agents still stationed abroad. Ibid. Bren, Paulina, 'Lustration in the Czech and Slovak Republics', pp. 19-20.

[25] *Prognosis*, No. 10, 22 November – 5 December 1992.

[26] Ibid. Bren, Paulina, 'Lustration in the Czech and Slovak Republics', p. 16.

[27] Ibid. Welsh, Helga, A., ' Dealing with the Communist Past', *Europe-Asia Studies*, p. 417.

[28] *OMRI Daily Digest*, No. 64, Part II, 30 March 1995.

A Democratic and Civil Society

their behaviour and whose commitment to transformation was questionable be removed from positions of power and influence. The specific implications of normalisation for the moral integrity of Czech society also meant confrontation with the Communist past was vital for the restoration of moral balance. Lustration provoked popular discussion and Parliamentary debate over how to deal with the Communist past. It therefore forced Czech society to confront the past by initiating a review of previous actions and in this way furthered the development of civil society.

5.1.3: Delayed Romanian Confrontation

The totalitarian nature of the Ceausescu regime and its violent opposition to transformation, means lustration and serious public examination of the Communist past in Romania is vital for the development of a civil society capable of furthering democratisation. However, the nebulous nature of the December Revolution facilitated the continued presence of the old elite in Romanian politics and state administration. This elite consisted of members of the former Party *apparat* and state administration who were responsible for the development of the Ceausescu regime and therefore particularly compromised by their activities. For this reason, critical examination of the past and exposure of individual collaboration was not in their interest.

Paradoxically, the prosecution and sentencing of some of the most prominent people associated with the Ceausescu regime occurred sooner than in either Hungary or the Czech Republic. In 1990, Ceausescu's brother, Nicolae Andreuta, the General in charge of the *Securitate's* Training College, was sentenced to fifteen years in prison. Ceausescu's son, Nicu, was sentenced to twenty years, but was released for treatment of his liver cirrhosis after serving only three months. In addition, 24 members of the Political Executive Committee were sentenced at a military tribunal in Bucharest. The Head of the *Securitate*, General Iulian Vlad, was also sentenced to three and a half years for detaining a UN official, four years for the mass arrests during the December Revolution, and nine years for genocide during the December Revolution[29]. But,

---

[29] Beckhern, Eberhard, *Tal der Wende*, Knaur 1991, pp. 94-96, p. 146.

the majority of those occupying less prominent positions in the regime's hierarchy were spared. The PDSR-led government passed legislation sealing the *Securitate's* secret files for a period of forty years[30]. It also encouraged state television to present the investigation of Human Right's violations under the Communist regime by a Truth Commission as a witch-hunt. The network of informers and collaborators in Romania was one of the most widespread in Central and Eastern Europe. Therefore, many ordinary people who had cooperated in one form or another with the former regime became afraid they would be implicated in the files and lose their jobs. The task of a Truth Commission is not the punishment of all those who worked within the regime, but rather the examination of the actions of individuals, especially those in influential positions, which led to serious abuses of Human Rights. Moreover, lustration does not entail the dismissal of all those who passed information to the *Securitate*, but ensures those most compromised by their activities under Ceausescu do not retain positions of power in state administration and the political establishment.

The PDSR's protection of members of the former political and administrative elite who would be dismissed or demoted as a result of lustration created a situation in which, as Dorin Tudoran stated:

'*...these abominable types [remained] in positions of authority in Romania, who would be unimaginable in almost any other country.*'[31]

The members of the former political and administrative elite, who enjoyed rather limited collective intellectual ability, were personally compromised by their ties to the Ceausescu regime. Such people were incapable of breaking their allegiance to the old regime. This was not necessarily based on ideological conviction, but the realisation, that they relied on the structures of the Stalinist command economy and the totalitarian political system to maintain their power. These factors limited their ability and willingness to

---

[30] Ibid. Welsh, Helga, A., ' Dealing with the Communist Past', p. 418.
[31] Carey, Henry, F., 'From Big Lie to Small Lies: State Mass Media Dominance in Post-Communist Romania', *East_European Politics and Societies*, Vol. 10, No. 1, Winter 1996, p. 35.

formulate and implement policies aimed at radical transformation and democratisation. The lack of personnel turnover was most obvious at local administrative level and in the presence of former members of the *Securitate* in the army special forces and the new Romanian secret service, the *SRI*[32].

The resistance of members of the former state administrative and prominent political elite to any form of lustration polarised the Romanian political landscape. The lack of personnel turnover and failure to confront the Communist past also limited the population's perception of regime transformation and disguised the nature of the former regime's mechanisms for retaining power, which facilitated their continued use by the PDSR. Some independent groups dedicated to exposing and analysing the truth did form, notably the journal *Memoria*, Memorial, but the lack of lustration and personnel turnover hindered the development of civil society and democratic consolidation.

Although not all members of the former elite are guilty of serious crimes, the PDSR's refusal to introduce a legal process of lustration meant there was no means of determining guilt or innocence. This enabled notorious figures to return to the political stage after the December Revolution. Thus, in November 1992, Adrian Paunescu, who had organised mass youth demonstrations to offer homage to Ceausescu as editor of the weekly, *Flacara*, was elected to the Parliamentary Cultural Commission. Corneliu Vadim Tudor, former editor of *Saptamina*, who had used information supplied by the *Securiate* to denounce those who disagreed with the regime, was also elected to the Committee. Eugen Barbu, who had been denounced by the Writer's Union for plagiarism and owed his former position as co-editor of *Saptamina* to Ceausescu's personal patronage, became a member of Parliament. All campaigned on a programme of chauvinistic nationalism with Fascist overtones. In addition to their Parliamentary careers, Tudor and Barbu re-emerged as editors of the anti-Semitic, extreme nationalist weekly,

---

[32] Of the estimated 14 259 members of the *Securitate*, one third left, 2841 were dismissed, and 2769 were accepted into the *SRI*. The Interior Ministry accepted 2896 former *Securitate* members and the Defence Ministry 449. Others have joined the army's quick reaction force. Ibid. Beckherrn, Eberhard, *Tal der Wende*, pp. 146-147.

România Mare[33]. Finally, the former Prime Minister, Nicolae Vacaroiu, had been a member of Ceausescu's State Planning Committee[34]. Thus, in contrast to Hungary, the continued presence of the old elite in state administration, political, managerial and university posts, placed successful transformation and democratisation in doubt; and in contrast to the Czech Republic, little attempt was made to remove the old guard.

The PDSR-led government continued to use some of the methods of manipulation employed by the previous regime. Despite their dubious reliability, the secret *Securitate* files were used to blackmail individuals and discredit the opposition. The trials of Communist officials which did occur were only linked to events in December 1989. Most importantly, the trial of Ceausescu himself resembled a political show trial and was a sham of legality. Although the concern to ensure Ceausescu's conviction and removal from power is understandable, the staging of a show trial did not promote transformation to a legal, democratic state.

The 1996 electoral success of the Democratic Convention of Romania led to a change in attitude towards lustration and confrontation with the Communist past. After a delay of three years, discussion of a bill drafted by Tichu Dumitrescu proposing full public access to secret files finally got underway in September 1997. Ion Diaconescu, the leader of the National Peasant Party and Chair of the Chamber of Deputies, proposed access to the secret police files be controlled by a Parliamentary Commission to prevent national controversy and social polarisation[35]. The extent of the informant network under the Ceausescu regime and the doubtful reliability of the files justifies some concern; but the need to review the past is more pressing. Only in this way can Romanians confront the past and assist the development of a democratic, civil society.

---

[33] Tismaneanu, Vladimir, 'The Quasi-Revolution and Its Discontents: Emerging Political Pluralism in Post-Ceausescu Romania', *East European Politics and Societies*, Vol. 7, No. 2, Spring 1993, pp. 319- 320.

[34] Altmann, Franz-Lothar, Hösch, Edgar, (Hrsg.), *Reformen und Reformer in Osteuropa*, Pustet 1994, p. 171.

[35] Dumitrescu and Diaconescu were imprisoned as political prisoners during the Communist regime. *RFE/RL Newsline*, Vol. 1, No. 111, Part II, 5 September 1997.

On 17 October, 1997, the Romanian government approved a draft law which requires officials from presidential to local government level to declare collaboration with the secret police and envisages public access to the secret police files. This represents the first official attempt to establish personal and moral accountability for past actions. Officials who admit collaboration, or are found to have made false declarations, will be requested to resign. If they refuse, their names will be published in the official government journal, *Monitorul oficial*. Public access to the secret files will be controlled by a nine member National Council supervised by Parliament. The names of informants will be concealed, but if an individual can prove he or she suffered as a result of the information in the files, the identity of the informant will be revealed[36]. In addition, the Military Prosecutor's Office in Timisoara started proceedings against Ceausescu's last Prosecutor General, Gheorghe Diaconescu, and the former Generals Victor Stanculescu and Mihai Chitac. They were all were sent to Timisoara by Ceausescu to put down the uprising and have been charged with complicity in and instigation to murder[37]. Stanculescu is already facing trial in the Bucharest Military Court for the embezzlement of $8 million in relation to the import of telephones for military use during his term as Defence Minister in 1990[38].

Such critical confrontation with Romania's Communist past augers well for the development of Romanian civil society and democratic consolidation. However, recent attempts to rehabilitate Marshal Antonescu, with whom Ceausescu was partial to being compared, and the initiation of legal procedures to rehabilitate members of Antonescu's government, demonstrate dealing with the Romanian past will be a complicated and difficult process[39].

---

[36] *RFE/RL Newsline*, Vol. 1, No. 142, Part II, 20 October 1997.
[37] *RFE/RL Newsline*, Vol. 1, No. 153, Part II, 5 November 1997.
[38] *RFE/RL Newsline*, Vol. 1, No. 157, Part II, 11 November 1997.
[39] *RFE/RL Newsline*, Vol. 1, No. 156, Part II, 10 November 1997. For an analysis of attempts to rehabilitate Antonescu, see Temple, Mark, 'The Politicization of History: Marshal Antonescu and Romania', *East European Politics and Societies*, Vol. 10, No. 3, Fall 1996.

5.2: The Media

A pluralist, independent media is essential if the population is to have access to sources of accurate information which are required for the effective exercise of civil society's controlling function over government and state. The Communist regimes' efforts to prevent the emergence of independent sources of information emphasise its importance for democratisation. The legacy of extensive state control exercised over the media consists of broadcasting monopolies, state control of licensing, distribution and advertising. Post-Communist governments may be tempted to use these remaining elements of control to limit the criticism which inevitably accompanies transformation, but limiting sources of information hinders the development of the informed public opinion necessary for the development of civil society and democratic consolidation. Although excessive criticism can consolidate the legacy of distrust towards the state which evolved under the Communist regimes, it is necessary to break the state's monopoly of information and create a pluralist, independent media.

5.2.1: The Hungarian Media

The Kádár regime in Hungary encouraged gradual reform and tolerated constructive criticism in the hope of improving the system. Limited media autonomy, which allowed a certain amount of critical news, was therefore permitted. Tolerance of critical opinion preserved elements of an official independent press, while *samizdat* publications maintained a network of contacts independent of state control. Thus, the Hungarian public was relatively well-informed and became accustomed to a de-ideologised media which was relatively reliable. In this way, elements of an autonomous public opinion were retained and the structures necessary for the development of civil society remained intact.

The Hungarian Democratic Forum (MDF), which led the first post-Communist government, was convinced of the validity of its historic mission to revive the Hungarian nation. In contrast to the pragmatism and de-ideologisation which had characterised the last years of the Communist regime, the MDF employed ideological terminology which alienated the population. Although the MDF's concern with the moral state of the Hungarian nation was justified, its vision of the nation's historic destiny was not compatible with contemporary reality. In addition, the means employed by the MDF to promote its ideology and the realisation of its vision were not always in keeping with the task of transformation and democratisation. This was exemplified by its treatment of the critical media.

The MDF interpreted media criticism as hindering its mission to rebuild the nation. Criticism of government policy contributed to the MDF's perception that the media was sympathetic to the opposition and biased in its reporting. The populist nationalists within the MDF called for more control over the media and started a campaign to remove critical, 'cosmopolitan' intellectuals and replace them with people more sympathetic to the MDF's national mission. This was not only an attack on the freedom of the press, but also had anti-Semitic overtones. After the 1991 dismissal of the Head of Hungarian Television, against the wishes of the President, the campaign culminated in 1994, when the government dismissed over a hundred employees of Hungarian Radio and Television[40]. Although it was alleged those dismissed had Communist affiliations, there was little doubt the government hoped their removal would lead to more sympathetic media presentation of its policies.

The attempt to control the media was directed by the MDF's messianic national ideology and was indicative of the increasing centralisation of power during its term of office. Centralisation was viewed as a means to increase the speed and ensure the effectiveness of transformation. But, state control of the press, while limiting criticism of transformation, also hinders the formation of critical public opinion which is vital for democratisation and democratic consolidation. In addition, the critical media was an expression of civil society's successful

---

[40] Bartlett, David, L., ' Democracy, Institutional Change, and Stabilisation Policy in Hungary', *Europe-Asia Studies*, Vol. 48, No. 1, January 1996, p. 63. See also Patkai, Judith, 'Controversy over Hungary's New Media War', *RFE/RL Research Report*, Vol. 3, No. 31, 12 August 1994, and Sukos, Miklos, 'The Media War', *East European Reporter*, March-April 1992.

development. Ironically, the debate triggered by the MDF's attempts to control the media increased public criticism and contributed to its electoral defeat.

The Hungarian 'media war' represented a threat to democratisation and civil society, but public response demonstrated the importance the population placed on an independent media and its role in a pluralistic, democratic system. Because of this, and its legal ties to the former regime, the Hungarian Socialist Party is extremely sensitive to accusations of media manipulation. On election, it reversed the centralisation of power which occurred under the MDF and accepted the autonomy of the Hungarian media. On 4 October, 1997, Hungary's first commercial television station began broadcasting and on 7 October, 1997, a second private station began operations[41].

The contrast between the MDF's clumsy attempts at media control and pragmatism of the media under the Kádár regime caused a public outcry which served to protect media autonomy. Thus, active civil society prevented manipulation of information by the state and furthered media autonomy in Hungary.

5.2.2: Czech Media Autonomy

In contrast to Hungary, where the official media was allowed to criticise aspects of the old system, as George Schöpflin noted, in Czechoslovakia:

> *'The official communications system, operating in a monopolistic and hierarchical manner, strove to socialise the population in the officially preferred values and to mould a public opinion in accord with official policy.'*[42]

This created a situation in which, according to Vaclav Havel:

---

[41] *RFE/RL Newsline*, Vol. 1, No. 132, Part II, 6 October 1997.
[42] Skilling, G., *Samizdat and an Independent Society in Eastern Europe*, Macmillan 1989, p. 37.

'...*the 'disorder of real history' is replaced by the 'orderliness of pseudo-history' which is determined not by the 'life of society' but by 'an official planner'.*'[43]

The lack of unbiased information in the official press hindered the formation of an autonomous public opinion capable of confronting the regime. Nevertheless, despite, or because of, the regime's strict control of all media publications, an active *samizdat* publishing network dedicated to publishing reliable information and critical analyses evolved. After the Velvet Revolution, the official media establishment's complicity with the policy of manipulation made it imperative an elite renewal occur. The *samizdat* organisation provided an established network of independent journalists and writers capable of replacing the old elite. The accessibility of western news programmes via satellite or terrestrial transmitter also acted to ensure accurate reporting. In addition, the Czech government's desire to distance itself from the Communist regime and affect a radical transformation actively furthered the development of an autonomous media. Official acceptance of a potentially critical independent media, even during the difficulties of transformation, was made easier by the Czech economy's relatively good performance, which limited public criticism of government policy. However, it does seem that, although political control was abandonned, polticians could ensure favourable media presentation by giving bribes to willing journalists[44].

Although the Czech Republic has a relatively low number of active civil groupings, the development of civil society has been furthered by the numerous sources of independent information to which individuals have access.

5.2.3: State Domination of Romanian Media

The level of state control and lack of accurate information was most serious in Romania. This was not only true for the media, but also for cultural publications. The last Writer's Union Congress

---

[43] Ibid. Skilling, G., *Samizdat and an Independent Society in Eastern Europe*, p. 99.
[44] See Vrba, Tomas, 'The Trade-offs of a Cozy Life', *Transitions*, Vol. 5, No. 3, March 1998, pp. 62-65.

under Ceausescu took place in 1981, after which the organisation vegetated[45]. To prevent the population gaining access to information, the regime systematically propagated mis-information, manipulated news and enforced strict censorship. Even the weather forecast was manipulated to ensure the official temperature did not drop to the level at which central heating systems were turned on. According to Pavel Câmpeanu, the media, in particular television, became:

> *'An amazing concentration of ideological messages... to transform the television schedule into a pure instrument of political ideology.'*[46]

The paltry entertainment schedule was further depleted when a secret survey in the late 1980's showed people preferred watching *Kojak* to Ceausescu[47]. After the 1989 December Revolution, the blatant lies characteristic of broadcasting under Ceausescu were terminated and the entertainment programme reinstated. But, an independent, pluralistic media capable of engaging in criticism of policies and political personalities was not in the interest of the elite faction which had gained power. The National Salvation Front therefore maintained state control of the mass media and thereby hindered the emergence of a critical civil society.

Although most Romanians possess a television, the majority can only receive the few state television channels. By the middle of 1995, only approximately 2 million households had cable television, while a mere 300 000 had satellite dishes[48]. Moreover, cable and satellite stations are dominated by entertainment and

---

[45] Ibid. Tismaneanu, Vladimir, 'The Quasi-Revolution and Its Discontents: Emerging Political Pluralism in Post-Ceausescu Romania', *East European Politics and Societies*, p. 321.

[46] Câmpeanu, Pavel, 'Romanian Television: From Image to History'. In Drummond, Philip, Paterson, Richard, Wilis, Janet, (Eds.), *National Identity and Europe: The Television Revolution*, BJF Publishing 1993, p. 111.

[47] Ibid. Carey, Henry, F., 'From big Lie to Small Lies: State Mass Media Domination in Post-Communist Romania', *East European Politics and Societies*, p. 25.

[48] Ibid. Carey, Henry, F., 'From Big Lie to Small Lies: State Mass Media Domination in Post-Communist Romania', p. 30.

foreign news. The majority of the Romanian population was therefore dependent on the one news programme offered by state television's main channel, *TvR*, for virtually all domestic news. *TvR's* coverage of the miners' first rampage in Bucharest in February, 1990 was indicative of continued media manipulation. Protests against the National Salvation Front were not broadcast, but the demonstrations which took place following *TvR's* appeal to the public to come and support the Front were transmitted. Moreover, *TvR* justified the violence perpetrated by the miners against the National Peasant and Liberal Parties[49]. In this way, the ruling elite attempted to discredit the opposition and create a favourable social consensus.

The PDSR's cooperation with extreme nationalist and neo-Communist parties led to the return of explicit chauvinism to Romanian broadcasting. In 1993, the chairman of *TvR*, Razvan Theodorescu, who had commissioned a weekly series, 'Memory of Sorrow', dealing with the Communist Gulag, was replaced by Paul Everac[50]. Throughout his period of office, Everac's weekly Saturday night editorials propagated chauvinistic nationalism and victimisation theories. *TvR* refrained from investigative journalism and, in its only news programme, alternated domestic and foreign news in no order of importance. Lack of integrity and dearth of professional journalistic reports presented a distorted impression of reality and furthered disinterest in politics. In this way, state control over television broadcasting was utilised to hinder the formation of an autonomous public opinion.

The PDSR-led government also presided over access to the limited number of independent television channel licences. The Audiovisual Council supervised the allocation of all radio and cable television licences, but restricted them to music, advertising, foreign news and domestic news headlines[51]. Only in 1996 did the Audiovisual Council award a national licence to *Tele 7 ABC*, a rival

---

[49] Ibid. Carey, Henry, F., 'From Big Lie to Small Lies: State Mass Media Dominance in Post-Communist Romania', p. 26.
[50] Each time Ceausescu announced a new policy, Everac had written a play to illustrate the *Conducator's* genius.
[51] Ibid. Carey, Henry, F., 'From Big Lie to Small Lies: State Mass Media Domination in Post-Communist Romania', p. 24.

for *TvR*. Various independent local television and radio stations gained licences, but they were reliant on state-owned transmitters and obliged to broadcast on low power after 9 p.m. or 10 p.m.[52]. This restriction limited audiences and forced such independent stations to focus on local programming. Although precarious finances and residual self-censorship often restrain independent radio stations from reporting national news, they promise to develop into an important source of information.

Despite initial difficulties in gaining access to state-controlled printing and distribution facilities, and obtaining advertising revenue from state-owned enterprises, the printed press has enjoyed relative freedom. The main daily newspapers are *Adevarul*, *Evenimentul Zilei* and *România Libera*. *Adevarul* has maintained the highest circulation, while *Evenimentul's* initial high circulation of between 600 000-800 000 was maintained by sensationalism and rumour mongering. *România Libera* is dedicated to facts and regularly prints corrections. In 1990, its first year, *România Libera's* circulation was between 300 000-1 000 000. The most independent daily newspaper, *Cotidianul*, has a tiny circulation of 10 000 and only survives due to the personal contributions made by émigré shipping magnate Ion Ratiu. Although interesting cultural articles appear in the weekly, *România Litera*, and in the monthly, *22*, their readership is limited to elite intellectual circles. In contrast, there are numerous party affiliated and extremist newspapers, although only *România Mare* has a mass weekly circulation, reputed to be oscillating between 50 00 to 500 000[53].

Interestingly, despite their diametrically opposed positions, both the state-controlled and independent media often shared a pattern of reporting. Although limited resources frequently reduced news to press conference statements and prevented informative reports on major topics, the independent press consistently failed to analyse the cause of government crises. Paradoxically, exposure of

---

[52] Transmission power for independent local radio stations was limited to 80 kilowatts, although those with their own transmitters broadcast at about 100 kilowatts. Ibid. Carey, Henry, F., 'From Big Lie to Small Lies: State Mass Media Dominance in Post-Communist Romania', p. 25.
[53] Ibid. Carey, Henry, F., 'From Big Lie to Small Lies: State Mass Media Dominance in Post-Communist Romania', pp. 32-33.

corruption was favourable to the PDSR because it justified both disgust with, and lack of involvement in, politics. In addition, no attempt was made to discover the real cause of the 1990 ethnic riots in Tîrgu Mures[54]. Moreover, the presentation of UDMR proposals for limited local autonomy as inevitably leading to secession, legitimated the ethnification of political discourse and discouraged compromise.

State-controlled mass media failed to investigate numerous contemporary issues such as Romania's covert support for Serbia; the dismissal and detention of over one hundred elected opposition Mayors between 1992 and 1996; the re-emergence of fascism; and the plight of the Roma population. The information it did provide reinforced cultural and ethnic stereotypes. Economic failure was blamed on hostile foreign forces and prejudice against the Roma and Magyar minorities fostered[55]. Mis-information and boring news bulletins successfully demobilised the majority of the population and promoted distrust towards and disillusion with state institutions amongst those active in civil society. The mass apathy and cynicism thus created prevented the formation of a critical public opinion and hindered the development of civil society.

The PDSR employed the state control of the mass media inherited from the former regime to consolidate existing social and ethnic cleavages and popular distrust of the state. This policy limited individual identification with the democratic system and threatened democratic consolidation. The 1996 electoral success of

---

[54] Between 19-20 March, 1990, violence broke out between the Hungarian and Romanian population of Tîrgu Mures. Three people were killed and 269 arrests were made. Unofficial reports claim eight dead and 300 injured. It seems supporters of *Vatra Românească* incited the violence by convincing rural peasants that the Romanian population in Tîrgu Mures was in danger. The peasants were given copious amounts of alcohol, supplied with clubs and driven in trucks to the town. Ibid. Beckherrn, Eberhard, *Tal der Wende*, pp. 329-330.

[55] In a survey of 1100 adult Romanians carried out in November 1993, 43% believed Romania's economic difficulties were caused by the International Monetary Fund. Despite the PDSR's limited commitment to privatisation, in a survey carried out in September 1994, 60% of those questioned believed the government was 'rather for', or '100% for' privatisation. Ibid. Carey, Henry, F., 'From Big Lie to Small Lies: State Mass Media Dominance in Post-Communist Romania', p. 42.

the Democratic Convention of Romania led to increased media autonomy and the development of a pluralistic press. By June 1997, the Audiovisual Council had approved 148 television licences, 1352 cable licences, and 235 radio licences (mostly for local radio stations). In addition, *PRO-TV*, a joint US-Romanian venture, now reaches 68% of Romanian territory. Other private television stations include *Amerom*, *Prima TV* and *Antena*, but they do not as yet have naitonal coverage[56]. However, it has proved difficult to change established patterns of reporting, and increased autonomy has also led to an increase in extremist press. But, although the media has the potential to both further and hinder the development of a democratic civil society in Romania, the emergence of a more varied, independent media landscape is a positive development.

5.3: The Role of the Church

The power of the Church, both institutional and spiritual, was a challenge to the Communist claim to represent absolute truth and knowledge. As a result, during the period of Communist rule, the Church suffered repression and was co-opted into supporting the system. The nature of this cooperation was not only dependent on the nature of the regime, but also on the Church confession. In contrast to the Roman Catholic Church, which has a non-national centre of power, the Orthodox Church relies on a national power base, and to consolidate its position encourages nationalism. The Orthodox Church also subordinated itself to the secular authority of the state in political matters. This fostered the evolution of a close relationship between the Orthodox Church and the national state. Thus, the Orthodox Church was more susceptible to pressure to cooperate with the Communist regime than the Roman Catholic. Whatever the form of cooperation, to provide moral guidance to society during the uncertainty of transformation, the Church must first come to terms with its own past. Only if this occurs can it present an example of moral integrity and tolerance which can help

---

[56] Gross, Peter, 'Inching toward Integrity', *Transitions*, Vol. 5, No. 3, March 1998, p. 82.

individuals regain a sense of moral balance and further the development of a tolerant civil society.

5.3.1: Roman Catholic Conservatism in Hungary

The majority of the Hungarian population, approximately 65%, are baptised Roman Catholics[57]. Five hundred thousand people, 0.2% of the population, belong to the Greek-Catholic Church, 5.3% are Calvinists, 4% are Lutherans, 2.6% belong to the Orthodox Church, and 43 000 are Jewish[58]. The Hungarian regime did not instrumentalise the Church, as happened in Romania, nor did it engage in systematic persecution, as occurred in Czechoslovakia. In contrast, the Hungarian authorities were prepared to allow the Church a certain amount of independence. Despite this, by 1980 there were only 3600 Catholic priests in Hungary, and of these, only 2800 were active. They served 2000 Latin rite parishes and 150 Uniate, or Greek-Catholic, parishes[59].

The Rabbinical Jewish Seminary in Budapest continued functioning and Hungary remains the only country in Europe to possess a Jewish Seminary authorised to train Rabbis. In 1980, the Seminary had one Czech, 3 Russian and 13 Hungarian students[60]. It was a centre of independent thought and maintained an important network of contacts both within and without Hungary. Roman Catholic schools were nationalised, but those staff who came from religious orders were retained and paid by the state[61]. Thus, Hungary was the only country in which the Church remained involved in the education system. It was also permitted to build new Churches, publish religious materials, increase contacts to western Churches and had freedom of appointment. However, in return for this relative independence, the Church was expected to refrain from openly challenging the regime. So, while individual priests and local committees offered support to conscientious objectors to military service, the Church refused to give official approval for

---

[57] Bugajski, Janusz, Pollack, Maxine, *East European Fault Lines*, Westview Press 1989, p. 149.
[58] *Der Fischer Weltalmanach 1990*, Fischer Taschenbuch Verlag 1989, p. 546.
[59] Ibid. Bugajski, Janusz, Pollack, Maxine, *East European Fault Lines*, p. 149.
[60] Ibid. Bugajski, Janusz, Pollack, Maxine, *East European Fault Lines*, p. 174.
[61] Ibid. Bugajski, Janusz, Pollack, Maxine, *East European Fault Lines*, p. 149.

such activities[62]. Indeed, in June 1982 the Church suspended Father Gyorgy Bulanyi, who had supported the founding of pacifist groups and assisted those who objected to military service[63]. Similarly, while Cardinal Mindszenty's ten year residence in the US Embassy in Budapest created a focus for opposition and demonstrated the limits of the regime's power, the Church did not prevent his exile to Austria in 1975[64].

The Catholic Church could play an important role in restoring moral standards, but its adherence to a rather old-fashioned, national-conservative view of society and nationhood has limited its relevance and thereby its potential to influence contemporary Hungarian society. The Church adheres to an outdated ideal of a Christian nation and society which is no longer applicable to modern Hungary. This is not only demonstrated by its ambiguous attitude towards anti-Semitism and the Roma population, but also by the compulsory religious education programme at school. In promoting compulsory religious education, the Church aimed to ensure Hungarian children were taught Christian morals as a means of reviving the Hungarian nation. This is legitimate, but in its promotion, the Church deliberately ignored the existence of other religions and nationalities. The exclusion of sections of the Hungarian population in this manner did nothing to further national understanding or tolerance.

In addition, the Church's links to the national-conservative Christian Democratic People's Party, KDNP, presents an opportunity to exercise political influence. The KDNP also aims to promote Christian values as a means of reviving the Hungarian nation. It draws most support from poor Catholic voters in rural eastern Hungary who are engaged in the most physical forms of labour. This voter base is stable, but limited[65]. The emphasis on

---

[62] Judt, Tony, 'The Dilemmas of Dissidence: The Politics of Opposition in East-Central Europe', *East European Politics and Societies*, Vol. 2, No. 2, Spring 1988, p. 210.
[63] Ibid. Bugajski, Janusz, Pollack, Maxine, *East European Fault Lines*, p. 150.
[64] Brown, J., F., *Eastern Europe and Communist Rule*, Duke University Press 1988, p. 73.
[65] In the 1990 elections, the KDNP gained 6.46% of the vote, and in the 1996 elections, 7.03%. Kipke, Rüdiger, 'Etabliert, aber nicht verwurzelt? Ungarns

Christian values and narrow voter base, means the KDNP is viewed by many as a Catholic lobby. Popular disapproval of a political role for the Church has further limited its ability to influence Hungarian society. The Hungarian Church leaders' request for representation in the Hungarian Parliament has been rejected by all parties[66].

In this way, the Church's potential to re-establish moral and spiritual balance in Hungarian society has been largely lost, but healthy scepticism and critical analysis are important elements of civil society. Although the Church's own actions may be somewhat ambiguous, public reaction to them has demonstrated civil society is active. In this limited sense, the Church has had a positive influence on the development of civil society in Hungary.

5.3.2: Czech Secularism

The majority of the Czech population are nominally Roman Catholic. However, the Protestant Hussite tradition has strongly influenced religious beliefs and the population is highly secularised. The Communist regime legally recognised eighteen Churches and religious communities, but it controlled all their activities. The State Office for Religious Affairs controlled Church finances, property, publications, contacts with western Churches, and also supervised religious education. All clerical appointments had to be approved by the Office, which could also withdraw licences[67]. The regime attempted to increase its control further by founding *Pacem in Terris*, a pro-regime group within the Catholic clergy. However, in March 1982 the Vatican proscribed the organisation and Cardinal Tomášek refused to recognise those priests who had joined it. The resultant collapse of relations between the regime and the Vatican led to an increase in the number of priests serving prison terms and 30 000 parish clergy positions being left vacant by 1985. In addition, only three out of thirteen diocese had Bishops[68].

Paradoxically, the continued persecution of the Church increased its popular support and awakened interest in religious

---

Parlamentsparteien und ihre Wähler', *Südosteuropa Mitteilungen*, Vol. 37, No. 2, 1997.
[66] *RFE/RL Newsline*, Vol. 2, No. 10, Part II, 16 January 1998.
[67] Ibid. Bugajski, Janusz, Pollack, Maxine, *East European Fault Lines*, p. 152.
[68] Ibid. Brown, J., F., *Eastern Europe and Communist Rule*, p. 310.

matters. Thus, the Czech Catholic *samizdat* was one of the most vigorous in Eastern Europe. As a result, at the start of transformation, the Catholic Church enjoyed respect and was in a position to play an important role in the reconstruction of the moral and spiritual balance in the Czech Republic.

The Czech population's perception of the Church's proper role has been strongly influenced by the Hussite movement and does not include a political role. Thus, the Church is reluctant to involve itself overtly in politics. The wide-spread perception of politics as an immoral pursuit has also tempered the Church's willingness to involve itself directly in Czech political life. Although the Christian Democratic Party draws most of its support from the Catholic vote, it does not represent a Church lobby. Its emphasis on a revival of Christian values is based on the generally accepted need to re-establish standards of behaviour in public life rather than on religious considerations. While absence from the political stage has limited the Church's potential to influence transformation directly, it ensures the Church's main concern remains the spiritual and physical well-being of the population. However, the Church's inability to combat popular intolerance towards the Roma population emphasises its limited possibilities to influence Czech society. Protests at the anti-Semitic elements contained in religious education also demonstrate the Church's rather ambiguous attitude towards intolerance of minority groups[69].

Despite this, the public refusal of prominent clerics, such as Cardinal Tomášek, to accept the authority of the Communist regime enabled the Church to preserve its independence and maintain its integrity. Some of the independent structures necessary for the development of civil society were therefore preserved amongst those who continued to support the Church during the Communist regime. The collapse of Communism caused confusion and exposed the moral vacuum present in Czech society. The necessity of filling the ideological and spiritual vacuum with meaning presented the Church with an opportunity to increase its influence over Czech

---

[69] *RFE/RL Newsline*, Vol. 1, No. 156, Part II, 10 November 1997. A student letter complaining about anti-Semitic elements in religious education was published in *Lidove Noviny* on 7 November, 1997.

society and politics. Ironically, the structures necessary for the development of civil society which the Church's resistance to the Communist regime helped preserve, now work to limit its influence. An excessive increase in influence has also been prevented by the population's secularism. Thus, the checks and balances inherent in civil society in the Czech Republic ensure the Church remains a spiritual, rather than politically orientated institution. The Church's acceptance of this role has furthered the development of civil society and democratic consolidation in the Czech Republic.

5.3.3: Romanian Orthodox Complicity

In contrast, the Romanian Orthodox Church has continued its active engagement in politics as a means of retaining its considerable power and influence. Romania has a population of approximately 22 million, of whom 90% are ethnic Romanians. Of these, 87% belong to the Romanian Orthodox Church and 1% to the Greek-Catholic Church. The 5% of the population who are Catholic are either Hungarian or Swabian Germans, while the 3.5% who belong to the Reformed, or Calvinist, Church, are all ethnic Hungarians[70]. Thus, in Romania, ethnic and religious divides combine to strengthen social cleavages. This represents a threat to the development of civil society and democratic consolidation. The Church can either contribute to divisions or try to limit these cleavages and therefore has a direct effect on democratic consolidation.

The Romanian Churches were generally compliant with the Communist regime and acceded to its wishes. The Patriarch of the Orthodox Church supported the regime from its inception and instigated a Purge to silence internal opposition[71]. Resistance was therefore left to individual pastors and priests, such as Father Gheorghe Calciu-Dumitreasa, who was imprisoned for a total of twenty years for subversion[72]. However, collaboration and complicity was not confined to the Orthodox Church. The

---

[70] Dutu, Alexandru, 'Kirche und Staat im heutigen Rumänien', *Südosteuropa Jahrbuch*, No. 25, 1994, p. 127.
[71] Brogan, Patrick, *Eastern Europe 1939-1989*, Bloomsbury 1990, p. 220.
[72] Ibid. Brown, J., F., *Eastern Europe and Communist Rule*, p. 288.

Reformed Church Bishop, Tibor Barth, and the Lutheran Bishop, Zoltan Kaldy, were both members of Ceausescu's government[73]. It is therefore ironic, but not surprising, that it was the dismissal of the non-conformist pastor László Tökés from the Timisoara parish by the Bishop of Oradea, Laszlo Papp, which provided the catalyst for the December Revolution[74].

Generally, the minority Churches offered more resistance to the regime. They were aided in this by their links to Churches outside Romania. In an attempt to abolish Papal jurisdiction over Romanian Catholics, the Law of Cults forbade religious bodies to have any connection with foreign religious communities[75]. The Catholic Church's refusal to accept the Law of Cults meant it was tolerated but not legally recognised. The assistance given to the Romanian Baptist Church by its fellow Church in the United States was also a vital link independent of state control. In order to disrupt this liaison, the regime confiscated Bibles sent by the American Baptist Church and recycled them into toilet paper[76]. In contrast, the Jewish community enjoyed relative independence. This was due to Ceausescu's desire to maintain a positive international image and the fact that the small number and advanced age of most indigenous Jews posed little threat to the regime. The Romanian Orthodox Church was unique among religious organisations in its subservience to the Communist regime.

The Orthodox Church has numerous elements in its services, for example the use of archaic language, which ordinary Church-goers cannot understand, and the priests' disappearance behind the Iconostasis for the most important parts of the service, which aim to maintain the mystical nature of religion and belief. In combination with the Orthodox emphasis on obedience and loyalty to the secular state, such mysticism has helped maintain the Church's omnipotent influence over the Romania population, especially in rural areas.

---

[73] Ibid. Bugajski, Janusz, Pollack, Maxine, *East European Fault Lines*, p. 163.
[74] Ironically, Pastor Tökés took over the Bishopric of Oradea from Papp after the Revolution. Ibid. Beckherrn, Eberhard, *Tal der Wende*, p. 285.
[75] Shafir, Michael, *Romania: Politics, Economics and Society*, Frances Pinter Publishers 1985, pp. 154-155.
[76] Ibid. Brown, J., F., *Eastern Europe and Communist Rule*, p. 288.

Such power is open to abuse and has often been employed to further the strategic interests of the state and the Church.

The Communist take-over and initial policy of sovietisation led to an onslaught of russification in all areas of Romanian life which did not spare the Orthodox Church. However, the Church's aim to be the sole spiritual representative for the whole Romanian nation tempted it into cooperation with the national Communist regime. The Church hoped this would ensure its predominate position and enable it to rid Romania of other religious confessions. The Orthodox Church's explicit Romanian nationalism was successfully combined with the chauvinistic national Communist ideology of the regime. The Orthodox Church complied with the persecution of the Greek-Catholic Church and, after its official reunification with the 'Mother Church', gained the majority of its possessions[77]. In addition, the anti-religious campaign of the 1980's was aimed at minority Churches rather than the Orthodox Church. Thus, in September 1984, the Second Baptist Church of Oradea, with a congregation of 2000, the largest in Europe, was demolished[78]. The Orthodox Church's close relationship with the regime was embarrassingly exposed by Patriarch Teoctist's public address on 19 December, 1989, in which he praised Ceausescu and the methods chosen to deal with the 'hooligans' in Timisoara. Although the 74 year old Patriarch abdicated on 18 January, 1990, he was reinstated on 4 April, 1990 during the Easter celebrations[79].

The Romanian Orthodox Church has yet to confront these aspects of its past or deal effectively with the problematic elements of its religious philosophy. Indeed, the Orthodox Church aims to retain its dominant position, political power and close relationship with the state. This is demonstrated by its plans to build a huge complex consisting of a cathedral, hotel and conference centre in Bucharest. The estimated cost of the project is $130 million, and the Church proposes using public funds to build it. Despite the

---

[77] For a detailed analysis, see Cipaianu, George, 'The Romanian Greek-Catholic Church under Communism', pp. 370-380. In Craciun, Maria, Ghitta, Ovidiu, (Eds.), *Ethnicity and Religion in Central and Eastern Europe*, Cluj University Press 1995.
[78] Ibid. Bugajski, Janusz, Pollack, Maxine, *East European Fault Lines*, p. 165.
[79] Ibid. Beckherrn, Eberhard, *Tal der Wende*, p. 285.

public outcry, the Church claims the proposed use of public funds is justified because 86% of Romanians are Orthodox[80].

This attitude is concurrent with the Orthodox Church's reluctance to reject its exclusive nationalist ideology and accept a role which restricts its political influence and limits its ties to the state. As a result, it does not preach tolerance of ethnic and religious minorities, supporting instead their assimilation into the Romanian nation and the Romanian Orthodox Church. Although the Orthodox Church was discredited by its links to Ceausescu's dictatorship, the moral confusion and search for spiritual guidance which accompanied the collapse of Communism revived its potential to influence Romanian society. However, the actions and teachings of the Romanian Orthodox Church have not furthered democratisation or the development of civil society. In view of this, its continued attempts to maintain political influence and consolidate its influence over sections of the population is a cause for concern and represents a threat to the development of civil society and democratic consolidation.

5.4: Ethnic Prejudice and Nationalism

The vacuum left behind by the collapse of Communism and the confusion and uncertainty caused by transformation has increased the attractiveness of nationalism for sections of the Hungarian, Czech and Romanian populations. This tendency has been encouraged by the necessity of national regeneration. Promoting national pride and unity can revitalise and unite populations during extraordinary situations, but it also offers extreme chauvinistic parties the opportunity to instrumentalise nationalism and consolidate existing ethnic prejudices and social tensions. The ethnic tapestry which makes up the states of Central and Eastern Europe means the exclusive nationalism propagated by such parties can only serve to divide society and isolate minority groups. Thus, solving the problem of ethnic prejudice and exclusive nationalism

---

[80] *Transitions*, Vol. 4, No. 6, November 1997, p. 11.

is vitally important for the development of civil society and long-term democratic consolidation.

5.4.1: The Roma

The Roma represent the largest minority group in the Central and East European region. They are subject to wide-spread intolerance and prejudice which contribute to their social isolation and prevent integration. The intolerance and ethnic exclusivity promoted by the discrimination of such a large section of society, and the social, political and economic exclusion this entails, hinders the cross-cutting social networks which are vital for the development of civil society and long-term democratic consolidation.

In comparison with Romania and Hungary, the Czech Roma population, numbering between 150 000-300 000, is relatively small[81]. But the Roma exist at the edge of Czech society; tolerated, but not accepted as an integral part of the Czech population. The Czech Citizenship Law resulted in approximately 110 000 Roma losing their citizenship rights[82]. Although modified, the Council of Europe has criticised the problems the law poses to some ethnic minorities and the discriminatory attitude of some bureaucrats[83]. The Roma in the Czech Republic occupy the margins of society and suffer daily, systematic discrimination. Unemployment rates are ten times higher for Roma than non-Roma. In addition, 80% of Roma children are automatically sent to special schools for children with learning difficulties, regardless of their actual academic performance[84]. The Roma's untenable position was reflected in the response to a television programme which implied asylum seekers in Canada enjoyed a better standard of living than in the Czech Republic. Following the programme, nearly 1100 Czech citizens, the vast majority Roma, requested refugee status in Canada. The

---

[81] Druker, Jeremy, 'Present but unaccounted for', *Transitions*, Vol. 4, No. 4, September 1997, p. 23.
[82] Petrova, Dimitrina, 'Get Out, You Stinking Gypsy', *Transitions*, Vol. 4, No. 4, September 1997, p. 21.
[83] *RFE/RL Newsline*, Vol. 1, No. 123, Part II, 23 September 1997.
[84] Helton, Arthur, C., 'Should the West open its Doors to the East's Roma?', *Transitions*, Vol. 4, No. 7, December 1997, p. 77.

Czech Republic now occupies third place among the countries of origin of people seeking asylum in Canada[85]. Indeed, in the eastern town of Ostrava, Czech officials seriously considered giving Roma families money for air tickets to leave the country[86]. Following international protest the plan was abandoned, but it demonstrates that prejudice against the Roma is socially acceptable in the Czech Republic.

For a long time, the problems associated with such wide-spread prejudice were not taken seriously by the Czech government. However, a survey published by the *Focus Agency* on 22 January, 1998, exposed the deep-seated ethnic prejudice present in Czech society. Of those asked, almost one-third were not in favour of co-existence with the Roma, and 14% believed the Roma should be expelled from the country. Two-thirds were satisfied with the way the Roma were depicted in the Czech media, although on the same day the survey was published, a petition entitled 'Several Words' was handed to the Council for National Minorities and the Council for Radio and Television complaining about the Roma's depiction and demanding the media help create a democratic society tolerant and protective of ethnic minorities[87].

The Roma's lack of integration has created an isolated group within the population which is prevented from taking part in Czech social and economic activity and has therefore fallen into a poverty trap. The exodus of the Roma population not only damages the Czech Republic's chances of joining the European Union, but also represents an irreplaceable loss of national potential. The potential for existing prejudice to develop into violent nationalism was demonstrated by the racially motivated killing of a Sudanese exchange student in Prague by two 'skinheads' on 8 November, 1997[88]. Indeed, since 1989, Czech 'skinheads' have caused the deaths of nine Roma. In one incident in the western Czech town of Pisek, at least 18 'skinheads' attacked a group of Roma. Four of the terrified Roma jumped into a river and one drowned after two of the attackers prevented him from leaving the water. The 1996 US State

---

[85] *RFE/RL Newsline*, Vol. 1, No. 122, Part II, 22 September 1997.
[86] *RFE/RL Newsline*, Vol. 1, No. 145, Part II, 23 October 1997.
[87] *RFE/RL Newsline*, Vol. 2, No. 15, Part II, 23 January 1998.
[88] *RFE/RL Newsline*, Vol. 1, No. 156, Part II, 10 November 1997.

A Democratic and Civil Society 485

Department country report on Human Rights noted that since 1994, assaults on Roma in the Czech Republic have increased six-fold[89]. However, the 5000 people, including Ministers and Deputies, who attended the demonstration called for 10 November, 1997, to protest the Prague killing, indicate the lack of support extreme, violent nationalism enjoys amongst the Czech population[90]. Furthermore, in an article published on 15 November, 1997, in *Dnes*, Vaclav Havel appealed to the Czech population to fight racism, calling it:

> '...*a destructive demon whose danger is being underestimated.*'[91]

He also urged the government to introduce legislation banning racist and xenophobic movements. The government's call on the Roma to stay in the Czech Republic and on the Czech population to improve relations with the Roma community bears witness to the state's increasing determination to combat ethnic discrimination. A special Commission of twelve Ministers has been called together to formulate plans aimed at integrating the Roma more successfully into Czech society[92]. Official acceptance of the necessity to overcome socially accepted prejudice and the introduction of government sponsored measures aimed at combating it will encourage the tolerance vital for the development of a tolerant civil society.

The Roma population in Hungary is larger than that in the Czech Republic. The 1990 Hungarian census gave the number of gypsies, according to mother tongue, as 48 072. However, minority organisations, using ethnicity, estimate the number at 600 000[93]. The true size of the Roma population lies between 550 000 and 800

---

[89] Four of the offenders have since been sentenced. Ibid. Petrova, Dimitrina, 'Get Out, You Stinking Gypsy', *Transitions*, p. 19.
[90] *RFE/RL Newsline*, Vol. 1, No. 157, Part II, 11 November 1997.
[91] *RFE/RL Newsline*, Vol. 1, No. 161, Part II, 17 November 1997.
[92] *RFE/RL Newsline*, Vol. 1, No. 149, Part II, 30 October 1997.
[93] Sterbling, Anton, 'Ethnische Strukturen und ethnische Parteien', *Südosteuropa*, Vol. 45, No. 8, 1996, p. 556.

000[94]. Interestingly, according to the official census, 98.5%, or 10 222 529 of the total Hungarian population of 10 347 823, can be viewed as Magyars[95]. This is higher than the estimated level of ethnic homogeneity of 92.0%, and leads to the conclusion that ethnic minorities in Hungary are highly linguistically and culturally assimilated[96]. Despite this, the Hungarian population remains prejudiced and intolerant towards the Roma.

In a public opinion survey, 28% of those asked stated 'criminal behaviour' was the main reason for their intolerance of the gypsy population. A further 21% gave begging, prodigality and parasitism as the main reason for their prejudice; while 11% named the high rate of alcoholism amongst the gypsy population. Indeed, a study carried out in Borsod-Abaiy County showed 40% of all burglaries, between 60-65% of all thefts, approximately half of all disturbances and rapes, and between 30-40% of all attempted homicides were carried out by members of the Roma community[97]. Although this would seem to vindicate the population's prejudice, the main reason behind the Roma's criminal activity is their continued social and economic marginalisation, which forces the majority to live a life of poverty.

The Roma population has a birth rate approximately twice as high as ethnic Hungarians. Approximately 75% of the Roma only speak Hungarian, but a survey in 1971 revealed 39% of all adult gypsies were illiterate. Furthermore, only 37% of gypsy children finish compulsory schooling. The Roma's low level of education and loss of traditional skills, caused by the Communist regime's settlement policy, forces the majority to accept unskilled work. Although unskilled workers account for only 12% of the total population, they account for 50% of the Roma population[98]. Thus, a

---

[94] Ibid. Jeremy, Druker, 'Present but unaccounted for', *Transitions*, p. 23.
[95] Ibid. Sterbling, Anton, 'Ethnische Strukturen und ethnische Parteien in Südosteuropa', *Südosteuropa*, p. 556.
[96] von Beyme, Klaus, *Systemwechsel in Osteuropa*, Suhrkamp 1994, p. 162.
[97] Toma, Peter, A., *Socialist Authority: The Hungarian Experience*, Praeger 1988, p. 251. Originally in Hann, Endre, 'Gypsies in Public Opinion', *Magyar Hirlap*, 6 July 1985, and Porlolov, Albert, 'The Situation of the Gypsy Population in Borsod-Abaiy-Zemplen County', *Borsod Review*, No. 1, 1985, pp. 72-78.
[98] Ibid. Toma, Peter, A., *Socialist Authority: The Hungarian Experience*, Praeger 1988, p. 250. Originally in *Mozgo_Vilag*, No. 6, 1985, pp. 74-77.

large section of the Roma population has experienced unemployment as a result of transformation, but, as unskilled workers, they have little prospect of finding a new job.

The emergence of over one hundred Roma organisations after 1989 was an example of the community's social organisation, but also indicated its divisions. The election of a national spokesman at the conference of Hungarian Roma organisations in April 1995, demonstrated the increasing cooperation between the Roma and the formation of the networks vital to civil society. State funding of two regular television and radio programmes, as well as three Roma newspapers, has also contributed to the Roma's increasing network of social, cultural and economic contacts[99].

Concern to present an example to neighbouring countries which have large Magyar minorities has led the Hungarian government to guarantee its minorities equal rights and collective participation in public life. On 13 December, 1994, the first elections for self-governing minorities were held. Out of a total of 639 elected persons, 423 were Roma[100]. However, the government decision to postpone the election of 13 minorities Deputies to the Hungarian Parliament from May 1998, when national elections are due to take place, until October 1998 or even the year 2001, has caused protest[101]. Self-governance has enabled the approximately 400 Roma councils to direct funds into education, health and training programmes, but has also consolidated social divisions and increase ethnic isolation[102]. Thus, more government sponsored education programmes are required to combat the Roma's social exclusion and public prejudice against them.

---

[99] Réti, György, 'Hungary and the Problem of National Minorities', *The Hungarian Quarterly*, Vol. 36, No. 139, August 1995, p. 77.

[100]. The Hungarian Constitution states that ethnic minorities, 'are a constituent element of the state'. It also provides for collective participation in public life and for wide-ranging use of minority languages in education and culture. Ibid, Réti, György, 'Hungary and the Problem of National Minorities', *The Hungarian Quarterly*, pp. 75-77.

[101] *RFE/RL Newsline*, Vol. 2, No. 10, Part II, 16 January 1998. Also *RFE/RL Newsline*, Vol. 2, No. 18, Part II, 28 January 1998.

[102] Roe, Sarah, 'Progressive Inaction in Hungary', *Transitions*, Vol. 4, No. 4, September 1997, p. 33.

The Hungarian government has embarked on programmes aimed at overcoming the Roma's disadvantaged social and economic position, with particular attention being paid to employment and welfare related programmes. However, the Labour Minister has admitted that more positive action is needed to provide jobs for the Roma[103]. The government has also initiated steps to improve the Roma's level of education and housing standards, but renovation is not always feasible and lack of alternative housing often forces resettlement into temporary accommodation[104]. Despite attempts to improve conditions, in his address to a Conference concerned with the situation of the Roma in Hungary, Prime Minister Gyula Horn admitted the position of the Roma has not substantially changed[105].

Romania describes itself as a unified Nation State, but its population is not ethnically homogenous. The 1992 census showed that 10.6% of the population belong to minority ethnic groups and communicate using a total of twenty six mother tongues[106]. The census gave the number of Roma as 409 723, approximately 1.8% of the population[107]. However, Roma representatives estimate the figure at between 2-2.5 million, approximately 7.5% of the total population[108]. Even according to official figures, the Roma population has almost doubled since 1977. Thus, the Roma probably constitute the largest ethnic minority in Romania.

The Roma are first mentioned in 1385 in a Certification of the Monastery Vodita, where they appear as a 'gift of un-free

---

[103] *RFE/RL Newsline*, Vol. 1, No. 168, Part II, 26 November 1997.

[104] Some 300 Roma demonstrated in Szekesfehervar to protest plans to remove 13 Roma families from a dilapidated building and place them in container homes. *RFE/RL Newsline*, Vol. 1, No. 166, Part II, 24 November 1997.

[105] *RFE/RL Newsline*, Vol. 1, No. 168, Part II, 26 November 1997.

[106] Remmel, Franz, 'Kei oh tschal – Wohin führt der Weg? Die Roma in Rumänien', *Südosteuropa Mitteilungen*, Vol. 36, No. 3, 1996, p. 229.

[107] An different official study estimated the number of Roma at 1 010 000. Ibid. Sterbling, Anton, 'Ethnische Strukturen und ethnische Parteien in Südosteuropa', pp. 553-554.

[108] Ibid. Remmel, Franz, 'Kei oh tschal – Wohin führt der Weg? Die Roma in Rumänien', *Südosteuropa Mitteilungen*, p. 230.

gypsies'[109]. They were serfs, or *robi*, and possessed no rights until their bound status was lifted in 1856. Originally, the Roma could gain freedom by marrying a Romanian but, in 1785, the law was changed so that Romanians entering into a mixed marriage also became serfs[110]. Since their arrival in Romania over 600 hundred year ago, the Roma have remained at the lower end of Romanian society, constituting the poorest and most disadvantaged social and ethnic group. It has been estimated that 87.4% of all Roma exist below what are considered 'normal' living standards in Romania and, of these, 63% live below the Romanian poverty line. Only 8.5% manage to 'put something' aside, and a mere 4.1%, commonly those who have returned from western Europe, claim they live well[111]. In view of this, it is not surprising that the Roma are involved in wide-spread criminal activity.

In the first quarter of 1995 the Romanian crime rate increased by 18%. But in contrast to popular belief, the Roma do not constitute the majority of criminals. In 1990, of the 44 298 criminals sentenced, only 3910 were Roma. This represents 0.21% of the whole population and a mere 0.15% of the Roma population. Although in 1994, 10% of all crime in Romania was committed by Roma, this figure is merely a reflection of the general increase in crime since the fall of Ceausescu. On 8 December, 1994, General Costica Voicu stated that, during 1994, there were four murders and four rapes reported each day[112].

The widely held belief that the Roma are primarily responsible for the dramatic increase in crime is simply not true. However, the type of crime with which Roma are most commonly associated; petty theft, such as stealing fire wood or flowers from graves to sell; accosting persons on the road; and disturbances such as fist

---

[109] Certificate from 3.10.1385. State Archives, Bucharest. Reg.-Nr. 6894. Ibid. Remmel, Franz, 'Kei oh tschal – Wohin führt der Weg? Die Roma in Rumänien', p. 230.
[110] Decree from Alexandru Mavrocordat, Slobornicescul hrisov, 23.12.1785. State Archives, Bucharest. Ibid. Remmel, Franz, 'Kei oh tschal – Wohin führt der Weg? Die Roma in Rumänien', p. 230.
[111] Ibid. Remmel, Franz, 'Kei oh tschal – Wohin führt der Weg? Die Roma in Rumänien', p. 240.
[112] Ibid. Remmel, Franz, 'Kei oh tschal – Wohin führt der Weg? Die Roma in Rumänien', p. 242.

fights in cemeteries or hospitals, are often topics of public discussion due to the irritation they cause. The extreme nationalist parties manipulate this to fuel prejudice against the Roma population. A study has shown that only 21% of the Romanian population is favourably inclined towards the Roma population, while 74% are negatively, or very negatively inclined[113]. Moreover, 24% of the Roma asked were not favourably inclined to other Roma[114].

The Roma's low level of education, desperate poverty, numerous children, no permanent work, or no employment at all, prevents social mobility and reinforces ethnic stereotypes. In Romania, 44% of adult Roma men and 43% of adult Roma women are illiterate. Of the Roma of school age up to the age of ten, 18.8% have never been to school, 15.5% only go to school occasionally, and 14.2% have stopped going to school all together. Lack of education reduces employment opportunities and has resulted in only 16.2% of all Roma working in a modern profession. But, only 3.95% of the Roma population still possess a traditional profession, such as blacksmith, carpenter, plumber or 'rag-and-bone' man. The majority, 79.95%, were employed as unskilled labourers on collective state farms which have been dissolved[115].

Without proper education it is impossible to find work and climb out of poverty. Roma children are prevented from attending school because they are needed to work to help feed the family. Roma girls tend to marry very young, often at 15 or 16, after which they cease to attend school. In addition, the head of the family has an almost despotic power of authority over other family members. Educated children find it easier to disregard such authority, which leads to a breakdown in the power structure of the extended family hierarchy. As a result, elder, less educated, members of the Roma

---

[113] Ibid. Remmel, Franz, 'Kei oh tschal – Wohin führt der Weg? Die Roma in Rumänien', p. 239.
[114] 'Sentimente nefavourabile fata de tigani', *Evenimentul Zilei*, No. 404, 19.10.93. Ibid. Remmel, Franz, 'Kei oh tschal – Wohin führt der Weg? Die Roma in Rumänien', p. 245.
[115] Ibid. Remmel, Franz, 'Kei oh tschal – Wohin führt der Weg? Die Roma in Rumänien', pp. 245-246. From 'Populatia Romilor I/II. Situatia socio-economica, Cu sprijinul Reprezentantei UNICEF in România, Bucaresti 1993'.

community tend to view education as a threat and do not always encourage the younger generation to excel at school.

However, the complex structures of contemporary society and economy make education essential. Lack of education has widened the social and economic gap between the Roma and the rest of the Romanian population. The wide-spread prejudice held against the Roma serves to maintain and consolidate this social and ethnic cleavage. This prevents the development of the tolerance and social networks which are vital elements of civil society.

Although the Roma community has never been politically or socially united, the political and social organisation demonstrated by the Democratic Union of the Roma in Romania bears witness to the increase in independent social networks. The exclusive ethnic nature of the organisation, however, tends to consolidate the ethnic and social cleavages it aims to overcome. In contrast, the Democratic Union of Roma and Gypsies, draws its members from the Romanian speaking Roma and the Hungarian speaking *cziganyok*, or gypsies[116]. Such cross-ethnic cooperation has the potential to positively influence the future development of Romanian civil society.

The reasons behind the wide-spread social rejection of the Roma, not only in Romania, but also in Hungary and the Czech Republic, are manifold. A history of disadvantage has trapped many Roma in a life determined by traditional structures of patriarchy which are incapable of adapting to the requirements of a modern society. Lack of education and loss of traditional skills following forced settlement by the Communist regimes meant the Roma took positions as unskilled labourers. It is precisely these positions which have been hardest hit by transformation. The miserable situation of the Roma leads to the conclusion that without long-term state financed programmes, they will remain caught in ever worsening poverty which will increase ethnic tension and social cleavages. Not only will this lead to an enormous loss of economic and cultural potential, but also to the slower development

---

[116] Ibid. Remmel, Franz, 'Kei oh drom tschal – Wohin führt der Weg? Die Roma in Rumänien', p. 237.

of a cohesive civil society, thus hindering long-term democratic consolidation.

5.4.2: The Magyar Minorities

The other large ethnic minority in Central and Eastern Europe are the Magyar populations who found themselves outside Hungary following the Treaty of Trianon in 1920 and the border changes after the Second World War. An estimated five million Magyar, one third of all ethnic Hungarians do not live in Hungary[117]. After the 1956 Revolution many Hungarians also fled the country. As a result, approximately 50 000 Hungarians live in Austria and between 1-1.5 million in the United States and the rest of western Europe[118]. Approximately 566 741 Magyars live in Slovakia, where they account for 10.8% of the total population, and 345 376 live in Serbia, mostly in the Vojvodina region, where they make up 20% of the local, and 3.5% of the total, population[119]. However, the largest Hungarian minority is found in Romania. In 1991, it was estimated that 1.6 million Magyars were resident in Romania, mostly in Transylvania. Indeed, the Magyar population represents 7.1% of the total Romanian population[120].

The national-Communist ideology propagated by Ceausescu and the regime's specific industrial and employment policies destroyed Transylvania's traditional ethnic structure and balance. The Romanian industrial workers sent into Transylvania from the Regat were especially susceptible to the regime's nationalist and anti-Hungarian propaganda. The Hungarian community was presented as innately revanchist and treated with suspicion.

The Hungarian minority's religion, the majority are Roman Catholic, also drew suspicion. Nearly all the Catholics in Moldavia are of Hungarian descent, and three quarters of all Catholics in Romania are ethnic Hungarians, mostly concentrated in Transylvania. Although the Hungarian minority's religious identity

---

[117] Ibid. Réti, György, 'Hungary and the Problem of National Minorities', p. 70.

[118] Joo, Rudolf, (Ed.), *The Hungarian Minority's Situation in Ceausescu's Romania*, Columbia University Press 1994, p. 27.

[119] Ibid. Sterbling, Anton, 'Ethnische Strukturen und ethnische Parteien', p. 557.

[120] Ibid. Sterbling, Anton, 'Ethnische Strukturen und ethnische Parteien', p. 553, p. 557.

helped preserve cultural identity, it also contributed to their isolation from Romanian society. The regime successfully isolated the Hungarian minority from the Romanian and neighbouring Hungarian population. The State Council Decree No. 225, from 6 December, 1974 was specifically aimed to restrict contacts between Hungary and Translyvania. It forbade Romanian citizens to offer lodgings to any foreigner except direct relatives, but foreigners of ethnic Romanian descent were permitted to stay with any relatives in Romania[121].

The Hungarian minority's crucial role in the December Uprising provided an opportunity to overcome the prejudice cultivated by the Communist regime, but demands for increased local autonomy and self-assured public appearances were perceived as threatening by many ethnic Romanians. Furthermore, the PDSR and extreme nationalist parties took advantage of the distorted nationalism which Ceasusescu had cultivated and continued its manipulation. The propagation of anti-Hungarian propaganda and extreme, chauvinistic nationalism was not only employed as a means to disguise weak economic policy, but also to maintain tension between the Hungarian and Romanian population. This has reached surreal extremes in the Transylvanian town of Cluj, where the extreme nationalist Mayor, Gheorghe Funar, has forbidden the Hungarian Consulate from flying the Hungarian flag and ordered park benches be painted red, yellow and blue, the colours of the Romanian national flag. Funar is also responsible for the pseudo-archaeological dig in front of the statue of the Hungarian King Mathias, which is itself surrounded by Romanian flags. The conflict such action provokes facilitates the maintenance of social and ethnic divisions formed under Ceausescu which prevent the cross-cutting networks required for the development of civil society.

Despite these problems, the Magyar community has successfully organised itself socially and politically. After the 1990 elections, the Democratic Federation of Hungarians in Romania was able to enter the Romanian Parliament as the second strongest opposition party. In the 1992 elections, the majority of the ethnic Hungarian

---

[121] Ibid. Roo, Rudolf, (Ed.), *The Hungarian Minority's Situation in Ceausescu's Romania*, p. 47.

community voted for the Federation and it gained 7.46% of the votes[122]. After the 1996 elections, the Hungarian minority fulfilled its potential to influence Romanian politics and became a member of the ruling government coalition. However, the ethnic nature of the organisation tends to consolidate the existing social and ethnic cleavages in Romanian society.

The situation of ethnic Hungarians living as ethnic minorities outside Hungary is a cause of concern for the Hungarian government. Indeed, former Prime Minister Antall stated:

> *'We never said that the minority question was the only factor in interstate relations, but we find it impossible to have good relations with a country that mistreats its Hungarian minority.'*[123]

The Hungarian government's interest in the fate of the minorities is construed as proof of Hungarian irredentism by extreme nationalist parties. Indeed, extreme nationalist Hungarian parties continually place the borders in doubt. In a recent interview, the deputy leader of the Independent Smallholders Party, Sandor Kavassy, stated:

> *'...ethnic borders and political borders must be bought into harmony sooner or later.'*[124]

Although this view is not shared by the majority of the Hungarian political class or population, it nevertheless represents an undercurrent in domestic Hungarian political debate. The Hungarian government's interest in the Magyar minorities is not motivated by irredentism or pure philanthropy, but mainly by concern to ensure European stability. The violation of minority rights in an area where so many ethnic minorities live together could potentially destabilise the entire region. The government also

---

[122] Ibid. Sterbling, Anton, 'Ethnische Strukturen und ethnische Parteien', p. 561.
[123] Cowen Karp, Regina, *Central and Eastern Europe: The Challenge of Transition*, Oxford University Press 1993, p. 135. Original from the Hungarian News Agency. *MTI*, 20.4.91.
[124] *RFE/RL Newsline*, Vol. 1, No. 156, Part II, 10 November 1997.

hopes that by involving itself, the minorities will be encouraged to remain where they are and will not emigrate to Hungary. The Hungarian government has only become involved in the minority debate when minority rights are threatened and is determined not to involve itself in national ethnic conflict. Hungarian involvement is also limited by an unwillingness to become sole protector for all the Hungarian minorities and the Diaspora's own rejection of excessive Hungarian interference. In addition, the domestic Hungarian population gives priority to democratic and economic transformation in Hungary rather than issues concerning the national minorities abroad.

In contrast to ethnic German communities, the Magyar minorities do not wish to return to Hungary[125]. The Hungarians' religious identity and linguistic uniqueness has helped maintain a strong ethnic identity. This is demonstrated by their constant numbers despite nearly seventy years of living as a minority. Therefore, regulation and guarantees ensuring their rights are essential. The suggestion of the Slovak Prime Minister, Vladimir Meciar, to resettle the 600 000 strong Magyar minority in Slovakia to Hungary was unconditionally rejected by the Hungarian government and led to a worsening of Hungarian-Slovak relations[126]. Increasing nationalism and agitation to limit minority rights, especially in Serbia, Slovakia and Romania, could provoke a concurrent increase of nationalism amongst both the Magyar minorities and the domestic Hungarian population. Such mutual escalation could cause regional de-stabilisation and represents a danger to democratic consolidation.

The Basic Treaties Hungary signed with Slovakia in March 1995, and Romania in 1996, regulate and normalise relations, as well as ensuring the rights of the Magyar minorities, and are therefore of great importance. Cooperation between the Hungarian and Romanian Ministries of Justice includes regular exchanges of information and mutual assistance in bringing nationality laws into line with European Union legislation[127]. Such cooperation

---

[125] As a result of emigration, the German community in Romania has decreased by more than 200 000 since 1977.
[126] *RFE/RL Newsline*, Vol. 1, No. 116, Part II, 12 September 1997.
[127] *RFE/RL Newsline*, Vol. 1, No. 124, Part II, 24 September 1997.

demonstrates increasing willingness to work together to deal with issues relating to the Hungarian minority and shows the positive influence efforts to achieve European Union membership can exert. On 3 October, 1997, Hungarian Foreign Minister Laszlo Kovacs stated, engaging in a war of words over minority rights is not in Hungarian interests as it would be:

> '...*unworthy of a country seeking integration in [Euro-Atlantic] organisations*'[128].

NATO and European Union membership can therefore contribute to regional stability and have a positive influence on long-term democratic consolidation.

5.5: NATO and European Union Expansion

Expanding NATO and the European Union (EU) to include the Czech Republic, Hungary and Romania requires the introduction of a democratic, institutional framework which is compatible with NATO and European Union norms. Thus, membership of NATO and the EU can provide the stability and institutional framework which guarantee the individual freedom essential for the development of civil society.

The events of 1989 bought the Cold War to an end, but new dangers and challenges for the democratic states in both Eastern and Western Europe have appeared. The possibility of violent social and ethnic conflict, and the spread of international organised crime are major causes of concern. In addition, the collapse of the Warsaw Pact robbed the military in the East of its only consultative and cooperative forum. Central and East European states feel particularly threatened by such developments and by the instability prevailing in the states of the former Soviet Union, but do not have the capability or resources to establish individual military structures capable of dealing with such threats.

---

[128] *RFE/RL Newsline*, Vol. 1, No. 132, Part II, 6 October 1997.

NATO is the only organisation capable of integrating the Central and East European military into an international security structure which can ensure European stability. Accession to NATO requires a commitment to increased military and defence spending, a difficult decision in the midst of a transformation which demands a general reduction in government spending. It also entails the abandonment of Soviet style military command structures and modernisation of military equipment to meet NATO standards. Thus, membership will place a considerable strain on those countries accepted into the Alliance.

Membership of the European Union offers the opportunity to join European political and economic structures. This not only promises economic benefits, but also increased possibilities of influencing European developments and international affairs. Membership of the European Union also symbolises the recognition of a shared European cultural identity, common values and aims. The prospect of European Union and NATO membership has also been used as a means of justifying the economic and social hardships which have accompanied transformation.

To join NATO and the EU, certain economic, political and democratic standards must be fulfilled. The prospect of membership therefore acts as an incentive to ensure certain standards are met. Thus, despite provocation, the Hungarian government refuses to be drawn into vitriolic debate over the future of the Magyar minority in Slovakia or Romania, as it rightly perceives this would be detrimental to its efforts to join the EU and NATO. Indeed, the prospect of membership has led the Hungarian and Romanian Justice Ministries to embark on cooperation to ensure their nationality laws conform to those required by the European Union. Such regional cooperation furthers the spread of internationally recognised legal standards. It also encourages potential members to exchange information and engage in consultation, both essential for the effective functioning of NATO and the EU, and the stability of the region.

On the other hand, accession to NATO and the EU has the potential to reduce regional cooperation as countries compete for membership. The awareness that neither institution can expand indefinitely may cause disillusion in those countries not accepted in the first or second rounds of expansion. Just as inclusion in European institutions furthers democratic consolidation, so rejection from them may threaten it. Although the decision of both the EU and NATO to invite groups of countries to join simultaneously has decreased competition between states, there remains no indication of when and where expansion will reach its outer limits. There is no doubt, that those countries with little prospect of accession will feel excluded from Europe. It also places them in the dilemma of whether to continue membership efforts or concentrate on other forms of cooperation. The Hungarian and Czech invitations to join NATO and the European Union in the first round of expansion vindicated their respective European policies. Romania's failure to be invited poses problems for the radical reform programme, whose centrepiece is successful European integration.

5.5.1: Czech and Hungarian Membership of NATO and the EU

On the 8 July, 1997, NATO announced that in 1999 it would accept Poland, the Czech Republic and Hungary as new members in a first round of expansion. During the Communist regime, the armed forces were placed under particular political pressure. While the Romanian military was relatively autonomous, the armed forces of Hungary and Czechoslovakia relied on Soviet made weapons and were subordinated to the Soviet Union via the Warsaw Pact Organisation. The Czechoslovak and the Hungarian Communist Parties also maintained an armed People's and Worker's Militia, respectively. The militias owed their allegiance solely to the Party and represented an armed force which the Party could rely on to maintain order. For the same reason, approximately 82% of all senior officers and 50% of all lower ranking officers in the Czechoslovak army were members of the Communist Party[129]. NATO membership requires democratisation and civilian control of the military. The Militias have been disbanded, but the military's Soviet-style structures must also be discarded and democratic convictions amongst military personnel furthered.

---

[129] Ibid. Beckherrn, Eberhard, *Tal der Wende*, p. 245.

A Democratic and Civil Society

Although the first post-Communist Hungarian government did not present a comprehensive military programme, it embarked on a policy of early retirement and encouraged all those over the age of 55 to leave the military. This was in many respects a continuance of the previous regime's policy of elite renewal and ensured those potentially most compromised by their activities under the Communist regime were removed from the military. The reduction of Generals, which had begun in 1988, was therefore continued. Between 1 January, 1988 and 31 December, 1991, 29 new Generals were appointed and 91 left the army. During the same period, 32 Colonels were appointed and 478 left. As a result of these policies, between 1 January, 1990 and 31 January, 1991, the number of professional soldiers in Hungary decreased by 5 942 persons, from 28 477 to 22 535[130]. On 1 January, 1991, military service was also reduced from 18 to 12 months[131].

The same process began in the Czech Republic in October 1991, when the 55 year old army General, Miroslav Vacek, was relieved of his position as Czech Defence Minister. He was replaced by the 58 year old civilian, and former dissident journalist, Lubos Dobrovsky[132]. Basic training was changed, active service time reduced and large numbers of older officers, including all the political appointees, left the military. Despite this, the Czech army is experiencing difficulty training and retraining the number of officers required as a NATO member[133]. In an attempt to overcome this problem, the United states has initiated a project to help the Czech army make optimal use of personnel. As a result, the Czech Defence Minister presented eight bills dealing with army organisation at the end of September 1997[134].

Integration into the Warsaw Pact also meant reliance on weapons produced by the Soviet Union or other members of the Pact. Czechoslovakia was the largest weapons producer, outside the

---

[130] Szabo, J., 'Die Streitkräfte und der Systemwandel'. In Kurtan, S., Sándor, P., Vass, L., (Hrsg.), *Politisches Jahrbuch Ungarns*, Budapest 1992, p. 376.

[131] Dunay, Pál, *Das alte Ungarn im neuen Europa?*, Hessishce Stiftung Friedens- und Konfliktforschung, HSFK Report, No. 2, March 1993, p. 6.

[132] Ibid. Beckherrn, Eberhard, *Tal der Wende*, p. 221.

[133] See *The Prague Post*, 25 June 1997.

[134] *RFE/RL Newsline*, Vol. 1, No. 136, 10 October 1997.

Soviet Union, in the Eastern Bloc. Three quarters of Czechoslovak military production was exported, making it the tenth largest arms exporter in the world. Approximately 80% of Hungarian military production was also exported. Three quarters of total Hungarian arms production was military surveillance equipment. Artillery and infantry weapons accounted for 12% of production, and repairs a mere 8%[135]. Despite this, the Hungarian and Czech armed forces were themselves poorly equipped. Declining economic performance forced the Hungarian regime to reduce military expenditure from 3.7% of GDP in 1986, to 1.9% of GDP in 1991[136]. Moreover, only 14% of the 1991 military budget was used to fund investment and acquisition. Thus, the vast majority of Hungarian military equipment is at least 20 years old[137]. The Hungarian airforce does possess 11 MiG 21 and MiG 23's, but they are old and do not conform to NATO norms[138]. In addition, the airforce is unable to fly more than 50% of them at any one time and pilots are therefore having difficulty fulfilling their minimum flight hours[139].

Full integration into NATO therefore requires modernisation of military equipment and infrastructure. The 50 000 Soviet troops who had been stationed in Hungary left behind a total of 149 barracks, 14 000 military flats, 6 airfields, and numerous hospitals and leisure facilities. The former Soviet Union claimed these installations to be worth a total of DM 8.1 billion[140]. On their departure on 30 June, 1991, the 60 000 Soviet troops stationed in the former Czechoslovakia left behind 64 army garrisons and 165

---

[135] Ibid. Beckherrn, Eberhard, *Tal der Wende*, pp. 238-239.
[136] Ibid. Cowen Karp, Regina, *Central and Eastern Europe: The Challenge of Transition*, p. 142.
[137] Ibid. Dunay, Pál, *Das alte Ungarn im neuen Europa?*, p. 21. Originally from Janza, K., 'Die Kosten der Militärreform', *Tarsadalnmi Szemle*, Vol. 46, No. 8-9, August-September 1991, p. 74.
[138] Ibid. Cowen Karp, Regina, *Central and Eastern Europe: The Challenge of Transition*, p. 144.
[139] McKinsey, Kitty, 'NATO: Brussels Tables Eastward Expansion this Month', *RFE/RL Report*. Http: //www.rferl.org.
[140] Ibid. Brown, J., F., *Eastern Europe and Communist Rule*, p. 37. Ibid. Beckherrn, Eberhard, *Tal der Wende*, pp. 229-230.

army barracks[141]. The former Soviet military bases are often highly polluted and in a severe state of disrepair; departing Soviet troops having removed all installations and often even structural material from buildings.

The renovation of such sites and facilities will be both expensive and time consuming, but is essential should NATO troops be stationed in the Czech Republic or Hungary. Since December 1995, between 2500-4000 American servicemen and women have established a logistics centre in the former Warsaw Pact military base in Taszar as part of the United Nation's Peacekeeping mission in former Yugoslavia. Taszar lies approximately half way between US bases in Germany and Bosnia. It is therefore crucial to US operations and continually provides accommodation for between 1200-1400 American troops in transit in and out of Bosnia. The stationing of American forces in Taszar has enabled the Hungarian military to become accustomed with the type of equipment used in NATO[142]. Hungarian participation in Peacekeeping operations in the former Yugoslavia, Albania and in the Gulf War have provided further experience of military cooperation. Such cooperation means the Hungarian military is the closest to fulfilling NATO standards and norms. The delivery of the first of 60 Mistral air-defence missiles and 15 Atlas launchers by the French *Marta Defence Company* in January 1998 also demonstrates Hungary's concerted effort to acquire NATO compatible military equipment. The delivery is part of a $100 million tender which was offered by the Hungarian government in 1997. A further 150 missiles are due to be delivered by the end of 1998[143].

Although a team of NATO experts discovered Hungary is capable of handling NATO aircraft, and the Czech Republic has modernised its communications network in line with NATO

---

[141] Ibid. Brown, J., F., *Eastern Europe and Communist Rule*, p. 37. Ibid. Beckherrn, Eberhard, *Tal der Wende*, p. 229.
[142] McKinsey, Kitty, 'Hungary: The Military Strive to Comply with NATO Criteria', *RFE/RL Report*. Http: //www.rferl.org. See also *The Presence of IFOR/SFOR in Hungary and the Hungarian Military Participation in Peace Operations in the Former Yugoslavia*, The Embassy of the Republic of Hungary, Washington DC. Http: // www.hungaryemb.org.
[143] *RFE/RL Newsline*, Vol. 2, No. 15, Part II, 23 January 1998.

requirements, integration will require an increase in military expenditure to ensure modernisation and compatibility. Current estimates suggest Hungary and the Czech Republic will have to spend between $1-1.3 billion annually for ten years to cover the costs of restructuring and modernisation. Czech defence expenditures will have to double and will reach 2% of GNP by the year 2000[144]. On 3 November, 1997, Vaclav Klaus announced new military budget allocations to cover the cost of modernisation and adaptation to NATO standards. A special Commission of Czech Ministers also approved an annual Czech contribution of 600 million Crowns, $18.3 million, to NATO after accession[145]. NATO itself will contribute a total of $315 million for Hungarian, and $265 million for Czech integration[146]. Modernisation of equipment must be accompanied by modernisation of training methods and new education programmes, especially courses in foreign languages. NATO officials have therefore encouraged Hungary and the Czech Republic to concentrate initially on education and training rather than the purchase of expensive military equipment.

Despite the costs of NATO membership, public support in Hungary has remained constant. Approximately 50% of the Hungarian population took part in the referendum on NATO membership which was held on 16 November, 1997. Of those, 85% were in favour of joining the Alliance[147]. On 18 November, 1997, the Hungarian Ambassador to NATO formally presented the Hungarian application for NATO membership[148]. The Czech Republic has not held a referendum, and indeed only approximately half the population support NATO membership[149]. The negative image of the Czech army under the Communist regime, as well as

---

[144] Winter, Sonia, 'Central Europe: New NATO Members are Willing and Able to Foot Bill', *RFE/RL Report*. Http: //www.rferl.org.
[145] *RFE/RL Newsline*, Vol. 1, No. 152, Part II, 4 November 1997.
[146] Ibid. McKinsey, Kitty, 'NATO: Brussles Tables Eastward Expansion this Month', *RFE/RL Report*.
[147] *RFE/RL Newsline*, Vol. 1, No. 161, Part II, 17 November 1997.
[148] *RFE/RL Newsline*, Vol. 1, No. 162, Part II, 18 November 1997.
[149] In a poll carried out amongst 1000 people in December 1997, only 25% were strongly in favour of, and 28% relatively in favour of, Czech membership of NATO. Obereigner, Dasa, 'Czech Republic: Focus on EU, NATO', *Transitions*, Vol. 5, No. 3, March 1998, p. 87.

that created by Jaroslav Hasek's parody, *Good Soldier Svejk*, combine to limit public trust in the military as an institution of national defence. The perception that the Czech Republic is surrounded by friendly states and the much publicised cost of NATO membership have also contributed to the public's lack of enthusiasm. The participation of Czech forces in the United Nation's Peacekeeping operations in Bosnia has therefore been a valuable demonstration of the necessity of international military cooperation to deal with potentially de-stabilising situations[150]. A survey published by the *Institute of Public Opinion Research* on 26 January, 1998, showed that support for NATO membership amongst the Czech population had increased from 47% in October 1997, to 54% at the time of the survey[151].

Reform of military personnel and command structures has ensured the democratisation of the military in Hungary and the Czech Republic. This process has been encouraged and accelerated by the prospect of NATO membership. Integration into an international, democratic military alliance will firmly bind Hungary and the Czech Republic into democratic European security structures. Military and political integration into NATO will also lessen the danger of regional conflict and increase ability to combat international security problems. NATO membership will assist in guaranteeing security in the Central and East European region and in this way can contribute to economic regeneration and democratic consolidation.

The security guarantee and stability provided by NATO membership will be complimented by membership of the European Union. However, continuing economic hardship and the delay in the start of accession negotiations have increased scepticism towards the EU in both Hungary and the Czech Repuiblic. This trend is most obvious in the Czech Republic where, in a poll carried

---

[150] On 2 December, 1997, 334 volunteers from a Czech mechanised brigade finished 3 months training and were sent for a 7 month tour of duty in Bosnia. Naegle, Jolyon, 'Czech Republic: Transformation of Military Progresses at Leisurely Pace', *RFE/RL Report*. Http: //www.rferl.org.

[151] The percentage of those against NATO membership fell from 54% in October 1997, to 24% at the time of the survey. *RFE/RL Newsline*, Vol. 2, No. 17, Part II, 27 January 1998.

out in September 1997, only 21% of those questioned were strongly in favour of and 37% somewhat in favour of EU membership. 54% had little or no interest at all in the EU[152]. On 15 July, 1997, the European Commission recommended that first round accession negotiations should begin in 1998 with Cyprus, the Czech Republic, Poland, Hungary, Slovenia and Estonia. Romania, Bulgaria, Latvia, Lithuania and Slovakia were named as candidates for a second wave of expansion[153]. Members of the European Union must also fulfil certain economic and political standards. For Hungary and the Czech Republic, membership will ensure economic transformation continues and further economic integration into European markets. It will open the European internal market to Czech and Hungarian products and make the EU's structural and regional funds readily available. Membership will also enable Hungary and the Czech Republic to play a role in the formulation of common European economic, foreign and security policies. Finally, it is symbolic of their 'return to Europe' and represents the recognition of their status as democratic European states. Thus, membership of the EU will have a positive influence on democratic consolidation. It is therefore vital that interest in the EU and support for membership be fostered.

5.5.2: Future Romanian Accession

Romania has not been invited to start accession negotiations with either NATO or the European Union in their first rounds of expansion. This decision was largely based on the fact that major economic and administrative reform only began in earnest after the PDSR's electoral defeat in November 1996. Until this date, the PDSR's ineffective policies had plunged the Romanian economy and society into an ever deepening crisis. Its ambiguous attitude towards democratisation and market reform damaged Romania's international standing and delayed economic and administrative restructuring. Despite this, Romania's chances of joining NATO and the EU in a second round of expansion are relatively good.

---

[152] Ibid. Obereigner, Dasa, 'Czech Republic: Focus on EU, NATO', *Transitions*, p. 87.
[153] Taken from the REE/RL Homepage. Http: //www.rferl.org.

Soviet troops left Romania in 1958, and after 1967 Romanian troops did not take part in any Warsaw Pact exercises. Nor did they participate in the 1968 Warsaw Pact invasion of Czechoslovakia. Although a member of the Warsaw Pact, Romania followed an independent, defensive military strategy[154]. Romanian autonomy also extended to military equipment, and approximately 80% of it was, and still is, produced domestically[155]. After the Six Day War between Israel and Egypt, Romanian enterprises recovered tanks from the desert and either stripped or repaired them to sell[156]. Despite such ingenuity, the Romanian active duty force, totalling 170 000 men, was poorly equipped[157].

Under Ceausescu, military expenditure was continually decreased, and at the 1982 Communist Party Conference was frozen at its 1982 level until 1985. At the same time, the economy was militarised. The army was employed to manage sections of the economy, such as harvesting and the construction of the Bucharest underground system, the Black Sea Canal and hydroelectric dams. In October 1985, Ceausescu declared a state of emergency and also placed the military in charge of power generation[158]. As a result, the standard of Romanian military equipment and morale in the armed forces rapidly declined.

The army's support of the December Revolution helped it regain its reputation amongst the population. Despite this, its role in the maintenance of the system of terror made reform of its command structures and replacement of numerous personnel imperative. Far-reaching personnel and institutional reform have also ensured the preparations for NATO integration are well underway. Romania's obligations for the CFE Treaty were met in November 1995, and the military has been placed under civilian and Parliamentary control. Immediately after the Revolution, the Political Committees,

---

[154] Marrese, Michael, Vanous, Jan, *Soviet Subsudization of Trade with Eastern Europe*, Institute of International Studies, Research Series, No. 52, University of California 1983, p. 69.
[155] *RFE/RL Newsline*, Vol. 1, No. 21, Part II, 29 April 1997.
[156] Ibid. Beckherrn, Eberhard, *Tal der Wende*, p. 239.
[157] Ibid. Cowen Karp, Regina, *Central and Eastern Europe: The Challenge of Transition*, p. 170.
[158] Nelson, Daniel, N., *Romanian Politics in the Ceausescu Era*, Gordon & Breach Science Publishers 1988, pp. 185-187.

which ensured officers' loyalty to the Party, were abolished and eighteen Generals who had been sent into reserve under Ceausescu recalled; amongst them General Militaru, who became Defence Minister, and General Nicolescu, his Deputy. A further 26 younger officers were promoted to the rank of General, while 28 existing Generals and the Chief of Ceausescu's Personal Guard were sent into retirement[159]. Since then, western training methods have been introduced and the modernisation of military equipment initiated.

The Romanian military has been fundamentally restructured. The ongoing programme requires the reduction of army personnel by a further 12 700 by the end of 1998. The government has approved compensation for those affected. The 2400 civilians made redundant at the Ministry of Defence in a parallel programme will also receive compensation[160]. The military has been reorganised to include brigades, battalions, several peacekeeping units and a rapid reaction force. Romania's commitment to international military cooperation and its ability to contribute to European security has been demonstrated by the successful participation of Romanian forces in United Nations peacekeeping operations in former Yugoslavia and in Albania. A total of 392 Romanian infantry men and eight officers have participated in the United Nation's mission in Albania, and Timisoara airport has been used as a supply base for the Albanian operation[161]. Participation in such missions has provided invaluable experience of international military cooperation and increased familiarity with NATO structures and equipment.

The Romanian Defence Ministry has estimated the cost of NATO membership, including the costs of military reform, acquisition and modernisation, at approximately $3 billion[162]. This includes the costs of upgrading military structure and command systems, estimated at $850 million; building operational interoperability and command procedures, $167 million; the

---

[159] Gabanyi, Anneli Ute, *Die unvollendete Revolution*, Piper 1990, pp. 63-65.
[160] *RFE/RL Newsline*, Vol. 2, No. 13, Part II, 21 January 1998.
[161] *Romania: Romania to sent Troops to join Albania Mission*, RFE/RL Homepage. Http:// www.rferl.org.
[162] *Romania: Bucharest Calculates NATO Admission Cost at $3 Billion*, RFE/RL Homepage. Http: //www.rferl.org.

modernisation of defence equipment and acquisition of new equipment, $1600 million; and the cost of upgrading military infrastructure to ensure full inter-operability, $1200 million[163]. The government has affirmed its ability to fund the cost itself and 2.87% of the 1997 budget was allocated to defence[164]. The Romanian military accepts NATO membership as a practical means of increasing regional security and military cooperation. Integration into NATO structures is also a means by which the military can regain its professionalism and will force the long-overdue modernisation and renovation of Romania's dilapidated military infrastructure and equipment. The majority of the Romanian military establishment is therefore highly supportive of NATO membership.

Romanian membership of NATO is also supported by its strategic importance for the linkage of regional NATO commands. Roland Asmus and Stephen Larabee, from the Rand Corporation, have defined three strategic areas necessary for NATO's regional command[165]. The East-Central area encompasses Poland, Hungary and the Czech Republic, as well as Slovenia and Slovakia. The North-East European area is comprised of the Baltic States, Finland, and Sweden. The South-Eastern area includes Romania, Bulgaria and the Balkans. However, the instability in the Balkans means in reality, only Romania and Bulgaria are possible candidates for NATO membership. With American aid, Germany and Denmark have begun various forms of regional military cooperation with Poland, the Baltic States, Finland and Sweden.

NATO's interest to avoid the spread of instability and conflict from the Balkans means that regional defence cooperation in the East-Central strategic area must include Romania, Moldova and Slovakia as well as Poland, Hungary, and the Czech Republic. The strategic importance of the Ukraine, which wants a strategic partnership with NATO, means cooperation between a Polish-

---

[163] The costs of accession were correlated with the perspective of achieveing 'initial capability' by 2001, and 'mature capability' by 2009. *Romania Today*, 'Costs of NATO Membership for Romania', No. 11, June 1997.
[164] Ibid. *Romania Today*, 'Costs of NATO Membership for Romania'.
[165] Molnár, Gusztáv, 'The Geopolitics of NATO Enlargement', *The Hungarian Quarterly*, Vol. 38, Summer 1997, pp. 11-12.

Hungarian-Romanian trio and the Ukraine acquires special importance. The countries link all three strategic areas are Poland, Hungary and Romania. Romanian membership would also provide NATO with increased access to the Black Sea, as well as control over more than 650 miles of the Danube's navigable course. Furthermore, Romania is the only country in region which has the air-lift capability, provided by its four C-130 planes, to deploy troops and dispense humanitarian aid[166]. Geostrategic considerations therefore dictate NATO's eastward expansion proceed through Poland, Hungary and Romania. Because NATO must take such considerations into account if it is to remain a functioning military alliance capable of guaranteeing the security of all its members, future Romanian accession is certain.

NATO membership will further political and military democratisation and help guarantee stability for the Romanian state. The prospect of membership was the decisive factor leading to Romania's final conclusion of Bilateral Treaties with Hungary, the Ukraine, Bulgaria and Moldova, which resolved long-standing conflicts. It can also ensure democratic norms and principles are adhered to. The recent decision of the Romanian Prosecutor-General's office to begin judicial proceedings to rehabilitate eight Ministers from Marshall Antonescu's government caused a strong protest from the United States, which stated rehabilitation:

> *'...would call into question the sincerity of Romania's commitment to the West's most fundamental shared values and is likely to trigger a reassessment of support for Romania's candidacy for membership of our economic and security institutions.'*[167]

The Prosecutor-General's Office has since found seven of the eight Ministers in question guilty of collective political responsibility for Antonescu's dictatorship, and halted the judicial rehabilitation process. The one exception is Toma Petre Ghitulescu,

---

[166] *Romania Today*, 'Romania's Views on NATO Enlargement', and 'Romani's Military Assets for the Alliance', No. 11, June 1997.
[167] *RFE/RL Newsline*, Vol. 1, No. 161, Part II, 17 November 1997.

who resigned from Antonescu's cabinet in May 1941, before the introduction of increasingly anti-Semitic policies[168]. However, a lawyer representing the Ghitulescu family has claimed to have found 'an article' which requires the Court to re-examine all eight cases[169]. The continuing Antonescu debate can only detract from attempts to create a democratic, civil society in Romania. During the particularly difficult Romanian transformation, the prospect of NATO and EU membership, and the commitment to common European values accession represents, can therefore contribute significantly to successful democratic consolidation.

The European Union has also decided not to include Romania in its first round of eastward expansion. The six years of government by the PDSR-led coalition were characterised by reluctance to transform the economic system and some of the fundamental economic and political structures from the Ceausescu regime. This has delayed economic transformation and political democratisation and is the main reason for the decision to exclude Romania from early membership.

Although both NATO and the EU have confirmed they plan further eastward expansion, Romania's failure to be accepted in the first round raised fears it was once more being excluded from Europe. NATO membership in particular was viewed as a matter of national dignity and a test of American commitment. The United States' announcement of the decision prior to the NATO meeting increased the sense of rejection and insult. The Romanian public found exclusion difficult to comprehend because over 90% of the population and the majority of the military supported NATO membership[170]. The coalition government led by the PNTCD had made NATO membership the centrepiece of its domestic and foreign policy. Exclusion from the first round of NATO expansion threatened to destabilise it.

---

[168] *RFE/RL Newsline*, Vol. 1, No. 166, Part II, 24 November 1997. See also Zsolt, Mato, 'Romania lets Sleeping Dogs Lie', *Transitions*, Vol. 5, No. 1, January 1998, pp. 10-11.
[169] *RFE/RL Newsline*, Vol. 2, No. 17, Part II, 22 January 1998.
[170] Gross, Peter, Tismaneanu, Vladimir, 'No NATO Shelter for Romania', *Transitions*, Vol. 4, No. 7, December 1997, p. 28. See also *Romania Today*, 'Romania's Views on NATO Enlargement'.

Although official Romanian reaction to NATO's decision was reserved, there can be no doubt that the decision provided extreme nationalist groupings with an opportunity to propagate and exacerbate national inferiority complexes, fears and phobias. These groups have emphasised the national degradation of rejection and preached increased animosity towards international cooperation. Although the vast majority of the population continue to support Romanian membership of NATO, the allure and popularity of those representing anti-democratic, xenophobic forces should not be underestimated. In a recent survey by the *Institute for the Quality of Life*, Vadim Tudor, leader of the extremist Party of Greater Romania, was the fifth most popular political leader, gaining the support of 28% of those who took part[171].

NATO and EU membership was not only perceived as a guarantee of stability, but also as representing Romania's acceptance as a democratic European state. Moreover, it was hoped early membership would promote investment and revive the failing economy. Exclusion from the first round of NATO and EU expansion is a set-back and may make the task of reforming the economy and democratising the political system, while at the same time confronting the popular attitudes formed under totalitarianism, more difficult. The Romanian President has admitted Romania's economic and political reforms lag behind those of Hungary and the Czech Republic, but awareness of failures and mistakes makes many Romanians sensitive to treatment which is perceived as different from that of other European countries undergoing transformation. On the other hand, the more realistic prospect of membership in a second round of expansion will help maintain the course of reform.

Romania's radical reform programme and improved relations with its neighbours, a result of NATO pressure to resolve conflict in regional political relations before membership, has increased its chances of being invited to join NATO and the European Union in the second round of expansion. If economic, political and military reforms continue successfully, Romania will no doubt be invited to

---

[171] Ibid. Gross, Peter, Tismaneanu, Vladimir, 'No NATO Shelter for Romania', *Transitions*, p. 30.

start accession negotiations in 1999, when NATO plans to review its expansion programme. Austria, Slovenia and the Baltic States are also expected to apply for NATO membership at this time. The European Union is likely to start preparations for a second round expansion, which would include Romania, after the first round in the year 2000. Early Hungarian and Czech membership of NATO and the EU reflects the more advanced state of their transformation. Romanian transformation has proved rather more difficult, but the prospect of accession to both organisations in a second round of expansion will ensure political and economic transformation continues and promote common democratic values.

5.6: Trust in State Institutions

Wide-spread popular trust in the ability of the state to carry out transformation is vital if civil society is to develop and the transformation process succeed. Under the Communist regimes, the Law was subordinated to the needs of ideology and the Communist Party. Thus, a democratic constitution, the establishment of the rule of Law and an independent judiciary are all vital if trust in state institutions is to be regained. Corruption amongst state officials must also be bought under control and eradicated.

After the 1989 Revolutions constitutional reform was undertaken in all three countries. This ensured the independence of the judiciary and respect for fundamental Human Rights. On 23 October, 1989, the Hungarian Parliament accepted a radically revised Constitution. The Constitution declares Hungary is an 'independent Republic' and a 'democratic *Rechtstaat*' in which the principle of the division of powers is recognised. Although the substantial revision means only a few passages of the original remain, the present Hungarian Constitution is based on the Communist Constitution, Law XX, from 1949[172]. In the light of this, political parties agree a new Constitution is desirable.

---

[172] Péter, László, 'Montinesquieu's Paradox on Freedom and Hungary's Constitutions 1790-1990', *The New Hungarian Quarterly*, Vol. 32, No. 123, Autumn 1991, p. 12. See also Hungarian Embassy, *Ungarn – parlamentarische Republik*, Fakten über Ungarn 1994.

However, the desire to retain the existing structure of public law and the difficulties of transformation have led to a waning of enthusiasm for a new Constitution. Thus, it seems Hungary will retain its current revised Constitution, but problems concerning the electoral law, the powers of the Constitutional Court, the President and the Public Prosecutor require clarification and further constitutional review.

The Czech Constitution came into effect on 16 December, 1992[173]. It was rewritten after the dissolution of the Czechoslovak Federation. The Romanian Constitution is based on the Communist Constitution, rather than that from 1923, to avoid the problem of the monarchy. The Constitution was revised using the French Constitution as a model and was accepted by the Chamber of Deputies on 8 December, 1991[174]. Both the Czech Republic and Hungary have retained remnants from the legal and administrative systems of the Austro-Hungarian Empire, but in comparative terms their Constitutions and legal systems are now most similar to those of the Federal Republic of Germany. The Austro-Hungarian administrative tradition facilitated the retention of certain bureaucratic elements, but also preserved certain standards of public morality and the sense of being a public servant. This tradition was absent in Romania where, under the influence of the Ottoman Empire, corruption amongst public officials was widely accepted. Corruption amongst public officials prevents the population trusting the state and its institutions and brings the democratic system into disrepute. It therefore represents a danger to democratic consolidation.

The Constitutions guarantee personal freedom, establish the rule of Law and the independence of the judiciary and law enforcement agencies. The Communist regimes employed the law to suit ideological goals. The judiciary was not independent and was expected to protect systemic norms and uphold socialist legality. The Romanian legal system, perhaps the most compromised, has been reformed and is now based on that of the fifth French

---

[173] For text, see Office of the Government of the Czech Republic. Http: //www.vlada.cz.
[174] For text, see Romanian Embassy, Washington DC. Http: //www.embassy.org/romania.

A Democratic and Civil Society

Republic. Judicial reform has not only included revision of legal statues and the establishment of a Constitutional Court, but those Judges who served under the Communist regime and disregarded the principles of legality have been removed and replaced. However, it is still necessary to appoint more Judges trained exclusively under the democratic system.

Under the Communist regimes the police force was employed as an instrument of control. To fulfil its proper role in a democratic state, the police must transform itself from an instrument of repression into an institution which serves the population and can competently engage in the fight against crime and corruption. The dissolution of the secret internal police represented the first step towards this goal. The Hungarian Secret Police, the *AS*, was dissolved in January 1990. The Czechoslovak Secret Police, the *StB*, which numbered 18 000, was dissolved on 1 February, 1990. At the same time, an Office for the Protection of the Constitution and Democracy was founded. The *StB* had been supported in its activities by a network of at least 120 000 informants. Such people were denied a Lustration Certificate during the lustration process. In March 1990, the notorious Romanian *Securitate* was also dissolved and replaced by the Romanian Security Service, SRI^{175}.

The Romanian police force has had particular difficulty shedding the negative image it acquired under the Ceausescu regime. The reform process is hampered by lack of resources, but long-term cooperation with the Devon and Cornwall Constabulary under the auspices of the 'British Know-How Fund', has provided numerous Romanian police officers with valuable experience and knowledge of the training and crime detection methods employed in the United Kingdom[176]. Indeed, the Director of the Bucharest police training academy is reorganising Romanian training programmes in line with those seen in the United Kingdom. Experience of community policing and the British police's aim to serve the population also influenced the decision to set up a police

---

[175] Ibid. Beckherrn, Eberhard, *Tal der Wende*, p. 147.
[176] See Devon and Cornwall Constabulary, *Romanian Police Know-How Fund*, April-July 1997, July-September 1997, September-November 1997.

station in the centre of Galati[177]. Most importantly, corruption amongst police officers must be reduced and the rule of Law apply to all equally. Only if this is achieved can the police protect the population and regain the trust required for individuals to report crime and assist with police enquiries.

Corruption amongst Parliamentary Deputies and state officials must be reduced. The Independent Commission of the Romanian Chamber of Deputies has recommended the Parliamentary immunity of Gabriel Bivolarv from the PDSR be lifted. He is charged with forging documents to gain personal and business credits[178]. The lifting of his immunity, and application to lift that of Vadim Tudor, the leader of the extremist Party of Greater Romania, represents an important step towards establishing acceptable standards of behaviour amongst Romanian Deputies and state officials[179]. This can help overcome the popular disillusion with Parliament and political parties which was demonstrated in a Romanian survey. In the survey, 50% of those questioned had no confidence in any political party, and 60% were disenchanted with the performance of Parliament and government[180].

Wide-spread disillusionment leads to apathy and hinders the development of a civil society capable of contributing to democratic consolidation. The crisis in the Czech Republic, which culminated in the government's resignation, was preceded by a period of indecision which damaged the standing of the country's democratic institutions. The government's resignation may lead to political renewal and the formulation of new policies more able to deal with the Czech Republic's economic difficulties, but it also threatens to delay economic transformation. The CSSD called for a

---

[177] Previously the Police Station was situated outside the city, inaccessible to those wishing to report a crime or ask for assistance. Conversation with D. J. Hollis O.B.E., Director of Finance and Administration, Devon and Cornwall Constabulary. 20.12.97.
[178] *RFE/RL Newsline*, Vol. 1, No. 164, Part II, 20 November 1997.
[179] For a summary of the events leading to the application to lift Tudor's Parliamentary immunity, see Shafir, Michael, 'Romania: Everybody seems to Love to Hate Tudor, Almost', *RFE/RL Report*. Http: //www.rferl.org.
[180] Ibid. Pridham, Geoffrey, Lewis, Paul, G., (Eds.), *Stabilising Fragile Democracies*, p. 223. The surveys were organised by and published in a Bucharest political journal. See *Sferu Politicii*, No. 10, October 1993.

halt to all privatisation and the Chamber of Deputies suggested the suspension of the privatisation of three major banks until the government crisis is solved[181]. The disruption incurred by political crisis and government immobility increases uncertainty and can lead to a decrease in support for transformation and democratic institutions.

5.6.1: Support for Transformation

Wide-spread corruption amongst state officials and constant bickering amongst political parties, rather than application to the task of transformation, has led to a certain amount of disillusion with the democratic system in all three countries. A survey carried out in Romania in 1993 showed that, of those asked, 27% had a preference for 'authoritarian, iron-fisted leadership'[182]. Disillusion with democratic institutions and Parliament is caused by poor standards of behaviour amongst Parliamentary Deputies and the inability of political parties to address the concerns of the population and deal effectively with the problems associated with economic transformation. If such problems are not dealt with, support for transformation will decline and democratic consolidation will be endangered.

The percentage of those opposed to privatisation is higher amongst the poor, elderly and those with a low level of education. It is precisely these groups who are most threatened by unemployment or who are already unemployed as a result of transformation. These groups are targeted by extremist parties, which often rely on a curious mixture of Communist and nationalist ideology to discredit liberalism, the market and privatisation. Policies of economic transformation and privatisation gain most support from the younger and more educated sections of the population. However, a survey carried out by a Hungarian-American research group into support for the market economy in Hungary showed that, although 73% of those asked were in favour of privatisation being carried out as quickly as possible, 60%

---

[181] *RFE/RL Newsline*, Vol. 1, No. 172, 4 December 1997.
[182] Shafir, M., 'Romanians and the Transformation to Democracy', *RFE/RL Report*, 30 April 1993, p. 47.

believed the new system only favoured a few rich citizens, and 75% thought it was impossible to make a decent living by honest work[183]. Such perceptions are influenced by the appearance of very wealthy individuals who are involved in dubious business dealings. If such perceptions continue, they can threaten the foundations of the legal, democratic state.

In Romania, poor standards of public behaviour, incessant bickering amongst political parties and the opposition's blocking tactics in Parliament, have increased the difficulties of economic transformation and exacerbated the fall in the standard of living. Thus, support for economic transformation amongst the population remains volatile. On 20 November, 1997, between 15 000 and 20 000 demonstrators from the Trade Union, *Fratia*, marched through Bucharest to protest against the government's market reforms[184]. Romania possesses the strongest Trade Union movement of all three countries, and it has continually striven to hinder and delay economic transformation. The 1990 miners' rampage in Bucharest demonstrated their violent potential and influence over political life. The threat to the development of civil society and democratic consolidation this represented was obvious in the miners' targeting of opposition political parties, the independent press and informal groups.

The Romanian Unions have engaged in numerous strikes and protests to try and halt the government's planned privatisation and closure of large state enterprises[185]. Although their concern to protect the social rights of workers is legitimate, the means chosen to achieve it are dubious. The Unions' attempts to halt the government's transformation programme are supported by the nationalist parties of the extreme right and the PDSR. These parties do not support radical economic transformation, nor are they unambiguously in favour of democratic transformation. The lack of support for economic transformation amongst the Romanian Trade Unions and their potential to influence government policy therefore

---

[183] Kiss, Yudit, 'Privatisation in Hungary – Two Years Later', *Soviet Studies*, Vol. 44, No. 6, 1992, p. 1015.
[184] *RFE/RL Newsline*, Vol. 1, No. 165, Part II, 21 November 1997.
[185] *Romanian Labor Movement, Trade Unions, Social and Economic Data*, Central European Online. Http: //www.centraleurope.com.

represent a danger to Romanian transformation and democratic consolidation.

Support for transformation can only be maintained if the population is aware of the advantages transformation brings. The Czech Republic has been most successful in maintaining a high level of support for transformation. This was facilitated by widespread trust in the government's ability to carry out economic transformation and the initial success of the transformation programme. However, since the government's collapse, trust in Parliament has decreased. In the daily, *Pravo*, Jiri Hanak, a political commentator, noted that, in contrast to the 70% of the population who trusted Vaclav Havel, only approximately 10-20% trusted Parliament[186].

Popular trust in the ability of state institutions to carry out transformation can only be gained if those responsible for the failed policies of the previous regime are removed from power and corruption amongst public servants is reduced. The guarantees of personal freedom and freedom of information contained in the new Constitutions help an informed public opinion develop, while religious and ethnic tolerance ensures all members of society have equal opportunity to fulfil their potential. As these factors are also vital for the development of civil society, support for transformation is inextricably linked to the development of such a society.

5.7: Civil Society and Democratic Consolidation

Although the scope of this study precludes coverage of all the factors related to the development of civil society, in particular educational reform, the factors examined are deemed of particular importance for democratic consolidation. However, during transformation not all aspects of civil society contribute to democratic consolidation. Furthermore, the ability to deal with the potentially de-stabilising effects which civil society can produce depends on the type of Communist regime which was in place, the

---

[186] Naegele, Jolyon, 'Havel Narrowly wins Re-election', *RFE/RL Newsline*, Vol. 2, No. 14, Part II, 23 January 1998.

nature of the democratic Revolution and the consequent transformation policies chosen.

Confrontation with the past, examination of the former system and acceptance of personal responsibility are essential for the re-establishment of moral standards and the development of a society capable of defending the democratic system from anti-democratic tendencies. An official lustration process can initiate elite rotation and also ensure those in public office accept personal responsibility and adhere to certain standards of behaviour.

In Hungary, the reformist nature of the Kádár regime meant citizens were not automatically compromised by their position or activities under it, especially as an elite rotation had already been initiated in the 1980's. The role the administrative and political elite had played in ensuring the success of the Negotiated Revolution also facilitated their retention in the new system. Therefore, the main aims of Hungarian lustration were to ensure accountability, transparency and that those in public office were not susceptible to blackmail. In this sens, the reconciliation that the inclusion of the former elite in the democratic system fostered furthered democratic consolidation in Hungary.

In contrast, the lustration process in the Czech Republic was specifically aimed at removing those involved in the maintenance of the former system from state administration and the political arena. This policy was justified by the repressive nature of the former regime and the resistance to change demonstrated by the administrative and political elite. It also helped re-establish certain moral standards, which had degenerated under the Communist regime. Strict lustration in the Czech Republic therefore furthered democratic consolidation, not only by ensuring elite rotation, but also by forcing Czech society to examine and accept responsibility for actions under the Communist regime.

The nature of the Romanian regime also made an elite rotation essential for the success of transformation. However, it was not in the interests of the previously marginalised faction of the Communist elite which initially gained power either to initiate radical systemic transformation, or to expose their own complicity in Ceausescu's reign of terror. Therefore, no serious attempt was made to initiate elite rotation, either in state administration or the political class. The refusal to accept personal responsibility, and the susceptibility to blackmail of those whose previous activities would be seriously damaging to them if revealed, created an atmosphere of intrigue and corruption which was not conducive to transformation or democratic consolidation.

Large-scale elite rotation in the political sphere was only initiated after the change of government following the 1996 elections. The new government introduced an official lustration process of Deputies and other public servants in an attempt to ensure those compromised by previous activities, and whose commitment to democratic transformation is ambiguous, are removed from office. The proposed public access to secret security files will also force individuals to examine their own role in the former system.

The course of events in Romania demonstrates that retaining members of the old elite in the new democratic system without vetting them represents a danger to transformation and democratic consolidation. The initiation of a lustration process, the examination of past actions and acceptance of personal responsibility is therefore an integral part of transformation and plays a vital role in democratic consolidation. However, the differences between the lustration process in the Czech Republic and Hungary demonstrate that the form of lustration and examination of the past can vary according to the nature of the former regime. Thus, as long as the former elite undergoes a vetting process, its inclusion in the new system does not necessarily hinder democratic consolidation.

Democratic consolidation is also furthered by the development of a critical public opinion, which in turn requires free access to reliable information. Only if the public is well informed can it be mobilised to support the democratic system and transformation. However, excessive criticism by an independent media can destabilise a newly formed democratic system and hinder the formation of trust in new state institutions.

Fear of the potentially de-stabilising effect of critical media coverage of transformation led the first post-Communist Hungarian government to embark on a 'media war'. Its aim was to ensure the government and its transformation policies were presented in a favourable light. This policy was a stark contrast to the de-ideologisation of the media which had occurred during the last years of the Communist regime and caused a public outcry. Indeed, the 'media war' was part cause of the MDF's 1994 electoral defeat. Hungarian civil society successfully defended the independent media, but critical media coverage of Parliament and political parties has served to decrease interest in democratic transformation and limit trust in state institutions.

In the Czech Republic, media freedom was ensured by the government's desire to effect a complete break with the former system. The potentially de-stabilising effect of an independent, critical media was limited by the early success of the government's radical transformation policies. Furthermore, the intellectual opposition and *samizdat* network, which operated under the former regime, had preserved elements of a critical public opinion. Thus, the Czech population was in a good position to effectively evaluate critical media reports concerning transformation. Freedom of information and a critical media therefore furthered the development of civil scoiety in the Czech Republic.

In contrast, the PDSR-led Romanian government manipulated the state-controlled media and tried to limit press freedom, especially in broadcasting. It employed the same methods used by the former regime to hinder the formation of a critical public opinion. The entertainment schedule, consisting largely of 'soap operas' and game shows, was increased, but reliable news and information programmes were few and far between. Moreover, state-controlled television propagated the same national inferiority complexes, xenophobia and contorted nationalism which had characterised the Ceausescu regime. The almost total destruction of civil society under Ceausescu meant that even the independent Romanian media shared some patterns of reporting with the state-controlled media, particularly in respect of the Hungarian and Roma minorities.

Continued media manipulation meant the population was systematically mis-informed and ensured suspicion towards ethnic minorities, foreign capital and economic and political transformation was maintained. Moreover, those who were active in civil society became disheartened and passive. Thus, civil society's potential to hinder democratic consolidation by consolidating social and ethnic cleavages, and distrust of the state was realised.

The radical transformation programme introduced by the PNTCD-led government can only succeed if the population is accurately informed about the true state of the economy, the nature of the former regime and the policies which need to be pursued. Freedom of information and the independence of the media are therefore crucial, but press freedom has also led to an increase in the extreme nationalist press. The developing civil society is still too weak to combat the potentially negative effect of the overtly critical and nationalist press on transformation and democratic consolidation, and this remains a problem in Romania.

During transformation, the critical media's potential to consolidate the distrust of state institutions, which formed under the Communist regime, can represent a danger to democratic consolidation. However, an independent media is vital for the development of an informed, critical public opinion, which can effectively combat this negative potential. Although developing civil society may have difficulty in dealing with this aspect of its critical function in the short-term, the vital role of an active, critical public opinion in civil society makes an independent media an essential ingredient of long-term democratic consolidation.

Religious belief can offer moral guidance and help re-establish standards of behaviour in the vacuum left by Communism and the confusion of transformation, but the Church as an institution has not always provided an example of tolerance, nor has it fully examined its own role under Communism.

In Hungary, the potential of the Roman Catholic Church to further democratic consolidation and civil society has been limited. Not only does the population reject a political role for the Church, but the Church's own national-conservative vision is inapplicable to contemporary Hungarian society. It also maintains a rather ambiguous attitude towards the Jewish and Roma population. While these factors have limited the Church's active role in democratic consolidation, the rejection of a political role for the Church is itself a demonstration of an active civil society and democratic consolidation in Hungary.

Although nominally Roman Catholic, the majority of the Czech population is highly secularised. It too rejects a political role for the Church, favouring instead the Church's provision of moral guidance. But, as in Hungary, the Church's ambiguous attitude towards anti-Semitism and discrimination against the Roma has limited its potential to contribute positively to democratic consolidation. Despite this, the Catholic Church's opposition to the former regime did maintain some of the independent networks required by civil society. However, as in Hungary, the Catholic Church's main contribution to the development of civil society and democratic consolidation lies in popular rejection of a political role for the Church.

The Romanian Orthodox Church neither provides an example of moral guidance, being the most subservient Church under the Communist regime, nor does it profess tolerance – aiming to assimilate the other religions within Romania. It has yet to examine its role within Ceausescu's system of terror and continues to preach the nationalism and intolerance characteristic of the former regime, into whose national-Communist ideology Romanian Orthodoxy assimilated itself. The Orthodox Church's continued influence over the Romanian population, especially in rural areas, is not, therefore, conducive to the development of civil society or democratic consolidation.

Intolerance and ethnic prejudice threaten the development of civil society and democratic consolidation because they deny a large section of the population the opportunity to play a full part in social, economic and political activity and thus benefit from transformation. This creates long-term domestic instability, hinders the development of the cross-cutting networks essential to civil society and prevents democratic consolidation. The problem ethnic intolerance and prejudice can cause for democratic consolidation has been widely underestimated. Discrimination against the Roma is socially accepted in Hungary, the Czech Republic and Romania, and is proving especially difficult to overcome. The Hungarian government has been most active in its attempts to better the social and economic position of the Roma by sponsoring numerous programmes aimed at improving the Roma's level of education and standard of housing, and overcoming popular prejudice. The government's concern to better the Roma's position is also linked to its desire to impress the exemplary treatment of Hungary's own ethnic minorities on those countries which themselves harbour large Magyar communities.

Although the Roma population in the Czech Republic is relatively small, Czech prejudice has increasingly expressed itself in violence. The recognition of the danger wide-spread ethnic discrimination represents to democratic consolidation has led to the formation of a Ministerial Commission charged with finding ways to overcome prejudice against the Roma and to further their social and economic integration.

In contrast to the Magyar community in Romania, which has successfully organised itself and become a member of the coalition government, the Roma remain impotent. However, while the Magyar community's exclusively ethnic organisation ensures their specific needs are taken into account, it has also deepened the ethnic cleavage between the Romanian and Magyar population. On the other hand, inclusion in government has forced the ethnic Hungarian organisation to address the problems of transformation for Romania as a whole. Nevertheless, at present, Romanian civil society is not strong enough to overcome all the potentially negative effects this type of ethnic organisation can have on democratic consolidation.

The difficulty the Roma in all three countries experience in forming effective pressure groups is directly linked to their low level of education and the absence of a substantial educated class within the Roma community. Lack of education forces the Roma to accept positions as unskilled labourers, but it is precisely these jobs which are most affected by transformation and which are less and less in demand. The problems associated with the Roma are so serious, and so threatening to long-term democratic consolidation, that they require sustained government programmes. These must increase the Roma's level of education and further their presence in the cultural, economic and political sphere, while encouraging tolerance and reducing prejudice amongst the general population.

The development of civil society and long-term democratic consolidation is also furthered by stability in the economic and political sphere. Membership of the European Union and NATO can help the attainment of such stability. Although prospective members must modernise military equipment and infrastructure, NATO membership will provide a forum and structure for military and political cooperation which can help ensure regional European stability and security. It also requires full civilian control of the military. Membership of the European Union will not only bring full access to European markets, but also include East European members in European political structures and ensure they have an influence on future European policy.

Hungary and the Czech Republic have been invited to begin accession negotiations for the first round of expansion of both NATO and the European Union. In their case, the justification of the sacrifices of transformation with the prospect of NATO and European membership was successful. The radical transformation programme in Romania was also justified as a means to gain accession of the European Union and NATO. Romania's failure to be accepted in the first round of expansion places its success in doubt. On the other hand, Romanian reform only began in earnest after the 1996 elections, and the realistic prospect of accession in a second round of expansion provides an attainable goal and therefore a secure framework within which to proceed with transformation. Despite this, the negative effect of rejection on Romanian transformation and democratic consolidation should not be underestimated.

Hungarian and Czech civil society is relatively well developed and has contributed positively to democratic consolidation. Civil society in Romania finds itself in a much earlier stage of development. Potentially negative effects on Romanian democratic consolidation, such as the consolidation of ethnic cleavages due to organisation according to ethnic criteria, and of distrust towards the state as a result of a critical media, are therefore much more difficult to overcome.

However, the continuing discrimination and social exclusion of the Roma represent obstacles to long-term democratic consolidation in all three countries. The initiation of government sponsored programmes can help to overcome this, but it will be a long and extremely difficult process. Hungary, the Czech Republic and Romania also suffer from a low level of popular trust in state institutions. The critical media, although vital to the development of an informed public opinion, has served to consolidate the distrust of the state which was engendered under the former regimes. If distrust of the state and public servants continues, the democratic system may fall into disrepute. To ensure the critical potential of civil society does not endanger democratic consolidation, it is essential measures be taken in all three countries to increase trust in the state. Such measures include enforcing the rule of Law, reducing corruption amongst officials and attaining economic and political stability; all of which also further the development of civil society and can therefore balance its critical potential.

The different nature of the Communist regimes left civil society in Hungary, the Czech Republic and Romania at various stages of development. During transformation, this differentiation has influenced civil scoiety's potential to hinder democratic consolidation. Despite this, current problems related to the further development of civil society are similar in all three countries. This indicates that the specific Communist legacy is less influential for long-term democratic consolidation than might be supposed.

CONCLUSION

> 'Not everything that exists is evident
> Nor can everything that exists be explained.'
> The warnings of a Mayan Priest.

*

Following the Revolutions of 1989, the countries under consideration, Hungary, the Czech Republic and Romania, all embarked on a process of political, economic and social transformation and democratisation. Their common aim was to create a democratic political system and market economy capable of fulfilling the economic, political and welfare expectations of the respective populations.

This study has analysed factors which were influenced by the legacy of Communist rule in Hungary, the Czech Republic and Romania and which were are essential components of democratic consolidation. The chief aspects examined were:
- the nature of the former regime,
- the type of democratic Revolution,
- the formation of political parties,
- the transformation of the economy,
- the level of development of civil society.

These accord closely with the main factors identified by Juan Linz and Alfred Stepan in their recently published book on democratic transition and consolidation[1]. They suggest that the three main areas which influence democratic consolidation are:
- the institutional framework,

---

[1] Linz, J., Stepan, A., *Problems of Democratic Transformation and Consolidation of Democracy*, John Hopkins University Press 1996.

- interest organisation (as represented by political parties),
- individual attitudes (as expressed in civil society).

As a result of this study, it seems that special emphasis must also be made of the major role that the organisation of economic institutions and economic performance plays in democratic consolidation.

Examination and evaluation of the way in which the Communist legacy influences these factors can help to determine the effect on democratic consolidation in other emerging democracies. This study has dealt with events up to March 1998, but general future trends can be discerned in developments which have taken place.

Although similar historical experience and development, and certain basic features common to Communist systems, mean that Hungary, the Czech Republic and Romania all face similar problems during transformation, it seems that the specific nature of the old regime and its individual legacy is vital in determining, not only the speed of transformation and democratisation, but also the ability to deal with the problems associated with transformation and democratic consolidation.

The 1989 democratic Revolutions represent the start of the transformation process and created the main institutional prerequisites for democratisation and democratic consolidation. However, the differences between the Revolutions demonstrate that, whatever its form, a democratic Revolution must eliminate the existing power structures and initiate elite rotation if long-term democratic consolidation is to occur.

Thus, the reformist regime in Hungary had been engaged in economic, and increasingly political, reform since the failed 1956 Uprising. Consequently, much of the legal framework required for transformation and democratisation was already in place by 1989. It also meant that those involved in state administration or the political sphere were not automatically compromised by their activities under the old regime, especially since the Party itself had initiated an extensive elite rotation during the 1980's. The willingness of the reformist Party leadership to negotiate systemic transformation with the opposition elite therefore facilitated a smooth transition, but prevented a complete break with the old system.

Conclusion

In contrast, the Czechoslovak and Romanian regimes left behind basically intact Stalinist systems. This meant transformation was a much more radical and difficult process. In Romania, transformation was further hindered by the specific form of despotic sultanism which evolved under Ceausescu. There was no reformist grouping within the Party and no organised dissident movement capable of steering the Revolution. This enabled a marginalised faction within the Party elite to take control; its complicity, continued ideological conviction and reliance on the structures created by Ceausescu to retain power prevented a complete break with the old system.

In Czechoslovakia, the neo-Stalinist regime's loss of ideological conviction and its own sense of legitimacy, together with the existence of an organised dissident movement, which was capable of taking control, combined to foster a radical break. The caesura was completed by the dissolution of the Czechoslovak Federation, which rid the Czech Republic of Slovakia, where many of the problems associated with an over-blown industrial and chronically under-funded agricultural sector are particularly acute.

The various forms of Revolution were a direct consequence of the specific regime types which had developed in Hungary, the Czech Republic and Romania. Gradual reform in Hungary facilitated a smooth transition, but the lack of a clear break with the previous system, has made it difficult for the population to form a clear identification with the new democratic system. The complete systemic break in the Czech Republic was emphasised in its transformation policies and helped to maintain support for the new democratic system. Despite its violence, the Revolution in Romania did not lead to a decisive break with the old system. The continued adherence to certain aspects of Communist ideology and use of the structures and methods which evolved under Ceausescu prevented the creation of a democratic institutional framework, and has engendered mistrust in the new system.

All three countries have introduced the formal institutions required for the functioning of a democratic system. The Czech experience of democracy during the inter-war years provided valuable memories of the compromise and consensus necessary in a functioning democratic system. This experience is totally absent in

Romania, where the lack of consensus amongst political parties over the basic political system provides for little hope of compromise on other matters. Hungarian democracy broke down during the inter-war period, but the Negotiated Revolution created the political consensus which forms the foundations of a democratic system.

The formation of democratic political parties and the holding of free elections was a direct consequence of the democratic Revolutions. However, the election process and political parties themselves have been influenced by the legacies of the former regimes and this has affected their ability to contribute to democratic consolidation. For example, the complicated election process in Hungary, a direct result of the Party and opposition elites' concern to ensure prominent political figures enter Parliament regardless of actual performance, has damaged its democratic legitimacy. The popular form of presidential election in Romania, combined with wide-ranging presidential powers, has resulted in the amount of political influence exerted by the President being dependent on individual taste. In both Hungary and Romania, some reform is necessary to ensure the democratic system maintains its legitimacy and can function more effectively.

Political parties in all three countries have found it difficult to orientate themselves in the new political landscape where concerns of the inter-war period are no longer pressing and the ideological cleavage between left and right is increasingly losing its meaning. To contribute to democratic consolidation, political parties must develop a spectrum of modern policies and offer acceptable choices to the electorate.

The inability of the conservative parties in Hungary to modernise their political agenda has alienated the majority of the population. The Hungarian Socialist Party's electoral success and transformation into a mass political party has been due to its political modernisation. This process was furthered by the successful removal of hard-line Communists after the dissolution of the Socialist Workers Party. The group of Party reformers who founded the Socialist Party had no nostalgia for the previous system; they had, after all, initiated its destruction. Furthermore, they realised they had to transform the party to maintain political attractiveness and to stand a chance of playing a role in the new political system they had helped create. The historical and conservative parties have been unable to follow this example and remain primarily concerned with issues related to traditional, rural Hungarian society and concerns over the state of the Christian Hungarian nation.

Ironically, these developments have led to a role reversal in which the Socialist Party defends liberal market-orientated policies, while the conservative opposition advocates more left-wing policies which support increased state intervention. In an attempt to offer a politically acceptable, modern conservative alternative, FIDESZ, originally a radical liberal party, has transformed itself into a moderate conservative party.

The Czech Republic also suffers from a narrow range of political alternatives – but on the left-wing of the political spectrum. Although Czech conservative parties are currently in a process of re-grouping, successful modernisation of their political programme and advocation of moderate liberal-conservatism convinced the majority of the Czech electorate that only a conservative government could ensure transformation. In contrast, the traditionally left-wing Social Democratic Party was disorientated by the total collapse of Communism and has found it difficult to modernise its political programme and find an agenda to suit the new political reality.

The lack of political alternatives in Romania is of a more elementary nature because currently, the only politically influential political groupings unconditionally in favour of democratisation and transformation are the Democratic Convention of Romania and the Democratic Party. The political alternatives to the strongest party in the CDR, the conservative National Peasant Party, are provided by extreme nationalist parties and the ambiguous policies of the PDSR. Indeed, the continuing political influence of extreme nationalist parties in Romania is one of the most unpleasant legacies of Ceausescu's regime.

Ceausescu's instrumentalisation of nationalism as a means to prevent the formation of a united popular opposition and maintain personal power distorted Romanian nationalism, and it is this distorted nationalism which the extreme parties propagate. They provide familiar scape-goats and offer simple solutions which appeal to large sections of the population thrown into uncertainty during transformation. The PDSR's failure to transform itself into a modern social democratic party stems from its inability to discard Communist ideology, a legacy of the lack of a reformist grouping within the Romanian Communist Party, and a continued reliance on authoritarian power structures formed under Ceausescu.

The specific Communist legacy has influenced the development of political parties in Hungary, the Czech Republic and Romania. Despite this influence, lack of a full range of acceptable political choices can be discerned in all three countries, although it is most extreme in Romania. This shortcoming represents a danger to democratic consolidation because those unhappy with the performance of one party may not be presented with a feasible political alternative. This can lead to disillusion with the democratic system and also to an increase in support for the more extreme parties as part of a protest vote.

Although this danger is most apparent in Romania, where the legacy of Communism is most complicated and difficult to overcome, it is also present in the Czech Republic, where the Social Democratic Party is finding it difficult to sever its ties with the Communist Party, and where the extreme right-wing Republican Party has also increased its level of support. In Hungary, however, the electorate showed its distaste for extremism when it elected the Socialist Party in 1994, and although the Socialist Party has to date maintained its status as a party of mass appeal, the lack of a political alternative which is acceptable to voters unhappy with its performance in government can lead to disenchantment with the political system and may increase support for the more extreme political parties.

The threat which a lack of political alternatives can have on democratic consolidation is even more pronounced in combination with economic transformation. If a political party cannot deliver the economic performance the population expects, the only political alternative may be to vote for an extreme party, not necessarily because it has a better strategy, but as the only means of registering discontent.

Conclusion

Economic transformation requires the restructuring of the entire system of economic relations and the introduction of new institutions designed to facilitate a free market economy. The initial effects of economic transformation, most importantly the decline in production resulting from the restructuring of old state subsidised industries and the resultant increase in unemployment, can hinder identification with the new system and endanger democratic consolidation. The legacy of state control and the inefficiency fostered under Communism has proved exceedingly difficult to overcome.

Thus, the large Hungarian foreign debt and budget deficit, which accumulated under the former regime, influenced the decision to initiate privatisation of state-controlled enterprises on a case-by-case basis, selling each enterprise to the highest bidder, in most cases foreign investors. But, despite previous reforms and the division of large monolithic enterprises, revenue was lower than expected because many enterprises were in a much worse economic position than had been presumed. The advantages of this form of privatisation were that, the lack of domestic capital available for investment was compensated by the high proportion of foreign investment attracted and that real owners took charge and initiated radical industrial restructuring. However, this policy led to an increased burden on the welfare state as the costs of social and unemployment benefits spiralled. In addition, this form of privatisation did not give the population a personal stake in the new economic system. Nevertheless, in lieu of participation in large enterprise privatisation, compensation policies enabled many ordinary people to obtain small private businesses, farms or housing and, in this way, increased their personal stake in the success of the new economic system.

The neo-Stalinist character of the former Czechoslovak regime made the exclusion of the former elites from the new system a vital element in the government's strategy for obtaining democratic legitimacy and encouraging systemic support. The means chosen to achieve this, corrective social justice and voucher privatisation, neglected economic imperatives, but gave the population a personal interest in the new system and so maintained a high level of support for transformation.

The Czech policy of restitution aimed to achieve corrective social justice. Property was returned to previous owners, rather than sold to present occupiers, as a means of destroying the pattern of social privileges which had evolved under Communism. Privatisation effectively destroyed the structure of Communist economic privileges by ensuring broad public access to the process. This also gave the population a high personal interest in the success of the new system and helped maintain a high level of support for transformation. Voucher privatisation entailed distributing vouchers which could be exchanged in return for shares in various state enterprises. However, it did not attract the foreign capital necessary for investment and restructuring, nor did it create real owners, because ownership was spread amongst the whole population. Consequently, economic rationality and industrial restructuring were delayed in favour of a programme aimed at destroying the pattern of Communist privileges and ensuring popular support for the new economic and democratic system.

The total lack of reform in Romania prior to 1989, and the retention of power by a section of the former elite combined to further complicate and delay economic transformation. The elite faction which gained power was not totally committed to privatisation; so privatisation policy was often contradictory and ineffective. In addition, the state of Romanian enterprises was so pitiable that in many cases there was little hope of effective restructuring or attracting foreign investment. The Stalinist gigantomania of the former regime left a legacy of out-dated industrial monoliths but, unlike the Czech government, the Romanian leadership was reluctant to destroy the structures of economic and social privilege formed under Ceausescu. Privatisation was often limited to a Manager/Worker Buyout, which changed none of the existing structures. Restitution of land was not supported by privatisation or de-monopolisation of ancillary companies connected with agriculture and was therefore aimed at ensuring the rural population's support for the power elite, rather than effective transformation. Economic restructuring has thus been hindered and the population's stake in the new system limited. As a consequence, the continued presence of structures from the old regime, poor economic performance and a low personal stake in the new system combine to limit popular support and delay democratic consolidation.

Transformation strategies in all three countries have, to a large extent, been determined by the policies of the previous regimes and the nature of their collapse; but all demonstrate the importance of providing the population with a personal interest in the new system. Where this fails, as in the initial stages of Romanian transformation, the disruption and unemployment inevitably caused by economic transformation may limit democratic consolidation because the population feels no sense of personal involvement in the necessary industrial, agricultural and property reform. The positive influence on democratic consolidation which obtaining economic stability and creating conditions suitable for sustainable economic growth, is demonstrated by the convergence of economic policy aims of all three countries. Austerity programmes and policies aimed at achieving industrial restructuring have been introduced in Romania and the Czech Republic, and the Hungarian austerity programme has been aimed at curbing government expenditure and restructuring the welfare state. While satisfactory economic performance is important, democratic consolidation is not dependent on economic stability alone.

The actions and opinions of individual citizens, as expressed in civil society, also play a vital role in furthering democratic consolidation. Although an active civil society is an essential ingredient of democratic consolidation, during transformation some aspects of civil society can actually work to hinder the process. A critical public opinion can tend to consolidate the mistrust of the state and its institutions which developed under the Communist regime, and ethnic organisation can widen current ethnic and social divisions. The ability to overcome civil society's negative potential and harness its positive influence on democratic consolidation is to a large extent dependent on the nature of the former Communist regime. A balanced, active civil society is dependent on a general systemic consensus, trust in the state to protect individual rights and uphold the rule of Law, freedom of association, free access to reliable information, and religious and ethnic tolerance.

The reformist Hungarian regime permitted constructive criticism of the system in the hope of improving its performance. It also refrained from demanding public displays of loyalty and did not interfere in the private sphere of its citizens, so the basic foundations of civil society remained intact. In Czechoslovakia, the neo-Stalinist regime forced public attestations of loyalty to convince itself of its legitimacy. The ability of a group of dissidents to resist the pressure of the regime to conform, exposed the moral corruption inherent in the system and in a society which acquiesced. So the foundations required for the development of a balanced civil society were preserved. In contrast, the Ceausescu regime succeeded in almost totally destroying civil society in Romania. The population was atomised and the regime exercised control over all aspects of social and private activity. Propaganda served to alienate nationalities and divide the workers from the intelligensia, thus making it an easy task to suppress individual attempts to organise a dissident movement.

The former Hungarian regime's programme of gradual reform facilitated reconciliation in society. However, those involved in the administration of the Communist system were vetted to ensure their previous activities did not bring the democratic system into disrepute or make individuals susceptible to blackmail. Hungarian civil society also benefited from the availability of relatively reliable sources of official information available under the previous regime. This fostered the development of critical, informed public opinion. The former regime's pragmatism and gradual reduction of ideology in everyday life, and ultimately in politics, has also limited the Catholic Church's ability to regain the political influence it enjoyed during the inter-War period. Despite these positive aspects, ethnic prejudice, especially against the Roma minority, is widespread and constitutes one of the most important factors hindering the development of a balanced civil society. The low level of trust in state institutions and consequent increasing political apathy apparent in Hungarian society is the other major factor which currently hinders democratic consolidation.

The neo-Stalinist Czechoslovak regime's normalisation policy created extreme moral disorientation in Czech society. The strict Czech Lustration Laws were an attempt to give the new system moral legitimacy by ensuring certain standards of behaviour were re-introduced into public life. The government's desire to achieve a radical break from the old regime fostered the development of a free, critical media. The Czech Hussite tradition and the secularisation which developed under Communism have prevented the Catholic Church from adopting an overtly political role. However, in common with Hungary, ethnic intolerance and prejudice against the Roma minority in the Czech Republic is widespread and increasingly hinders the development of a balanced civil society.

The development of Romanian civil society has proved most problematic. The problems have arisen from the severity of the Ceausescu regime and the subsequent policies of the PDSR government, which prevented an elite rotation and which continued manipulation of the media and nationalism in an attempt to create a favourable public opinion and discredit the opposition. Lack of acceptable standards of public behaviour has fostered corruption. Furthermore, the continued presence of those who are highly compromised by their activities under Ceausescu has caused disillusionment and apathy amongst those active in civil society and has tended to consolidate mistrust of the state and its institutions. In the light of the Orthodox Church's continued influence over sections of the Romanian population, the refusal of the Church to relinquish its political role and nationalist ideology also poses difficulties for the development of a tolerant civil society. In this situation, the wide-spread problem of socially accepted prejudice against the Roma and Magyar minorities is proving to be one of the main factors preventing the development of a balanced civil society in Romania. Indeed, social organisation according to specific ethnic criteria, while contributing to the development of an active civil society, also widens existing ethnic divisions and can actually hinder democratic consolidation.

The differentiated legacy of the Communist regimes has resulted in Hungarian and Czech civil society reaching a more advanced stage of development than in Romania. Although none of the three countries enjoys all the various intrinsic factors which contribute towards the development of civil society to the full, as long as civil society continues to develop its positive elements these can compensate for the more negative aspects which may be moderated as time goes by. Therefore, even though the specific Communist legacy may cause aspects of civil society to be problematic for democratic consolidation, a democratic civil society can still develop satisfactorily, albeit over a longer period of time.

Membership of NATO and the European Union can help such development by providing the stability and security required for economic growth and civil confidence. Membership criteria ensure certain standards are met, while acceptance into European institutions represents recognition as a democratic, European nation and may increase emphasis on a European, rather than purely national, identity.

However, all three countries suffer from an urban-rural divide; increasing regional tensions due to uneven economic development; disappointing economic performance for large sections of the population; low trust in state institutions; and wide-spread ethnic prejudice and intolerance – especially towards the Roma minority. These now represent the most important factors hindering the development of a balanced civil society and concerted government action is required if long-term democratic consolidation is not to be placed in jeopardy. This indicates the specific Communist legacy is not the main factor determining the outcome of long-term democratic transformation.

FINAL ANALYSIS

Analysis shows how specific Communist legacies in Hungary, the Czech Republic and Romania have been influential in determining the varied courses of transformation and current level of democratic consolidation. Thus, as indicated in this study, the current state of democratic consolidation in Hungary and the Czech Republic is generally more advanced than in Romania. However, whilst the factors determining transformation and democratic consolidation may be the same, the differentiated nature of the Communist legacy means their importance can vary. For example, in the Czech Republic, the destruction of the structures and patterns of economic and social privilege which had developed under the Communist regime took priority over immediate economic imperatives. There is, therefore, no inalienable blue-print for transformation which can ensure its success, but some specific elements are vital for a successful outcome and therefore essential for the process of change:

– The economic, social and political structures of privilege inherent in the former Communist regimes must be dismantled and standards of behaviour established which ensure the moral legitimacy of the system.
– The populace must gain a personal stake and individual interest in the development of the democratic system.
– Economic performance must be improved, leading to a higher standard of living, though because of the rigid, outdated controlled economies of the Communist systems, it seems inevitable that there will be economic hardship and an increase in unemployment in the short-term.
– It is important that a wide range of political choice is presented to the electorate by democratic political parties.
– The general conditions for the development of civil society must be created.

The order in which these elements are introduced depends on the nature of the Communist legacy, but it is not immediately necessary for all to be present during the initial period of transformation - indeed, this may be impossible to attain in the short-term. However, all the essential elements must be nurtured so that ultimately democratic consolidation becomes a reality.

Although the specific Communist legacy led to varied courses of action being taken to achieve democratic transformation and consolidation, the problems encountered and the policies chosen to deal with them in all three countries are increasingly similar. Hungary, the Czech Republic and Romania have all introduced austerity programmes in an attempt to create the conditions considered necessary for sustainable economic growth in a free market economy. Furthermore, all three suffer from a lack of comprehensive political choice; from a wide-spread mistrust of state institutions; and from a significant level of ethnic prejudice: all of which hinder the development of a balanced civil society capable of furthering democratic consolidation. Analysis indicates, therefore, that although the specific Communist legacies existing in the three countries influence the course and speed of transformation in various ways, and may further complicate the process, individually they do not necessarily determine the outcome. The Communist legacies have had a significant influence on the course of events in Hungary, the Czech Republic and Romania, but their effect may not be as crucial for long-term democratic consolidation as might be supposed from first impressions. Moreover, despite forty years differentiated development under their respective Communist regimes, and the specific influence of the Communist legacies on the course of transformation, a convergence of policy and national development, which bear more resemblance to West European patterns, can now be observed in Hungary, the Czech Republic and Romania.

APPENDIX I
Area and Population of East European Countries

Country	Population (millions)	Km^2	Miles^2	Density (per Km^2)
Albania	2.84	28 700	10 600	99
Bulgaria	8.94	110 912	43 325	81
Czech Republic and Slovakia	15.41	127 877	49 952	121
German Democratic Republic	16.7	108 178	42 257	154
Hungary	10.69	93 030	36 340	115
Poland	36.57	312 677	122 139	117
Romania	22.55	237 500	92 773	95
Yugoslavia	22.85	255 804	99 923	89

Source: Adapted from *UN Demographic Yearbook*, 1983.

APPENDIX II
Communist Party Membership in Eastern Europe, 1944-1948

Country	Date	No. Members	% Population
Bulgaria	9.1944	25 000	
	10.1944	50 000	
	1.1945	254 140	
	12.1946	490 000	
	6.1947	510 000	7.1
	12.1948	496 000	6.9
Czechoslovakia	3.1946	1 081 544	
	9.1947	1 172 000	9.4
	12.1947	1 281 131	
	2.1948	1 400 000	
	5.1948	2 150 000	
Hungary	12.1944	2500	
	2.1945	30 000	
	5.1945	150 000	
	7.1945	226 577	
	10.1945	508 801	5.7
	1.1946	608 72	
	9.1946	653 300	6.7
	1.1947	670 818	
	3.1947	708 646	
	12.1947	864 000	
	6.1948	887 472	9.6
Romania	8.1944	2000	
	10.1945	256 000	
	9.1947	710 000	4.4
	2.1948	806 000	5.0

Source: Adapted from Gati, Charles, *Hungary and the Soviet Bloc*, Duke University Press 1986, p. 82. Original in Borsi, Emil, *The European People's Democratic Revolutions*, Budapest 1975, pp. 47-52.

APPENDIX III
Radios, Televisions and Telephones in use in Eastern Europe in 1980

Countries	Radios (1000's)	Radios (per 1000 population)	Televisions (1000's)	Televisions (per 1000 population)	Telephones (1000's)	Telephones (per 1000 population)
Albania[1]	202	74	10	3.7	n.a.	n.a.
Bulgaria[2]	2149	242	1652	186	1255	141
Czech Republic and Slovakia[2]	4 693	307	4292	280	3150	206
Hungary	2700[1]	252	2766[2]	258	1261	118
Romania[2]	3205	144	3714	167	1196[3]	56[3]
Soviet Union[1]	130 000	490	81 000	305	23 707[4]	89
United States[1]	477 800	2099	142 000	624	180 424	788
United Kingdom[1]	53 000	947	22 600	404	26 651	477

1: Estimated number of Receivers in use.
2: Number of Licences issued or sets declared.
3: 1975
4: Excludes military telephone systems.

Source: Adapted from George Schöpflin, (Ed.), *The Soviet Union and Eastern Europe*, Muller, Blond and White 1986, p. 167. Original in *UNESCO Statistical Yearbook 1984*, *UN Statistical Yearbook 1981*.

APPENDIX IV
*Estimates of Gross and Net Hard Currency Debt
(in Billions of Dollars)*

	1971	1975	1976	1977	1978	1979	1980	1981	1982	1983
Soviet Union										
Gross	1.8	10.6	14.7	15.6	16.4	18.1	17.6	20.9	20.1	20.0
Net	0.6	7.5	10.0	11.2	10.4	9.3	9.3	12.4	10.1	8.4
Bulgaria										
Gross	0.7	2.6	3.2	3.7	4.3	4.4	3.5	3.1	2.8	2.5
Net	0.7	2.3	2.8	3.2	3.7	3.7	2.7	2.2	1.8	1.4
Czechoslovakia										
Gross	0.5	1.1	1.9	2.6	3.2	4.1	4.9	4.4	4.0	3.5
Net	0.2	0.8	1.4	2.1	2.5	3.1	3.6	3.5	3.3	2.6
GDR										
Gross	1.4	5.2	5.9	7.1	8.9	10.9	14.4	14.7	13.1	12.3
Net	1.2	3.5	5.0	6.2	7.5	9.0	11.8	12.5	11.1	8.9
Hungary										
Gross	1.1	3.1	4.1	5.7	7.5	8.5	9.1	8.7	7.7	8.3
Net	0.8	2.2	2.9	4.5	6.5	7.3	7.0	7.0	6.6	6.7
Poland										
Gross	1.1	8.0	11.5	14.0	17.8	22.7	25.1	25.5	25.2	26.4
Net	0.8	7.4	10.7	13.5	17.0	21.5	24.5	24.7	24.2	25.2
Romania										
Gross	1.2	2.9	2.0	3.6	5.2	7.0	9.4	10.2	9.8	8.9
Net	1.2	2.4	2.5	3.3	4.8	6.5	9.1	9.8	9.4	8.4
Yugoslavia										
Gross	-	-	-	8.4	10.7	13.5	17.4	19.0	18.5	18.9
Net	-	-	-	6.4	8.4	12.2	16.1	17.4	17.7	17.9

Source: Adapted from Economist Intelligence Unit, *Regional Review: Eastern Europe and the USSR: 1985*, EIU 1985, p. 16.

APPENDIX V

Comparative Economic Growth Rates (Percentages), 1960-1985
(compound annual rates of growth of total Gross National Product)

	1960-61	1965-70	1970-75	1976	1977	1978	1979	1980	1981	1982	1983	1984	1985
GDR	2.9	3.1	3.5	2.0	3.0	1.7	2.8	2.1	2.1	-0.4	1.8	3.2	2.4
Czechoslovakia	2.4	3.4	3.4	1.8	4.3	1.6	0.8	2.3	-0.5	2.0	1.5	2.7	1.7
Hungary	3.9	3.0	3.3	0.3	6.3	2.4	0.3	1.0	0.7	3.7	-1.0	2.7	-0.9
Poland	4.5	4.0	6.5	2.5	1.9	3.5	-1.8	-2.4	-5.3	-1.0	4.9	3.4	1.6
Bulgaria	6.4	5.1	4.7	3.0	-1.0	2.2	3.8	-2.9	2.7	3.2	-1.8	2.9	-0.8
Romania	5.4	4.9	6.7	10.8	2.5	4.7	3.6	-1.5	0.2	2.6	0.0	4.6	1.8
Eastern Europe:													
Total	3.8	3.7	4.9	3.2	2.8	2.8	1.0	-0.3	-1.0	0.9	1.8	3.3	1.4

Source: Adapted from Brown, J., F., *Eastern Europe and Communist Rule*, Duke University Press 1988, p. 504. Original in Lincoln, Gordon, *Eroding Empire: Western Relations with Eastern Europe*, Brookings Institution 1987, p. 331, Appendix, Table A-2.

APPENDIX VI
Average Annual Rates of Growth, 1951-1988 (Percentages)

	1951-1954	1955-1960	1961-1965	1966-1970	1971-1975	1976-1980	1981-1985	1986-1988
Bulgaria	12.2	9.7	6.7	8.8	7.8	6.1	3.7	5.6
Hungary	5.7	5.9	4.1	6.8	6.3	2.8	1.3	1.7
GDR	13.1	7.1	3.5	5.2	5.4	4.1	4.5	3.5
Poland	8.6	6.6	6.2	6.0	9.8	1.2	-0.8	3.9
Romania	14.1	6.6	9.1	7.7	11.4	7.0	4.4	5.1
Czech and Slovak Republics	8.2	7.0	1.9	7.0	5.5	3.7	1.7	2.4
CMEA as a whole	10.8	8.5	6.0	7.4	6.4	4.1	3.0	3.0

Source: Adapted from White, Stephen, Batt, Judy, Lewis, Paul, G., (Eds.), *Developments in East European Politics*, Macmillan Press Ltd 1993, p. 8. Original in *Statisticheskii ezhegodnik stran-chlenov SEV 1989*, Moscow: Finansy i statistika 1989, pp. 18-28.

APPENDIX VII
Economic Growth in Eastern Europe

	1981	1982	1983	1984	1985	1986	1987	1988	1989	1990	1991
Bulgaria	5.0	4.2	3.0	4.6	2.2	5.5	5.1	2.4	-0.4	-11.8	-23.0
											-20.2
Czechoslovakia	-0.1	0.2	2.3	3.5	3.0	3.1	2.1	2.3	0.7	-3.5	**-3.5**
East Germany	4.8	2.5	4.6	5.5	5.2	4.3	3.3	2.8	2.0	n.a.	
Hungary	2.5	2.6	0.3	2.5	-1.4	0.9	4.1	0.3	2.7	3.8	
						0.0	**2.4**	**3.8**			**-4.0**
Poland	-12.0	-5.5	6.0	5.6	3.4	4.9	1.9	4.9	-0.2	-15.8	-7.0
						4.2	**2.0**	**4.1**	**0.2**	**-11.6**	
Romania	-0.4	4.0	6.0	6.5	-1.1	3.0	0.7	-2.0	-7.9	-10.5	0.0
						2.1	**0.5**	**-0.3**	**-5.8**	**8.1**	**-15.0**

* 1991 figures are provisional or estimated.

Note: In the Communist period, the measure of economic growth was 'Net Material Product', which implies the value-added output of all physical production, transport and distribution. This differs from the normal Western measures, Gross Domestic Product or Gross National Product, in not counting the value of output in 'non-material' sectors such as health, education, administration, defence, banking, hotels and various other personal services. This means that NMP is smaller than the Western GNP or GDP, and the growth rates are likely to differ. The East Europeans are now changing or have already changed over to the Western GDP system as part of their economic transition. Where GDP figures are available, these are given in bold type.

Source: Adapted from White, Stephen, Batt, Judy, Lewis, Paul, G., (Eds.), *Developments in East European Politics*, Macmillan 1993, p. 212. Original in Economic Intelligence Unit and United Nations Economic Commission for Europe data.

APPENDIX VIII
Vilmos Farango's 1967 Survey on Nationalism amongst 125 Hungarian Secondary School Children

Questions:
- Are you proud of being a Magyar? If yes: why? If no: why?
- Apart from the Magyar nation, to which nation would you most like to belong?
- To which nation would you least like to belong?
- Do you accept marriage with negroes, gypsies or those of another colour?
- Is Hungary's independence endangered? If yes: form whom?

Answers:
- 83% were proud of being a Magyar
- 9% chose the Russian nation as the one they most wanted to belong to. Other nations chosen were France, the United Kingdom, Switzerland, Sweden and Germany.
- 37% accept mixed marriages, 45% disagree with them
- 47% perceived no danger to Hungary's independence
- 49% perceived a danger form 'imperialist powers', 4% perceived the Soviet Union as a threat.

Source: Adapted from Hartl, Hans, *Nationalismus in Rot*, Seewald Verlag 1968, pp. 60-61. Original in *Elet es Irodalom*, 7 January 1967.

APPENDIX IX
What is Better in Hungary when Compared with the West?
(% of Respondents)

	1986	1988	1988 Party Members	1988 Intelligensia
Possibility of bringing Children up satisfactorily	87	42	46	27
Right to Work	93	80	88	80
Level of Health Supply	66	47	45	23
Level of Social Morality	81	50	59	38
Balanced Family Life	73	36	40	24
Material Welfare	29	10	9	1
Equal Opportunities	69	38	49	29
Freedom to Express Views	67	43	50	29
Money keeps value	41	6	6	2
Chances of getting a Flat	39	16	19	5
Amount of Free Time	46	27	26	17

Source: Adapted from Swain, Nigel, *Hungary: The Rise and Fall of Feasible Socialism*, Verso 1992, p. 14. Original in Nagy, G., L., 'A ketteszakadt tarsadalom', *Jelkep*, Vol. X, No. 4, 1989, p. 55.

APPENDIX X
What would your ideal Hungarian society be like?
(Ranking Answers 1-10)

	Population as a whole	Party Members	Intellectuals
Incomes reflecting Performance	1	1	1
Human Rights	2	5	3
Jobs for All	3	10	12
Ending Poverty	4-5	11	10
Constant Economic Growth	4-5	4	4-5
Social Justice	6-7	3	4-5
No Inflation	6-7	6	7
Democracy	8	2	2
Free Medical System	10	12	15
Religious Freedom	13	14	13

Source: Adapted from Swain, Nigel, *Hungary: The Rise and Fall of Feasible Socialism*, Verso, 1992, p. 16. Original in Nagy, G., L., 'A ketteszakadt tarsadalom', *Jelkep*, Vol. X, No. 4, 1989, p. 61.

APPENDIX XI
Whose interests does the Hungarian Socialist Workers Party most represent?
(Ranking Answers 1-10)

	Population as a whole	Party Members	Intellectuals
Top Party leadership	1	1	1
Workers in Party Apparatus	2	2	2
Enterprise Managers	3	3	3
Party Members	4	5	4
Intellectuals	5	6	7
Workers	6	4	5
The Young	7	8	8
Peasants	8	7	6
The Old	9	10-11	11
Small Entrepreneurs	10-11	10-11	9
Non-Party Members	10-11	9	10

Source: Adapted from Swain, Nigel, *Hungary: The Rise and Fall of Feasible Socialism*, Verso 1992, p. 15. Original in Nagy, G., L., 'A ketteszakadt tarsadalom', *Jelkep*, Vol. X, No. 4, 1989, p. 56.

APPENDIX XII

Preliminary Survey from the Romanian National Commission for Statistics, February 1990 (based on incomplete data)

	Quantity Metric Tons 1000's			Imports used as % of total resources
	1980	1988	% increase	1988
Iron Ore				
Domestic	1460	2252	54	-
Imports	917	13900	1516	86
Coking Coal (Washed)				
Domestic	994	3608	363	-
Imports	416	4906	1179	58
Metallurgy Coke				
Domestic	820	5228	638	-
Imports	656	1099	68	17
Apatite Concentrates				
Domestic	0	0	0	-
Imports	73	873	1196	100
All Fuels				
Domestic	75 000	78 500	5	-
Imports	30 600	44 100	44	35

Source: Adapted from Ratesh, N., *Romania: The Entangled Revolution*, Praeger 1992, p. 159.

APPENDIX XIII
Central and East European Presidents

Country	System*	Term	Incumbent	Year Elected
Hungary	Indirect	5 Years	Arpad Göncz	1990
Czech Republic	Indirect	5 Years	Vaclav Havel	1993
Romania	Direct	4 Years	Ion Iliescu	1990
			Emil Constantinescu	1996

* Direct election of Presidents is through popular election, indirect election is election by Parliament.

Source: Adapted from Mcgregor, James, 'The Presidency in East Central Europe', *RFE/RL Research Report*, Vol. 3, No. 2, 14 January 1994.

APPENDIX XIV
Presidential Powers of Appointment

Appointment Powers	Hungary	Czech Republic	Romania
Prime Minister	•	•	x
Ministers on Prime Minister's suggestion	•	•	x
Constitutional Court	x	x	x
Supreme Court	x	x	
Judges	•	x	x
Prosecutor-General	x		
Central Bank Officials	x	x	
Security Council			
Senior Officers	•	x	•
Senior Commanders		•	
Ambassadors	x	x	x

- • Unqualified constitutional power
- x Partial, shared or qualified power

Source: Adapted from Mcgregor, James, 'The Presidency in East Central Europe', *RFE/RL Research Report*, Vol. 3, No. 2, 14 January 1994.

APPENDIX XV
Political Presidential Powers

Political Powers	Hungary	Czech Republic	Romania
Commander in Chief of Armed Forces	•	x	•
Chair National Security Council	•		•
Remands Laws for reconsideration	•	x	•
Sends Laws to Constitutional Court	•		•
Proposes Legislation	•		
Issues Decrees in non-emergencies			x
Proposes Amendments to Constitution			x
Calls special sessions of Parliament	•	x	•
Assumes special powers if Parliament not in session or unable to convene	x		•
Emergency Powers	•		•
Participates in Parliamentary Sessions	x	x	
May Addresses Parliament	•	•	•
Convenes Cabinet sessions			
Participates in Cabinet Sessions		•	x
May Request Government Reports		•	

- • Unqualified constitutional power
- x Partial, shared or qualified power

Source: Adapted from Mcgregor, James, 'The Presidency in East Central Europe', *RFE/RL Research Report*, Vol. 3, No. 2, 14 January 1994.

APPENDIX XVI
Symbolic, Ceremonial and Procedural Presidential Powers

Powers	Hungary	Czech Republic	Romania
Awards Titles, Decorations	x	x	x
Head of State	•	•	x
Convenes Parliamentary Session	x	x	x
Grants Pardons	x	•	x
Declares Amnesties		x	
Grants Citizenship	x		
Grants Asylum			
Expunges Convictions		•	
Accredits Foreign Ambassadors	•	x	•
Signs Laws	•	•	
Promulgates Laws	•		•
Dissolves Parliament	x	x	x
Calls Referendums	•	x	•
Calls Elections	•	•	
Signs Treaties	x	x	x
Receives Oaths of Office		x	x
Appoints Caretaker Government		x	

- • Unqualified constitutional power
- x Partial, shared or qualified power

Source: Adapted from Mcgregor, James, 'The Presidency in East Central Europe', *RFE/RL Research Report*, Vol. 3, No. 2, 14 January 1994.

APPENDIX XVII
Hungarian Parliamentary Elections, 25 March-8 April, 1990. Share of Vote on Regional List (%) and Number of Seats

Party	Regional List %	No. Seats
Hungarian Democratic Forum	24.73	165
Alliance of Free Democrats	21.39	91
Independent Smallholders	11.73	44
Hungarian Socialist Party	10.89	32
Alliance of Young Democrats	6.46	22
Christian Democratic Peoples' Party	6.46	21
Hungarian Socialist Workers' Party	3.86	
Hungarian Social Democratic Party	3.55	
Agrarian Alliance	3.13	1*
Others (including those jointly sponsored)	5.49	10*

* Candidates won seats in individual constituencies outright in the first round even though their parties did not cross the 4% of the total vote threshold to enter Parliament.

Source: Adapted from White, Stephen, Batt, Judy, Lewis, Paul, G., (Eds.), *Developments in East European Politics*, Macmillan Press Ltd 1993, p. 73. Original in *Magyar Kozlony*, No. 25, 1990.

APPENDIX XVIII
Hungarian Parliamentary Elections, 25 March-8 April, 1990

Party	% Votes	% MP's	No. MP's
Hungarian Democratic Forum (MDF)	24.73	42.7	165
Alliance of Free Democrats (SZDSZ)	21.39	23.	91 + 2*
Independent Smallholders (FKGP)	11.73	11.4	44
Hungarian Socialist Party (MSZP)	10.89	8.5	33
Alliance of Young Democrats (FIDESZ)	8.95	5.4	21 + 1*
Christian-Democratic Peoples' Party (KDNP)	6.46	5.4	21
Hungarian Socialist Workers' Party (MSZMP)	3.86		
Hungarian Social Democratic Party (MSZDP)	3.55		
Agrarian Union (ASZ)	3.13		
Entrepreneurs Party (VP)	1.89		

*Candidates supported by one or two parties.

Source: Adapted from Segert, Dieter, Machos, Csilla, *Parteien in Osteuropa*, Westdeutscher Verlag 1995, p. 43.

APPENDIX XIX
1990 Hungarian Parliamentary Elections

Party	No. Seats	% Seats
MDF	165	42.7
SZDSZ	94	24.4
FKGP	44	11.4
MSZP	33	8.5
FIDESZ	22	5.7
KDNP	21	5.5
Independents	7	1.8

1994 Hungarian Parliamentary Elections

Party	No. Seats	% Seats
MDF	38	9.8
SZDSZ	69	6.7
FKGP	26	6.7
MSZP	209	54.1
FIDESZ	20	5.2
KDNP	22	5.7
Others	2	0.3

MDF: Hungarian Democratic Forum
SZDSZ: Alliance of Free Democrats
FKGP: Independent Smallholders Party
MSZP: Hungarian Socialist Party
FIDESZ: Alliance of Young Democrats
KDNP: Christian Democratic Peoples Party

Source: Adapted from Merkel, Wolfgang, Sandschneider, Eberhard, Segert, Dieter, (Hrsg.), *Systemwechsel II: Die Institutionalisierung der Demokratie*, Leske & Budrich 1996, p. 237.

APPENDIX XX
Hungarian Parliamentary Elections, 8 May-29 May, 1994

Party	% Votes	% MP's	No. MP's
Hungarian Socialist Party (MSZP)	32.99	54.1	209
Alliance of Free Democrats (SZDSZ)	19.74	17.8	69
Hungarian Democratic Forum (MDF)	11.74	9.8	38
Independent Smallholders (FKGP)	8.82	6.7	26
Christian Democratic Peoples' Party (KDNP)	7.03	5.6	22
Alliance of Young Democrats (FIDESZ)	7.02	5.1	20
Hungarian Social Democratic Party (MSZDP)	0.95		
Agrarian Alliance (ASZ)	2.10		1
United Smallholders Party (EKGP)	0.82		1

Source: Adapted from Segert, Dieter, Machos, Csilla, *Parteien in Osteuropa*, Westdeutscher Verlag 1995, p. 98.

APPENDIX XXI
Elections to the Federal Assembly
of the Czech and Slovak Federative Republic
and the Czezch National Council, 8-9 June, 1990

Party	Federal Assembly % Votes	House of the Czech and Slovak Nations (People's Councils) % Votes	Czech National Council % otes
Civic Forum	53.1	50	49.5
Communist Party of Czechoslovakia	13.5	13.8	13.3
Christian and Democratic Union	8.7	8.7	8.4
Movement for Self-Governing Democracy-Society for Moravia and Silesia	7.9	9.1	10

Source: Adapted from Senechal, David, A., *Czechoslovakia*. Taken from the Internet on 29.2.96. Http: //www2.atrsci.wustl.edu/~ps4271/czs-ds.html.

APPENDIX XXII
Elections to the Federal Assembly of the Czech and Slovak Federative Republic, 5-6 June, 1992

Czech Republic

Party	House of the People % Votes	House of the People Seats (Total 150)	House of Nations % Votes	House of the Nations Seats (Total 150)
Civic Democratic Party and Christian Democratic Party	33.9	48	33.4	37
Left Bloc	14.3	19	14.5	15
Czechoslovak Social Democratic Party	7.7	10	6.8	6
Association for the Republican Party of Czechoslovakia	6.5	8	6.4	6
Christian Democratic Union-Czechoslovak People's Party	6	7	6.1	6
Liberal Social Union	5.8	7	6.1	5
Other Parties	25.8	0	26.7	0
Total	100	99	100	75

Source: Adapted from Senechal, David, A., *Czechoslovakia*. Taken from the Internet on 29.2.96. Http: //www2.artsci.wustl.edu/~ps4271/czs-ds.html.

APPENDIX XXIII
Constitution of Czech National Assembly, 1 January, 1993

Party	Czech National Council % Votes	Czech National Council Seats
Civic Democratic Party and Christian Democratic Party	29.7	76
Left Bloc	14.1	35
Czechoslovak Social Democratic Party	6.5	16
Liberal Social Union	6.5	16
Christian Democratic Union-Czechoslovak People's Party	6.3	15
Association for the Republic-Republican Party of Czechoslovakia	6	14
Civic Democratic Alliance	6	14
Movement for a Self-Governing Moravia and Sliesia	5.9	14
Other Parties	19	0
Total	100	200

Source: Adapted from Senechal, David, A., *Czechoslovakia*. Taken from the Internet on 29.2.96. Http: //www2.artsci.wustl.edu/~ps4271/czs-ds.html.

APPENDIX XXIV
Czech Local Elections, 18-19 November, 1994

Party	% votes	% mandates
Union of Independent Candidates	7.1	39.1
Christian Democratic Union-Czechoslovak People's Party (KDU-CSL)	7.5	12.4
Civic Democratic Party (ODS)	28.7	11
Independent Candidates		10.6
Communist Party of Bohemia and Moravia (KSCM)	13.4	9.2
Czech Social Democratic Party (CSSD)	8.1	2.4
Movement of Agricultural Workers		1.1

Due to the different size of constituencies and the number of voters in them, the percentage of mandates won by the respective political parties does not correspond to the actual percentage of votes.

Source: Adapted from *Czech The News*, Newsletter of the Embassy of the Czech Republic, Washington. Taken from the Internet. Http: //www.czech.cz/washington.

APPENDIX XXV
Czech Parliamentary Elections, 31 May-1 June, 1996

Party	Votes %	No. Seats
Civic Democratic Party (ODS)	29.62%	68
Social Democratic Party (CSSD)	26.44	61
Communist Party of Bohemia and Moravia (KSCM)	10.33	22
Christian Democratic Union-Czechoslovak People's Party (KDU-CSL)	8.08	18
Civic Democratic Alliance (ODA)	6.36	13
Assembly of the Republic-Czechoslovak Republican Party (SPR-RSC)	8.01	18
Left Bloc (LB)	1.40	
Free Democrats-Liberal National Socialist Party (SD-LSNS)	2.05	
Democratic Union (DEU)	2.80	
Party of the Democratic Left (SDL)	0.13	
Pensioners for Long-Term Certainty (DZJ)	3.08	
Independents	0.50	
Moravian National Party-Movement of Moravian Silesian Unification (MNS-HSMS)	0.27	
Movement of Self-Governing Moravia and Silesia-Moravian National Unification (HSMS-MSNJ)	0.42	

Source: Open Media Research Institute (OMRINet). Taken from the Internet on 13.6.96. Http: \\www.omri.cz.

APPENDIX XXVI
Czech Senatorial Elections Final Round, 23 November, 1996

Party	Seats
Civic Democratic Party (ODS)	32
Czech Social Democratic Party (CSSD)	25
Christian Democratic Union-People's Party (KDU-CSL)	13
Civic Democratic Alliance (ODA)	7
Communist Party of Bohemia and Moravia (KSCM)	2
Democratic Union (DEU)	1
Independents	1
Total	81

Source: Embassy of the Czech Republic, Press Department.

APPENDIX XXVII
1993 Czech Presidential Elections

First Ballot

Candidate	Chamber of Deputies	
	Votes For	Votes Against
Vaclav Havel	109	81

Czech Presidential Elections, 20 January, 1998

First Ballot

Candidate	Chamber of Deputies		Senate	
	Votes For	Votes Against	Votes For	Votes Against
Vaclav Havel	91	109	39	42

Second Ballot

Candidate	Chamber of Deputies		Senate	
	Votes For	Votes Against	Votes For	Votes Against
Vaclav Havel	99	98	47	34

Source: Adapted from Naegele, Jolyon, 'Havel narrowly wins Re-election', *RFE/RL Newsline*, Vol. 2, No. 14, Part II, 22 January 1998.

APPENDIX XXVIII
Romanian Parliamentary and Senatorial Elections, 20 May, 1990

Party	No. Seats Assembly of Deputies	No. Seats Senate
National Salvation Front	263	92
Democratic Federation of Hungarians in Romania	29	12
Liberal Party	29	9
National Peasant Party	12	1
Romanian Ecological movement	12	1
Alliance for Unity of Romanians	9	2
Democratic Agrarian Party	9	-
Romanian Ecological Party	8	1
Independent	-	1
Romanian Social Democratic Party	5	-
Social Democratic Party of Romania	2	-
Labour Democratic Party	1	-
Free Exchange Party	1	-
National Reconstruction Party	1	-
Party of Democratic Youth	1	-
'Bratianu' Liberal Union	1	-
German Democratic Forum	1	-
Roma Democratic Forum	1	-
Ethnic Representation for 9 National Minorities	9	-
Others	2	-
Total	396	119

Source: Adapted from Staar, Richard, F., (Ed.), *The 1991 Yearbook on International Communist Affairs*, Hoover Institute Press 1991, p. 337. Also Grey, Jason, *Romania*. Http: //www2.artsci.wustl.edu/~ps4271/rom-jg.html.

APPENDIX XXIX
Romanian Assembly of Deputies, 20 May, 1990

Party	No. Seats	% Seats
National Salvation Front	263	65.8
Democratic Federation of Hungarians in Romania	29	7.3
National-Liberal Party	29	7.3
National Peasant Party	12	3
Romanian Ecological Movement	12	3
Party of Romanian National Unity	9	2.3
Democratic Peasant Party	9	2.3
Romanian Ecological Party	8	2
Social Democratic Party	5	1.3
Others	11	2.8

Source: Adapted from Merkel, Wolfgang, Sandschneider, Eberhard, Segert, Dieter, (Hrsg.), *Systemwechsel II: Die Institutionalisierung der Demokratie*, Leske & Budrich 1996, p. 245.

APPENDIX XXX
1992 Romanian Assembly of Deputies

Party	No. Seats	% Seats
Democratic Front of National Salvation	117	35.7
Romanian Democratic Convention	82	25
National Salvation Front	43	13.1
Democratic Federation of Hungarians in Romania	27	8.2
Party of Romanian National Unity	30	9.1
Greater Romania Party	16	4.9
Socialist Workers Party	13	4.0
Ethnic Minorities	13	-

Source: Adapted from Merkel, Wolfgang, Sandschneider, Eberhard, Segert, Dieter, (Hrsg.), *Systemwechsel II: Die Institutionalisierung der Demokratie*, Leske & Budrich 1996, p. 245.

APPENDIX XXXI
Romanian Local Elections, 2 June, 1996

Party	Mayor % Votes	No. ayors	% of ayors	Local Council % Votes	No. Local Councils ontrolled	% of Local Councils
PDSR	26.49	868	33.6	16.28	290	16.88
CDR	13.15	447	16.30	11.27	199	11.58
USD	13.15	251	9.15	3.55	61	3.57
Independent	7.52	251	9.15	3.55	61	3.57
UDMR	4.43	104	3.79	7.06	133	7.74
PSM	4.12	104	3.79	5.15	98	5.70
PUNR	4.05	141	5.14	5.40	95	5.24
PDAR	3.33	178	6.49	3.20	63	3.57
PL93	2.77	59	2.15	2.81	53	3.08
PAC	2.53	36	11.31	3.16	56	3.26
PRM	1.44	54	1.97	4.03	71	4.13

PDSR: Party of Social Democracy in Romania
CDR: Democratic Convention of Romania
USD: Social Democratic Union
UDMR: Democratic Federation of Hungarians in Romania
PSM: Socialist Party of Work
PUNR: Party of Romanian National Unity
PDAR: Democratic Agrarian Party of Romania
PL93: Liberal Party 93
PAC: Civic Alliance Party
PRM: Greater Romania Party

Source: Press Department of the Romanian Embassy, Bonn.

APPENDIX XXXII
Romanian Parliamentary and Senate Elections, 3 November, 1996

Party	% Votes Senate	No. Seats Senate	% Votes Chamber of Deputies	No. Seats Chamber of Deputies
CDR	30.70	53	30.17	122
PDSR	23.08	41	21.52	91
USD	13.16	23	12.93	53
UDMR	6.81	11	6.64	25
PRM	4.54	8	4.46	19
PUNR	4.22	7	4.36	18
PS	2.26		2.29	-
PSM	2.16		2.15	-
ANL	1.92		1.57	-
PPR	1.45		1.44	-
PSMR	1.33		1.73	-

CDR: Democratic Convention of Romania
PDSR: Party of Social Democracy in Romania
USD: Social Democratic Union
UDMR: Democratic Federation of Hungarians in Romania
PRM: Greater Romania Party
PUNR: Party of Romanian National Unity
PS: Socialist Party
PSM: Socialist Labour Party
ANL: National-Liberal Alliance
PPR: Pensioners Party in Romania
PSMR: Romanian Socialist Labour Party

In addition, fifteen minority organisations each received a seat in the Chamber of Deputies:
Federation of Jewish Communities in Romania
Turkish Democratic Union of Romania
'Bratstvo' Community of Bulgarians in Romania
Hellenic Union of Romania
Union of Poles in Romania
Democratic Union of Czechs and Slovaks in Romania
Roma Party (*Partida Romilor*)
Italian Community of Romania
Democratic Union of the Turco-Muslim Tartars in Romania
Cultural Union of Albanians in Romania
Community of Lipovenian Russians in Romania
Democratic Union of Serbs and Carasovenians in Romania
Union of Armenians in Romania
Union of Ukrainians in Romania
German Democratic Forum of Romania.

Source: Press Department of the Romanian Embassy, Bonn. Also adapted from *Open Media Research Institute (OMRINet)* data. Taken from the Internet on 26.11.96. Http: //www.omri.cz.

APPENDIX XXXIII

*Romanian Presidential Election: First Round,
3 November, 1996*

Candidate	Party	% Votes
Ion Iliescu	PDSR	32.25
Emil Constantinescu	CDR	28.21
Petre Roman	USD	20.54
Gyorgy Fruda	UDMR	6.02
Corneliu Vadim Tudor	PRM	4.72
Gheorghe Funar	PUNR	3.22
Tudor Mohara	PS	1.27
Nicolae Manolescu	ANL	0.71
Adrian Paunescu	PSM	0.69
Radu Campeanu	Independent	0.35
Nicolae Militaru	Independent	0.22

PDSR: Party of Social Democracy in Romania
CDR: Democratic Convention of Romania
USD: Social Democratic Union
UDMR: Democratic Federation of Hungarians in Romania
PRM: Greater Romania Party
PUNR: Party of Romanian National Unity
PS: Socialist Party
ANL: National-Liberal Alliance
PSM: Socialist Labour Party

Romanian Presidential Election: Run-Off, 17 November, 1996

Candidate	Party	% Votes
Ion Iliescu	PDSR	45.59
Emil Constantinescu	CDR	54.41

Source: Adapted from *Open Media Research Institute (OMRINet)* data. Taken from the Internet. Http: //www.omri.cz.

APPENDIX XXXIV
Structure of Czechoslovak Steel Output by Type of Process (% shares in Total Production)

Method of Production	1970 World Average	1970 CSSR	1980 World average	1980 CSSR
Siemens-Martin	39.4	68.3	23.8	61.3
Electrical Furnaces	14.7	11.7	22.0	12.8
Oxygen Converters	41.1	18.0	53.3	25.9
Continuously Cast Steel	4.2	0.4	30.0	1.5[*]

[*] The share of continuously cast steel was planned to increase to 8% by 1985, but this was still below the world average, which had already reached approximately 40% by 1982.

Source: Adapted from Sobell, Vlad, 'Czechoslvoakia: The Legacy of Normalization', *East European Politics and Societies*, Vol. 2, No. 1, Winter 1988, p. 48. Original in Miksa, Josef, 'Ferrous Metallurgy: Which Direction to Go?' *Hospodárské Noviny*, No. 24, 1985, pp. 8-9.

APPENDIX XXXV
The Impact of Economic Transition on the Economies of Hungary and Czechoslovakia (Annual Change)

Country	Industrial Output	Agriculture	Retail prices	Unemployment (% of Labour Force)
Hungary				
1990	-9.2	-3.8	28.9	1.7
1991	-21.5	2.0	35.0	8.3
1992*	-15.0	-3.0	17.5	11.4 (a)
Czechoslovakia				
1990	-3.7	-3.5	10.0	0.3
1991	-32.1	-8.8	53.6	6.6
1992*	-9.0	-10.0	12.0	6.0

* Estimate
(a) September 1992 actual.

Source: Adapted from White, Stephen, Batt, Judy, Lewis, Paul, G., *Developments in East European Politics*, Macmillan 1993, p. 218. Original in Economist Intelligence Unit Data.

BIBLIOGRAPHY

AAREBROT, Frank, H., BAKKA, Pal, H., 'Die vergleichende Methode'. Chapter 1, in BERG-SCHLOSSER, Dirk, MÜLLER-ROMMEL, Ferdinand, *Vergleichende Politikwissenschaft*, Opladen 1992.

ACZEL, György, 'The Challenge of our Age and the Response of Socialism', *The New Hungarian Quarterly*.

ACZEL, Tamas; MERAY, Tibor, *Die Revolte des Intellekts*, Langen-Müller 1961.

ADAM, Jan, 'The Transition to a Market Economy in Hungary', *Europe-Asia Studies*, Vol. 47, No. 6, 1995.

ADAM, Jan, 'Transformation to a Market Economy in the former Czechoslovakia', *Europe-Asia Studies*, Vol. 45, No. 4, 1993.

ÁGH, Attila, KURTÁN, Sándor, (Eds.), *Democratization and Europeanization in Hungary: The First Parliament (1990-1994)*, Hungarian Centre for Democracy Studies 1995.

ÁGH, Attila, KURTÁN, Sándor, *The First Parliament (1990-1994)*, Hungarian Centre for Democracy Studies 1995.

AKOS, Valentinyi, 'Monetary Policy and Stabilisation in Hungary', *Soviet Studies*, Vol. 44, No. 6, 1992.

ALMOND, Mark, 'Romania Since the Revolution', *Government and Opposition*, Vol. 25, No. 4, Winter 1990.

ALMOND, Mark, *The Rise and Fall of Nicolae and Elena Ceausescu*, Chapmans 1992.

ALTHAMMER, Walter 'Soziale Marktwirtschaft – ein Modell für Osteuropa?' *Südosteuropa Mitteilungen*, Vol. 35, No. 4, 1995.

ALTHAMMER, Walter, 'Was ist zu tun in Südosteuropa?' *Südosteuropa Mitteilungen*, Vol. 37, No. 2, 1997.

ALTMANN, Franz-Lothar, HOESCH, Edgar, (Hrsg.), *Reformen und Reformer in Osteuropa*, Verlag Friedrich Pustet 1994.

Amnesty International, *Rumänien: Zur politischen Verfolgung seit 1970*, Nomos Verlag 1978.

ANDERSON, Andy, *Die ungarische Revolution 1956*, Verlag Association 1977.

ANKERL, Géza, 'The Native Right to speak Hungarian in the Carpathian Basin', *The Hungarian Quarterly*, Vol. 35, No. 133, Spring 1994.

ANTALL, J., 'Remembering the Revolution', *Current Policy*, No. 41, 1991.

ANTALL, József, 'Spiegel Interview', *Der Spiegel*, No. 21, 1990.

APPEL, Hilary, 'Justice and the Reformation of Property Rights in the Czech Republic', *East European Politics and Societies*, Vol. 9, No. 1, 1995.

ARATO, Andrew, 'Bruch oder Kontinutiät?' *Transit*, No. 9, Summer 1995.

ARATO, Andrew, 'Election, Coalition and Constitution in Hungary', *The Hungarian Quarterly*, Vol. 35, No. 135, Autumn 1994.

ARATO, Andrew, 'Revolution, *civil society* und Demokratie', *Transit*, No. 1, Autumn 1990.

ARENDT, Hannah, *Die ungarische Revolution und der totalitäre Imperialismus*, R. Piper & Co. Verlag 1958.

ARMSTRONG, John, A., 'Toward a Framework for Considering Nationalism in East Europe', *East European Politics and Societies*, Vol. 2, No. 2, Spring 1988.

ASCHENBRENNER, Viktor, *Böhmen: Herzland Europas*, Würzburg Verlag 1994.

ASH, Timothy Garton, 'Central Europe: The Present Past', *The New York Review of Books*, 13 July 1995.

ASH, Timothy Garton, 'Mitteleuropa?', *Daedalus*, Vol. 119, No. 1, Winter 1990.

ASH, Timothy Garton, 'Prag: Intellektuelle und Politiker', *Transit*, No. 10, Autumn 1995.

ASH, Timothy Garton, *The Uses of Adveristy*, Penguin Books 1991.

ASH, Timothy Garton, *We the People*, Granata Books 1990.

ASLUND, Anders, *Post-Communist Economic Revolutions: How Big a Bang?* Center for Strategic and International Studies, Washington D.C. 1992.

AXENCIUC, Viktor, TIBERIAN, Ioan, *The Making of the Unitary Romanian National State*, The Academy of Social and Political Sciences of the Socialist Republic of Romania 1989.

AXT, Heinz-Jürgen, 'Der Beitrag der Europäischen Union zur Modernisierung südosteuropäischer Staaten', *Südosteuropa Mitteilungen*, Vol. 35, No. 2, 1995.

BACIU, Nicolas, *Verraten und Verkauft*, Universitas Verlag 1986.

BACKHAUS, Jürgen, (Hrsg.), *Systemwandel und Reform in östlichen Wirtschaften*, Metropolis 1991.

BAKKA, Pál, H., *Imperial Breakdown, Political Fragmentation and State-Building*, Paper, 16 World Congress of the International Political Science Association, Berlin, August 21-25 1994.

BAKOS, Gabor, 'Hungarian Transition after Three Years', *Europe-Asia Studies*, Vol. 46, No. 7, 1994.

BALAN, Dodu, Ion, *Cultural Policy in Romania*, UNESCO Press 1975.

BALÁZS, Peter, 'How can the European Community be Expanded?' *The New Hungarian Quarterly*, Vol. 33, No. 125, Spring 1992.

BANAC, Ivo, *Eastern Europe in Revolution*, Cornell University Press 1992.

BANGO, Jenö, *Die post-sozialistische Gesellschaft Ungarns*, Trofenik Verlag 1991.

BARBARIA, Frank, A., *Modern 'Asiatic' Despotism ~ Masquerading in Communist Workers' Ideology*, IDEAS 1980.

BART, István, 'Transition and Privatisation in Publishing', *The Hungarian Quarterly*, Vol. 36, No. 140, Winter 1995.

BARTLETT, David, 'The Political Economy of Privitization: Property Reform and Democracy in Hungary', *East European Politics and Societies*, Vol. 6, No. 1, Winter 1992.

BARTLETT, David, L., 'Democracy, Institutional Change and Stabilisation Policy in Hungary', *Europe-Asia Studies*, Vol. 48, No. 1, 1996.

BATT, Judy, 'The End of Communist Rule in East-Central Europe: A Four Country Comparison', *Government and Opposition*, Vol. 26, No. 3, Autumn 1991.

BAUER, Tamás, 'Hungarian Economic Reform in East European Perspective', *East European Politics and Societies*, Vol. 2, No. 3, Fall 1988.

BAUER, Tamás, 'The Hungarian Alternative to Soviet-Type Planning', *Journal of Comaprative Economics*, Vol. 7, No. 3, 1983.

BAYER, József, 'Zur Kontinuität der Legitimationskrise in Ungarn', *Südosteuropa*, Vol. 44, No. 11-12, 1995.

BAYER, Jozsef, DEPPE, Rainer, (Hrsg.), *Der Schock der Freiheit*, Suhrkamp 1993.

BECKHERRN, Eberhard, *Tal der Wende: Wohin steuert Osteuropa?* Knaur 1991.

BÉKÉS, Csaba, 'The 1956 Revolution and World Politics', *The Hungarian Quarterly*, Vol. 36, No. 138, Summer 1995.

BENDA, Kálmán, 'From St. Stephen to Post-Ceausescu', *The Hungarian Quarterly*, Vol. 35, No. 133, Spring 1994.

BERECZ, János, *1956: Counter-Revolution in Hungary*, Budapest 1956.

BEREND, Ivan, T., RANKI, György, *Economic Development in East Central Europe in the Nineteenth and Twentieth Centuries*, Columbia University Press 1974.

BERG-SCHLOSSER, Dirk, QUENTER, Sven, 'Makro-Quantitative vs. Makro-Qualitative Methoden', *Politisches Vierteljahresheft*, Vol. 37, No. 1, März 1996.

BERG-SCHLOSSER, Dirk, MÜLLER-ROMMEL, Ferdinand, *Vergleichende Politikwissenschaft*, Opladen 1992.

BERG-SCHLOSSER, Dirk, MÜLLER-ROMMEL, Ferdinand, *Vergleichende Politikwissenschaft (3. Auflage)*, Leske & Budrich 1997.

BERGLUND, Sten, DELLENBRANT, Jan Aake, (Eds.), *The New Democracies in Eastern Europe (Second Edition)*, Edward Elgar 1994.

BERGMANN, Theodor, *Ketzer im Kommunismus*, Decaton Verlag 1993.

BERINDEI, Dan, 'Pro und Kontra Ion Antonescu: Eine Geschichtsdebatte in Rumänien', *Südosteuropa*, Vol. 45, No. 11-12, 1996.

BERMEO, Nancy, (Ed.), *Liberalization and Democratization*, John Hopkins University Press 1992.

BERNTZEN, Einar, 'Values Count but Institutions Decide: The Stein Rokkan Approach in Comparative Political Sociology', *Scandinavian Political Studies*, Vol. 15, No. 4, 1992.

BEYRAM, D., BOCK, I., (Hrsg.), *Das Tauwetter und die Folgen*, Temmen 1988.

BIBÓ, István, *Democracy, Revolution, Self-Determination*, Columbia University Press 1991.

BIBÓ, István, *Die Misere der osteuropäischen Kleinstaaterei*, Verlag Neue Kritik 1992.

BIDELUX, Robert, *Communism and Development*, London 1985.

BIGLER, Robert, M., 'Back in Europe and Adjusting to the New Realities of the 1990's in Hungary', *East European Quarterly*, Vol. 30, No. 2, Summer 1996.

BINGEN, Dieter, *Die revolutionäre Umwälzung in Mittel- und Osteuropa*, Göttinger Arbeitskreis Papier No. 10, Duncker & Humblot 1993.

BLOMMESTEIN, Hans, MARESSE, Michael, (Eds.), *Transformation of Planned Economies*, OECD 1991.

BOCK, Ivo, SCHLOTT, Wolfgang, TATUR, Melanie, *Kollektive Identitäten in Ostmitteleuropa*, Temmen 1994.

BOGETIC, Zeljko, 'The Role of Employee Ownership in Privatisation of State Enterprises in Eastern and Central Europe', *Europe-Asia Studies*, Vol. 45, No. 3, 1993.

BOSSÁNYI, Katalin, 'Taking Stock of Economic Transition', *The Hungarian Quarterly*, Vol. 36, No. 138, Summer 1995.

BOSSÁNYI, Katalin, 'Two-Thirds Country: Income Inequality in Hungary in the Nineties', *The Hungarian Quarterly*, Vol. 38, No. 146, Summer 1997.

BOTOS, Katalin, 'Financial Aspects of Agricultural Policies in Hungary', *Soviet Studies*, Vol. 42, No. 1, January 1990.

BOURGIN, Simon, 'The Well of Discontent: A Senior American Correspondent's Briefings on Budapest, 1956. Part I', *The Hungarian Quarterly*, Vol. 37, No. 142, Summer 1996.

BOURGIN, Simon, 'The Well of Discontent: A Senior American Correspondent's Briefings on Budapest, 1956. Part II', *The Hungarian Quarterly*, Vol. 37, No. 143, Autumn 1996.

BOZÓKI, András, 'Censorship in the 1980's', *The Hungarian Quarterly*, Vol. 36, No. 139, Autumn 1995.

BOZÓKI, András, 'Democracy Across the Negotiating Table', *The New Hungarian Quarterly*, Vol. 33, No. 125, Spring 1992.

BOZÓKI, András, 'Hungary's Road to Systemic Change: The Opposition Roundtable', *East European Politics and Societies*, Vol. 7, No. 2, Spring 1993.

BOZÓKI, András, 'Intellectuals in a New Democracy: The Democratic Charter in Hungary', *East European Politics and Societies*, Vol. 10, No. 2, Spring 1996.

BOZÓKI, András, 'Post-Communist Transition: Political Tendencies in Hungary', *East European Politics and Societies*, Vol. 4, No. 2, Spring 1990.

BRAHAM, Randolph, L., 'The Jews of Translyvania: Opportunistic Historical Accounts', *East European Quarterly*, Vol. 31, No. 4, Winter 1997.

BRAHM, Heinz, *Die neue Parteienlandschaft in Osteuropa*, Bundesinstitut für Ostwissenschaftliche und Internationale Studien, Bericht No. 35, 1993.

BREN, Paulina, 'Lustration in the Czech and Slovak Republics', *RFE/RL Research Report*, Vol. 2, No. 29, 16 July 1993.

BRINE, Jenny, *Comecom: The Rise and Fall of an International Socialist Organisation*, Clio Press 1992.

BROGAN, Patrick, *Eastern Europe 1939-1989*, Bloomsbury 1990.

BROM, Karla, ORENSTEIN, Mitchell, 'The Privatised Sector in the Czech Republic: Government and Bank Control in a Transitional Economy', *Europe-Asia Studies*, Vol. 46, No. 6, 1994.

BROWN, James, F., *Challenges to Soviet Control in Eastern Europe*, Rand 1984.

BROWN, James, F., *Eastern Europe and Communist Rule*, Duke University Press 1988.

BROWN, James, F., *Surge to Freedom*, Duke University Press 1991.

BRUNNER, Georg, (Hrsg.), *Ungarn auf dem Weg der Demokratie*, Bouvier Verlag 1993.

BRUSZT, Laszlo, 'Transformative Politics: Social Costs and Social Peace in East Central Europe', *East European Politics and Societies*, Vol. 6, No. 1, Winter 1992.

BRZEZINSKY, Z., K., *The Soviet Bloc: Unity and Conflict*, Harvard University Press 1974.

BRZEZINSKY, Zbigniew, 'A Plan for Europe', *Foreign Affairs*, Vol. 74, No. 1, January-February 1995.

BUCH, Claudia, M., *Bank Behaviour and Bad Loans*, Kiel Working Paper No. 679.

BUCH, Claudia, M., *Dealing with Bad Debt – Lessons from Eastern Europe*, Kiel Working Paper, No. 642, July 1994.

BUCH, Claudia, M., *Monetary Policy and the Transformation of the Banking System in Eastern Europe*, Kiel Working Paper No. 676, February 1995.

BUCH, Claudia, M., *Overcoming Obstacles to Successful Reforms in Economies in Transition*, Kiel Studies No. 261, 1994.

Budapest University Research Group, *Human Right's in Today's Hungary*, Mezon 1990.

BUGAJSKI, Janusz, POLLACK, Maxine, *East European Fault Lines: Dissent, Opposition and Social Activism*, Westview Press 1989.

BUNCE, Valerie; CSANÁDI, Maria, 'Uncertainty in the Transition: Post-Communism in Hungary', *East European Politics and Societies*, Vol. 7, No. 2, Spring 1993.

Bundesinsitut für Ostwissenschaftliche und Internationale Studien, *Aufbruch im Osten Europas: Chancen für die Demokratie und Marktwirschaft nach dem Zerfall des Kommunismus,* Carl Hanser Verlag 1993.

Bundesinsitut für Ostwissenschaftliche und Internationale Studien, *Zwischen Krise und Konsolidierung,* Carl Hanser Verlag 1995.

BURGER, Josef, 'The Politics of Restitution in Czechoslovakia', *East European Politics,* Vol. 31, No. 4, Winter 1992.

BUSCH, Ulrich, VARGA, József, 'Finanzierungsprobleme des Budgets in Ungarn', *Südosteuropa,* Vol. 46, Bo. 1-2, 1997.

BUSCH, Ulrich, VARGA, Jozsef, 'Konsolidierungsbemühungen in monetären Sektor Ungarns', *Südosteuropa,* Vol. 45, No. 4-5, 1996.

BUTNARU, I., C., *The Silent Holocaust,* Greenwood Press 1992.

CALINESCU, Matei, TISMANEANU, Vladimir, 'The 1989 Revolution and Romania's Future', *Problems of Communism,* Vol. 40, No. 1-2, January-April 1991.

CAPEK, Ales, SAZAMA, Gerald, W., 'Czech and Slovak Economic Relations', *Europe-Asia Studies,* Vol. 45, No. 2, 1993.

CAREY, Henry, F., 'From Big Lie to Small Lies: State Mass Media Dominance in Post-Communist Romania', *East European Politics and Societies,* Vol. 10, No. 1, Winter 1996.

CASTELLAN, Georges, *A History of the Balkans,* Boulder 1992.

CEBULAK, Wojciech, 'Social Turmoil in Post-Socialist Eastern Europe: A Revolution gone Astray?' *East European Quarterly,* Vol. 31, No. 1, March 1997.

Central European Online, *Alliance of Free Democrats.*

Central European Online, *Alliance of Young Democrats – Hungarian Civic Party.*

Central European Online, *Czech Budget Still $465 million in the Hole.*

Central European Online, *Czech Cabinet to Discuss National Property Fund.*

Central European Online, *Hungarian Democratic People's Party.*

Central European Online, *Hungarian Economic Index Charts.*

Central European Online, *Latest Figures from the Hungarian Economy.*

Central European Online, *Main Figures from the Hungarian Economy.*

Central European Online, *Romania: Economy.*

Central European Online, *Romanian Labor Movement, Trade Unions, Social and Economic Data.*

CERNOHORSKY, Ivan, *Monetäre Aspekte des Transformationsprozesses in Mittel- und Osteuropa am Beispiel der Tschechoslowakei*, Würzburg 1992.

CHAN, Claude, 'An Ordinary Pogrom', *Transitions*, Vol. 4, No. 4, September 1997.

CHARLTON, Michael, *The Eagle and the Small Birds*, BBC 1984.

CHAVANCE, Bernard, *The Transformation of Communist Systems*, Westview Press 1994.

CHINYAEVA, Elena, 'Hostages of Their own music', *Transitions*, Vol. 4, No. 4, September 1997.

CHIROT, D., *The Origins of Backwardness in Eastern Europe*, University of California Press 1988.

CHRUSCHTCHOW, Nikita, *Die Geheimrede Chruschtchows: ZK der KPdSU, 20. Parteitag, 25 Februar 1956*, Dietz Verlag 1990.

CIA World Fact Book 1993.

CICHY, Ulrich, E., 'Ungarn: Teilerfolge bei der wirtschaftlichen Transformation', *Vierteljahresberichte*, No. 132, Juni 1993.

CLARK, Ed, SOUSLSBY Anna, 'The Re-formation of the Managerial Elite in the Czech Republic', *Europe-Asia Studies*, Vol. 48, No. 2, 1996.

CLAWSON, P., 'Promoting Democracy Abroad', *Orbis*, Vol. 37, No. 4, Fall 1993.

CLEMENT, Rolf, 'Das Ziel ist mehr Sicherheit', *Europäische Sicherheit*, Vol. 46, No. 2, February 1997.

COLLIER, D., 'The Comparative Method', in **FINIFTER, A., W.,** (Ed.), *Political Science: The State of the Discipline II*, Washington DC 1993.

COMISSO, Ellen, 'Market Failures and Market Socialsim: Economic Problems of the Transition', *East European Politics and Societies*, Vol. 2, No. 3, Fall 1988.

CONNELLY, John, 'Foundations for Reconstructing Elites: Communist Higher Education Policies in the Czech Lands, East Germany and Poland, 1945-1948', *East European Politics and Societies*, Vol. 10, No. 3, Fall 1996.

Constanza Port Administration, *Constanza Port*, 1996.

COPOSU, Corneliu, 'Interview', *Südosteuropa*, Vol. 42, No. 7-8, 1993.

COULTER, Fiona, HEADY, Christopher, LAWSON, Colin, SMITH, Steven, 'Fiscal Systems in Transition: The Case of the Czech Income Tax Law', *Europe-Asia Studies*, Vol. 47, No. 6, 1995.

COWEN KARP, Regina, *Central and Eastern Europe: The Challenge of Transition*, Oxford University Press 1993.

COX, Terry, FURLONG, Andy, (Eds.), *Hungary: The Politics of Transition*, Frank Cass & Co. Ltd. 1995.

COX, Terry, FURLONG, Andy, *Hungary: The Politics of Transition*, Frank Cass 1995.

CRACIUN, Maria, GHITTA, Ovidiu, (Eds.), *Ethnicity and Religion*, Cluj University Press 1995.

CRAMPTON, R., J., *Eastern Europe in the Twentieth Century,* Routledge 1994.

CRANE, Keith, *The Romanian Economic Mess after Ceausescu,* The Rand Corporation, December 1988.

CREMONA, Marise, 'Community Relations with the Visegrad Group', *Current Survey,* 1992.

CROAN, Melvin, 'The Lands In-Between: The Politics of Cultural Identity in Contemporary Eastern Europe', *East European Politics and Societies,* Vol. 3, No. 2, Spring 1989.

CSABA, Gombar, *Balance: The Hungarian Government 1990-1994,* Budapest 1994.

CSABA, László, 'A Convalescent Economy', *The New Hungarian Quarterly,* Vol. 33, No. 126, Summer 1992.

CSABA, László, 'Macroeconomic Policy in Hungary: Poetry versus Reality', *Soviet Studies,* Vol. 44, No. 6, 1992.

CSABA, László, 'Ripeness is All: From Comecon to the European Union', *The Hungarian Quarterly,* Vol. 36, No. 137, Spring 1995.

CSALOG, Zsolt, "We offer our Love': Gypsies in Hungary', *The New Hungarian Quarterly,* Vol. 33, No. 127, Autumn 1992.

CSEPELI, György, 'The Social Psychology of a Changeover', *The Hungarian Quarterly,* Vol. 36, No. 132, Spring 1995.

CSEPELI, György, ÖRKÉNY, Antal, *Ideology and Political Beliefs in Hungary,* Pinter Publishers 1992.

CSEPELI, György, ÖRKÉY, Antal, 'From Unjust Equality to Just Inequality', *The New Hungarian Quarterly,* Vol. 33, No. 126, Summer 1992.

CSEPELI, György, *Structure and Contents of Hungarian National Identity,* Peter Lang 1989.

CSONTOS, L., 'Fiscal Illusions, Decision Theory and Public Sector Reform', *Acta Oeconomica*, Vol. 47, No. 3-4, 1995.

CUNNINGHAM, F., *Democratic Theory and Socialism*, Cambridge University Press 1987.

Czech Trade and Industry Ministry, *Tschechische Republik: Wirtschaftshandbuch_1997*, Prague 1997.

CZERWINSKI, E., J., PIELKALKIEWICZ, J., (Eds.), *The Soviet Invasion of Czechoslovakia: Its Effects on Eastern Europe*, Praeger 1972.

d'ESTAING, Valéry Giscard, 'The Two halves of Europe', *International Affairs*, Vol. 65, No. 4, Autumn 1989.

DAHRENDORF, Ralf, 'Übergänge: Politik, Wirtschaft und Freiheit', *Transit*, No. 1, Autumn 1990.

DANIELS, R., V., *A Documentary History of Communism: Volume 2*, University Press New England 1984.

DANIELS, Robert, V., *The End of the Communist Revolution*, Routledge 1993.

DAVIDSON, Ian, 'The Search for A New Order in Europe', *International Affairs*, Vol. 66, No. 2, April 1990.

DAWISHA, Karen, *Eastern Europe, Gorbachev and Reform*, Cambridge University Press 1990.

DAWISHA, Karen, PARROT, Bruce, *Politics, Power and the Struggle for Democracy in South-East Europe*, Cambridge University Press 1997.

DAWISHA, Karen, PARROT, Bruce, *The Consolidation of Democracy in East-Central Europe*, Cambridge University Press 1997.

de CANDOLE, James, *Czechoslovakia: The End of an Illusion*, Institute for European Defence and Strategic Studies 1993.

de NÈVRE, Dorothée, 'Die Parlamentarische Opposition in Rumänien', *Südosteuropa*, Vol. 35, No. 4, 1995.

DEÁK, István, 'Uncovering Eastern Europe's Dark History', *Orbis*, Vol. 34, No. 1, Winter 1990.

DELAPINA, Franz, HOFBAUER, Hannes, KOMLISY, Andrea, MELINZ, Gerhard, ZIMMERMANN, Susan, *Ungarn im Umbruch*, Verlag für Gesellschaftskritik 1991.

DELVIN, Kevin, 'Are the East Blocs Reformable?' *RFE/RL Background Report*, No. 3, November 1993.

Der Fischer Weltalmanach 1990, Fischer Taschenbuch Verlag 1989.

DESAI, Padama, 'Is the Soviet Union Subsidizing Eastern Europe?', *European Economic Review*, Vol. 30, No. 1, January 1986.

DEUBNER, Christian, KRAMER, Heinz, 'Die Erweiterung der Europäischen Union nach Mittel- und Osteuropa', *Aus Politik und Zeitgeschichte*, No. 18-19, 6 Mai 1994.

Deutsche Bank Research, *Fokus Osteuropa*, 10 March 1997.

Devon and Cornwall Constabulary, *Romanian Police Know-How Fund*, April-July, July-September, September-November 1997.

DJILAS, Milovan, 'A Revolutionary Democratic Vision of Europe', *International Affairs*, Vol. 66, No. 2, April 1990.

DOBSZAY, János, 'Back to the Future: The 1994 Elections', *The Hungarian Quarterly*, Vol. 35, No. 134, Summer 1994.

DODD, Thomas, 'Genossenschaften – ein Modell für Osteuropa?' *Aussenpolitik*, Vol. 45, No. 2, 1994.

DONGES, Jürgen, B., *Zur Wirtschaftsreform in Osteuropa*, Frankfurter Institut für wirtschaftliche Forschung e.V., No. 24, January 1992.

DÖRLER, Bernd, 'Alle wollen weg – Sofort', *Der Spiegel*, No. 4, 1990.

DRUKER, Jeremy, 'Present but Unaccounted for. How many Roma live in Central and Eastern Europe depends on who you ask', *Transitions*, Vol. 4, No. 4, September 1997.

DRUMMOND, Philip, PATERSON, Rishard,WILIS, Janet, *National Identity and Europe*, BJF Publishing 1993.

DRUWE, Ulrich, *Osteuropa im Wandel: Szenarien einer ungewissen Zukunft*, Beltz Quadriga 1992.

DUBRAVCIC, Dinko, 'Entrepreneurial Aspects of Privatisation in Transition Economies', *Europe-Asia Studies*, Vol. 47, No. 2, 1995.

DUFFEK, Karl, *Die demokratischen Revolutionen in Mittel- und Osteuropa*, Passagen Verlag 1991.

DUNAY, Pál, *Das alte Ungarn im neuen Europa?* Hessische Stiftung für Friedens- und Konfliktforschung No. 2, 1993.

DUNCAN, Peter, J., S., RADY, Martyn, (Eds.), *Culture and Politics in Post-Totalitarian Europe*, LIT Verlag 1993.

DUNCAN, Peter, J., S., RADY, Martyn, (Eds.), *Towards a New Community*, LIT 1993.

DUTU, Alexandru, 'Kirche und Staat im heutigen Rumänien', *Südosteuropa Jahrbuch*, No. 25, 1994.

DUTU, Alexandru, 'National Identity and Tensional Factors in South Eastern Europe', *East European Quarterly*, Vol. 31, No. 2, Summer 1997.

DVORÁKOVÁ, Vladimíra, VORÁCEK, Emil, (Eds.), *The Legacy of the Past as a Factor of the Transformation Process in Postcommunist Countries of Central Europe*, Papers from a Conference organised by the Department of Political Science, University of Economics Prague, 7-9.12.93.

DYKER, David, A., 'Learning the Game: Technological Factors of Economic Transformation', *Europe-Asia Studies*, Vol. 49, No. 3, May 1997, pp. 445-461.

East European Politics and Societies, 'Post-1989 Intellectual Cooperation and Intellectual Property Rights: A Romanian Case', Vol. 10, No. 2, Spring 1996.

EAST, Roger, *Revolutions in Eastern Europe*, Pinter Publishers 1992.

East-West, 'Romania Reschedules 1986-87 Commercial Debt', No. 391, July 1986.

EIS, Zdeněk, 'Tradition und Gegenwart in der politischen Kultur der Tschechoslowakei', *Zeitschrift für Politik*, Vol. 39, No. 2, 1992.

ELLINGSTRAD, Marc, 'The Maquiladora Syndrome: Central European Prospects', *Europe-Asia Studies*, Vol. 49, No. 1, 1997.

Embassy of Romania, *Econoic Bulletin: April 1997.*

Embassy of Romania, *Economic Bulletin: February 1997.*

Embassy of Romania, *Economic Bulletin: January 1997.*

Embassy of Romania, *Economic Bulletin: March 1997.*

Embassy of Romania, *Economic Bulletin: May 1997.*

Embassy of Romania, *Privatization in Romania.*

Embassy of the Czech Republic, *Wirtschaftsbrief Tschechien*, April 1997.

Embassy of the Czech Republic, *Wirtschaftsbrief Tschechien*, March 1997.

Embassy of the Republic of Hungary, *The Presence of IFOR/SFOR in Hungary and the Hungarian Military Participation in Peace Operations in the Former Yugoslavia.*

Embassy of the Republic of Hungary, *Ungarn – parlamentarische Republik*, Fakten über Ungarn 1994.

ESTRIN, Saul, HARE, Paul, SURÁNYI, Marta, 'Banking in Transition: Development and Current Problems in Hungary', *Soviet Studies*, Vol. 44, No. 5, 1992.

EVANS, Geoffry, WHITEFIELD, Stephen, 'Social and Ideological Cleavage Formation in Post-Communist Hungary', *Europe-Asia Studies*, Vol. 47, No. 7, 1995.

FAHIDI, Gergely, 'Paying for the Past', *The Hungarian Quarterly*, Vol. 35, No. 136, Winter 1994.

FÉHÉR, Ferenc, 'On Making Central Europe', *East European Politics and Societies*, Vol. 3, No. 3, Fall 1989.

FÉNYES, Dr. S., *Revisionist Hungary*, Romanian Historical Studies 1988.

FENYO, Mario, D., 'Literature and Society: Hungary and the Millennium', *East European Quarterly*, Vol. 30, No. 4, Winter 1996.

FERREIRA, Margarida, 'The Liberalisation of East-West Trade: An Assessment of its Impact on Exports from Central and Eastern Europe', *Europe-Asia Studies*, Vol. 47, No. 7, 1995.

FETJÖ, François, 'A Curtain of Indifference to Follow the Iron Curtain?' *The Hungarian Quarterly*, Vol. 136, No. 139, Autumn 1995.

FINE, C., R., 'The Diminishing Real Wage: Tripartism's Balance of Power in Hungary', *East European Quarterly*, Vol. 31, No. 2, Summer 1997.

FINK, Gerhard, *Rumänien: Wirtschafts- und Systempolitik*, Bundesinstitut für Ostwissenschaftliche und Internationale Studien, Bericht No. 51, 1984.

FISCHER, Klemens, H., 'Die Europäische Union – Zwischen Erweiterung und Vertiefung', *Europäische Sicherheit*, Vol. 46, No. 1, January 1997.

FISCHER-GALATI, Stephen, *Communist Parties of Eastern Europe*, Columbia University Press 1979.

FISCHER-GALATI, Stephen, *Twentieth Century Romania*, Columbia University Press 1970.

FIW SYMPOSIUM, *Mittel und Osteuropa im marktwirtschaftlichen Umbruch*, No. 142, Carl Heymans Verlag 1991.

FLOROR, P., (Hrsg.), *State, Economy and Society in Eastern Europe 1815-1975*, Campus 1983.

FOWKES, Ben, *Aufstieg und Niedergang des Kommunismus in Osteuropa*, Decaton Verlag 1994.

FRENKIN, Anatoli, 'Rußlands mögliche Reaktionen auf die Osterweiterung der NATO', *Europäische Sicherheit*, Vol. 46, No. 2, February 1997.

FRENTZEL-ZAGORSKA, Janina, 'Civil Society in Poland and Hungary', *Soviet Studies*, Vol. 42, No. 4, 1990.

FRIEDRICH, Clemens, MENZEL, Birgit, (Hrsg.), *Osteuropa im Umbruch*, Peter Lang 1994.

FRYDMAN, Roman, RAPACZYNSKI, Andrzej, 'Wieviel Staat braucht der Markt?' *Transit*, No. 3, Winter 1991/92.

FUNKE, Norbert, 'Timing and Sequencing of Reforms: Competing Views and the Role of Credibility', *Kyklos*, Vol. 46, 1993.

GABANYI, Anneli Ute, 'Ceausescu's Personality Cult', *RFE/RL Reseach: Romanian Situation Report*, 6 February 1987.

GABANYI, Anneli Ute, 'Kommunalwahlen in Rumänien', *Südosteuropa*, Vol. 45, No. 11-12, 1996.

GABANYI, Anneli Ute, 'Politische Parteien in Rumänien nach der Wende', *Südosteuropa*, Vol. 44, No. 112, 1994.

GABANYI, Anneli Ute, 'Rumänien zwischen Revolution und Restauration', *Aus Politik und Zeitgeschichte*, Vol. 42, No. 14.

GABANYI, Anneli Ute, 'Rumänien: Die Wende als institutioneller Wandel', *Südosteuropa Jahrbuch*, No. 25, 1994.

GABANYI, Anneli Ute, 'Rumäniens Sicherheit und die NATO', *Südosteuropa*, Vol. 43, No. 1-2, 1994.

GABANYI, Anneli Ute, 'Systemwandel in Rumänien: Verfassung und neue Institutionen', *Südosteuropa*, Vol. 44, No. 9-10, 1995.

GABANYI, Anneli Ute, 'Ungarn und die rumänische Sicherheit: Perzeption und Politik', *Südosteuropa*, Vol. 42, No. 9, 1993.

GABANYI, Anneli Ute, *Die unvollendete Revolution*, Piper 1990.

GÁBOR, R., I., 'Small Entrepreneuership in Hungary – Ailing or Prospering?' *Acta Oeconomica*, Vol. 46, No. 3-4, 1994.

GABRISCH, Hubert, 'Eastern Enlargement of the European Union: Macroeconomic Effects in New Member States', *Europe-Asia Studies*, Vol. 49, No. 4, June 1997, pp. 567-590.

GALLAGHER, Tom, *Romania after Ceausescu*, Edinburgh University Press 1995.

GATI, Charles, *Hungary and the Soviet Bloc*, Duke University Press 1986.

GATI, Charles, *The 'oc that Failed*, Indiana University Press 1990.

GEDEON, Péter, 'Hungary: Social Policy in Transition', *East European Politics and Societies*, Vol. 9, No. 3, Fall 1995.

GEORGESCU, Vlad, 'Romania in the 1980's: The Legacy of Dynastic Socialism', *East European Politics and Societies*, Vol. 2, No. 1, Winter 1988.

GERLICH, Peter, PLASSER, Fritz, ULRAM, Peter, (Hrsg.), *Regimewechsel*, Böhlau 1993.

GERÖ, András, *Modern Hungary Society in the Making*, Central European University Press 1995.

GHERMANI, Dionisie, 'Stagnation und Hoffnungszeichen: Rumänien fünf Jahre nach dem Sturz Ceausescus', *Herder Korrespondenz*, Heft 2, Vol. 48, November 1994.

GIBNEY, Mark, 'Prosecuting Human Rights Violations from a Previous Regime: The East European Experience', *East European Quarterly*, Vol. 31, No. 1, March 1997.

GILBERG, Trond, *Modernization in Romania since World War II*, Preager 1975.

GLAESSNER, Gert-Joachim, *Demokratie nach dem Ende des Kommunismus*, Westdeutscher Verlag 1994.

GLIGOROV, Vladimir, 'Gradual Shock Therapy', *East European Politics and Societies*, Vol. 9, No. 1, Winter 1995.

GLOTZ, Peter, 'Die Einheit und die Spaltung Europas', *Aus Politik und Zeitgeschichte*, No. 6, 30 Januar 1992.

GOLAN, Galia, *Reform Rule in Czechoslovakia*, Cambridge University Press 1973.

GOLEA, Traian, *Romania: Beyond the Limits of Endurance*, Romanian Historical Studies 1988.

GOMA, Paul, *Lumea Libera*, New York, 16 June 1990.

GOMULKA, Stanislav, *Growth, Innovation and Reform in Eastern Europe*, Wheatsheaf.

GÖNCZ, Árpád, 'Intellectual or Politician?' *The Hungarian Quarterly*, Vol. 35, No. 136, Winter 1994.

GÖNCZ, Árpád, 'The Least Expensive Way to Guarantee Security', *Transitions*, Vol. 4, No. 7, December 1997.

GREBING, Helga, *Der Revisionismus: von Bernstein bis zum Prager Frühling*, Verlag C. H. Beck 1977.

GREGORI, Ilina, SCHASER Angelika, (Hrsg.), *Rumänien im Umbruch*, Verlag Dr. Dieter Winkler 1993.

GREY, Jason, *Hungary*.
Http: //ww2.artsci.wustl.edu/~ps4271/hungary.html.

GREY, Jason, *Romania*.
Http: //ww2.artsci.wustl.edu/~ps4271/rom-jg.html.

GRIFFITH, (Ed.), *Central and Eastern Europe: The Opening Curtain?*

GROSFELD, Irena, 'Privatisation of State Enterprises in Eastern Europe: The Search for a Market Environment', *East European Politics and Societies*, Vol. 5, No. 1, Winter 1991.

GROSS, Peter, 'Inching toward Integrity', *Transitions*, Vol. 5, No. 3, March 1998.

GROSS, Peter, TISMANEANU, Vladimir, 'No NATO Shelter for Romania', *Transitions*, Vol. 4, No. 7, December 1997.

GROTHAUSEN, Klaus-Detlev, (Hrsg.), *Südosteuropa Handbuch Band II*, Vandenhoek & Ruprecht 1977.

GUELLETTE, Agota, 'Financing the Acquisition of Western Technology in the Context of Hungarian Reform', *Soviet Studies*, Vol. 41, No. 4, October 1989.

GUMPEL, Werner, 'Makroökonomische Stabilisierung: Ihre sozialen Probleme und die Kosten der Transformation in Südosteuropa', *Südosteuropa*, Vol. 45, No. 4-5, 1996.

GUMPEL, Werner, 'Ungarns Wirtschaft nach der politischen Wende: Der Anschluß an Europa', *Südosteuropa*, Vol. 43, No. 11-12, 1994.

GZOWSKI, Alison, *Facing Freedom: The Children of Eastern Europe*, Viking 1992.

HAJEK, Igor, 'Czech Culture in the Cauldron', *Europe-Asia Studies*, Vol. 46, No. 1, 1994.

HALÁSZ, Gábor, 'Schooling and Social Change', *The Hungarian Quarterly*, Vol. 35, No. 135, Autumn 1994.

HAMMOND, T., T., (Ed.), *The Anatomy of Communist Takeovers*, Yale University Press 1975.

HAMPEL, Adolf, 'Schwierige Nachbarn', *Die Politische Meinung*, Vol. 40, No. 307, Juni 1995.

HANÁK, Péter, 'Central Europe: An Alternative to Disintegration', *The New Hungarian Quarterly*, Vol. 33, No. 127, Autumn 1992.

HANÁK, Péter, (Hrsg.), *Die Geschichte Ungarns*, Reimar Hobbing Verlag 1988.

HANCOCK, Ian, 'The Struggle for the Control of Identity', *Transitions*, Vol. 4, No. 4, September 1997.

HANKISS, Elemér, 'Zwischen zwei Welten: Wertewandel in Ungarn', *Transit*, No. 1, Autumn 1990.

HANKISS, Elmer, 'In Search of a Paradigm', *Deadalus*, Vol. 119, No. 1, Winter 1990.

HARRINGTON, Joseph, F., COURTNEY, Bruce, J., *Tweaking the Nose of the Russians*, Columbia University Press 1991.

HARRISON, Mark, 'Comment: Stalinism in Post-Communist Perspective', *Europe-Asia Studies*, Vol. 49, No. 3, May 1997, pp. 499-502.

HARTL, Hans, 'Das Nationalismus-Syndrom des Kommunismus', *Südosteuropa Jahrbuch*, No. 16, 1986.

HARTL, Hans, (Hrsg.), *Nationalismus in Rot*, Seewald Verlag 1968.

HARTMANN, Jürgen, *Politik und Gesellschaft in Osteuropa*, Campus Verlag 1983.

HATSCHIKJAN, Magarditsch, A., 'Die außenpolitischen Neuorientierungen in Ostmitteleuropa', *Aussenpolitik*, Vol. 45, No. 1, 1994.

HATSCHIKJAN, Magarditsch, A., 'Minen, Enträumung, Modernisierung: Anmerkungen zu Transformation und Nationalismus in Südosteuropa', *Südosteuropa*, Vol. 43, No. 5, 1994.

HATSCHIKJAN, Magarditsch, A., WEILEMANN, Peter, R., (Hrsg.), *Parteienlandschaften in Osteuropa*, Schöningh 1994.

HAVAS, Gábor, KERTESI, Gábor, KEMÉRLY, István, 'The Statistics of Deprivation', *The Hungarian Quarterly*, Vol. 36, No. 138, Summer 1995.

HAVEL, Havel, MICHNIK, Adam, 'Die unvollendete Revolution', *Transit*, No. 4, Summer 1992.

HAVEL, Vaclav, 'A Chance to Stop Exporting Wars and Violence', *Transitions*, Vol. 4, No. 7, December 1997.

HAVEL, Vaclav, 'Intellektuelle in die Politik!' *Transit*, No. 10, Autumn 1995.

HAVEL, Vaclav, 'Interview', *Der Spiegel*, No. 48, 1989.

HAVEL, Vaclav, *Am Anfang war das Wort*, Rowohlt 1990.

HAVEL, Vaclav, *Summer Meditations on Politics, Morality and Civility in a Time of Transition*, Facer & Faber Ltd. 1992.

HAVEL, Vaclav, *Versuch in der Wahrheit zu Leben*, Rowohlt Taschenbuch Verlag 1989.

HAX, H., KLENNER, W., KRAUS, W., MATSUDA, T., NAKAMURA, T., (Eds.), *Economic Transformation in Eastern Europe and East Asia*, Springer 1996.

HEIMANN, Erwin, *Ein Volk sucht seinen Weg: Erfahrungen in Rumänien*, Verlag SOI Bern 1969.

HEINRICH, Hans-Georg, *Hungary: Politics, Economic and Society,* Pinter 1986.

HEJZLAR, Zdenek, *Reform Kommunismus,* Europäische Verlagsanstalt 1976.

HELD, Joseph, *The Columbia History of Eastern Europe in the Twentieth Century,* Columbia University Press 1992.

HELLER, Agnes, FEHÉR, Ferenc, *Ungarn 1956,* VSA Verlag 1982.

HELLER, Mikhail, *Cogs in the Wheel,* Alfred A. Knopf Inc. 1988.

HELTAI, György, 'Reform to Revolution: Interview given to a US Journalist, 12 December, 1956', *The Hungarian Quarterly,* Vol. 37, No. 142, Summer 1996.

HERR, Hansjörg, WESTPHAL, Andreas, (Hrsg.), *Transformation in Mittel- und Osteuropa,* Campus 1993.

HICKS, Andrew, 'Havel's Presidential Pulpit', *Transitions,* Vol. 5, No. 2, February 1998.

HODOS, Georg, Hermann, *Schauprozesse,* Campus Verlag 1988.

HOENSCH, Jörg, K., *Geschichte der Tschechoslowakischen Republik 1918-1978,* Kohlhammer 1978.

HOGG, QC. MP., Rt. Hon., Douglas, 'Central Europe: The New Security Relationships', *RUSI Journal,* Vol. 139, No. 4, 1994.

HÖHMANN, Hans-Hermann, 'Zunehmende wirtschaftliche Schwierigkeiten in Osteuropa', *Die Internationale Politik,* 1979-1980.

HÖHMANN, Hans-Hermann, MEIER, Christian, *Systemic Transformation in the East of Europe,* Bundesinstitut für Ostwissenschaftliche und Internationale Studien, Bericht No. 4, 1994.

HÖHMANN, Hans-Hermann, NOVE, Alec, VOGEL, Heinrich, (Eds.), *Economics and Politics in the USSR,* Westview Press 1986.

HÖHMANN, Hans-Hermann, *Wirtschaftsreform in Osteuropa: Was ist neu an neuen Entwicklungen?* Bundesinstitut für Ostwissenschaftliche und Internationale Studien, Bericht No. 41, 1985.

HÖHMANN, Hans-Hermann, *Zu Interdependenz und Interaktion von wirtschaftlicher und politischer Reform in der sowjetischen Perestrojka*, Bundesinstitut für Ostwissenschaftliche und Internationale Studien, Bericht No. 23, 1989.

HOMANN, Harald, ALBRECHT, Clemens, 'Die Wiederentdeckung Osteuropas', *Zeitschrift für Politik*, Vol. 40, No. 1, 1993.

HOPPE, Hans-Joachim, 'Die Lage der mittel- und südosteuropäischen Länder', *Aussenpolitik*, Vol. 45, No. 2, 1994.

HORN, Gyula, *Freiheit, die ich meine*, Hoffmann & Campe 1991.

HORSKY, Vladimir, *Die sanfte Revolution in der Tschechoslowakei 1989*, Bundesinstitut für Ostwissenschaftliche und Internationale Studien, Bericht No. 14, 1990.

HÖSCH, Edgar, 'Die Entstehung des Nationalstaates in Südosteuropa', *Südosteuropa*, Vol. 42, No. 10, 1993.

HOWARD, Dick, A., E., 'Drafting Constitutions for the New Democracies', *Problems of Communism*, Vol. 41, No. 1-2, January-April 1992.

HOWARD, Dick, A., E., *Constitution Making in Eastern Europe*, Woodrow Wilson Press 1993.

HRUBY, Peter, *Czechoslovakia between East and West: The Changing Role of Communist Intellectuals, 1948-1968*, University of Geneva, Dissertation No. 302, Western Australian Institute of Technology 1979.

HUNT, Swannee, 'Women's Vital Voices', *Foreign Affairs*, Vol. 76, No. 4, July/August 1997.

HUNYA, Gábor, 'The Romanian Economy in 1993/1994: From Stagnation with Inflation to Stagnation with Stabilization', *Südosteuropa,* Vol. 43, No. 11-12, 1994.

IGNATIEFF, Michael, 'On Civil Society', *Foreign Affairs,* Vol. 74, No. 2, March-April 1995.

IGNATOW, Assen, *Instrumentilisierung des orthodoxen Christentums in Osteuropa heute,* Bundesinstitut für Ostwissenschaftliche und Internationale Studien, Bericht No. 28, 1994.

IGNATOW, Assen, *Psychologie des Kommunismus,* Johannes Berchmans Verlag 1985.

ILIESCU, Ion, *Aufbruch nach Europa,* Böhlau 1995.

ILINCIOIU, Ion, *The Great Romanian Peasant Revolt of 1907,* The Romanian Academy 1991.

INOTAI, András, 'Ausländische Direktinvestitionen in Ungarn', *Südosteuropa,* Vol. 44, No. 11-12, 1995.

INOTAI, Andras, 'Transforming the East: Western Illusions and Strategies', *The Hungarian Quarterly,* Vol. 35, No. 133, Spring 1994.

International Social Science Journal, *Democratic Transition in the East and the South,* Basil Blackwell 1991.

IONESCU, Dan, 'The Romanian-Hungarian Basic Treaty', *Open Media Reseach Institute (OMRINet),* Analytical Brief No. 334.

JAMES, Robert, Rhodes, *The Czechoslovak Crisis 1968,* Weidenfeld & Nicolson 1969.

JANN, Olaf, 'Fundamentalismus und die Moderne. Eine globale Problemkonstellation mit zentraler Bedeutung für Südosteuropa', *Südosteuropa Mitteilungen,* Vol. 37, No. 1, 1997.

JANOS, Andrew, C., *Authoritarian Politics in Communist Europe,* University of California Press 1976.

JEDLICKI, Jerzy, 'The Revolution of 1989: The Unbearable Burden of History', *Problems of Communism*, Vol. 34, No. 4, July-August 1990.

JESZENSZKY, Géza, 'Interview', *Südosteuropa*, Vol. 42, No. 6, 1993.

JESZENSZKY, Gezá, 'More Bosnias? National and ethnic Tensions in the Post-Communist World', *East European Quarterly*, Vol. 31, No. 3, Fall 1997.

JOHNSON, William, T., YOUNG, Thomas-Durell, 'NATO Expansion and Partnership for Peace: Assessing the Facts', *RUSI Journal*, Vol. 139, No. 6, December 1994.

JOO, Rudolf, (Ed.), *The Hungarian Minority's Situation in Ceausescu's Romania*, Columbia University Press 1994.

JÓZSA, Gyula, *Von der Implosion des politbürokratischen Systems in Ungarn zum Rechtstaat und zum Parteipluralismus*, Bundesinstitut für Ostwissenschaftliche und Internationale Studien, Bericht No. 23, 1992.

JUDT, Tony, 'Die Linke links liegen lassen?', *Transit*, No. 4, Summer 1992.

JUDT, Tony, 'The Dilemmas of Dissidence: The Politics of Opposition in East-Central Europe', *East European Politics and Societies*, Vol. 2, No. 2, Spring 1988.

JUDT, Tony, 'The Dilemmas of Dissidence: The Politics of Opposition in East-Central Europe', *East-European Politics and Societies*, Vol. 2, No. 2, Spring 1988.

JUDT, Tony, 'The Rediscovery of Central Europe', *Daedalus*, Vol. 119, No. 1, Winter 1990.

KABBE, Georgy, *Die Privatisierung in Osteuropa*, Conference Paper, Friedrich-Ebert Stiftung Fachtagung, 23-27 September 1996, 'Der schwierge Weg der osteuropäischen Länder zur Demokratie und Marktwirtschaft'.

KÁDÁR, Béla, 'Central Europe Again', *The New Hungarian Quarterly*, Vol. 32, No. 121, Spring 1991.

KÁDÁR, Béla, 'Economic Strategies before Integration', *The Hungarian Quarterly*, Vol. 38, No. 146, Summer 1997.

KÁDÁR, Béla, 'Timing Entry into the EU', *The Hungarian Quarterly*, Vol. 37, No. 141, Spring 1996.

KALDOR, Mary, VEJVODA, Ivan, 'Democratization in Central and East European Countries', *International Affairs*, Vol. 73, No. 1, January 1997.

KAPLAN, Frank, L., 'Changes in Czechoslovak and Czech Mass Media since 1989: A U.S. Perspective', *East European Quarterly*, Vol. 30, No. 1, Spring 1996.

KAPLAN, Karel, 'Reflections on the Political Trials', *Nova Mysl*, Nos. 6-8, 1968.

KAPLAN, Karel, *Anatomie einer regierenden kommunistischen Partei*, Bundesinstitut für Ostwissenschaftliche und Internationale Studien, Bericht No. 19, 1989.

KARSAI, Judit, WRIGHT, Mike, 'Accountability, Governance and Finance in Hungarian Buy-Outs', *Europe-Asia Studies*, Vol. 46, No. 6, 1994.

KASER, Micheal, 'Securing the Market System after Transition', *Europe-Asia Studies*, Vol. 49, No. 3, May 1997, pp. 463-467.

KAWCZYNSKI, Rudko, 'The Politics of Romani Politics', *Transitions*, Vol. 4, No. 4, September 1997.

KEIL, Thomas, J., AUSTIN, Mark, D., ANDREESCU, Viviana, 'Concerns about Neighbourhood Safety in Two Romanian Cities: Copsa Mica and Bucaresti', *East European Quarterly*, Vol. 30, No. 1, Spring 1996.

KELETI, György, 'Hungary and Euro-Atlantic Integration', *RUSI Journal*, Vol. 140, No. 3, June 1995.

KELETI, György, 'Ungarns Sicherheit und der NATO-Beitritt', *Europäische Sicherheit*, Vol. 46, No. 2, February 1997.

KEMME, David, M., 'The Chronic Shortage Model of Centrally Planned Economies', *Soviet Studies,* Vol. 41, No. 3, July 1989.

KENWAY, Peter, KLVACOVÁ, Eva, 'The Web of Cross-Ownership among Czech Financial Intermediaries: An Assessment', *Europe-Asia Studies,* Vol. 48, No. 5, 1996.

KERTESZ, Stephen, *Between Russia and the West,* University of Notre Dame Press 1984.

KIELINGER, Thomas, 'Waking up in the new Europe – with a Headache', *International Affairs,* Vol. 66, No. 2, April 1990.

KILENYI, Geza, *New Tendencies in the Hungarian Economy,* Budapest 1990.

KILLICK, Thomas, STEVENS, Christopher, 'Eastern Europe and the Third World', *International Affairs,* Vol. 67, No. 4, October 1991.

KING MICHAEL OF ROMANIA, 'Romania and NATO: The Time for a Real Partnership', *RUSI Journal,* Vol. 142, No. 2, April 1997.

KING MICHAEL OF ROMANIA, 'The Future of Democracy in Eastern Europe', *RUSI Journal,* Vol. 135, No. 4, Winter 1990.

KIPKE, Rüdiger, 'Etabliert aber nicht verwurzelt? Ungarns Parlamentsparteien und ihre Wähler', *Südosteuropa Mitteilungen,* Vol. 37, No. 2, 1997.

KIRÁLY, J., 'The Hungarian Fisher Cycle, or a possible interpretation of the capital loss of Hungarian banks', *Acta Oeconomica,* Vol. 47, No. 3-4, 1995.

KIRKPATRICK, Jeane, J., 'After Communism, What?' *Problems of Communism,* Vol. 41, No. 1-2, January-April 1992.

KISS, Janos, 'Verfassungsgebung in zwei Schritten', *Transit,* No. 9, Summer 1995.

KISS, Yudit, 'Cost Illusions? Defence Industry Conversions in Czechoslovakia 1989-1992',. *Europe-Asia Studies*, Vol. 45, No. 6, 1993.

KISS, Yudit, 'Privatisation in Hungary – Two Years Later', *Soviet Studies*, Vol. 44, No. 6, 1992.

KLAUS, Vaclav, JEZEK, Tomáš, 'Liberalism and Recent Changes in Czechoslovakia', *East European Politics and Societies*, Vol. 5, No. 1, Winter 1991.

KLEIN, Günter, 'Rumäniens Minderheitenpolitik im Kontext internationaler Beziehungen und der Empfehlungen des Europarates', *Südosteuropa*, Vol. 45, No. 11-12, 1996.

KLEININGER, Nikolaus, 'Rumänien', *Südosteuropa Jahrbuch*, No. 24, 1993.

KLIGMAN, Gail, 'Reclaiming the Public: A Reflection on Creating Civil Society in Romania', *East European Politics and Societies*, Vol. 4, No. 3, Fall 1990.

KLIGMAN, Gail, 'The Politics of Reproduction in Ceausescu's Romania', *East European Politics and Societies*, Vol. 6, No. 3, Fall 1992.

KLIGMAN, Gail, *The Wedding of the Dead*, University of California Press 1988.

KOCSIS, György, SZÁNTÓ, Anikó, 'The Economic State of the Nation', *The Hungarian Quarterly*, Vol. 38, Spring 1997.

KOCSIS, Györgyi, 'Growth vs. Equilibrium: Interim Reports', *The Hungarian Quarterly*, Vol. 36, No. 140, Winter 1995.

KOCSIS, Györgyi, 'How to Uncook Fish Soup: Strategies for Privatisation', *The New Hungarian Quarterly*, Vol. 32, No. 123, Autumn 1991.

KOCSIS, Györgyi, 'Light for the Economy?' *The New Hungarian Quarterly*, Vol. 33, No. 125, Spring 1992.

KOCSIS, Györgyi, 'Stabilization through Restriction', *The Hungarian Quarterly,* Vol. 36, No. 138, Summer 1995.

KOCSIS, Györgyi, 'The Distant Lights of the European Union', *The Hungarian Quarterly,* Vol. 35, No. 135, Autumn 1994.

KOCSIS, Györgyi, 'The Uncertain State of Privatisation', *The New Hungarian Quarterly,* Vol. 33, No. 128, Winter 1992.

KOLOSI, Tamás, SÁGI, Matild, 'Social Changes in Postcommunist Societies', *The Hungarian Quarterly,* Vol. 38, no. 146, Summer 1997.

KOLTAY, J., 'Unemployment and Employment Policy in Central and Eastern Europe: Similarities and Differences', *Acta Oeconomica,* Vol. 43, No. 3-4, 1994.

KONRAD, György, *Antipolitik,* Suhrkamp 1985.

KOPITS, G., 'Hungary's Preannounced Crawling Peg', *Acta Oeconomica,* Vol. 47, No. 3-4, 1995.

KOPITS, G., 'Midway in the Transition', *Acta Oeconomica,* Vol. 46, No. 3-4, 1994.

KORALKA, J., *Tschechen im Habsburgerreich und in Europa 1815-1914,* Oldenburg Verlag 1991.

KORBONSKI, Andrzej, 'The Politics of Reforms in Eastern Europe: The Last Thirty Years', *Soviet Studies,* Vol. 41, No. 4, January 1989.

KORNAI, János, 'A Steep Road', *The Hungarian Quarterly,* Vol. 36, No. 138, Summer 1995.

KORNAI, János, 'Socialist Transformation and Privatisation: Shifting form a Socialist System', *East European Politics and Societies,* Vol. 2, No. 4, Spring 1990.

KORNAI, János, 'The Dilemmas of Hungarian Economic Policy', *Acta Oeconomica,* Vol. 47, No. 3-4, 1995.

KORNAI, János, 'The Dilemmas of Hungarian Economic Policy', *Acta Oeconomica*, Vol. 47, No. 3-4, 1995.

KORNAI, János, 'The Evolution of Financial Discipline under the Postsocialist System', *Kyklos*, Vol. 46, 1993.

KORNAI, János, 'The Social Issue in the Era of Transition', *The Hungarian Quarterly*, Vol. 37, No. 141, Spring 1996.

KORNAI, János, *The Road to a Free Economy*, W. W. Norton & Co. 1990.

KÖRÖSÉNYI, András, 'The Reasons for the Defeat of the Right in Hungary', *European_Politics and Societies*, Vol. 9, No. 1, Winter 1995.

KOUBA, K., 'Systemic Changes in the Czech Economy after Four Years (1990-1993)', *Acta Oeconomica*, Vol. 46, No. 3-4, 1994.

KOVÁCS, János Mátyás, 'Das Große Experiment des Übergangs', *Transit*, No. 1, Autumn 1990.

KOVÁCS, János Mátyás, 'Paradigmen des Übergangs', *Transit*, No. 9, Summer 1995.

KOVÁCS, János, Mátyás, 'From Reformation to Transformation: Limits to Liberalism in Hungarian Economic Thought', *East European Politics and Societies*, Vol. 5, No. 1, Winter 1991.

KOVÁCS, János, Mátyás, TURDOS, Marton, *Reform and Transformation in Eastern Europe*, Routledge 1992.

KOVACSIS, J., 'Die wichtigsten Charakteristiken des ungarischen Siedlungsnetzes', *Südosteuropa Jahrbuch*, No. 18, 1988.

KÖVES, A., 'After the Bokros Package: What Next?' *Acta Oeconomica*, Vol. 47, No. 3-4, 1995.

KOVRIG, Bennet, *Communism in Hungary*, Hoover Institute Press 1979.

KREJCÍ, Jaroslaw, *Czechoslovakia at the Crossroads of European History*, I. B. Tauris & Co. Ltd. 1990.

KRETSCHMER, Hans Jörg, 'Das Verhältnis der Länder Südosteuropas zur Europäischen Union', *Südosteuropa Mitteilungen*, Vol. 37, No. 2, 1997.

KRÓL, Marcin, 'Revolution, Restauration, Amnesie', *Transit*, No. 2, Summer 1991.

KRYSTUFEK, Z., *The Soviet Regime in Czechoslovakia*, East European Monographs 1981.

KUCZI, Tibor, VAJDA, Agnes, 'Privatisation and the Second Economy', *The New Hungarian Quarterly*, Vol. 33, No. 126, Summer 1992.

KUKORELLI, István, 'The Birth, Testing and Results of the 1989 Hungarian Electoral Law', *Soviet Studies*, Vol. 43, No. 1, 1991.

KUN, Joseph, *Hungarian Foreign Policy: The Experience of a New Democracy*, Praeger 1993.

KUNDERA, M., 'The Tragedy of Central Europe', *The New York Review of Books*, 26 April 1984.

KUPKA, Martin, 'The Transformation of Ownership in Czechoslovakia', *Soviet Studies*, Vol. 44, No. 2, 1992.

KURÓN, Jacek, *Glaube und Schuld*, Aufbau Verlag 1991.

KURTÁN, Sándor, 'Systemwechsel, Institutionen und Eliten in Ungarn', *Südosteuropa Jahrbuch*, No. 25, 1994.

KURTÁN, Sándor, P., VASS, L., (Hrsg.), *Politisches Jahrbuch Ungarns*, Budapest 1992.

KUSIN, Vladimir, V., 'Husak's Czechoslovakia and Economic Stagnation', *Problems of Communism*, Vol. 31, No. 3, May-June 1982.

KUX, Ernst, 'Revolution in Eastern Europe – Revolution in the West?' *Problems of Communism*, Vol. 40, No. 3, May-June 1991.

KWASNIEWSKI, Aleksander, 'Isolationism is an Anachronism', *Transitions*, Vol. 4, No. 7, December 1997.

LAKI, Mihály, 'Chances for the Acceleration of Transition: The Case of Hungarian Privatisation', *East European Politics and Societies*, Vol. 7, No. 3, Fall 1993.

LAKI, Mihály, 'Economic Programs of the Ex-Opposition Parties in Hungary', *East European Politics and Societies*, Vol. 5, No. 1, Winter 1991.

LAKI, Mihály, 'Opportunities for Workers' Participation in Privatisation in Hungary: The Case of the Eger Flour Mill', *Europe-Asia Studies*, Vol. 47, No. 2, 1995.

LAMPE, John, R., 'Economic Dilemmas of Eastern Europe', *East European Politics and Societies*, Vol. 2, No. 3, Fall 1988.

LANE, David, 'The Gorbachev Revolution: The Role of the Political Elite in Regime Disintegration', *Political Studies*, Vol. 44, No. 1, March 1996.

LASKY, Melvin, J., *Die ungarische Revolution*, Colloquium Verlag 1958.

LATAWSKI, Paul, 'Central and Eastern Europe: Exporting Instability?' *RUSI Journal*, Vol. 140, No. 4, August 1995.

LAUTH, Hans-Joachim, MERKEL, Wolfgang, 'Zivilgesellschaft und Transformation', *Forschungsjournal Neue Soziale Bewegungen*, Vol. 10, No. 1, 1997.

LEFTER, Ion, 'Romania: Details of Economic Reforms Expected Today', *RFE/RL News*, 27.6.97.

LEMKE, Christiane, 'Nachholende Mobilisierung und politischer Protest in postkommunistischen Gesellschaften', *Aus Politik und Zeitgeschichte*, 24 January 1997.

LENDVAI, Paul, 'There is no such Thing as Eastern Europe', *The Hungarian Quarterly,* Vol. 36, No. 140, Winter 1995.

LENDVAI, Paul, *Hungary: The Art of Survival,* I. B. Tauris & Co. Ltd. 1988.

LENGYEL, Gyoergy, *Hungarian Economy and Society during World War Two,* Columbia University Press 1993.

LENGYEL, László, 'Europe through Hungarian Eyes', *International Affairs,* Vol. 66, No. 2, April 1990.

LENGYEL, Zsolt, K., 'Warten auf das Wunder: Dilemmata des Systemwandels in Ungarn 1990-1992', *Zeitschrift für Politik,* Vol. 40, No. 3, 1993.

LEVCIK, Friedrich, 'Czechoslovakia: Economic Performance in the Post-Reform Period and Prospects for the 1980's', *East European Assessment: Part I,* U.S Congress Joint Economic Committee, Washington D.C. 1981.

LEVY, Robert, 'Did Ana Pauker Prevent a 'Rajk Trial' in Romania?' *East European Politics and Societies,* Vol. 9, No. 1, Winter 1995.

LEWIN, Moshe, *The Making of the Soviet System,* The New Press 1994.

LEWIS, Paul, G., *Central Europe since 1945,* Longman 1994.

LEWIS, Paul, G., *Eastern Europe,* Croom Helm 1984.

LINZ, J., STEPAN, A., *Problems of Democratic Transition and Consolidation of Democracy,* John Hopkins University Press 1996.

LIPSET, Seymour, ROKKAN, Stein, *Party Systems and Voter Alignments: Cross-National Perspectives,* The Free Press 1967.

LITVAN, György, '1957 – The Year After', *The Hungarian Quarterly,* Vol. 37, No. 143, Autumn 1996.

LONGWORTH, Philip, *The making of Eastern Europe,* Macmillan 1992.

LORINC, Hanja Istvanffy, 'Foreign Debt, Debt Management Policy and Implications for Hungary's Development', *Soviet Studies*, Vol. 44, No. 6, 1992.

LOTSPEICH, Richard, 'Crime in the Transition Economies', *Europe-Asia Studies*, Vol. 47, No. 4, 1995.

LUKACS, John, 'The Concept and Symbol of Eastern Europe', *The New Hungarian Quarterly*, Vol. 32, No. 124, Winter 1991.

LUKS, Leonid, 'Abschied von Leninismus – zur ideologischen Dynamik der Perestrojka', *Zeitschrift für Politik*, Vol. 37, No. 4, 1990.

MACHOS, Csilla, 'Elitenbildung und Elitenwandel in der Ungarischen Sozialistischen Partei (1989-1996)', *Südosteuropa*, Vol. 46, No. 1-2, 1997.

MACHOS, Csilla, 'FIDESZ – Der Bund Junger Demokraten', *Südosteuropa*, Vol. 42, No. 1, 1993.

MACHOS, Csilla, 'Stationen eines Imageverlusts: Der ungarische Bund Junger Demokraten im Jahr 1993', *Südosteuropa*, Vol. 43, No. 1-2, 1994.

MACHOS, Csilla, 'Von der Staatspartei zur 'Volkspartei'?' Überlegungen am Beispiel der Ungarischen Sozialistischen Partei', *Südosteuropa*, Vol. 44, No. 11-12, 1995.

MADERTHANER, M., SCHAFRANEK, H., UNFRIED, B., (Hrsg.), *Ich habe den Tod verdient*, Verlag für Gesellschaftskritik 1991.

MAGAS, István, 'Reforms under Pressure: Hungary', *East European Quarterly*, Vol. 24, No. 1, Spring 1990.

MAIER, Hans, 'Totalitarismus und Politische Religionen', *Vierteljahresheft für Zeitgeschichte*, Vol. 43, No. 3, Juli 1995.

MAJOR, I., 'From Credit Vouchers to the Small Investors' Share-Purchase Programme', *Acta Oeconomica*, Vol. 46, No. 3-4, 1994.

MALCOLM, Neil, 'The 'Common European Home' and Soviet European Policy', *International Affairs*, Vol. 65, No. 4, Autumn 1989.

MANDELBAUM, Michael, 'Preserving the New Peace: The Case Against NATO Expansion', *Foreign Affairs*, Vol. 74, No. 3, May-June 1995.

MANER, Hans-Christian, 'Rumänien nach den Novemberwahlen 1996 – die ersten 100 Tage der neuen Machthaber', *Südosteuropa Mitteilungen*, Vol. 37, No. 2, 1997.

MARGA, Andrei, 'Cultural and Political Trends in Romania Before and After 1989', *East European Politics and Societies*, Vol. 7, No. 1, Winter 1993.

MARKÓ, Béla, 'Transylvania: Managing within a Nation-State', *The Hungarian Quarterly*, Vol. 36, No. 140. Winter 1995.

MÁRKOS, György, G., *Party System and Political Cleavage Translation in Hungary*, Hungarian Papers of Political Science No. 3, Hungarian Academy of Sciences 1996.

MÁRKOS, György, *Lateinamerika in Ungarn?* Paper presented at the Friedrich-Ebert Stiftung 23-27 September 1996, 'Fachtagung: Der schwierige Weg der osteuropäischen Länder zur Demokratie und Marktwirtschaft'.

MARRESE, Michael, VANOUS, Jan, *Soviet Subsidization of Trade with Eastern Europe*, Institute of International Studies Research Series No. 52, University of California 1983.

MARTINSEN, Kare Dahl, 'Vaclav Klaus und die politische Stabilität in der Tschechishcen Republik', *Osteuropa*, Vol. 44, No. 11, November 1994.

MARTONYI, János, 'The EC and Central Europe', *The New Hungarian Quarterly*, Vol. 33, No. 128, Winter 1992.

MASON, David, S., 'Attitudes toward the Market and Political Participation in the Postcommunist States', *Slavic Review*, Vol. 54, No. 2, Summer 1995.

MASON, David, S., 'Glasnost, Perestrioka and Eastern Europe', *International Affairs*, Vol. 64, No. 3, Summer 1988.

MATO, Zsolt-Istvan, 'Iliescu and His Party Play the Nationalist Card', *Open Media Research Institute (OMRINet)*, Analytical Brief No. 461.

McDONALD, Jason, 'Transition to Utopia: A Reinterpretation of Economics, Ideas, and Politics in Hungary, 1984-1990', *East European Politics and Societies* Vol. 7, No. 2, Spring 1993.

McGREGOR, James, 'The Presidency in East-Central Europe', *RFE/RL Research Report*, Vol. 3, No. 2, 14 January 1994.

McKINSEY, Kitty, 'Hungary: The Military Strive to Comply with NATO Criteria', *RFE/RL Report*.

McKINSEY, Kitty, 'NATO: Brussels Tables Eastward Expansion this Month', *RFE/RL Report*.

MELESCANU, Teodor, 'Romania's Option for the European and Atlantic Integration. The Significance of the Romanian-German Partnership', *Südosteuropa*, Vol. 45, No. 11-12, 1996.

MEND, Vojtéch, 'Die Unterdrückung des Prager Frühlings', *Aus Politik und Zeitgeschichte*, No. 36, 28 August 1992.

MERKEL, Wolfgang, (Hrsg.), *Systemwechsel 1: Theorien, Ansätze und Konzeptionen*, Opladen 1994.

MERKEL, Wolfgang, SANDSCHNEIDER, Eberhard, (Hrsg.), *Systemwechsel III: Parteien im Transfromationsprozeß*, Leske & Budrich 1997.

MERKEL, Wolfgang, SANDSCHNEIDER, Eberhard, SEGERT, Dieter, (Hrsg.), *Systemwechsel II: Die Institutionalisierung der Demokratie*, Leske & Budrich 1996.

MERKES, Michael, *Europa ohne Kommunismus*, Europa Union Verlag 1990.

MERKL, Wolfgang, 'Systemwechsel: Probleme der demokratischen Konsolidierung in Ost- Mitteleuropa', *Aus Politik und Zeitgeschichte*, No. 18-19, 6 Mai 1994.

MEYER, Gerd, "Zwischen Haben und Sein' Psychische Aspekte des Transformationsprozesses in postkommunistischen Gesellschaften', *Aus Politik und Zeitgeschichte*, 24 January 1997.

MICHNIK, Adam, 'Verborgene Ungeheuer', *Der Spiegel*, No. 28, 1990.

MIHAILESCU, Ioan, 'Mental Stereotypes in the First Year of Post-Totalitarian Romania', *Government and Opposition*, Vol. 28, No. 3, Autumn 1993.

MIHÁLYI, P. , 'Common Patterns and Peculiarities in Privatisation: A Progress Report on the Transition Economies', *Acta Oeconmica*, Vol. 46, No. 1-2, 1994.

MIHÁLYI, P., 'Common Patterns and Particularities in Privatisation: A Progress Report on the Transition Economies', *Acta Oeconomica*, Vol. 46, No. 1-2, 1994.

MIHOK, Brigitte, *Ethnostratifikation im Sozialismus: Aufgezeigt an den Beispielländern Ungarn und Rumänien*, Peter Lang 1990.

MILIN, Miodrag, *Timisoara – 15-21 December 1989*, Timisoara 1990.

MILLER, Tilly, *Der Prager Frühling und Reformpolitik Heute*, Olzog Verlag 1989.

MINOGUE, Kenneth, *Alien Powers: The Pure Theory of Ideology*, St. Martin's Press 1985.

MIZSEI, Kalman, 'From Goulash Socialism to Vichyssoise Capitalism', *Transitions*,
Vol. 4, No. 3, August 1997.

MIZSEI, Kálmán, 'Privitisation in Eastern Europe: A Comparative Study of Poland and Hungary', *Soviet Studies*, Vol. 44, No. 2, 1992.

MIZSEI, Kálmán, 'Recipes for Growth', *The Hungarian Quarterly*, Vol. 35, No. 135, Autumn 1994.

MLYNÁR, Zdeněk, (Hrsg.), *Der Prager Frühling*, Bund Verlag 1983.

MLYNÁR, Zdeněk, *Nachtfrost*, Europäische Verlagsanstalt 1978.

MOÏSI, Dominique, MERTES, Michael, 'Europe's Map, Compass and Horizon', *Foreign Affairs*, Vol. 74, No. 1, January-February 1995.

MOLNÁR, Gusztáv, 'A Turning Point in Hungarian Foreign Policy', *The Hungarian Quarterly*, Vol. 37, No. 141, Spring 1996.

MOLNÁR, Gusztáv, 'The Geopolitics of NATO Enlargement', *The Hungarian Quarterly*, Vol. 38, No. 146, Summer 1997.

MOLNÁR, Patricia, 'Unemployment: The Hard Facts', *The New Hungarian Quarterly*, Vol. 33, No. 127, Autumn 1992.

MOMMSEN, Margareta, *Nationalismus in Osteuropa*, Verlag C. H. Beck 1992.

MOORHOUSE, Jacqui, 'Ostmitteleuropa auf dem Weg in die Europäische Union', *Aussenpolitik*, Vol. 47, 4th. Quarter 1996.

MORRISON, John, *The Czech and Slovak Experience*, Macmillan 1992.

MORVAI, Krisztina, 'Retroactive Justice based on International Law: A Recent Discussion by the Hungarian Consitutional Court', *East European Consitutional Review*, Vol. 2, No. 3, 1993/1994.

MÜLLER, Stephan, 'Flüchtling- und Asylpolitik in Ungarn', *Südosteuropa*, Vol. 42, No. 7-8, 1993.

MUNGIU, Alina, 'Intellectuals as Political Actors in Eastern Europe: The Romanian Case', *East European politics and Societies*, Vol. 10, No. 2, Spring 1996.

MUNGIU, Alina, PIPPIDI, Andrei, 'Letter from Romania', *Government and Opposition*, Vol. 29, No. 3, Autumn 1994.

MURAVCHIK, Joshua, 'Exporting Democracy', *Orbis*, Vol. 37, No. 4, Fall 1993.

MURELL, Peter, 'Evolutionary and Radical Approaches to Economic Reform', *Economics of Planning*, Vol. 25, No. 1, 1992.

MURRELL, Peter, 'Conservative Political Philosophy and the Strategy of Economic Transition', *East European Politics and Societies*, Vol. 6, No. 1, Winter 1992.

MUSIL, Jirí, 'Czech and Slovak Society', *Government and Opposition*, Vol. 28, No. 4, Winter 1993.

NAEGELE, Jolyon, 'Czech Republic: Transformation of Military Progresses at Leisurely Pace', *RFE/RL Report*.

NAGY, Boldizsár, 'The Danube Dispute: Conflicting Paradigms', *The New Hungarian Quarterly*, Vol. 33, No. 128, Winter 1992.

NARKIEWICZ, Olga, A., *Petrification and Progress: Communist Leaders in Eastern Europe 1956-1988*, Harvester Wheatsheaf 1990.

National Agency For Privatization, *Reform in Roumania*, Bucharest 1997.

NEAGOE, Stelian, *Istoria Guvernelor Romaniei: de la inceputuri – 1859 pana in zilele noastre – 1995*, Machiavelli 1995.

NELSON, Daniel, N., *Romanian Politics in the Ceausescu Era*, Gordon & Breach Science Publishers 1988.

O'NEIL, Patrick, 'Revolution from Within', *World Politics*, Vol. 48, No. 4, July 1996.

OBEREIGNER, Dasa, 'Czech Republic: Focus on EU and NATO', *Transitions*. Vol. 5, No. 3, March 1998.

OBLATH, G., 'Macroeconmic Effects of Fiscal Deficits in Hungary', *Acta Oeconomica*, Vol. 47, No. 3-4, 1995.

OBLATH, Gábor, 'Macroeconomic Developments between 1990-1994', *The Hungarian Quarterly,* Vol. 35, No. 134, Summer 1994.

OECD, *Review of the Labour Market in the Czech Republic,* OECD 1995.

OECD, *Wirtschaftsausblick,* December 1993.

Office of the Government of the Czech Republic, *Correction of Economic Policy and other Transforamtion Measures,* 16 March 1997.

Office of the Government of the Czech Republic, *CZ Government Coalition Stabilization and Recuperative Programme,* 28 May 1997.

Official Monitor, No. 125, 19 June 1997.

OLDENBURG, Fred, *Moskau und der Zusammenbruch des Kommunismus in Osteuropa,* Bundesinstitut für Ostwissenschaftliche und Internationale Studien, Bericht No. 62, 1990.

OLDSON, William, O., 'Background to Catastrophe: Romanian Modernization Policies and the Environment', *East European Quarterly,* Vol. 30, No. 4, Winter 1996.

OLTAY, Edith, 'A Profile of Istvan Csurka', *RFE/RL Research Report,* 9 October 1992.

OLTAY, Edith, 'Hungary's Screening Law', *RFE/RL Research Report,* No. 3, 15 April 1994.

Open Media Research Institute (OMRINet), *Czech Election Results.*

Open Media Research Institute (OMRINet), *Romanian Election Results.*

OPLATA, Andreas, *Der Eiserne Vorhang reißt,* Verlag Neue Zürcher Zeitung 1990.

ORBMAN, Jan, 'Czech Opposition Parties in Disarray', *RFE/RL Research Report,* Vol. 2, No. 16, 16 April 1993.

OSCHLIES, Wolf, 'Zur politischen Rolle Orthodoxer Kirche auf dem Balkan', *Südosteuropa*, Vol. 42, No. 10, 1993.

OSCHLIES, Wolf, *Soziale Mobilisierung in Rumänien*, Bundesinstitut für Ostwissenschaftliche und Internationale Studien, Bericht No. 47, 1973.

OSCHLIES, Wolf, *Wirtschaftsreform und Reformdebatten in Rumänien*, Bundesinstitut für Ostwissenschaftliche und Internationale Studien, Bericht No. 42, 1994.

Osteuropa Forum, *Prager Frühling – Reformen Gestern und Heute*, Jurius 1989.

OTAHÁl, Milan, *Der rauhe Weg zur 'samtenen Revolution'*, Bundesinstitut für Ostwissenschaftliche und Internationale Studien, Bericht No. 25, 1992.

PACEPA, Ion, *Red Horizons*, Coronet Books 1989.

PALEI, L., V., 'How to Carry out Economic Reform: Points of View and Reality', *Soviet Studies*, Vol. 42, No. 1, January 1990.

PAPALEKAS, Johannes, Chr., 'Theoretische Ansätze zum Verständnis der Revolution in Ostmittel- und Südosteuropa', *Südosteuropa Jahrbuch*, No. 24, 1993.

PATAKI, Judith, 'Controversy over Hungary's new Media War', *RFE/RL Research Report*, Vol. 3, No. 31, 12 August 1994.

PATAKI, Judith, 'Istvan Csurka's Tract: Summary and Reactions', *RFE/RL Research Report*, 9 October 1992.

PATOCKA, Jan, 'Was sind die Tschechen?', *Transit*, No. 2, Summer 1991.

PEHE, Jiri, 'Czechs Fall from their Ivory Tower', *Transitions*, Vol. 4, No. 3, August 1997.

PÉTÉR, Làszló, ' The National Community and its Past: Reflections on the History of Transylvania', *The New Hungarian Quarterly*, Vol. 33, No. 125, Spring 1992.

PÉTÉR, László, 'Montenesquieu's Paradox on Freedom and Hungary's Constitutions 1790-1990', *The New Hungarian Quarterly*, Vol. 32, No. 123, Autumn 1991.

PETROVA, Dimitrina, 'Get Out, You Stinking Gypsy', *Transitions*, Vol. 4, No. 4, September 1997.

PFAFF, Dieter, 'Stand der politischen und rechtlichen Ausgangsvoraussetzungen für die Wirtschaftsentwicklung in Albanien, Bulgarien und Rumänien', *Südosteuropa*, Vol. 45, No. 2, 1996.

PICK, Milos, 'Quo Vadis? – Homo Sapiens? Results and Alternatives for the Transformation Strategy of the CSFR', *Europe-Asia Studies*, Vol. 45, No. 1, 1993.

PIKE, David, 'Georg Lukács on Stalinism and Democracy: Before and After Prague, 1968', *East European Politics and Societies*, Vol. 2, No. 2, Spring 1988.

PLASSER, F., ULRAM, P., *Transformation oder Stagnation?* Signum Verlag 1993.

PLASSER, Fritz, PRIBERSKY, Andreas, (Eds.), *Political Culture in East Central Europe*, Avebury 1996.

POKSTEFL, Josef, *Die ideologische Bewältigung des Prager Frühlings in der CSSR (1969-1976)*, Bundesinstitut für Ostwisenschaftliche und Internationale Studien, Bericht No. 33, 1978.

Politische Eliten in Ostmitteleuropa im 20. Jahrhundert. Systemwechsel -Elitenwechsel? Internationale Fachtagung des Herderinstituts und des J. G. Herder-Forschungsrates, Vortragssaal Herder-Institut, 27-29 March 1996.

POMOGÁTS, Béla, 'After the Change', *The Hungarian Quarterly*, Vol. 35, No. 133, Spring 1994.

POZNANSKI, Kazimierz, 'Market Alternative to State Activism in Restoring the Capitalist Economy', *Economics of Planning*, Vol. 25, No. 1, 1992.

PRIDHAM, Geoffry, LEWIS, Paul, G., *Stabilising Fragile Democracies*, Routledge 1996.

PRIEß, Lutz, WILKE, Manfred, 'Die DDR und die Besetzung der Tschechoslowakei am 21. August 1968', *Aus Politik und Zeitgeschichte*, No. 36, 28 August 1992.

PRYBYLA, Jan, S., 'The Road form Socialism: Why, Where, What and How?' *Problems of Communism*, Vol. 40, No. 1-2, January-April 1991.

PRZEWORSKI, Adam, TEUNE, Henry, *The Logic of Comparative Social Inquiry*, Malaber 1982.

RACZ, Barnabas, 'Political Pluralism in Hungary: The 1990 Elections', *Soviet Studies*, Vol. 43, No. 1, 1991.

RACZ, Barnabas, 'The Socialist-Left Opposition in Post-Communist Hungary', *Europe-Asia Studies*, Vol. 45, No. 4, 1993.

RACZ, Barnabas, KUKORELLI, Istvan, 'The 'Second Generation' Post-Communist Elections in Hungary 1994', *Europe-Asia Studies*, Vol. 47, No. 2, 1995.

RADOS, Antonia, *Die Verschwörung der Securitate*, Hoffmann & Campe 1990.

RAFAEL, Edgar, R., *Entwicklungsland Rumänien*, Oldenbourg Verlag 1994.

RAGIN, Charles, BERG-SCHLOSSER, Dirk, DE MEUR, Gisèle, *Political Methodology: Macro-Qualitative Comparative Methods*, Manuscript.

RAINER, János, 'The Reprisals', *The New Hungarian Quarterly*, Vol. 33, No. 127, Autumn 1992.

RAINER, János, M., 'The Road to Budapest, 1956: New Documentation on the Kremlin's Decision to Intervene. Part II', *The Hungarian Quarterly*, Vol. 37, No. 143, Autumn 1996.

RAINER, János, M., 'The Road to Budapest, 1956: New Documentation on the Kremlin's Decision to Intervene. Part I', *The Hungarian Quarterly*, Vol. 137, No. 142, Summer 1996.

RAISER, Martin, *Ein Tschechisches Wunder?* Kiel Discussion Papers No. 233, June 1994.

RAISER, Martin, *Governing the Transition to a Market Economy*, Kiel Working Papers No. 592, August 1993.

RAISER, Martin, NUNNENKAMP, Peter, *Output Decline and Recovery in Central Europe*, Kiel Working Papers No. 601, October 1993.

RAISER, Martin, *Soft Budget Constraints*, Kiel Working Papers No. 549, December 1992.

RAKOWSA-HARMSTONE, Teresa, *Perspectives for Change in Communist Societies*, Westview Press 1979.

RATESH, Nestor, *Romania: The Entangled Revolution*, Praeger 1992.

RAUTSI, Inari, *The Eastern Question Revisited*, Helsinki 1993.

REMMEL, Franz, 'Kei oh drom tschal? – Wohin führt der Weg? Die Roma in Rumänien', *Südosteuropa Mitteilungen*, Vol. 36, No. 3, 1996.

RENNEBERGER, Franz, (Hrsg.), *Zwischen Zentralisierung und Selbstverwaltung*, Südosteuropa Gesellschaft 1989.

RENNER, Hans, *A History of Czechoslovakia since 1945*, Routledge 1989.

RÉTI, György, 'Hungary and the Problem of National Minorities', *The Hungarian Quarterly*, Vol. 36, No. 139, Autumn 1995.

RÉVESZ, Gabor, *Perestroika in Eastern Europe*, Westview Press 1990.

RFE/RL News, *Romania: Bucharest calculates NATO Admission Cost at $3 Billion.*

RFE/RL News, *Romania: Romania to send Troops to Join Albania Mission.*

RFE/RL News, *Romania: Senate Approves Foreign Property Ownership.*

RFE/RL Research Report, 'Hungarian Situation Report', 16 May 1985.

RFE/RL Situation Report on Romania, 'An Underground Essay on Urban and Rural Development', 3 February 1986.

RICHTER, Sándor, 'Hungary's Changed Patterns of Trade and Their Effects', *Soviet Studies*, Vol. 44, No. 6, 1992.

RICHTER, Sándor, (Ed.), *The Transition from Command to Market Economies in East-Central Europe*, Westview Press 1992.

ROBEJSEK, Peter, *Europapolitische Vorstellungen und Konzepte in der DDR, in Polen, der CSSR und Ungarn*, Bundesinstitut für Ostwissenschaftliche und Internationale Studien, Bericht No. 6, 1996.

ROE, Sarah, 'Progressive Inaction in Hungary', *Transitions*, Vol. 4, No. 4, September 1997.

ROMAN, Petre, 'Interview', *Der Spiegel*, No. 2, 1990.

ROMAN, Petre, 'Interview', *Der Spiegel*, No. 37, 1990.

RÓNA-TAS, Ákos, 'The Selected and the Elected: The making of the New Parliamentary Elite in Hungary', *East European Politics and Societies*, Vol. 5, No. 3, Fall 1991.

RONNAS, Per, 'Turning the Romanian Peasant into a new Socialist Man', *Soviet Studies*, Vol. 41, No. 4, October 1989.

ROPER, Stephen, D., 'From Opposition to Government Coalition: Unity and Fragmentation with the Democratic Convention of Romania', *East European Quarterly*, Vol. 31, No. 4, Winter 1997.

ROPER, Steven, D., 'The Romanian Party System and the Catch-All Party Phenomenon', *East European Quarterly*, Vol. 93, No. 4, Winter 1994.

ROSE, Richard, 'Contradictions Between Micro- and Macro-Economic Goals in Post-Communist Societies', *Europe-Asia Studies*, Vol. 45, No. 3, 1993.

ROSE, Richard, HAERPFER, Christian, 'Mass Response to Transformation in Post-Communist Societies', *Europe-Asia Studies*, Vol. 46, No. 1, 1994.

ROSKIN, Michael, G., 'The Emerging Party Systems of Central and Eastern Europe', *East European Quarterly*, Vol. 32, No. 1, Spring 1992.

ROSKIN, Michael, G., *The Rebirth of East Europe (2nd Edition)*, Prentice Hall 1994.

ROSTOWSKI, Jacek, 'Problems of Creating Stable Monetary Systems in Post-Communist Economies', *Europe-Asia Studies*, Vol. 45, No. 3, 1993.

ROTHCHILD, Donald, GROTH, Alexander, J., 'Pathological Dimensions of Domestic and International Ethnicity', *Political Science Quarterly*, Vol. 110, No. 1, Spring 1995.

ROTHSCHILD, Joseph, *East-Central Europe Between the Two World Wars*, University of Washington Press 1974.

ROTHSCHILD, Joseph, *Return to Diversity*, Oxford University Press 1989.

ROUSSO, Henry, "Säuberungen' Gestern und Heute', *Transit*, No. 2, Summer 1991.

ROYEN, Christoph, 'Die Befreiung Mittel-Ost-Europas von der Sowjetischen Vorherrschaft', *Die Internationale Politik*, 1989-1990.

RUDOLF, Peter, 'Die USA und die NATO-Erweiterung', *Aussenpolitik*, Vol. 47, 4th. Quarter 1996.

RUPNIK, Jacques, 'Eisschrank oder Fegefeuer: Das Ende des Kommunismus und das Wiederwachen der Nationalismen in Osteuropa', *Transit,* No. 1, Autumn 1990.

RUPNIK, Jacques, MOÏSI, Dominique, '1989 in historischer Perspektive', *Transit,* No. 2, Summer 1991.

RUSI JOURNAL, *Focus – Security through NATO in the 21st Century – Vision into Reality,* Vol. 142, No. 6, December 1997.

RUST, Val, D., KNOST, Peter, WICHMANN, Jürgen, (Hrsg.), *Education and the Values Crisis in Central and Eastern Europe,* Peter Lang 1984.

SAKWA, Richard, *Gorbachev and His Reforms 1985-1990,* Philip Allan 1990.

SÁRKÖZY, Tamás, 'Die Eigentumsverhältnisse und das ungarische Gesellschaftsrecht', *Südosteuropa Jahrbuch,* No. 21, 1990.

SÁRKÖZY, Tamás, (Ed.), *Foreign Investments in Hungary,* Budapest 1989.

SAVITT, Ronald, 'Privatization and the Consumer', *The New Hungarian Quarterly,*
Vol. 33, No. 128, Winter 1992.

SCHAPIRO, Leonard, *The Communist Party of the Soviet Union,* Methuen & Co. Ltd. 1963.

SCHEWARDNADSE, Eduard, 'Wer hat Osteuropa verloren?' *Der Spiegel,* No. 27, 1990.

SCHIRRMACHER, Frank, (Hrsg.), *Im Osten erwacht die Geschichte,* Deutsche Verlagsanstalt 1990.

SCHMIDT, Andreas, S., 'Die politischen Auseinandersetzungen am 'Nationalen Runden Tisch' in Ungarn (1989)', *Südosteuropa,* Vol. 46, No. 1-2, 1997.

SCHMIDT, Jochen, *Populismus oder Marxismus,* Tübingen 1992.

SCHMIDT-HARTMANN, Eva, *Kommunismus und Osteuropa,* Oldenbourg 1994.

SCHMIDT-SCHWEIZER, Andreas, S., 'Die Öffnung der ungarischen Westgrenze für DDR-Bürger im Sommer 1989', *Südosteuropa Mitteilungen,* Vol. 37, No. 1, 1997.

SCHMIEDING, Holger, BUCH, Claudia, *Better Banks for Eastern Europe,* Kiel Discussion Papers No. 197, December 1992.

SCHMIEDING, Holger, KOOP, Michael, *Privatisierung in Mittel- und Osteuropa: Konzepte für der Hindernislauf zur Marktwirtschaft,* Kiel Discussion Papers No. 165, February 1991.

SCHÖNFELD, Roland, 'Das Südöstliche Europa nach dem Ende der Sowjetischen Hegemonie', *Die Internationale Politik,* 1989-1990.

SCHÖNFELD, Roland, 'Wandel der Wirtschaftssysteme in Ostmittel- und Südosteuropa', *Südosteuopa Jahrbuch,* No. 24, 1993.

SCHÖNFELD, Ronald, (Hrsg.), *Reform und Wandel in Südosteuropa,* Oldenbourg 1985.

SCHÖNFELD, Ronald, *Nationalitätenprobleme in Südosteuropa,* Oldenbourg 1987.

SCHÖPFLIN, George, 'Conservatism and Hungary's Transition', *Problems of Communism,* Vol. 40, No. 1-2, January-April 1991.

SCHÖPFLIN, George, 'Konservative Politik und konservative Faktoren in den Postkommunistischen Gesellschaften', *Transit,* No. 4, Summer 1992.

SCHÖPFLIN, George, 'Post-Communism: Constructing New Democracies in Central Europe', *International Affairs,* Vol. 67, No. 2, April 1991.

SCHÖPFLIN, George, 'The Condition of Post-Communism', *The New Hungarian Quarterly,* Vol. 122, No. 32, Summer 1991.

SCHÖPFLIN, George, 'The End of Communism in Eastern Europe', *International Affairs*, Vol. 66, No. 1, January 1990.

SCHÖPFLIN, George, 'The Political Traditions of Eastern Europe', *Daedalus*, Vol. 119, No. 1, Winter 1990.

SCHÖPFLIN, George, WOOD, Nancy, (Eds.), *In Search of Central Europe*, Polity Press 1989.

SCHWARTZ, H., *Prague's 200 Days*, Frederick A. Preager Publishers 1969.

SEBÖK, László, 'The Demography of a Minority', *The Hungarian Quarterly*, Vol. 35, No. 133, Spring 1994.

SEGERT, Dieter, MACHOS, Csilla, *Parteien in Osteuropa*, Westdeutscher Verlag 1995.

SEISANU, Romulus, *Rumania*, Romanian Historical Studies 1987.

SELUCKY, Radoslav, *The Plan that Failed*, Nelson 1970.

SENECHAL, David, *Czechoslovakia*.
Http: //ww2.artsci.wustl.edu/~ps4272/czs-ds.html.

SEVERIN, Adrian, 'Interview', *Südosteuropa*, Vol. 42, No. 10, 1993.

SEVERIN, Adrian, 'The Strategic Outlook for South-East Europe', *RUSI Journal*, Vol. 142, No. 4, August 1997, pp. 7-11.

SHAFIR, Michael, 'Ceausescu's Overthrow: Popular Uprising or Moscow-Guided Conspiracy?' *Report on Eastern Europe*, No. 13, 19 January 1990.

SHAFIR, Michael, 'Is the Party of Romanian National Unity Disintegrating?' *Open Media Research Institute (OMRINet)*, Analytical brief No. 414.

SHAFIR, Michael, 'Is the Romanian Opposition heading for Victory?' *Open Media Research Institute (OMRINet)*, Analytical Brief No. 260.

SHAFIR, Michael, 'Light at the end of the Hungarian-Romanian Tunnel?' *Open Media Research Institute (OMRINet)*.

SHAFIR, Michael, 'Mini-Reshuffle of Romanian Government', *Open Media Research Institute (PMRINet)*, Analytical Brief No. 295.

SHAFIR, Michael, 'Romania's 'Different' Presidential Candidate: Nicolae Manolescu', *Open Media Research Institute (OMRINet)*, Analytical Brief No. 227.

SHAFIR, Michael, 'Romania Opts for Political Change', *Open Media Research Institute (OMRINet)*, Analytical Brief No. 436.

SHAFIR, Michael, 'Romania: Everybody seems to Love to Hate Tudor, Almost', *RFE/RL Report*.

SHAFIR, Michael, 'Romanians and the Transition to Democracy', *RFE/RL Research Report*, Vol. 2, No. 18, 30 April 1993.

SHAFIR, Michael, 'The Romanian Coalition Breaks', *Open Media Research Institute (OMRINet)*, Analytical Brief No. 314.

SHAFIR, Michael, 'Victor Ciorbea: Romania's Prime Minister Designate', *Open Media Research Insitute (OMRINet)*, Analytical Brief No. 482.

SHAFIR, Michael, *Romania: Politics, Economics and Society*, Frances Pinter Publishers Ltd. 1985.

SIEBERT, Horst, (Ed.), *The Transformation of Socialist Economies*, Institüt für Weltwirtschaft, Kiel 1992.

SIEGEL, Achim, 'Totalitarismus', *Zeitschrift für Politik*, Vol. 43, No. 2, June 1996.

ŠÍK, Ota, 'What Czechoslovakia expects from Gorbachev', *Government and Opposition*, Vol. 25, No. 4, Winter 1990.

SIMAI, Mihály, 'Hungarian Problems', *Government and Opposition*, Vol. 27, No. 1, Winter 1992.

SIMON, Gerhard, 'Das Ende der Sowjet Union', *Aussenpolitik*, Vol. 47, Winter 1996.

SIMON, János, 'Freiheit oder Wohlstand? Zum Demokratieverständnis der ungarischen Bürger', *Südosteuropa*, Vol. 44, No. 11-12, 1995.

SIMONS, Thomas, W., Jr., *Eastern Europe in the Postwar World*, Macmillan 1991.

SIMONTEI, Marko, 'A Comparative Review of Privatisation Strategies in Four Former Socialist Countries', *Europe-Asia Studies*, Vol. 45, No. 1, 1993.

SINGER, Ladislav, *Der ungarische Weg*, Seewald Verlag 1978.

SINGHOFEN, S., *Die Spaltung der CSFR und die Bedeutung nationalistischer Strömungen*, Magisterarbeit, Christian-Albrechts Universität, Kiel 1994.

SIPUR, Elena, 'Von Bessarabien zur Republik Moldau – Die historischen Wurzeln eines Konflikts', *Südosteuropa*, Vol. 43, No. 3-4, 1993.

SÎRBU, Marina-Cristina, 'Towards a Market Economy: The Romanian Effort', *East European Quarterly*, Vol. 93, No. 4, Winter 1994.

SITZLER, Kathrin, 'Parteiensystem und Gesellschaft in Ungarn', *Südosteuropa*, Vol. 41, No. 3-4, 1992.

SITZLER, Kathrin, 'Ungarns politische Reformen im Spiegel der neuen Verfassungskonzeptionen', *Aus Politik und Zeitgeschichte*, No. 23, 2 Juni 1989.

SKILLING, Gordon, H., 'Independent Currents in Czechoslovakia', *Problems of Communism*, January-February 1985.

SKILLING, Gordon, H., (Ed.), *Czechoslovakia 1918-1988*, Macmillan 1991.

SKILLING, Gordon, H., *Charter 77 and Human Rights in Czechoslovakia*, George Allen & Unwin 1981.

SKILLING, Gordon, H., *Czechoslovakia's Interrupted Revolution*, Princeton University Press 1976.

SKILLING, Gordon, H., *Samizdat and an Independent Society in Eastern Europe*, Macmillan 1989.

SMOLAR, Aleksander, 'Durch die Wüste: Die Dilemma des Übergangs', *Transit*, No. 1, Autumn 1990.

SMUTNÝ, Pavel, 'Die Tschechoslowakei – eine Rückkehr zu sich selbst', *Aus Politik und Zeitgeschichte*, No. 6, 31 Januar 1992.

SOBELL, Vlad, 'Czechoslovakia: The Legacy of Normalization', *East European Politics and Societies*, Vol. 2, No. 1, Winter 1988.

SPIROIU, Nicolae Constantin, 'The Balkans and European Security', *RUSI Journal*, Vol. 136, No. 3, Autumn 1991.

STAAR, Richard, F., (Ed.), *East-Central Europe and the USSR*, St. Martin's Press 1991.

STAAR, Richard, F., *The 1991 Yearbook on International Communist Affairs*, Hoover Institution Press 1991.

STAAR, Richard, F., *The Communist Regimes in Eastern Europe*, Hoover Institute Press 1971.

STANISZKIS, Jadwiga, 'Patterns of Change in Eastern Europe', *East European Politics and Societies*, Vol. 4, No. 1, Winter 1990.

STARK, David, 'Das Alte im Neuen: Institutionenwandel in Osteuropa', *Transit*, No. 9, Summer 1995.

STARK, David, 'Path, Dependence and Privatisation Strategies in East Central Europe', *East European Politics and Societies*, Vol. 6, No. 1, Winter 1992.

STARK, David, 'Privatisierungsstrategien in der CSFR, Ostdeutschland, Polen und Ungarn', *Transit*, No. 3, Winter 1991/92.

STARK, David, 'Privatization in Hungary: From Plan to Market of from Plan to Clan?' *East European Politics and Societies*, Vol. 4, No. 3, Fall 1990.

STARK, David, 'Transforming the Economies of East and Central Europe: Introduction', *East European Politics and Societies*, Vol. 6, No. 1, Winter 1992.

STEMPLOWSKI, Ryszard, 'Sailing in the same Direction', *RUSI Journal*, Vol. 140, No. 1, February 1995.

STERBLING, Anton, 'Ethnische Strukturen und Ethnische Parteien in Südosteuropa', *Südosteuropa*, Vol. 45, No. 8, 1996.

STERBLING, Anton, 'Überlegungen zum 'Wiederwachen der Geschichte'', *Südosteuropa*, Vol. 42, No. 3-4, 1993.

STERBLING, Anton, *Aufbruch oder Konfusion?* Universität der Bundeswehr, Hamburg No. 5, 1994.

STERBLING, Anton, *Ethnische Probleme in Rumänien*, Universität der Bundeswehr, Hamburg No. 6, 1995.

STERBLING, Anton, *Traditionale Strukturen und Agrawirtschaftliche Probleme in den Gesellschaften Südosteuropas*, Universität der Bundeswehr, Hamburg No. 2, 1993.

STOKES, Gale, 'Lessons of the East European Revolutions of 1989', *Problems of Communism*, Vol. 40, No. 5, September-October 1991.

STOKES, Gale, *From Stalinism to Pluralism*, Oxford University Press 1991.

STOKES, Gale, *The Walls came Tumbling Down*, Oxford University Press 1993.

STRÖBINGER, R., *Schicksalsjahre an der Moldau*, Casimir Katz Verlag 1990.

STUTH, Reinhard, 'Europa – Müde vom Wandel?' *Aussenpolitik*, Vol. 45, No. 1, 1995.

Südosteuropa Mitteilungen, 'Strukturwandel und Europäische Union. Ruhrgebiet, Osterweiterung und Reform der Strukturpolitik', Internationale Konferenz der Südosteuropa Gesellschaft und der Universität Duisburg, 5.5.97-6.5.97, *Südosteuropa Mitteilungen*, Vol. 37, No. 2, 1997.

SUGAR, Peter, F., *A History of Hungary*, Indiana University Press 1991.

SUKOSD, Miklos, 'The Media War', *East European Reporter*, March-April 1992.

SUTTNER, Ernst, Chr., 'Das religiöse Moment in seiner Bedeutung für Gesellschaft, Nationsbildung und Kultur Südosteuropas', *Südosteuropa Mitteilungen*, Vol. 37, No. 1, 1997.

SVETOZAR, Pejovich, 'Der Markt der Institutionen: Osteuropa zwischen Nationalismus und Liberalismus', *Transit*, No. 9, Summer 1995.

SVITÁK, Ivan, *The Czechoslovak Experiment 1968-1969*, Columbia University Press 1971.

SVITÁK, Ivan, *The Unbearable Burden of History: The Sovietization of Czechoslovakia*, Academia Praha 1990.

SWAAN, Wim, 'Prices and Market Behaviour in the Early Stages of the Transition to a Market Economy', *Soviet Studies*, Vol. 43, No. 3, 1991.

SWAIN, G., SWAIN, N., *Eastern Europe since 1945*, Macmillan 1993.

SWAIN, Nigel, *Hungary: The Rise and Fall of Feasible Socialism*, Verso 1992.

SZABÓ, Maté, 'Probleme der Demokratisierung in Ungarn', *Aus Politik und Zeitgeschichte*, No. 6, 31 Januar 1992.

SZANYA, T., S., 'Ultra-Nationalism in Central Europe', *Orbis*, Vol. 37, No. 4, Fall 1993.

SZELENYI, Ivan, 'Alternative Futures for Eastern Europe: The Case of Hungary', *East European Politics and Societies*, Vol. 4, No. 2, Spring 1990.

SZELENYI, Ivan, 'Hungary 1989: Introduction', *East European Politics and Societies*, Vol. 4, No. 2, Spring 1990.

SZELENYI, Ivan, *Socialist Entrepreneurs: Embourgeoisement in Rural Hungary*, University of Wisconsin Press 1988.

SZELEYNI, Ivan, *Urban Inequalities under State Socialism*, Oxford University Press 1983.

SZIRÁCZKI, György, 'Employment Policy and Labour Market in Transition: From Labour Shortage to Unemployment', *Soviet Studies*, Vol. 42, No. 4, October 1990.

SZÖNYI, István, 'Hungary and NATO: What is at Stake?' *Südosteuropa*, Vol. 43, No. 9-10, 1994.

SZÖNYI, István, 'Minorities and NATO: The Twin Emphasis of Hungarian Foreign Policy', *Südosteuropa*, Vol. 42, No. 11-12, 1993.

TABORSKY, Edward, *President Benes Between East and West*, Hoover Institution Press 1981.

TAKÁCS, Albert, 'Staatliche Verwaltung und lokale Gesellschaft', *Südosteuropa Jahrbuch*, No. 18, 1988.

TEMPLE, Mark, 'The Politicization of History: Marshal Antonescu and Romania', *East_European Politics and Societies*, Vol. 10, No. 3, Fall 1996.

TERRY, S., M., (Ed.), *Soviet Policy in Eastern Europe*, Yale University press 1984.

The National Christian Democratic Peasant Party, *Synthesis of the Political Programme (Draft)*, Bucharest, January 1996.

The New Hungarian Quarterly, 'György Aczel Answers Questions on Hungarian Society', No. 22, Summer 1981.

The Romanian Digest, 'Bank Privatisation Law Update', Vol. 2, No. 6, 6 June 1997.

The Romanian Digest, *Discharged Employees to Have Imposed Social Protection,* Vol. 2, No. 6, June 1997.

The Romanian Digest, *Proposed Revisions to Foreign Investment Laws,* Vol. 2, No. 6, June 1997.

The Romanian Digest, *State Ownership Fund Subordinated to Government,* Vol. 2, No. 6, June 1997.

The Romanian Embassy, *The Romanian Business Environment: General Data.*

The World Bank Economic Review, Vol. 6, No. 1, 1992.

TILLY, Charles, *Die europäischen Revolutionen,* Verlag C. H. Beck 1993.

TIMÁR, János, 'Particular Features of Employment and Unemployment in the Present Stage of Transformation of the Post-Socialist Countries', *Europe-Asia Studies,* Vol. 47, No. 4, 1995.

TIMMERMANN, Heiner, *Ungarn nach 1945,* Dadder 1990.

TIMMERMANN, Heinz, *Die KP Nachfolgeparteien in Osteuropa,* Bundesinstitut für Ostwissenschaftliche und Internationale Studien, Bericht No. 31, 1994.

TIMMERMANN, Heinz, *Die Volksrevolutionen in Osteuropa: Charakter, Probleme und Perspektiven,* Bundesintsitut für Ostwissenschaftliche und Internationale Studien, Bericht No. 22, 1990.

TISMANEANU, Vladimir, 'Ceausescu's Socialism', *Problems of Communism,* January-February 1985.

TISMANEANU, Vladimir, 'Personal Power and Political Crisis in Romania', *Government and Opposition,* Vol. 24, No. 2, Summer 1989.

TISMANEANU, Vladimir, 'The Quasi-Revolution and Its Discontents: Emerging Political Pluralism in Post-Ceausescu Romania', *East European Politics and Societies*, Vol. 7, No. 2, Spring 1993.

TISMANEANU, Vladimir, 'The Tragicomedy of Romanian Communism', *East European Politics and Societies*, Vol. 3, No. 2, Spring 1989.

TISMANEANU, Vladimir, *In Search of Civil Society*, Routledge 1990.

TISMANEANU, Vladimir, *Reinventing Politics: Eastern Europe from Stalin to Havel*, The Free Press Inc. 1992.

TISMANEANU, Vladimir, *The Crisis of Marxist Ideology in Eastern Europe*, Routledge 1988.

TÖKÉS, László, 'Interview', *Der Spiegel*, No. 3, 1990.

TÖKÉS, Rudolf, L., 'From Visegrad to Krakow: Cooperation, Competition, and Coexistence in Central Europe', *Problems of Communism*, Vol. 40, No. 6, November-December 1991.

TÖKÉS, Rudolf, L., 'Hungary's New Political Elites: Adaptation and Change, 1989-1990', *Problems of Communism*, Vol. 34, No. 6, 1990.

TÖKÉS, Rudolf, L., 'Vom Post-Kommunismus zur Demokratie: Politik, Parteien und Wahlen in Ungarn', *Aus Politik und Zeitgeschichte*, No. 45, 2 November 1990.

TOMA, Peter, A., *Socialist Authority: The Hungarian Experience*. Praeger 1988.

TONTSCH, Günther, H., 'Das persönliche Grund- und Wohnungseigentum in Rumänien', *Südosteuropa Jahrbuch*, No. 21, 1990.

TONTSCH, Günther, H., 'Probleme des Zentralismus und der Dezentralisieung im rumänischen Verwaltungssystem', *Südosteuropa Jahrbuch*, No. 18, 1988.

TONTSCH, Günther, H., 'Wandel der politischen Systeme Südosteuropas unter besonderer Berücksichtigung der Verfassungsordnungen', *Südosteuropa Jahrbuch*, No. 24, 1993.

TONTSCH, Günther, H., *Partei und Staat in Rumänien*, Verlag Wissenschaft und Politik 1985.

TOTH, Andras, 'The Social Impact of Restructuring in Rural Areas of Hungary: Disruption of Security or the End of Rural Socialist Middle Class Society?' *Soviet Studies*, Vol. 44, No. 6, 1992.

TOTOK, William, *Die Zwänge der Erinnnerung*, Jurius 1988.

Transitions, 'Counterpoint: Is Czech Voucher Privatization a Success?' **SVENJAR, Jan,** 'A Good Start to a Yet-Unfinished Economic Revolution', **MLADEK, Jan,** 'A Too Costly Social Engineering Project', Vol. 4, No. 4, September 1997.

Transitions, 'Counterpoint: Should the West Open its Doors to the East's Roma?' **HELTON, Arthur, C.,** 'Romani Refugees Deserve International Protection', **WIDGREN, Jonas,** 'Asylum Can't Replace Improvements at Home', Vol. 4, No. 7, December 1997.

Transitions, 'Counterpoint: What to Do with Gabcikovo?' **LANYI, Andras,** 'Hungary: A Case of Ecological Aggression', **JENCIK, Gabriel,** 'Slovakia: A Response to Broken Promises', Vol. 4, No. 1, June 1997.

Transitions, 'Horn blasted over Roma issues', Vol. 5, No. 3, March 1998.

TROND, Gilberg, *Coalition Strategies of Marxist Parties*, Duke University Press 1989.

TSATOS, Dimitris, Th., KEDZIA, Zdzislaw, (Hrsg.), *Parteienrecht in mittel- und osteuropäischen Staaten*, Nomos Verlag 1994.

TUCKER, R., C., (Ed.), *Stalinism: Essays in Historical Interpretation*, W. W. Norton & Co. Inc. 1977.

TURNOCK, David, *The Making of Eastern Europe: From the Earliest Times to 1815*, Routledge 1988.

TYSON, Laura, 'Economic Adjustment in Eastern Europe', *Rand*, September 1984.

U.S. State Department, *Romania: Human Rights Practices 1995.*

ULC, Otto, 'The Bumpy Road of Czechoslovakia's Velvet Revolution', *Problems of Communism*, Vol. 41, No. 3, May-June 1992.

VALENTA, J., *Soviet Intervention in Czechoslovakia 1968*, John Hopkins University Press 1991.

VALKI, László, 'NATO Enlargement: The Hungarian Interests', *The Hungarian Quarterly*, Vol. 37, No. 141, Spring 1996.

VÁMOS, Tibor, 'Life After Socialism: Abacus and ICBM', *The New Hungarian Quarterly*, Vol. 33, No. 125, Spring 1992.

van FRAUSUM, Yves, G., 'Industrial Restructuring in Romania: Diagnosis and Strategies', *Europe-Asia Studies*, Vol. 47, No. 1, 1995.

van FRAUSUM, Yves, G., GEHMANN, Ulrich, GROSS, Jürgen, 'Market Economy and Economic Reform in Romania: Macroeconomic and Microeconomic Perspectives', *Europe-Asia Studies*, Vol. 46, No. 5, 1994.

VANJA, Tamás, 'The Business of Survival', *The Hungarian Quarterly*, Vol. 35, No. 136, Winter 1994.

VARGA, Gyula, 'Die landwirtschaftliche Kleinproduktion in Ungarn', *Südosteuropa Jahrbuch*, No. 21, 1990.

VÁRKONYI, Anna, 'A Catalogue of Woe: The Environment', *The New Hungarian Quarterly*, Vol. 33, No. 126, Summer 1992.

VASKO, V., *The Unsilenced*, Zvon 1990.

VASS, László, 'Europeanisation and Interest Groups in the new Hungarian Political System', *Südosteuropa*, Vol. 42, No. 5, 1993.

VASS, László, 'Interessengruppen in Ungarn', *Südosteuropa*, Vol. 42, No. 5, 1993.

VEEN, Hans-Joachim, *Wandel im Kommunismus,* Edition Interform 1979.

VERDERY, Katherine, *National Ideology under Socialism,* University of California Press 1991.

VERES, Ella, 'The Mixed Towns of Transylvania', *Transitions,* Vol. 4, No. 7, December 1997.

VIDA, István, 'János Kádár and the Czechoslovak Crisis of 1968', *The Hungarian Quarterly,* Vol. 35, No. 135, Autumn 1994.

VODOPIVEC, Milan, 'The Persistence of Job Security in Reforming Socialist Economies', *Soviet Studies,* Vol. 43, No. 6, 1991.

von BEYME, Klaus, *Systemwechsel in Osteuropa,* Suhrkamp 1994.

VRBA, Tomas, 'The Trade-offs of a Cozy Life', *Transitions,* Vol. 5, No. 3, March 1998.

WÄDEKIN, Karl-Eugen, 'East European Trends and Prospects: A European Perspective', *East European Economies,* Vol. 1.

WALLER, Michael, COPPTIERS, Bruno, DESCHOUWER, Kris, (Eds.), *Social Democracy in a Post-Communist Europe,* Frank Cass & Co. Ltd. 1994.

WASKO, Janet, MOSCO, Vincent, (Eds.), *Democratic Communications in the Information Age,* Garamond Press 1992.

WEIDENFELD, Werner, (Hrsg.), *Demokratie und Marktwirtschaft in Osteuropa,* Verlag Bertelsmann Stiftung 1993.

WEINER, Elaine, 'Assessing the Implications of Political and Economic Reform in the Post-Socialist Era: The Case of Czech and Slovak Women', *East European Quarterly,* Vol. 31, No. 4, Winter 1997.

WELSH, Helga, A., 'Dealing with the Communist Past: Central and East European Experiences after 1990', *Europe-Asia Studies,* Vol. 48, No. 3, 1996.

WETTIG, Gerhard, *Die Sowjetunion und die Entwicklungsperspektiven des Kommunismus in Osteuropa,* Bundesinstitut für Ostwissenschaftliche und Internationale Studien, Bericht No. 44, 1990.

WETTIG, Gerhard, *Nation und Konflikt in Osteuropa nach dem Zusammenbruch des Kommunismus,* Bundesinstitut für Ostwissenschaftliche und Internationale Studien, Bericht No. 28, 1992.

WHEATCROFT, Stephen, G., 'A Further Note of Clarification on the Famine, the Camps and Excess Morality', *Europe-Asia Studies,* Vol. 49, No. 3, May 1997, pp. 503-505.

WHEATON, Bernard, KAVAN, Zdenek, *The Velvet Revolution,* Westview Press 1992.

WHITE, S., BATT, J., LEWIS, P., G., *Developments in East European Politics,* Macmillan 1993.

WHITE, Stephen, (Ed.), *Ideology and Soviet Politics,* Macmillan Press 1988.

WHITE, Stephen, PRAVDA, Alex, GITELMAN, Zvi, (Eds.), *Developments in Soviet and Post-Soviet Politics,* The Macmillan Press Ltd. 1992.

WILLIAMS, Kieran, 'New Sources on Soviet Decision Making during the 1968 Czechoslovak Crisis', *Europe-Asia Studies,* Vol. 48, No. 3, 1996.

WINDERL, Thomas, 'Machteliten im Systemwechsel: über Wandel und Kontinutiät osteuropäischer Eliten', *Südosteuropa,* Vol. 43, No. 11-12, 1994.

WINDSOR, Philip, ROBERTS, Adam, *Czechoslovakia 1968,* Columbia University Press 1969.

WINIECKI, Jan, 'East-Central Europe: A Regional Survey – The Czech Republic, Hungary, Poland and Slovakia in 1993', *Europe-Asia Studies,* Vol. 46, No. 5, 1994.

WINIECKI, Jan, 'The Inevitability of a Fall in Output in the Early Stages of Transition to the Market: Theoretical Underpinnings', *Soviet Studies*, Vol. 43, No. 4, 1991.

WINTER, Sonia, 'Central Europe: New NATO Members are Willing and Able to Foot the Bill', *RFE/RL Report*.

WOLCHIK, Sharon, L., *Czechoslovakia in Transition*, Pinter Publishers 1991.

WOLKOW, Wladimir, K., 'Die Sowjetische Parteiherrschaft und der Prager Frühling 1968', *Aus Politik und Zeitgeschichte*, No. 36, 28 August 1992.

WOLLE, Stefan, 'Die DDR Bevölkerung und der Prager Frühling', *Aus Politik und Zeitgeschichte*, No. 36, 28 August 1992.

WOLLMANN, Hellmut, 'Der Systemwechsel in Ostdeutschland, Ungarn, Polen und Rußland', *Aus Politik und Zeitgeschichte*, 24 January 1997.

WÖRNER, Manfred, 'The State of the Alliance', *RUSI Journal*, Vol. 133, No. 3, Autumn 1988.

ZELLNER, Wolfgang, DUNAÝ, Pál, 'Die Außenpolitik Ungarns im ersten Jahr der Regierung Horn', *Südosteuropa*, Vol. 44, No. 11-12, 1995.

ZEMAN, Z., A., B., *Pursued by a Bear: The Making of Eastern Europe*, Charto & Windus 1989.

ZIELONKA, Jan, *Security in Central Europe*, Adelphi Paper No. 272, 1993.

ZIEMER, Klaus, 'Ausgangsbedingungen für den politischen und wirtschaftlichen Transformationsprozeß in Südosteuropa', *Südosteuropa*, Vol. 45, No. 2, 1996.

ZINNER, Paul, E., *National Communism and Popular Revolt in Eastern Europe*, Columbia University Press 1956.

Further Sources

Press Department of the Czech Embassy, Bonn.
Press Department of the Hungarian Embassy, Bonn.
Press Department of the Romanian Embassy, Bonn.
Central European Online. Http: //www.centraleurope.com.
OMRI Daily Digest. Http: //www.rferl.org.
Open Media Reseach Insitute (OMRINet). Http: //www.omri.cz.
RFE/RL Reports, News and Newsline. Http: //www.rferl.org.
Der Spiegel
Die Zeit
Frankfurter Allgemeine Zeitung
Newsweek
The Prague Post

JN
96
.A91
H65
1999